APPEAL

COUNTER THE COUNTERFEIT & BUILD A STRONG FOUNDATION FOR SUCCESS

Books are our best friends, is the adage we have grown up with. However, the pirates of piracy are continuously forging 'our best friends'. Our books and their supplementary online resources are copyrighted, and we don't lend any right-to-copy. Piracy is synonymous to stealing books.

Knowledge comes real, let's not encourage its counterfeit. Therefore, we appeal all our readers to discourage pirated books and **choose authentic ones**.

HOW TO IDENTIFY THE PIRATED BOOKS?

1 COVER AND SPINE

- Look and feel (new or used book)
- Blurred images on the cover
- Hologram pasted on front
- Defective spine (wrinkles) or air pocket at its bottom
- Unclear ISBN/bar codes
- Missing/non-operational Unique Coupon Code for exclusive access to McGraw Hill Edge

2 TEXT/PRINTING/BINDING

- Uneven inking of pages
- Poor quality or blurred photographs/images/charts
- Substandard paper quality and opacity
- Misaligned pages
- Missing pages
- Inferior binding quality

You can further watch this video on How to identify a pirated book

For more information about identifying piracy, visit **https://www.mheducation.co.in/piracy**

To report a pirated book, send 'Hi' on WhatsApp code given on the back cover or write to us at **support.india@mheducation.com**.

Reported pirated books are examined to combat their piracy.

Let's fight the Pirates of Piracy and resolve to go for original!

About the Authors

Sumesh Chahal has been mentoring and guiding students for the most prestigious Civil Services Examination for more than 10 years and has guided many IAS toppers over the years, including All India Ranks-1, 2 & 3. With over 10 years of experience, he specialises in guiding aspirants through the pivotal phase of personality development, the most crucial aspect of the Civil Services Examination. With his profound understanding of the Civil Services Examination, he stands as one of the foremost mentors in this field.

Animesh Pradhan an alumnus of NIT Rourkela, exemplifies dedication and excellence. He has secured an All-India Rank-2 in his very first attempt in the prestigious civil services examination. Animesh has set a benchmark for aspirants across the country. His journey is a testament to perseverance, hard work, and strategic preparation, making him a true role model for future civil servants.

Virupaksh Singh is an accomplished IAS officer and a remarkable achiever, having cracked the civil services examination twice with notable ranks. He secured AIR-49 in CSE 2023 and AIR-392 in CSE 2022. A graduate of the prestigious National Law University (NLU) Delhi, Virupaksh's dedication and resilience have set a high standard for civil services aspirants.

Shubham Jain is an esteemed IPS officer who secured AIR-152 in the CSE 2022. A graduate of the National Law University (NLU) Delhi, Shubham's academic excellence is complemented by his professional experience as an advocate. Before joining the Indian Police Service, he practiced law at the Supreme Court and various appellate fora in Delhi.

Comprehensive Coverage of both Old & New NCERTs from

Class 6th to 12th

NCERT COMPENDIUM

Indian & World Geography

One Stop Solution for UPSC & STATE-PSCs

Sumesh Chahal

Animesh Pradhan (AIR-2, CSE-2023)

Virupaksh Singh (AIR-49, CSE-2023)

Shubham Jain (AIR-152, CSE-2022)

Mc Graw Hill

McGraw Hill Education (India) Private Limited

Published by McGraw Hill Education (India) Private Limited
Registered Office: Anjana Complex No: 5/90 A, Butt Road, St. Thomas Mount, Chennai – 600016

NCERT Compendium - Indian & World Geography

Print Edition

ISBN (13): 978-93-5532-820-5
ISBN (10): 93-5532-820-6

E-Book Edition

ISBN (13): 978-93-5532-828-1

ISBN (10): 93-5532-828-1

1 2 3 4 5 6 7 8 9 28 27 26 25 24

Printed and bound in India

Typeset at 22-B, Ground Floor, Near Karol Bagh Metro Pillar No. 112, Old Rajinder Nagar, New Delhi-110060 and printed at Magic International Pvt. Ltd., Plot No. 26E, Sector-31, (Industrial), Site-IV, Greater Noida 201306

Cover Source: Shutterstock

Cover Designer: Gyanendra Swamy

Visit us at: www.mheducation.co.in

Write to us at: support.india@mheducation.com

CIN: U80302TN2010PTC111532

Toll Free Number: 1800 103 5875

Preface

As authors, having spent several years researching geography and thoroughly investigating UPSC and State-PSC exams, we are proud to introduce **NCERT Compendium-Indian and World Geography**. This book is carefully designed for aspiring civil servants, offering a thorough understanding of geography for both the preliminary and main examination. This compendium is built on the rich knowledge found in NCERT textbooks from Classes VI to XII, covering the entire geography syllabus for UPSC and State PSC exams. We have closely adhered to the NCERT framework; however, our approach extends beyond just textbook content.

Each chapter is enhanced with analysis, interpretations, and perspectives to encourage deeper understanding rather than just memorisation. This focus on analysis empowers you to develop a deeper understanding of geographical events and processes, enabling you to answer the questions effectively. Each section of this book ends with carefully crafted MCQs which are meant to prepare you for the Prelims. Furthermore, there are also thought-provoking main examination questions which will make sure that you can frame good answers that are full of insights and are well-structured.

We have no doubt that if utilised properly during your preparation for UPSC CSE or any other State PSC examinations; then this NCERT Compendium- Indian and World Geography shall serve as a great guide towards achieving success. With dedication alongside having such an all-inclusive study material like this one by your side, there's nothing else left other than being confident enough because success will be yours.

Preface

The authors, having spent several years researching geography and thoroughly investigating UPSC and State PSC exams, we are proud to introduce NCERT Compendium: Indian and World Geography. This book is carefully designed for aspiring civil servants, offering a thorough understanding of geography for both the preliminary and main examinations. This compendium is built on the vast knowledge found in NCERT textbooks from Classes VI to XII, covering the entire geography syllabus for UPSC and State PSC exams. We have closely adhered to the NCERT framework. However, our approach extends beyond just textbook content.

Each chapter is enhanced with analyses, interpretations, and perspectives to encourage deeper understanding rather than just memorisation. This focus on analysis empowers you to develop a deeper understanding of geographical events and processes, enabling you to answer the questions effectively. Each section of the book ends with carefully crafted MCQs, which are meant to prepare you for the Prelims. Furthermore, there are also thought-provoking main examination questions, which will make sure that you can frame good answers that are full of insight and are well-founded.

We have no doubt that if utilised properly during your preparation for UPSC CSE or any other State PSC examination, then this NCERT Compendium: Indian and World Geography shall serve as a great guide towards achieving success. With dedication alongside having such an all-inclusive study material like this one by your side, there's nothing else left other than being confident enough because success will be yours.

Acknowledgements

The completion of this NCERT Compendium-Indian and World Geography fills us with immense gratitude. This project wouldn't have been possible without the invaluable contributions of several remarkable individuals. Sincere thanks to the geographers and researchers whose insightful perspectives enriched the analysis and interpretations within this book. A special thanks also goes out to the countless UPSC and State PSC aspirants whose unwavering pursuit of knowledge continues to inspire educators like us. A heartfelt appreciation is extended to Shivam Kumar and Vikas Bhankhar for their thorough review and editing.

We are grateful for the support of our parents, family, and friends in our endeavours. We owe our special thanks to the team at McGraw Hill including Lalit Singh, Tanweer Ahmad, Nikhil Wadhera, Raman Vashisth, Suhaib Ali and others for their effort and unstinted cooperation in bringing out this book.

Contents

UNIT 1 The Origin and Evolution of The Earth

In This Unit

Comprehensive and profound coverage of the following NCERT's chapters:

- ✓ NCERT Class- 6th (The Earth: Our Habitat), Chapters- 1, 3 and 5
- ✓ NCERT Class- 11th (Fundamentals of Physical Geography), Chapters- 2 and 3

Early Theories

Origin of the Earth

- One of the earlier and popular arguments regarding the origin of the earth was given by German philosopher **Immanuel Kant.**
- **Mathematician Laplace** revised it in 1796. It is known **as Nebular Hypothesis.**
- **Nebular Hypothesis**- The hypothesis considered that the planets were formed out of a cloud of material associated with a youthful sun, which was slowly rotating. Later in 1900, **Chamberlain and Moulton** considered that a wandering star approached the sun. Consequently, an extension of material in the shape of a cigar was split off from the solar surface. The material that had detached from the solar surface continued to rotate around the sun as the passing star moved away, gradually condensing into planets.
- **This argument was backed by Sir James Jeans and later by Sir Harold Jeffrey.**
- This argument that the Earth is a companion to the Sun and coexisted with it has existed since a long time and is called the **Binary Theory.**
- In 1950, Carl Weizascar in Germany and Otto Schmidt in Russia made several revisions to the **"Nebular Hypothesis."** They believed that solar nebula, which is primarily composed of hydrogen and helium with some dust, encircling the sun. A disk-shaped cloud was created by particle collisions and friction, and the planets formed due to **accretion.**

Modern Theories

Origin of the Universe

- The Big Bang theory, also known as the **Expanding Universe Hypothesis,** is the most widely accepted theory explaining the origin of the universe.
- **Edwin Hubble, in 1920**, provided evidence that the universe is expanding. As time passes, galaxies move further and further apart.

The Big Bang Theory considers the following stages in the development of the universe:

1. In the beginning, all matter forming the universe existed in one place in the form of a "tiny ball" (singular atom) with an unimaginably small volume, infinite temperature and infinite density.
2. At the Big Bang the "tiny ball" exploded violently. This led to a huge expansion. It is now generally accepted that the event of the big bang took place, 13.7 billion years before the present.
3. After the Big Bang, the temperature fell to 4,500 K (Kelvin) in 300,000 years, which is when atomic matter first evolved. The universe became transparent.

The expansion of the universe means an increase in space between the galaxies. An alternative to this was **Hoyle's concept of Steady State.** It considered the universe to be roughly the same at any point of time , however this has been refuted by the Scientific community.

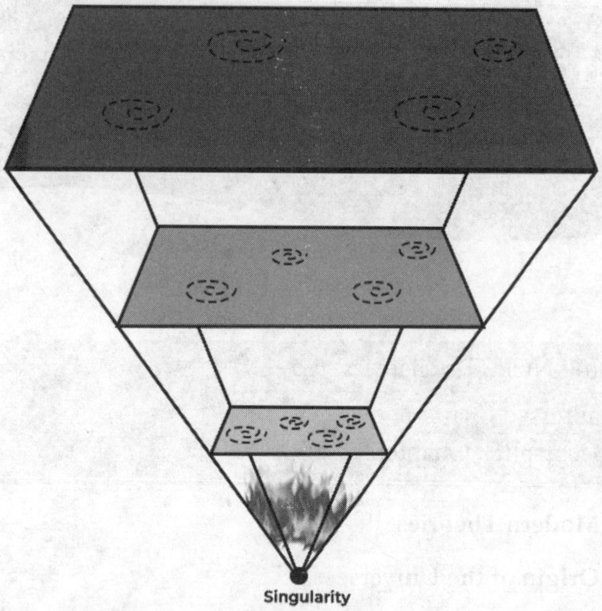

The Big Bang Theory

The Star Formation

- The distribution of matter and energy was not even in the early universe. These initial density differences gave rise to differences in gravitational forces and it caused the matter to get drawn together. These formed the bases for the development of **Galaxies**.
- A galaxy contains a large number of stars. Galaxies spread over vast distances that are measured in thousands of **light-years.**
- **The diameters of individual galaxies range from 80,000-150,000 light years.**
- The formation of a galaxy begins with the buildup of hydrogen gas in the form of a massive cloud known as a **nebula**.
- Eventually, growing nebula develop localised clumps of gas. These clumps continue to grow into even denser gaseous bodies, giving rise to formation of **stars**.
- The formation of stars is believed to have taken place some **5-6 billion years ago**.

Constellations- Constellations are the diverse patterns created by distinct **star clusters. Big Bear, or Ursa Major**, is one such constellation. **The Saptarishi (Sapta-seven, rishi-sages)** constellation is among the easiest to recognise. It is a constellation that is made up of seven stars and is a component of Ursa Major.

Pole Star- The stars were once employed by people to help them discern their path at night. The direction of the north is shown by the North star. There is another name for it: **the Pole Star**. It never moves from its spot in the sky. With the aid of the **Saptarishi,** we can determine the Pole Star's location.

> **A light year** is not a measure of time, but rather of distance. The speed of light is 300,000 km/second. Given this, it is assumed that a light year is the distance that a light source will travel in a year. This is 9.461×10^{12} kilometres. The earth and the sun are separated by 149,598,000 km on average. It takes 8.311 minutes in light years.

Formation of Planets

The following are considered to be the stages in the development of planets:

1. The stars are localised lumps of gas within a **Nebula.** A huge revolving disc of gas and dust forms around the gas core of the gas cloud as a result of the gravitational pull within the lumps.
2. **The gas cloud** begins to condense in the next stage, and the material surrounding the core transforms into tiny, spherical particles. Through the process of cohesion, these small, circular objects grow into what are known as **planetesimals.**
3. Larger bodies begin to form through collisions, and the material adheres to one another due to gravitational pull. A lot of smaller bodies come together to become planetesimals.
4. **During the last stage**, a great number of tiny planetesimals combine to produce fewer large bodies known as **planets.**

> The sun, the moon and all those objects shining in the night sky are called **Celestial Bodies.**

> 'Sol' in Roman mythology is the 'Sun-God'. 'Solar' means 'related to the sun'. The family of the sun is, therefore, called the **Solar System.**

Our Solar System

- There are **eight planets** in our solar system. The planets originated approximately **4.6 billion years** ago, while the nebula that is thought to have generated our solar system began to collapse and form its core around 5-5.6 billion years ago.
- The Sun (the star), eight planets, sixty-three moons, millions of smaller entities such as comets and asteroids, and an enormous amount of dust particles, and gases are included in our solar system.
- Out of the eight planets, Mercury, Venus, Earth and Mars are called the **Inner Planets** as they lie between the sun and the belt of asteroids. The other four planets are called the **Outer Planets.**
- Alternatively, the first four are called **Terrestrial,** meaning earth-like as they are made up of rock and metals, and have relatively high densities. The rest four are called **Jovian or Gas Giant planets**. Jovian means Jupiter -like.
- Most of them are much larger than the terrestrial planets and have a thick atmosphere, mostly of **Helium and Hydrogen**. Our planets all formed around the same time, about 4.6 billion years ago. **Pluto used to be considered one of them, but not anymore.**
- In **2006, the International Astronomical Union** decided that Pluto might be referred to as a **"Dwarf Planet,"** much like other recently discovered celestial bodies.

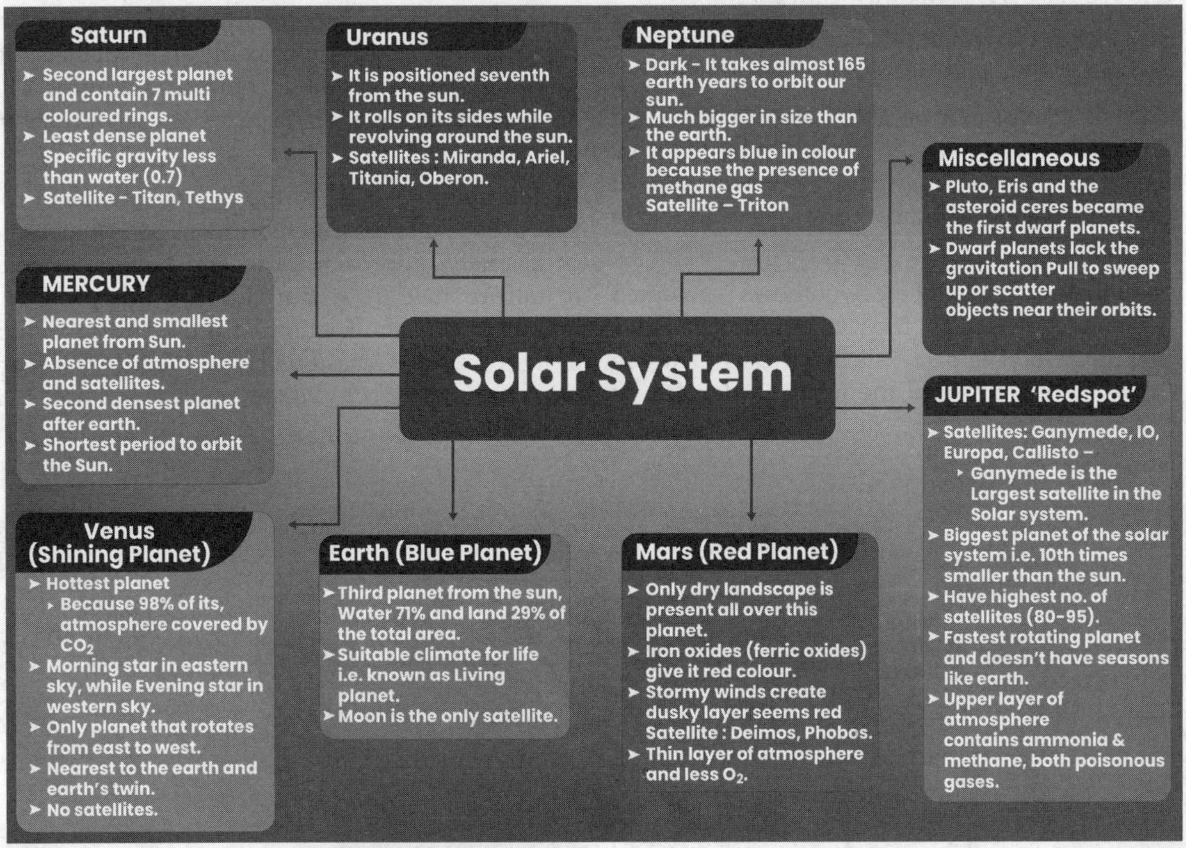

> An easy way to memorise the name of the planets in order of their distance from the sun is:
>
> **M**y **V**ery **E**fficient **M**other **J**ust **S**erved **U**s **N**uts.

The following circumstances explain how terrestrial and Jovian planets differ from each other:

1. In the immediate region of the parent star, when it was too warm for gases to condense into solid particles, the terrestrial planets were born. The formation of Jovian planets took place at a great distance.
2. The solar wind blasted off a lot of gas and dust from the terrestrial planets because it was closest

to **the Sun**. The Jovian planets' gases were not similarly removed by the solar winds since they were not that strong.

3. Because the terrestrial planets are smaller, the escaping gases could not be contained by their reduced gravity.

Giant Planets like Jupiter, Saturn, and Uranus are surrounded by rings made of small debris and dust. You can even see them from Earth with a powerful telescope.

The Moon

- The only natural satellite of the earth is the moon. Its diameter is only one-quarter that of the earth. It is about 3,84,400 km away from us.
- **Sir George Darwin** implied in **1838** that the earth and moon were once a single, fast-rotating body.
- The whole mass took the shape of a dumbbell and ultimately broke down. It was also proposed that the material that makes up the moon was isolated from the Pacific Ocean's current location in a depression.
- Nonetheless, neither of the hypotheses is accepted by modern scientists. Most people today agree that the **"Giant Impact,"** also known as **"The Big Splat,"** is what caused the moon to develop as Earth's satellite.
- Not too long after the earth was created, a body around **1 to 3 times the size of Mars** crashed with the planet. A sizeble portion of the earth fell into space. After that, this piece of blasted material orbited the earth and eventually coalesced into the current moon approximately 4.44 billion years ago.
- The Moon takes around **27 days** to complete one revolution of the Earth, that is exactly same as time that it takes to complete one spin. This is the reason why we can see only one side of the moon from the Earth.
- There are no conducive circumstances for life on the moon. Its surface is made up of plains, mountains, and depressions.

Asteroids- There are many small bodies that orbit the sun in addition to the stars, planets, and satellites. We refer to these bodies as **Asteroids**. They are majorly located in the space between Jupiter and Mars' orbits.

Meteoroids- We refer to the tiny fragments of rock that orbit the sun as **meteoroids**. These meteoroids occasionally approach Earth and have a tendency to fall upon it. They burn during this process as an outcome of the friction with the air. It produces a light burst. Occasionally a meteor hits Earth without burning completely and leaves a hole in its footprints.

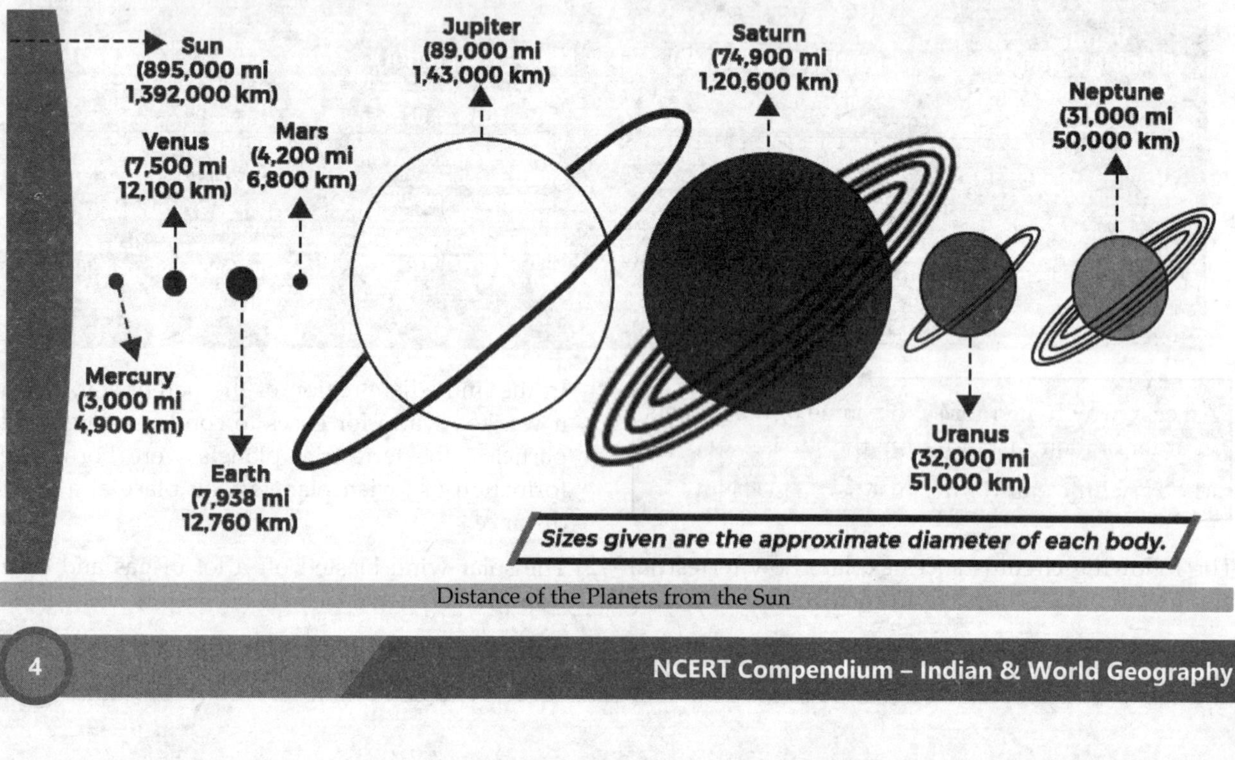

Distance of the Planets from the Sun

Revolution and Rotation of the Planets			
S.No.	**Planet**	**Period of Rotation**	**Period of Revolution**
1	Mercury	58 ½ Days	88 days
2	Venus	243 days	224 days
3	Earth	24 hrs	365 ¼ days
4	Mars	24 ½ days	687 days
5	Jupiter	10 hrs	12 years
6	Saturn	10 ¾ hrs	29 ½ yrs
7	Uranus	17 ¼ hrs	84 years
8	Neptune	16 hrs	165 yrs
9	Pluto (Dwarf planet)	6.4 days	248 yrs

A celestial body that orbits a planet in the same way that planets orbit the Sun is called a **Satellite.**

Neil Armstrong was the first man to step on the surface of the moon on 20 July 1969.

Evolution of the Earth

- At first, the Earth was a hot, rocky, and barren planet with a thin layer of hydrogen and helium in its atmosphere. This is not the same as the modern image of the earth. Therefore, certain processes or events must have occurred for the earth to change from a rocky, arid, and hot planet to a lovely one with plenty of water and an atmosphere that is favourable to life.
- The structure of the Earth is **layered.** The material that is present varies from the earth's centre to the furthest point of the atmosphere.
- The least dense material is found in the atmosphere. The earth's interior is divided into zones that extend from the surface to deeper depths, and each zone includes distinct materials.

The speed of light is around 300,000 km/s. Nevertheless, it still takes the sun's light eight minutes to reach Earth at this speed.

Evolution of Lithosphere

- During its early stages, the Earth was primarily in an unstable state. The temperature inside had risen as a result of the density gradually increasing. Consequently, the materials within began to segregate based on their densities.
- As a result, **lighter materials** gravitated **towards the surface,** and **heavier minerals,** like iron, **sank into** the earth's centre.
- Over time, it cooled even more, hardened, and shrank in size. Eventually, as a result, a crust began to form on the outer surface.
- The earth heated up much more as a result of the massive impact during **the formation of the moon.** The earth-forming material was divided into several layers by the process of **differentiation.**
- We have layers such as the crust, mantle, outer core, and inner core that go from the surface to the inner core. The density of the substance rises from the crust to the core.

Evolution of Atmosphere and Hydrosphere

- The two main elements that make up the earth's atmosphere currently are **Nitrogen and Oxygen.**
- The current atmosphere has undergone **three stages of evolution.** The disappearance of the **original atmosphere** characterises the initial step. The earth's heated interior played a role in the **atmosphere's evolution during the second stage. Lastly, the process of photosynthesis** is the reason how the living world changed the makeup of the atmosphere.
- The early atmosphere, which contained helium and hydrogen, is supposed to have been destroyed **by the solar winds.** This was the case not only for Earth but for all terrestrial planets as well, since solar winds were supposed to have caused them to lose their original atmosphere.
- Water vapour and gases were expelled from the solid earth's interior as it was cooling down. This marked the **beginning of the current atmosphere's evolution.**
- The majority of the elements in the early atmosphere were nitrogen, carbon dioxide, water vapour, ammonia, methane, and very little free oxygen. **Degassing** is the process by which the gases were released from the interior.
- Volcanic eruptions that occurred on a regular basis added gases and water vapour to the atmosphere. The water vapour that had been discharged began to condense as the earth was cooling.

- The temperature dropped and carbon dioxide from the atmosphere began to get dissolved in the rain. This led to increasing condensation and precipitation.
- **Oceans** were created as precipitation fell on the surface and gathered in the depressions. The formation of Earth and its oceans occurred within **500 million years.**
- This indicates that the age of the oceans may reach 4,000 million years. Life started to evolve about **3,800 million years** ago. However, the process of photosynthesis emerged around 2,500–3,000 million years ago.
- Through the process of photosynthesis, oxygen first entered the oceans. Oceans eventually became oxygen-rich, and the atmosphere started to fill with oxygen **2,000 million years ago.**

Origin of Life

- The final stage of Earth's evolution concerns the beginnings and development of life. It is obvious that the early conditions on Earth, or even in the Earth's atmosphere, were not favourable for the emergence of life.
- According to contemporary scientists, complex organic molecules were first created and then formed as a result of some sort of **chemical reaction** that **gave rise to life**.
- Because of their composition, they were able to replicate and turn lifeless objects into living things. Fossils are the remnants of life that once inhabited this planet and can be found in rocks.
- Microstructures that bear a strong resemblance to the current type of blue algae have been discovered in geological strata that date back over 3,000 million years. It is reasonable to suppose that 3,800 million years ago is when life first started to evolve.

Eons	Era	Period	Epoch	Age/ Years Before Present	Life/Major Events
	Cainozoic (From 65 Million years to the present times)	Quaternary	Holocene	0-10,000	Modern Man
			Pleistocene	10,000-2 Million	Homo Sapiens
		Tertiary	Pliocene	2-5 Million	Early Human Ancestor
			Miocene	5-24 Million	Ape: Flowering Plants and Trees
			Oligocene	24-37 Million	Anthropoid Ape
			Eocene	37-58 Million	Rabbits and Hare
			Palaeocene	57-65 Million	Small Mammals : Rats - Mice
	Mesozoic 65-245 Million Mammals	Cretaceous		65-144 Million	Extinction of Dinosaurs
		Jurassic		144-208 Million	Age of Dinosaurs
		Triassic		208-245 Million	Frogs and turtles
	Palaeozoic 245-570 Million	Permian		245-286 Million	Reptile dominate-replace amphibians
		Carboniferous		286-360 Million	First Reptiles: Vertebrates; Coal beds Amphibians
		Devonian		360-408 Million	First trace of life on land: Plants
		Silurian		408-438 Million	First Fish
		Ordovician		438-505 Million	No terrestrial Life : Marine Invertebrate
		Cambrian		505-570 Million	
Proterozoic	Pre-Cambrian 570 Million -4,800 Millionn			570-2,500 Million	Soft-bodied arthropods
Archean				2,500-3,800 Million	Blue green Algae: Unicellular bacteria
Hadean				3,800-4,800 Million	Oceans and Continents form - Ocean and Atmosphere are rich in Carbon dioxide
Origin of Stars	5,000-13,700 Million			5,000 Million	Origin of the sun
Supernova				12,000 Million	
Big Bang				13,700 Million	Origin of the universe

Geological Time Scale

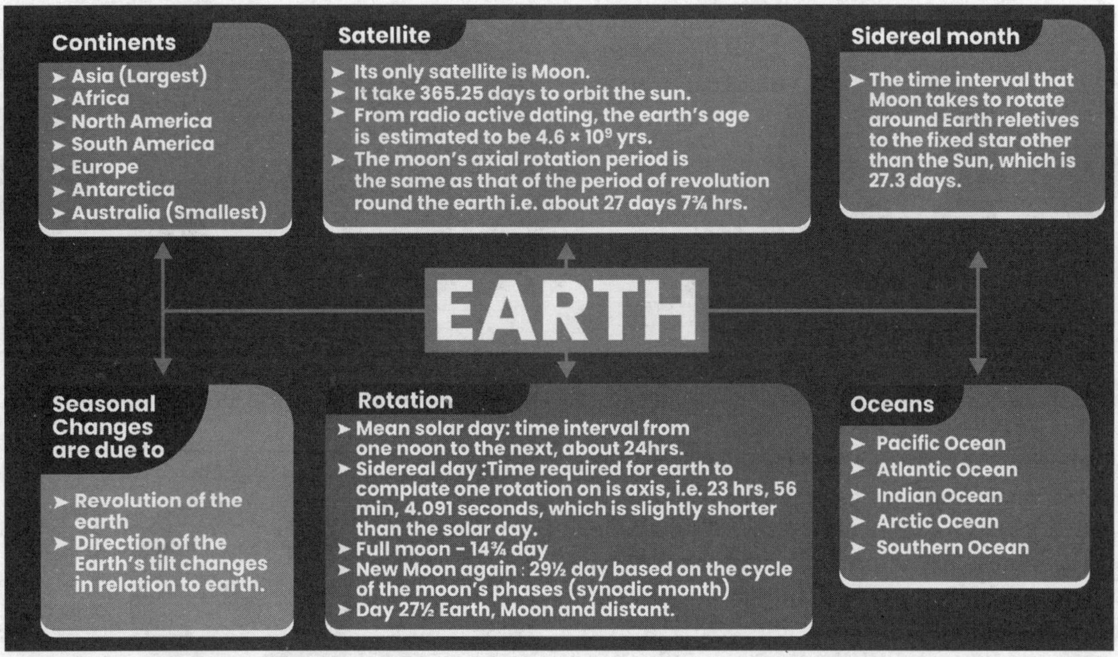

Interior of the Earth

The processes taking place inside the earth have a significant impact on how the surface of the planet is arranged. Both **endogenic and exogenic processes are continuously reshaping the landscape**.

Sources of Information about the Interior

The **radius of the Earth is 6,370 kilometres.** Nobody is able to make observations or get material samples from the Earth's core. Our understanding of the earth's interior is primarily derived from estimates and deductions. However, some of the data is gathered by means of in-person observations and material examination.

Direct Sources

- The easiest solid earth material to obtain is surface rock, or the rocks that are extracted from **mining regions.**
- In addition to mining, scientists are working on other initiatives to reach lower depths and investigate the conditions in the crust. Two significant programmes, the **"Deep Ocean Drilling Project" and the "Integrated Ocean Drilling Project,"** are being worked on by scientists worldwide.
- A further direct information source is **volcanic eruptions.** During a volcanic eruption, the molten material (magma) falls onto the earth's surface and becomes accessible for laboratory investigation. It is challenging to determine the depth of the magma's source, though.

Indirect Sources

- **Temperature, Pressure and density-** As a consequence of our mining operations, we are aware that as we descend farther into the interior, both temperature and pressure rise. Furthermore, it is well known that the material's density rises with depth. The rate at which these properties change can be determined. Scientists have estimated the temperature, pressure, and material density at various depths by using knowledge of the earth's overall thickness.
- **Meteors- The meteors** that occasionally get to Earth are another source of knowledge. It should be highlighted, however, that the material that meteors provide for study does not originate from the earth's interior. The composition and structure of the meteors are comparable to those of Earth. These are solid bodies made of materials either identical to or comparable to those of our planet. As a result, this **adds another source of knowledge about the earth's innards.**

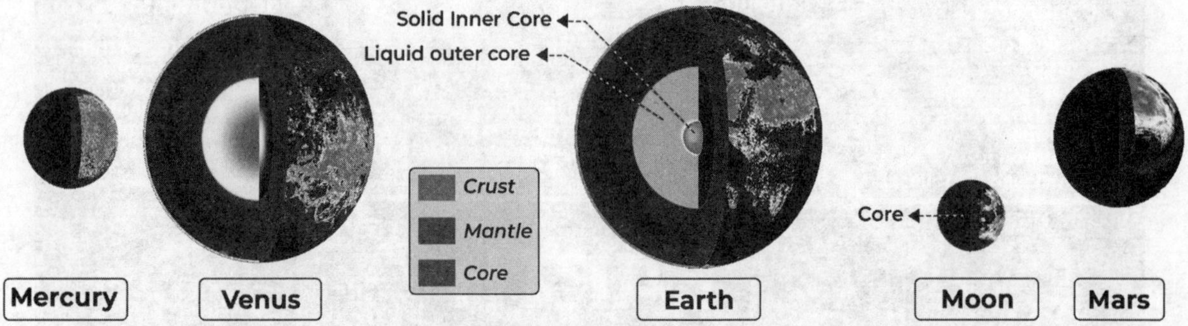

Interior Structure of the Planets

- **Gravitation-** At various surface latitudes, **the gravitational force (g)** is not constant. At the equator, it is less and increases towards the poles. This is because of the distance from the centre at the equator being greater than that at the poles. The mass of the substance affects the gravity measurements as well. This number is influenced by the unequal distribution of material mass within the planet. Numerous other factors also affect the gravity reading at different locations. The readings do not match the predicted values. We can learn more about the distribution of mass in the earth's crust from gravity anomalies.
- **Magnetic field-** In addition to providing information about the distribution of materials in the crust, magnetic surveys also reveal information about the distribution of magnetic materials in this region.
- **Seismic activity-** One of the most significant sources of knowledge about the earth's interior is seismic activity. Seismic wave research offers a comprehensive view of the interior's layers.

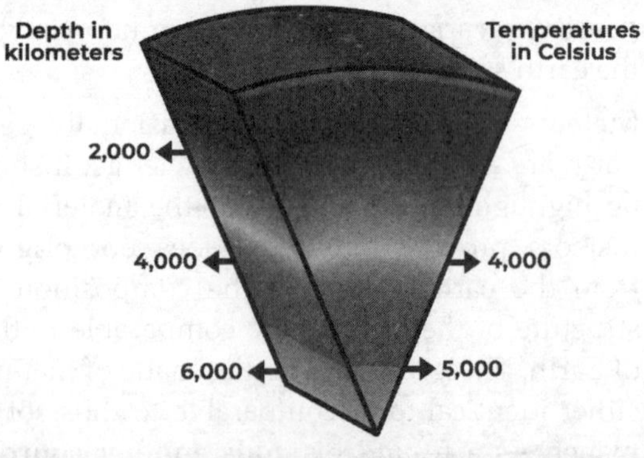

Temperatures in the Earth

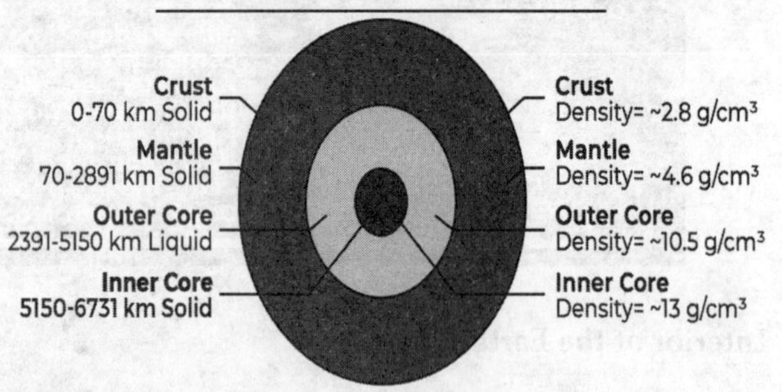

Increasing Density from Crust to Core

Earthquake

An earthquake in simple words is the shaking of the earth. It is a natural event. It is caused due to release of energy, which generates waves that travel in all directions.

Why does the Earth Shake?

The release of energy occurs along a **fault**. A fault is a sharp break in the crustal rocks. Rocks along a fault tend to move in opposite directions. As the overlying rock strata press them, the friction locks them together. However, their tendency to move apart at some point of time overcomes the friction. As a result, the blocks get deformed and eventually, they slide past one another abruptly. This causes a release of energy, and the energy waves travel in all directions. The point where the energy is released is called the **focus** of an earthquake, alternatively, it is called the **hypocentre**. The energy waves travelling in different directions reach the surface. The point on the surface, nearest to the focus, is called **epicentre**. It is the first one to experience the waves. It is a point directly above the focus.

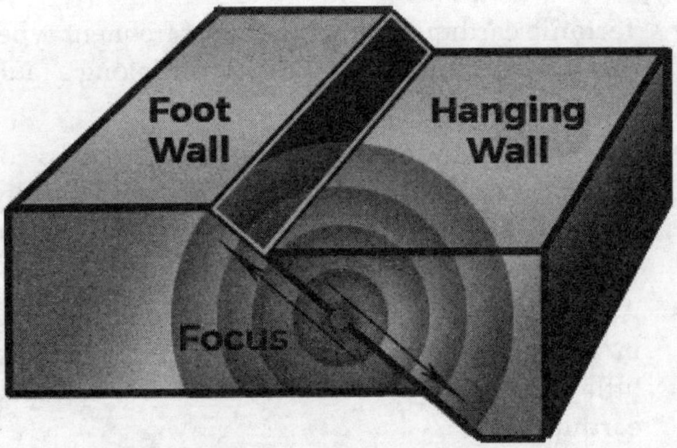

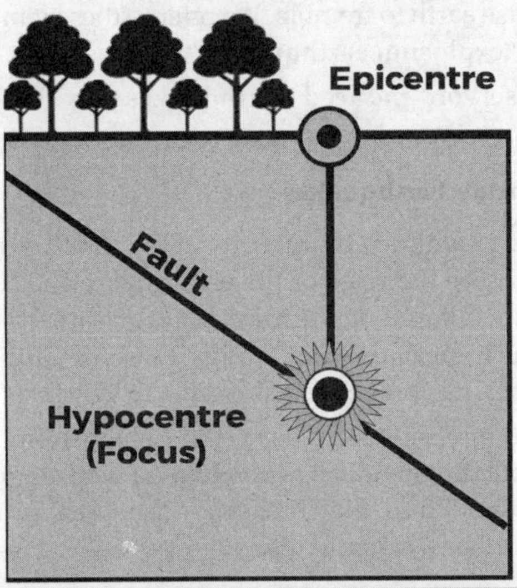

Focus & Epicentre

Earthquake Waves

All natural earthquakes take place in the lithosphere. The waves that reach the surface are recorded by a device known as a **"Seismograph."**

There are essentially two types of earthquake waves: surface waves and body waves.

- **Body waves** flow through the earth's body in all directions as a result of energy being released at the focus. Thus, they are called body waves. There are two types of body waves, **P and S-waves**.
  - **P-waves** move faster and are the first to arrive at the surface. These are also called **'Primary Waves'**. The P-waves are similar to sound waves. They travel through gaseous, liquid and solid materials.
  - **S-waves** take some time to reach the surface. We refer to these as **Secondary Waves**. One crucial aspect of S-waves is their limited ability to pass through only solid objects. This is a very significant S-wave property. It has aided scientists in their understanding of the composition of the earth's interior.
- **Surface waves** are created when the body waves interact with the rocks on the surface. These waves travel parallel to the top layer.
  - When waves pass through various densities of materials, their velocity changes. The velocity increases with the increase in material density.
  - When they come into contact with materials that have varying densities, their orientation also shifts due to reflection or refraction.
  - Waves move in different directions when they are refracted, whereas they come back when they are reflected.
  - The waves at the surface are the last to register on the seismograph. These waves cause more damage. They result in the shifting of rocks, which leads to the collapse of buildings.

Propagation of Earthquake Waves

- Different types of earthquake waves travel in different manners. **P-waves** vibrate in a direction parallel to the wave. In the direction of propagation, this applies pressure to the material. Consequently, it causes variations in the material's density, which causes the material to stretch and compress.
- Other waves vibrate in a direction that is **perpendicular** to the direction of propagation. **S-wave** vibrations occur perpendicular to the direction of waves in the vertical plane. As a result, they cause crests and troughs in the material they move through.

Emergence of Shadow Zone

Seismographs, which are situated in far areas, record the waves produced by earthquakes. There are, nevertheless, several localities where the waves are not recorded. We refer to this area as the **"Shadow Zone."**

- Seismographs at any distance within 105° of the epicentre, were found to record the arrival of both P and S-waves. Seismographs farther 145° away from the epicentre, however, register the arrival of P-waves but not S-waves. This means that the **shadow zone for both wave types was found to be between 105° and 145° from the epicentre**.
- S-waves are not received in the entire zone above 105°. Compared to P-waves, the shadow zone of an S-wave is substantially larger. The earth's shadow zone for P-waves is a band that extends from 105° to 145° from the epicentre. Not only is the S-wave shadow zone more expansive, but it also makes up somewhat more than 40% of the earth surface.

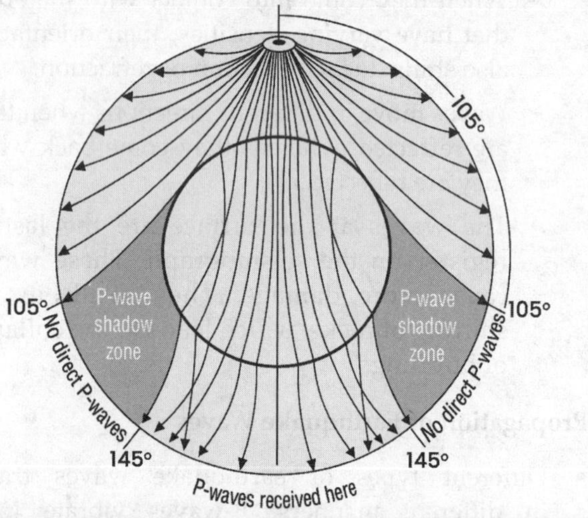

P- wave Shadow Zone

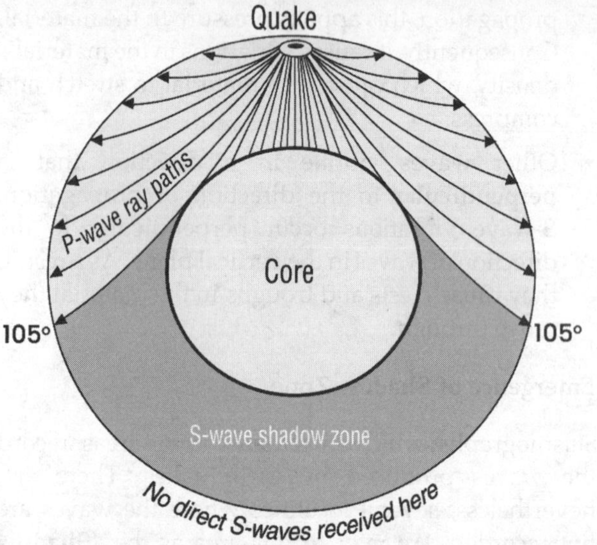

S- wave Shadow Zone

Types of Earthquakes

- **Tectonic** earthquakes are the most frequent type. These are produced when rocks slide along a fault plane.
- **Volcanic earthquakes** are a specific class of tectonic earthquakes that are occasionally recognised. These are limited to regions where **volcanoes are still active**, though.
- At times, the roofs of underground mines fall in regions with high mining activity, creating little tremors. We refer to these as **collapse earthquakes**.
- Chemical or nuclear device explosions can also cause earth to tremble. We refer to these vibrations as **"explosion earthquakes."**
- **Reservoir induced earthquakes** are those that happen near large reservoirs.

Measuring Earthquakes

- The magnitude or intensity of the shock is used to measure the scale of the earthquake. The **Richter scale** is based on the magnitude of the earthquake which **measures the energy released** during the earthquake. The scale is from **1 to 10.**
- The intensity scale bears the Italian seismologist **Mercalli's name**. The event's evident damage is factored into the intensity scale. **The intensity** scale has a range of **1 to 12**.

Effects of Earthquake

Earthquake is a natural hazard. The following are the immediate hazardous effects of earthquake:

1. Ground Shaking
2. Differential ground settlement
3. Land and mudslides
4. Soil liquefaction
5. Ground lurching
6. Avalanches
7. Ground displacement
8. Floods from dam and levee failures
9. Fires
10. Structural collapse
11. Falling objects
12. Tsunami

EARTHQUAKE

- An earthquake is a sudden shaking or trembling of a part of the earth's crust which results in tremors and vibrations. An earthquake can be either a volcanic earthquake or a tectonic earthquake.
- Volcanic earthquakes occur along with a volcanic eruption and the tectonic earthquakes are caused by their deformation or displacement in rocks.
- Focus is the point of origin of the earthquake and also called Hypocentre.
- Epicentre is the point above the focus on the surface where the waves are first felt.

Measurements

1 Richter Scale

The strength of an earthquake is known as its magnitude, which is measured in Richter scale. Magnitude is the amount of energy released during the earthquake.

2 Mercalli Scale

The intensity of an earthquake is measured using this device. Intensity is the visible amount of damage caused by the earthquake.

PRIMARY WAVES

- They are also called P- Waves.
- They're the first to be recorded on seismograph.
- Particles vibrate parallel to the direction of propagation of the wave.
- It travels at a speed of 8 Km/sec.

SECONDARY WAVES

- They are also called S-Waves
- They're recorded after the P-Waves.
- Particles vibrate perpendicular to the direction of propagation of the wave
- It travels at a speed of 5 Km/sec.

SURFACE WAVES

- They're also called L- Waves.
- They're the last to be recorded on the seismograph.
- These waves are responsible for the wide scale visible damage on the surface of the earth.
- It travels at a speed of 4 Km/sec.

Causes for Earthquake

- Volcanicity
- Anthropogenic Effect
- Tectonic Causes (Folding & Faulting)
- Impact of Meteorite

Only when the earthquake's epicentre is below oceanic waters and its magnitude is large enough a tsunami would arise. Waves caused by earthquakes are known as **tsunami**. Even though the actual seismic activity only lasts a few seconds, if the quake's magnitude is more than 5, its consequences can be disastrous.

	Continental Drift	See Floor Spreading	Plate Tectonics
Explained by	Put forward by **Alfred Wegener** in 1920s	**Arthur Holmes** explained Convectional Current Theory in the 1930s. Based on convection current theory, **Harry Hess** explained See Floor Spreading in the 1940s	In 1967, **McKenzie and Parker** suggested the theory of plate tectonics. **Morgan** later outlined the theory in 1968
Theory	Explains the Movement of Continents only	Explains the Movement of Oceanic Plates only	Explains the Movement of Lithospheric plates that include both continents and oceans.
Forces for movement	Buoyancy, gravity, pole-fleeing force, tidal currents, tides	Convection currents in the mantle drag crustal plates	Convection currents in the mantle drag crustal plates
Evidence	Apparent affinity of physical features, botanical evidence, fossil evidence, Tillite deposits, placer deposits, rocks of same age across different continents etc.	Ocean bottom relief, Palaeomagnetic rocks, distribution of earthquakes and volcanoes etc.	Ocean bottom relief, Palaeomagnetic rocks, distribution of earthquakes and volcanoes, gravitational anomalies at trenches, etc.
Drawbacks	Too general and sometimes illogical evidence.	Doesn't explain the movement of continental plates	-----------------
Acceptance	Discarded	Not complete	Most widely accepted
Usefulness	Helped in the evolution of convection current theory and seafloor spreading theory	Helped in the evolution of plate tectonics theory	Helped us understand various geographical features.

Volcanoes and Volcanic Landforms

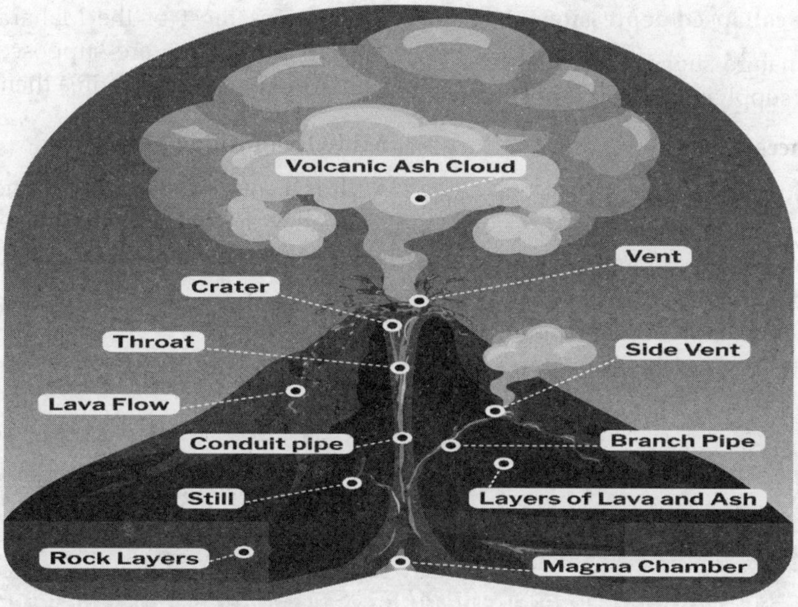

Volcanoes

- A volcano is a place where gases, ashes and/or molten rock material, lava, escape to the ground.
- **A volcano is called an active volcano** if the materials mentioned are being released or have been released in the recent past.
- The layer below the solid crust is mantle. It has a higher density than that of the crust. The mantle contains a weaker zone called the **asthenosphere**.
- It is from **asthenosphere** that the molten rock materials find their way to the surface. The material in the upper mantle portion is called **magma**. Once it starts moving towards the crust or it reaches the surface, it is referred to as **lava**.
- Lava flows contain various things which are carried to the ground like: pyroclastic debris, volcanic bombs, ash, dust, and gases like nitrogen and sulphur compounds. Trace amounts of hydrogen, argon, and chlorine, are among the materials that carry it to the ground.

Classification of Volcanoes

Volcanoes are classified on the grounds of the nature of eruption and the form developed at the surface. Important types of volcanoes are as follows:

Shield Volcanoes

- The shield volcanoes are the biggest volcanoes on earth, excluding the basalt flows. The most well-known examples are the **volcanoes in Hawaii**.
- The majority of the lava in these volcanoes is basalt, which erupts with great fluidity. Because of this, these volcanoes are not steep.
- They usually have low-explosivity, becoming explosive only if water manages to enter inside the vent. The approaching lava flows like a fountain, ejected from the top of the vent, and eventually turns into a **cinder cone**.

Composite Volcanoes

- Lavas that are **more viscous and colder** than basalt, emerge from these volcanoes. These volcanoes frequently erupt catastrophically. Massive amounts of pyroclastic debris and ashes fall to the ground with the lava.
- The material builds up near the vent entrances, resulting in the creation of layers that give the mounts the appearance of **composite volcanoes**.

Caldera

- Of all the volcanoes on Earth, these are the most explosive. Because they are typically so explosive, when they erupt, they usually collapse on themselves rather than building any tall structure. **Calderas are the collapsed depressions**.

- Their explosive nature suggests that the massive magma chamber supplying the lava is not far away.

Flood Basalt Provinces

- The lava ejected by these volcanoes is extremely fluid and flows across great distances. **Thick basalt lava** flows spanning thousands of square kilometres cover-up many regions of the planet. A sequence of floods may occur, some of which may reach thicknesses of over 50 m. Flows can be hundreds of km long.
- **The Deccan Traps** in India are a significantly larger province of flood basalt that currently occupies most of the Maharashtra plateau. The trap formations are supposed to have formerly covered a far greater area than they do now.

Mid-Ocean Ridge Volcanoes

- It is a continuous range of underwater volcanoes that wraps around the globe, stretching nearly 70,000 kilometers.
- Frequent eruptions occur in the centre portion of this ridge.

VOLCANOES

A volcano is a vent or an opening on the earth's crust, through which hot molten materials erupt from the interior. The eruption of materials from the interior of the earth's crust may occur with huge explosions or quietly in nature.

There are three types of volcanoes
This classification is based on the frequency of eruption

Active Volcanoes

It erupts frequently. Most of the active volcanoes are formed along the mid oceanic ridges. Mauna Loa in Hawaii island is the largest active volcano of the world. The Barren island is the only active volcano in India.

Dormant Volcanoes

They are called sleeping volcanoes. These volcanoes were active in the past, stopped ejecting lava now, but it can erupt at any time in the future. Ex: Vesuvius of Italy, Mauna Kea of Hawaii.

Extinct Volcanoes

They are also called dead volcanoes. They erupted in the past but they did not do so recently & in future it is expected there will not be any eruptions. Ex: Mt. Kilimanjaro of Africa, Narcondam Island of Andaman island, Tiruvannamalai hills of Tamil Nadu, Panaka hills of Andhra Pradesh.

Volcanic Landforms

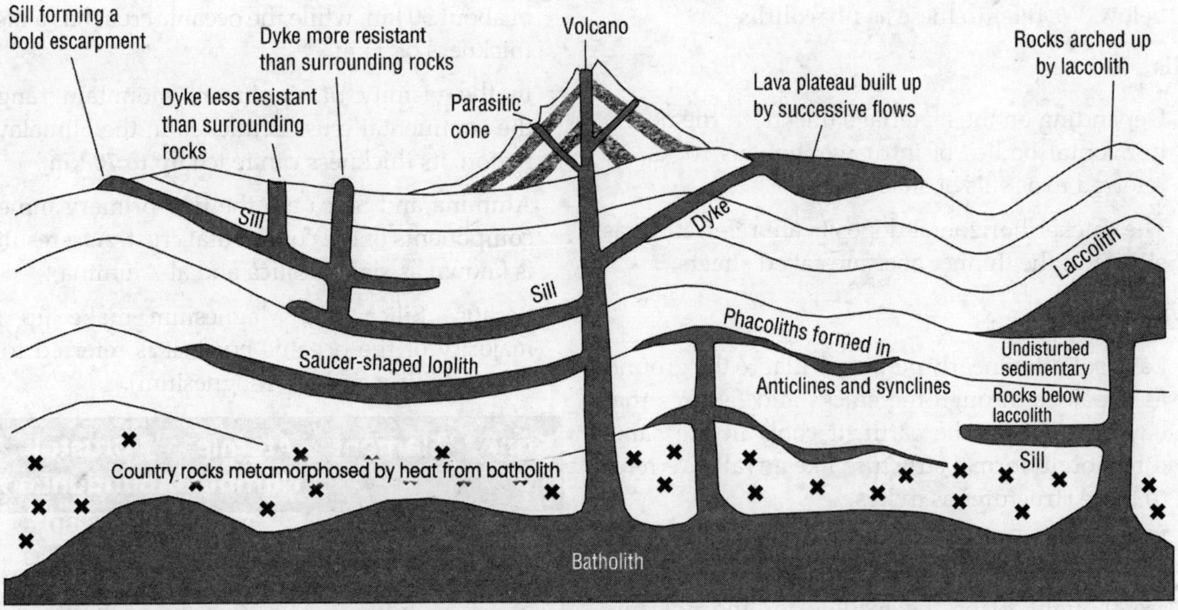

Volcanic Landforms

Intrusive Forms

- When the lava cools down inside the crust, it takes on various shapes. We refer to these kinds as **invasive (intrusive) forms.**
- **Igneous rocks** are formed when the lava spilled during volcanic eruptions cools down. Either when the lava reaches the surface or while it is still under the crust, cooling may occur.
- Igneous rocks are categorised as **volcanic rocks** (cooling at the surface) or **plutonic rocks** (cooling in the crust) based on where the lava is cooling.

Batholiths

- Huge domes arise when a substantial mass of **magmatic material cools** at the crust's lower depths.
- Only until the overlaying materials are removed by denudational processes do they become visible on the surface.
- They are spread over vast areas and occasionally go down to depths of many kilometres. These entities are granitic. The **cooled part of magma chambers is called a batholith**.

Lacoliths

- These are enormous, invasive, dome-shaped bodies that are connected from below by a conduit that resembles a pipe.
- It is similar to the volcanic domes on the surface of composite volcanoes, but it is situated at a **greater depth**. You may think of it as the confined source of lava that rises to the surface.
- There are scattered granite rock hills of dome shape on the **Karnataka plateau**. The majority of them, which have left their outermost layer, are lacoliths or batholiths.

Lapolith

- Wherever it encounters a weak plane, some of the lava may have a tendency to travel horizontally as it flows higher.
- It may take on several forms. If it becomes concave to the sky body and takes on the shape of a saucer, it is referred to as a **lapolith**.

Phacolith

- In folded igneous land, an undulating mass of intrusive rocks can occasionally be found at the top of anticlines or at the base of synclines.

- These wavy materials have a distinct channel to the magma chambers (later evolved as batholiths) below. We refer to these as **phacoliths**.

Sills

- Depending on the material's thickness, the nearly horizontal bodies of intrusive igneous rocks are referred to as sills or sheets.
- The thicker horizontal deposits are referred to as **sills**, and the thinner ones are called **sheets.**

Dykes

- Lava solidifies nearly perpendicular to the ground as it passes through the cracks and fissures that have formed in the earth. It cools in the same direction to form a structure like a wall. We refer to these structures as **dykes**.
- In the Western Maharashtra region, these are the most frequently observed invasive types. These are thought to be the feeders for the volcanic eruptions that gave rise to the Deccan traps.

STRUCTURE OF THE EARTH

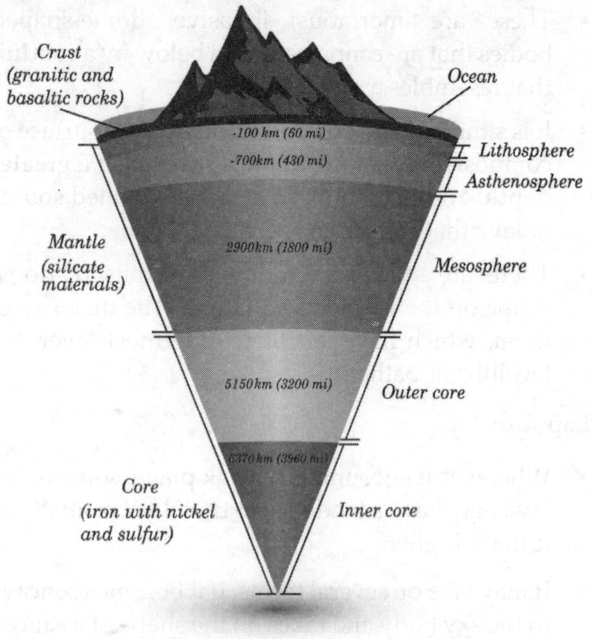

Structure of the Earth

The Crust

- It is the earth's outermost solid region. Its nature is **Brittle**. Beneath the marine and continental regions, the crust has **different thicknesses.**
- **The oceanic crust** is **less thick** than the **continental crust**. The continental crust has a mean thickness of about 30 km, while the oceanic crust has a mean thickness of 5 km.
- In the vicinity of significant mountain ranges, the continental crust is thicker. In the Himalayan region, its thickness can reach **up to 70 km**.
- Alumina and Silica are the two primary mineral components of the continental crust. As a result, it is known as **sial** (si-Silica and al-Alumina).
- Because Silica and Magnesium make up the majority of the oceanic crust, it is referred to as **sima** (si-Silica and ma-Magnesium).

Rank	Element	Atomic Number	Crustal Abundance %
1	Oxygen	8	46.60
2	Silicon	14	27.70
3	Aluminium	13	8.13
4	Iron	26	5.00
5	Calcium	20	3.63
6	Sodium	11	2.83
7	Magnesium	12	2.59
8	Potassium	19	2.09
9	Titanium	22	0.44
10	Hydrogen	1	0.14
10+	Others		0.85

The Mantle

- The mantle is the term for the part of the interior that is located below the crust. From **Moho's discontinuity**, the mantle descends to a **depth of 2,900 kilometres.**
- **The asthenosphere** is the term for the uppermost part of the mantle. Astheno is the term for **weak.** It is projected to extend up to **400 kilometres.** During volcanic eruptions, it is the **primary source** of magma that rises to the surface.
- The term "lithosphere" refers to the crust and the topmost portion of the mantle. Its thickness is **between 10 and 200 km.** Beyond the asthenosphere lies the lower mantle. It is **in solid state.**

The Core

- The earth's core's existence was clarified by the earthquake wave velocities. The depth of the **core-mantle boundary is 2,900 kilometres.**

- The inner core is solid, whereas the outer core is in liquid state. **Iron and Nickel** make up the majority of the extremely heavy material that makes up the core. It is also known as the **nife** layer at times.

Nearly 1% of the earth's volume is formed from the crust; the remaining 84% is formed from the mantle, and the remaining 15% is the core.

Motions of the Earth

The two distinct motions of the earth include rotation and revolution.

- The earth moves on its axis during **rotation**.
- **Revolution** is the term used to describe the earth's fixed orbit or route around the sun.
- The imaginary axis of the earth forms an angle of **66 1/2°** with the plane of its orbit. **The orbital plane is the plane that the orbit forms.**
- The sun provides light for the earth. Only half of the planet receives light from the sun at a time due to its spherical form.
- Half of it faces the sun seen as **day**, while the other half faces the opposite direction, which is seen as **night**.
- The **circle of illumination** is the line that, on a globe, separates day from night. **The axes and this circle do not align.**
- About twenty-four hours is needed for the earth to complete one rotation on its axis. **The Earth day** is the name given to the time of rotation. This shows how the earth moves daily.

What Would Happen if the Earth Stopped Rotating?

The part of the earth that faces the sun would constantly be bright, providing constant warmth to that area. The other half would always be in the dark and extremely cold. Under such harsh circumstances, life would not have been feasible.

The ancient Indian astronomer Aryabhata had stated that 'the earth is round and rotates on its own axis'.

- **Revolution** refers to the earth's second motion in its orbit around the sun. A year, or 365 1/4 days, is needed for one orbit around the sun.
- For convenience's sake, we disregard six hours and count a year as having 365 days. **Over the course of four years, six hours saved annually are added to create one day (24 hours). The month of February is extended by one day. As a result, February has 29 days rather than 28 every fourth year. Leap years are those with 366 days in a year.**
- The orbit of the earth around the sun is **elliptical**. The earth is **tilted** in the same direction throughout its orbit.
- The seasons of summer, winter, spring, and autumn often comprise a year. The earth's tilted rotation around the sun causes the seasons to change.

Summer Solstice

- The Northern Hemisphere is inclined towards the sun **on June 21**. The **Tropic of Cancer** is directly exposed to solar radiation. These regions thus experience increased heat. Because the sun's beams are slanted, the regions close to the poles receive less heat.
- Because the **North Pole** is oriented towards the sun, areas outside of the **Arctic Circle** receive constant daylight for almost half the year.
- It is summer in the areas **north of the equator** because the sun shines on a huge chunk of the Northern Hemisphere. June 21 is the day with the **longest day and the shortest night** in these locations.
- All of these circumstances are currently inverted in the **Southern Hemisphere**. There, winter is in full swing. The days are shorter than the nights. The **Summer Solstice** occurs at this point in the earth's orbit.

Winter Solstice

- On **December 22**, the South Pole tilts towards the **Tropic of Capricorn**, bringing direct sunlight to the region. A greater area of the Southern Hemisphere receives light when solar radiation falls vertically at the Tropic of Capricorn (23 and 1/2° S).
- As a result, the **Southern Hemisphere** is experiencing **summer**, which brings **longer days and shorter nights**.
- In the Northern Hemisphere, the opposite occurs. This is called the **Winter Solstice.**

Equinox

- The equator receives direct sunlight on **March 21 and September 23**. Since neither pole is oriented towards the sun in this configuration, the duration of day and night is equal on the entire planet. We refer to this as an **equinox.**

- **Autumn in the Northern Hemisphere** and **spring in the Southern Hemisphere** begin on September 23. On March 21, however, it is the opposite it is fall in the Southern Hemisphere and spring in the Northern Hemisphere.

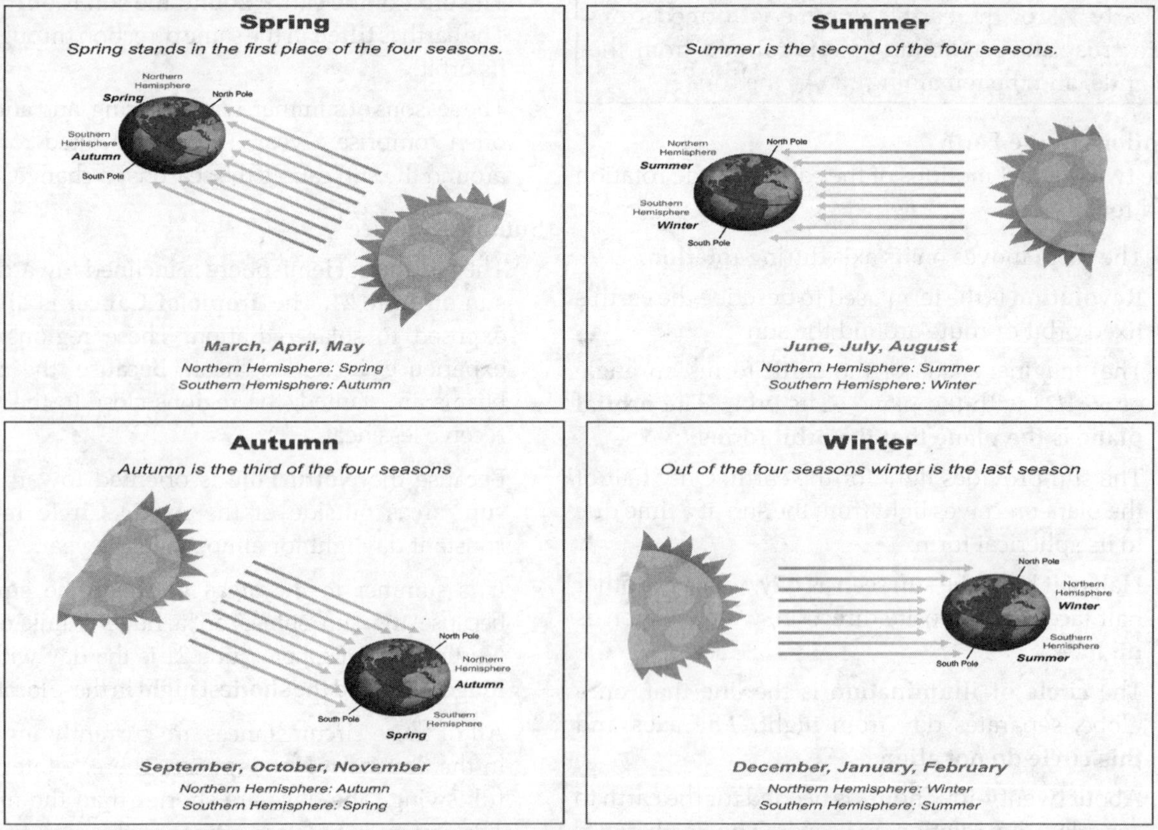

Equinox

Major Domains of the Earth

The surface of the earth is a complicated zone in which three major aspects of the environment meet, overlap and interact.

- The **Lithosphere** is the solid part of the earth where living beings reside.
- The **Atmosphere**, which consists of layers of gases surrounding the planet earth, contains nitrogen, carbon dioxide, oxygen, and other gases.
- The **Hydrosphere** is the vast region of the earth's surface that is covered in water. All kinds of water, including **ice, water, and water vapour**, are included in the hydrosphere.
- **The Biosphere** is the little area that consists of air, water, and land that is home to all living forms.

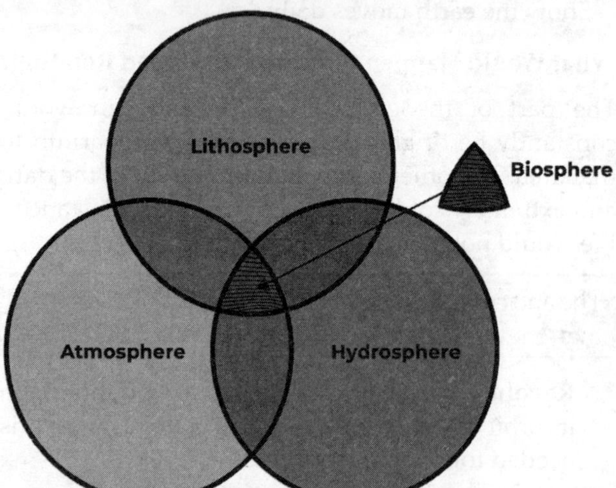

Components of the Environment

Continents and Oceans

The seven main continents are Asia, Europe, Africa, North America, South America, Australia, and Antarctica. These continents are separated by huge bodies of water.

Asia

- The largest continent is Asia. It makes up around one-third of the planet's land area.
- The **Eastern Hemisphere** is where the continent is located. This continent is crossed by the **Tropic of Cancer**.
- The **Ural Mountains divide Asia from Europe** on the western side. **Eurasia (Europe + Asia)** refers to the combined landmass of Europe and Asia.

Europe

- **Asia** is **bigger than Europe**. Europe is located towards the West of Asia.
- The **Arctic Circle** traverses it. It is surrounded on **three sides by bodies of water.**

Africa

- **After Asia, Africa is the second largest continent**.
- The Equator, often known as 0° latitude, nearly passes through the centre of the continent. Africa is mostly located in the Northern Hemisphere.
- The Tropic of Cancer, the Equator, and the Tropic of Capricorn **all pass through this continent**.
- Africa is home to the world's largest hot desert, the **Sahara Desert**. The oceans and seas encircle the continent on all sides.
- Africa is home to the **Nile, the longest river in the world**.

North America

- The third-largest continent on the planet is North America. **The Isthmus of Panama** is a very small land strip that connects it to South America.
- The entirety of the continent is located in both the **Northern and Western Hemispheres.**
- This continent is surrounded by three oceans. These three oceans are the **Pacific, Atlantic, and Arctic**.

South America

- **Southern Hemisphere** includes major portion of South America in it.
- **It is bordered by two oceans,** to the west and east, respectively, which are **the Pacific and Atlantic oceans.**
- Its entire length is passed by the **Andes mountain** range from north to south, which is the longest in the world.
- **The Amazon**, the largest river in the world, is located in South America.

Australia

- The Southern Hemisphere includes complete Australia continent which is smallest of all other continents.
- The oceans and seas cover it from all sides. It is also known as an **island continent.**

Antarctica

- Antarctica is a large continent that lies completely in the Southern Hemisphere.
- This continent has the South Pole at its middle point. Because of its location in the **South Polar Region**, heavy **ice sheets cover it permanently**.
- No human settlements exist permanently.
- **In Antarctica, numerous nations maintain their research centers including India's Maitri and Dakshin Gangotri** research stations.

TEST YOURSELF

Multiple Choice Questions

Q1. The age of the Earth is estimated to be approximately:

(a) 4.5 billion years (b) 1 billion years

(c) 10 million years (d) 100,000 years

Q2. The theory that explains the origin of the universe and the Earth as a result of a massive explosion is known as:

(a) Big Bang Theory

(b) Plate Tectonics Theory

(c) Evolution Theory

(d) Continental Drift Theory

Q3. The process by which the Earth's continents have moved over time is known as:

(a) Tectonic plate movement (b) Erosion

(c) Weathering (d) Volcanism

Q4. The outermost layer of the Earth is known as the:

(a) Crust (b) Mantle

(c) Core (d) Lithosphere

Q5. The movement of tectonic plates is driven by:

(a) Convection currents in the mantle

(b) Earth's rotation

(c) Volcanic activity

(d) Magnetic forces

Q6. The current era in the geologic time scale, characterised by the presence of humans and their impact on the Earth's ecosystems, is called the:

(a) Mesozoic Era (b) Paleozoic Era

(c) Cenozoic Era (d) Precambrian Era

Q7. Which is the thinnest layer of the Earth?

(a) Crust (b) Mantle

(c) Outer Core (d) Inner Core

Q8. The asthenosphere is a part of which layer of the Earth?

(a) Crust (b) Mantle

(c) Outer Core (d) Inner Core

Q9. The outer core of the Earth is primarily composed of:

(a) Liquid iron and nickel

(b) Solid iron and nickel

(c) Magma

(d) Silicate minerals

Q10. The inner core of the Earth is primarily composed of:

(a) Liquid iron and nickel

(b) Solid iron and nickel

(c) Magma

(d) Silicate minerals

Q11. The layer of the Earth responsible for generating the magnetic field is:

(a) Crust (b) Mantle

(c) Outer Core (d) Inner Core

Q12. Which layer of the Earth is directly responsible for volcanic activity?

(a) Crust (b) Mantle

(c) Outer Core (d) Inner Core

Q13. The depth of the Earth's inner core from the crust is approximately:

(a) 5,000 kms (b) 6,000 kms

(c) 7,000 kms (d) 8,000 kms

Q14. Which layer of the Earth is thickest?

(a) Crust (b) Mantle

(c) Outer Core (d) Inner Core

Q15. What is the primary cause of an earthquake?

(a) Volcanic eruption

(b) Plate tectonic movement

(c) Underground mining activities

(d) Groundwater extraction

Q16. The point within the Earth where an earthquake originates is called the:

(a) Centre (b) Epicentre

(c) Focus (d) Seismic wave

Q17. The point on the Earth's surface directly above the focus of an earthquake is called the:

(a) Hypocentre (b) Epicentre

(c) Focus (d) Seismic wave

Q18. The instrument used to measure the intensity of an earthquake is called a:

(a) Seismograph (b) Barometer

(c) Thermometer (d) Anemometer

Q19. The scale used to measure the magnitude of an earthquake is called the:

(a) Richter scale (b) Mercalli scale

(c) Beaufort scale (d) Celsius scale

Q20. Which type of seismic wave arrives first at a seismograph station?

(a) P-waves (b) S-waves

(c) Surface waves (d) L-waves

Q21. Which type of seismic wave causes the most damage to buildings and infrastructure?

(a) P-waves (b) S-waves

(c) Surface waves (d) L-waves

Q22. Which of the following regions is most prone to earthquakes?

(a) Coastal areas

(b) Plateau regions

(c) Mountainous regions

(d) All regions have equal risk

Q23. The study of earthquakes is known as:

(a) Seismology (b) Volcanology

(c) Geomorphology (d) Meteorology

Q24. Which ocean is the largest on Earth?

(a) Pacific Ocean (b) Atlantic Ocean

(c) Indian Ocean (d) Southern Ocean

Q25. The continents are primarily located in which hemisphere of the Earth?

(a) Northern Hemisphere

(b) Southern Hemisphere

(c) Eastern Hemisphere

(d) Western Hemisphere

Q26. Which of the following is not considered one of the seven continents?

(a) Africa (b) Australia

(c) Antarctica (d) Greenland

Q27. The boundary between the North American and South American continents is defined by which geographic feature?

(a) The Isthmus of Panama

(b) Panama City

(c) Amazon River

(d) Andes Mountains

Q28. The largest oceanic ridge system on Earth is known as:

(a) Mid-Atlantic Ridge (b) East Pacific Rise

(c) Mariana Trench (d) Himalayan Range

Q29. The Red Sea is a narrow sea that separates which two continents?

(a) Africa and Europe

(b) Africa and Asia

(c) Asia and Europe

(d) North America and South America

Q30. What is a volcano?

(a) A large body of water

(b) A mountain made of rocks

(c) A vent in the Earth's crust through which molten rock and gases escape

(d) A deep trench in the ocean floor

Q31. Which type of volcano has a broad, gently sloping cone?

(a) Composite volcano (b) Shield volcano

(c) Cinder cone volcano (d) Stratovolcano

Q32. Which type of volcano is characterised by alternating layers of lava and pyroclastic materials?

(a) Composite volcano (b) Shield volcano

(c) Cinder cone volcano (d) Stratovolcano

Q33. Which type of volcano is relatively small in size and has steep sides?

(a) Composite volcano (b) Shield volcano

(c) Cinder cone volcano (d) Stratovolcano

Q34 The opening at the top of a volcano is called:

(a) Crater (b) Magma chamber

(c) Caldera (d) Vent

Q35. Which type of volcano is known for its explosive eruptions and steep slopes?

(a) Composite volcano (b) Shield volcano

(c) Cinder cone volcano (d) Stratovolcano

Q36. The molten rock beneath the Earth's surface is called:

(a) Lava (b) Magma

(c) Pyroclastic materical (d) Ash

Q37. What is the term for an eruption that involves the ejection of a mixture of hot gases, ash, cinders, and bombs?

(a) Pyroclastic flow (b) Lava flow

(c) Lahar (d) Ash cloud

Q38. The largest volcano on Earth is:

(a) Mount Kilimanjaro (b) Mount Vesuvius

(c) Mauna Loa (d) Mount St. Helens

Q39. The study of volcanoes is called:

(a) Vulcanology (b) Seismology

(c) Geomorphology (d) Petrology

Answer Key

Q1.	a	Q2.	a	Q3.	a	Q4.	a
Q5.	a	Q6	c	Q7.	a	Q8	b
Q9	a	Q10.	b	Q11.	c	Q12.	b
Q13.	b	Q14.	b	Q15.	b	Q16	c
Q17.	b	Q18.	a	Q19.	a	Q20.	a
Q21.	c	Q22.	c	Q23.	a	Q24.	a
Q25.	a	Q26.	d	Q27.	a	Q28.	a
Q29.	b	Q30.	c	Q31.	b	Q32.	a
Q33.	c	Q34	a	Q35.	a	Q36.	b
Q37.	a	Q38.	c	Q39.	a		

Model Questions for Main Examination

Q1. Write a short note on theories related to the origin and evolution of earth.

Q2. Discuss the evolution of the layered structure of the Earth along with the formation of the lithosphere, hydrosphere and atmosphere. (UPSC 2020)

UNIT 2

Globe: Latitudes and Longitudes

In This Unit

Comprehensive and profound coverage of the following NCERT's chapters:

- ✓ NCERT Class- 6th (The Earth: Our Habitat), Chapters- 2 and 6
- ✓ NCERT Class- 9th (Contemporary India), Chapter- 1
- ✓ NCERT Class- 11th (India Physical Environment), Chapter- 1

- **Globe** is a true model (miniature form) of the earth. **The axis** is a needle that is fixed through the globe at some tilt. **The North and South Poles** are the two points on planet Earth that the needle passes through.
- The globe can be rotated around this needle in the same **west-east direction** as the earth moves. But keep in mind there is a significant distinction. There is no such needle on the real planet. It revolves around an imaginary line known as its axis.
- Partitioned into two equal sections, the globe is segmented by another imaginary line. We refer to this line as the **equator**.
- The terms **"Northern Hemisphere"** and **"Southern Hemisphere"** refer to the two halves of our planet, respectively the Northern part and the Southern part. Both of them are equal parts, divided by the equator which is an imaginary circular line.
- All circles that are parallel from the equator to the poles are referred to as **latitude parallels. Degrees** are used to measure latitudes.
- **The equator denotes the latitude of zero degrees.** The equator and either poles are at a distance one-fourth of a circle around the planet, hence the distance between them is one-fourth of 360 degrees, or 90°. **The North Pole** is therefore located at **90 degrees north latitude**, and the **South Pole** is located at **90 degrees south latitude.**
- **"North latitudes"** are all parallels that are located north of the equator. Likewise, any parallel that lies south of the equator is referred to as a **"south latitude."**

By measuring the angle of the Pole Star from your place, you can know the latitude of your place.

Our Country – India

India is a country of large geographical area. It is surrounded by the mighty Himalayas in the North, and in the west by the Arabian Sea. In the east it is bound by the Bay of Bengal and the Indian Ocean in the south, along the Indian Peninsula's coastlines.

Locational Setting

- India is situated in the northern hemisphere. **The Tropic of Cancer (23°30′N)** cuts across the country.
- Mainland of India spreads from **South to North**, between **8°4′N** and **37°6′N** latitudes. India spreads, between **68°7′E** and **97°25′E** longitudes from **west to east**.
- Because of its extensive longitudinal extent of around 29°, locations situated at India's two extremes may experience a broad variety of variations in local time.
- Consequently, there is a two-hour gap between these two places. The sun rises about two hours earlier in the east (Arunachal Pradesh) than in the west (Gujarat).

- The national standard time for the entire country is determined by measuring the length of the **Standard Meridian** of India, which passes through Mirzapur, Uttar Pradesh, at 82°30′E.

> The southernmost point of the Indian Union **'Indira Point'** in the Great Nicobar group of Islands is not visible anymore after the 2004 Indian Ocean Tsunami.

> Large countries which stretch extensively from east to west do not have a single Standard Time for the whole country. The USA and Canada have seven and six time zones respectively

Size

- The land mass of India has an area of **3.28 million square km**. India's total area accounts for **about 2.4 per cent** of the total geographical area of the world.
- **India is the seventh largest country in the world.**
- India has a land boundary of about 15,200 km and the total length of the coastline of the mainland, including Andaman and Nicobar and Lakshadweep, is 7,516.6 km.
- It stretches roughly 3,200 km **north-south** from Ladakh to Kanyakumari and 2,900 km **east-west** from Arunachal Pradesh to Kachchh.
- India has a population of over one hundred-forty crore in mid-2023, surpassing China as the most populous country in the world according to UN data.

India and the World

- The Indian landmass has a central location between East and West Asia. India is a southward extension of the Asian continent.
- **The trans Indian Ocean routes**, which connect the countries of Europe in the West and the countries of East Asia, provide a strategic central location to India.
- The **Deccan Peninsula** protrudes into the Indian Ocean, thus helping India to establish close contact with West Asia, Africa and Europe from the western coast and with Southeast and East Asia from the eastern coast.
- India is the only nation with a longer coastline in the Indian Ocean, and its prominent position in the region allows the naming of an ocean after it.

> Since the opening of the Suez Canal in 1869, India's distance from Europe has been reduced by 7,000 km.

India's Neighbours

- There are seven countries that share land boundaries with India. They are **Pakistan and Afghanistan in the northwest, China, Nepal, and Bhutan in the North and Myanmar and Bangladesh in the east.**
- **Sri Lanka and Maldives** are our island neighbours lying on the south across the sea. The Palk Strait divides India and Sri Lanka.
- Only one ocean bears the name of a country, India, the **Indian Ocean**. The ocean is nearly trapezoidal in shape. Its borders are with Asia to the north, Africa to the west, and Australia to the east.
- The **Southern Ocean** stretches north to 60 degrees south latitude, surrounding the continent of Antarctica.
- **The Arctic Ocean** encircles the North Pole and is situated inside the Arctic Circle. Berring Strait, a slender, shallow water channel, connects it to the Pacific Ocean. It is bounded by Eurasia's and North America's northern shores.

Important Parallels of Latitudes

In addition to the equator (0°), the North and South Poles (90°N and 90°S), there are four significant latitude parallels:

- **Tropic of Cancer** (23-1⁄2° N) in the Northern Hemisphere.
- **Tropic of Capricorn** (23-1⁄2° S) in the Southern Hemisphere.
- **Arctic Circle** at 66-1⁄2° north of the equator.
- **Antarctic Circle** at 66-1⁄2° south of the equator.

Heat Zones of the Earth

Torrid Zone

- At least once a year, the midday sun crosses over at all latitudes between the Tropics of Cancer and Capricorn.

- As a result, this region, known as **the Torrid Zone**, experiences the most heat.

Temperate Zones

- Any latitude north of the **Tropics of Cancer and Capricorn** will never see the midday sun.
- The sun's rays continue to decrease in angle as they approach the poles. Consequently, mild temperatures are experienced in the areas bounded by the Tropic of Cancer and the Arctic Circle in the North Hemisphere and the Tropic of Capricorn and the Antarctic Circle in the South Hemisphere. That's why these are referred to as **temperate zones.**

Frigid Zones

- Extreme cold can be found in regions that are located between the **Antarctic Circle and the South Pole** in the **Southern Hemisphere** and the **Arctic Circle and the North Pole** in the **Northern Hemisphere.**
- This is due to the sun's limited ascent above the horizon in this location. As a result, its rays are constantly **slanted** and produce less heat. Hence, these are referred to as **"Frigid Zones" (very cold).**

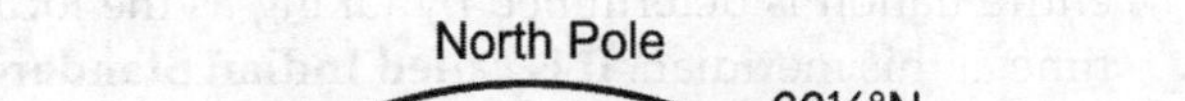

Important Latitudes and Heat Zones

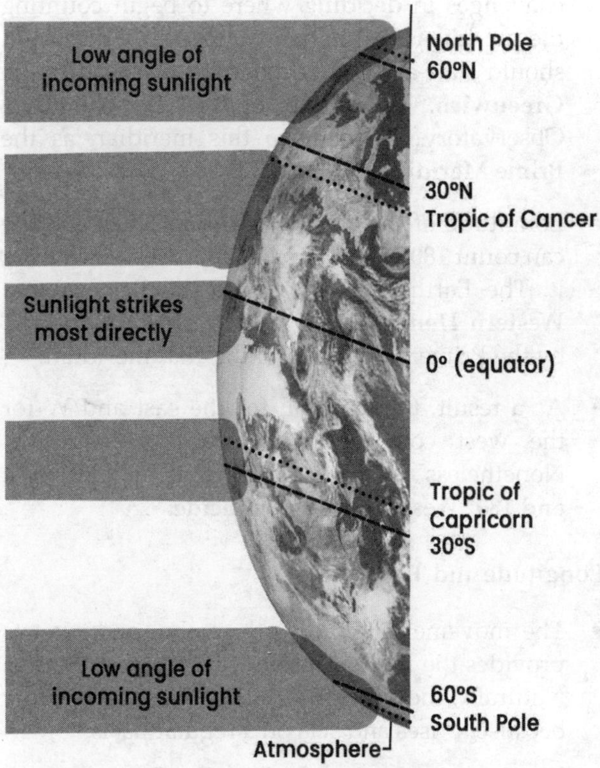

Angle of Incoming Sunlight

Longitudes

- In order to precisely define a location, additional information is required beyond just its latitude. For instance, the latitudes of the Mauritius Islands in the Indian Ocean and the Tonga Islands in the Pacific Ocean are the same, at 20° S. It now needs to be determined how far east or west these locations are from a specific line of reference that runs from the North Pole to the South Pole in order to accurately locate them. The distances between these lines of reference are expressed in **"degrees of longitude,"** and they are referred to as the **meridians of longitude**.
- There are additional divisions for each degree into minutes and minutes into seconds. Since they are semi-circles, the distance between them gradually gets smaller as one moves poleward until it reaches zero at the poles, the meeting point of all the meridians.
- In contrast to latitude parallels, all longitudinal meridians have the same length. This created

challenges in deciding where to begin counting the meridians. All nations agreed that the count should start at the meridian that passes through **Greenwich**, the home of the British Royal Observatory. We refer to this meridian as the **Prime Meridian.**

- Longitude of the **Prime Meridian is 0°,** and we can count 180° eastward and 180° westward from it. The Earth is **divided into the Eastern and Western Hemispheres**, which are equal in size, by the Prime Meridian and the 180° meridian.
- As a result, the letters E for the east and W for the west come after a location's longitude. Nonetheless, it is noteworthy that the **180° East and 180° West meridians coincide.**

Longitude and Time

- The movement of the earth, moon, and planets provides the most accurate way to measure time. Naturally, the sun is the world's best timekeeper because it rises and sets on a regular basis.
- **The sun's shadow**, which is longest at sunrise and sunset and shortest at noon, can be used **to determine local time.**
- Every location along the Greenwich Prime Meridian will experience midday or noon when the sun is at its zenith in the sky.
- The places east of Greenwich will be **ahead** of Greenwich time, while the places west of **Greenwich will be behind** it, as the earth rotates from west to east.
- Here is how to determine the rate of difference. The planet rotates 360 degrees in roughly 24 hours, or 15 degrees every hour or 1 degree every four minutes. As a result, at 15° east of Greenwich, the time at 12 noon on that day will be 15 × 4 = 60 minutes, or one hour ahead of Greenwich time, or 1 p.m. However, the time will be one hour behind Greenwich time at 15° west of Greenwich, or 11:00 a.m. Similarly, when it is 12 noon at Greenwich, it will be midnight at 180°.
- When midday arrives and the sun is at its zenith in the sky, any location can set a watch to read 12 o'clock. Such a watch will display the local time for that location.

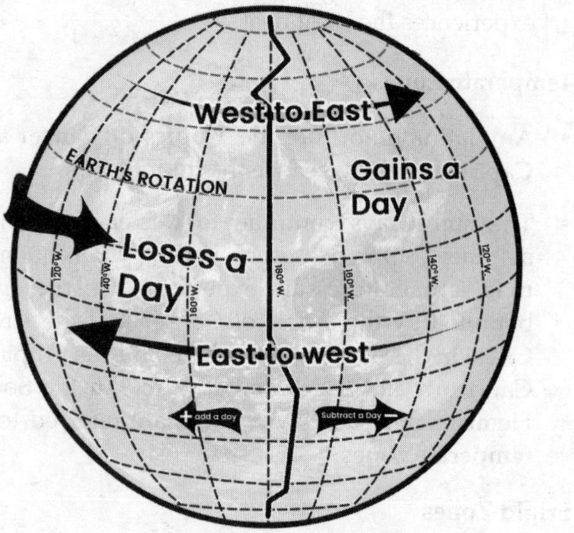

International Date Line

Time Zones of the World

Why do we have Standard Time?

- Locations that are on different meridians will inevitably have different local times. For instance, creating a schedule for trains which cover multiple longitudes will be challenging.
- **India uses 82 1/2°E, or 82° 30′E,** as its standard meridian of longitude. The standard time for the entire nation is determined by taking as the local time at this meridian. **It is called Indian Standard Time (IST).**
- **For examples,** Kabir resides in a tiny village close to Bhopal. He informs his friend Alok that they would not be able to get some sleep tonight. India and England were playing cricket match in London, since 2 p.m. This implies that the game would start in India at 7.30 p.m. and go on far into the night because India is five hours and thirty minutes ahead of GMT and is situated at 82°30′E, east of Greenwich. Therefore, when it is 2:00 p.m. in London, it will be 7:30 p.m. in India.
- Because of their extensive longitudinal history, certain countries have chosen multiple standard times. For example, there are up to **eleven standard times in Russia.**
- There are **twenty-four time zones on earth**, each lasting an hour. Thus, each zone **encompasses 15°** of longitude.

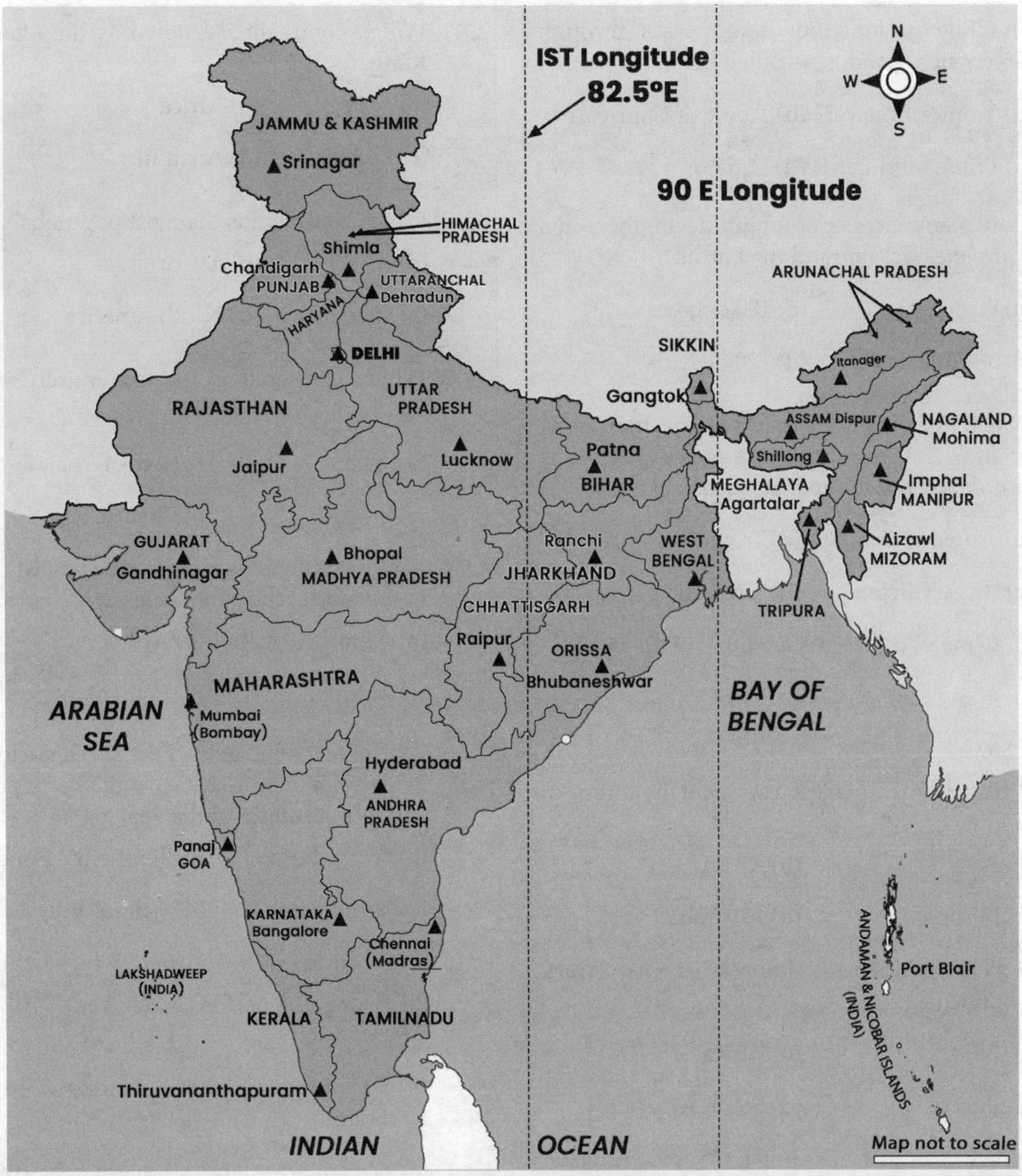

Indian Standard Meridian

TEST YOURSELF

Multiple Choice Questions

Q1. The equator is an example of which type of latitude?

(a) Prime Meridian (b) Tropic of Cancer

(c) Tropic of Capricorn (d) None of the above

Q2. The line of latitude that is approximately 23.5 degrees south of the equator is called the:

(a) Tropic of Cancer (b) Tropic of Capricorn

(c) Prime Meridian (d) International Date Line

Q3. The line of longitude that passes through Greenwich, London, is called the:

(a) Tropic of Cancer (b) Tropic of Capricorn

(c) Prime Meridian (d) Equator

Q4. How many degrees of longitude are there in a complete circle around the Earth?

(a) 90 degrees (b) 180 degrees

(c) 360 degrees (d) 720 degrees

Q5. Which line of latitude marks the northernmost point where the Sun appears directly overhead at noon on the summer solstice?

(a) Tropic of Cancer (b) Tropic of Capricorn

(c) Arctic Circle (d) Antarctic Circle

Q6. How many continents are there in the world?

(a) 4 (b) 5

(c) 6 (d) 7

Q7. Which is the smallest continent in terms of land area?

(a) Asia (b) Africa

(c) Europe (d) Australia

Q8. Which continent is known as the "Dark Continent"?

(a) Asia (b) Africa

(c) Europe (d) South America

Q9. Which continent is home to the Amazon Rainforest?

(a) Asia (b) Africa

(c) Europe (d) South America

Q10. Which continent is known as the "Old World"?

(a) Asia (b) Africa

(c) Europe (d) North America

Q11. Which continent is known as the "Land of Kangaroos"?

(a) Asia (b) Africa

(c) Europe (d) Australia

Q12. Which continent is the most populous?

(a) Asia (b) Africa

(c) Europe (d) North America

Q13. Which continent is located entirely in the Southern Hemisphere?

(a) Asia (b) Africa

(c) Europe (d) Antarctica

Q14. Which continent is home to the largest desert in the world, the Sahara Desert?

(a) Asia (b) Africa

(c) Europe (d) South America

Q15. Which heat zone of the Earth is characterised by extreme temperatures and receives direct sunlight throughout the year?

(a) Frigid Zone (b) Temperate Zone

(c) Torrid Zone (d) Polar Zone

Q16. The Torrid Zone lies between which latitudes?

(a) 0 degrees and 23.5 degrees North and South

(b) 23.5 degrees and 66.5 degrees North and South

(c) 66.5 degrees and 90 degrees North and South

(d) 0 degrees and 90 degrees North and South

Q17. Which heat zone of the Earth experiences moderate temperatures and is located between the Torrid Zone and the Polar Zones?

(a) Frigid Zone (b) Temperate Zone

(c) Torrid Zone (d) Polar Zone

Q18. Which heat zone of the Earth is characterised by extremely low temperatures and receives indirect sunlight?

(a) Frigid Zone (b) Temperate Zone

(c) Torrid Zone (d) None of the above

Q19. Which heat zone experiences the least amount of sunlight throughout the year?

(a) Frigid Zone (b) Temperate Zone

(c) Torrid Zone (d) None of the above

Q20. The Temperate Zone lies between which latitudes?

(a) 0 degrees and 23.5 degrees North and South

(b) 23.5 degrees and 66.5 degrees North and South

(c) 66.5 degrees and 90 degrees North and South

(d) 0 degrees and 90 degrees North and South

Q21. The Frigid Zone lies between which latitudes?

(a) 0 degrees and 23.5 degrees North and South

(b) 23.5 degrees and 66.5 degrees North and South

(c) 66.5 degrees and 90 degrees North and South

(d) 0 degrees and 90 degrees North and South

Q22. The Polar Zones are located around the:

(a) Equator

(b) Tropic of Cancer

(c) Tropic of Capricorn

(d) Poles (North and South)

Q23. The region near the Equator experiences which type of climate?

(a) Tropical climate

(b) Continental climate

(c) Mediterranean climate

(d) Polar climate

Q24. The heat zones of the Earth are primarily determined by:

(a) Elevation (b) Longitude

(c) Latitude (d) Precipitation

Answer Key

Q1.	d	Q2.	b	Q3.	c
Q4.	c	Q5.	a	Q6.	d
Q7.	d	Q8.	b	Q9.	d
Q10.	c	Q11.	d	Q12.	a
Q13.	d	Q14.	b	Q15.	c
Q16.	a	Q17.	b	Q18.	a
Q19.	a	Q20.	b	Q21.	c
Q22.	d	Q23.	a	Q24.	c

Model Question for Main Examination

Q. Briefly discuss about the heat zones present on the Earth.

UNIT 3

Distribution of Oceans and Continents

In This Unit

Comprehensive and profound coverage of the following NCERTs' chapter:

✓ NCERT Class- 11th (Fundamentals of Physical Geography), Chapter- 4

Continental Drift

- **Dutch cartographer Abraham Ortelius** initially proposed that the continents might have been joined as early as 1596. A map created by **Antonio Pellegrini** combined the three continents.
- But in 1912, German meteorologist **Alfred Wegener** presented a thorough argument known as **"the continental drift theory."** This was connected with how the continents and oceans are distributed.
- Wegener stated that the mega ocean encircled the single continental mass that all of the continents made up of. The name of the supercontinent, **PANGAEA**, corresponds to **"all of the earth"**, while Panthalassa meant **"all water,"** **PANTHALASSA** was the name given to the mega-ocean. According to his theory, Pangaea, the supercontinent, started to divide about 200 million years ago. When Pangaea initially split into two sizable continental masses, the northern and southern components were formed by Laurasia and Gondwanaland, respectively. Later, Laurasia and Gondwanaland kept splitting off into the smaller continents that are still there today.

Evidence in Support of the Continental Drift

- **The Matching of Continents (Jig-Saw-Fit):** The coastlines of South America and Africa that face each other are very similar. It should be mentioned that **Sir Edward Crisp Bullard** provided a map in 1964 that was created using a computer algorithm to determine the best match of the Atlantic margin. It turned out to be just right.
- **Rocks of Same Age Across the Oceans:** The recent development of radiometric dating techniques has made it easier to correlate the rock formations from several continents separated by a large ocean. The 2,000-million-year-old rocks from the coast of Brazil align with those found in western Africa. The Jurassic period is represented by the oldest marine sediments found along the coasts of South America and Africa. This implies that there was no ocean before that point.
- **Tillite:** It is the sedimentary rock that was created by glacial deposits. It is known that six distinct landmasses in the Southern Hemisphere have deposits similar to the **Gondawana system** found in India. The system's thick tillite near the base indicates widespread and persistent glaciation. Africa, Falkland Island, Madagascar, Antarctica, and Australia are home to counterparts of this succession.
- **Placer Deposits:** It is a remarkable fact that there are **abundant placer gold deposits** along **Ghana's coast** yet that there is not a single source rock in the area. When the two continents were lying side by side, it is clear that Ghana's gold reserves originated from the Brazil plateau because of the **gold-bearing veins** located there.
- **Distribution of Fossils:** Lemurs have been observed in Madagascar, Africa, and India. This has led some people to propose the idea of a contiguous landmass called "Lemuria" that connects these three landmasses. Mesosaurus and other small reptiles were well adapted to brackish, shallow water. The remains of these are found only at two places: the **Southern Cape province**

of South Africa and **Iraver formations of Brazil**. The two locations are currently separated by an ocean at a distance of 4,800 kilometers.

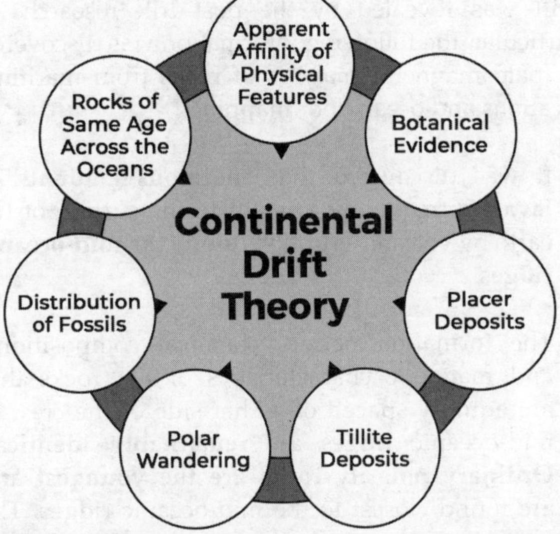

Evidence for Continental Drift Theory

Force for Drifting

Wegener proposed that **tidal and pole-fleeing forces** were the sources of the movement that caused the continents to drift apart.

- The earth's rotation has an impact on the polar-fleeing force which leads to creations of a bulge near the equator.
- Wegener also proposed the **tidal force**, which is caused by the sun's and moon's attraction to oceanic waters, resulting in tides. Still, the majority of academics believed these factors to be insufficient.

Post-Drift Studies

Convectional Current Theory

Arthur Holmes in the 1930s discussed the mantle convection currents are produced by the mantle's temperature fluctuations brought in by radioactive materials. Holmes contended that the entire mantle portion contains a system of these currents.

Mapping of the Ocean Floor

An in-depth analysis of the ocean's structure has shown that the ocean floor is not just a huge plain but also a relief zone. Following World War II, missions to survey the ocean floor gave scientists a clear image of the ocean relief and revealed the presence of deep trenches and submerged mountain ranges, primarily found in the nearby continents. Volcanic eruption activity was determined to be highest around the mid-oceanic ridges. The rocks from the oceanic crust are substantially younger than those from the continental regions, according to rock dating. It was discovered that rocks with equally spaced locations from the crest of oceanic ridges and on either side of the ridge shared remarkably alike ages and compositions.

Ocean Floor Configuration

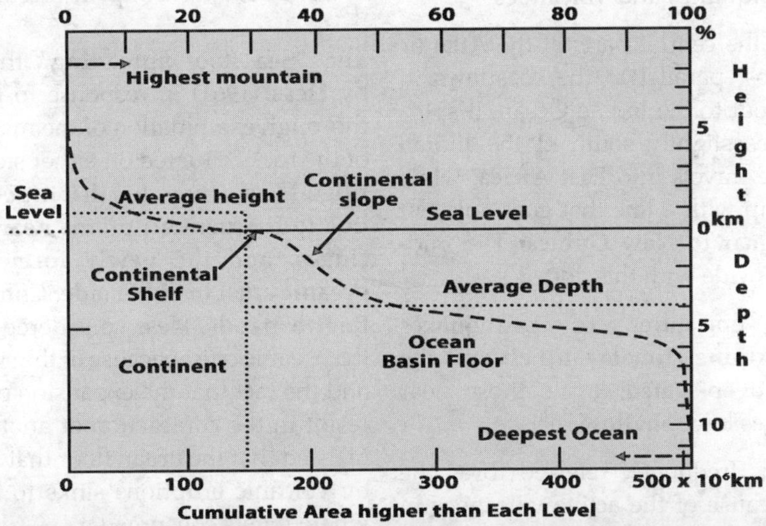

Ocean Floor

We will discuss a few aspects of ocean floor arrangement in this part that are relevant to our familiarity with how continents and oceans are distributed. The depth and the types of relief allow for the segmentation of the ocean floor into three main sections. These sections are **continental margins, deep-sea basins and mid-ocean ridges.**

Continental Margins

These define the boundary that separates deep-sea basins from continental shorelines. **Deep-oceanic trenches, continental shelf, continental slope, and continental rise** are a few of them. When it comes to the dispersion of oceans and continents, the deep-oceanic trenches are the regions of notable importance.

Abyssal Plains

These vast plains are situated between the mid-oceanic ridges and the continental edges. The regions where the continental sediments that drift past the edges end up are known as the **abyssal plains**.

Mid-Oceanic Ridges

This creates a network of connected mountains inside the water. Despite being covered by ocean waters, it is the longest mountain range on Earth's surface. At the crest it is designated by a central rift system, fragmented plateau, and a flank zone which runs the entire length of it. The area of active volcanoes is the rift system at the crest.

Distribution of Earthquakes and Volcanoes

- A line of dots in the central parts of the Atlantic Ocean runs almost parallel to the coastlines. It goes all the way out to the Indian Ocean. It splits into two branches slightly south of the Indian subcontinent: one travels into **East Africa**, while the other meets up with a line that goes adjacent to it from **Myanmar to New Guinea**. The mid-oceanic ridges coincide with this dotted line.
- Normally, the epicentres of earthquakes throughout the **Alpine-Himalayan belt and the Pacific rim are deep-seated**, while those near **mid-oceanic ridges** have **shallow foci.**
- The Pacific rim is frequently referred to as the **"ring of fire"** because of the active volcanoes in this region.

Concept of Sea Floor Spreading

Considerable information that was unavailable when Wegener first proposed the idea of continental drift was revealed by the post-drift research. In particular, the following information was discovered by paleomagnetic analyses of rocks from maritime locations and ocean floor mapping:

1. It was discovered that **enormous amounts of lava** are frequently brought to the surface of the earth by volcanic eruptions **along the mid-oceanic ridges**.
2. The formation period, chemical compositions, and magnetic characteristics of the rocks that are **equally spaced** on either side of the crest of mid-oceanic ridges are **remarkably identical. Ordinary polarity rocks are the youngest** and are found closest to the mid-oceanic ridges. The farther one travels from the crest, the older the rocks get.
3. Compared to continental rocks, the rocks, that make up the ocean crust are far younger. Continental rock formations date as far back as 3200 millon years while Earth does not have rocks older than 200 million years.
4. While the quake foci in the mid-oceanic ridge zones have shallow depths, the deep trenches have deep-seated earthquake occurrences.

The **"Sea floor spreading"** theory was put forth by **Hess (1961)** in response to these findings and a thorough examination of the magnetic characteristics of the rocks situated on either side of the mid-oceanic ridge. **Hess contended that the oceanic crust ruptures due to frequent eruptions near the crest of oceanic ridges, and the newly formed lava pushes the oceanic crust to either side. Consequently, the ocean floor expands.** Hess considered the consumption of the oceanic crust because of the shorter age of the crust and the fact that the expansion of one ocean does not result in the contraction of another. Additionally, he insisted that the ocean floor that is pushed to the crest by volcanic eruptions sinks to the oceanic trenches where it gets consumed.

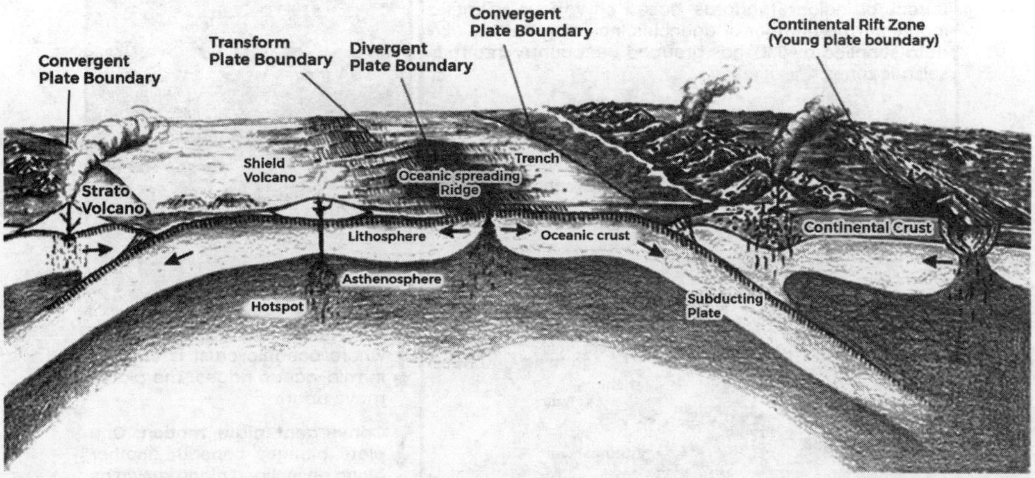

Sea Floor Spreading

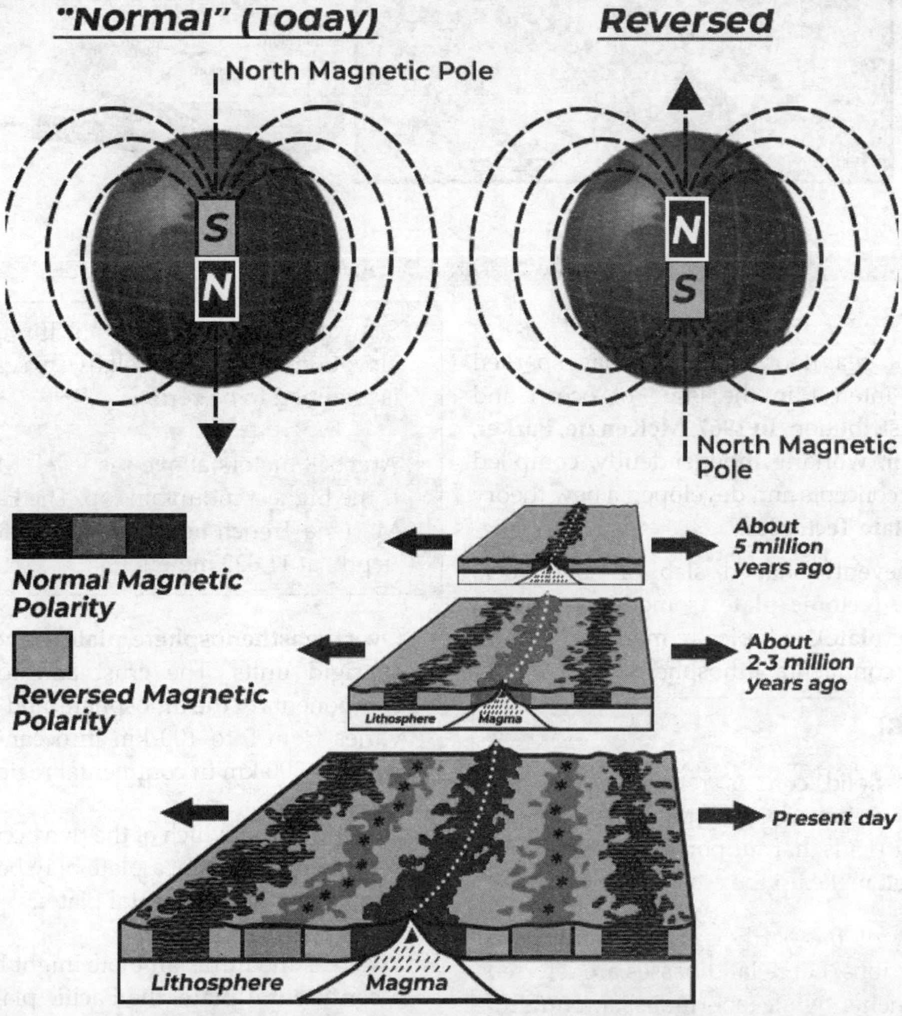

Normal and Reversed Magnetic Polarity

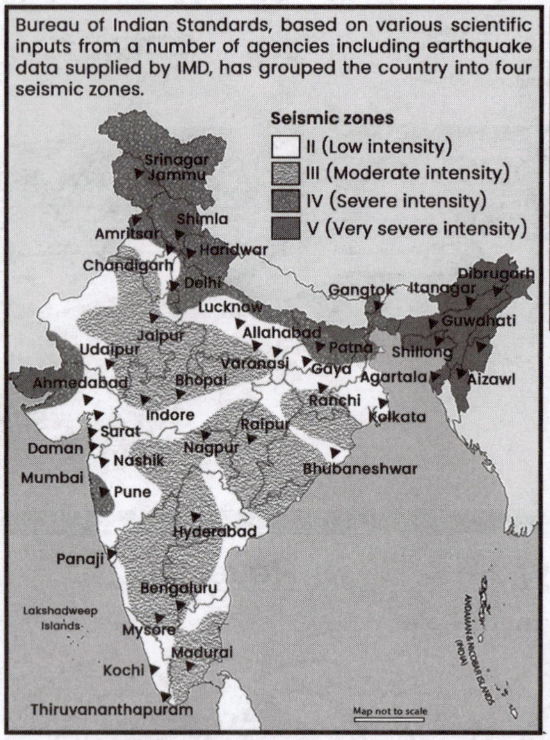

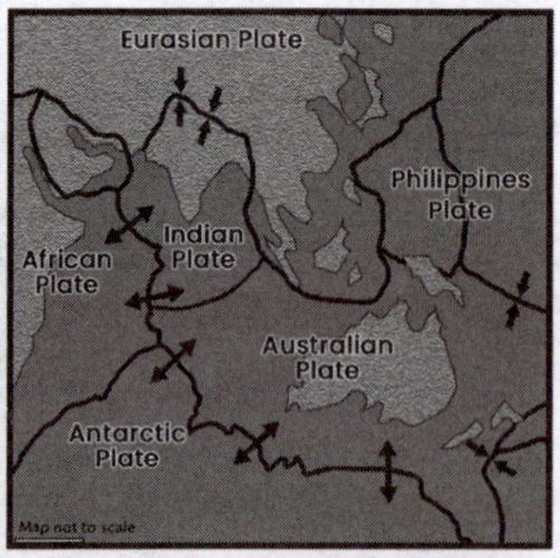

Divergent plate motion: Occurs where oceanic crust is created in mid-ocean ridges. The plates move apart.

Convergent plate motion: One plate plunges beneath another along an inclined plane known as a subduction zone.

Convergent plate movement

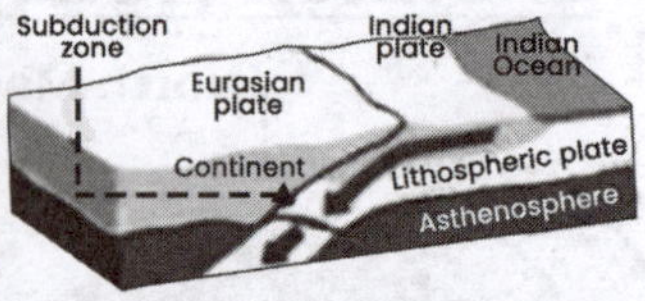

Plate Tectonics

- The idea of sea floor spreading has sparked a renewed interest in the issue of ocean and continent distribution. **In 1967, McKenzie, Parker, and Morgan,** working independently, compiled the existing concepts and developed a new theory known as **Plate Tectonics**.
- A vast, unevenly shaped slab of solid rock, known as a **tectonic plate** (sometimes called a **lithospheric plate**), is typically made up of both oceanic and continental lithosphere.

LITHOSPHERE

- The earth's solid core is referred to as the **Lithosphere**. It is made up of the thin soil layers that hold nutrients that support life on Earth and the rocks that make up the crust of the planet.
- The surface of the earth is divided into two primary sections. Large landmasses are referred to as continents, while enormous amounts of water are known as ocean basins.
- Seawater levels are constant throughout. Land elevation is measured relative to sea level, which is assumed to be zero.
- At 8,848 meters above sea level, Mount Everest is the highest mountain top. The Pacific Ocean's Mariana Trench holds the record for the lowest depth, at 11,022 meters.

- Over the **asthenosphere, plates travel horizontally** as rigid units. The crust and top mantle are components of the lithosphere, and their thickness varies from 5 to 100 km in oceanic regions and roughly 200 km in continental regions.
- Depending on which of the two occupies a greater portion of the plate, a plate may be referred to as the oceanic or continental plate.
- Whereas the Eurasian plate might be classified as a **continental plate**, the Pacific plate is primarily an **oceanic plate.**

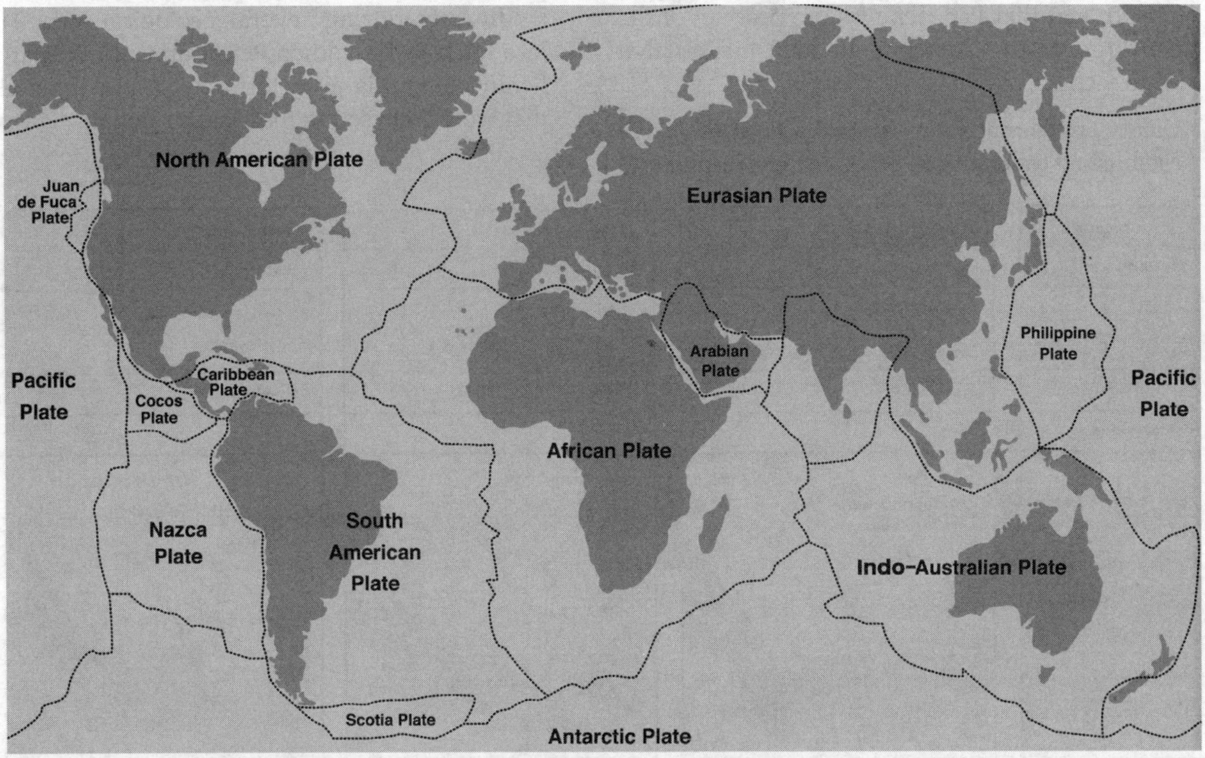

Major and Minor Plates of the World

- According to the theory of plate tectonics, the lithosphere of the earth is separated into **seven major plates and a few minor ones**. These major plates are surrounded by young fold mountains, faults, and/or trenches. **The major plates are as given below:**
  - ➢ Antarctica and the surrounding oceanic plate
  - ➢ North American (along the Caribbean islands, the western Atlantic floor is divided from the South American plate) plate
  - ➢ South American (alongside the Caribbean islands, the western Atlantic floor divides from the North American plate) plate
  - ➢ Pacific plate
  - ➢ India-Australia-New Zealand plate
  - ➢ Africa with the eastern Atlantic floor plate
  - ➢ Eurasia and the adjacent oceanic plate.
- **Some minor plates are as follows:**
  - ➢ **Cocos plate**: Lies in between Pacific plate and Central America
  - ➢ **Nazca plate**: Lies in between Pacific plate and South America
  - ➢ **Arabian plate**: Mainly lies in the Saudi Arabian landmass
  - ➢ **Philippine plate**: Found in between Pacific and the Asiatic plate
  - ➢ **Caroline plate**: Found in between the Indian (North of New Guinea) and Philippine plate
  - ➢ **Fuji plate**: Lies in North-east of Australia

Types of Plate Boundaries

- Throughout Earth's history, these plates have been in constant motion over the planet.
- A plate is made up of continents, and the plate itself travels. Furthermore, it may be mentioned that, without exception, every plate has moved at some point in the geological past and shall do so continuously in the future.
- Wegener first believed that **Pangaea**, the supercontinent, had once comprised all of the continents.
- Subsequent discoveries, however, show that the continental masses that rest on the plates have been moving throughout the geological

period, and that Pangaea was the product of the convergence of various continental masses that were sections of one or the other plates.

- Using **paleomagnetic data**, scientists have established the positions of the current continental landmasses during several geological eras. The location of the Indian subcontinent, primarily Peninsular India, is determined using the rocks that were analysed in the Nagpur region.

Type of Margin	Divergent	Convergent	Transform
Motion	Spreading	Subduction	Lateral Sliding
Effect	Constructive (Oceanic lithosphere created)	Destructive (Oceanic lithosphere destroyed)	Conservative (lithosphere neither created or destroyed)
Topography	Ridge/Rift	Trench	No Major effect
Volcanic activity	Yes	Yes	No

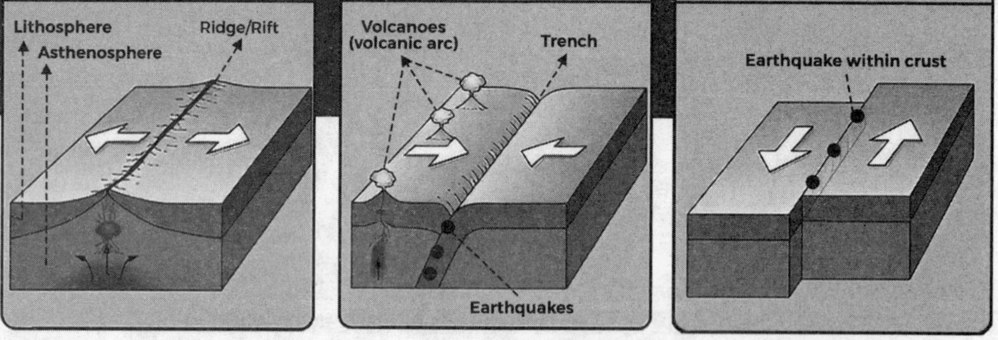

Types of Plate Boundaries

1. Divergent Boundaries

- Where crust is formed when plates separate from one another. **Spreading sites** are locations when plates diverge from one another.
- The most well-known illustration of divergent borders is the **Mid-Atlantic Ridge**.

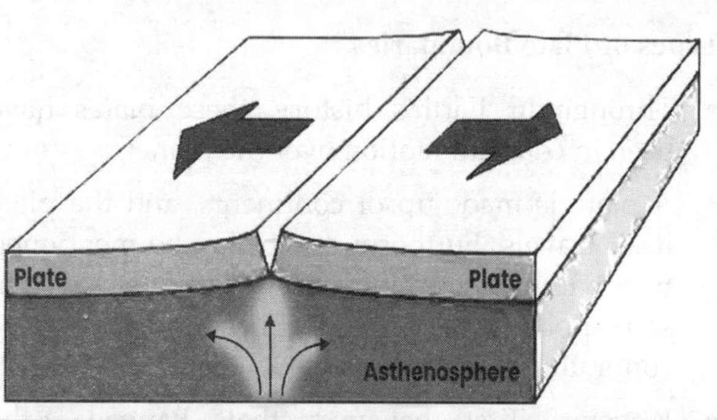

Divergent Boundary

2. Convergent Boundaries

- When one plate subducts beneath another, the crust is destroyed and a **subduction zone** is created.
- **Convergence can happen in three different ways**. These are the following: (i) between two oceanic plates; (ii) between two continental plates; and (iii) between an oceanic plate and a continental plate.

3. Transform Boundaries

- When plates slide along one another horizontally, there is neither creation nor destruction of the crust.
- The planes of separation known **as transform faults** are usually perpendicular to the mid-oceanic ridges.
- There is a differential movement of a part of the plate away from the earth's axis since the eruptions do not occur along the entire crest at same time. Blocks of the plate segments that have split are impacted by the earth's rotation.

Rates of Plate Movement

- Scientists can determine the rates of plate movement by observing the strips of normal and reverse magnetic field that run parallel to the mid-oceanic ridges.

- These rates differ significantly. The **East Pacific Rise alongside Easter Island**, in the South Pacific, approximately 3,400 km west of Chile, has the **quickest rate** (more than 15 cm/year), while the **Arctic Ridge** has the **slowest of movement** (less than 2.5 cm/year).

Force for the Plate Movement

- The principles of **sea floor spreading and the unified theory of plate tectonics** has demonstrated the dynamic nature of both the earth's interior and surface.

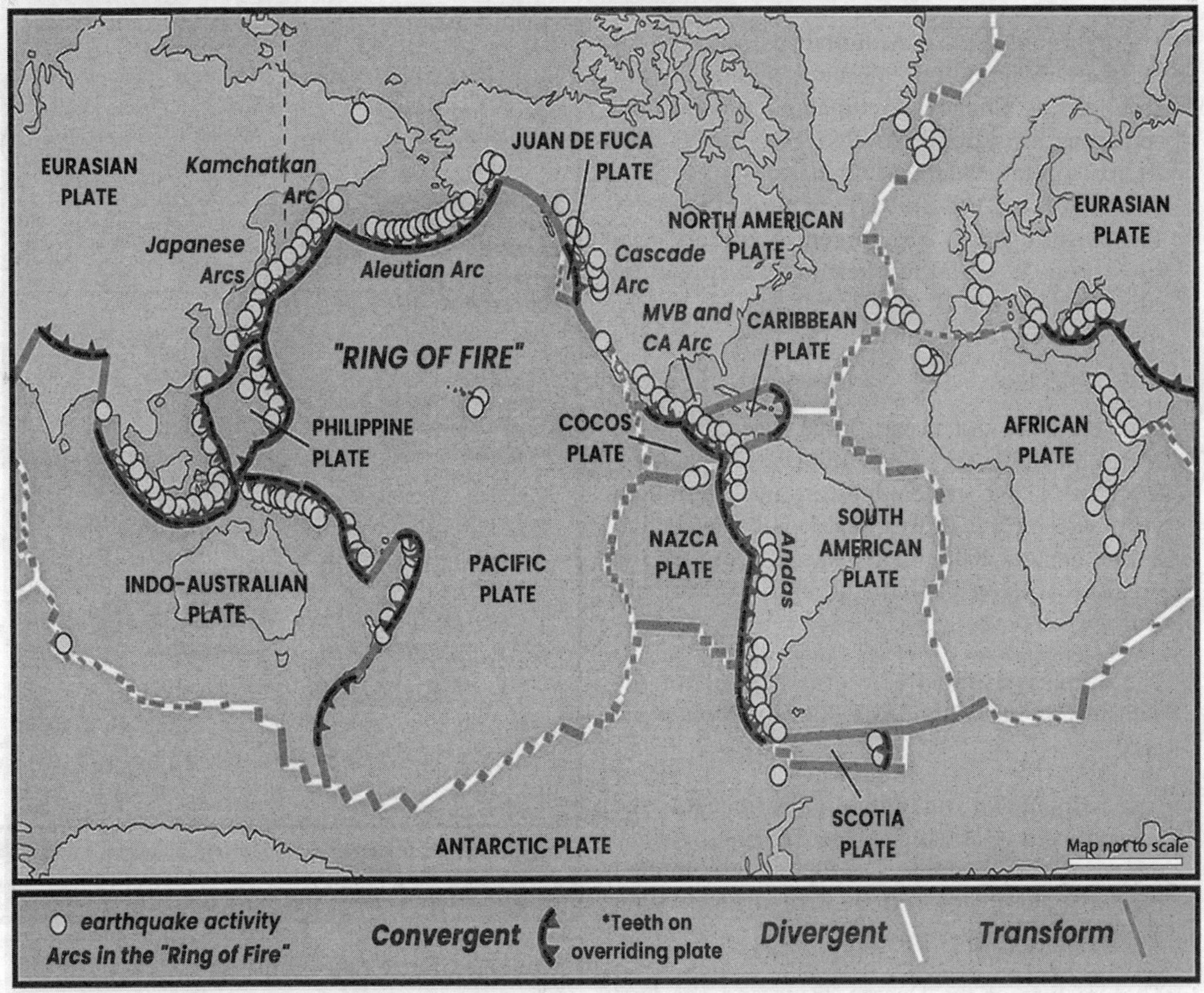

Ring of Fire

- It is speculated that the moveable rock underlying the inflexible plates is moving in a circular pattern. The heated material rises to the surface, distributes, and starts to cool, and finally dives once more into the deeper depths. Scientists refer to this repeatedly occurring cycle as a **convection cell or convective flow**.
- **Radioactive decay and residual heat** are the two main sources of heat in the earth. The force that drives behind plate movement is the slow movement of the hot, softened mantle beneath the rigid plates.

Movement of the Indian Plate

- Peninsular India and the continental parts of Australia are included in the Indian plate. The northern plate boundary is formed by the subduction zone along the Himalayas, which is the convergence of two continents.

- It connects to the island arc in **the east** by passing via the **Java Trench** and the **Rakinyoma Mountains in Myanmar**.
- The **eastern margin** is a spreading site in the SW Pacific that is located east of Australia and corresponds to an oceanic ridge.
- The Pakistani **Kirthar Mountain** is followed by the **western margin**. It continues southeastward around the **Chagos Archipelago**, joining the spreading site from the Red Sea rift. It also stretches parallel to the **Makrana coast**.
- The oceanic ridge, a divergent boundary that runs about **W-E and merges** into the spreading site a little south of New Zealand, also marks the boundary between India and the Antarctic plate.
- Situated in a vast ocean, India was a massive island off the **coast of Australia**. It was isolated from the Asian continent until around 225 million years ago by the **Tethys Sea**. It is believed that approximately 200 million years ago, **during the breakup of Pangaea**, India began her northward journey.
- The Himalayas rapidly rose as a result of the collision of India and Asia 40–50 million years ago.
- Approximately 140 million years ago, the subcontinent was situated as far south as 50 degrees South latitude. The Tethys Sea divided the two major plates, with the Tibetan block being closer to the Asian continent.
- The creation of the Deccan Traps and the lava outpouring that took place during the shift of the Indian plate towards the Eurasian plate was a significant occurrence. This lasted for a very long time, beginning about 60 million years ago.
- The subcontinent was still near the equator. The creation of the Himalayas began 40 million years ago and continued till then. It is believed that the process is still ongoing and that the **Himalayas are continually growing in height**.

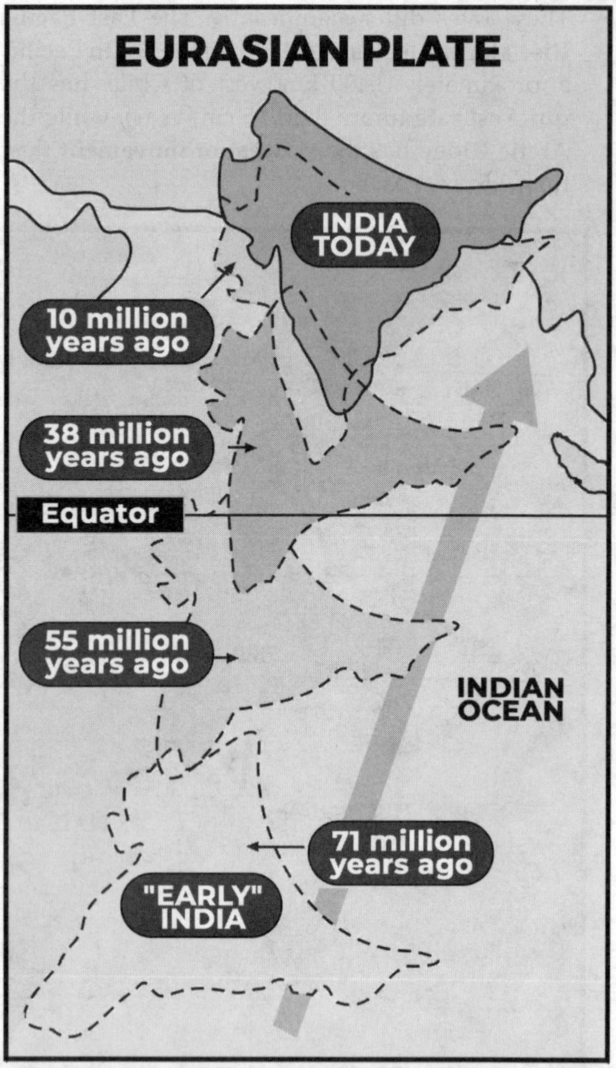

Movement of the Indian Plate

TEST YOURSELF

Multiple Choice Questions

Q1. Which ocean is the largest and covers about one-third of the Earth's surface?

(a) Atlantic Ocean (b) Indian Ocean
(c) Pacific Ocean (d) Southern Ocean

Q2. The world's busiest and most important ocean trade route is:

(a) Atlantic Ocean (b) Indian Ocean
(c) Pacific Ocean (d) Arctic Ocean

Q3. Consider the following pairs:

S.N.	List I	List II
1.	Continental Margins	It is the regions where the continental sediments that drift past the edges end up.
2.	Abyssal Plains	It defines the boundary that separates deep-sea basins from continental shorelines.
3.	Mid-Oceanic Ridges	It is a network of connected mountains inside the ocean.

How many of the above pairs are correctly matched?

(a) Only one (b) Only two

(c) All three (d) None

Q4. Which of the following statement(s) is/are correct?

1. The epicentre of earthquakes throughout the Alpine-Himalayan belt and the Pacific rim are deep-seated, while those near mid-oceanic ridges have shallow foci.
2. Compared to continental rocks, the rocks that make up the ocean crust are much older.

Select the correct answer using the code given below:

(a) 1 only (b) 2 only

(c) Both 1 and 2 (d) Neither 1 nor 2

Q5. With reference to Plate Tectonics Theory, which one of the following is correct about Divergent Boundaries?

(a) The planes of separation known as transform faults are usually perpendicular to the mid oceanic ridges.

(b) During the process, the lithospheric crust is destroyed and a subduction zone is created.

(c) The most common example of divergent plate movement is the Mid-Atlantic Ridge.

(d) The Himalayas are formed due to the divergence of Eurasian Plate from Indian Plate.

Q6. The ocean that is known for its rich biodiversity, including the Great Barrier Reef, is the:

(a) Atlantic Ocean (b) Indian Ocean

(c) Pacific Ocean (d) Southern Ocean

Q7. Consider the following statements:

1. The Himalayas are continually growing in height.
2. Deccan Traps was formed during the shift of the Indian plate towards the Eurasian plate.

Which of the statements given above is/are correct?

(a) 1 only (b) 2 only

(c) Both 1 and 2 (d) Neither 1 nor 2

Q8. Which one of the following is a minor tectonics plate?

(a) Pacific plate

(b) Philippine plate

(c) Africa with the eastern Atlantic floor plate

(d) India-Australia-New Zealand plate

Answer Key					
Q1.	c	Q2.	a	Q3.	a
Q4.	a	Q5.	c	Q6.	c
Q7.	c	Q8.	b		

Model Questions for Main Examination

Q1. Critically examine the Continental Drift Theory.

Q2. What factors might contribute to the distribution of oceans and continents on Earth?

Q3. How do you think the distribution of oceans and continents affects the climate and weather patterns across the planet?

UNIT 4

Minerals and Rocks

In This Unit

Comprehensive and profound coverage of the following NCERTs' chapter:

✓ NCERT Class- 11th (Fundamentals of Physical Geography), Chapter- 5

Introduction

The earth is composed of various kinds of elements. The exterior layer of the earth has these elements in solid form, whereas the interior is heated and molten. Approximately 98% of the Earth's crust is made up of eight elements: oxygen, silicon, aluminum, iron, calcium, sodium, potassium, and magnesium. The other components include titanium, hydrogen, phosphorus, manganese, sulphur, carbon, nickel, and other elements. The elements in the Earth's crust are rarely found exclusively but are usually combined with other elements to make various substances. These substances are recognised as **minerals.**

Thus, a **mineral is a naturally occurring inorganic substance**, having an orderly atomic structure and a definite chemical composition and physical properties. **A mineral is composed of two or more elements. But, sometimes single element minerals like sulphur, copper, silver, gold, graphite etc. are found.**

Earth's interior contains hot magma, which is the fundamental source of all minerals. A systematic sequence of minerals forms when the lava cools, crystallising and solidifying one after the other to form rocks. **Organic compounds can be found in solid, liquid, and gaseous forms in minerals including coal, petroleum, and natural gas.**

Physical Characteristics of Minerals

- **External crystal form:** It is determined by internal arrangement of the molecules like cubes, octahedrons, hexagonal prisms, etc.
- **Cleavage:** It is the tendency to break in given directions producing relatively plane surfaces as a result of internal arrangement of the molecules, may rupture at any angle to each other in one or more directions.
- **Fracture:** It is the internal molecular arrangement so complex there are no planes of molecules; the crystal will break in an irregular manner, not along planes of cleavage.
- **Lustre:** It is the appearance of a material without regard to colour; each mineral has a distinctive lustre like metallic, silky, glossy etc.
- **Colour:** Some minerals have characteristic colour determined by their molecular structure malachite, azurite, chalcopyrite etc., and some minerals are coloured by impurities. For example, because of impurities quartz may be white, green, red, yellow etc.
- **Streak:** It is the colour of the ground powder of any mineral. It may be of the same colour as the mineral or may differ- malachite is green and gives green streak, fluorite is purple or green but gives a white streak.
- **Transparent**: Whether rays pass through so that objects can be seen plainly.
- **Translucent:** Light rays pass through but will get diffused so that objects cannot be seen through it.
- **Opaque:** Light will not pass at all.
- **Structure:** It is defined as the particular arrangement of the individual crystals; fine, medium or coarse grained; fibrous-separable, divergent, radiating.
- **Hardness:** It denotes the relative resistance being scratched; ten minerals are selected to measure

the degree of hardness from 1-10. They are: 1. Talc; 2. Gypsum; 3. Calcite; 4. Fluorite; 5. Apatite; 6. Feldspar; 7. Quartz; 8. Topaz; 9. Corundum; 10. Diamond.

- **Specific gravity:** It is the ratio between the weight of a given object and the weight of an equal volume of water; object weighed once in air, once in water, and its weight in air divided by the difference between the two weights.

Some Major Minerals and their Characteristic

Feldspar

Every form of feldspar has **silicon and oxygen**, although certain variants contain additional elements such as sodium, potassium, calcium, aluminum, etc. About half of the earth's composition feldspar mineral is present. It is light cream to salmon pink in colour. It is used in ceramics and glass-making processes.

Quartz

It is one of the most important components of sand and granite. It is made up of silica. This mineral is a hard mineral and almost insoluble in water. It is utilised in radio and radar processing systems and is either white or colourless. It is known to be an important component of granite.

Pyroxene

Pyroxene consists of calcium, aluminium, magnesium, iron and silica. Around 10% of the earth's crust is made up of Pyroxene. It is found in meteorites. It is green or black in colour.

Amphibole

Aluminium, calcium, silica, iron, magnesium are major elements of Amphibole. Around 7% of the earth crust is made up of this mineral. It is in green or black colour and used in asbestos industry. Hornblende is another form of amphiboles.

Mica

It contains minerals including silica, potassium, magnesium, iron, and magnesium. 4% of the earth's crust is made up of it. Commonly, igneous and metamorphic rocks contain mica. It is used in electrical appliance making industry.

Olivine

Major components of olivine include silica, iron, and magnesium. Jewellery is made with it. It is often a greenish crystal that is frequently discovered in basaltic rocks. Besides these main minerals, other minerals like chlorite, calcite, magnetite, haematite, bauxite and barite are also present in some quantities in the rocks.

Metal-based Minerals These minerals fall into three categories based on the amount of metal they contain:

(i) Precious metals, such as platinum, silver, and gold.

(ii) Ferrous metals: To create different types of steel, iron and other metals are frequently combined.

(iii) Non-ferrous metals: These comprise metals such as aluminium, copper, zinc, lead, tin, and so on.

Non-Metallic Minerals: There is no metal content in these minerals. Nitrates, phosphates, and sulphur are a few non-metallic mineral examples. Cement is a composition of non-metallic minerals.

Rocks

The earth's crust is composed of rocks. A rock is an aggregate of **one or more minerals**. Rock may be hard or soft and in varied colours. For Example, granite is hard, soapstone is soft. Quartzite can have a milky white colour, while gabbro is a dark brown. The mineral components that make up rocks are not explicitly stated. The most prevalent minerals in rocks are feldspar and quartz.

Petrology is the science of rocks. A petrologist studies rocks in all their aspects viz., mineral composition, alteration, structure, occurrence, texture, origin and relationship with different rocks.

There are many different kinds of rocks which are categorised into three categories on the basis of their process of formation. As mentioned below:

1. **Igneous Rocks:** solidified from magma and lava;
2. **Sedimentary Rocks:** the result of deposition of fragments of rocks by exogenous processes;
3. **Metamorphic Rocks:** formed out of existing rocks undergoing recrystallisation.

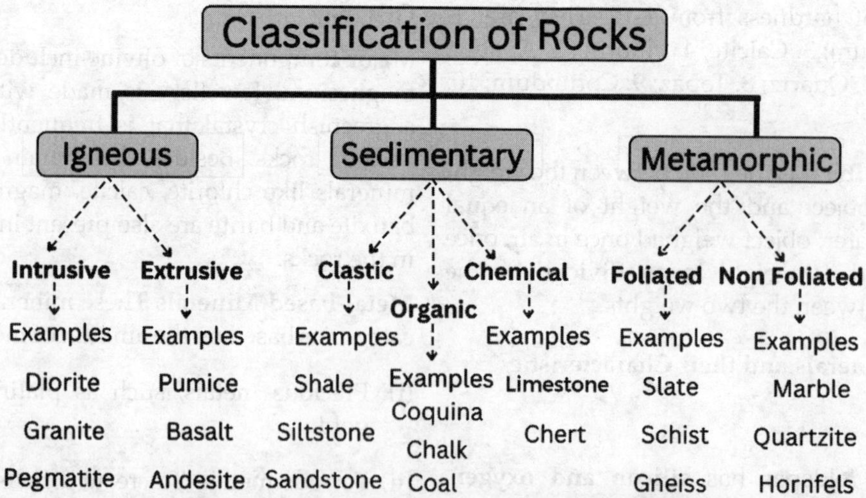

Classification of Rocks

Igneous Rocks

- As igneous rocks form out of magma and lava from the interior of the earth, they are known **as primary rocks.** The igneous rocks (Ignis –in Latin means 'Fire') are formed when magma cools and solidifies.
- Molten lava quickly cools and solidifies upon contact with the earth's surface. These are called **extrusive igneous rocks.**
- Occasionally, the molten lava in the earth's crust cools down. We refer to these solid rocks as **intrusive igneous rocks.**
- Based on their texture, igneous rocks are categorised. The physical properties of the materials, such as their size and grain arrangement, determine their texture.
- Large mineral grains may result from the gradual cooling of molten material at very deep depths.
- Small, smooth grains are the product of sudden cooling (at the surface).
- Igneous rocks are composed of grains with intermediate sizes due to intermediate cooling conditions.
- Igneous rocks include granite, gabbro, pegmatite, basalt, volcanic breccia, and tuff.

Sedimentary Rocks

- The Latin term sedimentum, which means settling, is the source of the English word **"sedimentary"**.
- Rocks on the surface of the earth, whether igneous, sedimentary, or metamorphic, are fractured into a variety of sizes by forces that cause **denudation**.
- These pieces are moved and placed by various other agencies. These sediments become rocks by **compaction**. We term this process **lithification.**
- The depositional layers in many sedimentary rocks hold onto their properties long after lithification. Because of this, sedimentary rocks like sandstone and shale have a variety of layers with different thicknesses.
- Sedimentary rocks are categorised into three main types based on the **method of formation:**
  - ➢ Mechanically formed: sandstone, loess, limestone, shale, conglomerate etc. are examples;
  - ➢ Organically formed: limestone, chalk, geyserite, coal etc.
  - ➢ Chemically formed: chert, limestone, halite, potash etc.

Metamorphic Rocks

- The word metamorphic means 'change of form'.
- Under extreme heat and pressure, igneous and sedimentary rocks can transform into metamorphic rocks. For instance, limestone turns into marble and clay becomes slate.
- Rocks undergo metamorphism when they are pushed to lower levels by tectonic forces, when molten magma rising through the crust comes in touch with the crustal rocks, or when the rocks

above exert significant pressure on the underlying rocks.

- A process known as metamorphism causes previously consolidated rocks to recrystallize and reorganise their parent rocks.
- **Dynamic metamorphism** is the term used to describe the mechanical disruption and reorganisation of the original minerals within rocks as a result of breaking and crushing without any noticeable chemical changes.
- Rock materials undergo chemical transformation and recrystallization as a result of **thermal metamorphism.**
- Thermal metamorphism can be classified into two categories: contact metamorphism and regional metamorphism.
- During **contact metamorphism**, heated magma and lava collide with the rocks, causing the minerals to recrystallize at elevated temperatures.
- In **regional metamorphism**, rocks recrystallize as a result of deformation brought on by tectonic shearing, high pressure, or both.
- Certain rocks undergo metamorphism, which causes the rock grains or minerals to arrange into layers or lines. We refer to this type of mineral or grain arrangement in metamorphic rocks as **foliation or lineation**.
- Occasionally, substances or minerals from several groups are layered alternately, thin to thick, and appear in both light and dark colours. The term "banding" refers to this type of structure found in metamorphic rocks, and rocks that exhibit **banding** are referred to as **banded rocks**.
- There are two main categories of metamorphic rocks: foliated rocks and non-foliated rocks.
- Metamorphic rocks include quartzite, gneissoid, granite, syenite, slate, schist, marble, and others.

Rock Cycle

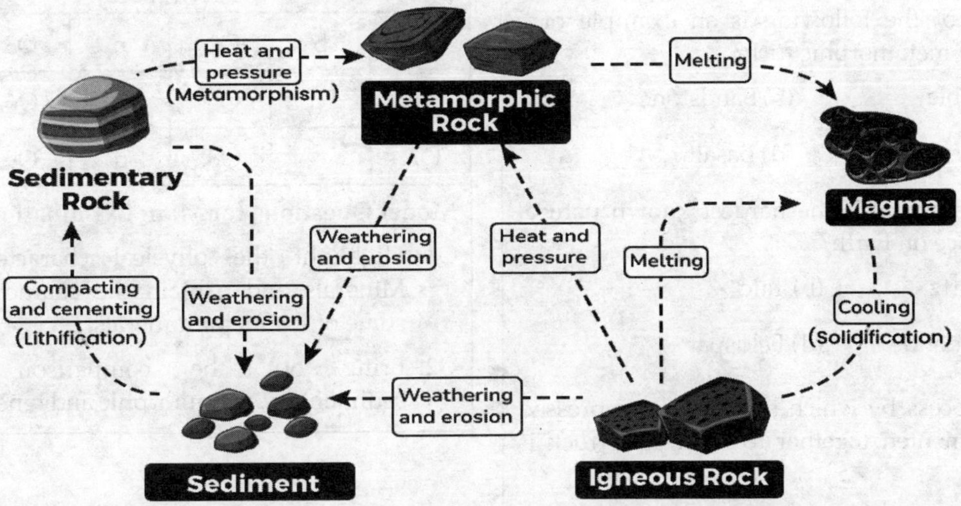

Rock Cycle

Rocks can change over time and never stay in one place for very long. The process of turning old rocks into new ones is known as the "Rock Cycle." Primary rocks are igneous rocks, from which secondary and metamorphic rocks are formed. Metamorphic rocks can be formed from igneous rocks. Sedimentary rocks are created by the pieces of igneous and metamorphic rocks. Even sedimentary rocks themselves can fracture and become fragments, which can then serve as a starting point for the development of new sedimentary rocks. When crustal rocks (igneous, metamorphic, and sedimentary) are formed, they can be carried into the mantle (the interior of the earth) by the subduction process, which is the process by which portions or entirety of crustal plates descend beneath one another in plate convergence zones. There, the elevated temperature causes the crustal rocks to melt and transform into molten magma, which is the original source of igneous rocks.

TEST YOURSELF

Multiple Choice Questions

Q1. Which of the following is NOT a characteristic of minerals?

(a) Naturally occurring

(b) Organic composition

(c) Definite chemical composition

(d) Ordered atomic arrangement

Q2. Which mineral is composed of silicon dioxide (SiO2)?

(a) Calcite (b) Quartz

(c) Feldspar (d) Gypsum

Q3. Which type of rock is formed by the solidification of molten magma or lava?

(a) Sedimentary rock (b) Metamorphic rock

(c) Igneous rock (d) None of the above

Q4. Which of the following is an example of a foliated metamorphic rock?

(a) Marble (b) Sandstone

(c) Gneiss (d) Basalt

Q5. Which mineral is the hardest known natural substance on Earth?

(a) Quartz (b) Talc

(c) Diamond (d) Feldspar

Q6. The process by which sediments are pressed and cemented together to form solid rock is called:

(a) Weathering (b) Erosion

(c) Compaction (d) Deposition

Q7. Which type of rock is formed by the alteration of existing rocks due to heat and pressure?

(a) Sedimentary rock (b) Igneous rock

(c) Metamorphic rock (d) None of the above

Q8. Which of the following is NOT a characteristic of igneous rocks?

(a) Formed from cooled and solidified magma or lava

(b) Often contain visible grains or crystals

(c) Classified based on texture and mineral composition

(d) Frequently contain fossils

Q9. How are rocks classified in the rock cycle?

(a) By colour (b) By size

(c) By origin and formation (d) By weight

Answer Key

Q1.	b	Q2.	b	Q3.	c
Q4.	c	Q5.	c	Q6.	c
Q7.	c	Q8.	d	Q9.	c

Model Questions for Main Examination

Q1. Highlight the physical characteristics of Minerals and explain the characteristics of some of the major minerals.

Q2. Bring out the comparison between sedimentary, metamorphic and igneous rocks.

UNIT 5

Geomorphic Processes

In This Unit

Comprehensive and profound coverage of the following NCERTs' chapter:

✓ NCERT Class- 11th (Fundamentals of Physical Geography), Chapter- 5

The earth's surface is being continuously subjected to external forces originating within the earth's atmosphere and by internal forces from within the earth. The **external forces are** referred to as **exogenic forces** and the **internal forces** are referred to as **endogenic forces.**

- **Exogenic forces** cause the earth's surface to undergo **degradation** (wearing down) of relief/ elevations and **aggradation** (filling up) of basins/ depressions. The phenomenon of wearing down of relief variations of the surface of the earth through erosion is known as **gradation.**
- As a result of the **endogenic forces'** constant elevation or buildup of certain regions of the earth's surface, exogenic processes are unable to balance out the relief variations on the planet's surface. Thus, variances persist as long as exogenic and endogenic factors continue to function in opposition to one another.
- Generally speaking, **exogenic processes are mostly land-wearing forces, whereas endogenic forces are primarily forces that construct land.**

Geomorphic processes are the result of **endogenic and exogenic forces** that exert physical and chemical forces on earth's materials, changing the structure of the planet's surface.

- Volcanism and diastrophism are examples of **endogenic geomorphic processes.**
- **Exogenic geomorphic** processes include erosion, deposition, mass wasting, and **weathering.**

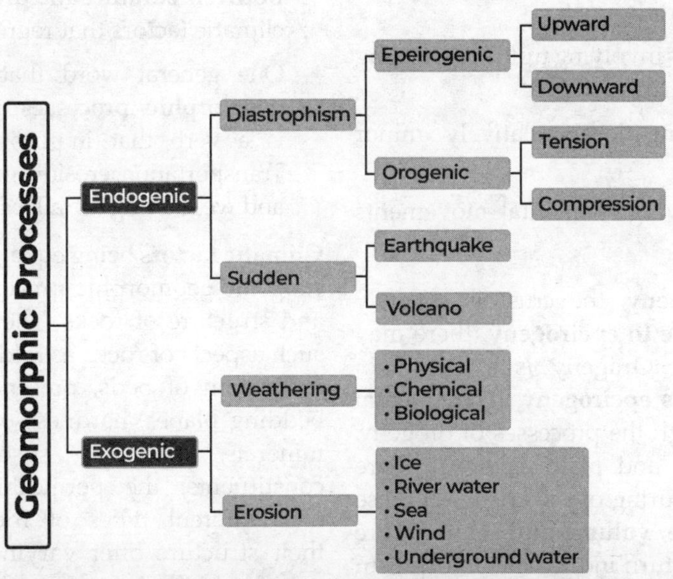

Geomorphic Processes

- **A geomorphic agent** is any exogenic factor of nature (such as water, ice, wind, etc.) that has the ability to gather and move earth materials.
- **Gravity** besides being a directional force activating all downslope movements of matter also causes stresses on the earth's materials. Indirect gravitational stresses activate wave and tide induced currents and winds.
- Without gravity and gradients there would be **no mobility** and hence no erosion, transportation and deposition are possible. So, gravitational stresses are as important as the other geomorphic processes.

Endogenic Processes

The energy emanating from within the earth is the main force behind endogenic geomorphic processes. This energy is mostly generated by radioactivity, rotational and tidal friction and primordial heat from the origin of the earth. This energy due to geothermal gradients and heat flow from within induces **diastrophism** and **volcanism** in the lithosphere.

Diastrophism

All processes that move, elevate or build up portions of the earth's crust come under diastrophism. They include:

1. **Orogenic processes** involving mountain building through severe folding and affecting long and narrow belts of the earth's crust.
2. **Epeirogenic processes** involving uplift or warping of large parts of the earth's crust.
3. **Earthquakes** involving local relatively minor movements.
4. **Plate tectonics** involving horizontal movements of crustal plates.

In the process of orogeny, the crust is severely deformed into folds. **Due to epeirogeny**, there may be simple deformation. **Orogeny** is a mountain building process whereas **epeirogeny** is continental building process. Through the processes of orogeny, epeirogeny, earthquakes and plate tectonics, there can be faulting and fracturing of the crust. All these processes cause **pressure, volume and temperature** (PVT) changes which in turn induce metamorphism of rocks.

Exogenic Processes

The exogenic processes derive their energy from the atmosphere determined by the ultimate energy from the sun and also the gradients created by tectonic factors.

- All earthly materials with a sloping surface are subject to **gravitational force**, which tends to cause matter to move in a downward direction along the slope. Force applied per unit area is called **stress**. Stress is produced in a solid by pushing or pulling. **This induces deformation.**
- Forces acting along the faces of earth materials are **shear stresses** (separating forces). It is this stress that breaks rocks and other earth materials. The shear stresses result in angular displacement or slippage.
- Earth materials are subject to **molecular stresses** in addition to gravitational stress. These can be induced by a variety of processes, with the most common being temperature variations, crystallisation, and melting.
- **Chemical reactions** generally result in the dissolution of soluble minerals or cementing agents, as well as the loosening of grain bonds.
- Thus, the buildup of strains in the earth's material body is the fundamental cause of weathering, mass motions, and erosion.
- **Both temperature and precipitation** are significant climatic factors that regulate different processes.
- One general word that describes **all exogenic geomorphic processes is denudation. Denude** is a verb that implies to expose or strip off. Transportation, erosion, mass wasting / movements, and weathering are all examples of denudation.

Climatic factors being equal, the intensity of action of exogenic geomorphic processes depends upon type and structure of rocks. The term structure includes such aspects of rocks as folds, faults, orientation and inclination of beds, presence or absence of joints, bedding planes, hardness or softness of constituent minerals, chemical susceptibility of mineral constituents; the permeability or impermeability etc. Different types of rocks with differences in their structure offer varying resistances to various geomorphic processes.

Some of the exogenic geomorphic processes are given below:

Weathering

Weathering is defined as mechanical disintegration and chemical decomposition of rocks through the actions of various elements of weather and climate.

As very little or no motion of materials takes place in weathering, **it is an in-situ or on-site process.**

There are three major groups of weathering processes:

1. Chemical
2. Physical or mechanical
3. Biological

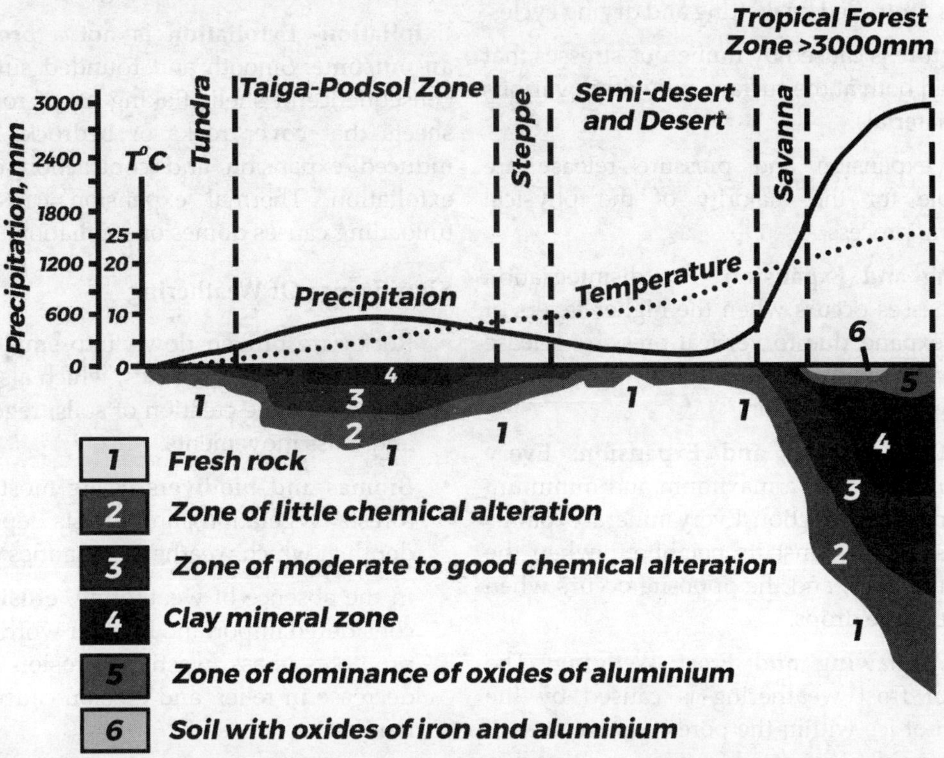

Climatic Regimes and Depth of Weathering Mantles

Chemical Weathering Processes

- **A group of weathering processes** viz; solution, carbonation, hydration, oxidation and reduction act on the rocks to decompose, dissolve or reduce them to a fine clastic state through chemical reactions by oxygen, surface and/or soil water and other acids.
- **Water and air (oxygen and carbon dioxide)** along with heat must be present to speed up all chemical reactions.
- **Solution:** When something is dissolved in water or acids, the water or acid with dissolved contents is known as solution.
- **Carbonation:** Carbonation is the reaction of carbonate and bicarbonate with minerals and is a common process helping the breaking down of feldspars and carbonate minerals.
- **Hydration:** Hydration is the chemical addition of water. Minerals take up water and expand; this expansion causes an increase in the volume of the mineral itself or rock.
- **Oxidation and Reduction:** Oxidation means a combination of a mineral with oxygen to form oxides or hydroxides in the presence of atmosphere and oxygenated waters. When oxidised minerals are placed in an environment where oxygen is absent, **reduction** takes place. Such conditions exist usually below the water table, in areas of stagnant water and waterlogged ground.

Physical Weathering Processes

- **Physical or mechanical weathering processes depend on some applied forces. The applied forces could be:** (i) gravitational forces such as overburden pressure, load and shearing stress; (ii) expansion forces due to temperature changes, crystal growth or animal activity; (iii) water pressures controlled by wetting and drying cycles.
- Rock fracture is caused by numerous stresses that are applied both at the surface and within various earthly materials.
- Thermal expansion and pressure release are responsible for the majority of the physical weathering process.
- **Unloading and Expansion:** The disintegration of rock masses occurs when the higher layers of the rock expand due to vertical pressure release caused by the removal of the underlying rock load caused by ongoing erosion.
- **Temperature changes and Expansion:** Every mineral in a rock has a maximum and minimum expansion and contraction. Every mineral expands and presses up against its neighbour when the temperature rises, and the opposite occurs when the temperature drops.
- **Freezing, Thawing and Frost Wedging:** The process of frost weathering is caused by the formation of ice within the pores and crevices of rocks as a result of repeated freezing and thawing cycles. Every day, frost freezes in glacial zones.
- **Salt Weathering:** Salts in rocks expand due to thermal action, hydration and crystallisation. Salt crystallisation is most effective of all salt-weathering processes.

Biological Weathering Processes

- The removal or addition of minerals and ions from the weathering environment, as well as physical alterations brought on by the growth or migration of organisms, are all examples of **biological weathering**.
- The act of earthworms, termites, rats, and other similar species **burrowing and wedging** helps expose the newly exposed surfaces to chemical attack and facilitates the entrance of moisture and air.
- Humans contribute to the mixing and creation of new contacts between air, water, and minerals in earth materials by **affecting vegetation, ploughing, and cultivating soils.**
- **Plant roots** exert a tremendous pressure on the earth materials mechanically breaking them apart.

Special Effects Of Weathering

Exfoliation- Exfoliation is not a procedure; it is an outcome. Smooth and rounded surfaces are the consequence of shells flaking off of roughly curved sheets that cover rocks or bedrock. Temperature-induced expansion and contraction can result in exfoliation. Thermal expansion causes tors and unloading causes domes of exfoliation.

Significance Of Weathering

- Rocks are broken down into smaller fragments by **weathering processes**, which also prepare the ground for the creation of soils, regolith, erosion, and mass movements.
- **Biomes and biodiversity** are mostly caused by forests (vegetation), and forests depend upon the depth at which weathering mantles occur.
- In the absence of weathering, **erosion** cannot be considered important. In other words, weathering promotes mass wasting, erosion results in a decrease in relief, and erosion causes changes to landforms.
- The enrichment and concentrations of some precious ores, such as copper, iron, manganese, aluminium, and so on, are aided by **weathering of rocks and deposits** and are crucial to the country's economy.
- **As rocks weather**, certain minerals are eliminated by groundwater's chemical or physical leaching, **increasing** the concentration of the valuable materials that are still present. In the absence of this kind of weathering, there may not be enough of the valuable material present to make its extraction, processing, and refinement economically feasible. This is referred to as **enrichment**.

Mass Movements

- Because of these movements, the mass of rock debris is directly affected by gravity as it descends the slopes. This means that while debris may take the air, water, or ice with it, air, water, or ice do not carry debris from one place to another.

- **The mass movements**, such as **creep, flow, slide, and fall,** can affect shallow to deep columns of materials at slow to rapid speeds.
- All substances, including bedrock and weathered materials, are subject to **gravity**. Therefore, although it facilitates large movements, weathering is **not a need** for mass movements.
- Compared to unweathered materials, mass movements occur more frequently on slopes that have seen weathering.
- **Gravity is the primary force** behind mass movements; **no other geomorphic agent**, such as flowing water, glaciers, wind, waves, or currents, influences mass movement processes.
- This indicates that while there is a transfer of materials from one location to another (facilitated by gravity), mass movements are not subject to erosion.
- The following factors, among others, promote mass movements: weak, unconsolidated materials; thinly bedded rocks; faults; steeply dipping beds; vertical cliffs or steep slopes; plentiful precipitation, torrential rains; lacking of vegetation, etc.
- Many activating reasons precede mass movements. They are as mentioned below:

a. Removal of support using artificial or natural methods from below to materials above.

b. Increase in height and gradient of slopes.

c. Overloading by using artificial or naturally occurring fillers.

d. Overloading brought on by persistent rain, saturation, and lubricating of the slope materials.

e. Material or load removal from above the primary slope surfaces.

f. Occurrence of explosions or machinery, earthquakes.

g. An **excessive** amount of natural seepage.

h. Water from lakes, reservoirs, and rivers is heavily drawn down, which causes the discharge of water from beneath slopes and riverbanks to be slow.

i. Indiscriminate removal of natural vegetation.

Landslides

- These are perceptible movements that happen rather quickly. The materials are comparatively dry.
- The kind of discontinuities in the rock, the level of weathering, and the slope's steepness all affect the detached mass size and shape.

Based upon the type of movement of materials several types are identified in this category:

- **Slump-** A slump occurs when one or more units of rock debris slip and rotate backward relative to the slope that the movement is occurring on.
- **Debris slide** is the term for the rapid rolling or sliding of earth debris without mass rotation backward.
- When earth **debris falls** from a vertical or overhanging face, it almost falls freely.
- **A rockslide** is the movement of a single mass of rock down a bedding, fault, or joint surface. Rock sliding is destructive and quite rapid over steep slopes.
- The free falling of rock blocks over a steep slope while maintaining their distance from the slope is known as **rock fall**. In contrast to rockslides, which affect materials down to a significant depth, rock falls originate from the rock face's superficial layers.

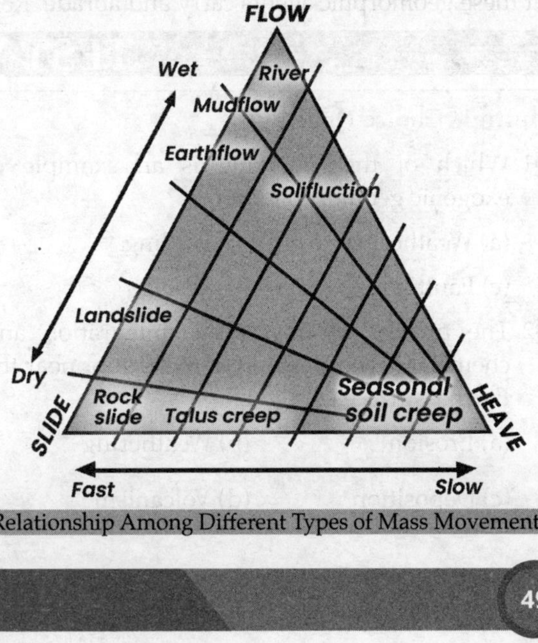

Relationship Among Different Types of Mass Movements

In our nation, the Himalayas frequently see **landslides and debris avalanches**. This is due to many factors. One is that because the Himalayas are **tectonically active**. Sedimentary rocks and unconsolidated and semi-consolidated deposits comprise the majority of them. The hill slopes are quite steep. The frequency of lanslides in Himalayas are higher than in the Nilgiris, which border Tamil Nadu, Karnataka, Kerala, and the Western Ghats.

Nilgiris are mostly composed of very hard and relatively tectonically stable rocks compared to the Himalayas. However, Nilgiris also experience direct rock falls due to nearly vertical cliffs and escarpments.

Temperature ranges and fluctuations cause pronounced mechanical weathering. For short periods of time, they experience significant rainfall. Thus, in addition to landslides and debris avalanches, almost direct rock fall occurs regularly in these locations.

Erosion and Deposition

Erosion is the process of **acquisition and transportation** of rock debris. The fragmentation of big rocks into smaller pieces due to weathering and other processes is removed and transported to different locations by erosional geomorphic agents such as groundwater, running water, glaciers, wind, and waves, depending on the dynamics of each of these agents.

Erosion is also significantly **aided by the rock debris** that these geomorphic agents carry and abrade. Relief deteriorates due to erosion; that is, the landscape is worn down. This indicates that while weathering contributes to erosion, it is not essential for erosion to occur. Degradation processes include erosion, weathering, and mass-wasting. The earth's surface is constantly changing, and erosion is mostly responsible for this. Kinetic energy governs deluge processes including transportation and erosion. Groundwater, waves, glaciers, wind, and moving water all contribute to the erosion and movement of earth's elements. The first three of these agents are governed by the weather. They stand for three different states of matter: solid (glacier), liquid (flowing water), and gaseous (wind). The other two causes of erosion, groundwater, and waves, are not influenced by the climate.

While the work of ground water is primarily governed by the lithological characteristics of the region, the work of waves is determined by their location along the interface between the lithosphere and hydrosphere, or the coastal region. Karst topography only forms if water is accessible and the rocks are soluble and porous. Erosion leads to deposition. On softer slopes, the erosional agents lose energy and velocity, causing the materials they carry to begin to settle on their own.

To put it another way, no agent really performs depositions. Finer materials are deposited later, after the coarser ones are deposited. Depressions are filled by deposition. Running water, glaciers, wind, waves, and groundwater are examples of the same erosional agents that also function as aggradational or depositional agents.

TEST YOURSELF

Multiple Choice Questions

Q1. Which of the following is an example of exogenic geomorphic process?

(a) Weathering (b) Folding

(c) Faulting (d) Uplift

Q2. The process of physical disintegration and chemical decomposition of rocks at or near the Earth's surface is called:

(a) Erosion (b) Weathering

(c) Deposition (d) Volcanism

Q3. The process of wearing away and removal of rocks and soil by natural agents such as water, wind, and ice is known as:

(a) Weathering (b) Erosion

(c) Deposition (d) Transportation

Q4. The process by which sediment is dropped or deposited by water, wind, or ice is called:

(a) Weathering (b) Erosion

(c) Deposition (d) Transportation

Q5. The downslope movement of rock, soil, and debris under the influence of gravity is called:

(a) Weathering (b) Erosion

(c) Deposition (d) Mass wasting

Q6. The process of gradual wearing away of the Earth's surface through the action of water, wind, or ice is known as:

(a) Abrasion (b) Corrosion

(c) Attrition (d) Erosion

Q7. The process of chemical decomposition of rocks due to the action of water, oxygen, and acids is called:

(a) Mechanical weathering

(b) Biological weathering

(c) Chemical weathering

(d) Physical weathering

Q8. The process of breaking and fragmentation of rocks does not happen due to temperature changes is known as:

(a) Exfoliation (b) Frost action

(c) Thermal expansion (d) Hydrolysis

Q9. The process of erosion in which fine particles of rock and soil are lifted and carried away by wind is called:

(a) Fluvial erosion (b) Glacial erosion

(c) Aeolian erosion (d) Coastal erosion

Answer Key					
Q1.	a	Q2.	b	Q3.	b
Q4.	c	Q5.	d	Q6.	d
Q7.	c	Q8.	a	Q9.	c

Model Questions for Main Examination

Q1. Explain the role of weathering in shaping landforms. Discuss the different types of weathering processes and their significance in the formation of specific landforms.

Q2. Describe the process of erosion and its impact on landscape development. Provide examples of erosional landforms formed by rivers, glaciers, and wind, highlighting the distinctive features and mechanisms involved in each case.

UNIT 6 Soil

In This Unit

Comprehensive and profound coverage of the following NCERTs' chapters:

- ✓ NCERT Class- 8th (Resource and Development), Chapter- 2
- ✓ NCERT Class- 11th (India Physical Environment), Chapter- 6

Soil is the thin layer of **granular substances** that covers the earth's surface. It is mainly associated to land. Type of soils is determined by the underlying landforms. Soil is the formation of earthly weathered rocks, minerals, and organic materials. **Weathering** is the process that causes this to occur. **Fertile soil** has the proper **balance** of minerals and organic materials.

Process of Soil Formation

Weathering is primarily responsible for Soil formation (pedogenesis). The primary ingredient needed for soil formation is this weathering mantle, or the depth of the weathered material. A thin layer of soil has been created by the source rock material being subjected to different weathering and gradation processes. **First,** bacteria and other inferior plant bodies, such as mosses and lichens, colonise the weathered debris or transported deposits. The decomposing bodies of plants and other organisms aid in the **buildup of humus**. **Small grasses and ferns** might sprout, and eventually, seeds carried by birds and the wind will give rise to **shrubs and trees.** Plant roots pierce the ground, animals that burrow raise particles, and eventually the mass of material becomes porous and sponge-like, allowing air to pass through and retaining water. This mature soil is a complex mixture of mineral and organic materials.

Factors of Soil Formation

The major factors of soil formation are:

Parent Material- In the formation of soil, **parent material** acts as a **passive control factor**. Parent materials might be **any weathered rock debris or transported deposits**, either **on-site or in situ**. The mineral and chemical composition of the rock deposits and debris, as well as their texture and structure, all influence the development of soil. Important factors to be taken into account under parent materials are the kind, rate, and depth of the weathering mantle.

Topography- Topography has an impact on how much sunlight a surface covered in parent materials receives as well as how much surface and subsurface drainage flows over and through the parent materials. Over flat upland areas, soils will be thick, while on steep slopes, they will be thin. Soil formation is advantageous over gentle slopes where water percolates well and erosion is slow. In locations with flat terrain, the soil may accumulate a substantial amount of organic matter and a thick layer of clay, giving the soil a dark colour.

Climate- In soil development, the following climatic factors are involved: (i) moisture as measured by humidity, evaporation, and precipitation intensity, frequency, and duration; (ii) seasonal and diurnal fluctuations in temperature.

Rainfall contributes to the soil's moisture content, which enables chemical and biological processes. Abundant water facilitates the downward movement of soil particles through the soil **(eluviation)** and deposits them below **(illuviation)**. In regions with high rainfall, such as **wet equatorial regions**, a significant portion of the **silica** in the soil is also taken, along with **calcium, sodium, magnesium, and potassium**. **Desilication** is the process of removing silica from the soil.

Due to **high temperatures in dry climates**, where evaporation exceeds precipitation, groundwater is drawn to the surface through capillary action. As a result, salts are left behind in the soil as the water evaporates. **A crust known as "hardpans" is formed by these salts in the soil.** Kanker, or calcium carbonate nodules, are found in tropical climates and regions with **moderate precipitation.** There are two ways that temperature might affect **chemical and biological activity: either in increasing or decreasing manner.**

With the exception of carbonation, **chemical activity** increases at higher temperatures, decreases at lower ones, and stop completely at freezing temperatures. Because of this, the profiles of tropical soils with higher temperatures are deeper, while the soils in the frozen tundra are primarily composed of components that have been mechanically broken.

Biological Activity: The amount of bacterial activity in soil reveals variations between **cold and warm regions**. Because bacterial growth is sluggish in frigid regions, humus builds up there. In humid tropical and equatorial regions, there is very little humus in the soil due to rapid oxidation of dead plants and high bacterial development and action. Moreover, gaseous nitrogen from the air is taken up by bacteria and other soil organisms, who then transform it into a chemical form that plants can use. We call this process **"nitrogen fixation."** Leguminous plants have a type of bacteria called rhizobium that resides in their root nodules and fixes nitrogen that is good for the host plant. Large animals, such as rodents, termites, ants, and earthworms, etc also impact soil.

Time- The third major component influencing the formation of soil is time. The maturation of soils and profile development are determined by the duration of the soil formation processes. When all soil-forming processes operate for a long enough period of time to generate a profile, the soil is considered mature.

Human activities also influence it to a large extent.

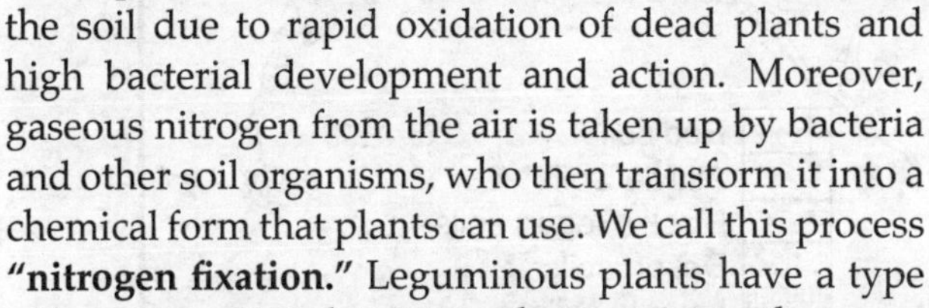

Factors that Influence Soil Formation

Layers of Soil

Soil profile is the arrangement of **three layers** which are called horizons. They are:

- **'Horizon A'** is the highest zone, where organic materials have combined with water, nutrients, and mineral matter—all essential for plant growth.
- A zone of transition between "horizon A" and "horizon C," represents **"horizon B"** is made up of both above- and below-ground materials. Although the mineral content is clearly worn, there is some organic stuff present.
- The loose parent material is what makes up **"Horizon C"**. The soil creation process starts with this layer, which later gives rise to the two layers mentioned above.

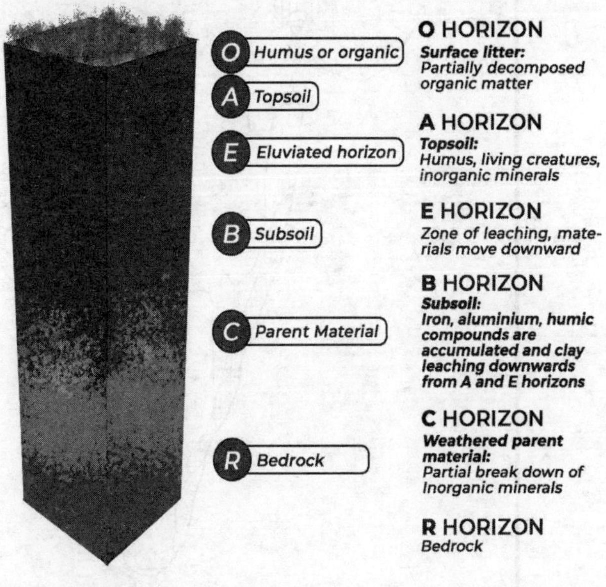

Classification of Soils

In the past, **soils** were divided into **two major categories**: **Usara and Urvara**, which were respectively **sterile** and **fertile**. Soils were categorised in the **sixteenth century A.D. according** to both their internal properties and exterior attributes, such as soil moisture content, texture, and colour. The primary soil types were classified as sandy, clayey, silty, and loam, among others, based on texture. They were classified as red, yellow, black, etc. based on colour.

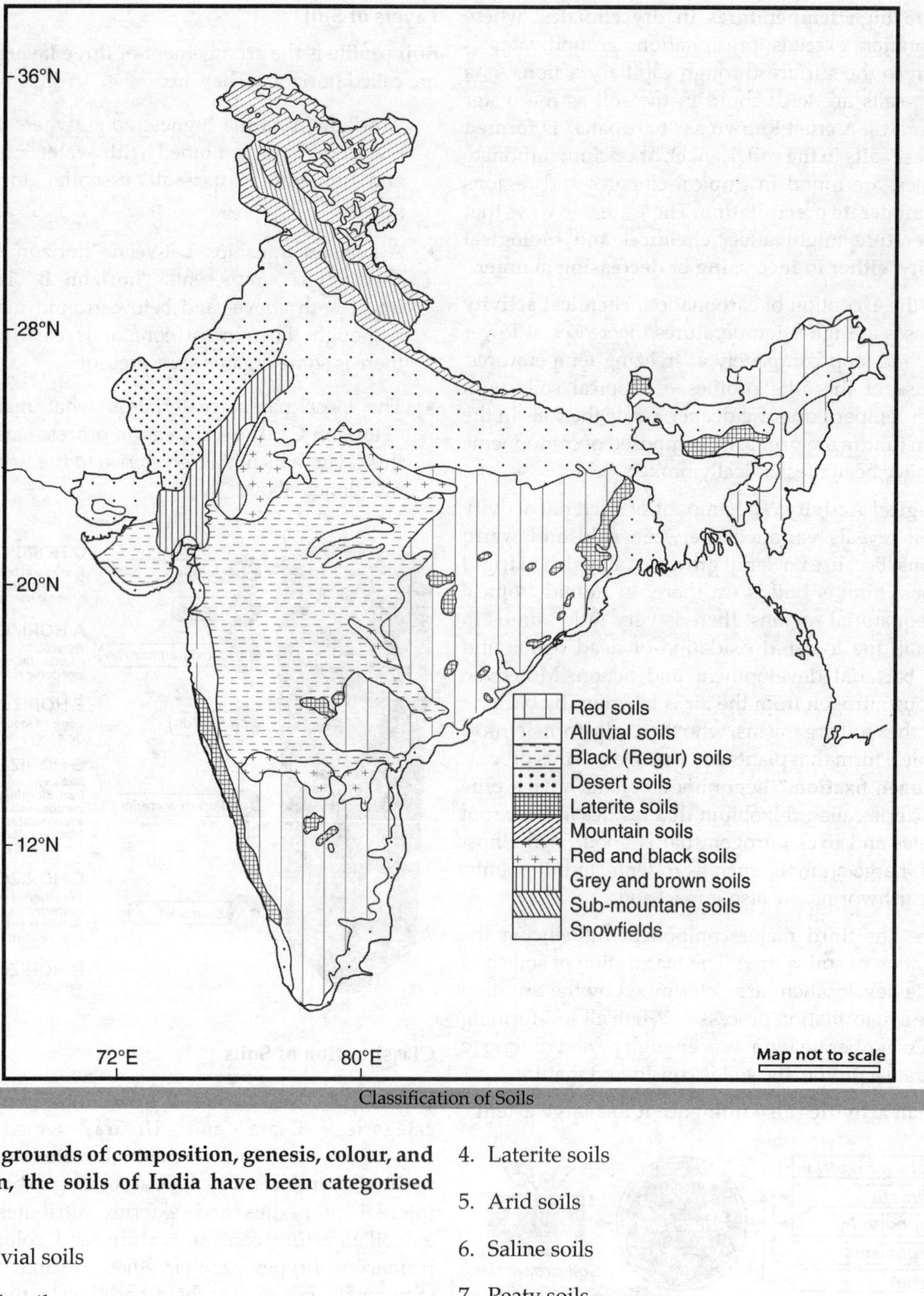

Classification of Soils

On the grounds of composition, genesis, colour, and location, the soils of India have been categorised into:

1. Alluvial soils
2. Black soils
3. Red and Yellow soils
4. Laterite soils
5. Arid soils
6. Saline soils
7. Peaty soils
8. Forest soils

Alluvial Soils

- The northern plains and river basins are largely covered by **alluvial soils**. Approximately 40% of the country is covered by these soils. These have been deposited by three important Himalayan-river systems– the **Indus, the Ganga and the Brahmaputra.**
- Through a narrow corridor in Rajasthan, they extend into the plains of Gujarat. The eastern coastal plains also have alluvial soil, especially in the deltas of the Krishna, Godavari, Mahanadi, and Kaveri rivers.
- There are different ratios of sand, silt, and clay in the alluvial soil. Soil particles appear to be slightly larger as we travel inlands towards the river valleys. The soils are coarser around the location of the slope break, or in the higher portions of the river valley. Piedmont plains like the **Duars, Chos, and Terai** are more likely to have these types of soils.
- Soils are classified according to their age in addition to the size of their grains or other constituents. Alluvial soils are categorised as **Bangar or Khadar** based on their age.
- Floods deposit fine silts called **khadar**, the new alluvium, on the soil every year, enriching it. Separated from the flood plains, the **Bhangar** system is an older alluvium deposit. **Kankars, or calcareous concretions, are present in the soils of both Khadar and Bhangar**. In comparison to the Khadar soil, the bangar soil contains **more kankar** nodules.
- In general, they have low phosphorus content but high potash content. The lower and middle Ganga plains as well as the **Brahmaputra valley** have **more-loamy, clayey soils**. From the west to the east, the amount of sand diminishes.
- The alluvial soils range in colour from **light grey to ash grey.** The depth of the deposition, the materials' textures, and the maturity period all affect the shade.
- Alluvial soil regions are **highly fertile** and **densely populated** due to their extensive cultivation.

Black Soil

- These soils are black in colour and are also known as **regur soils**. Black soil is ideal for growing cotton and is also known as **black cotton soil**. It is believed that climatic conditions along with the parent rock material are the important factors for the formation of black soil.
- This kind of lava-flow-based soil is typical of the **Deccan trap (Basalt) region**, which is **distributed across the northwest Deccan plateau**. They stretch southeast along the **Godavari and Krishna valleys**, encompassing the plateaus of Maharashtra, Saurashtra, Malwa, Madhya Pradesh, and Chhattisgarh.
- **The very fine, or clayey, material** makes up the **black soils**. Their **ability** to **retain moisture is well-known.**
- They **shrink when they are dry**, and **swell** and become **sticky when they are wet**. Thus, these soils get large cracks during the dry season. Thus, a process similar to **"self-ploughing"** takes place. Black soil holds moisture for a very long time due to its slow absorption and loss of moisture, which allows crops especially those fed by rain to survive even during the dry season.
- The black soils are high in lime, iron, magnesium, and alumina chemically. They contain potash as well. But they are deficient in organic matter, nitrogen, and phosphorus. The colour of the soil ranges from deep black to grey.

Red and Yellow Soil

- In the eastern and southern regions of the Deccan Plateau, **red soil** is found due to presence of crystalline igneous rocks in areas that receive little rainfall. A considerable distance is covered with red loamy soil along the Piedmont zone of the Western Ghat.
- Additionally, some areas of Odisha, Chhattisgarh, and the southern portion of the middle Ganga plain have **yellow and red soils.**
- **The soil develops a reddish colour** due to a wide diffusion of iron in crystalline and metamorphic rocks. It looks yellow when it occurs in a hydrated form.
- The fine-grained red and yellow soils are normally fertile, whereas coarse-grained soils found in dry upland areas are poor in fertility. They are generally poor in nitrogen, phosphorous and humus.

Laterite Soil

- The name **"laterite"** comes from the Latin word "later," which meaning brick. High rainfall and temperatures are favourable to the development of laterite soils. This soil is the product of intensive leaching due to heavy rain.
- Rain removes silica and lime from the soil, leaving behind soils that contain iron oxide and aluminum compounds. Bacteria that are tolerant of high temperatures quickly destroy the humus from the soil.
- These soils have an **abundance of iron oxide and potash** but a **deficiency of organic matter, nitrogen, phosphate, and calcium**. **Laterites** are therefore **unsuitable for cultivation**; however, in order to make the **soil useful for farming manure and fertiliser needs to be used.**
- **The hilly regions** of Odisha and Assam, Karnataka, Kerala, Tamil Nadu, Madhya Pradesh, and other states are **frequently home to laterite soils**. **Tree crops like cashew nuts** do better on **red laterite soils**, which are found in Tamil Nadu, Andhra Pradesh, and Kerala.
- The construction of houses often uses bricks made from **laterite soils**. These soils are often found in the highest regions of the Peninsular plateau.

Arid Soils

- Colour of **Arid soils** varies from red to brown. They are often saline in nature and have a sandy texture. Certain regions have extremely high salinity levels, and common salt is made by letting water evaporate.
- The soil lacks humus and moisture due to the dry environment, high temperatures, and quicker evaporation. There is not enough nitrogen present, and the phosphate amount is normal.
- Since the amount of calcium in the soil increases downhill, **Kankar occupies the lower horizons.** Water infiltration is restricted by rocks known as the Kankar layer in the lowest horizons.
- These soils become cultivable with adequate irrigation, as in western Rajasthan.

Saline Soils

- **Usara soils** is another name for them. Because **saline soils have higher concentrations** of magnesium, potassium, and sodium, they are **infertile** and cannot support vegetative development.
- The dry environment and inadequate drainage are the main causes for their higher salt content. They operate in environments that are swampy and water-logged as well as arid and semi-arid climates.
- They have a sandy to loamy structure. They are deficient in calcium and nitrogen. Saline soils are more common in the **Sundarban regions** of West Bengal, the eastern coast deltas, and western Gujarat.
- Saline soils are emerging in **fertile alluvial soils** in places associated with **intensive farming** and **excessive irrigation**, particularly in places where the green revolution occured.
- When dry weather and excessive irrigation are combined, capillary action is encouraged and salt accumulates on the top layer of the soil. Farmers are **encouraged to add gypsum** to these areas, particularly in **Punjab and Haryana**, in order **to address the issue of salinity** in the soil.

Peaty Soils

- They are found in regions with high humidity, a lot of rainfall, and healthy vegetation growth. As a result, a significant amount of dead organic matter builds up in these places, giving the soil a rich humus and organic content. These soils may contain as much as 40–50% organic matter.
- These soils are often black in colour and heavy. They are also alkaline in several areas.
- It is widely distributed in the coastal regions of West Bengal, Odisha, and Tamil Nadu, as well as the northern part of Bihar and the southern part of Uttarakhand.

Forest Soils

- These soils are found in hilly and mountainous regions with an adequate supply of rainforests. Depending on the mountain environment in which they form, the soil texture varies.

- On the valley sides, they are loamy and silty, whereas on the upper slopes, they are coarse-grained. These acidic, low-humus soils undergo denudation in the snow-covered regions of the Himalayas.
- The soils found in the lower parts of the valleys particularly on the river terraces and alluvial fans are fertile.

Soil Degradation

The term **"degradation of soil"** refers to the reduction in soil fertility that occurs when the soil's depth and nutritional state decrease as a result of misuse and erosion.

Soil Erosion

- The destruction of the soil cover is described as **soil erosion.**
- Due to their capacity to both carry and remove soil, wind and water are potent factors of soil erosion.
- Significant **wind erosion** occurs in arid and semi-arid areas. Erosion from **flowing water is particularly important** in areas with steep slopes and high rainfall.
- The most significant type of **erosion caused by water** is known as **sheet and gully** erosion, and it occurs widely throughout India.
- **Sheet erosion** takes place on level grounds after a heavy rainfall with minimal soil removal, that is not easily noticeable. But it is harmful since it removes the finer and more fertile top soil.
- On steep hillsides, **gully erosion** is frequent. The agricultural areas become unsuitable for cultivation as gullies grow deeper with rains and split them into tiny fragments.
- **Bad land topography** is a region that has a lot of deep ravines or gullies. Ravines are widespread in the Chambal basin. Besides this, they are also found in Tamil Nadu and West Bengal.
- **Human activities** too are responsible for soil erosion to a great extent. As the human population increases, the demand on the land also increases. Forest and other natural vegetation is removed for human settlement, for cultivation, for grazing animals and for various other needs.
- **Deforestation** is one of the major causes of soil erosion. Plants keep soils bound in locks of roots, and thus, prevent erosion. They also add humus to the soil by shedding leaves and twigs. Forests have been denuded practically in most parts of India but their effect on soil erosion are more in hilly parts of the country

Impact of soil erosion on agriculture: For Indian agriculture, soil erosion is a major issue that has detrimental repercussions in other areas as well. When debris from erosion is pushed down to rivers, it reduces the rivers' carrying capacity, increases the frequency of floods, and damages agricultural lands.

Over-irrigation in India's irrigated zones is turning a sizeable portion of arable land salty. The fertility of the soil is destroyed when salt that gets trapped in its lower profiles rises to the surface. When organic manures are absent, chemical fertilisers are likewise detrimental to the soil. Chemicals harden the soil and eventually lower its fertility if it does not obtain adequate humus. Since the River Valley Projects were the first to benefit from the Green Revolution, this issue is common in these regions.

Soil Conservation Measures

A methodology known as "soil conservation" aims to keep the soil fertile, stop soil erosion and depletion, and restore the damaged state of the soil.

Some measures of soil conservation are listed below:

- **Regulation of over-grazing and shifting cultivation:** In many areas of India, overgrazing and shifting agriculture have impacted the natural land cover and caused significant erosion. Villagers should be educated and made aware of the potential effects to be able to regulate and control it.
- **Mulching**: An organic material layer, like straw, covers the bare ground in between plants. Soil moisture retention is aided by it.
- **Contour barriers**: Along contours, barriers are constructed with soil, grass, and stones. Water is collected by creating trenches in front of the barriers.
- **Rock dam**: The water flow is slowed down by piling up rocks. This stops more soil erosion and gullies.

- **Terrace farming**: To create flat surfaces for growing crops, steep slopes are marked with wide, level steps or terraces. They lessen erosion of the soil and surface runoff.
- **Intercropping**: To prevent soil erosion caused by rain, crops are sown at different times and arranged in alternating rows.
- **Contour ploughing**: Forming a natural barrier to prevent water from flowing down a hillside by ploughing parallel to its contours.
- **Shelter belts**: To prevent wind movement and preserve soil cover, rows of trees are planted in arid and coastal areas.
- By creating **tree shelter belts** and practicing **agroforestry**, efforts should be taken to **prevent sand dunes from encroaching** on agricultural land in **arid and semi-arid regions**. The conversion of unsuitable land for farming into **grazing pastures** is recommended.

The people who use the land and benefit from it will ultimately bear the responsibility for its conservation.

TEST YOURSELF

Multiple Choice Questions

Q1. Which type of soil is rich in lime, iron, magnesia and alumina, also contain potash, but they lack in phosphorous, nitrogen and organic matter?

(a) Laterite soil (b) Black soil

(c) Alluvial soil (d) Peaty soil

Q2. Which soil covers 40% of the total area of India?

(a) Peaty soil (b) Laterite soil

(c) Forest soil (d) Alluvial soil

Q3. For which soil, farmers of Punjab and Haryana are advised to add gypsum?

(a) Peaty soil (b) Arid soil

(c) Red and Yellow soil (d) Saline soil

Q4. A region with a large number of deep gullies or ravines is called?

(a) Gully topography (b) Sheet topography

(c) Arid topography (d) Bad-land topography

Q5. Which soil occurs widely in the northern part of Bihar, southern part of Uttarakhand and the coastal areas of West Bengal, Odisha and Tamil Nadu?

(a) Peaty soil (b) Black soil

(c) Alluvial soil (d) Arid soil

Q6. Which factor plays a significant role in soil formation?

(a) Climate (b) Topography

(c) Parent material (d) All of the above

Q7. Soil erosion caused by wind is known as:

(a) Sheet erosion (b) Rill erosion

(c) Gully erosion (d) Wind erosion

Q8. Which soil horizon contains the most organic matter?

(a) A horizon (b) B horizon

(c) C horizon (d) D horizon

Q9. Soil texture refers to:

(a) The colour of the soil

(b) The smell of the soil

(c) The size of mineral particles in the soil

(d) The fertility of the soil

Q10. Soil pH below 7 indicates:

(a) Acidic soil (b) Alkaline soil

(c) Neutral soil (d) None of the above

Q11. Which technique is used for soil conservation on hilly slopes?

(a) Contour ploughing (b) Crop rotation

(c) Mulching (d) Drip irrigation

Q12. Soil degradation refers to:

(a) Improvement in soil quality

(b) Increase in soil fertility

(c) Decline in soil quality

(d) None of the above

Q13. Humus is formed by the decomposition of:

(a) Rocks (b) Water

(c) Plants and animals (d) Air

Q14. The process of nutrient leaching occurs in which soil horizon?

(a) A horizon (b) B horizon

(c) C horizon (d) D horizon

Q15. The main objective of soil conservation is to:

(a) Increase soil erosion

(b) Improve soil fertility

(c) Deplete soil nutrients

(d) None of the above

Q16. The black cotton soil of India has been formed due to the weathering of: (UPSC 2021)

(a) Brown forest soil (b) Fissure volcanic rock

(c) Granite and schist (d) Shale and limestone

Answer Key

Q1.	b	Q2.	d	Q3.	d
Q4.	d	Q5.	a	Q6.	d
Q7.	d	Q8.	a	Q9.	c
Q10.	a	Q11.	a	Q12.	c
Q13.	c	Q14.	a	Q15.	b
Q16.	b				

Model Questions for Main Examination

Q1. Write about the practices through which soil erosion occurs? Mentions ways how to solve it?

Q2. Describe formation and features of Alluvial soil?

UNIT 7

Major Landforms of The Earth

In This Unit

Comprehensive and profound coverage of the following NCERTs' chapters:

- ✓ NCERT Class- 6th (The Earth: Our Habitat), Chapter- 6
- ✓ NCERT Class- 11th (Fundamentals of Physical Geography), Chapter- 6

There are countless types of landforms on Earth. The lithosphere may have flat and rough areas. Two mechanisms lead to the formation of these landforms. The earth's surface rises and falls in different places due to the first process, which is **internal in nature.** The ongoing **erosion and rebuilding** of the ground surface is the second process, sometimes known as the **external process**. The processes of **erosion and deposition** are lowering and rebuilding the surface, respectively. The flowing water, ice, and wind are responsible for these two processes.

Landforms can be classified as mountains, plateaus, and plains based on their slope and elevation.

> A Hill is a land surface that rises higher than the surrounding area. Generally, a steep hill with an elevation of more than 600 metres is termed as a mountain.

Mountains

- Any naturally occurring height on Earth is referred to as a mountain. The mountains usually have a wide base and a tiny summit.
- In some mountains, there are permanently frozen rivers of ice. They are called **glaciers**.
- Mountains are very useful. The mountains are a storehouse of water.
- Mountains may be arranged in a line known as **range**.
- There are three types of mountains- **Fold Mountains, Block Mountains and the Volcanic Mountains.**

Fold Mountains

- The **Alps and the Himalayas** are new fold mountains featuring steep peaks and a rough terrain.
- One of the world's oldest fold mountain systems is **the Aravali range** in India. Erosion has caused significant degradation to the range.
- Ural Mountains in Russia and the Appalachians in North America have low elevation and rounded features as these are incredibly ancient.

Block Mountains

- When vast areas are split up and moved vertically, block mountains are formed. The lowered blocks are referred to as **graben,** and the raised blocks are called **horsts.**
- Such mountain systems can be found in Europe in the **Vosges Mountain and the Rhine Valley.**

Volcanic mountains

- Volcanic activity is the cause of the formation of volcanic mountains.
- Such mountains are **Mt. Fujiyama in Japan and Mt. Kilimanjaro in Africa.**

> **Mauna Kea** (Hawaii) in the Pacific Ocean is an under-sea mountain. It is higher than Mount Everest being 10,205 metres high.

Plateaus

- A plateau is a flat area of raised ground. It is a level **tabletop ground** that rises over the surroundings.
- A plateau could have one or more steeply sloping sides. Plateaus typically range in height from a few hundred to several thousand metres.
- Like mountains, plateaus can be young or old. One of the oldest plateaus is the **Deccan plateau** in India.
- Other examples include the Western Plateau of Australia and the East African Plateau, which includes Kenya, Tanzania, and Uganda.
- At **4 to 6 thousand metres** above mean sea level, the **Tibetan plateau** is the highest in the world.
- Plateaus have abundant mineral resources, which makes them highly valuable. Because of this, the plateau regions are home to a large number of mining sites worldwide.
- **The African plateau** is well-known for its **diamond and gold mining. Huge coal, manganese, and iron reserves can be discovered in India's Chota Nagpur plateau.**
- As the river drops from a **considerable height** in the plateau areas, there could be multiple waterfalls. Examples of such waterfalls in India are the **Jog falls** in Karnataka and the **Hundru falls** in the Chota Nagpur plateau on the river **Subarnarekha**.
- The **lava plateaus** are rich in black soil that are fertile and good for cultivation.

Plains

- **A plain** is a broad area of level ground. Generally speaking, they are no more than 200 metres above mean sea level. Certain plains are levelled incredibly whereas some can be swaying gently.
- The majority of the plains are created by rivers and their offshoots.
- Mountains are eroded by rivers that run down their slopes. They then leave their cargo, which is made up of silt, sand, and stones, in the valleys and along their paths. These sediments are what give rise to plains.
- Plains are generally quite fruitful. It is simple to construct a transportation network. As a result, the world's plains are densely populated.
- In North America and Asia, there are some of the biggest river-made plains. For instance, the Yangtze in China and the Ganga and Brahmaputra in India are responsible for creating these plains in Asia.
- The area is extremely productive for agriculture due to its rich soils. The Indo-Gangetic plains are also the most heavily populated areas of India.

Landforms and Their Evolution

Landforms are created by variations in temperature and the vertical or horizontal movement of land masses; these processes can also fluctuate in intensity, resulting in new modifications to the landforms. In this context, evolution refers to phases in which a landform changes after it has first developed, or in which a portion of the earth's surface changes from one landform to another.

Running Water

- In humid regions, which receive heavy rainfall, running water is considered the most important of the geomorphic agents in bringing about the degradation of the land surface.
- There are **two components** of running water. One is **Overland Flow** on the general land surface as a sheet. Another is **Linear Flow** as streams and rivers in valleys.
- Most of the **erosional landforms** made by running water are associated with vigorous and youthful rivers flowing along gradients.
- With time, stream channels over **steep gradients turn gentler** due to continued erosion, and as a consequence lose their velocity, facilitating active deposition. There may be depositional forms associated with streams flowing over steep slopes.
- The amount of deposition increases with the gentler the gradient or slope of the river channels.
- When the stream beds turn gentler due to continued erosion, downward cutting becomes less dominant and lateral erosion of banks increases and as a consequence the hills and valleys are reduced to plains.

- The divides between drainage basins are likewise lowered until they are almost completely flattened leaving finally, a lowland of faint relief with some low resistant remnants called **monadnocks** standing out here and there. This type of plain forming as a result of stream erosion is called a **peneplain** (an almost plain).

The characteristics of each of the stages of landscapes developing in running water regimes may be summarised as follows:

Youth: Streams are few during this stage with poor integration and flow over original slopes showing shallow V-shaped valleys with no floodplains or with very narrow floodplains along trunk streams. Streams divide are broad and flat with marshes, swamp and lakes. Meanders if present develop over these broad upland surfaces. These meanders may eventually entrench themselves into the uplands. Waterfalls and rapids may exist where local hard rock bodies are exposed.

Mature: During this stage streams are plenty with good integration. The valleys are still V-shaped but deep; trunk streams are broad enough to have wider floodplains within which streams may flow in meanders confined within the valley. The flat and broad inter stream areas and swamps and marshes of youth disappear and the stream divides turn sharp. **Waterfalls and rapids disappear.**

Old: In old age, there are few, smaller tributaries with gentle gradients. Vast floodplains featuring oxbow lakes, natural levees, and other features are traversed by **meandering** streams. Divides are broad and flat with lakes, swamps and marshes. Most of the landscape is at or slightly above sea level.

> There are thousands of small waterfalls in the world. The highest waterfall is **Angel Falls of Venezuela in South America**. Some other waterfalls are **Niagara Falls** located on the border between Canada and USA in **North America** and **Victoria Falls** on the borders of Zambia and Zimbabwe in **Africa**.

Ground Water

- In this case, groundwater as a resource is not of interest. We concentrate on the **role that groundwater plays in the erosion of land masses** and the development of landforms.
- It is **well-permeable**, sparsely bedded, heavily jointed, and cracked rocks that allow surface water to **percolate**. When the water below the surface descends to a certain depth vertically, it flows horizontally through the bedding planes, joints, or materials themselves. The erosion of the rocks is brought on by the water's downward and horizontal motion.
- When creating landforms, **the mechanical or physical removal of materials** by shifting groundwater is negligible. This is the reason that not all kinds of rocks exhibit the effects of groundwater. However, in calcium carbonate-rich rocks like limestones or dolomites, surface and groundwater undergo chemical reactions that result in solution and precipitation deposits, which gives rise to a variety of landforms.
- Both of these processes—**solution and precipitation**—are present in dolomites and limestones, which can be found either alone or intermingled with other rocks. **Karst Topography**, named for the typical topography found in the limestone rocks of the Karst region in the Balkans next to the Adriatic Sea, refers to any limestone or dolomitic region exhibiting typical landforms created by the action of groundwater through the processes of solution and deposition.
- Additionally, erosional and depositional landforms are characteristic of the karst topography.

Glaciers

- Glaciers are masses of moving ice that flow either as broad trough-like valleys when they flow down the slopes of mountains, as in the case of mountain and valley glaciers, or as sheets over the land, known as **piedmont glaciers or continental glaciers** if a massive sheet of ice is spread across the plains at the foot of mountains.
- In contrast to water flow, glaciers move slowly. There could be a daily shift of a few centimetres to a few metres, or perhaps less or more. The primary factor behind the movement of glaciers is gravity.
- Numerous glaciers are moving down the Himalayan valleys and slopes in our nation. Some of these can be seen in the **upper regions of Uttarakhand, Himachal Pradesh, and Jammu and Kashmir**. Meltwaters originating beneath

the Gangotri glacier's snout (Gaumukh) mostly feed Bhagirathi. The Alakananda River receives its water supply from the Alkapuri glacier. Near Devprayag, the rivers Bhagirathi and Alkananda merge to form the Ganga.

- The sheer weight of the ice causes friction, which greatly accelerates glacial erosion. Glaciers remove large-sized, sharp rocks and bits of land, which are then dragged over valley floors or sides, causing severe damage from plucking and abrasion.
- Even unweathered rocks may experience severe damage from glaciers, which can also turn high mountains into low hills and plains. The debris that is cleared and the divides that are lowered as glaciers move forward eventually cause the slope to become so low that the glaciers cease to move, leaving behind a mass of low hills and large outwash plains together with other depositional characteristics.

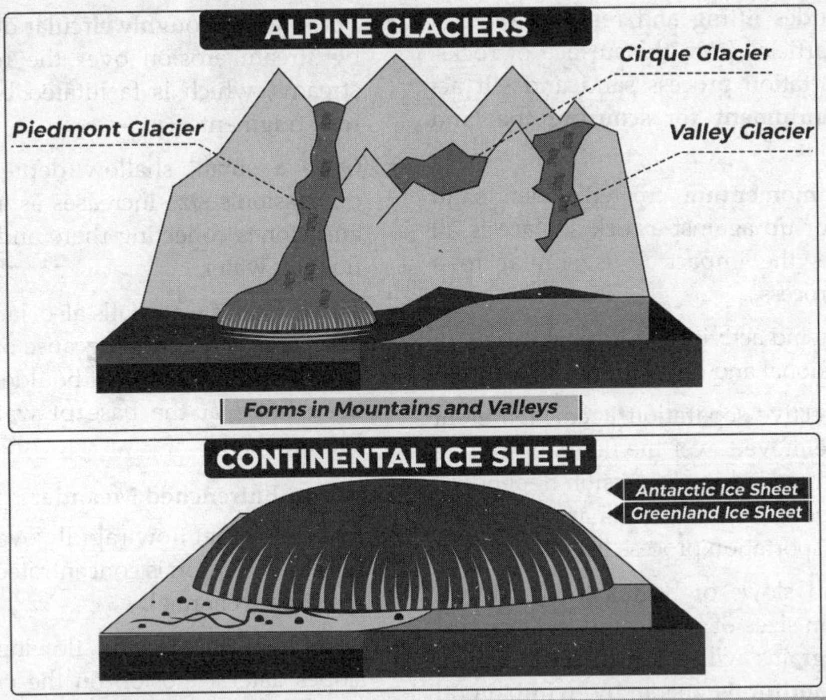

Types of Glaciers

Waves and Currents

- The most destructive and dynamic processes are those that occur around the coast. Along the coast, certain changes happen extremely quickly. There may be **erosion in one season and deposition in another at a certain location.**
- Waves are responsible for the majority of the changes that occur near coasts. There is a significant churning of sediments on the sea floor as waves break and throw water onto the shore with tremendous force.
- Coastal areas are significantly impacted by the continuous breaking waves. More quickly than regular breaking waves, storm and tsunami waves can have far-reaching effects.
- Coastal landforms are influenced by two factors, **apart from wave action**: (i) the **structure of the sea floor and land**; and (ii) Whether the coast is **retreating (submerging) landward or moving forward (emerging) seaward.**
- **By considering constant sea level, coasts can be classified into two types as:**
  - ➢ High, rocky coasts **(submerged coasts)**
  - ➢ Low, smooth and gently **sloping sedimentary coasts (emergent coasts)**

Winds

- In hot deserts, **wind** is one of the two main factors. The dry and barren nature of the desert floors causes them to heat up excessively and rapidly.

- The air just above the heated floors heats up due to turbulence, pushing hot, lighter air upward. This creates **Eddies, Whirlwinds, Updrafts, and Downdrafts** when obstacles get in the way of the air movement.
- Additionally, winds travel quickly across the desert floors, creating turbulence when they encounter obstacles.
- There are storm winds that can cause a lot of damage.
- **Deflation** includes lifting and removal of dust and smaller particles from the surface of rocks. In the transportation process sand and silt act as effective **equipment for scouring** the land surface.
- The **force of momentum** created when sand is blown into or up against a rock surface is all that constitutes the impact. It is similar to a sandblasting process.
- In the deserts, wind activity produces a variety of fascinating erosional and depositional structures.
- Wind is an effective separation agent. Different sized grains are moved over the floors by rolling or saltation and carried in suspension depending on the wind speed. The materials are separated during the transportation process itself.
- When the wind slows or begins to die down, depending upon sizes of grains and their critical velocities, the grains will begin to settle. So, in **depositional landforms** made **by wind**, good sorting of grains can be found.

Erosional Landforms

Running Water

Valleys

- Valleys originate from small, narrow rills that progressively grow into long, wide gullies. The gullies then continue to deepen, expand, and lengthen until they eventually form valleys.
- Depending upon dimensions and shape, many types of valleys like V-shaped valley, gorge, canyon, etc. can be recognised.
- A **Gorge** is a deep valley with very steep to straight sides and a **canyon** is characterised by steep step-like side slopes and may be as deep as a gorge.
- A gorge is almost equal in width at its top as well as its bottom. In contrast, a **Canyon** is wider at its top than at its bottom. In fact, a canyon is a variant of gorge.
- **The kinds of valleys** are determined by the type and composition of the rocks that give rise to them. For example, gorges form in hard rocks whereas canyons often form in sedimentary rocks that are bedded horizontally.

Potholes and Plunge Pools

- **Potholes** are roughly circular depressions created by stream erosion over the rocky beds of hill streams, which is facilitated by the abrasion of rock fragments.
- Once a small, shallow depression occurs, the depression's size increases as a result of pebbles and stones collecting there and being rotated by flowing water.
- At the foot of waterfalls also, large potholes, quite deep and wide, form because of the sheer impact of water and rotation of boulders. Such large and deep holes at the base of waterfalls are called **Plunge Pools.**

Incised or Entrenched Meanders

- In streams that flow rapidly over steep gradients, normally erosion is concentrated on the bottom of the stream channel.
- Compared to streams flowing on low, gentle slopes, lateral erosion on the valley sides occurs less frequently in the case of steep gradient streams.
- Streams that flow over mild slopes acquire meandering or sinuous channels due to active lateral erosion.
- It is common to find meandering courses over floodplains and delta plains where stream gradients are very gentle. But very deep and wide meanders can also be found cut in hard rocks. Such meanders are called **Incised** or **Entrenched Meanders.**

River Terraces

- Surfaces known as **river terraces** indicate old floodplain or valley floor levels. They could be alluvial terraces made up of stream deposits or bedrock surfaces without of any alluvial cover.

- In essence, river terraces are the outcome of erosion since the stream erodes vertically into its own depositional floodplain.
- The term **"paired terraces"** refers to the river terraces that appear at the same elevation on both sides of the rivers.

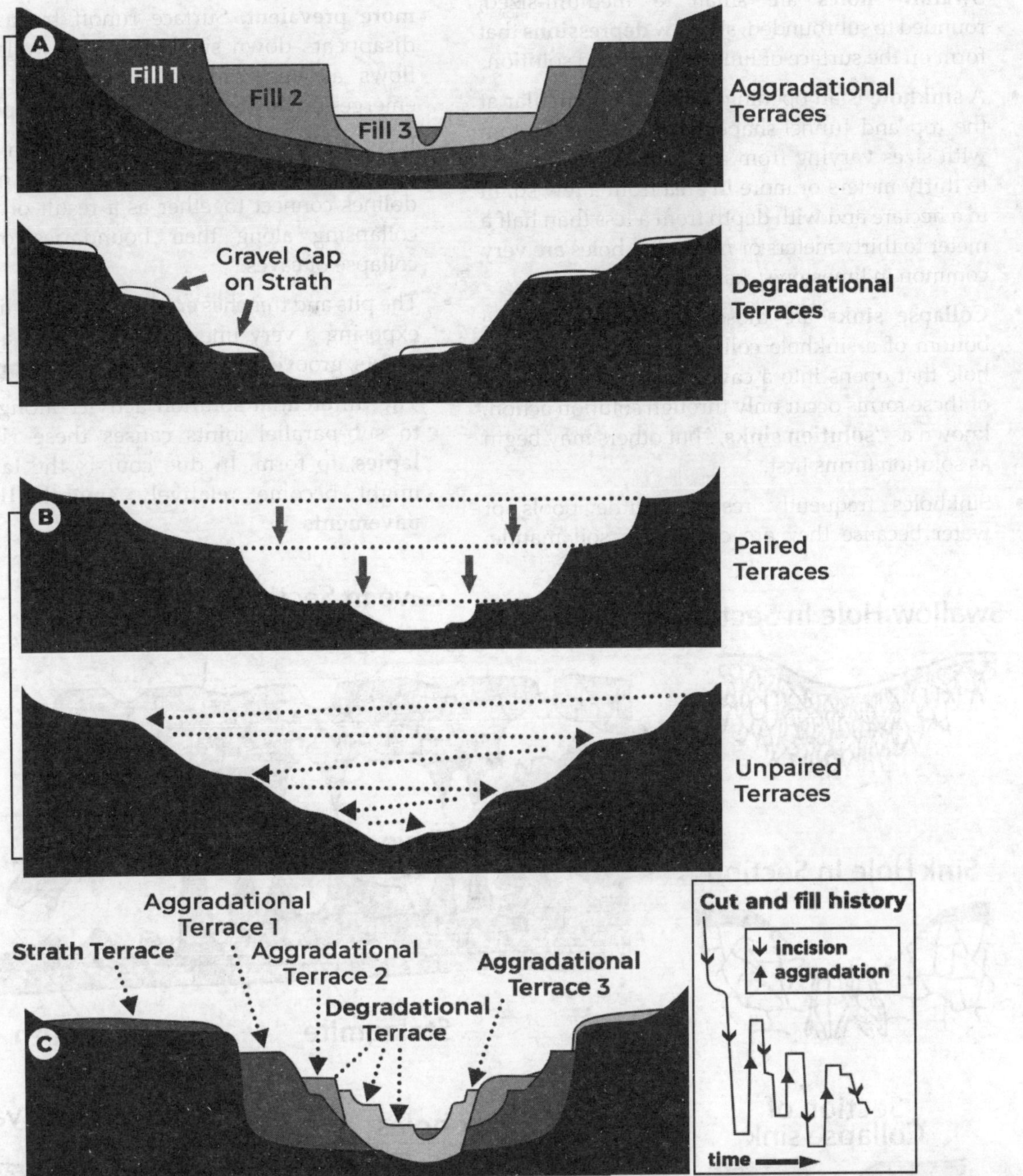

Paired, Unpaired, Degradational and Aggradational Terraces

When one side of the stream has terraces and the other has none or terraces at significantly different elevations, the terraces are called **Non-Paired Terraces**. Unpaired terraces are common in places where the soil is slowly rising or where the variations in the water column are not consistent along both the banks. The terraces may result **due to** (i) receding water after a peak flow; (ii) change in hydrological regime due to climatic changes; (iii) tectonic uplift of land; (iv) sea level changes in case of rivers closer to the sea.

Pools, Sinkholes, Lapies And Limestone Pavements

- **Swallow holes** are small to medium-sized, rounded to subrounded, **shallow depressions** that form on the surface of limestones due to solution.
- A **sinkhole** is an opening more or less circular at the top and funnel-shaped towards the bottom with sizes varying from a less than half a meter to thirty meters or more in area from a few sq. m to a hectare and with depth from a less than half a meter to thirty meters or more. Sinkholes are very common in limestone/ karst areas.
- **Collapse sinks** are those that form when the bottom of a sinkhole collapses, producing a big hole that opens into a cave or void below. Some of these forms occur only through solution action, known as **"solution sinks,"** but others may begin as solution forms first.
- Sinkholes frequently resemble little pools of water because they are covered in soil mantle. Sometimes, the **collapse sinks** are referred to as **"dolines."**.
- Compared to collapse sinks, solution sinks are **more prevalent**. Surface runoff frequently just disappears down sinkholes and swallow holes, flows as underground streams, and then re-emerges downstream through a cave opening.
- Long, narrow to wide trenches known as **valley sinks or uvalas emerge** when sink holes and dolines connect together as a result of materials collapsing along their boundaries or ceiling collapse of caves.
- The pits and trenches erode away at the limestone, exposing a very uneven surface with a maze of points, grooves, and ridges known as **lapies.**
- The differential solution activity along parallel to sub-parallel joints causes these **ridges, or lapies**, to form. In due course, the **lapie** field might become relatively **smooth limestone pavements**.

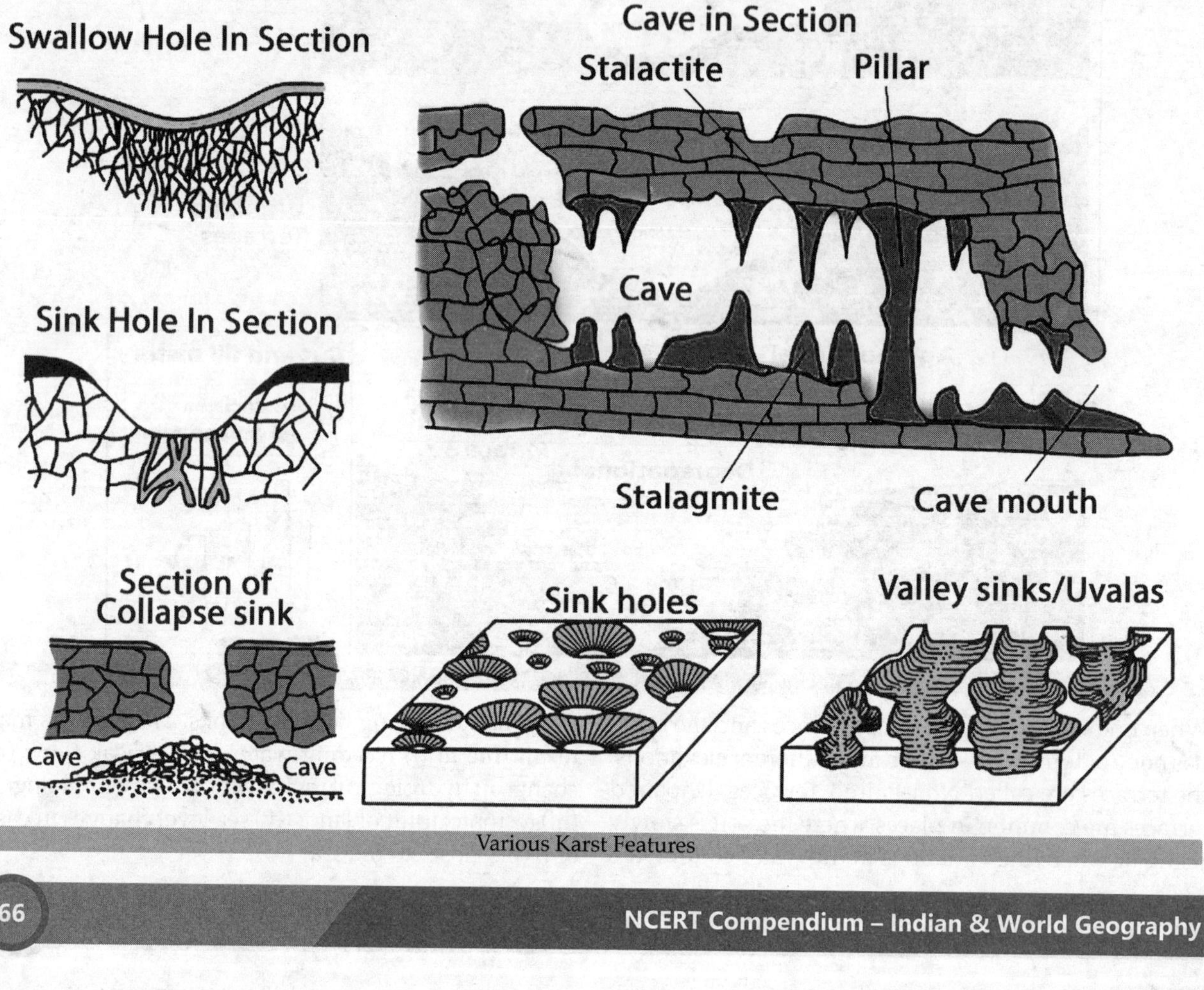

Various Karst Features

Caves

- **Cave** formation is common in locations where there are alternating beds of rocks **(shale, sandstone, quartzite)** with limestones or dolomites in between, or where limestones are massive, dense, and occur in thick strata.
- Water travels horizontally along bedding planes when it seeps through the materials or fractures and joints. The limestone dissolves along these bedding planes, creating long, narrow, to broad openings that are known as **caves.**
- Depending on the limestone beds and surrounding rocks, there may be a maze of caverns at various elevations.
- In general, **cave** streams emerge through an opening in the cave. **Tunnels** are caves with entrances on both ends.

Glaciers

Cirque

- In mountains covered by glaciers, **cirques** are the most prevalent landform. At the headwaters of glacier valleys, cirques are frequently encountered. As the ice builds up and goes down the mountain peaks, it creates appealing cirques.
- These are broad, deep troughs or basins with steep walls at both the head and sides that descend precipitously. Following the glacier's retreat, cirques frequently contain a lake of water.
- We refer to these lakes as **tarn lakes or cirque lakes.** It is possible for there to be several **cirques,** each one stepping into the next below.

Horns And Serrated Ridges

- The cirque walls erode headward, forming **horns**. When three or more radiating glaciers meet at their cirques, they form horns, which are tall, sharply pointed peaks with steep sides.
- Due to gradual erosion, the gaps between the headwalls or side walls of cirques become narrower and eventually transform into **saw-toothed or serrated ridges**, known as aretes, with a very pointed crest and a zigzag pattern.
- In actuality, the tallest peaks in the **Alps (Matterhorn)** and the **Himalayas (Everest)** are horns created by headward erosion of radiating cirques.

Glacial Valleys/Troughs

- **Glaciated valleys** have large floors, relatively smooth sides, and a U-shaped, trough-like shape. Debris that has been left behind in the valleys may be scattered in the form of swampy-looking moraines.
- There might be lakes created by debris in the valleys or gouged out of the stony bottom. On one or both sides of the main glacial valley, there may be elevated hanging valleys.
- Often, the sides of divides or spurs of these **hanging valleys** that open into main glacier valleys are truncated, giving the impression that they have triangular dimensions. **Fjords or fiords** are very deep glacial troughs that form shorelines (in high latitudes) and are filled with seawater.

Waves and Currents

Cliffs, Terraces, Caves and Stacks

- **Terraces and wave-cut cliffs** are two types that are typically found in areas where shoreline erosion is the main mechanism.
- The majority of **sea cliffs** are quite steep, with some reaching heights of up to 30 metres or more. There may be a level or slightly sloping platform at the base of these cliffs, covered in granite fragments from the sea wall behind. A **wave-cut terrace** is a platform that appears at a height higher than the typical wave height.
- **Sea caves** are formed when waves smash into the base of a cliff and the rock debris that is thrown against it, creating hollows that eventually enlarge and deepen.
- The sea cliffs slide farther inland, and cave ceilings crumble. Rock fragments that remain isolated as tiny islands just offshore could indicate the cliff's retreat. **Sea stacks** are sturdy rock formations that were formerly a component of a hill or cliff.
- **Sea stacks** are also temporary; over time, wave erosion may cause coastal cliffs and hills to

disappear, creating flat coastal plains. An influx of sediment from the surrounding land may cover sea stacks with alluvium or cover them with sand or pebbles to create a **broad beach.**

Winds

Pediments And Pediplains

- **Pediments** are gently sloping stone floors around the base of mountains, sometimes covered in a thin layer of debris. These stony floors are created when the mountain front is eroded by a mix of sheet flooding and stream erosion.
- The steep edges of the landmass or the steep sides of the tectonically controlled steep incision features onto the landmass are where erosion begins.
- The steep wash slope and free face retreat backwards when pediments with a cliff or free face above them are developed. The erosion process known as **Parallel Retreat of Slopes** by **Back-Wasting** is the result of this technique.
- The pediments stretch rearward at the expense of the mountain front due to parallel retreat of slopes, and the mountain progressively diminishes, leaving behind an inselberg that is a vestige of the mountain. In this way, the high topography of desert regions is diminished to **Pediplains**, which are low, featureless plains.

Playas

- In the deserts, plains are by far the most recognised landform. When there are hills and mountains all around a basin, the water flows towards its middle, where a nearly level plain gradually forms as a result of silt from the basin boundaries gradually depositing there.
- A shallow body of water covers this plain when there is enough water. These kinds of shallow lakes are known as **playas**, and they frequently have good salt deposition. Playas are areas where water is only temporarily retained due to evaporation. **Alkali flats** are the playa plain coated in salt deposits.

Deflation Hollows and Caves

- Wind currents that flow continuously in one direction sweep away weathered mantle that was once covering the rocks or bare earth. **Deflation Hollows** are small, shallow depressions that could be produced by this process. Numerous **small voids or pits** are also produced throughout the surface of rocks by deflation.
- Sand carried by the wind abrasives and impacts the rock walls, creating **blow outs,** which are initially shallow depressions that grow deeper and wider enough to be referred to as **caves.**

Mushroom, Table and Pedestal Rocks

- Many of the desert's rock outcrops are quickly worn down by wind deflation and abrasion, leaving behind some exquisitely polished relics of resistant rocks that appear to be **mushrooms** with a broad, rounded pear-shaped cap above and a slender stem below.
- Occasionally, the upper surface is wide, like a tabletop, and frequently, the remnants are prominent, resembling **pedestals.**

Depositional Landforms

Running Water

Alluvial Fans

- Low-gradient foot slope plains are the source of **alluvial fans,** which are created when streams from higher elevations meet.
- Generally, streams that run across steep slopes have a fairly coarse load. An extensive low-to-high cone-shaped deposit known as an alluvial fan is created when this load becomes too great for the streams to carry over gentler gradients.
- Usually, streams that flow over fans don't stay in their original channels for very long; instead, they move around the fan to form a number of channels known as **distributaries.**
- In humid climates, alluvial fans often have low cones that slope gently from head to toe; in **arid and semi-arid climates,** on the other hand, they appear to be **high cones with steep slopes.**

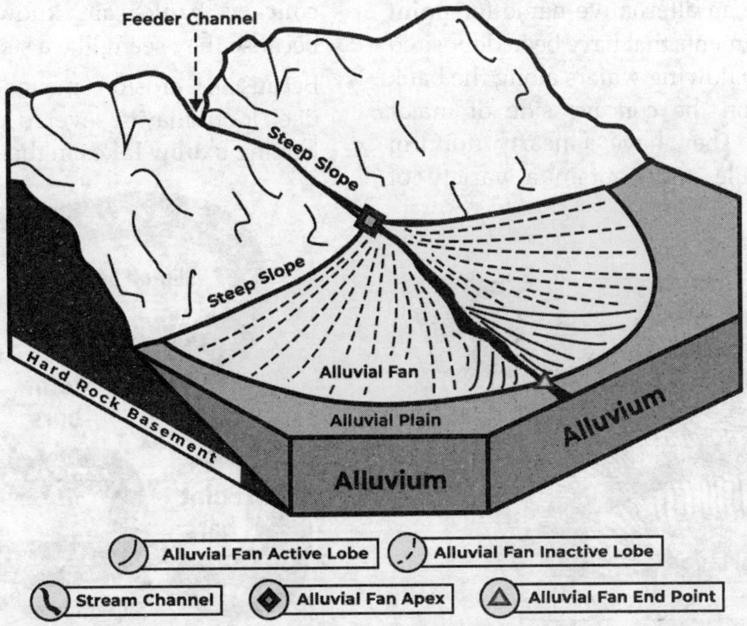

Alluvial Fans

Deltas

- Deltas are similar to allivial fans, but develop in a different location. Here, the weight that the rivers carry is dumped into the ocean.
- The load spreads and builds up as a **low cone** if it is not dispersed along the coast or moved far out to sea.
- The deposits that comprise deltas are finely stratified and very well sorted, in contrast to alluvial fans.
- The finer fractions, such as silts and clays, are carried out into the sea whereas the coarsest materials settle out first.

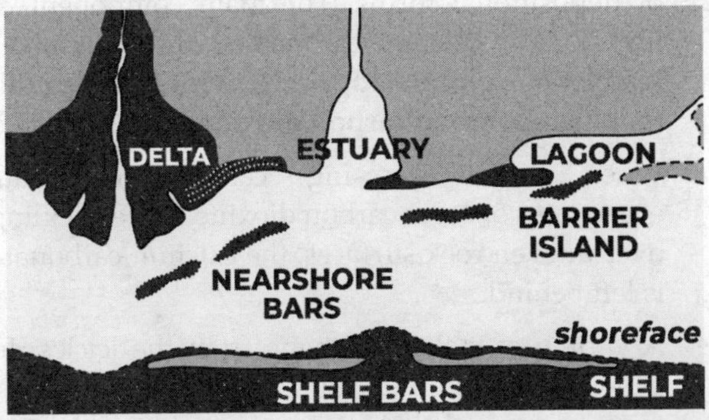

Deltas

Floodplains, Natural Levees And Point Bars

- A significant landform formed by river deposition is the **floodplain.**
- At the point where the stream channel slopes gently, large-sized sediments are deposited first.
- Sand, silt, and clay are examples of fine-sized sediments that are usually carried by slower-moving streams in kinder channels that are typically found on plains and deposited over the bed when the waters overflow their banks during flooding above the bed.
- The **active floodplain** is an area of river deposits used as a river bed. The floodplain situated above the bank is **inactive floodplain.**
- There are basically, two types of deposits found in **inactive floodplains** above the banks: **channel deposits and flood deposits**.
- **Delta plains** are the floodplains found in deltas.
- Among the significant landforms connected to **floodplains** are **natural levees and point bars.**
- The banks of large rivers often have **natural levees**. Usually divided into several mounds, these are low, parallel, linear ridges of coarse deposits along riverbanks.

- **Meander bars** are an alternative name for **point bars**. They are sediments that have been deposited in a linear form by flowing waters along the bank and are located on the concave side of major rivers' meanders. They have a nearly uniform breadth and profile and contain a variety of sediment sizes.

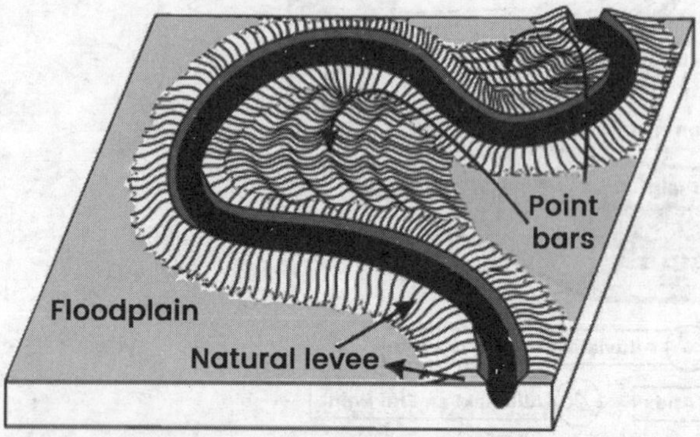

Natural Levee and Point Bars

Meanders

- Rivers rarely flow in straight lines amid vast flood and delta plains. Over flood and delta plains, **meanders**—loop-like channel patterns—develop.
- Meander is a kind of channel pattern, not a landform. That's because of (i) water's tendency to work laterally on the banks when it flows over very gentle gradients; (ii) the irregularities and unconsolidated nature of the alluvial deposits that make up the banks, which can be exploited by water applying lateral pressure; (iii) The water is being deflected by the Coriolis force, which acts on it similarly to how the wind is deflected.
- Water flows pleasantly and begins to work laterally when the channel's gradient drops significantly.
- Little irregularities along the banks gradually give way to a modest curvature; the curvature grows as a result of erosion along the outside of the bank and deposition on the inside of the curve.
- The propensity to meander is **lessened** in the absence of deposition, erosion, and undercutting.
- In meanders of large rivers, undercutting occurs along the convex bank while active deposition occurs along the concave bank.
- **Convex banks** have a long, gentle profile, while **concave banks** are known as **cut-off banks** because they seem like a steep scarp.
- Because of erosion, meanders that develop into deep loops may be severed at the sites of inflection, leaving **oxbow lakes** in their place.

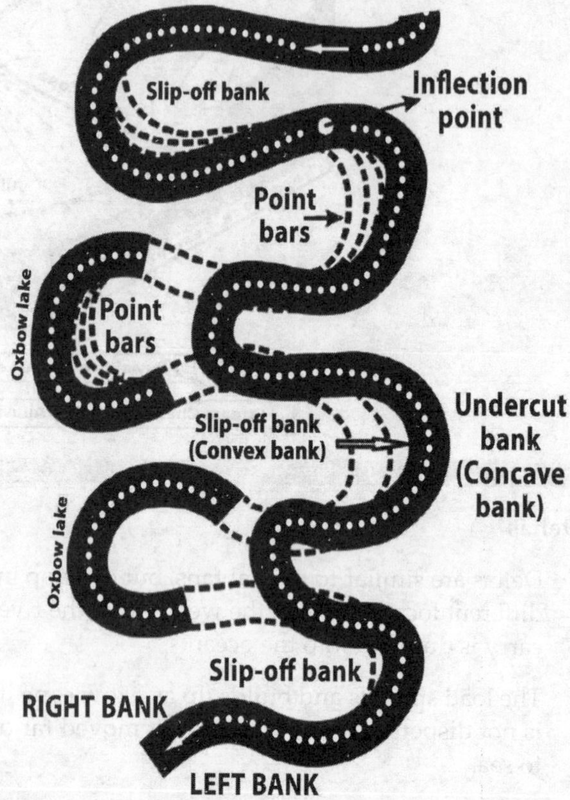

Meander Growth and Cut-off Loops and Slip-off and Under-cut Banks

Ground Water

Stalactites, Stalagmites And Pillars

- The limestone caves are home to a wide variety of depositional forms. The main component of limestone is calcium carbonate, which dissolves readily in **carbonated water, which is rainfall that has absorbed carbon dioxide.**
- When water carrying calcium carbonate evaporates or loses carbon dioxide while trickling over uneven rock surfaces, the calcium carbonate is left behind.
- A variety of **stalactites** hang from the icicles. In general, they exhibit a range of shapes and sizes, tapering towards the free ends from broad bases.

- From the cave floors, **stalactites rise**. Actually, stalagmites originate from water trickling through the stalactite's small conduit or from the surface.
- **Stalagmites** can be shaped like a **disc or a column, and they can have a little depression** that resembles a crater or a smooth, rounded bulging end.
- **Columns and pillars** with **varying diameters** emerge from the eventual fusion of stalactites and stalagmites.

Glaciers

Moraines

- **Glacial till** is the **unsorted mixture** of fine and coarse particles left behind by melting glaciers. Long ridges made by glacial till deposits are called **moraines.**
- Long ridges of debris called **terminal moraines** are deposited at the tip (toe) of the glaciers. Along the sides that run parallel to the glacial troughs, **lateral moraines** develop.
- **A horse-shoe shaped ridge** can be formed when lateral moraines unite with a terminal moraine.
- Numerous glaciers that rapidly recede onto valley floors leave behind an uneven layer of till. **Ground moraines** are deposits with such variations in thickness and surface topography.
- The term **"Medial Moraine"** refers to the moraine located in the middle of the glacier valley, surrounded by lateral moraines.

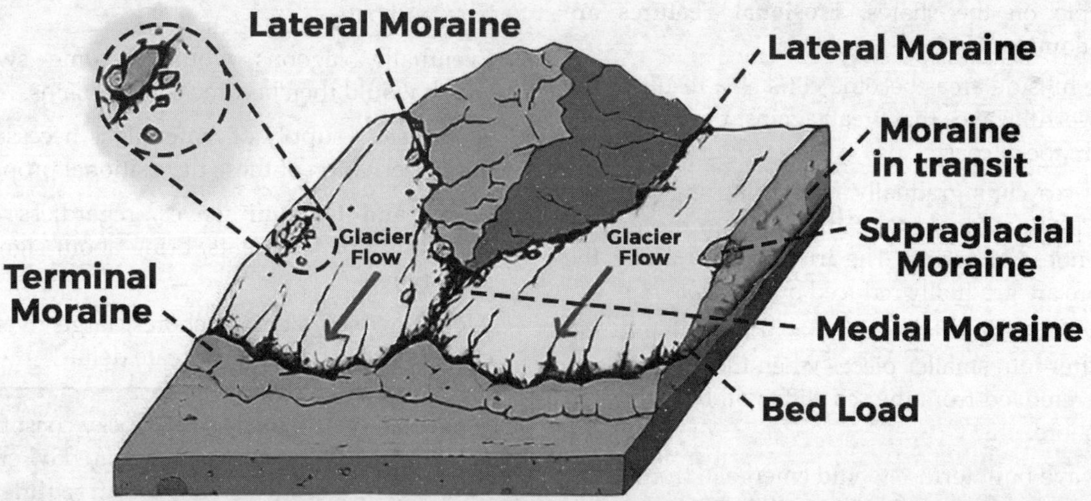

Types of Moraines

Eskers

- Water moves through holes in the ice, seeps down the edges, and flows on the surface of the ice when glaciers melt in the **summer**.
- These liquids build up beneath the glacier and move via a channel beneath the ice like streams. These streams have ice forming their banks as they flow over the ground rather than through a valley. When the ice melts, very coarse materials like boulders and blocks, combined with a small fraction of rock debris, settle in the valley beneath the glacier and become an **esker**, which is a **sinuous ridge**.

Outwash Plains

- Broad, flat alluvial fans, known as glacio-fluvial deposits, cover the plains at the base of glacial mountains and beyond the edge of continental ice sheets. These fans can combine to create outwash plains composed of **gravel, silt, sand, and clay.**

Drumlins

- **Drumlins** are smooth, oval-shaped, ridge-like formations that are mostly made of glacial till, with some sand and gravel masses mixed in.
- Drumlins' long axes go parallel to the direction in which the ice is moving. They can be as long as one kilometre and as tall as thirty metres or so.

- **The stoss end**, or one end of the drumlins facing the glacier, is steeper and blunter than the **tail, or other end**.
- Drumlins give an indication of direction of glacier movement.

Waves and Currents

High Rocky Coasts

- The rivers seem to have been submerged along the high, rocky shorelines, leaving a highly uneven coastline.
- The coastline looks to be heavily indented, with **fjords** (glacial valleys) extending water into the surrounding terrain.
- The hill sides drop off abruptly into the water bodies. Depositional landforms are not first visible on the shores. **Erosional Features are predominant.**
- The hillside areas become cliffs as a result of the powerful waves that break against the land along high, rocky coasts.
- The sea cliffs gradually retreat, leaving a wave-cut platform in front of them due to the waves' relentless battering. The irregularities along the shore are gradually reduced by waves.
- The materials that roll to a round shape and shatter into smaller pieces when they fall off and are removed from the sea cliffs will be deposited offshore.
- A wave-built terrace would emerge in front of the wave-cut terrace following a protracted period of **cliff development and retreat** when the coastline becomes considerably smoother and additional material is added to this offshore deposit.
- As the coast erodes, longshore currents and waves have access to a plentiful supply of material, which they deposit as beaches along the shore and bars in the nearshore zone, which are long ridges of sand and/or shingle ridges running parallel to the coast.
- Bars are submerged objects that are referred to as **barrier bars** when they emerge above the sea.
- **A spit** is a barrier bar that is keyed up to a bay's headland.
- **Lagoons** arise when spits and barrier bars obstruct the entrance to a bay.
- Over time, sediments from the surrounding land would cover the lagoons, creating a coastal plain.

Low Sedimentary Coasts

- The rivers create coastal plains and deltas along low sedimentary beaches, giving the impression that they are longer.
- The shoreline seems to be smooth, with occasional water intrusions in the form of **tidal creeks and lagoons.**
- The ground gradually dips down to the water. Along the beaches, marshes and swamps could be abundant. Most prominent are depositional traits.
- The bottom sediments get disturbed and easily move when waves break over a slightly sloping sedimentary coast, creating spits, lagoons, barrier bars, and bars.
- Eventually, lagoons would become swamps, which would then become coastal plains.
- A consistent supply of materials is necessary for the preservation of these depositional properties.
- **Storm and tsunami** waves, regardless of the availability of sediments, bring about significant alterations.
- Along low sedimentary shores, large rivers that carry in a lot of sediment create deltas.

Our nation's **west coast** is steep, rocky coast that is retreating. The west shore is dominated by eroded features. India's east coast has a **low sedimentary** shore. On the east coast, depositional features predominate.

Beaches and Dunes

- **Beaches** are found in areas along even the rugged shorelines and are characteristic of shorelines where deposition is predominant.
- The majority of the silt found on beaches is either the result of wave erosion or land that is carried by rivers and streams.
- The beach is a **temporary phenomenon**. In another season, the seemingly permanent stretch of sand could be reduced to a very thin strips of coarse pebbles.

- Sand-sized materials make up the majority of the beaches. **Pebbles and even cobbles that are exceptionally tiny** can be found on beaches known as **shingle beaches.**
- **Sand dunes** will be formed just **behind the beach from the sands that have been removed and winnowed** from over the beach surfaces.
- Low sedimentary beaches are prone to lengthy, parallel ridges **formed by sand dunes.**

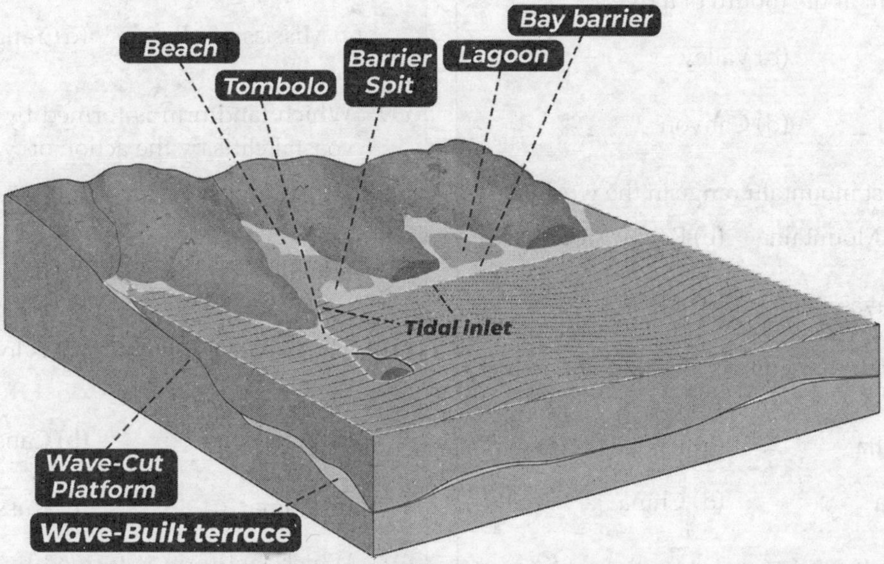

Bars, Barriers and Spits

> Since the majority of a storm or tsunami's destructive force is absorbed by the coastal offshore bars, they provide the first line of defence against them. Next, in order to neutralise the destructive power of storm and tsunami waves, come barriers, beaches, beach dunes, and mangroves, if any. The **"sediment budget"** and the mangroves along the shore will therefore be disturbed by human activity, eroding these coastal formations and leaving human settlements vulnerable to storm and tsunami waves.

Winds

Sand dunes

- Sand is lifted and carried from one location to another by wind. Sand falls and accumulates in low, hill-like structures when the wind ceases. We refer to these as **sand dunes**. The wind may carry sand across great distances when the grains are light and fine. **Loess** is the term for this type of sand that forms across vast expanses.

There can be a great variety of dune forms:

- **Barchans are crescent-shaped dunes** that form where the original surface over which sand is moving is nearly uniform and the wind direction is consistent and moderate. The points or wings of the dunes are oriented away from the wind direction, or downwind.
- When vegetation partially covers sandy areas, **parabolic dunes** are formed. Hence, parabolic dunes are barchans that are inverted when the wind is blowing in the same direction.
- With a minor exception, Seif is comparable to Barchan. **Seif** is a single wing, single point. This occurs when the wind conditions change. Seifs' single wings can get incredibly long and tall.
- When there is a limited quantity of sand and a consistent wind direction, **longitudinal dunes** are formed. They appear to be lengthy, low-lying ridges that are quite long.
- The orientation of **transverse dunes** is perpendicular to the direction of the wind. When there is a consistent wind and an extended feature that is perpendicular to the wind direction, sand is produced, forming dunes. They could have a low height and be very lengthy.

TEST YOURSELF

Multiple Choice Questions

Q1. Which landform is formed by the deposition of sediment at the mouth of a river?

(a) Delta (b) Valley

(c) Plateau (d) Canyon

Q2. The highest mountain range in the world is:

(a) Andes Mountains (b) Rocky Mountains

(c) Himalayas (d) Alps

Q3. The Grand Canyon is located in which country?

(a) Australia (b) United States

(c) Canada (d) China

Q4. Which landform is formed by the collision of two tectonic plates?

(a) Volcano (b) Plain

(c) Rift valley (d) Fold mountains

Q5. The Great Barrier Reef is located off the coast of which country?

(a) Australia (b) Brazil

(c) Indonesia (d) Mexico

Q6. The Sahara Desert is located in which continent?

(a) Africa (b) Asia

(c) South America (d) Europe

Q7. Which landform is characterised by a flat, elevated surface with steep sides?

(a) Plateau (b) Valley

(c) Peninsula (d) Archipelago

Q8. The largest river in South America is:

(a) Amazon River (b) Nile River

(c) Mississippi River (d) Yangtze River

Q9. Which landform is formed by the erosion of coastal cliffs by the action of waves?

(a) Cape (b) Gulf

(c) Fjord (d) Bay

Q10. The Great Dividing Range is located in which country?

(a) Australia (b) Canada

(c) China (d) Russia

Q11. Which landform is formed by the erosion of river valleys by glaciers?

(a) Canyon (b) Delta

(c) Fjord (d) Plateau

Q12. The formation of stalactites and stalagmites is associated with which landform?

(a) Cave (b) Dune

(c) Volcano (d) Mesa

Q13. The process of weathering and erosion is primarily responsible for the formation of which landform?

(a) Plateau (b) Valley

(c) Mesa (d) Canyon

Q14. The process of deposition by wind is responsible for the formation of which landform?

(a) Delta (b) Moraine

(c) Meander (d) Barrier island

Q15. The formation of karst topography is associated with the dissolution of which type of rock?

(a) Igneous rock (b) Metamorphic rock

(c) Sedimentary rock (d) Volcanic rock

Q16. The process of uplift and folding of rock layers is responsible for the formation of which landform?

(a) Rift valley (b) Fold mountains

(c) Coastal plain (d) Escarpment

Q17. The formation of sand dunes is primarily associated with which agent of erosion?

(a) Wind (b) Water

(c) Ice (d) Gravity

Q18. The erosion of a coastline by the action of waves results in the formation of which landform?

(a) Peninsula (b) Estuary

(c) Sea cliff (d) Oxbow lake

Q19. The formation of a volcanic island is associated with which geological process?

(a) Faulting (b) Folding

(c) Volcanism (d) Weathering

Q20. The deposition of sediment at the mouth of a river forms which landform?

(a) Delta (b) Canyon

(c) Escarpment (d) Fjord

Answer Key

Q1.	a	Q2.	c	Q3.	b	Q4.	d
Q5.	a	Q6.	a	Q7.	a	Q8.	a
Q9.	a	Q10.	a	Q11.	c	Q12.	a
Q13.	d	Q14.	d	Q15.	c	Q16.	b
Q17.	a	Q18.	c	Q19.	c	Q20.	a

Model Questions for Main Examination

Q1. How do you think landforms are shaped and evolved over time? Provide examples to support your answer.

Q2. In your opinion, what role does the external forces, such as water and wind erosion, play in the formation and transformation of landforms? Discuss with relevant illustrations or case studies.

UNIT 8
Physical Features of India

In This Unit

Comprehensive and profound coverage of the following NCERTs' chapter:

- ✓ NCERT Class- 9th (Contemporary India-I), Chapter- 2
- ✓ NCERT Class- 11th (India Physical Environment), Chapter- 2

Current estimation shows that the earth is approximately 460 million years old. Over these long years, it has undergone many changes brought about primarily by the endogenic and exogenic forces. These forces have played a significant role in giving shape to various surfaces and subsurface features of the earth. It is primarily through the interplay of these endogenic and exogenic forces and lateral movements of the plates that the present geological structure of the Indian subcontinent has been created. **India** can be classified into **three geological divisions based on differences in its geological formations** and **structure**. These geological regions are:

1. The Peninsular Block.
2. The Himalayas and other Peninuslar Mountains.
3. Indo-Ganga-Brahmaputra Plain.

The Peninsular Block

- The northern boundary of the Peninsular Block may be taken as an irregular line running from Kachchh along the western flank of the Aravali Range near Delhi and then roughly parallel to the Yamuna and the Ganga as far as the Rajmahal Hills and the Ganga delta.
- Apart from these, the Karbi Anglong and the Meghalaya Plateau in the northeast and Aravalli in the west are also extensions of this block.
- The northeastern parts are separated by the Malda fault in West Bengal from the Chotanagpur plateau.
- In Rajasthan, the desert and other desert–like features overlay this block.

Formation of Peninsula

- The Peninsula is formed essentially by a great complex of very ancient **gneisses and granites,** which constitutes a major part of it.
- **Since the Cambrian period,** the Peninsula has been standing like a rigid block with the exception of some of its western coast which is submerged beneath the sea and some other parts changed due to tectonic activity without affecting the original base.
- As a part of the Indo-Australian Plate, it has been subjected to various vertical movements and block faulting.
- The rift valleys of the Narmada, Tapi and the Mahanadi and the Satpura block mountains are some examples.
- The Peninsula mostly consists of relict and residual mountains like the Aravali hills, the Nallamala hills, the Javadi hills, the Veliconda hills, the Palkonda range and the Mahendragiri hills, etc. The river valleys here are shallow with low gradients.

The Himalayas and Other Peninsular Mountains

- The Himalayas along with other Peninsular mountains are young, weak and flexible in their geological structure unlike the rigid and stable Peninsular Block.
- Consequently, they are still subjected to the interplay of exogenic and endogenic forces,

resulting in the development of faults, folds and thrust plains.

- These mountains are tectonic in origin, dissected by fast-flowing rivers which are in their youthful stage.
- Various landforms like gorges, V-shaped valleys, rapids, waterfalls, etc. are indicative of this stage.

Indo-Ganga-Brahmaputra Plain

- The plains created by the rivers Indus, Ganga, and Brahmaputra make up **India's third geological division.**
- It was originally a geo-synclinal depression that reached its peak development about 64 million years ago, during the third stage of the construction of the Himalayan Mountains.
- Since then, sediments from the Peninsular and Himalayan rivers have been progressively filling it. In these plains, the alluvial deposits are 1,000–2,000 metres deep on average.

Physiography

The results of structure, process, and developmental stage determine an area's **physiography**. The physical attributes of the Indian subcontinent are remarkably diverse. Huge, expanses of rugged landscape, including numerous mountain ranges with diverse peaks, beautiful valleys, and deep gorges, can be found in the north. A sequence of developed scarps, sharply divided plateaus, and stripped rocks make up the stable table land in the south. The large plain of North India is located between these two.

India can be classified into the following physiographic categories based on these macro differences:

1. The Northern and North Eastern Mountains
2. The Northern Plain
3. The Peninsular Plateau
4. The Indian Desert
5. The Coastal Plains
6. The Islands

The North and Northeastern Mountains

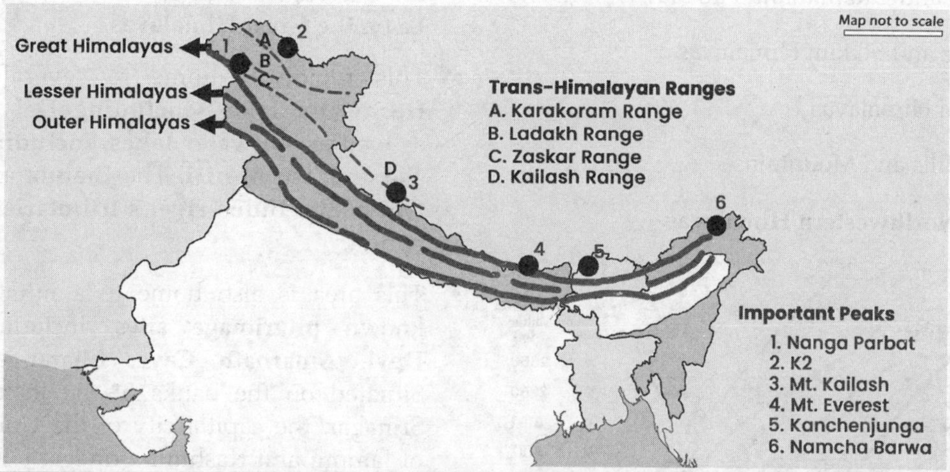

Himalayan Ranges

- The Northeastern hills and the Himalayas are part of the North and Northeastern Mountains.
- A collection of parallel mountain ranges forms the Himalayas. **The Greater Himalayan range, which comprises the Great Himalayas and the Shiwalik**, is one of the significant ranges.
- These ranges are located in the northwest region of India, generally oriented from northwest to southeast. The Himalayas in Arunachal Pradesh stretch from southwest to northwest, however in Darjeeling and Sikkim they are oriented east-west. They are located in the north-south direction in Nagaland, Manipur, and Mizoram.
- The Great or Inner Himalayas also called Himadri is the name given to the northernmost range. With an average height of 6,000 metres, it is the most

continuous range made up of the highest peaks. It includes every notable Himalayan peak.

- The Great Himalayan range, also referred to as **the central axial range**, is roughly 2,500 km long from east to west and 160–400 km wide from north to south.
- The Great Himalayas are characterised by asymmetrical folds. Granite makes up this region of the Himalayas' core. It is always covered in snow, and several glaciers flow down from these mountain ranges.
- The Himalayas form a formidable and elongated barrier separating the Indian subcontinent from the nations of Central and East Asia. The Himalayas represent a barrier not just in terms of geography but also in terms of climate, drainage, and cultural differences.
- The Himalayas have significant regional differences. Based on various geomorphological features, range alignment the Himalayas can be further subdivided into the following groups:

1. Kashmir or Northwestern Himalayas
2. Himachal and Uttarakhand Himalayas
3. Darjeeling and Sikkim Himalayas
4. Arunachal Himalayas
5. Eastern Hills and Mountains

Kashmir or Northwestern Himalayas

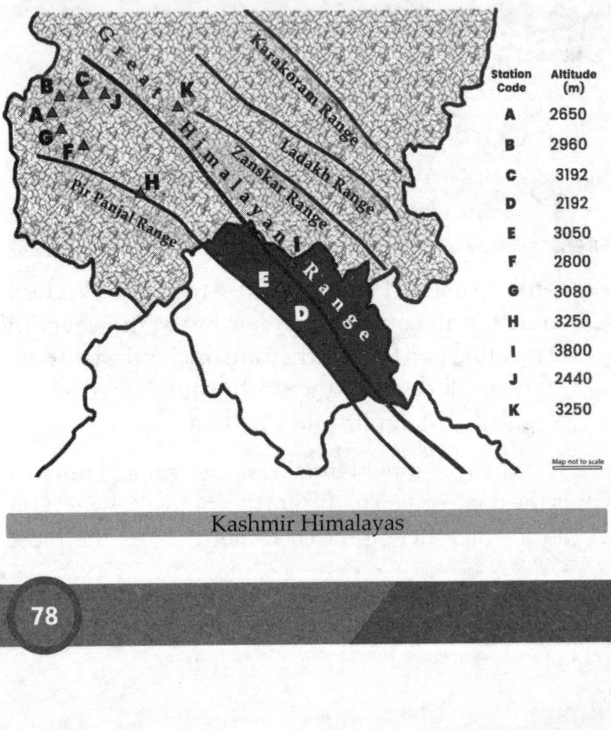

Kashmir Himalayas

- It is made up of several ranges, including the **Pir Panjal, Ladakh, Zaskar, and Karakoram**. Situated between the Karakoram ranges and the Greater Himalayas, the northeastern region of the Kashmir Himalayas is a frigid desert.
- The world-famous **Kashmir Valley and Dal Lake** are located **between the Pir Panjal range and the Great Himalayas**. This area is also home to significant South Asian glaciers like the **Baltoro and Siachen.**
- Another notable feature of the Kashmir Himalayas is the **Karewa formations**, which are helpful for growing **Zafran,** a regional kind of saffron.

> **Karewas**
>
> Karewas are the thick deposits of glacial clay and other materials embedded with moraines. These are unconsolidated lacustrine deposits. Lacustrine means "associated with lakes".

- Several noteworthy passes in the area are **Khardung La on the Ladakh range, Photu La on the Zaskar, Banihal on the Pir Panjal, and Zoji La on the Great Himalayas.**
- This region is home to several significant **freshwater lakes, including Dal and Wular**, as well as **saltwater lakes, including Pangong Tso and Tso Moriri**. The **Jhelum and Chenab, two of the Indus river's tributaries**, drain this region.
- This area is also home to a number of well-known **pilgrimage sites**, including **Vaishno Devi, Amarnath Cave, Charar-e-Sharif, etc.** Situated on the banks of the Jhelum River is Srinagar, the capital city of the Union Territory of Jammu and Kashmir. Srinagar's Dal Lake is a noteworthy natural feature. Even though Jhelum in the Kashmir Valley is still in its early stages of development, it has meandering features, which are typical of **the mature stage of the evolution of a fluvial landform.**
- This region's southernmost portion is made up of longitudinal valleys called **"duns."** Important examples include the duns of Jammu and Pathankot.

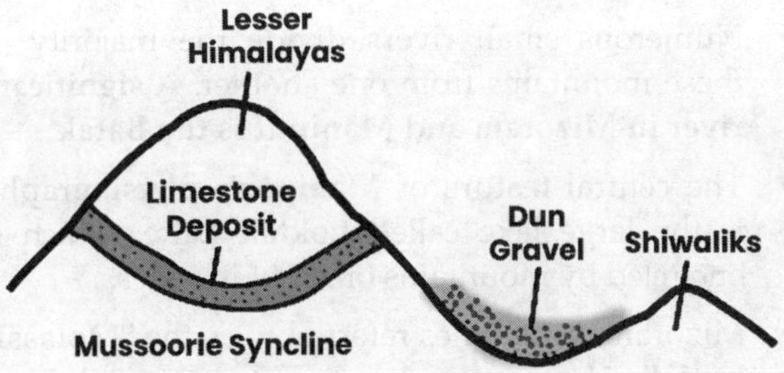

Duns

The meandering of the Jhelum River in Kashmir Valley is a result of the local base level of sediments provided by a larger lake, existed millions of year ago, of which the present Dal Lake is a small part.

The Himachal and Uttarakhand Himalayas

- The most rugged mountain range, referred to as **Himachal or the lesser Himalaya**, is found to the south of the Himadri. Rocks that have been changed and compacted a great deal make up the ranges.
- This section is roughly located between the Kali, a tributary of Ghaghara, in the east and the Ravi in the west. It is drained by the Indus and Ganga, two of India's principal river systems. Rivers Ravi, Beas, and Satluj are tributaries of the Indus, while the Yamuna and Ghaghara are tributaries of the Ganga that run through this area.
- The Ladakh cold desert, which is located in the Spiti subdivision of the district Lahaul and Spiti, extends into the northernmost region of the Himachal Himalayas.
- The Himalayan mountain ranges are all prominently featured in this section. These are the Shiwalik range from the north to the south, the **Lesser Himalayas (known locally as Dhauladhar in Himachal Pradesh and Nagtibha in Uttarakhand**), and the **Great Himalayan range**.
- Some of the most significant hill stations, including Dharamshala, Mussoorie, Shimla, and Kaosani, as well as cantonment towns and health resorts, including Shimla, Mussoorie, Kasauli, Almora, Lansdowne, and Ranikhet, were created in the Lesser Himalayan area (1,000–2,000 m).
- From a physiographic perspective, this region is distinguished by two features: the **"Shiwalik" and the "Dun formation."**
- The Harike Dun, the Chandigarh-Kalka Dun, the Nalagarh Dun, the Dehra Dun, the Kota Dun, and others are some of the significant duns in this area. **The largest dun of them is Dehra Dun**, which is roughly 35–45 km long and 22–25 km wide.
- **The Bhotia people** are the majority inhabitants of the valleys of the Great Himalayan range. These are **nomadic groups** that travel in the summer to the **"Bugyals"** (summer grasslands in the higher regions) and return to the valleys in the winter.
- There is also the well-known **"Valley of Flowers"** in this area. This region is also home to several pilgrimage sites, including Hemkund Sahib, Kedarnath, Badrinath, Gangotri, and Yamunotri.
- Additionally, the area is renowned for having **five well-known Prayags**, or river confluences: **Vishnuprayag, Nandaprayag, Karnaprayag, Rudraprayag, and Devprayag.**

The Shiwalik

The word "shiwalik" comes from the geological formation in and around Sivawala, a village close to Dehra Dun that was formerly the Imperial Survey's headquarters before the organisation moved to Dehra Dun for permanent headquarters.

The Darjeeling and Sikkim Himalayas

- The Himalayas of Bhutan in the east and Nepal in the west encircle them.
- Even though it is a small portion of the Himalayas, it is quite important. There are deep valleys and high mountain peaks like Kanchenjunga (Kanchan Giri) in this region, which is well-known for its **fast-flowing rivers like Tista**.
- Lepcha tribes live in the region's higher reaches, while a mixed population of Nepalis, Bengalis, and Central Indian tribals populate the southern portion of the region, especially the Darjeeling Himalayas.

- The British introduced tea plants in this area because of its favourable physical characteristics, which included a moderate slope, a thick layer of soil with a high organic content, evenly spaced annual rainfall, and warm winters.
- These, along with the Arunachal Himalayas, are notable for missing the Shiwalik formations in comparison to the other parts of the Himalayas.
- The **'duar formations'**, which have also been exploited to build tea gardens, are significant in place of the Shiwaliks in this area. In addition to their natural beauty, the Himalayan states of **Sikkim and Darjeeling are renowned for their abundant wildlife, especially orchids.**

The Arunachal Himalayas

- These stretch from the eastern Himalayas of Bhutan to the **eastern Diphu Pass**. The mountain range runs generally from **southwest to northeast**.
- **Namcha Barwa and Kangtu** are two of the region's significant mountain peaks. Rivers which flow quickly cut through these ranges from north to south, creating deep gorges.
- Bhramaputra crosses Namcha Barwa and then runs into a deep gorge. The **Kameng, Subansiri, Dihang, Dibang, and Lohit** are a few of the significant rivers.
- These have the greatest potential for hydroelectric power generation in the country because they are perennial and fall at a high rate.
- The diverse ethnic tribal people who call the Arunachal Himalayas home are a significant feature of these regions. From west to east, some of the notable ones are the **Nagas, Mishmi, Abor, Monpa, and Nyishi.**
- **Jhumming** is a common practice in these communities. Another name for it is **slash** and **burn cultivation or shifting cultivation.**

The Eastern Hills and Mountains

- These belong to the Himalayan Mountain range, which is generally oriented from **north to south.**
- Different local names are used to refer to them. They are referred to as **Mizo or Lushai hills in the south, Patkai Bum, Naga hills, and the Manipur hills in the north**.
- Several tribal communities that practise **Jhum cultivation** reside on these low hills.
- Numerous small rivers divide the majority of these mountains from one another. A **significant river in Mizoram and Manipur is the Barak.**
- The central feature of **Manipur's physiography** is the large lake called **Loktak Lake**, which is encircled by mountains on all of its sides.
- Mizoram, sometimes referred to as the **"Molassis basin"** is composed of soft unconsolidated deposits.
- The majority of **Nagaland's rivers** flow into the **Brahmaputra as tributaries**. The rivers in the eastern portion of Manipur are **tributaries of Chindwin**, which is a tributary of the Irrawady of Myanmar, whereas two rivers in Mizoram and Manipur are tributaries of the Barak River, which is a tributary of Meghna.

Some Highest Peaks of the Himalayas

Peak	Country	Height (in meters)
Mt. Everest	Nepal	8848.86
Kanchenjunga	India	8598
Makalu	Nepal	8485
Dhaulagiri	Nepal	8172
Nanga Parbat	India	8126
Annapurna	Nepal	8091
Nanda Devi	India	7818
Namcha Barwa	India	7782
Kamet	India	7756
Gurla Mandhata	Nepal	7728

The Northern Plains

- The **alluvial deposits** delivered by the **Indus, Ganga, and Brahmaputra rivers form the northern plains.**
- The **silt deposits** caused the rivers to break into **multiple courses** in their lower course. These are called Distributaries.
- The plains span over 3,200 kilometres from east to west. These plains range in breadth from 150 to 300 kilometres on average. Alluvium deposits can reach maximum depths of 1,000–2,000 metres.

- There are **three** main divisions of the Northern Plain. **The Punjab Plains** are the Western portion of the Northern Plain. The majority of this plain, which was formed by the Indus and its tributaries, is in Pakistan.

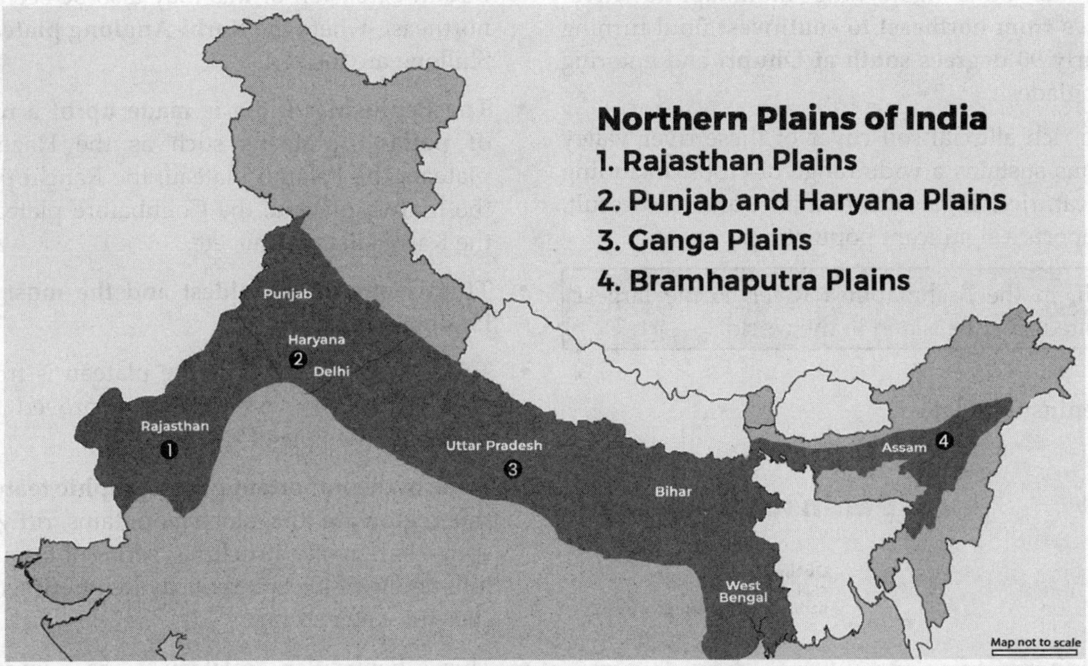

Northern Plains of India

- **The Himalaya** is the **source** of the **Indus and its tributaries**, which include the Jhelum, Chenab, Ravi, Beas, and Satluj. The **doabs**, which are named after the combination of the words **"do,"** which means **"two,"** and **"ab,"** which means **"water,"** dominate this area of the plain.
- **The Ganga plain stretches between the rivers Teesta and Ghaggar**. It is dispersed over North India, primarily in West Bengal, Delhi, Uttar Pradesh, Bihar, and parts of Jharkhand. The Brahmaputra plain is in the East, namely in Assam.
- In general, the northern plains are characterised as level terrain with no relief differences. Diverse relief characteristics can also be found in these huge plains.
- **The Northern Plains can be classified into four regions** based on differences in **relief features**.
- Following their descent from the mountains, the rivers deposit pebbles in a narrow strip that runs parallel to the Shiwaliks' slopes and is between 8 and 16 kilometers wide. We call it **Bhabar**. In the Bhabar Belt, all streams vanish.
- The rivers and streams reappear south of this belt, creating the **terai**, a wet, **marshy and swampy area**. There was a lot of wildlife in this densely forested area. This area is home to Uttar Pradesh's Dudhwa National Park.
- The northern plain is primarily composed of older alluvium. It is situated above the river floodplains and has a feature like a terrace. **Bhangar** is the name for this section. This area's soil has calcareous deposits, referred to locally as **kankar**.
- **Khadar** is the term for the more recent, younger deposits found in the floodplains.
- Sand bars, meanders, oxbow lakes, and braided channels are some of the typical characteristics of mature stage river erosional and depositional landforms seen in these plains.
- Riverine islands and sandbars are features of the **Brahmaputra plains**. Floods occur frequently in most of these places, and the river courses change over time, creating braided streams.
- The mouths of these powerful rivers also create some of the world's biggest deltas, like the well-known **Sundarbans delta**.

- The Indus and Ganga River systems are separated by the states of **Haryana and Delhi.**
- On the other hand, the Brahmaputra River flows **from northeast to southwest** until turning nearly **90 degrees south at Dhubri** and entering Bangladesh.
- The rich alluvial soil cover of these river valley plains sustains a wide range of crops, including wheat, rice, sugarcane, and jute, and as a result, supports a significant population.

> Majuli, in the Brahmaputra River, is the largest inhabited riverine island in the world.

The Peninsular Plateau

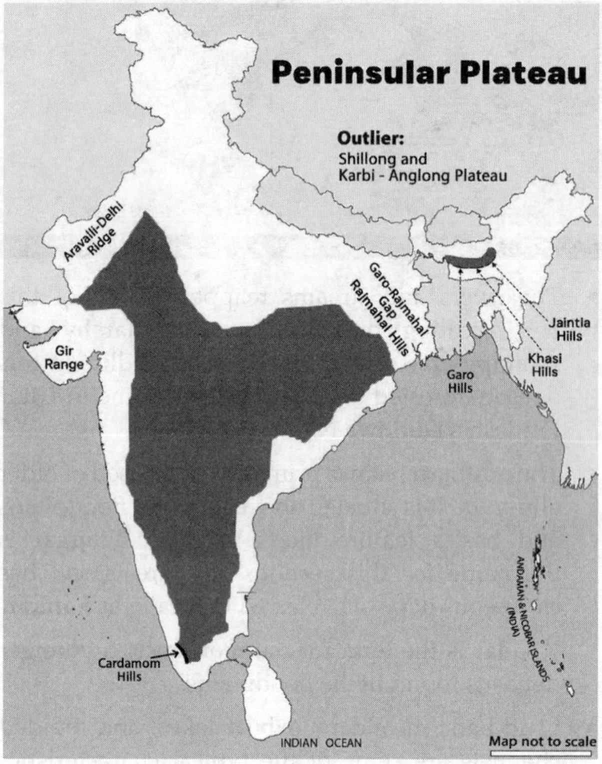

- **The Peninsular plateau** is an irregular triangle that rises from 150 metres above the river plains to 600–900 metres above sea level.
- The Peninsular plateau is a tableland composed of the old crystalline, igneous and metamorphic rocks.
- The outer boundaries of the **Peninsular plateau** are constituted by the **Gir range in the west**, the **Rajmahal hills in the east**, the **Delhi ridge (an extension of the Aravalis) in the northwest**, and the **Cardamom hills in the south**.
- But an extension of this may also be seen in the northeast, where the **Karbi-Anglong plateau** and Shillong are located.
- **The Peninsular India is made up of a number of patland plateaus** such as the Hazaribagh plateau, the Palamu plateau, the Ranchi plateau, the Malwa plateau, the Coimbatore plateau and the Karnataka plateau, etc.
- **This is one of the oldest and the most stable landmass of India.**
- The general elevation of the plateau is from the west to the east, which is also proved by the pattern of the flow of rivers.
- Some of the **important physiographic features of this region are** tors, block mountains, rift valleys, spurs, bare rocky structures, series of hummocky hills and wall-like quartzite dykes offering natural sites for water storage.
- This Peninsular plateau has undergone recurrent phases of upliftment and submergence accompanied by crustal faulting and fractures. The **Bhima fault** is known for its recurrent seismic activities.
- The northwestern part of the plateau has a complex relief of ravines and gorges. The ravines of Chambal, Bhind and Morena are some of the well-known examples.
- One of the distinct features of the Peninsular plateau is the black soil area known as **Deccan Trap.** This is of volcanic origin hence the rocks are igneous.

On the basis of the prominent relief features, the Peninsular plateau can be divided into three broad groups:

1. The Deccan Plateau
2. The Central Highlands
3. The Northeastern Plateau

The Deccan Plateau

- This is bordered by the Western Ghats in the west, Eastern Ghats in the east and the Satpura, Maikal range and Mahadeo hills in the north. The Deccan

Plateau is higher in the west and slopes gently eastwards.

- The **Western Ghats** and the **Eastern Ghats** mark the western and the eastern edges of the Deccan Plateau respectively.
- Western Ghats lie parallel to the western coast. They are continuous and can be crossed through **passes** like the Thal, Bhor and Pal Ghats.
- The Western Ghats cause orographic rain by facing the rain bearing moist winds to rise along the western slopes of the Ghats.
- **Western Ghats** are locally known by different names such as Sahyadri in Maharashtra, Nilgiri hills in Karnataka and Tamil Nadu and Anaimalai hills and Cardamom hills in Kerala.
- Western Ghats are comparatively higher in elevation and more continuous than the Eastern Ghats. Their average elevation is 900– 1600 metres as against 600 metres of the Eastern Ghats.
- **'Anaimudi' (2,695 m),** the highest peak of the Peninsular plateau, is located on the Anaimalai hills of the Western Ghats followed by **Dodabetta** (2,637 m) on the Nilgiri hills.
- **Most of the Peninsular rivers have their origin in the Western Ghats.**
- **The Eastern Ghats** stretch from the Mahanadi Valley to the Nigiris in the south.
- Eastern Ghats comprising the discontinuous and low hills are highly eroded by the rivers such as the Mahanadi, the Godavari, the Krishna, the Kaveri, etc.
- Some of the important ranges include the **Javadi hills, the Palconda range, the Nallamala hills, the Mahendragiri hills, etc.**
- The Eastern and the Western Ghats meet each other at the Nilgiri hills.

The Central Highlands

- The part of the Peninsular plateau lying to the north of the Narmada River, covering a major area of the Malwa plateau, is known as the Central Highlands.
- The Vindhyan range is bounded by the Satpura range on the south and the Aravallis on the northwest.
- The **Satpura range** is formed by a series of scarped plateaus on the south, generally at an elevation varying between 600-900 m above the mean sea level. This forms the northernmost boundary of the Deccan plateau.
- It is a classic example of the relict mountains which are highly denuded and form discontinuous ranges.
- The extension of the Peninsular plateau can be seen as far as Jaisalmer in the West, where it has been covered by the longitudinal sand ridges and crescent-shaped sand dunes called **barchans**.
- The Central Highlands are wider in the west but narrower in the east. The eastward extensions of this plateau are locally known as the **Bundelkhand** and **Baghelkhand**.
- This region has undergone metamorphic processes in its geological history, which can be corroborated by the presence of metamorphic rocks such **as marble, slate, gneiss, etc.**
- The general elevation of the Central Highlands ranges between 700-1,000 m above the mean sea level and it slopes towards the north and northeastern directions.
- The Vindhyan and Kaimur ranges are the source of the majority of the Yamuna river's tributaries.
- The only notable tributary of the river Chambal that rises from the western Aravalli is called Banas.
- The Rajmahal hills represent an eastern extension of the Central Highland, and the Chota Nagpur Plateau, to the south, contains a substantial stock of mineral resources.

The Northeastern Plateau

- It is primarily a continuation of the main Peninsular plateau.
- The Meghalaya plateau and the Rajmahal hills are separated by a massive fault that is thought to have been caused by the force of the Indian plate moving northeastward during the Himalayan origin.
- Subsequently, the deposits from the several rivers filled in this depression.

- The Meghalaya and the Karbi Anglong plateau are now separated from the Peninsular Block.
- **The Meghalaya plateau is bifurcated into three distinct regions, namely the (i) Garo Hills, (ii) Khasi Hills, and (iii) Jaintia Hills**. These regions are called after the ethnic communities that occupy them.
- There's also an extension of this in the **Assamese Karbi Anglong highlands.**
- Likewise, the **Chotanagpur plateau, the Meghalaya plateau** is abundant in mineral resources, including **limestone, coal, iron ore, coal, sillimanite, and uranium.**
- The region experiences the most amount of rainfall due to the south-west monsoon. This has led to a heavily degraded surface on the Meghalaya plateau. **With no permanent vegetation cover, Cherrapunji exhibits a clear rocky surface.**

The Indian Desert

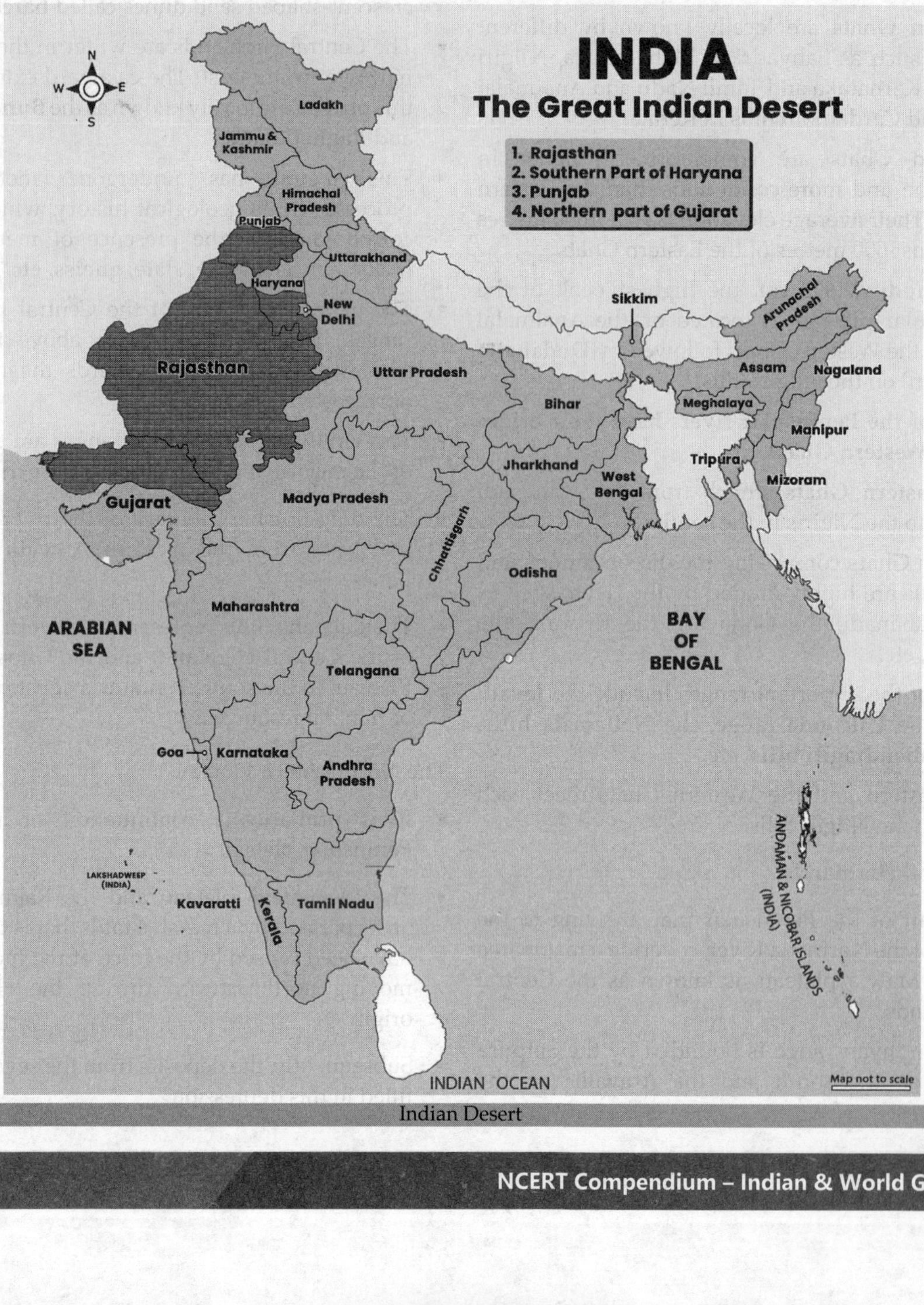

Indian Desert

- The Great Indian desert is located to the northwest of the Aravali hills. It's a topographically undulating region with **longitudinal dunes and barchans** scattered throughout.
- This area has an arid climate with little vegetation cover since it receives little rainfall less than 150 mm annually.
- This is sometimes referred to **as Marusthali** due to these distinguishing characteristics.
- It is thought that this area was beneath the sea **during the Mesozoic era**. The evidence found at the wood fossil park at Aakal and the marine deposits around Brahmsar, near Jaisalmer, support this (the wood fossils are estimated to be 180 million years old).
- **An oasis, shifting dunes**, and **mushroom rocks** are some of the prominent desert land features found here (primarily in its southern portion).
- The desert can be separated into two halves based on their orientation: the **northern section slopes towards Sindh**, while the **southern part faces the Rann of Kachchh**.
- The majority of the rivers in this area are temporary. There is **considerable significance to the Luni River,** which flows **through the southern portion** of the desert.
- Certain streams disappear after a certain distance and join a **lake or playa**, illustrating a classic example of inland drainage. From the brackish water of the lakes and playas, salt is mostly obtained.

The Coastal Plains

On the basis of the location and active geomorphological processes, the Coastal Plains can be broadly divided into two: **(i) the western coastal plains; (ii) the eastern coastal plains.**

The Western Coastal Plains

- One example of a submerged coastal plain is the western coastal plains.
- Dwaraka, a city on the west coast of India that was formerly a part of the continent, is said to be underwater.
- It is a narrow zone due to this submergence, which creates **ideal conditions** for the growth of ports and harbours like **Kandla, Mazagaon, JLN port Nhava Sheva, Marmagao, Mangalore, Cochin, etc.**
- The Arabian Sea and the Western Ghats encircle the narrow plain that forms the western coast.
- It is divided into **three parts**. The northern portion of the coast is known as the **Konkan** (Mumbai Goa), its central portion as the **Kannad Plain**, and its southern portion as the **Malabar coast**.
- The western coastal plains are broad in the north and south but narrow in the middle. This coastal plain's rivers do not create any deltas as they run through it.
- The backwaters, or "Kayals," that are utilised for inland navigation and fishing are one of the Malabar coast's distinctive features. Another is its unique tourist attraction.
- The renowned **Nehru Trophy Vallamkali**, a **boat race**, takes place in **Punnamada Kayal, Kerala, annually.**

The Eastern Coastal Plain

- As compared to the western coastal plain, the eastern coastal plain is broader and is an example of an emergent coast.
- In the northern part, it is referred to as the **Northern Circar,** while the southern part is known as the **Coromandel Coast.**
- There are well developed deltas here, formed by the rivers flowing eastward into the Bay of Bengal. These include the deltas of the Mahanadi, the Godavari, the Krishna and the Kaveri.
- **Because of its emergent nature**, it has less, number of ports and harbours. The continental shelf extends up to 500 km into the sea, which makes it difficult for the development of good ports and harbours.

> The largest saltwater lake in India is called **Chilika Lake.** It is located in the southern part of the Mahanadi delta in the state of Odisha.

The Islands

There are two important island groups in India as given – (i) The Bay of Bengal and (ii) The Arabian Sea.

Island Groups of Bay of Bengal

- There are **roughly 572 islands** or islets in the **Bay of Bengal** island groups. These are located approximately **between 92°E and 94°E and 6°N and 14°N**.

- The Ritchie's archipelago and Labrynth Island are the two main groups of islets.
- The **Andaman Islands in the north and the Nicobar Islands in the south** make up the two main categories into which the entire collection of islands falls. A body of water known as the **Ten-degree channel** divides them.
- It is believed that these islands are an elevated portion of submarine mountains. However, some smaller islands are volcanic in origin. **Barren island, the only active volcano in India is also situated** in the **Nicobar Islands.**
- **Some important mountain peaks in Andaman and Nicobar Islands** are **Saddle peak** (North Andaman – 738 m), **Mount Diavolo** (Middle Andaman – 515 m), **Mount Koyob** (South Andaman – 460 m) and **Mount Thuiller** (Great Nicobar – 642 m).
- The coastal line has some coral deposits, and beautiful beaches. These islands receive convectional rainfall and have an equatorial type of vegetation.

Island Groups of the Arabian sea

- The **islands of the Arabian sea** include Lakshadweep and Minicoy.
- These are scattered between 8°N-12°N and 71°E -74°E longitude. These islands are located at a distance of 280 km-480 km off the Kerala coast.
- The entire group of islands is composed of coral deposits. 11 of the roughly 36 islands are inhabited.
- **Minicoy** is the largest island with an area of 453 sq. km.
- **Kavaratti island** is the administrative headquarters of Lakshadweep. The Pitti island, which is uninhabited, has a bird sanctuary.
- The **Eight Degree Channel** separates the islands of Minicoy and Maldives, the **Nine Degree Channel** separates the island of Minicoy from the main Lakshadweep archipelago.
- On the eastern seaboard, **the islands in this archipelago include storm beaches made up of rocks, shingles, cobbles, and unconsolidated pebbles.**

Corals

Coral polyps are small, short-lived creatures that inhabit colonies. They function best in warm, shallow, mud-free waters. They release carbonate of calcium. Reefs are formed of secreted coral and their skeletons, which are classified into three primary types: atolls, fringing reefs, and barrier reefs. An excellent illustration of the first type of coral reef is the Great Barrier Reef in Australia. **Atolls** are coral reefs that are built like a horseshoe or circular.

TEST YOURSELF

Multiple Choice Questions

Q1. Which is the highest peak in the Indian Himalayas?

(a) Mount Kanchenjunga (b) Nanda Devi

(c) Mount Everest (d) Annapurna

Q2. The Aravalli Range is located in which part of India?

(a) Western India (b) Eastern India

(c) Southern India (d) Northern India

Q3. The Deccan Plateau is located between which two mountain ranges?

(a) Western Ghats and Eastern Ghats

(b) Vindhya Range and Aravalli Range

(c) Himalayas and Karakoram Range

(d) Satpura Range and Aravalli Range

Q4. Which is the largest river basin in India?

(a) Ganga-Brahmaputra-Meghna (b) Godavari

(c) Krishna (d) Narmada

Q5. The Thar Desert is located in which state of India?

(a) Rajasthan (b) Gujarat

(c) Madhya Pradesh (d) Punjab

Q6. Which river forms the famous Dudhsagar Falls in India?

(a) Ganga (b) Yamuna

(c) Brahmaputra (d) Mandovi

Q7. The Palk Strait lies between India and which country?

(a) Sri Lanka (b) Maldives

(c) Bangladesh (d) Myanmar

Q8. The Gulf of Khambhat is located in which state of India?

(a) Gujarat (b) Maharashtra

(c) Tamil Nadu (d) Odisha

Q9. Which of the following is a group of islands located in the Bay of Bengal?

(a) Andaman and Nicobar Islands

(b) Lakshadweep Islands

(c) Maldives

(d) Seychelles

Q10. The Great Indian Desert is another name for:

(a) Thar Desert (b) Rann of Kutch

(c) Sundarbans (d) Deccan Plateau

Q11. Consider the following pairs: (UPSC 2022)

	Peak		Mountains
1.	Namcha Barwa	—	Garhwal Himalaya
2.	Nanda Devi	—	Kumaon Himalaya
3.	Nokrek	—	Sikkim Himalaya

Which of the pairs given above is/are correctly matched?

(a) 1 and 2 (b) 2 only

(c) 1 and 3 (d) 3 only

Q12. The largest island in the world is:

(a) Greenland (b) Borneo

(c) Madagascar (d) New Guinea

Answer Key

Q1.	a	Q2.	a	Q3.	a	Q4.	a
Q5.	a	Q6.	d	Q7.	a	Q8.	a
Q9.	a	Q10.	a	Q11.	b	Q12.	a

UNIT 9

Drainage

In This Unit

Comprehensive and profound coverage of the following NCERTs' chapters:

- ✓ NCERT Class- 9th (Contemporary India-I), Chapter- 3
- ✓ NCERT Class- 11th (India Physical Environment), Chapter- 3

"Drainage" refers to the movement of water through clearly defined channels, while **"drainage system"** refers to the network of these channels. The geological time period, the nature and composition of the rocks, the topography, the slope, the volume of water moving, and the flow's periodicity all affect an area's drainage pattern. A river's **"catchment area"** is the area from which it draws its water supply. A **drainage basin** is the region that is drained by a river and its tributaries.

Contribution of Water by Rivers in India

River	% Contribution of Water
Brahmaputra	40
Ganga	25
Godavari	6.4
Mahanadi	3.5
Krishna	3.4
Narmada	2.9
Rest	20

The term **"watershed"** refers to the border that divides a drainage basin from another. While the catchments of little rivulets and rills are sometimes referred to **as watersheds**, the catchments of large rivers are known as **river basins**. However, there is a **small difference** between a **watershed and a river basin**. Whereas **basins** encompass **wider areas**, **watersheds** are **smaller** in size.

> The world's largest drainage basin is of the **Amazon River**.

There are several ways to differentiate the Indian drainage system.

On the grounds of discharge of water (directed towards the sea), it may be categorised into:

1. The **Arabian Sea drainage**
2. The **Bay of Bengal drainage**

The Delhi Ridge, the Aravallis, and the Sahyadris separate them from one another. **The Bay of Bengal receives around 77%** of the drainage area from the **Ganga, Brahmaputra, Mahanadi, Krishna, and other rivers**, while the **Arabian Sea receives 23%** of the water from the **Indus, Narmada, Tapi, Mahi, and Periyar systems.**

On the grounds of the size of the watershed, the drainage basins of India are categorised into three categories:

1. **Major river basins with catchment areas larger than 20,000 square kilometres**. There are fourteen drainage basins in all, including the Ganga, Brahmaputra, Krishna, Tapi, Narmada, Mahi, Pennar, Sabarmati, Barak, and others.
2. **Medium river basins**, which include 44 river basins including the Kalindi, Periyar, Meghna, and others, and have a **catchment area of 2,000–20,000 sq. km.**
3. A respectable number of rivers run in the region of low rainfall are found in **minor river basins,** which have a catchment area of **less than 2,000 square kilometres.**

Drainage Systems Based on the Size of the Catchment Area

Division	Size of catchment area in sq km
Major river	20,000
Medium river	20,000–2,000
Minor river	2,000 and below

On the basis of the mode of origin, nature and characteristics, the Indian drainage may also be classified into two categories:

1. The **Himalayan drainage**
2. The **Peninsular drainage**

While generally, the large rivers belong to Himalayan drainage, there are two exceptions. These are Narmada and the Tapi of the Peninsular Drainage which release their water into the Arabian Sea, together with several smaller rivers.

Drainage Systems In India

The drainage system in India is made up of numerous small and large rivers. It is the result of precipitation's nature and properties as well as the evolution of the three main physiographic units.

The Himalayan Drainage

The major Himalayan rivers are the **Indus, the Ganga and the Brahmaputra**. Because the rivers in this system receive water from both precipitation and snowmelt, they are **perennial.**

- These rivers flow through the big gorges created by erosion that occurred in tandem with the Himalayan uplift.
- Along with creating deep gorges, these rivers meander across steep terrain, creating V-shaped valleys, rapids, and waterfalls. They create depositional features along the way into the plains, including as braided channels, flood plains, oxbow lakes, deltas close to the river mouth, and level valleys.
- These rivers run greatly meandering throughout the plains, changing direction often, but they are extremely tortuous in the Himalayan reaches.
- The Kosi River, referred to as the **"sorrow of Bihar,"** is infamous for its propensity to alter its path. Massive amounts of silt are brought down from the upper reaches of the Kosi and deposited on the lowlands. The river alters its route as a result of the obstruction in its path.

Evolution of The Himalayan Drainage

- Geologists speculate that during the Miocene epoch, approximately 5–24 million years ago, a powerful river known as Shiwalik or Indo-Brahma flowed along the whole length of the Himalaya, from Assam to Punjab and then to Sind, before emptying into the Gulf of Sind close to lower Punjab. This opinion is supported by the Shiwalik's extraordinary continuity, its lacustrine origin, and the alluvial deposits that are made up of sands, silt, clay, boulders, and conglomerates.
- **Over time, it is believed that the Indo-Brahma River split into three primary drainage systems:** (i) the Ganga and its Himalayan tributaries in the central region; (ii) the Indus and its five tributaries in the western region; and (iii) the eastern portion of the Brahmaputra stretch in Assam and its Himalayan tributaries. The Pleistocene upheaval in the western Himalayas, particularly the elevation of the Potwar Plateau (Delhi Ridge), which served as the water divide between the Indus and Ganga drainage systems, is most likely what caused the fragmentation.
- Similar to this, the Ganga and Brahmaputra systems were redirected to flow towards the Bay of Bengal during the **mid-Pleistocene era** due to the down-thrusting of the Malda gap area between the **Rajmahal hills** and the Meghalaya plateau.

The River Systems of The Himalayan Drainage

There are several river systems in the Himalayan drainage basin, but the following are the main ones:

The Indus River System

- With a total length of 2,880 km (in India 1,114 km) and an area of 11,65,000 sq. km (in India, 321 289 sq. km), it is one of the world's largest river basins.
- The westernmost of India's Himalayan rivers is the **Indus, also referred to as the Sindhu**. It comes from a glacier in the Kailash Mountain range, 4,164 metres high, close to Bokhar Chu in the Tibetan area.
- **In Tibet,** it is known as **'Singi Khamban' or Lion's mouth**. After flowing in the northwest direction between the Ladakh and Zaskar ranges, it passes through Ladakh and Baltistan.
- It cuts across the Ladakh range, forming a spectacular gorge near Gilgit in Jammu and Kashmir. It enters Pakistan near Chilas in the Dardistan region.
- The Indus receives a number of Himalayan tributaries such as the Zaskar, the Nubra, the Shyok, the Hunza, Shigar, the Gasting and the Dras. It finally emerges out of the hills near Attock where it receives the Kabul River on its right bank.
- The other important tributaries joining the right bank of the Indus are the Khurram, the Tochi, the Gomal, the Viboa and the Sangar. They all originate in the Sulaiman ranges.

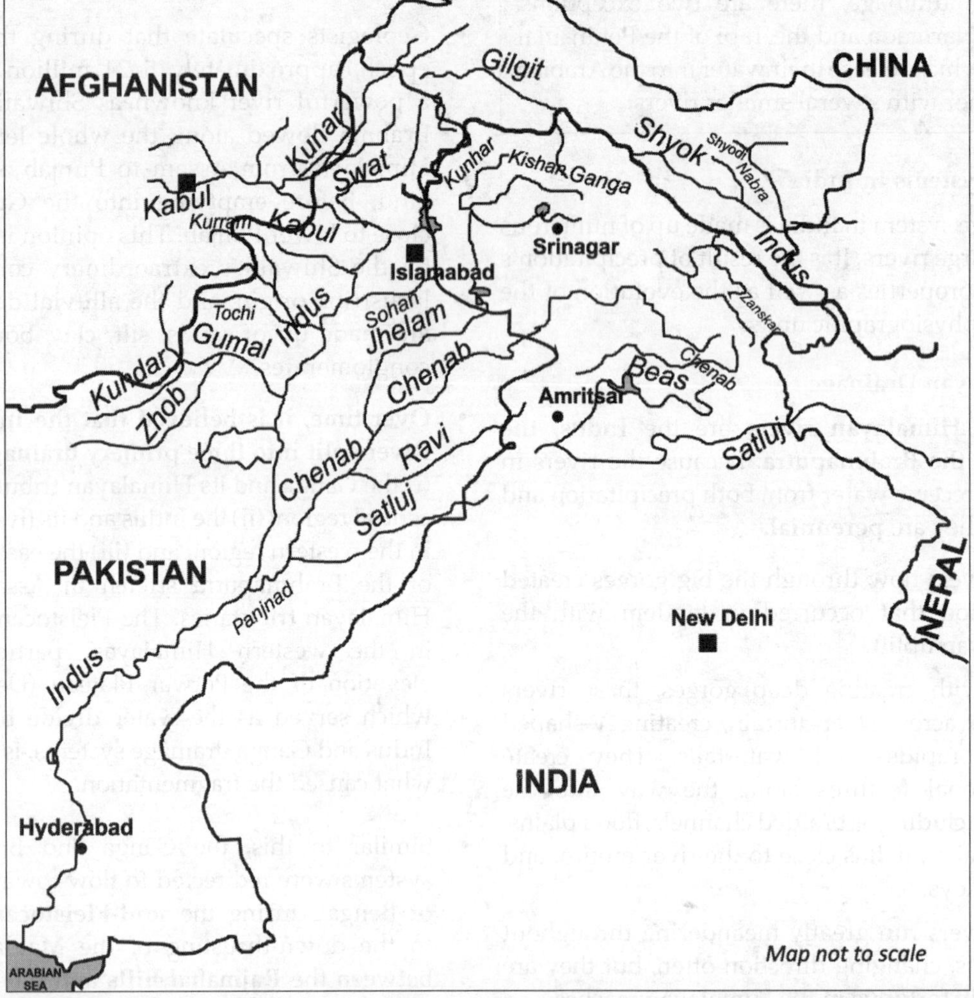

Indus River System

- The river flows southward and receives '**Panjnad**' a little above Mithankot. The Panjnad is the name given to the five rivers of Punjab, namely the Satluj, the Beas, the Ravi, the Chenab and the Jhelum.
- It finally discharges into the Arabian Sea, east of Karachi. **The Indus flows in India only through Jammu and Kashmir.**
- **The Jhelum,** an important tributary of the Indus, rises from a spring at Verinag situated at the foot of the Pir Panjal in the south-eastern part of the valley of Kashmir. It flows through Srinagar and the Wular lake before entering Pakistan through a deep narrow gorge. It joins the Chenab near Jhang in Pakistan.
- **The Chenab** is the largest tributary of the Indus. It is formed by two streams, the Chandra and the Bhaga, which join at Tandi near Keylong in Himachal Pradesh. Hence, it is also known as **Chandrabhaga.** The river flows for 1,180 km before entering into Pakistan.
- **The Ravi** is another important tributary of the Indus. It rises west of the Rohtang pass in the Kullu hills of Himachal Pradesh and flows through the Chamba valley of the state. Before entering Pakistan and joining the Chenab near Sarai Sidhu, it drains the area lying between the southeastern part of the Pir Panjal and the Dhauladhar ranges.
- **The Beas** is another important tributary of the Indus, originating from the Beas Kund near the Rohtang Pass at an elevation of 4,000 m above the mean sea level. The river flows through the Kullu valley and forms gorges at Kati and Largi in the Dhauladhar range. It enters the Punjab plains where it meets the Satluj near Harike.
- **The Satluj** originates in the '**Raksas tal**' near Mansarovar at an altitude of 4,555 m in Tibet where it is known as Langchen Khambab. It flows almost parallel to the Indus for about 400 km before entering India, and comes out of a gorge at Rupar. It passes through the Shipki La on the Himalayan ranges and enters the Punjab plains. It is an **antecedent river.** It is a very important tributary as it feeds the canal system of the Bhakra Nangal project.

According to the regulations of the **Indus Water Treaty (1960),** India can use only 20 percent of the total water carried by the Indus River system. This water is used for irrigation in Punjab, Haryana and the southern and the western parts of Rajasthan.

The Ganga System

- The Ganga is the most important river of India both from the point of view of its basin and cultural significance. It rises in the Gangotri glacier near Gaumukh (3,900 m) in the Uttarkashi district of Uttarakhand. Here, it is known as the **Bhagirathi.**
- It cuts through the Central and the Lesser Himalayas in narrow gorges. At **Devprayag,** the **Bhagirathi** meets the Alaknanda; hereafter, it is known as the Ganga.
- The Alaknanda has its source in the Satopanth glacier above Badrinath. The Alaknanda consists of the Dhauli and the Vishnu Ganga which meet at Joshimath or **Vishnu Prayag.**
- The other tributaries of Alaknanda such as the Pindar joins it at **Karna Prayag** while Mandakini or Kali Ganga meets it at **Rudra Prayag.** The Ganga enters the plains at Haridwar. From here, it flows first to the south, then to the south-east and east before splitting into two distributaries, namely the Bhagirathi and the Padma.
- The river has a length of 2,525 km. It is shared by Uttarakhand (110 km) and Uttar Pradesh (1,450 km), Bihar (445 km) and West Bengal (520 km). The Ganga basin covers about 8.6 lakh sq. km area in India alone. The Ganga River system is the largest in India having a number of perennial and non-perennial rivers originating in the Himalayas in the north and the Peninsula in the south, respectively.
- The Son is its major right bank tributary. The important left bank tributaries are the Ramganga, the Gomati, the Ghaghara, the Gandak, the Kosi and the Mahananda.
- Ambala is located on **the water divide** between the Indus and the Ganga River systems. The plains from Ambala to the Sundarban stretch over nearly 1800 km, but the fall in its slope is hardly 300 meters. In other words, there is a fall of just one meter for every 6 km. Therefore, the river develops large meanders.

- The river finally **discharges itself into the Bay of Bengal near the Sagar Island**. The delta formed by these rivers is known as the Sundarban Delta.
- **The Yamuna,** the western most and the longest tributary of the Ganga, has its source in the Yamunotri glacier on the western slopes of Banderpunch range (6,316 km). It joins the Ganga at Prayag (Allahabad). It is joined by the Chambal, the Sind, the Betwa and the Ken on its right bank which originates from the Peninsular plateau while the Hindan, the Rind, the Sengar, the Varuna, etc. join it on its left bank. Much of its water feeds the western and eastern Yamuna and the Agra canals for irrigation purposes.

The **Sundarban Delta** derived its name from the Sundari tree, which grows well in marshland. It is the world's largest and fastest growing delta. It is also the home of the Royal Bengal tiger.

- **The Chambal** rises near Mhow in the Malwa plateau of Madhya Pradesh and flows northwards through a gorge up wards of Kota in Rajasthan, where the Gandhisagar dam has been constructed. From Kota, it traverses down to Bundi, Sawai Madhopur and Dholpur, and finally joins the Yamuna. **The Chambal is famous for its bad land topography called the Chambal ravines.**
- **The Gandak** comprises two streams, namely Kaligandak and Trishulganga. It rises in the Nepal Himalayas between the Dhaulagiri and Mount Everest and drains the central part of Nepal. It enters the Ganga plain in Champaran district of Bihar and joins the Ganga at Sonpur near Patna.
- **The Ghaghara** originates in the glaciers of Mapchachungo. After collecting the waters of its tributaries – Tila, Seti and Beri, it comes out of the mountain, cutting a deep gorge at Shishapani. The river Sarda (Kali or Kali Ganga) joins it in the plain before it finally meets the Ganga at Chhapra.

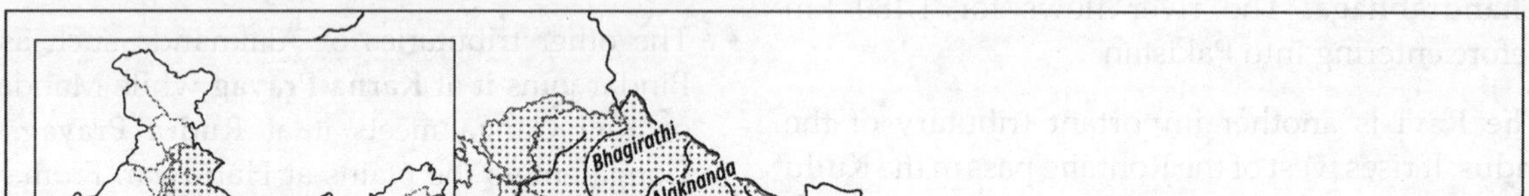

Ganga River System

- **The Kosi** is an **antecedent river** with its source to the north of Mount Everest in Tibet, where its main stream Arun rises. After crossing the Central Himalayas in Nepal, it is joined by the **Son Kosi** from the West and the Tamur Kosi from the east. It forms **Sapt Kosi** after uniting with the river Arun.

- **The Ramganga** is comparatively a small river rising in the Garhwal hills near Gairsain. It changes its course to the southwest direction after crossing the Shiwalik and enters into the plains of Uttar Pradesh near Najibabad. Finally, it joins the Ganga near Kannauj.
- **The Damodar** occupies the eastern margins of the Chotanagpur Plateau where it flows through a rift valley and finally joins the Hugli. The Barakar is its main tributary. Once known as the **'sorrow of Bengal'**, the Damodar has been now tamed by the Damodar Valley corporation, a multipurpose project.
- **The Sarda or Saryu River** rises in the Milam glacier in the Nepal Himalayas where it is known as the Goriganga. Along the Indo-Nepal border, it is called Kali or Chauk, where it joins the Ghaghara.
- The **Mahananda** is another important tributary of the Ganga rising in the Darjiling hills. It joins the Ganga as its last left bank tributary in West Bengal.
- **The Son** is a large south bank tributary of the Ganga, originating in the Amarkantak plateau. After forming a series of waterfalls at the edge of the plateau, it reaches Arrah, west of Patna, to join the Ganga.

'Namami Gange Programme', is an Integrated Conservation Mission, approved as **"Flagship Programme"** by the Union Government in June 2014 with the twin objectives of effective abatement of pollution, conservation and rejuvenation of the National River Ganga.

Main pillars of the Namami Gange Programme are:

- Sewerage Treatment Infrastructure
- River-Front Development
- River -Surface Cleaning
- Biodiversity
- Afforestation
- Public Awareness
- Industrial Effluent Monitoring
- Ganga Gram

The Brahmaputra River System

- The Brahmaputra, one of the largest rivers of the world, has its origin in the **Chemayungdung glacier** of the Kailash range near the Mansarovar lake.
- From here, it traverses eastward longitudinally for a distance of nearly 1,200 km in a dry and flat region of southern Tibet, where it is known as the **Tsangpo, which means 'the purifier**.' The Rango Tsangpo is the major right bank tributary of this river in Tibet.
- It emerges as a turbulent and dynamic river after carving out a deep gorge in the Central Himalayas near **Namcha Barwa** (7,755 m).
- The river emerges from the foothills under the name of **Siang or Dihang**. It enters India west of Sadiya town in Arunachal Pradesh. Flowing southwest, it receives its main left bank tributaries, viz., Dibang or Sikang and Lohit; thereafter, it is known as the Brahmaputra.
- The Brahmaputra receives numerous tributaries in its 750 km long journey through the Assam valley. Its major left bank tributaries are the Burhi Dihing and Dhansari (South) whereas the important right bank tributaries are the Subansiri, Kameng, Manas and Sankosh.
- The Subansiri which has its origin in Tibet, is an antecedent river. The Brahmaputra enters into Bangladesh near Dhubri and flows southward.
- In Bangladesh, the Tista joins it on its right bank from where the river is known as the **Jamuna.** It finally merges with the river Padma, which falls in the Bay of Bengal.
- In Tibet, the river carries a smaller volume of water and less silt as it is a cold and a dry area. In India, it passes through a region of high rainfall. Here the river carries a large volume of water and considerable amount of silt. The Brahmaputra has a braided channel in its entire length in Assam and forms many riverine islands. The world's largest riverine island named **Majuli** is formed by the Brahmaputra.
- The Brahmaputra is well-known for floods, channel shifting and bank erosion.
- It is slightly longer than the Indus, and most of its course lies outside India.

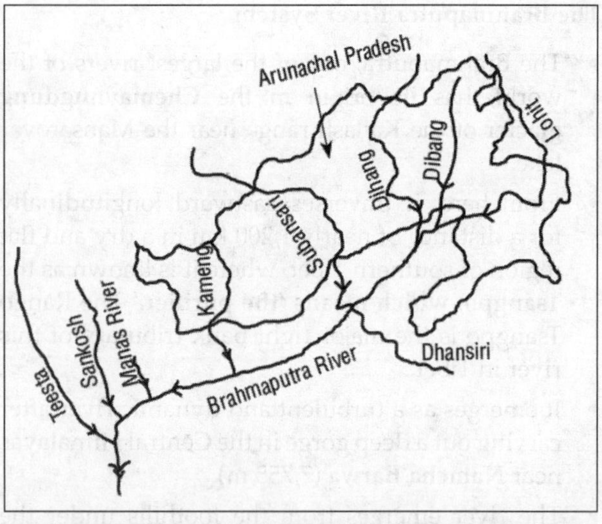

Brahmaputra River System

The Peninsular Drainage System

The Peninsular drainage system is older than the Himalayan one. This is evident from the broad, largely-graded shallow valleys, and the maturity of the rivers. The Western Ghats running close to the western coast act as the water divide between the major Peninsular rivers, discharging their water in the Bay of Bengal and as small rivulets joining the Arabian Sea. Most of the major Peninsular rivers except **Narmada and Tapi** flow from west to east. The Chambal, the Sind, the Betwa, the Ken, the Son, originating in the northern part of the Peninsula belong to the **Ganga River System.** The other major river systems of the Peninsular drainage are – the Mahanadi, the Godavari, the Krishna and the Kaveri. Peninsular rivers are characterised by fixed course, absence of meanders and non-perennial flow of water. The Narmada and the Tapi which flow through the rift valley are, however, exceptions.

The Evolution of Peninsular Drainage System

Three major geological events in the distant past have shaped the present drainage systems of Peninsular India:

1. Subsidence of the western flank of the Peninsula leading to its submergence below the sea during the early tertiary period. Generally, it has disturbed the symmetrical plan of the river on either side of the original watershed.
2. Upheaval of the Himalayas when the northern flank of the Peninsular block was subjected to subsidence and the consequent trough faulting. The Narmada and The Tapi flow in trough faults and fill the original cracks with their detritus materials. Hence, there is a lack of alluvial and deltaic deposits in these rivers.
3. Slight tilting of the Peninsular block from northwest to the southeastern direction gave orientation to the entire drainage system towards the Bay of Bengal during the same period.

River Systems of the Peninsular Drainage

A brief account of the major Peninsular River systems is given below:

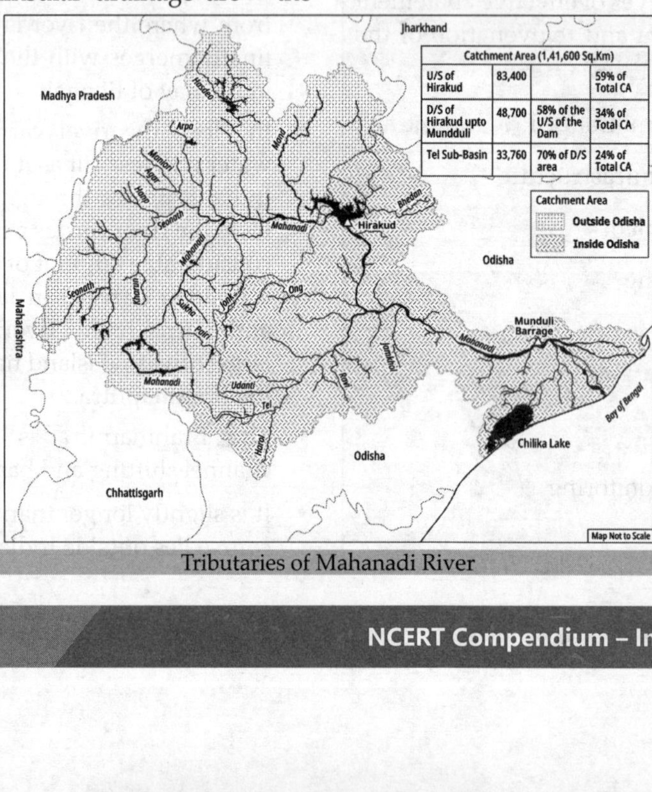

Catchment Area (1,41,600 Sq.Km)			
U/S of Hirakud	83,400		59% of Total CA
D/S of Hirakud upto Mundduli	48,700	58% of the U/S of the Dam	34% of Total CA
Tel Sub-Basin	33,760	70% of D/S area	24% of Total CA

Tributaries of Mahanadi River

- **The Mahanadi Basin-** The Mahanadi rises near Sihawa in Raipur district of Chhattisgarh and runs through Odisha to discharge its water into the Bay of Bengal. It is 851 km long and its catchment area spreads over 1.42 lakh sq. km. Some navigation is carried on in the lower course of this river. 53 per cent of the drainage basin of this river lies in Madhya Pradesh and Chhattisgarh, while 47 per cent lies in Odisha.
- **The Godavari Basin- The Godavari is the largest Peninsular River system**. It rises in the Nasik district of Maharashtra and discharges its water into the Bay of Bengal. Its tributaries run through the states of Maharashtra, Madhya Pradesh, Chhattisgarh, Odisha and Andhra Pradesh. It is 1,465 km long with a catchment area spreading over 3.13 lakh sq. km. 49 per cent of this, lies in Maharashtra, 20 per cent in Madhya Pradesh and Chhattisgarh, and the rest in Andhra Pradesh. The Penganga, the Indravati, the Pranhita, and the Manjra are its principal tributaries. The Godavari is subjected to heavy floods in its lower reaches to the south of Polavaram, where it forms a picturesque gorge. It is navigable only in the deltaic stretch. The river after Rajamundri splits into several branches forming a large delta. Because of the length and area it covers, it is also known as the **Dakshin Ganga.**

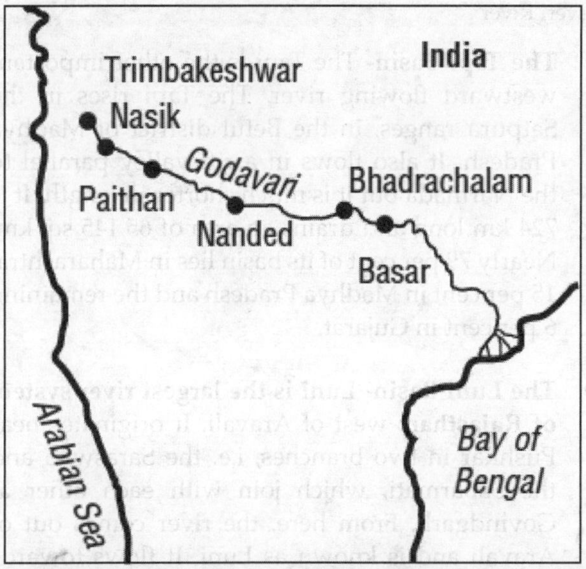

Tributaries of Godavari River

- **The Krishna Basin-** The Krishna is the **second largest east- flowing** Peninsular River which rises near Mahabaleshwar in Sahyadri. Its total length is 1,401 km. The Koyna, the Ghatprabha, the Musi, the Tungabhadra and the Bhima are its major tributaries. Of the total catchment area of the Krishna, 27 per cent lies in Maharashtra, 44 per cent in Karnataka and 29 per cent in Andhra Pradesh and Telangana

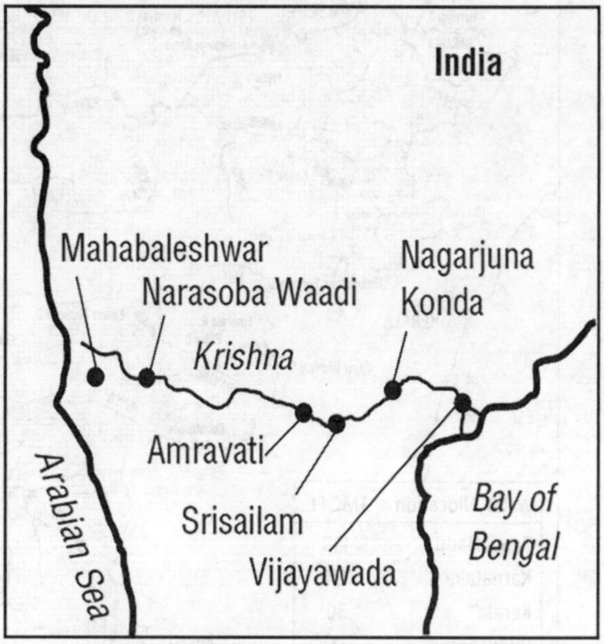

Tributaries of Krishna River

- **The Kaveri Basin-** The Kaveri rises in Brahmagiri hills (1,341m) of Kodagu district in Karnataka and it reaches the Bay of Bengal in south of Cuddalore in Tamil Nadu. Its length is 800 km and it drains an area of 81,155 sq. km. Since the upper catchment area receives rainfall during the southwest monsoon season (summer) and the lower part during the northeast monsoon season (winter), the river carries water throughout the year with comparatively less fluctuation than the other Peninsular rivers. About 3 percent of the Kaveri basin falls in Kerala, 41 per cent in Karnataka and 56 per cent in Tamil Nadu. Its important tributaries are the Kabini, the Bhavani, Hemavati and the Amravati. The river Kaveri makes the second biggest waterfall in India, known **as Shivasamudram Falls.** The hydroelectric power generated from the falls is supplied to Mysuru, Bengaluru and the Kolar Gold Field.

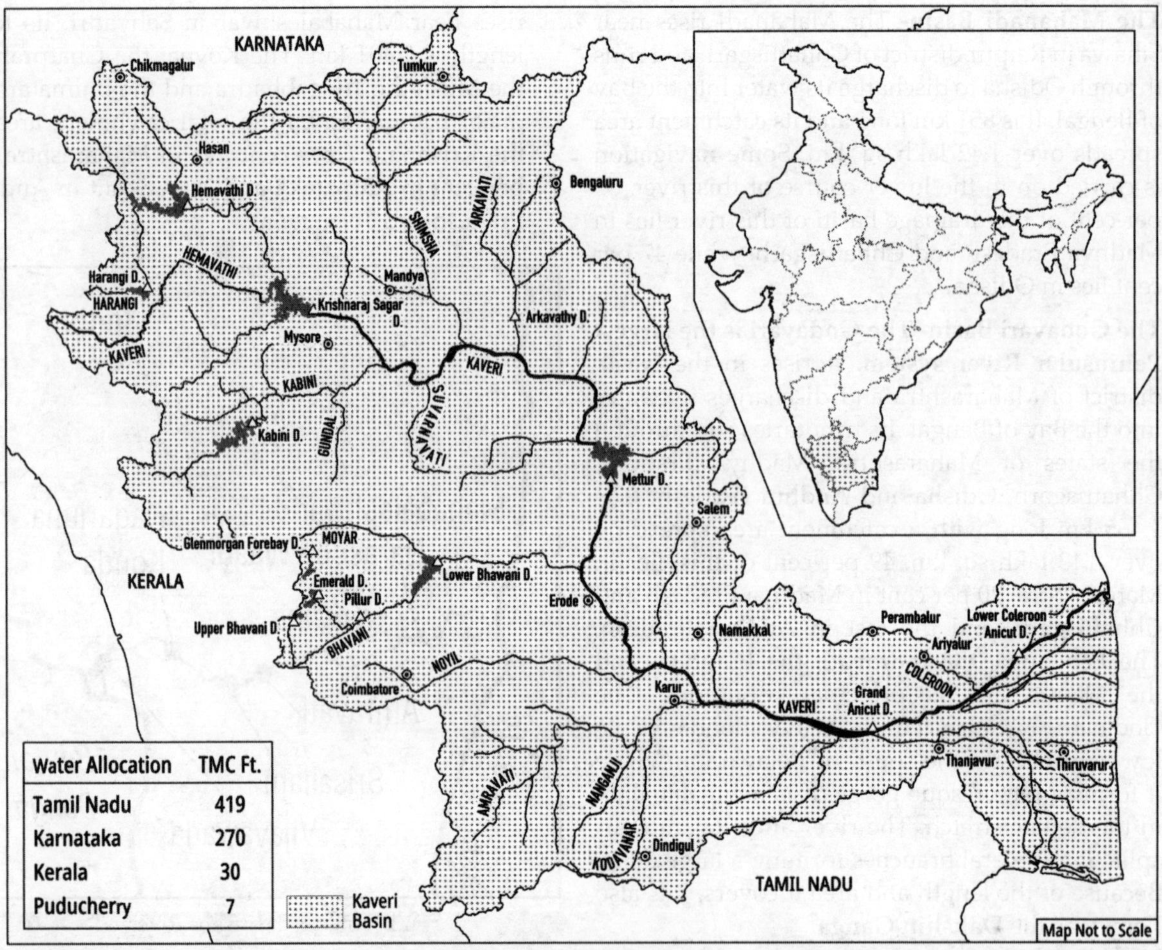

Tributaries of Kaveri River

- **The Narmada Basin-** The Narmada originates on the western flank of the Amarkantak plateau at a height of about 1,057 m in Madhya Pradesh. Flowing in a rift valley between the Satpura in the south and the Vindhyan range in the north, it forms a picturesque gorge in marble rocks and Dhuandhar waterfall near Jabalpur. After flowing a distance of about 1,312 km, it meets the Arabian sea south of Bharuch, forming a broad 27 km long estuary. Its catchment area is about 98,796 sq. km. The Sardar Sarovar Project has been constructed on this river. The Narmada basin covers parts of Madhya Pradesh and Gujarat.

- **The Narmada River conservation mission has been undertaken by the government of Madhya Pradesh by a scheme named Namami Devi Narmade.**

- **The Tapi Basin-** The Tapi is the other important westward flowing river. The Tapi rises in the Satpura ranges, in the Betul district of Madhya Pradesh. It also flows in a rift valley parallel to the Narmada but it is much shorter in length. It is 724 km long and drains an area of 65,145 sq. km. Nearly 79 per cent of its basin lies in Maharashtra, 15 per cent in Madhya Pradesh and the remaining 6 per cent in Gujarat.

- **The Luni Basin- Luni is the largest river system of Rajasthan**, west of Aravali. It originates near Pushkar in two branches, i.e. the Saraswati and the Sabarmati, which join with each other at Govindgarh. From here, the river comes out of Aravali and is known as Luni. It flows towards the west till Telwara and then takes a southwest direction to join the Rann of Kuchchh. The entire river system is ephemeral.

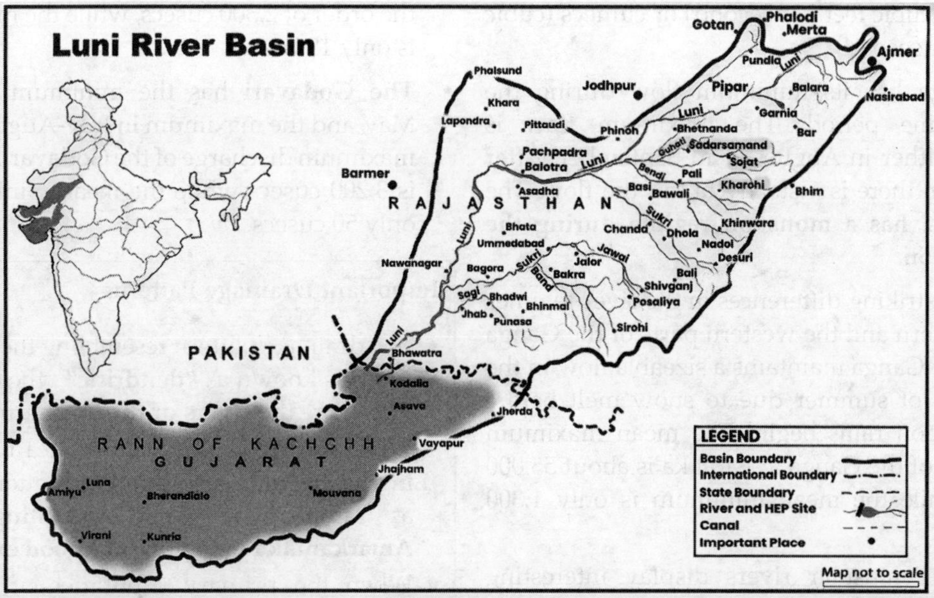

Luni River Basin

Smaller Rivers Flowing Towards the West (Arabian Sea)

- **Rivers of Gujarat**- The Shetrunji is one such river which rises near Dalkahwa in Amreli district. The Bhadra originates near Aniali village in Rajkot district. The Dhadhar rises near Ghantar village in Panchmahal district. Sabarmati and Mahi are the two famous rivers of Gujarat.
- The Vaitarna rises from the Trimbak hills in Nasik district at an elevation of 670 m.
- **Rivers of Karnataka**- The Kalinadi rises from Belgaum district and falls in the Karwar Bay. The source of the Bedti river lies in Hubli Dharwar and traverses a course of 161 km. The Sharavati is another important river in Karnataka flowing towards the west. The Sharavati originates in Shimoga district of Karnataka and drains a catchment area of 2,209 sq. km.
- **Rivers of Goa**- Goa has two important rivers. One is Mandovi and the other is Juari.
- **Rivers of Kerala**- Kerala has a narrow coastline. The longest river of Kerala, **Bharathapuzha** rises near Annamalai hills. It is also known as Ponnani. It drains an area of 5,397 sq. km. The Periyar is the second largest river of Kerala. Its catchment area is 5,243 sq. km. Another river of Kerala worth mentioning is the Pamba river which falls in the Vembanad lake after traversing a course of 177 km.

Small Rivers Flowing towards the East (Bay of Bengal)

- The Subarnrekha, the Baitarni, the Brahmani, the Vamsadhara, the Penner, the Palar and the Vaigai are important rivers that flow towards the east.

River Regimes

The pattern of flow of water in a river channel over a year is known as its **regime**.

- The north Indian rivers originating from the Himalayas are perennial as they are fed by glaciers through snow melt and also receive rainfall water during the rainy season.
- The rivers of South India do not originate from glaciers and their flow pattern witnesses fluctuations. The flow increases considerably during monsoon rains. Thus, the regime of the rivers of South India is controlled by rainfall which also varies from one part of the Peninsular plateau to the other.
- The **discharge** is the volume of water flowing in a river measured over time. It is measured either

in cusecs (cubic feet per second) or cumecs (cubic meters per second).

- The Ganga has its minimum flow during the January-June period. The maximum flow is attained either in August or in September. After September, there is a steady fall in the flow. The river, thus, **has a monsoon regime during the rainy season.**
- There are striking differences in the river regimes in the eastern and the western parts of the Ganga Basin. The Ganga maintains a sizeable flow in the early part of summer due to snow melt before the monsoon rains begin. The mean maximum discharge of the Ganga at Farakka is about 55,000 cusecs while the mean minimum is only 1,300 cusecs.
- The two Peninsular rivers display interesting differences in their regimes compared to the Himalayan rivers.
- **Narmada** has a very low volume of discharge from January to July but it suddenly rises in August when the maximum flow is attained. The flow of water in the Narmada, as recorded at Garudeshwar, shows that the maximum flow is of the order of 2,300 cusecs, while the minimum flow is only 15 cusecs.
- **The Godavari** has the minimum discharge in May, and the maximum in July-August. The mean maximum discharge of the Godavari at Polavaram is 3,200 cusecs while the mean minimum flow is only 50 cusecs.

Important Drainage Patterns

- The drainage pattern resembling the branches of a tree is known as **"dendritic"** , the examples of which are the **rivers of the northern plain.**
- When the rivers originate from a hill and flow in all directions, the drainage pattern is known as **'radial'. The rivers originating from the Amarkantak range present a good example of it.**
- When the primary tributaries of rivers flow parallel to each other and secondary tributaries join them at right angles, the pattern is known as **'trellis'**.
- When the rivers discharge their waters from all directions in a lake or depression, the pattern is known as **'centripetal'**.

SL.NO.	ASPECTS	Himalayan River	Peninsular River
1.	Place of origin	Himalayan mountain covered with glaciers	Peninsular plateau and central highland
2.	Nature of flow	Perennial; receive water from glacier and rainfall	Seasonal; dependent on monsoon rainfall
3.	Type of drainage	Antecedent and consequent leading to dendritic pattern in plains	Superimposed, rejuvenated resulting in trellis, radial and rectangular patterns
4.	Nature of river	Long course, flowing through the rugged mountains experiencing headward erosion and river capturing; In plains meandering and shifting of course.	Smaller, fixed course with well-adjusted valleys.
5.	Catchment area	Very large basins	Relatively smaller basin
6.	Age of the river	Young and youthful, active and deepening in the valleys	Old rivers with graded profile, and have almost reached their base levels

Comparison between the Himalayan and the Peninsular River System

Role of Rivers in the Economy

Using rivers for irrigation, navigation, hydro-power generation is of special significance — particularly to a country like India, where agriculture is the major source of livelihood of the majority of its population.

River Pollution

- The growing domestic, municipal, industrial and agricultural demand for water from rivers naturally affects the quality of water. As a result, more and more water is being drained out of the rivers reducing their volume.
- On the other hand, a heavy load of untreated sewage and industrial effluents are emptied into the rivers. This affects not only the quality of water but also the self-cleansing capacity of the river. For example, given the adequate streamflow, the Ganga water is able to dilute and assimilate pollution loads within 20 km of large cities. But the increasing urbanisation and industrialisation do not allow it to happen and the pollution level of many rivers has been rising.
- Most of the cremation grounds are on the banks of rivers and the dead bodies are sometimes thrown in the rivers. On the occasion of some festivals, the flowers and statues are immersed in the rivers. Large scale bathing and washing of clothes also pollute river waters.

National River Conservation Plan (NRCP)

The river cleaning programme in the country was initiated with the launch of the **Ganga Action Plan (GAP)** in 1985. The Ganga Action Plan was expanded to cover other rivers under the National River Conservation Plan (NRCP) in 1995. The objective of the NRCP is to improve the water quality of the rivers, which are major water sources in the country, through the implementation of pollution abatement works.

Lakes

India has many lakes. These differ from each other in size and other characteristics. Most lakes are permanent; some contain water only during the rainy season, like the lakes in the basins of inland drainage of semi-arid regions. There are some lakes which are the result of the action of glaciers and ice sheets, while others have been formed by wind, river action and human activities.

- A meandering river across a floodplain forms cut-offs that later develops into **ox-bow lakes.** Spits and bars form lagoons in the coastal areas, e.g., the Chilika lake, the Pulicat lake and the Kolleru lake.

Lakes of large extent are called seas, like the Caspian, the Dead and the Aral seas.

- Most of the freshwater lakes are in the Himalayan region. They are of glacial origin. In other words, they formed when glaciers dug out a basin, which was later filled with snowmelt.
- The Wular lake in Jammu and Kashmir, in contrast, is the result of tectonic activity. It is the largest freshwater lake in India.
- **The Dal Lake, Bhimtal, Nainital, Loktak and Barapani** are some other important freshwater lakes.
- Apart from natural lakes, the damming of the rivers for the generation of hydel power has also led to the formation of lakes, such as Guru Gobind Sagar (Bhakra Nangal Project).
- Lakes are of great value to human beings. A lake helps to regulate the flow of a river. During heavy rains, it prevents flooding and during the dry season, it helps to maintain an even flow of water. Lakes can also be used for developing hydel power. They moderate the climate of the surroundings; maintain the aquatic ecosystem, enhance natural beauty, help develop tourism and provide recreation.

TEST YOURSELF

Multiple Choice Questions

Q1. Which one of these does not belong to the 'panjnad'?

(a) Beas (b) Yamuna

(c) Ravi (d) Chenab

Q2. Where does Bhagirathi meets Alaknanda?

(a) Vishnu Prayag (b) Rudra Prayag

(c) Devprayag (d) Prayag

Q3. Which river is the largest tributary of Indus?

(a) Chenab (b) Jhelum

(c) Ravi (d) Satluj

Q4. Which river originates from the glaciers of Mapchachungo?

(a) Gandak (b) Damodar

(c) Sarda (d) Ghaghara

Q5. By what name Brahmaputra river is known in Bangladesh?

(a) Jamuna (b) Rango Tsangpo

(c) Dihang (d) Sikang

Q6. Which river forms the largest delta in India?

(a) Narmada (b) Ganga

(c) Godavari (d) Mahanadi

Q7. Which of the following rivers does not flow into the Arabian Sea?

(a) Narmada (b) Tapi

(c) Sindhu (d) Mahanadi

Q8. The river system that drains into the Bay of Bengal is known as:

(a) The Peninsular River system

(b) The Himalayan River system

(c) The Coastal River system

(d) The Plateau River system

Q9. The Indus River originates from:

(a) Mansarovar Lake (b) Karakoram Range

(c) Satluj Glacier (d) Yamunotri

Q10. The river that flows through the Rift Valley in Peninsular India is:

(a) Krishna (b) Narmada

(c) Kaveri (d) Mahanadi

Q11. The river basin of the Ganga River is the largest in India and covers how many states?

(a) 4 (b) 6

(c) 11 (d) 10

Q12. The Godavari River is also known as:

(a) Gandak (b) Dakshin Ganga

(c) Both a and b (d) None of the above

Q13. Which of the following is not a tributary of the Brahmaputra River?

(a) Tista (b) Subansiri

(c) Dibang (d) Yamuna

Q14. The East flowing rivers of the Peninsular India mainly drain into:

(a) The Bay of Bengal

(b) The Arabian Sea

(c) The Gulf of Khambhat

(d) The Gulf of Mannar

Q15. The river basin of the Mahanadi River is located in which states of India?

(a) Odisha and Chhattisgarh

(b) Madhya Pradesh and Maharashtra

(c) Rajasthan and Gujarat

(d) Bihar and Uttar Pradesh

Q16. With references to India, Didwana, Kuchaman, Sargol and Khatu are the names of? (UPSC 2021)

(a) Glaciers (b) Mangrove areas

(c) Ramsar sites (d) Saline lakes

Answer Key

Q1.	b	Q2.	c	Q3.	a	Q4.	d
Q5.	a	Q6.	b	Q7.	d	Q8.	a
Q9.	a	Q10.	b	Q11.	c	Q12.	b
Q13.	d	Q14.	a	Q15.	a	Q16.	d

Model Questions for Main Examination

Q1. Write about the evolution of peninsular drainage system in India and how is it different from the Himalayan drainage system?

Q2. There are tensions going on between India and China, so write about the origin and importance of Brahmaputra River for India?

UNIT 10 Composition and Structure of Atmosphere

In This Unit

Comprehensive and profound coverage of the following NCERTs' chapter:

✓ NCERT Class- 11th (Fundamentals of Physical Geography), Chapter- 7

- **The atmosphere** is a layer of gas that envelops the entire earth. The earth's thin layer of air is an essential and noteworthy feature. It supplies us with oxygen to breathe and shields us from the sun's damaging rays.
- The atmosphere reaches a height of **around 1,600 kilometres.**
- **About 99 percent of the clean, dry air** in the atmosphere is made up of **nitrogen and oxygen.** 78% of the gas is nitrogen, 21% is oxygen, and 1% comprises other gases such as argon, carbon dioxide, and others.
- The atmospheric density changes as altitude increases. It reaches its maximum at sea level and quickly drops as we move up. The climbers' struggle to breathe is caused by this drop in air density.
- Going upward also results in a drop in temperature. The earth is under pressure from the atmosphere. This changes according to their location. There are places with low pressure and places with high pressure. From high pressure to low pressure, air flows. **Wind** can be described as **moving air**.

Composition of the Atmosphere

The atmosphere is composed of gases, water vapour and dust particles. The ratio of gases in the upper atmosphere varies to the point where oxygen is nearly non-existent at a height of 120 km. Similarly, carbon dioxide and water vapour are found only up to 90 km from the surface of the earth.

Gas	Percentage by Volume
Nitrogen (N_2)	78.084
Oxygen (O_2)	20.946
Argon (Ar)	0.934
Carbon dioxide (CO_2)	0.037
Neon (Ne)	0.00182
Helium (He)	0.00052
Methane (CH_4)	0.00015
Krypton (Kr)	0.00011

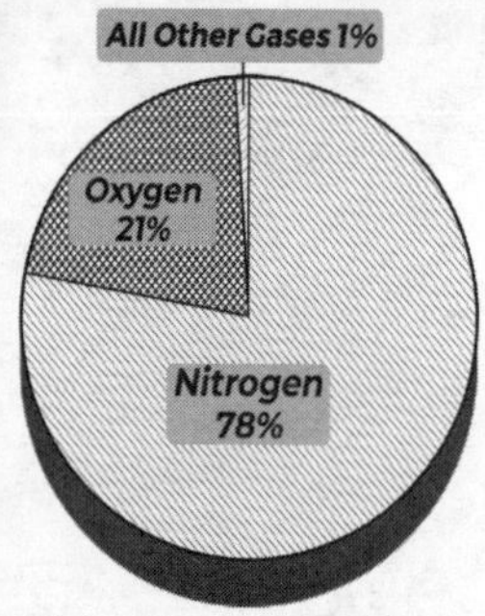

Composition of Atmosphere

Gases

1. Nitrogen

- It is the most abundant gas in the atmosphere. A certain amount of nitrogen enters our lungs during inhalation and is exhaled. However, nitrogen is necessary for plants to survive. They cannot directly absorb nitrogen from the atmosphere. Certain bacteria found in soil and plant roots extract nitrogen from the surrounding air and convert it into a form that plants can use.

2. Oxygen

- In the atmosphere, it is the second most abundant gas. Oxygen is taken in by both people and animals from the surrounding air.
- Green plants create oxygen through the process of photosynthesis. The air's oxygen concentration stays constant in this way. This balance is upset when we cut down trees.

3. Carbon dioxide

- Carbon dioxide is used by green plants to produce food and oxygen. Carbon dioxide is released by either humans or animals.
- There seems to be a perfect balance between the amount of carbon dioxide stored by plants and the amount exhaled by animals or humans.
- However, burning fuels like coal and oil disturbs the equilibrium. Every year, they contribute billions of tonnes of carbon dioxide to the atmosphere. Consequently, the earth's climate and weather are being impacted by the growing amount of carbon dioxide.
- Since it is opaque to outgoing terrestrial radiation but transparent to incoming solar radiation, this gas is extremely significant to meteorology.
- It takes up a portion of terrestrial radiation and reflects back some portion of it towards the earth's surface. **The Green House Effect** can be attributed primarily to it.

4. Ozone

- It is an additional significant component of the atmosphere that is situated between 10 and 50 km above the surface of the planet. It serves as a filter, absorbing solar ultraviolet radiation and keeping them from reaching the earth's surface.

5. Water Vapour

- Another changeable gas in the atmosphere that reduces with altitude is water vapour. It might make up four percent of the air by volume in the warm, humid tropics, but less than one percent of the air in the polar regions and dry and cold desert regions.
- As one moves from the equator to the poles, water vapour also decreases. In addition, it retains some of the heat that the planet radiates by absorbing solar radiation.
- Hence, it functions as a blanket, preventing extreme temperatures on Earth. The stability and instability of the air are also influenced by water vapour.

Dust Particles

- The atmosphere can hold onto small solid particles that come from a variety of sources, such as dust, pollen, sea salts, fine soil, smoke-soot, ash, and broken-down meteorite fragments.
- Despite being mostly concentrated in the **lower layers of the atmosphere; dust particles** can be carried to extremely high altitudes by convectional air currents.
- Due to dry winds, subtropical and temperate regions have larger concentrations of dust particles than equatorial and polar regions.
- Particles of salt and dust function as hygroscopic nuclei around which condensed water vapour forms clouds.

Structure of the Atmosphere

The temperature and density of the various layers that make up the atmosphere fluctuate. Density is lowest at higher altitudes and is highest close to the earth's surface. Based on temperature conditions, the atmosphere is separated into five distinct layers. They are: **troposphere, stratosphere, mesosphere, thermosphere and exosphere.**

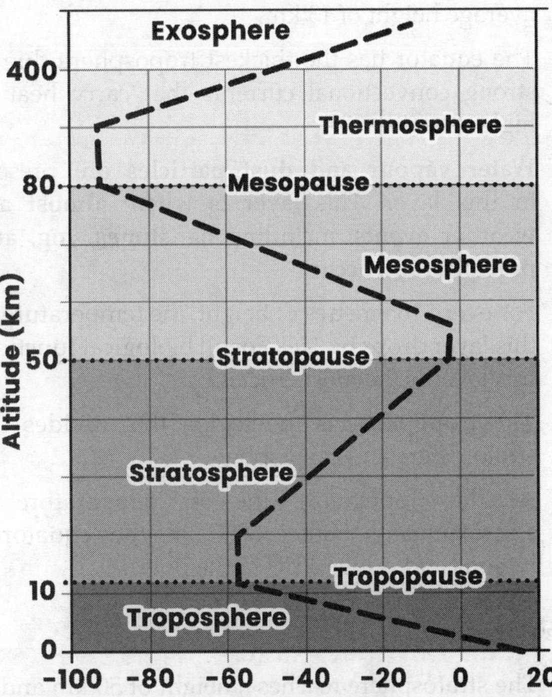

Layers of the Atmosphere

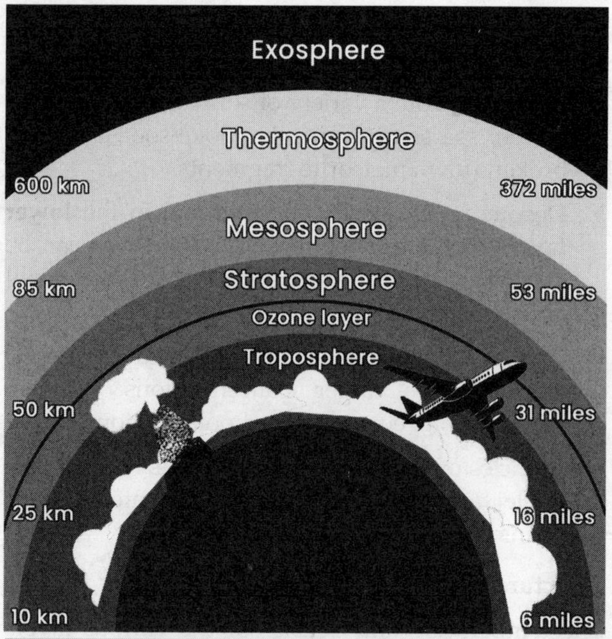

Structure of the Atmosphere

Troposphere

- The lowest layer of the atmosphere is called the troposphere. Its height ranges from around 8 km at the poles to about 18 km at the equator, with an average height of 13 km.
- The equator has the thickest troposphere due to strong convectional currents that carry heat to high altitudes.
- **Water vapour and dust particles** are present in this layer. This layer is where **almost all-weather events**, including **hailstones, fog, and precipitation, occur.**
- For every 165 metres of height, the temperature in this layer drops by 1°C. For all biological function, this layer is the most crucial.
- **The tropopause** is the region that divides the stratosphere and troposphere.
- At the tropopause, the air temperature is approximately minus 80°C in the equatorial regions and minus 45°C in the poles.

Stratosphere

- The stratosphere reaches a height of 50 km and is situated above the tropopause.
- This layer of the atmosphere is nearly free of clouds and related climatic phenomena, providing the perfect environment for aircraft flight.
- **The presence of the ozone layer within the stratosphere** is a crucial characteristic.
- Life on planet Earth is protected from strong and hazardous forms of energy by this layer, which absorbs ultraviolet light.

Mesosphere

- Situated at an altitude of 80 km, the mesosphere lies above the stratosphere.
- The temperature in this layer drops once more as altitude rises, reaching **-100°C at 80 km.**
- When meteorites enter this layer from space, they burn up.
- **The mesopause** is the upper boundary of the mesosphere.

Ionosphere

- The range of the ionosphere **above the mesopause is 80–400 km.**
- It is referred to as the ionosphere because it **includes electrically charged particles known as ions.**
- This layer reflects radio waves that are transmitted from the earth back to it.
- In this place, the temperature rises with height.

Exosphere

- The exosphere is the highest layer of the atmosphere above the thermosphere.
- There is very little air in this layer. From here, light gases such as **hydrogen and helium move into space.**
- Though not much is known about it, this layer is the highest.
- Any contents present are highly rarefied within this layer, eventually merging into outer space.

ATMOSPHERE

- Atmosphere is a mixture of gases and solids that surrounds the Earth. It contains life giving gases like Oxygen.
  - Air is essential for the survival of all organisms and integral part of the mass of Earth.
  - 99% of the total mass of the atmosphere is confined to 32 Km from the earth's surface.
- Composition of the atmosphere: The atmosphere is a mixture of gases, water vapour and dust particles.
  - The proportion of gases changes in higher layers of the atmosphere.
  - As the height increases Oxygen decreases in atmosphere.
  - Carbon dioxide and water is found only up to 90 km from the surface of the Earth.

Constituent	N_2	Oxygen	Argon	CO_2	Neon	He	Krypton	Xenon	H_2
% by Volume	78.08	20.95	0.93	0.036	0.002	0.0005	0.001	0.00009	0.00005

Layers of the Atmosphere

1. Troposphere

- From the surface of the Earth it extends up to 8 kms at the poles and 18 kms at the equator.
- Responsible for weather changes such as temperature, pressure, winds, cloud formation and rainfall.
- The temperature decreases with increasing height in this layer.
- The tropopause is a thin layer that lies between the troposphere and the stratosphere.

2. Stratosphere

- Stratosphere extends approximately for about 50 km.
- Temperature increases with height.
- This is the layer where most jet planes fly, owing to the lack for weather phenomena.
- The top edge of the stratosphere is rich in Ozone (20-50 %) that protect us from UV rays.
- This zone is also called as Isothermal layer and Ozonosphere.
- After the stratosphere, there is again a buffer layer called Stratopause.

3. Mesosphere

- Mesosphere: It extends approximately for about 80 km.

4. Ionosphere

- Ionosphere: It extends from 80 kms to 500 kms.
- Named ionosphere because in this part of the atmosphere the sun's radiation gets ionized.
- It reflects the radio waves back to the earth which help in modern communications.

5. Exosphere

- It is the uppermost layer of the atmosphere.
- The main gases within the exosphere are the lighter gases, mainly Hydrogen and Helium, sometimes considered a part of outer space.

TEST YOURSELF

Multiple Choice Questions

Q1. Which of the following gases is the most abundant in Earth's atmosphere?

(a) Oxygen (b) Nitrogen

(c) Carbon dioxide (d) Hydrogen

Q2. The ozone layer is located in which layer of the atmosphere?

(a) Troposphere (b) Stratosphere

(c) Mesosphere (d) Thermosphere

Q3. The atmospheric layer where weather phenomena occur, such as clouds and rainfall, is called the:

(a) Troposphere (b) Stratosphere

(c) Mesosphere (d) Thermosphere

Q4. What percentage of the Earth's atmosphere is composed of nitrogen?

(a) Approximately 21% (b) Approximately 50%

(c) Approximately 78% (d) Approximately 95%

Q5. The greenhouse effect is primarily caused by:

(a) Oxygen in the atmosphere

(b) Nitrogen in the atmosphere

(c) Carbon dioxide in the atmosphere

(d) Water vapour in the atmosphere

Q6. Which of the following layers of the atmosphere contains the highest concentration of ozone?

(a) Troposphere (b) Stratosphere

(c) Mesosphere (d) Thermosphere

Q7. The process by which water vapour changes into liquid water is called:

(a) Condensation (b) Evaporation

(c) Transpiration (d) Precipitation

Q8. The atmospheric layer closest to the Earth's surface is called:

(a) Troposphere (b) Stratosphere

(c) Mesosphere (d) Thermosphere

Q9. The international unit for measuring atmospheric pressure is:

(a) Pascal (Pa) (b) Newton (N)

(c) Joule (J) (d) Kilogram (kg)

Answer Key

Q1.	b	Q2.	b	Q3.	a	Q4.	c
Q5.	c	Q6.	b	Q7.	b	Q8.	a
Q9.	a						

Model Questions for Main Examination

Q1. Describe the compositions of the atmosphere and briefly explain any one component of it.

Q2. Explain the structure of atmosphere and explain the role of the layer that protects us from UV rays.

UNIT 11 Solar Radiation, Heat Balance and Temperature

In This Unit

Comprehensive and profound coverage of the following NCERTs' chapter:

✓ NCERT Class- 11th (Fundamentals of Physical Geography), Chapter- 8

Solar Radiation

- The majority of energy that reaches the earth's surface is in short wavelengths. The energy that the earth receives is referred to as **insolation**, or incoming solar radiation.
- Because the earth is a geoid that resembles a sphere, very little of the sun's energy is intercepted by the earth because its rays fall obliquely at the top of the atmosphere. At the top of its atmosphere, the planet receives 1.94 calories per square centimetre each minute on average.
- The variations in the earth-sun distance cause a modest variation in the solar output received at the top of the atmosphere over the course of a year.
- On July 4, the earth is at its furthest point from the sun (152 million km) during its revolution around the sun. The term **"aphelion"** refers to this location of Earth.
- The earth is at its closest point to the sun (147 million km) on January 3. We refer to this point as **perihelion**. As a result, the planet receives somewhat **more annual insolation on January 3rd than it does on July 4th**.
- However, additional factors like land and sea distribution and air circulation obscure the impact of this variation in solar output.
- As a result, daily weather variations on Earth's surface are not significantly impacted by this variation in solar output.

Variability of Insolation at the Surface of The Earth

- The quantity and intensity of insolation change **during the day, season, and year**. These fluctuations in insolation are **caused by the following factors:**
  - ➢ The earth's rotation around its axis
  - ➢ The sun's beams' angle of inclination
  - ➢ The duration of the day
  - ➢ The atmosphere's transparency
  - ➢ The way the land is arranged concerning its aspect
- The angle formed by the Earth's axis with the plane of its orbit around the sun, which is 66 1/2°, has a bigger effect on the amount of insolation received at different latitudes.
- The angle at which the rays are inclined determines the amount of insolation received. This is dependent upon a location's latitude. Sunlight rays slant as latitude increases because of the decreasing angle which they create with the earth's surface.
- The area that vertical rays cover is consistently smaller than that of slanting rays. The net energy received per unit area reduces as more space is covered, distributing the energy.
- Furthermore, **more absorption, scattering, and diffusion occur** because the slant rays are **required to penetrate a deeper layer of the atmosphere.**

The Solar Radiation Passing Through the Atmosphere

- Short wave solar radiation can pass through the atmosphere quite easily. Before reaching the surface of the earth, the incoming solar energy travels through the atmosphere. A large portion of the near-infrared light is absorbed by water vapour, ozone, and other gases in the troposphere.
- The visible spectrum is scattered both towards space and the earth's surface by very small-suspended particles in the troposphere. The sky gains colour from this process. The dispersion of light within the atmosphere is responsible for the blue colour of the sky and the red colour of the rising and setting sun.

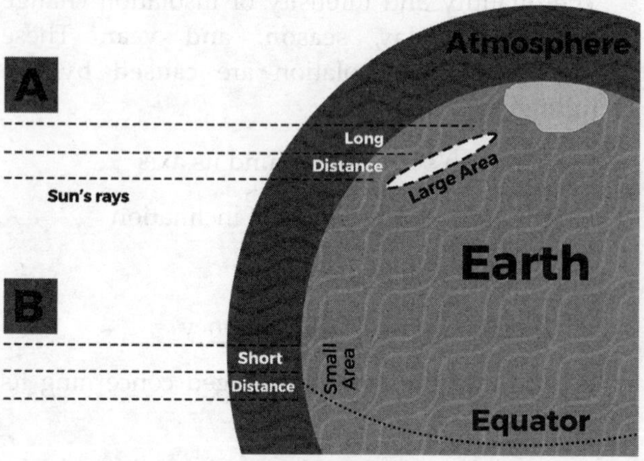

Variation of Insolation on Earth

Spatial Distribution of Insolation at The Earth's Surface

- At the surface, the insolation varies from approximately 70 Watt/m^2 in the poles to approximately 320 Watt/m^2 in the tropics. The subtropical deserts receive the most insolation and the least amount of cloud cover. Compared to the tropics, the Equator receives relatively less insolation.
- At a given latitude, the insolation tends to be higher over land than it is over sea. The intermediate and higher latitudes receive less radiation in the winter than they do in the summer.

Heating and Cooling of Atmosphere

There are different ways of heating and cooling of the atmosphere.

Conduction

- The earth transfers heat in the form of long waves to the nearby air layers once it has been heated by insolation. Heat builds up gradually in the air that comes into touch with the ground, as well as in the upper layers that come into contact with the lower levels. We refer to this procedure as **conduction**.
- When two bodies with different temperatures come into touch, conduction occurs, which is the movement of energy from the warmer to the colder body. Heat is transferred until the temperature of both bodies reaches the same point or the contact is severed. The lower atmosphere is heated in large part by conduction.

Convection

- The air that comes into contact with the earth warms up vertically as a result of currents, which further transfers the atmosphere's heat. **Convection** is the term for this **vertical heating** of the atmosphere.
- **The troposphere** is the only place where convective energy transfer occurs.

Advection

- **Advection** is the term used to describe the transmission of heat by **horizontal air movement**.
- The air's horizontal movement is comparatively more significant than its vertical movement.
- Advection alone accounts for the majority of the **diurnal (day and night) variation** in daily weather in middle latitudes.
- During the summer, in **tropical places**, especially in northern India, advection results in the formation of local winds known **as "loo."**

Terrestrial Radiation

- The earth receives brief waves of insolation, which heat the surface of the planet. After heating up, the earth turns into a radiating body that sends long waves of energy into the atmosphere. The atmosphere is heated from below by this energy. We call this process **"terrestrial radiation."**
- The atmospheric gases, especially carbon dioxide and other greenhouse gases, absorb **long wave radiation**. As a result, radiation from the earth indirectly heats the atmosphere.

- Heat is subsequently radiated and transmitted into space via the atmosphere. In the end, the earth's surface and atmosphere remain at a constant temperature because the sun's heat is reflected back into space.

Heat Budget of the Planet Earth

Heat is neither gained or lost by the earth as a whole. It sustains its own temperature. This can only occur when the **heat lost by** the earth through **terrestrial radiation** is equal to the **heat absorbed** in the form of **insolation.**

Assume that there is 100% insolation at the top of the atmosphere. A certain quantity of energy is absorbed, dispersed, and reflected as it travels through the atmosphere. Only the residual portion reaches the surface of the earth. Even before they reach the surface of the earth, around 35 units are reflected back into space. 2 units of these come from regions of the earth covered in snow and ice, while the remaining 27 units are reflected back from the tops of the clouds. The term **"earth's albedo"** refers to the amount of radiation reflected back.

The earth's surface absorbs 51 of the remaining 65 units, with **14 of those units being absorbed by the atmosphere. Terrestrial radiation is the 51 units** that the earth emits back into space. Of these, **34 are absorbed by the atmosphere** (6 through direct absorption, 9 through convection and turbulence, and 19 through latent heat of condensation). Of these, **17 are straight away radiated into space.**

Additionally, 48 units of radiation (14 from insolation and 34 from terrestrial radiation) that are absorbed by the atmosphere are reflected back into space. Therefore, the total radiation coming back from the earth and the atmosphere, respectively, is 17+48=65 units, which balances the total radiation coming back from the sun, which is 65 units. This is known as the **earth's heat budget or heat balance.**

This explains why, despite the immense heat transfer that occurs, the earth never warms nor cools.

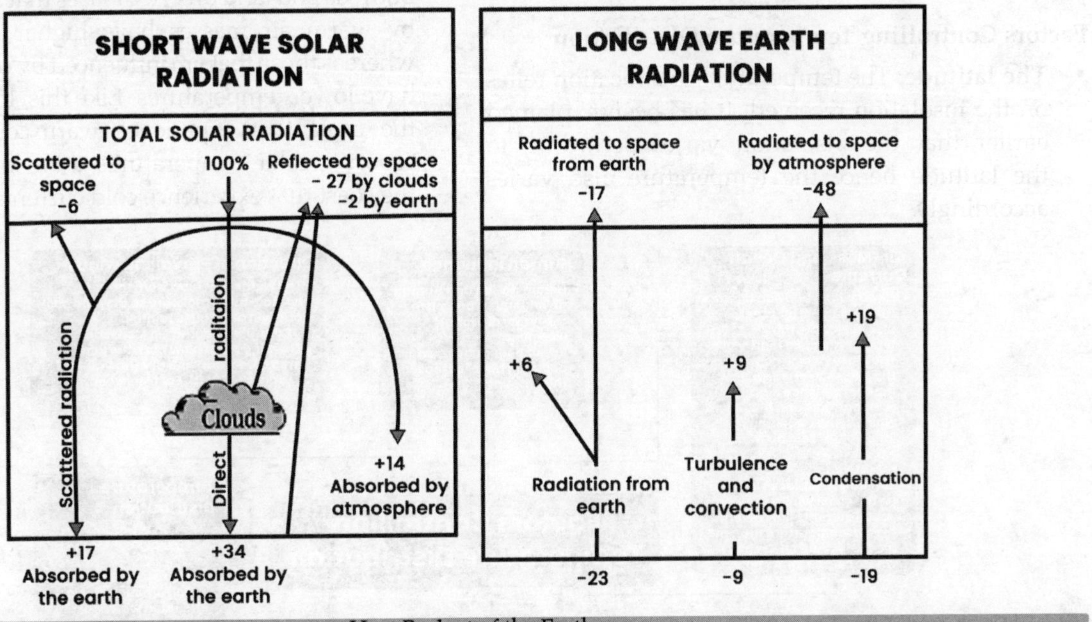

Heat Budget of the Earth

Variation in The Net Heat Budget at The Earth's Surface

The quantity of radiation received at the surface of the earth varies. There is a surplus of radiation in certain portions of the earth and a deficit in other parts.

The latitudinal fluctuation in the net radiation balance of the earth's atmospheric system is shown in the following Figure. According to the diagram, there is a **net radiation balance surplus between 40 degrees north and south, and a deficit in the areas closest to the poles.** Because the extra heat energy from the tropics is redistributed poleward, the high latitudes do not permanently freeze owing to excess deficiency, nor do the tropics gradually warm up as a result of the buildup of excess heat.

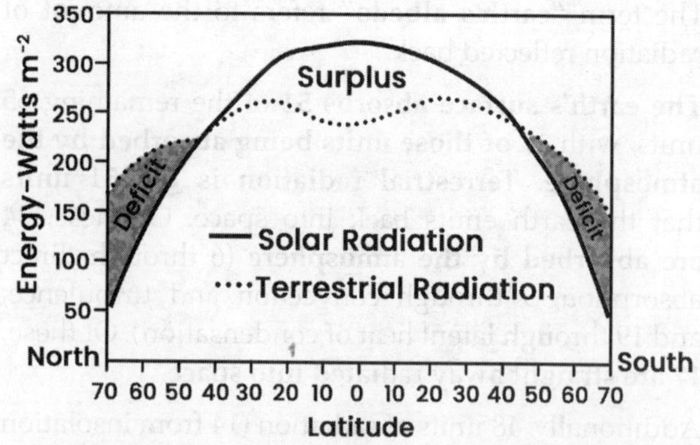

Latitudinal Variation in Net Radiation Balance

Temperature

Heat, which is expressed in terms of temperature, is produced by the interaction of insolation with the atmosphere and the earth's surface. Temperature is the measurement of how hot (or cold) something (or somewhere) is in degrees, whereas heat is the molecular movement of the particles that comprise a substance.

Factors Controlling Temperature Distribution

- **The latitude:** The temperature of a location relies on the insolation received. It has been explained earlier that the insolation varies according to the latitude hence the temperature also varies accordingly.
- **The altitude:** The atmosphere is not directly heated by terrestrial radiation from below. Therefore, the places near the sea-level record higher temperature than the places situated at higher elevations. In other words, the temperature generally decreases with increasing height. The rate of decrease of temperature with height is termed as the normal lapse rate. It is 6.5°C per 1,000 m.
- **Distance from the sea:** Another aspect that affects the temperature is the location of a place with respect to the sea. Compared to land, the sea gets heated slowly and loses heat slowly. Land heats up and cools down quickly. Therefore, the variation in temperature over the sea is less compared to land. The places situated near the sea come under the moderating influence of the sea and land breezes which moderate the temperature.
- **Air-mass and Ocean currents:** The movement of air masses influences temperature in a similar way as both sea and land breezes. Places that are influenced by warm air masses have higher temperatures, whereas those that are influenced by cold air masses have lower temperatures. Like this, locations along the coast that experience warm ocean currents report greater temperatures than locations along the coast that experience cold currents.

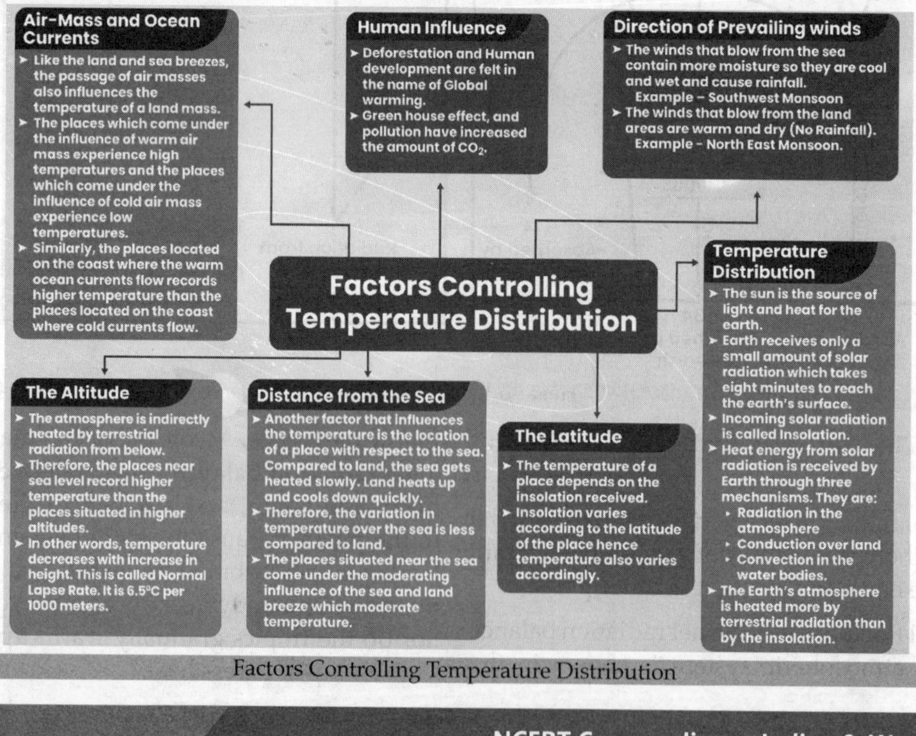

Factors Controlling Temperature Distribution

Distribution of Temperature

The global distribution of temperature can well be understood by studying the temperature distribution in January and July.

- Since the isotherms on the map are typically parallel to the latitude, the latitude normally has a noticeable impact on temperature. Particularly in the northern hemisphere, the January deviation from this overall trend is more noticeable than the July deviation.
- The land surface area of the **northern hemisphere** is **significantly greater** than that of the **southern hemisphere**. Because of this, the effects of ocean currents and land mass are readily apparent.
- **The isotherms diverge** in January, moving **northward across the ocean** and **southward across the continent**. **The North Atlantic Ocean** is where you may observe this.
- The Northern Atlantic Ocean is warmer due to the existence of warm ocean currents, such as the Gulf Stream and North Atlantic drift, and the isotherms bend northward. In Europe, the isotherms lean southward and the temperature drops rapidly over the landscape.
- In the **southern hemisphere, the ocean's influence is particularly noticeable**. In comparison to the northern hemisphere, the temperature variation is more gradual here, with the isotherms roughly parallel to the latitudes.
- The isotherms in July often run parallel to the latitude. Over 27°C is the recorded temperature in the equatorial oceans. In the subtropical continental region of Asia, at the 30° N latitude, over 30°C is observed over land.
- The temperature range between January and July is depicted in the figure, with more than 60°C representing the greatest variation over the northeastern region of the continent of Eurasia. The cause of this is **continentality.**

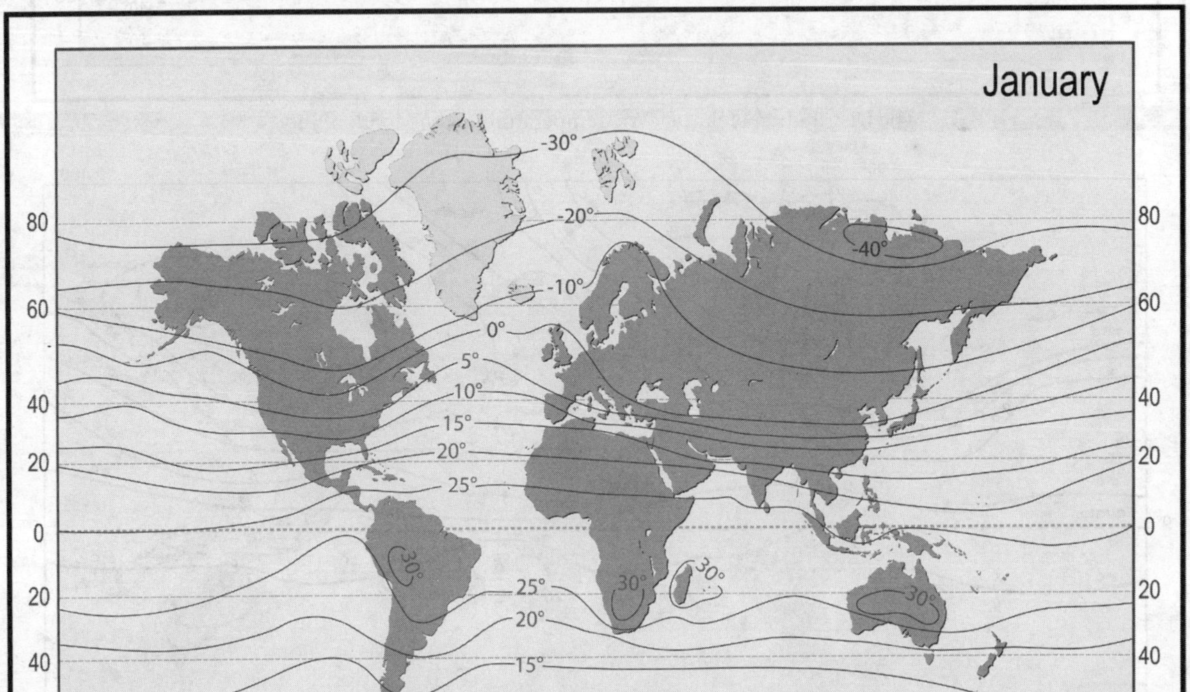

The Distribution of Surface Air Temperature in the Month of January

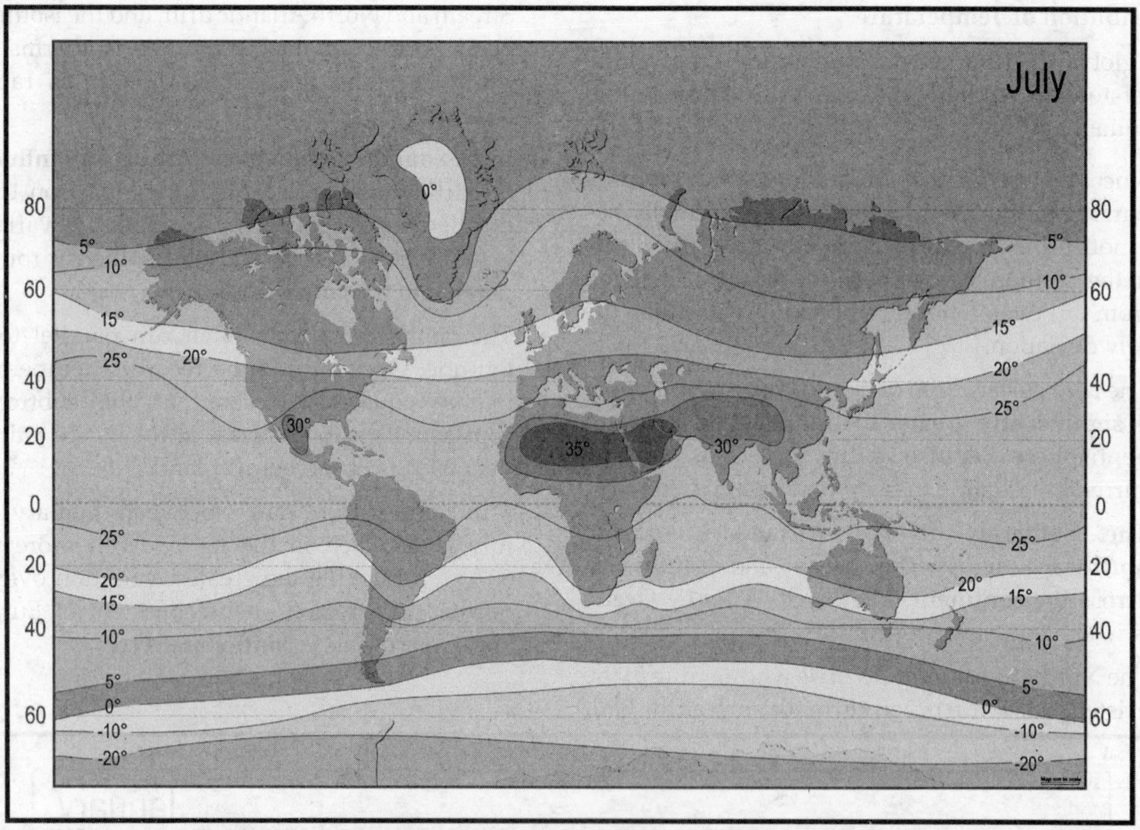

The Distribution of Surface Air Temperature in the Month of July

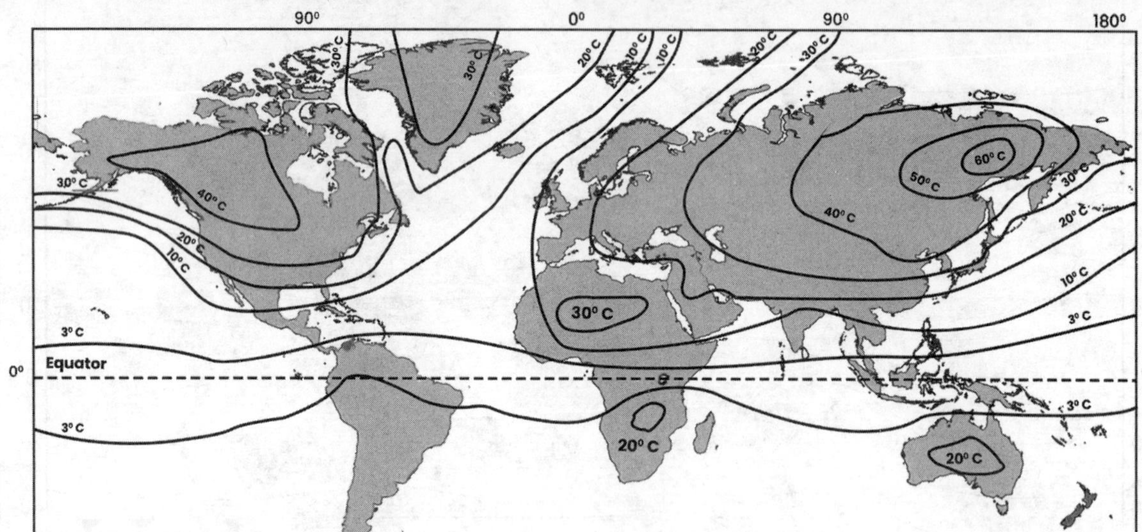

The Range of Temperature Between January and July

Inversion of Temperature

- In general, as elevation rises, temperature falls. The term for it is referred to as **normal lapse rate**. Occasionally, the normal lapse rate is inverted when circumstances are reversed. The term for it is **temperature inversion**.
- **Inversions** are generally of lesser duration, but they do occur frequently. An extended winter night with clear skies and still air is perfect for inversion.
- During the night, the earth radiates off the heat of the day, making the early morning hours colder than the air above. Temperature inversion is common all year long over polar regions.
- **Stability in the lower atmosphere** is encouraged by **surface inversion**. Particles of dust and smoke gather underneath the inversion layer and propagate horizontally to occupy the lower atmospheric layers.
- It is not unusual to have a **dense fog** in the mornings, particularly in the winter. Until the sun rises and starts to warm the earth, this inversion usually lasts a few hours.
- Because of air drainage, inversion occurs in hills and mountains. Gravity causes the cold air, that is produced at night in the highlands and mountains, to flow.
- **The cold air** travels down the slope in pockets and valley bottoms, piling up deeply with warm air above, because it is **heavy and dense, almost like water**. It is known as air drainage. It shields plants against the damaging effects of frost.

- According to **Plank's law**, a body that is hotter will radiate more energy with a shorter wavelength.
- The energy required to increase a 1 gram of a substance's temperature by one degree Celsius is known as **specific heat**.

TEST YOURSELF

Multiple Choice Questions

Q1. Solar radiation is the radiant energy emitted by the:

(a) Moon (b) Earth

(c) Sun (d) Stars

Q2. Which layer of the Earth's atmosphere absorbs most of the incoming solar radiation?

(a) Troposphere (b) Stratosphere

(c) Mesosphere (d) Thermosphere

Q3. The process by which the Earth's surface and lower atmosphere absorb and re-radiate infrared radiation is known as:

(a) Conduction (b) Convection

(c) Radiation (d) Greenhouse effect

Q4. The balance between incoming solar radiation and outgoing terrestrial radiation determines the:

(a) Temperature of the atmosphere

(b) Humidity of the atmosphere

(c) Pressure of the atmosphere

(d) Wind speed of the atmosphere

Q5. The region around the equator receives the highest amount of solar radiation, resulting in:

(a) Low temperatures

(b) High temperatures

(c) Moderate temperatures

(d) Constant temperatures

Q6. Which of the following factors affects the intensity of solar radiation received at the Earth's surface?

(a) Latitude (b) Altitude

(c) Cloud cover (d) All of the above

Q7. The instrument used to measure air temperature is

(a) Barometer (b) Hygrometer

(c) Thermometer (d) Anemometer

Q8. The average weather conditions of a place over a long period of time is called:

(a) Climate (b) Weather

(c) Temperature (d) Precipitation

Q9. The line joining places that have the same average annual temperature is known as:

(a) Isotherm (b) Isobar

(c) Isohyet (d) Isoline

Q10. The movement of air from areas of high pressure to areas of low pressure is known as:

(a) Convection (b) Advection

(c) Radiation (d) Conduction

Answer Key

Q1.	c	Q2.	b	Q3.	d	Q4.	a
Q5.	b	Q6.	d	Q7.	c	Q8.	a
Q9.	a	Q10.	a				

Model Questions for Main Examination

Q1. Write a short note on the ways of heating and cooling of the atmosphere.

Q2. Write a short note on the Heat Budget of the Earth surface.

UNIT 12 Atmospheric Circulation and Weather Systems

In This Unit

Comprehensive and profound coverage of the following NCERTs' chapter:

✓ NCERT Class- 11th (Fundamentals of Physical Geography), Chapter- 9

- Air expands when it gets hot and contracts when it cools. Variations in atmospheric pressure are the outcome of this. Air is consequently set in motion and moves from a high to a low-pressure area. The wind is created as Air moves horizontally.
- Atmospheric pressure plays a crucial role in determining when Air will rise or sink. This global phenomenon helps to maintain a consistent temperature on Earth, as the wind carries heat and moisture across the planet.
- Moist air rises upward, cools, forms clouds, and produces precipitation.

Atmospheric Pressure

- **The atmospheric pressure** is the **weight of an air** column confined **in a unit area**, ranging from mean sea level to the top of the atmosphere.
- **Millibar is the unit** for expressing atmospheric pressure. The average atmospheric pressure at sea level is 1,013.2 millibar.
- The air at the surface has a higher pressure because of its density due to gravity. A **mercury barometer** or an aneroid barometer is used to measure air pressure.
- **With height, the pressure drops**. It fluctuates from location to location at any elevation, and this variation is what primarily drives air motion, that is, wind, which travels from high-pressure regions to low-pressure regions.

Vertical Variation of Pressure

- The pressure in the lower atmosphere drops quickly as altitude increases. For every 10 metres of height gain, there is a drop of roughly one mb. However, it does not always decrease at the same pace.
- Compared to the horizontal pressure gradient, the vertical pressure gradient forces are substantially greater. However, a roughly equal but opposing gravitational force usually balances it out. As a result, there are not many powerful upward breezes.

Horizontal Distribution of Pressure

- Variations in pressure can significantly impact the direction and speed of the wind. Isobars drawn at constant levels are used to study the horizontal distribution of pressure.
- Lines joining locations with equal pressure are called **isobars**. Pressure is recorded at any station after being lowered to sea level for comparison purposes to remove the impact of elevation.

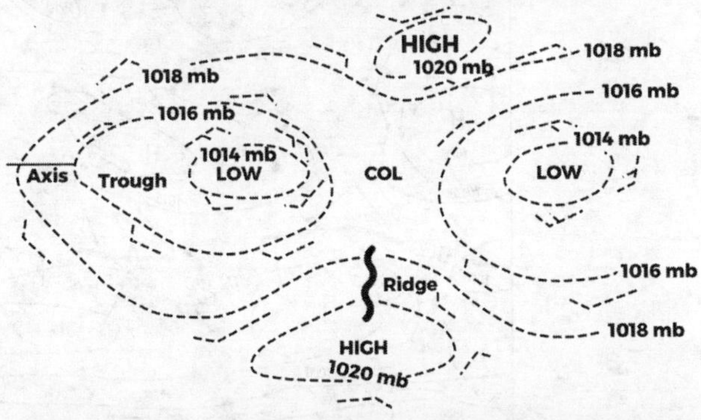

Isobars, Pressure and Wind System in the Northern Hemisphere

- The above image depicts the pressure system-corresponding isobar patterns. One or more isobars enclose the low-pressure system, with the lowest pressure in the centre isobar. One or more isobars with the highest pressure in the centre encircle the high-pressure system.

World Distribution of Sea Level Pressure

- The region known as the **"equatorial low"** has low sea level pressure close to the equator.
- **The subtropical highs**, or high-pressure zones, are between **30° N and 30° S**.
- The low-pressure belts extending further poleward along 60° N and 60° S are called **subpolar lows.**
- **"Polar high"** refers to the high pressure near the poles.
- In nature, these pressure belts are not permanent. They move in sync with the sun's **apparent motion**. They move **northward in the summer** and **southward in the winter** in the northern hemisphere.

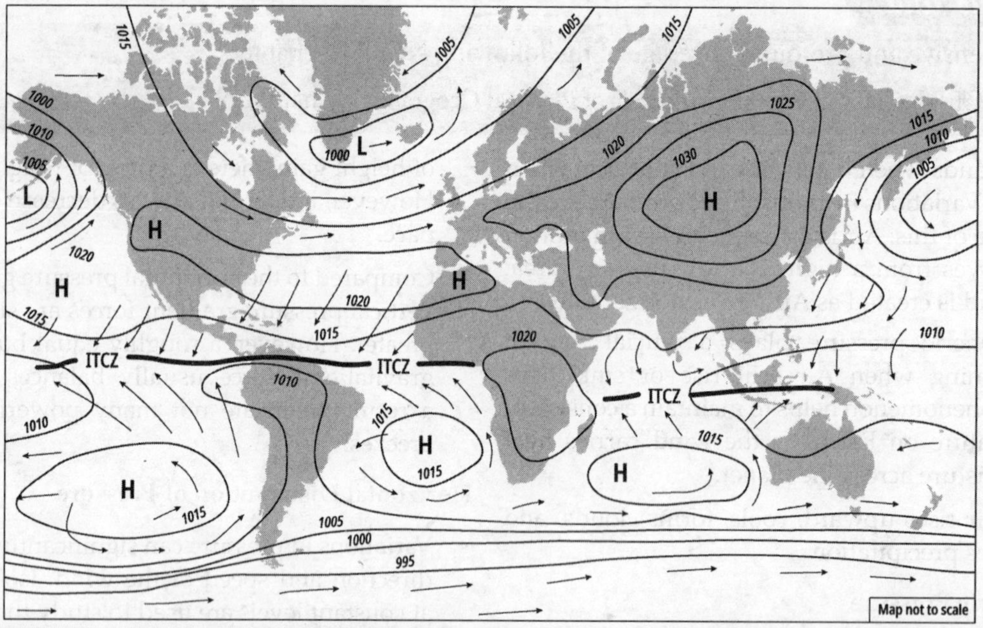

Distribution of Pressure (in millibars) – January

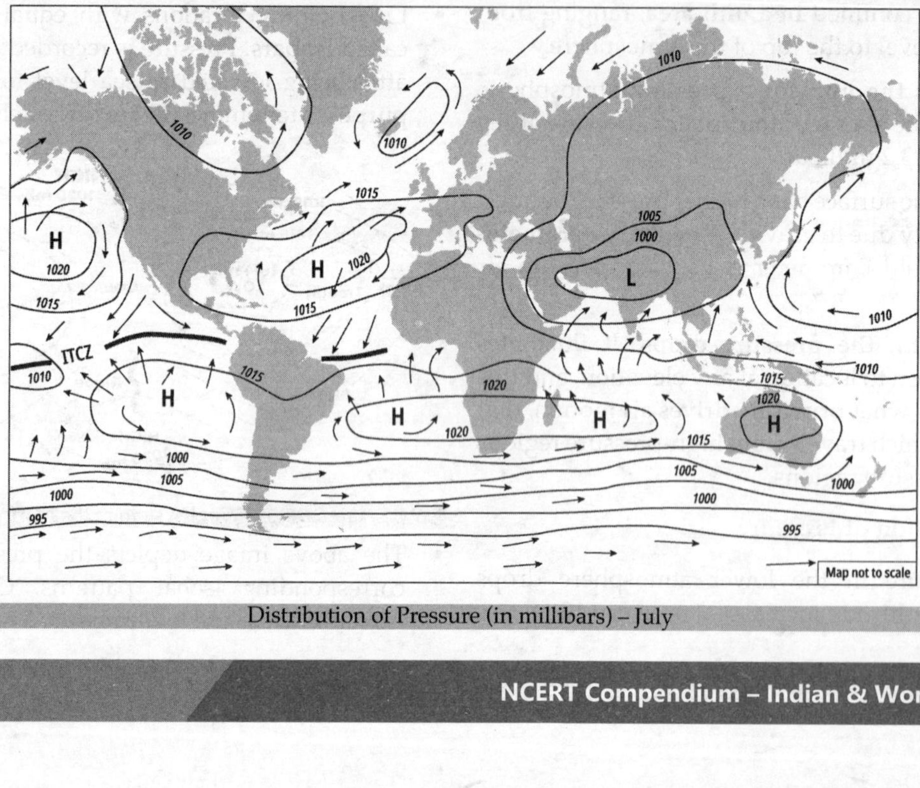

Distribution of Pressure (in millibars) – July

PRESSURE BELTS

Pressure Belts

- Air pressure is defined as the pressure thrust by the weight of the air on the earth's surface.
- The average air pressure at the sea level is 1,013 millibars.
- The atmospheric pressure is always inversely related to the atmospheric temperature.
- High Pressure Belts are formed in the areas of low temperature.

Equatorial Low Pressure Belt

- The sunrays are vertical over here throughout the year. Due to high temperature, the air become lighter and starts rising and causes low pressure conditions.
- This zone is otherwise called as "a belt of Calm" or "Doldrums".

Subtropical High Pressure Belt

- This zone lies between 25° and 35° latitudes in both the hemispheres.
- The rising air from the tropics is getting cooled due to low temperature so the air descends at about 30°- 35° latitudes.
- In ancient times, the merchants carrying horses in their ships had to throw some of them out while passing through this zone in order to lighten the ship. Hence, this zone is called "Horse Latitudes".

Polar High Pressure Belt

- This pressure belt forms at the poles.
- The sunrays fall in a slanting manner at the poles and as a result the temperature is low and heavy air accumulates and produces high pressure.

Sub Polar Low Pressure Belt

- This belt lies between 60°- 65° latitudes in both the hemispheres
- The air spreads outward from this zone due to the rotation of the earth so the low pressure is produced.

General circulation of the atmosphere

- The pattern of planetary winds largely depends on:
  - (i) Latitudinal variation of atmospheric heating.
  - (ii) Emergence of pressure belts.
  - (iii) The migration of belts following apparent path of the sun.
  - (iv) The distribution of continents and oceans.
  - (v) The rotation of earth.
- The pattern of the movement of the planetary winds is called the General Circulation of the Atmosphere.
- Air in horizontal motion is called wind. Air generally moves from high pressure area to the low pressure area. The speed of the wind is generally mentioned in kilometers or miles on land and in knots at sea.

Forces Affecting the Velocity and Direction of Wind

The variations in atmospheric pressure cause the **air to move.** The wind is the motion of the air. From **high pressure to low pressure, the wind blows.** At the surface, friction is experienced by the wind. Furthermore, the earth rotation influences the wind's movement. **The Coriolis force** is the force generated by the earth's rotation. As a result, three forces work together to influence the horizontal winds close to the earth's surface: the Coriolis, frictional, and pressure gradient forces. Furthermore, the gravitational force acts downward.

Pressure Gradient Force

Variations in atmospheric pressure generate a force. **The pressure gradient** is the rate at which pressure changes with respect to distance. When the isobars are close to one another, the pressure gradient is strong; when they are farther apart, it is weak.

Frictional Force

It influences the wind's speed. Its effect is highest at the surface and typically reaches elevations between 1 and 3 km. Friction is negligible above the sea surface.

Coriolis Force

- The direction of the wind is influenced by the earth's rotation around its axis. Because it was first described by a French physicist in 1844, this force is also known as the Coriolis force. **It deflects the wind to the right and left in the northern and southern hemispheres respectively.**
- A higher wind velocity results in a more significant deflection. The angle of latitude and the Coriolis

force are precisely proportional. **At the equator, it is absent** and reaches its **maximum at the poles.**

- The force of the pressure gradient is perpendicular to the Coriolis force. An isobar is perpendicular to the pressure gradient force. More wind speed and more significant wind deflection in the direction of flow are directly related to pressure gradient force.
- The wind blows around it in low-pressure areas because of these two forces acting perpendicular to one another. The wind blows perpendicular to the isobars at the equator, where the Coriolis force is zero. Rather than intensifying, the low-pressure fills. For this reason, **tropical cyclones do not form close to the equator.**

Pressure and Wind

- The combined effects of the wind-generating forces determine the wind's direction and velocity. The Coriolis force and the pressure gradient primarily govern the winds in the upper atmosphere, located two to three kilometres above the surface and accessible from the frictional influence of the surface.
- In the **absence of friction** and with straight isobars, the **Coriolis force balances the pressure gradient force**, causing the wind to blow parallel to the isobar. We refer to this wind as the **geostrophic wind.**

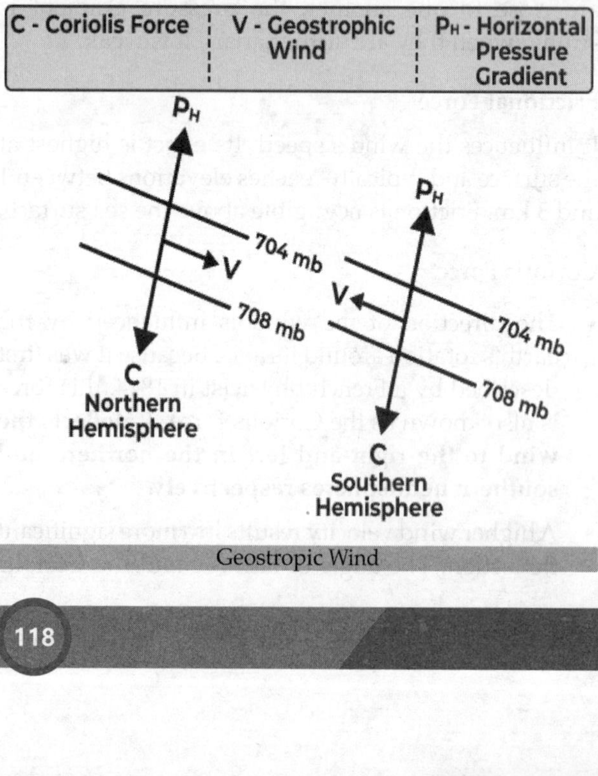

Geostropic Wind

- A cyclonic circulation is the wind circulation surrounding **a low**, while anti-cyclonic circulation occurs **around a high**. The winds surrounding them change direction depending on where these systems are located in the hemisphere.
- There is often a close relationship between the wind circulation at higher levels and the wind circulation at the earth's surface near low and high points.
- Generally, air will converge and rise over an area of low pressure. When there is high pressure, the air will descend from above and split at the surface.
- In addition to convergence, air rises due to **eddies, convection currents, orographic uplift, and uplift along fronts.** This rise in air is necessary for the development of clouds and precipitation.

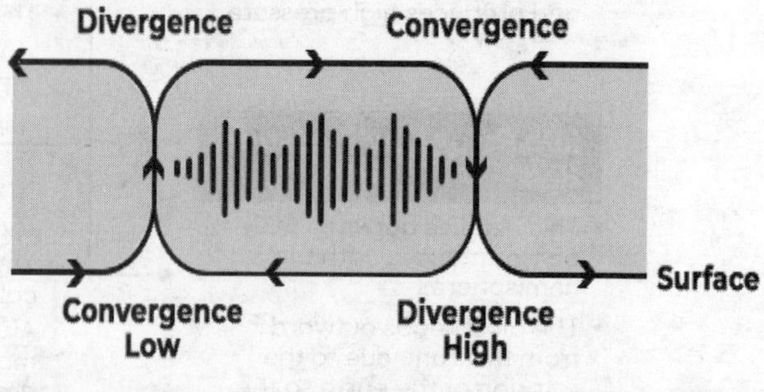

Convergence and Divergence of Winds

General Circulation of The Atmosphere

- **The pattern of planetary winds largely depends on:**

(i) Latitudinal variation of atmospheric heating;

(ii) Emergence of pressure belts;

(iii) The migration of belts following apparent path of the sun;

(iv) The distribution of continents and oceans;

(v) The rotation of earth.

- **The atmosphere's general circulation is the movement pattern of the planetary winds.** It also triggers ocean water circulation, which affects the earth's climate.

Pattern of Wind Direction in Cyclones and Anticyclones

Pressure System	Pressure Condition at the Centre	Pattern of Wind Direction in Northern Hemisphere	Pattern of Wind Direction in Southern Hemisphere
Cyclone	Low	Anticlockwise	Clockwise
Anticyclone	High	Clockwise	Anticlockwise

- Convection culminating from high insolation raises the air at the **Inter Tropical Convergence Zone (ITCZ),** resulting in the formation of low pressure.
- This low-pressure area is where the tropical winds converge. **The convective cell** rises with the convergent air and travels towards the poles after reaching the top of the troposphere at a height of 14 km.
- Air accumulates as a result at roughly 30° N and S. A subtropical high is created when some of the stored air sinks to the earth's surface.
- Another reason the air sinks is that it cools down when it approaches 30° N and S latitudes. The air below, close to the surface, moves toward the equator in the easterlies.
- The Inter Tropical Convergence Zone (ITCZ) is the convergence point for easterlies originating from both sides of the equator. **Cells are defined** as such circulations that go from the surface downward and vice versa. **Hadley Cell** is the name given to such a cell in the tropics.
- Circulation in the middle latitudes is caused by warm air rising from the subtropical high and sinking cold air coming from the poles. At the surface, these winds are referred to as **westerlies,** and the cell is named the **Ferrel Cell**.
- At polar latitudes, the polar easterlies, which blow towards middle latitudes, cause the cold, thick air to subside close to the poles. We refer to this cell as the **polar Cell.**
- The general circulation of the atmosphere is patterned after these three cells. It is sustained by heat energy moving from lower latitudes to higher latitudes.

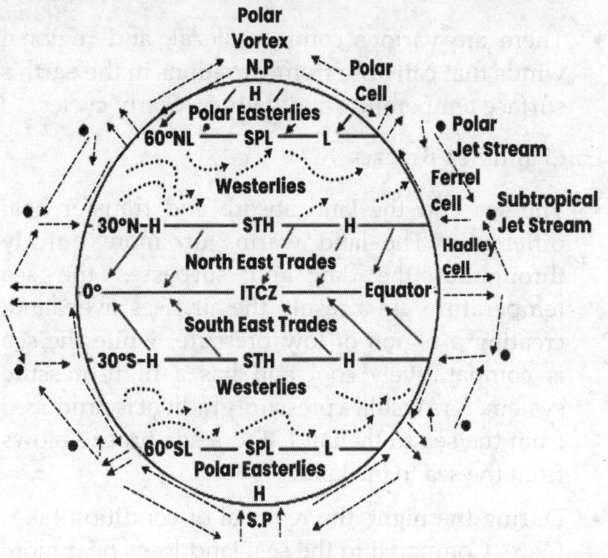

Simplified General Circulation of the Atmosphere

General Atmospheric Circulation and its Effects on Oceans

In terms of overall atmospheric circulation, the warming and cooling of the Pacific Ocean is most significant. Warm water from the central Pacific Ocean gradually replaces the cool Peruvian current as it moves towards the coast of South America. **The El Nino** is the name for this warm water occurrence off the coast of Peru. Pressure variations in **Australia and the Central Pacific** are closely related to the El Nino occurrence. **The Southern Oscillation** is the name given to this shift in the pressure pattern over the Pacific. ENSO is the term used to describe the combined effects of El Nino and the Southern Oscillation. Global weather patterns undergo significant changes during years with a strong ENSO. Heavy rainfall falls on the arid west coast of South America, Australia has droughts, and sometimes India and China experience floods. In many regions of the world, this phenomenon is closely watched and utilised for long-term weather forecasting.

Seasonal Wind

- The Wind circulation pattern altered as changes in seasons due to the shifting of places of maximum heating, wind belts and pressure. Especially throughout Southeast Asia, the monsoons exhibit the most noticeable impact of this change.

Local Winds

- There are various common, local, and regional winds that can arise from variations in the earth's surface temperature and daily or yearly cycles.

Land and Sea Breezes

- The sea and the land absorb and transfer heat differently. The land warms up more quickly throughout the day and surpasses the sea temperature. As a result, the air rises over land, creating a region of low pressure, while the sea is comparatively cool and has a high-pressure system. As a result, a pressure gradient is produced from the sea to the land, and a **sea breeze** blows from the sea to the land.
- During the night, the reversal of condition takes place. Compared to the sea, land loses heat more quickly. There is a pressure gradient from the land to the sea, which causes a **land breeze.**

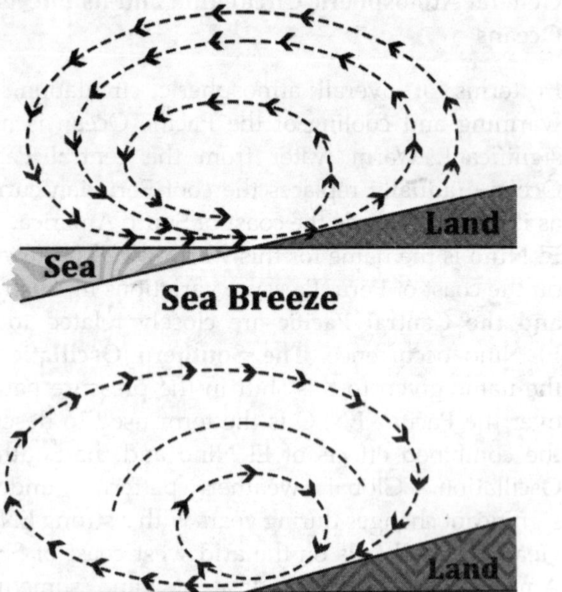

Land and Sea Breezes

Mountain and Valley Winds

- In mountainous areas, air travels upslope during the day as the slopes heat up, creating a gap filled by valley air blowing up the valley. **The valley breeze** is the name given to this wind.
- **The mountain wind** brings the dense air down into the valley when the slopes cool during the night. **"Katabatic Wind"** refers to the cool air draining into the valley from high plateaus and glacier fields.
- There is a different kind of warm breeze on the leeward side of mountain ranges. As these winds traverse mountain ranges, their moisture condenses and becomes precipitation.
- **An adiabatic process** warms the dry air as it descends the leeward side of the slope.

Air Masses

- The air takes on the characteristics of the location when it is above it for a long enough period. The large expanses of plains or oceans can be considered homogeneous zones.
- **An airmass** is a collection of air with certain properties related to temperature and humidity. It is described as a vast body of air with minimal horizontal temperature and moisture variation. **The source regions** are the uniform surfaces across which air masses develop.
- The air masses are divided according to the source regions. **There are five major source regions.** These are:

(i) Warm tropical and subtropical oceans;
(ii) The subtropical hot deserts;
(iii) The relatively cold high latitude oceans;
(iv) The very cold, snow-covered continents in high latitudes;
(v) Permanently ice covered continents in the Arctic and Antarctica.

- **Accordingly, following types of air- masses are recognised:**

(i) Maritime tropical (mT);
(ii) Continental tropical (cT);
(iii) Maritime polar (mP);
(iv) Continental polar (cP);
(v) Continental arctic (cA).

- Tropical air masses are warm and polar air masses are cold.

Fronts

- **A front** is the boundary zone formed when two distinct air masses collide. **Frontogenesis** is the term used to describe the process by which fronts form. There are four primary categories of fronts, as given below:
    - ➢ **Stationary front:** The front is referred to as stationary when it **stays still.**
    - ➢ **Cold front:** The cold front is the contact zone formed when cold air advances towards a warm air mass.
    - ➢ **Warm front:** A warm front is created when warm air moves in the direction of cold air.
    - ➢ **Occluded front:** An air mass is referred to as an **occluded front** when it is **completely** raised **above the ground**.
- The fronts, which have high temperature and pressure gradients and are found in middle latitudes, produce sudden temperature fluctuations, air rises, clouds **form, and precipitation occurs.**

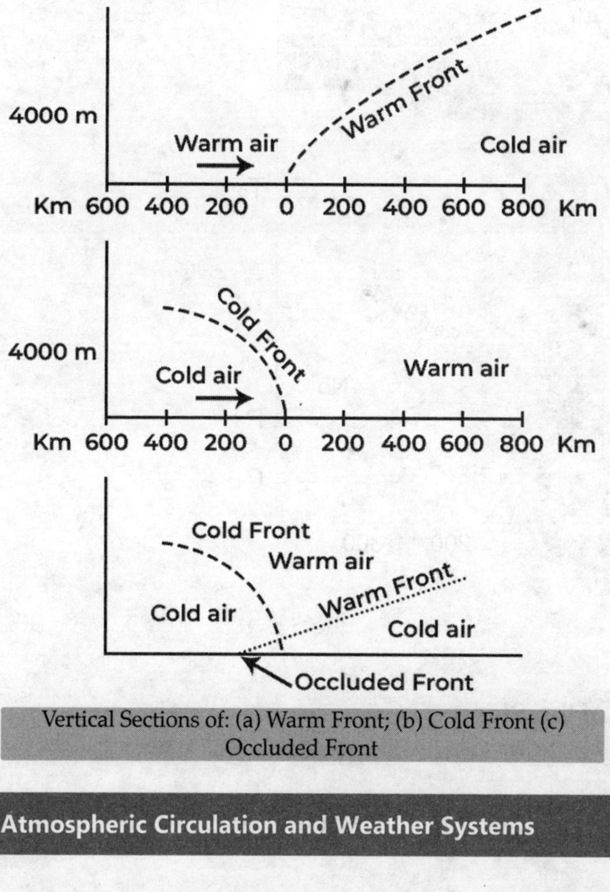

Vertical Sections of: (a) Warm Front; (b) Cold Front (c) Occluded Front

Extra Tropical Cyclones

- **Middle latitudes or extra tropical cyclones** are the systems that develop in the mid and high latitudes outside the tropics. The weather over the region in the middle and high latitudes changes suddenly when the front passes through.
- **Extratropical cyclones** develop beside the polar front, which is motionless at first. Warm air rises from the south, and cold air from the north of the front in the northern hemisphere.
- Warm air goes northward, and cold air moves southward as the pressure drops along the front, initiating an **anticlockwise cyclonic circulation.**
- A well-developed extratropical cyclone with a warm front and a cold front is produced by the **cyclonic circulation.**
- Between the cold air or cold sector in the rear and the forward direction are pockets of warm air or warm sector. A series of clouds form in the sky ahead of the warm front, causing precipitation as the warm air slides over the cold air.
- The warm air is forced upward by the cold front as it approaches from behind, and cumulus clouds consequently form along the cold front.
- The cold front advances more quickly than the warm front, eventually surpassing it. The front is obscured, the warm air is entirely lifted, and the cyclone evaporates.

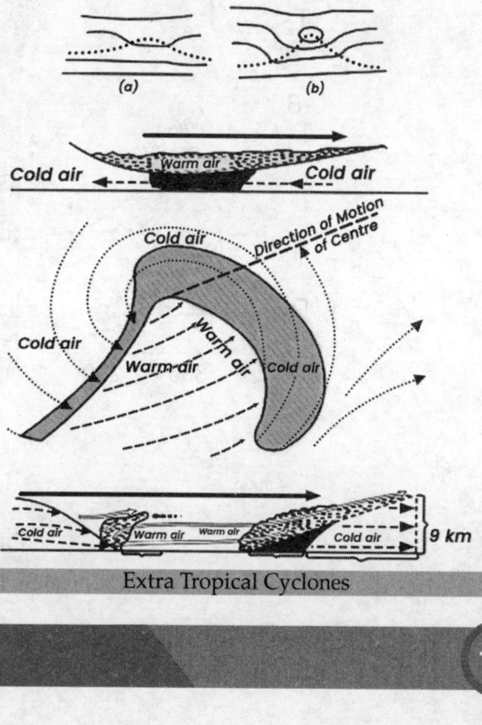

Extra Tropical Cyclones

Tropical Cyclones

- **Tropical cyclones** are violent storms that originate over oceans in tropical areas and move over to the coastal areas, bringing about large-scale destruction caused by violent winds, very heavy rainfall, and storm surges.
- This is one of the most dreadful natural calamities. **They are known as Cyclones in the Indian Ocean, Hurricanes in the Atlantic, Typhoons in the Western Pacific and South China Sea, and Willy-willies in Western Australia.**
- Tropical cyclones develop over warm tropical oceans. Tropical storms are more likely to form and intensify under the following conditions:
  - ➢ A large portion of the ocean that is warmer than 27°C.
  - ➢ The Coriolis force exists.
  - ➢ Minimal fluctuations in the vertical wind velocity.
  - ➢ An area of weak low pressure or low-level cyclonic circulation that already exists.
  - ➢ Upper divergence above the system of sea level.
- The condensation process in the tall cumulonimbus clouds encircling the storm's centre produces the energy that strengthens the storm.
- With continuous supply of moisture from the sea, the storm is further strengthened. On reaching the land the moisture supply is cut off, and the storm dissipates.
- The place where a tropical cyclone crosses the coast is called the **landfall of the cyclone**. Cyclones that cross 20° N latitude generally recurve and are more destructive.

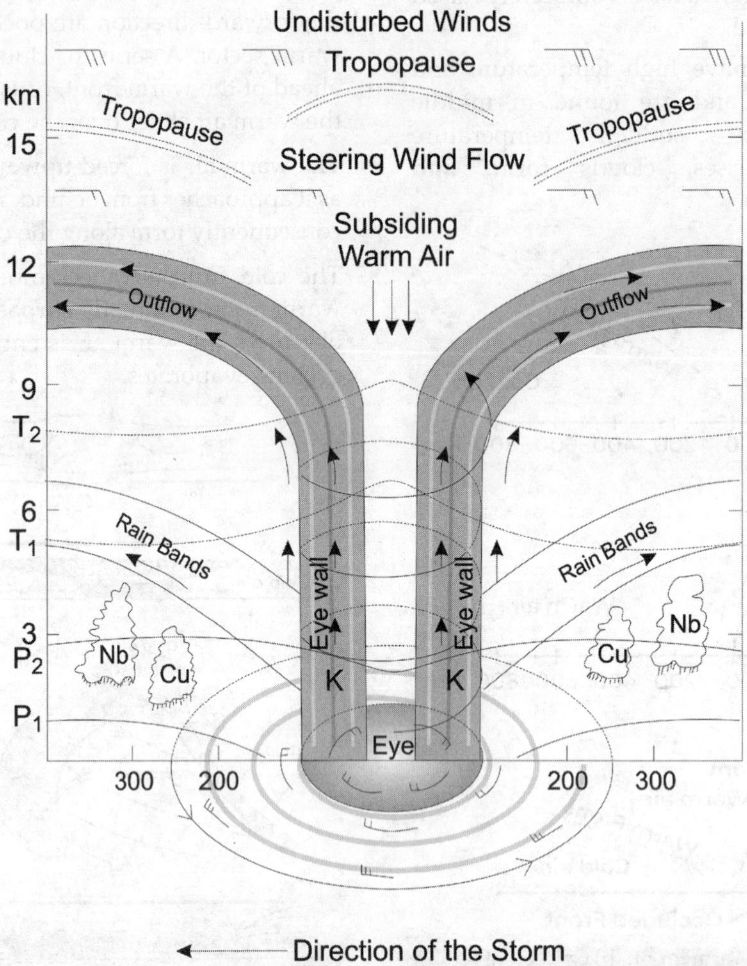

Vertical Section of the Tropical Cyclone

- A **mature tropical cyclone** is characterised by the strong spirally circulating wind around the centre, called the **eye.** The diameter of the circulating system can vary between 150 and 250 km.
- The eye is a region of calm with subsiding air. Around the eye is the **eye wall,** where there is a strong spiralling ascent of air to greater height reaching the tropopause.
- The wind reaches maximum velocity in this region, reaching as high as 250 km per hour. Torrential rain occurs here. From the eye wall, rain bands may radiate, and trains of cumulus and cumulonimbus clouds may drift into the outer region.
- The diameter of the storm over the Bay of Bengal, Arabian Sea and Indian Ocean is between 600 - 1200 km. The system moves slowly, about 300 - 500 km per day. The cyclone creates storm surges and they inundate the coastal lowlands. The storm peters out on the land.

Difference between Tropical Cyclone and Extra Tropical Cyclone

Extra Tropical Cyclones	Tropical Cyclones
They have a clear frontal system.	They have no clear frontal system.
They can come from both the land and the sea, and they encompass a greater area.	Tropical cyclones only form over the oceans, and they break up as soon as they come on land.
They affect a much larger area.	They do not affect much larger area as extra tropical cyclones affects.
The wind velocity in an extra tropical cyclone is lower.	The wind velocity in a tropical cyclone is much higher and it is more destructive.
The extra tropical cyclones move from west to east.	The tropical cyclones move from east to west.

Thunderstorms

Formation of Thunderstorm

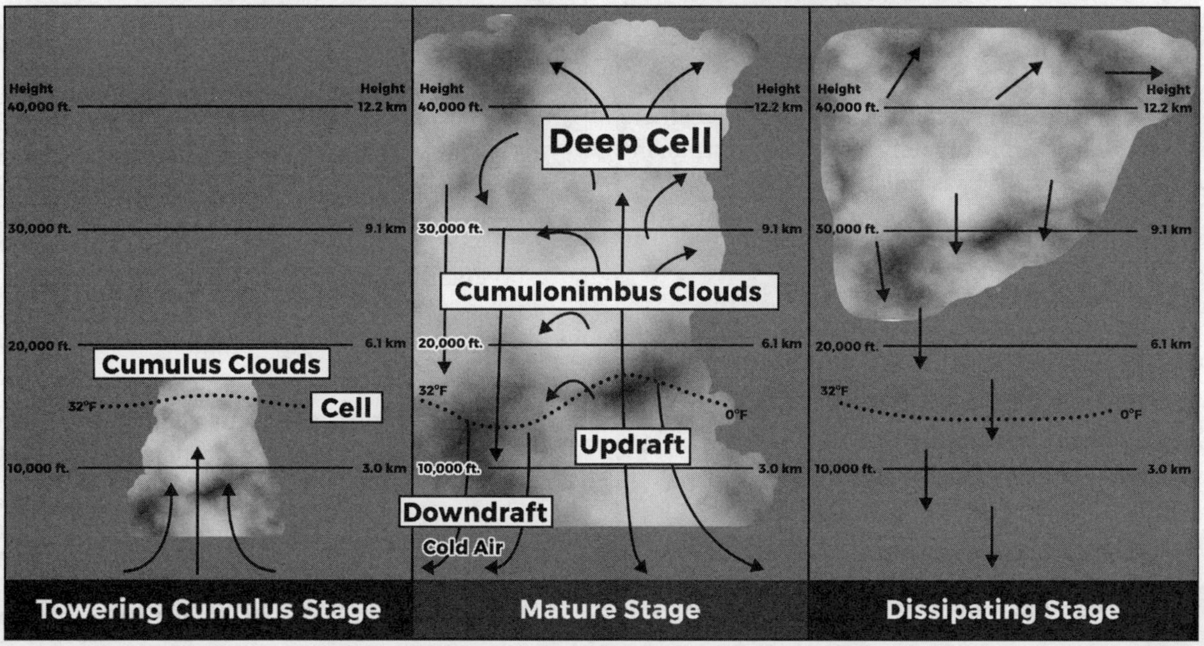

- **Tornadoes and thunderstorms** are two more violent local storms. They happen quickly and cover a little region, yet they are intense.
- Strong convection produces **thunderstorms** on humid, warm days. A mature cumulonimbus cloud that produces lightning and thunder is called a thunderstorm.
- Hails form and descend in the form of **hailstorms** when clouds reach altitudes where temperatures are below zero.
- **Dust storms** can occur during a thunderstorm if there is not enough moisture in the air.
- An intense updraft of warm air ascending to a greater height is what gives rise to a thunderstorm and makes the clouds larger—precipitation results from this. Afterwards, rain and cool air descend to Earth by the downdraft.

Tornadoes

- Sometimes, during intense thunderstorms, the swirling wind falls with enormous velocity, wreaking catastrophic destruction along its path, like an elephant's trunk with extremely **low pressure at its centre**. We refer to this type of event as a tornado. The majority of **tornadoes** occur in middle latitudes. **Water spouts** are the name for the tornado over the sea.
- In these storms, the heat and potential energies are transformed into kinetic energy, causing the restless atmosphere to return to its stable state.

TEST YOURSELF

Multiple Choice Questions

Q1. The atmospheric circulation cell that occurs between the equator and 30 degrees latitude in both hemispheres is called the:

(a) Polar cell (b) Ferrel cell
(c) Hadley cell (d) Jet stream

Q2. The low-pressure belt at the equator is known as the:

(a) Polar front (b) Trade winds
(c) Doldrums (d) Subtropical high

Q3. The belt of calm winds and variable weather located at approximately 30 degrees latitude in both hemispheres is called the:

(a) Polar front (b) Trade winds
(c) Doldrums (d) Subtropical high

Q4. The meeting point of the northeast trade winds and the southeast trade winds is known as the:

(a) Polar front
(b) Inter Tropical Convergence Zone (ITCZ)
(c) Subtropical jet stream
(d) Subtropical high

Q5. The belt of strong westerly winds found between 30 degrees and 60 degrees latitude in both hemispheres is known as the:

(a) Polar front (b) Trade winds
(c) Doldrums (d) Westerlies

Q6. The boundary between two air masses with different temperatures and moisture content is called a:

(a) Cold front (b) Warm front
(c) Occluded front (d) Stationary front

Q7. The area of low atmospheric pressure that develops and moves along the polar front is known as a:

(a) Polar front (b) Cyclone
(c) Anticyclone (d) Tornado

Q8. The boundary between two air masses with similar temperatures and moisture content that is not moving is called a:

(a) Cold front (b) Warm front
(c) Occluded front (d) Stationary front

Q9. The area of high atmospheric pressure that forms over the oceans and brings clear skies and calm winds is known as a:

(a) Polar front (b) Cyclone

(c) Anticyclone (d) Tornado

Q1.	c	Q2.	c	Q3.	d
Q4.	b	Q5.	d	Q6.	a
Q7.	b	Q8.	d	Q9.	c

Model Questions for Main Examination

Q1. Explain the division of the atmosphere into layers based on temperature classification and how each layer is significant for us?

Q2. Discuss in detail the tri-cellular model of atmospheric circulation. (UPSC 2019)

UNIT
13 Water in The Atmosphere

In This Unit

Comprehensive and profound coverage of the following NCERTs' chapter:

✓ NCERT Class- 11th (Fundamentals of Physical Geography), Chapter- 10

The atmosphere contains three distinct forms of water: gaseous, liquid, and solid. Water bodies release moisture into the atmosphere through evaporation, while plants release moisture into the environment through transpiration. Thus, water is constantly exchanged between the atmosphere, the oceans, and the continents through the processes of evaporation, transpiration, condensation, and precipitation.

- The amount of water vapour in the air is referred to as **humidity**. It is expressed in several ways using quantitative methods.
- **Absolute humidity** is the measure of the actual amount of water vapour in the atmosphere. It is measured in **grams per cubic metre** and represents the weight of water vapour per unit volume of air.
- The temperature of the air determines how much water vapour it can contain. On Earth's surface, the absolute humidity varies from location to location.
- **Relative humidity** is the amount of moisture in the atmosphere as a percentage of its total capacity at a particular temperature.
- The ability to hold onto moisture changes as air temperature does, and it also impacts relative humidity. It is less on continents and greater over oceans.
- **At a specific temperature**, **saturated air has the maximum** amount of **moisture**. This indicates that the air cannot hold any more moisture at that point at the specified temperature.
- **The dew point** is the temperature at which saturation happens in a specific air sample.

Evaporation and Condensation

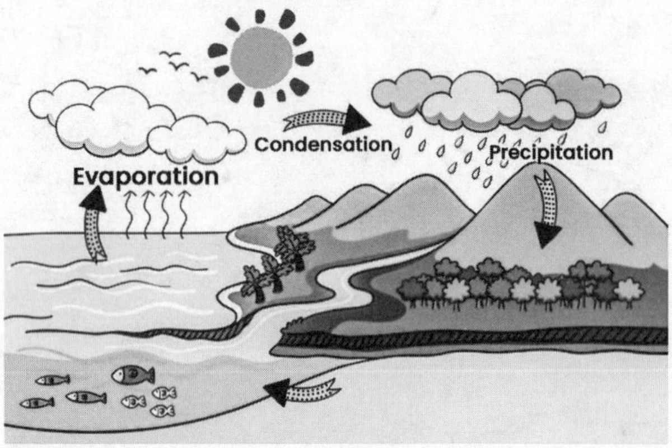

Evaporation and Condensation

Evaporation

- Water changes from a liquid to a gas through a process called **evaporation**. Evaporation is mostly caused by heat. **Latent heat of vaporisation** is the term used to describe the temperature at which water begins to evaporate.
- A rise in temperature enhances the ability of the air parcel to absorb and hold water.
- Similarly, air has the ability to absorb and hold moisture if the moisture level is low. The saturated layer is replaced with the unsaturated layer by air movement. As a result, evaporation increases with increased air movement.

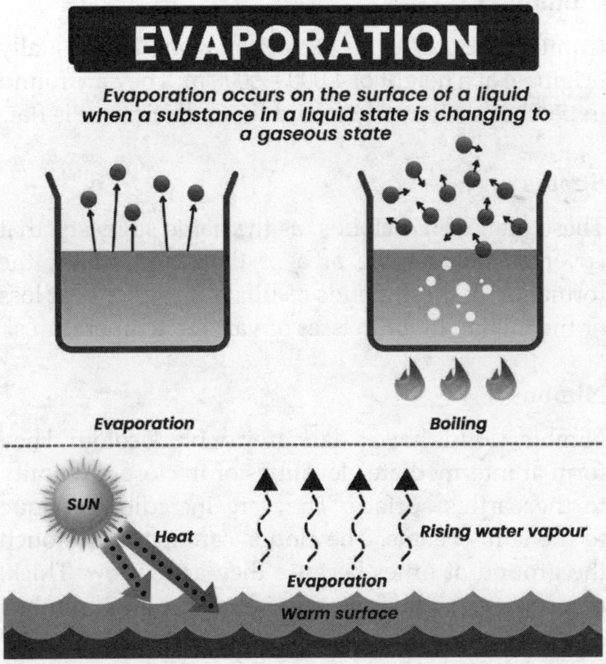

Condensation

- **Condensation** is the process by which water vapour changes into actual water. Heat loss results in condensation. Moist air may cool to the point that it can no longer hold water vapour. The surplus water vapour then condenses into liquid.
- **Sublimation** is the process when it directly condenses into a solid state.
- Condensation occurs in free air when very small particles known as **hygroscopic condensation nuclei** cool down. Particles of dust, smoke and salt from the ocean are particularly good nuclei because they absorb water.
- Condensation can also occur when the temperature is **near the dew point** or when moist air comes into contact with a colder surface.
- Thus, the quantity of cooling and the air's relative humidity affect condensation.
- The amount of air, temperature, pressure, and humidity all affect condensation.
- Condensation takes place in following conditions:
  - ➢ when the air's volume stays constant but its temperature drops to the dew point;
  - ➢ when the temperature and volume are both reduced;
  - ➢ When evaporation adds moisture to the air.
- However, the drop in air temperature is the most conducive factor for condensation.
- Following condensation, atmospheric moisture, or water vapour, can take on the following forms: **dew, frost, fog, and clouds.**
- When the dew point is both greater and lower than the freezing point, condensation occurs. If there is sufficient moisture and dew point is lower than freezing point, it will directly turn in to ice crystals. While, if dew point is higher than freezing point it will turn in to water droplets through condensation.

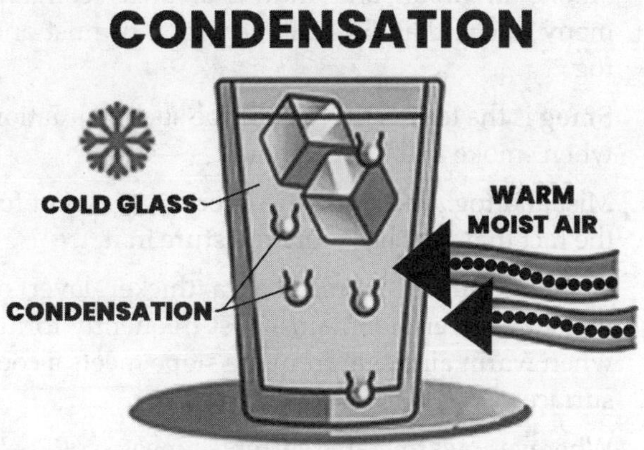

Condensation

Dew

- **Dew** is the term for moisture that forms as droplets of water on the colder surfaces of solid objects, such as leaves, grass blades and stones, instead of being a condensation from air above the surface.
- A clear sky, calm air, high relative humidity, and long, cold nights are optimal for its creation. **For dew to occur, the dew point needs to be higher than the freezing point**.

Frost

- When condensation occurs below freezing point (0°C), that is, when the **dew point is at or below freezing point, frost** develops on cold surfaces.
- Rather than being deposited as water droplets, the extra moisture takes the shape of tiny ice crystals.

- The optimal conditions for the creation of white frost are identical to those for the formation of dew, with the exception that the air temperature needs to be **at or below the freezing point.**

Fog and Mist

- Condensation occurs internally on fine dust particles when the temperature of an air mass containing a significant amount of water vapour suddenly drops.
- Therefore, **a cloud with a base at or close to the ground is considered a fog**. The visibility drops to almost nil due to the fog and mist.
- Smoke in urban and industrial areas contains many nuclei that aid in the creation of mist and fog.
- **Smog** is the term used to describe such a situation when smoke and fog combine.
- Mist and fog are identical in every way except for the fact that mist has more moisture in it.
- Each nucleus in a mist has a thicker layer of moisture. Over mountains, mist frequently forms when warm air rising from the slope meets a cool surface.
- Wherever warm air currents meet cold air currents, fogs arise, which are more dry than mist.
- Fogs are tiny clouds formed by condensation surrounding nuclei presented by smoke, dust, and salt particles.

Clouds

A cloud is a collection of small water droplets or ice crystals that are created when water vapour condenses in free air at high elevations. Clouds take on **different shapes** when they **form at different heights** above the earth's surface.

Four categories are used to classify clouds based on factors such as **height, expanse, density, transparency, and opaqueness: (i) cirrus, (ii) cumulus, (iii) stratus, and (iv) nimbus.**

Cirrus

Cirrus clouds are developed at high altitudes (8,000 - 12,000m). They are thin and detached clouds having a feathery appearance. Their colour is always white.

Cumulus

Cumulus clouds seems like cotton wool. They usually originate at a height of 4,000 - 7,000 m. They are found in patches scattered here and there. Their base is flat.

Stratus

These are layered clouds, as the name suggests, that cover a considerable area of the sky. Usually, the formation of these clouds results from either heat loss or the mixing of air masses of varying temperatures.

Nimbus

Nimbus clouds have a dark grey or black colour. They form at intermediate elevations or in close proximity to the earth's surface. They are incredibly opaque to the sun's beams. The clouds can appear to touch the ground at times because they are so low. Thick, amorphous clouds of vapour are called nimbus clouds.

A combination of these four basic types can give rise to the following types of clouds: high clouds – cirrus, cirrostratus, cirrocumulus; middle clouds – altostratus and altocumulus; low clouds – stratocumulus and nimbostratus and clouds with extensive vertical development – **cumulus** and **cumulonimbus.**

Precipitation

- The process of continuous condensation in free air helps the condensed particles to grow in size. When the resistance of the air fails to hold them against the force of gravity, they fall onto the earth's surface.
- Therefore, precipitation is the discharge of moisture that occurs when water vapour condenses. This could happen in a **liquid or solid state**. When precipitation occurs in the form of fine snowflakes and is below freezing, it is referred to as **snowfall**. When precipitation occurs in the form of water, it is known as **rainfall.**
- Hexagonal crystals that represent moisture are released. These crystals condense into snowflakes. Other than rain and snow, additional types of precipitation include **sleet and hail**, albeit the latter are rare and sporadic in terms of both timing and location.

- **Snowfall** consists of frozen precipitation, and re-frozen melted snow. **Sleet** is the result of precipitation that occurs when a layer of air that is warmer than freezing falls on top of a layer that is below freezing close to the ground. Raindrops hit the colder air below as they descend from the warmer air above. Consequently, they thicken and descend to the earth as minuscule ice pellets, no more significant than the droplets that gave rise to them.
- **Hailstones** are the drops of rain that, after being released by the clouds, become solidified into small rounded solid pieces of ice which reach the surface of the earth. These are formed by the rainwater passing through the colder layers. Hailstones have several concentric layers of ice one over the other.

Types of Rainfall

Rainfall can be categorised into three primary types according to where it originates: convectional, orographic or relief, and cyclonic or frontal.

Convectional Rain

- As air temperature rises, it becomes lighter and rises by convection currents. It expands and loses heat as it rises, which causes condensation to occur and the formation of cumulus clouds.
- Heavy rain occurs during lightning and thunder, but it passes quickly. In the summer or during the hottest part of the day, this kind of rain is typical. It is quite prevalent in the inner regions of the continents and the equatorial regions, especially in the northern hemisphere.

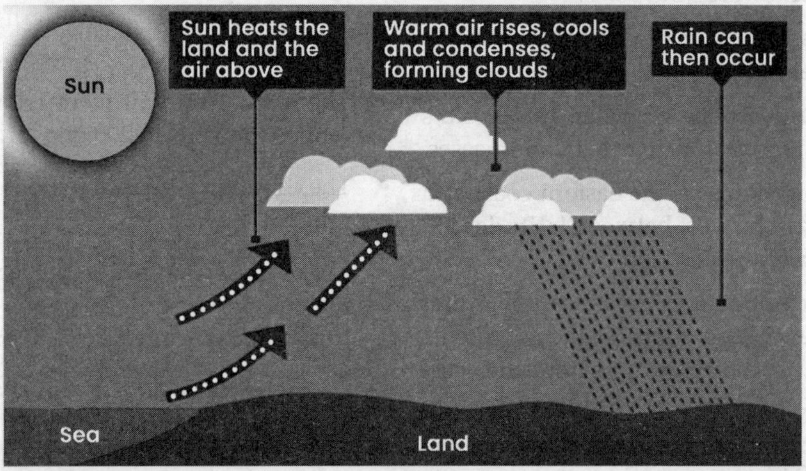

Convectional Rain

Orographic Rain

- The saturated air mass is compelled to ascend when it encounters a mountain; during its ascent, it expands, the temperature drops, and the moisture condenses.
- The main feature of this type of rain is that it pours more heavily on the windward slopes. When these winds reach the opposite slope, they descend and the temperature rises after providing rain on the windward side.
- Afterward, as a result of their increased ability to absorb rainwater, these leeward slopes continue to be dry and rainless. **The rain-shadow area** is the portion of the leeward side that receives less rainfall. Another name for it is the **relief rain**.

Cyclonic or Frontal Rain

- This occurs due to the convergence of different air masses with different temperatures, density, and humidity. The turbulent conditions are produced, and cyclonic rain occurs along the fronts of the cyclone. **The layer separating them is known as a front.**
- A front is the boundary zone formed when two distinct air masses meet. **Frontogenesis** is the term for the process by which the fronts form.
- **At the warm front**, the lighter warm air that is less dense is usually forced to rise over denser cold air and thereby leading to cyclonic rain.

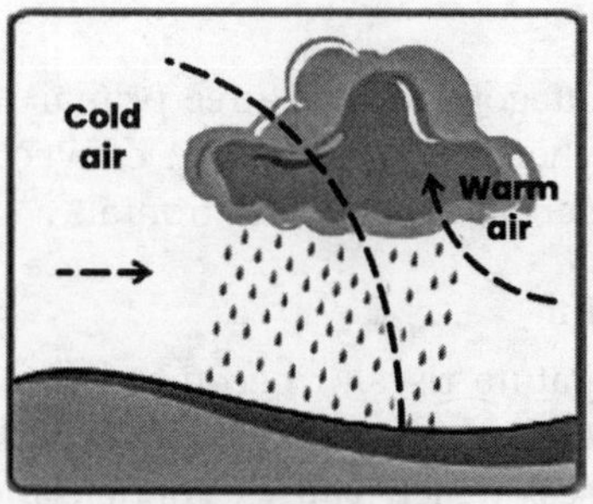

Cyclonic Rainfall

Relief (Orographic) Rainfall

Convectional Rainfall

World Distribution of Rainfall

The amount of rainfall that falls in different parts of the earth's surface throughout the year varies as well, depending on the season.

- Rainfall often decreases significantly as one moves from the **equator** towards the poles.
- **The world's coastal regions** receive more rainfall than the continents' interiors do.
- Due to their large supply of water, the world's oceans receive more rainfall than their landmasses.
- The rainy season begins on the eastern coast and decreases towards the west **between latitudes 35° and 40° N and S of the equator**.
- However, because of the westerlies, rainfall is first obtained on the western edges of the continents and continues to decrease towards the east between 45° and 65° N and S of the equator.
- Rainfall is more on the windward side of the coastal plain and lessens towards the leeward side **where mountains run parallel to the coast**.

The following list of significant precipitation regimes is based on the overall amount of precipitation that occurs each year:

- Heavy rainfall exceeding 200 cm annually falls in the equatorial belt, the monsoon land's coastal regions, and the windward slopes of the mountains along the western shores in the cold temperate zone.
- The annual rainfall in interior continental areas ranges from 100 to 200 cm.
- The continents' coastal regions experience modest rainfall.
- The annual rainfall in the eastern and interior regions of temperate areas and the central parts of tropical lands varies from 50 to 100 cm.
- Regions located in the rain shadow zone of high latitudes and the interior of continents receive extremely little precipitation annually—less than 50 cm.

TEST YOURSELF

Multiple Choice Questions

Q1. Consider the following statements:

1. High clouds primarily reflect solar radiation and cool the surface of the Earth.
2. Low clouds have a high absorption of infrared radiation emanating from the Earth's surface and thus cause warming effect.

Which of the statements given above is / are correct? (UPSC 2022)

(a) 1 only (b) 2 only

(c) Both 1 and 2 (d) Neither 1 nor 2

Q2. Water vapour in the atmosphere is primarily derived from:

(a) Evaporation of ocean water

(b) Condensation of groundwater

(c) Melting of glaciers

(d) Precipitation from clouds

Q3. The process by which water vapour changes into liquid water is called:

(a) Evaporation (b) Condensation

(c) Precipitation (d) Transpiration

Q4. The temperature at which air becomes fully saturated with water vapour called

(a) Dew point (b) Boiling point

(c) Freezing point (d) Melting point

Q5. The process by which plants release water vapour into the atmosphere is called?

(a) Evaporation (b) Condensation

(c) Precipitation (d) Transpiration

Q6. The conversion of water vapour directly into ice crystals without passing through the liquid phase is called:

(a) Evaporation (b) Sublimation

(c) Condensation (d) Precipitation

Q7. The visible form of water droplets or ice crystals suspended in the atmosphere is known as:

(a) Humidity (b) Dew

(c) Fog (d) Clouds

Q8. The process by which water falls from the atmosphere to the Earth's surface in the form of rain, snow, sleet, or hail is called:

(a) Evaporation (b) Condensation

(c) Transpiration (d) Precipitation

Q9. The layer of the atmosphere where clouds and weather phenomena occur is called

(a) Troposphere (b) Stratosphere

(c) Mesosphere (d) Thermosphere

Q10. The measurement of the amount of water vapour present in the air is known as:

(a) Humidity (b) Temperature

(c) Pressure (d) Precipitation

Q11. The difference between the actual amount of water vapour present in the air and the maximum amount it can hold at a given temperature is called:

(a) Relative humidity (b) Absolute humidity

(c) Dew point (d) Condensation point

Q1.	d	Q2.	a	Q3.	b
Q4.	a	Q5.	d	Q6.	b
Q7.	d	Q8.	d	Q9.	a
Q10.	a	Q11.	a		

Model Questions for Main Examination

Q1. Critically analyse the forms of water present in the atmosphere.

Q2. Briefly discuss about clouds and highlight its various types.

UNIT 14

World Climate and Climate Change

In This Unit

Comprehensive and profound coverage of the following NCERTs' chapter:

✓ NCERT Class- 11th (Fundamentals of Physical Geography), Chapter- 11

Basis	Weather	Climate
Meaning	Weather is the atmospheric condition which changes daily. It can even change within a day.	Climate indicates the standard pattern of weather condition of a particular area or place over a long period.
Duration	It is a short period analysis that changes daily or even within a day.	It changes over a long period. It can be months or years.
Study	It needs a minute by minute study of atmosphere in an area over a short period (climatology).	It is an average of the weather over a long period (meteorology).
Affecting components	Temperature, humidity, air pressure, cloudiness, precipitation etc.	Temperature, wind pattern, ocean surface temperature and precipitation.
Variability	It varies constantly.	Its variability is relatively less.

Difference between Weather and Climate

There are three main methods used to categorise climate. They are applied, genetic, and empirical.

Observed data, especially those on temperature and precipitation, serve as the foundation for **empirical classification.** Climates are arranged based on their causes through **genetic classification. Applied classification** is for a specific purpose.

Weather and Climate

Weather

The day-to-day condition of the atmosphere at a place with respect to the temperature, humidity, rainfall, windspeed, etc. is called Weather at that place.

The temperature, humidity, and other factors are called Elements of the Weather.

Climate

The word 'Climate' is defined as the weather averaged over a long period of time and over a large area. The standing average period is 30 years.

Factors determining Weather and Climate

A. Latitude:
- The equator receives vertical rays which fall over a small area.
- In contrast, the polar regions receive slanting sunrays and they fall over a wide area.
- As a result of this, places near the equator are hotter than the poles.

B. Altitude:
- The places located on higher altitudes are always cooler than those on the plains.
  - This is because the air becomes thinner and it absorbs less heat.
- Secondly, the atmosphere can be heated upwards by the Earth's surface.
  - The air near the surface of the earth is denser and contains more carbon dioxide, water vapour, dust and other impurities. Hence, it absorbs more heat than the thin and clear air in the upper layers.
- Normal Lapse Rate: Temperature decreases at the rate 6.5°C for every 1000 metres high on the earth's surface. This is known as Normal Lapse Rate.

C. Distance from the Sea:
- Water is a bad conductor of heat i.e. it takes longer time to heat and longer time to cool.
- Due to this moderating effect of the sea, places near the coast have low range of temperature and high humidity.
- The places in the interior of the continents do not experience this moderating effect of the sea.
- These places have extreme temperatures. The places far from the sea have higher range of diurnal (daily) and annual temperatures.

D. Ocean Currents:
- Warm currents make the coastal area warm, wet, and free from ice.
- Cold current makes the coastal area cool, dry and bring in icebergs.

E. Direction of prevailing winds:
- The winds that blow from the sea to land contain more moisture so they are cool and wet.
- The winds blowing from land are warm and dry.

F. El Nino effect:
- El Niño, which affects wind and rainfall patterns, has been blamed for droughts and floods in countries around the Pacific Rim.
- El Niño refers to the irregular warming of surface water in the Pacific.
- The warmer water pumps energy and moisture into the atmosphere, altering global wind and rainfall patterns.

G. Human Influence:
- Result of Industrial Revolution- Deforestation, Transportation, Concrete buildings and many industries.
  Impacts- Global Warming, Greenhouse Effect, Urban Heat Island and Pollution, which have increased the amount of CO_2.

Koeppen's Scheme of Classification of Climate

The empirical climate classification scheme created in 1918 **by Vladimir Petrovich Koeppen** is the most extensively used classification system for climate. Koeppen found a close connection between climate and vegetation distribution. He classified the climates using specific temperature and precipitation values that he had chosen, connected to the spread of flora. It is an empirical classification based on mean monthly and mean annual temperature and precipitation data.

Four of the five major climatic groupings identified by Koeppen are based on temperature, while one is based on precipitation. Later on, the last **Highland classification** was introduced.

Climatic Groups According to Koeppen

Group	Characteristics
A-Tropical	Average temperature of the coldest month is 18° C or higher
B-Dry Climates	Potential evaporation exceeds precipitation
C-Warm Temperate	The average temperature of the coldest month of the (Mid-latitude) climate year is higher than minus 3°C but below 18°C
D-Cold Snow Forest Climates	The average temperature of the coldest month is minus 3° C or below
E-Cold Climates	Average temperature for all months is below 10° C
H- High Land	Cold due to elevation

The climatic groupings are further classified into different types, denoted by small letters, according to temperature and precipitation seasonality features. The small letters f, m, w, and s stand for the **seasons of dryness**; f for no dry season; m for monsoon climate; w for winter dry season; and s for summer dry season. **The small letters** a, b, c, and d indicate the temperature severity. The capital letters S for steppe or semi-arid regions, B-Dry Climates and W for desert regions are used to categorise.

Climatic Types According to Koeppen

Group	Type	Letter Code	Characteristics
A-Tropical Humid Climate	Tropical wet	Af	No dry season
	Tropical monsoon	Am	Monsoonal, short dry season
	Tropical wet and dry	Aw	Winter dry season
B-Dry Climate	Subtropical steppe	BSh	Low-latitude semi arid or dry
	Subtropical desert	BWh	Low-latitude arid or dry
	Mid-latitude steppe	BSk	Mid-latitude semi arid or dry
	Mid-latitude desert	BWk	Mid-latitude arid or dry
C-Warm temperate (Mid-latitude) Climates	Humid subtropical	Cfa	No dry season, warm summer
	Mediterranean	Cs	Dry hot summer
	Marine west coast	Cfb	No dry season, warm and cool summer
D-Cold Snow forest Climates	Humid continental	Df	No dry season, severe winter
	Subarctic	Dw	Winter dry and very severe
E-Cold Climates	Tundra	ET	No true summer
	Polar ice cap	EF	Perennial ice
H-Highland	Highland	H	Highland with snow cover

Koppen' Climate Classification Scheme Symbols Description		
1st	**2nd**	**3rd**
A (Tropical)	f (Rainforest) m (Monsoon) w (Savanna, dry winter) s (Savanna, dry summer)	
B (Dry)	W (Arid Desert) S (Semi-Arid or steppe)	h (Hot) k (Cold)
C (Temperate)	w (Dry winter) f (No dry season) s (Dry summer)	a (Hot summer) b (Warm summer) c (Cold summer)
D (Continental)	w (Dry winter) f (No dry season) s (Dry summer)	a (Hot summer) b (Warm summer) c (Cold summer) d (Very cold winter)
E (Polar)		T (Tundra) F (Ice cap)

Detailed Classification of Major Climatic Types according to the Modified Koppen-Geiger scheme			
Letter Symbol			**Criterion**
1st	2nd	3rd	
A			temperature of coolest month 18 °C or higher
	f		precipitation in driest month at least 60 mm
	m		precipitation in driest month less than 60 mm but equal to or greater than 100 – (r/25)[1]
	w		precipitation in driest month less than 60 mm and less than 100 – (r/25)
B[2]			70% or more of annual precipitation falls in the summer half of the year and r less than 20t + 280, or 70% or more of annual precipitation falls in the winter half of the year and r less than 20t, or neither half of the year has 70% or more of annual precipitation and r less than 20t + 140[3]
	W		r is less than one-half of the upper limit for classification as a B type (see above)
	S		r is less than the upper limit for classification as a B type but is more than one-half of that amount
		h	t equal to or greater than 18 °C
		k	t less than 18 °C
C			temperature of warmest month greater than or equal to 10 °C, and temperature of coldest month less than 18 °C but greater than –3 °C

	s		precipitation in driest month of summer half of the year is less than 30 mm and less than one-third of the wettest month of the winter half
	w		precipitation in driest month of the winter half of the year less than one-tenth of the amount in the wettest month of the summer half
	f		precipitation more evenly distributed throughout year; criteria for neither s nor w satisfied
		a	temperature of warmest month 22 °C or above
		b	temperature of each of four warmest months 10 °C or above but warmest month less than 22 °C
		c	temperature of one to three months 10 °C or above but warmest month less than 22 °C
D			temperature of warmest month greater than or equal to 10 °C, and temperature of coldest month –3 °C or lower
	s		same as for type C
	w		same as for type C
	f		same as for type C
		a	same as for type C
		b	same as for type C
		c	same as for type C
		d	temperature of coldest month less than –38 °C (d is used instead of a, b, or c)
E			temperature of warmest month less than 10 °C
	T		temperature of warmest month greater than 0 °C but less than 10 °C
	F		temperature of warmest month 0 °C or below
H[4]			temperature and precipitation characteristics highly dependent on traits of adjacent zones and overall elevation—highland climates may occur at any latitude

[1]In the formulas above, r is average annual precipitation total (mm), and t is average annual temperature (°C). All other temperatures are monthly means (°C), and all other precipitation amounts are mean monthly totals (mm).

[2]Any climate that satisfies the criteria for B type is classified as such, irrespective of its other characteristics.

[3]The summer half is April–Sept. for the Northern Hemisphere and October–March for the Southern Hemisphere.

[4]Most modern climate schemes include altitude. The highland zone has been taken from G.T. Trewartha

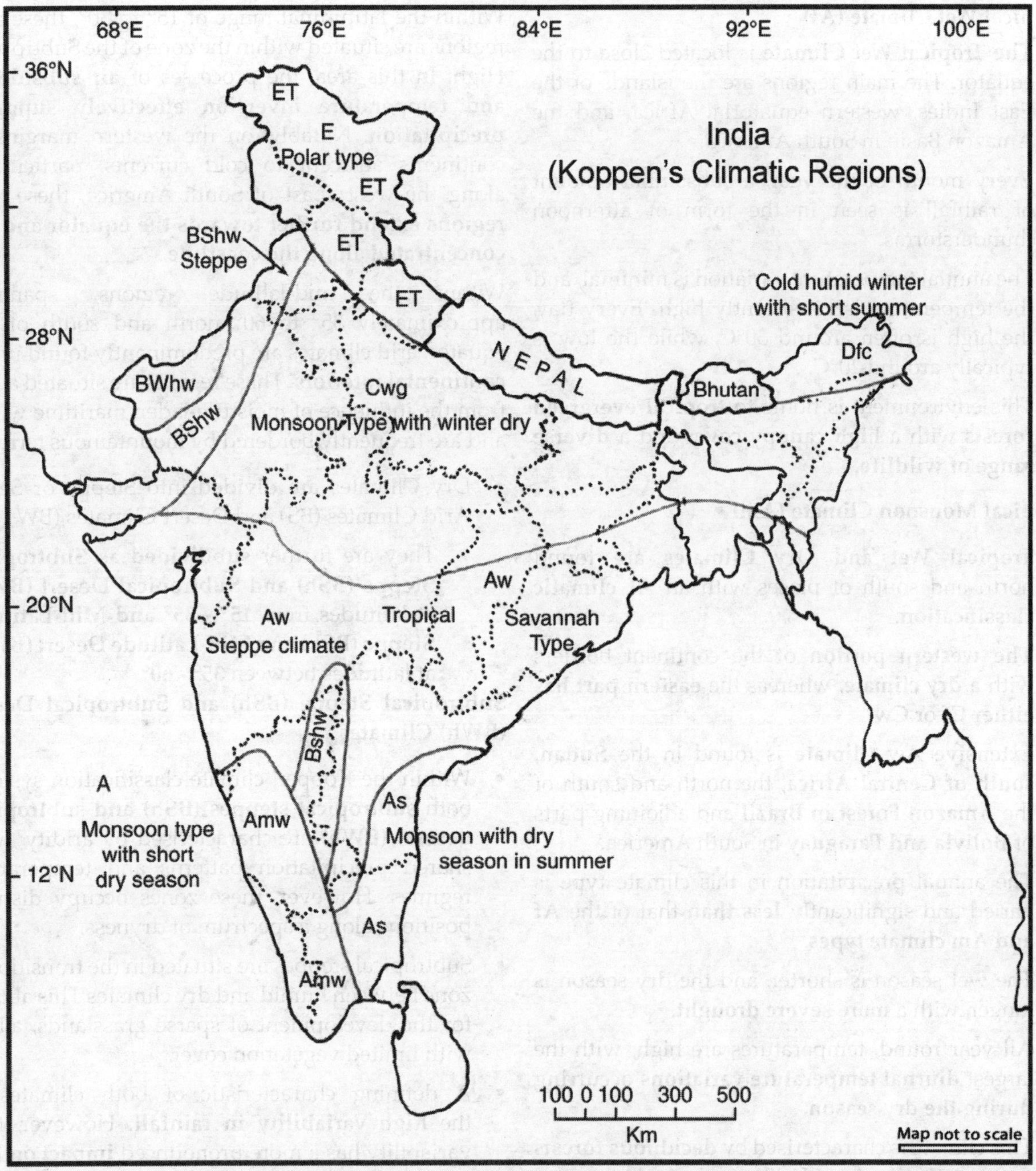

Climatic Classification of India according to Koeppen

Group A: Tropical Humid Climates

There are **tropical humid climates** located between the Tropics of Cancer and Capricorn. The Inter Tropical Convergence Zone (ITCZ) and the year-round presence of the sun contribute to the hot and muggy environment. There is an extensive annual rainfall range and a minimal annual temperature range. There are **three classifications** within the tropical group:

- Af- Tropical Wet Climate
- Am - Tropical Monsoon Climate
- Aw- Tropical Wet and Dry climate

Tropical Wet Climate (Af)

- **The Tropical Wet Climate** is located close to the equator. The main regions are the islands of the East Indies, western equatorial Africa, and the Amazon Basin in South America.
- Every month of the year, a substantial amount of rainfall is seen in the form of afternoon thunderstorms.
- The annual temperature variation is minimal, and the temperature is consistently high. Every day, the high is often around 30°C, while the low is typically around 20°C.
- This environment is home to **tropical evergreen forests** with a **high canopy** cover and a **diverse range of wildlife.**

Tropical Monsoon Climate (Am)

- **Tropical Wet and Dry Climates** are found north and south of places with an **Af climatic classification.**
- **The western portion** of the continent borders with **a dry climate,** whereas the **eastern part has either Cf or Cw.**
- **Extensive Aw Climate** is found in the **Sudan, south of Central Africa,** the north and south of the **Amazon Forest in Brazil** and adjoining parts of **Bolivia and Paraguay** in South America.
- The annual precipitation in this climate type is varied and significantly **less than** that of the **Af and Am climate types.**
- The wet season is shorter, and the dry season is longer, with a **more severe drought.**
- All year round, temperatures are high, with the largest **diurnal temperature variations occurring during the dry season.**
- This climate is characterised by **deciduous forests and grasslands shredded by trees.**

Group B: Dry Climates

Regions classified as **dry climates** are characterised by **exceptionally low levels of precipitation,** which are **insufficient to support** the flourishing of **plant life.** These arid environments encompass a vast expanse of the Earth's surface, distributed across a wide latitudinal range, extending from **15 degrees to 60 degrees north and south of the equator.**

Within the latitudinal range of 15° to 30°, these arid regions are situated within the zone of the Subtropical High. In this area, the processes of **air subsidence and temperature inversion effectively suppress precipitation.** Notably, on the western margins of continents adjacent to cold currents, particularly along the west coast of South America, these **arid regions extend further towards the equator and are concentrated along the coastline.**

Within the mid-latitude regions, spanning approximately 35° to 60° north and south of the equator, arid climates are predominantly found in the **continental interiors.** These regions are situated away from the influence of moisture-laden maritime winds and are frequently bordered by mountainous terrain.

- Dry Climates are divided into Steppe or Semi-Arid Climates (BS) and Desert Climates (BW).
  - They are further **subdivided as Subtropical Steppe (BSh) and Subtropical Desert (BWh)** at latitudes from **15° - 35° and Mid-Latitude Steppe (BSk) and Mid-Latitude Desert (BWk)** at latitudes between **35° - 60°.**

Subtropical Steppe (BSh) and Subtropical Desert (BWh) Climates

- Within the Koppen climate classification system, both **subtropical steppes (BSh) and subtropical deserts (BWh)** are characterised by aridity, with shared precipitation patterns and temperature regimes. However, these zones occupy distinct positions along a spectrum of dryness.
- Subtropical steppes are situated in the transitional zone between humid and dry climates This allows for the development of sparse grasslands, albeit with limited vegetation cover.
- A defining characteristic of both climates is the **high variability in rainfall.** However, this variability has a more pronounced **impact on life in the steppe.** The erratic nature of precipitation events in steppes can more readily **lead to periods of famine** compared to the consistently arid desert environment.
- Desert regions are further distinguished by the occurrence of **short, intense thunderstorms.** While these downpours may appear dramatic, they are often ineffective in replenishing soil moisture due to rapid evaporation.

- In coastal deserts bordering cold currents, **fog is a relatively common phenomenon.**
- Summer temperatures in these regions soar to exceptional highs. Notably, the record for the highest shade temperature ever recorded was set at **Al Aziziyah, Libya, on September 13th, 1922, at a staggering 58°C**. Both **annual and diurnal temperature** variations are significant within these subtropical dry zones.
- Case of India
    - ➢ **BWhw**, in Western Rajasthan, indicates **Hot Desert with Dry Winter i.e. Thar.**
    - ➢ **BShw**, in the Central Rajasthan, indicates **Steppe or Semi-Arid Climate with Dry Winter.**

Group C: Warm Temperate (Mid-Latitude) Climates

Warm Temperate (Mid-Latitude) Climates encompass a latitudinal band ranging from **30° to 50°** primarily concentrated on the **eastern and western margins of continents**. These climatic regimes are characterised by **summers with warm temperatures and winters with mild conditions**. They can be further subdivided into four distinct classifications.

- Humid Subtropical, i.e., dry in winter and hot in summer (Cwa)
- Mediterranean (Cs)
- Humid Subtropical, i.e., no dry season and mild winter (Cfa)
- Marine West Coast Climate (Cfb)

Humid Subtropical Climate (Cwa)

- Found mostly in the interior plains of South China and North India, this climate zone is poleward of the Tropics of Cancer and Capricorn.
- The climate is **similar to the Aw** climate, **except for the warm winter.**

Mediterranean Climate (Cs)

- As the name suggests, **the Mediterranean climate** occurs around the Mediterranean Sea, along the **west coast** of continents in **subtropical** latitudes between **30° - 40°** latitudes, e.g., **Central California, Central Chile,** along the **coast in southeastern and southwestern Australia.**
- These areas are under the **influence of subtropical highs** in **summer** and **westerly winds** in **winter.** Hence, the climate is characterised by **a hot, dry summer and mild, rainy winter.**
- Monthly average temperature in **summer is around 25° C** and in **winter below 10°C**. The **annual precipitation** ranges between **35 - 90 cm.**

Humid Subtropical (Cfa) Climate

- **Humid Subtropical Climate** lies on the **eastern parts** of the continent in **subtropical latitudes.**
- In this region, the **air masses** are generally **unstable** and cause **rainfall throughout the year.**
- They occur in **the eastern United States of America, southern and eastern China, southern Japan, northeastern Argentina, coastal South Africa and the eastern coast of Australia.**
- The annual averages of precipitation vary from **75-150 cm. Thunderstorms** in summer and **frontal precipitation** in winter are common.
- The mean monthly temperature in **summer is around 27°C**, and in **winter,** it varies from **5°-12° C.** The **daily range** of temperature is **small.**

Marine West Coast Climate (Cfb)

- **Marine West Coast Climate** is located **poleward** from the Mediterranean climate on the west coast of the continents.
- The main areas are **Northwestern Europe, the west coast of North America, north of California, southern Chile, southeastern Australia and New Zealand.**
- Due to marine influence, the **temperature is moderate** and **warmer in winter.**
- The mean temperature in summer months ranges from **15°-20°C** and in winter **4°-10°C.**
- The **annual and daily ranges** of temperature are **small.** Precipitation occurs throughout the year. Precipitation varies greatly from **50-250cm.**

Group D: Cold Snow Forest Climates

Cold snow forest climates occur in **large continental areas** in the northern hemisphere between **40°-70° North** latitudes in **Europe, Asia and North America.** Cold snow forest climates are divided into two types:

1. Df- Cold Climate with Humid Winter
2. Dw- Cold Climate with Dry Winter

Cold Climate with Humid Winters (Df)

- **Cold Climate with Humid Winter** occurs **poleward of marine west coast** climate and **mid-latitude steppe.**
- The winters are **cold and snowy**. The **frost-free** season is **short**.
- The **annual ranges** of temperature are **large**.
- The weather **changes are abrupt and short**. Poleward, the winters are **more severe**.

Cold Climate with Dry Winters (Dw)

- **Cold climate with dry winters** occurs mainly over **Northeastern Asia**.
- The development of a pronounced **Winter Anticyclone** and its weakening in summer sets in monsoon-like **'reversal of wind'** in this region.
- Poleward summer temperatures are lower and winter temperatures are extremely low with many locations experiencing **below freezing point temperatures** for up to **seven months** in a year.
- **Precipitation** occurs in **summer**. The annual precipitation is low, from **12-15 cm**.

Group E: Polar Climates

Polar Climates exist poleward **beyond 70° latitude.** Polar climates consist of **two types**:

- Tundra (ET)
- Ice Cap (EF)

Tundra Climate (ET)

- The vegetation, which includes **flowering plants, lichens, and low-growing mosses, gives rise to the name "Tundra Climate" (ET).** This is the permafrost area where the subsurface remains frozen all the time.
- Only low growing plants are supported by the short growth season and water logging. In the tundra, daytime hours are unusually lengthy in the summer.

Ice Cap Climate (EF)

- **The ice cap climate (EF)** is present over Antarctica and interior Greenland. The temperature is below freezing even in the summer. Extremely little precipitation falls in this location.
- As snow and ice build-up, the increasing pressure causes the ice sheets to distort and eventually break. They drift like floating icebergs through the waters of the Arctic and Antarctic. This climate is seen at Plateau Station, Antarctica, located at 79°S.

Group H: Highland Climates

Topography determines the climate in the Highlands. Large variations in mean temperature over short distances are observed in high mountains. The kinds and amounts of precipitation differ geographically throughout the highlands. In the environment of mountains, there is vertical zonation or layering of climatic types with elevation.

Climate Change

Our current environment may have prevailed for the past 10,000 years, with occasional large shifts. Since the beginning of time, the climate of the planet Earth has seen numerous fluctuations. Glacial and interglacial periods have changed, according to geological data. The geomorphological features show evidence of glacier advances and retreats, particularly at high latitudes and altitudes. Periods of warmth and cold are also evident in the sediment deposits found in glacial lakes. There are hints about wet and dry seasons in the tree rings. The whims of climate are documented in historical accounts. These pieces of evidence collectively suggest that climate change is an ongoing, natural phenomenon.

India saw alternating dry and wet seasons as well. According to archaeological discoveries, the Rajasthan desert had a cool, moist climate approximately 8,000 B.C. There was more rainfall between 3,000 and 1,700 B.C. This area served as the Harappan civilisation's core from roughly 2,000 to 1,700 B.C. Since then, the dry conditions have gotten worse.

Around 500–300 million years ago, during the Cambrian, Ordovician, and Silurian periods of geological time, the world was warm. There were glacial and interglacial phases throughout the Pleistocene epoch; the most recent significant peak glacial period ended roughly 18,000 years ago, with the beginning of the current interglacial period 10,000 years ago.

Climate in The Recent Past

The climate is constantly changing. Extreme weather events were common during the 1990s and the previous century. The decade of the 1990s saw some of the worst floods in global history, as well as the highest temperatures of the century. The worst devastating drought in the Sahel region, south of the Sahara Desert, from 1967-1977 is one such variability. During the 1930s, **a severe drought** occurred in the southwestern Great Plains of the United States, described as the **Dust Bowl**. Historical records of crop yield or crop failures, of floods and migration of people tell us about the effects of changing climate. A number of times, Europe witnessed warm, wet, cold and dry periods; the significant episodes were the warm and dry conditions in the tenth and eleventh centuries when the Vikings settled in Greenland. Europe witnessed the **"Little Ice Age"** from 1550 to about 1850. From about 1885 to 1940, the world temperature showed an upward trend. **After 1940**, the rate of increase in temperature **slowed down**. However, it has been increasing again since the mid-1970s, when global temperatures have risen by **0.5 °C** over a period of 25 years. According to the **Intergovernmental Panel on Climate Change (IPCC),** since 1970, the global average temperature has been rising at the **rate of 1.7°C per century**, as compared to a long-term decline over the past 7000 years at a baseline rate of 0.01°C per century.

Even a **one-degree *global* rise** in temperature is significant because it takes a vast amount of heat to warm all of the oceans, the atmosphere, and the land masses by that much. In the past, a **one- to two-degree drop** was all it took to plunge the Earth into the **Little Ice Age**. A **five-degree drop** was enough to bury a large part of North America under a towering mass of ice 20,000 years ago.

Causes of Climate Change

The causes of climate change are many. They can be grouped into Astronomical and Terrestrial causes.

- **Astronomical causes** are the changes in solar output associated with sunspot activities. **Sunspots** are dark and cooler patches of the sun, which increase and decrease in a cyclical manner.
  - ➢ According to some meteorologists, when the **number of Sunspots** increases, cooler and wetter weather and greater storminess occur. A decrease in sunspot numbers is associated with warm and drier conditions.
  - ➢ Another astronomical theory is **Millankovitch Oscillations**, which infer cycles in the **variations in the earth's orbital characteristics** around the sun, the **wobbling** of the earth and the changes in the earth's **axial tilt**. All these alter the amount of insolation received from the sun, which in turn, might have a bearing on the climate.
- **Under Terrestrial causes, Volcanism** is considered as another cause for climate change. Volcanic eruption throws up lots of aerosols into the atmosphere. These aerosols remain in the atmosphere for a considerable period of time, reducing the amount of sun's radiation reaching the Earth's surface.
  - ➢ After the recent **Pinatoba and El Cion volcanic eruptions**, the average temperature of the Earth fell to some extent for some years.
  - ➢ The most important anthropogenic effect on the climate is the increasing trend in the **concentration of greenhouse gases** in the atmosphere which is likely to cause global warming.

Global Warming

- Due to the presence of greenhouse gases, the atmosphere is behaving like a greenhouse. The atmosphere also transmits the incoming solar radiation but **absorbs the vast majority of long wave radiation** emitted upwards by the Earth's surface.
- The gases that absorb long-wave radiation are called **greenhouse gases**. The processes that warm the atmosphere are often collectively referred to as the **Greenhouse Effect.**
- **Global Warming** is the **long-term warming** of the planet's overall temperature.
  - ➢ Though this warming trend has been **going on for a long time**, its pace has significantly increased in the **last hundred years** due to the **burning of fossil fuels**. As the human

population has increased, so has the volume of fossil fuels burned. **Fossil fuels include coal, oil, and natural gas**, and burning them causes what is known as the **"Greenhouse Effect" in Earth's atmosphere.**

The term **'Greenhouse'** is derived from the analogy to a greenhouse used in cold areas for preserving heat. A greenhouse is made up of glass. The glass, which is transparent to incoming shortwave solar radiation, is opaque to outgoing long-wave radiation. The glass, therefore, allows in more radiation and prevents the long wave radiation from going outside the glass house, causing the temperature inside the glasshouse structure to be warmer than outside. When you enter a car or a bus, during summer, when windows are closed, you feel more heat than outside. Likewise, during winter, the vehicles with closed doors and windows remain warmer than the temperature outside. This is another example of the greenhouse effect.

Green House Gases (GHGs)

- **The primary GHGs of concern** today are **Carbon Dioxide (CO_2), Chlorofluorocarbons (CFCs), Methane (CH_4), Nitrous Oxide (N_2O) and Ozone (O_3).** Some other gases such as **Nitric Oxide (NO) and Carbon Monoxide (CO)** easily react with GHGs and affect their concentration in the atmosphere. **Water Vapour** which is responsible overall for about half of all atmospheric gas forcing. Water vapour and clouds are more dynamic atmospheric constituents and contribute strong climate change feedback influences.
- Other **short-lived gases (e.g. carbon monoxide, NO)** and **aerosols (e.g. mineral dust, black carbon)** that also vary more strongly over location and time.
- **Ozone** has warming influences comparable to nitrous oxide and CFCs, and is **longer lived and more abundant** in the **stratosphere** than in the troposphere.
- Many **refrigerants and other halogenated gases** also cause GHG effect. The **Chloro-fluorocarbons (CFCs)** are highly effective. These are products of human activity.

Physical Drivers of Climate Change

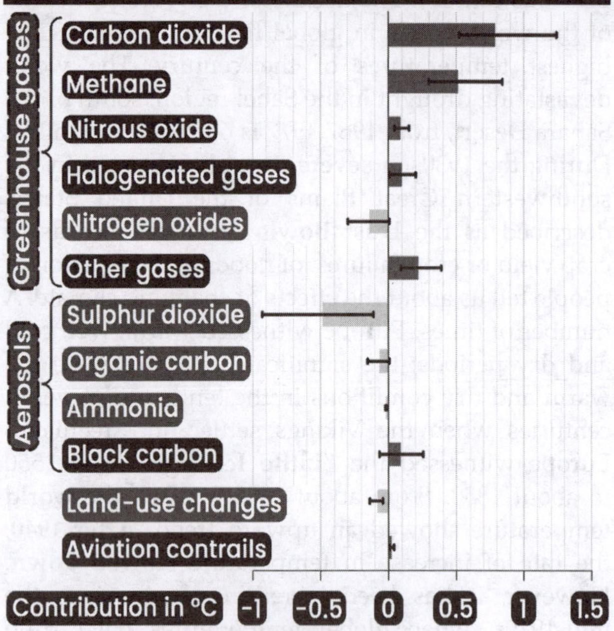

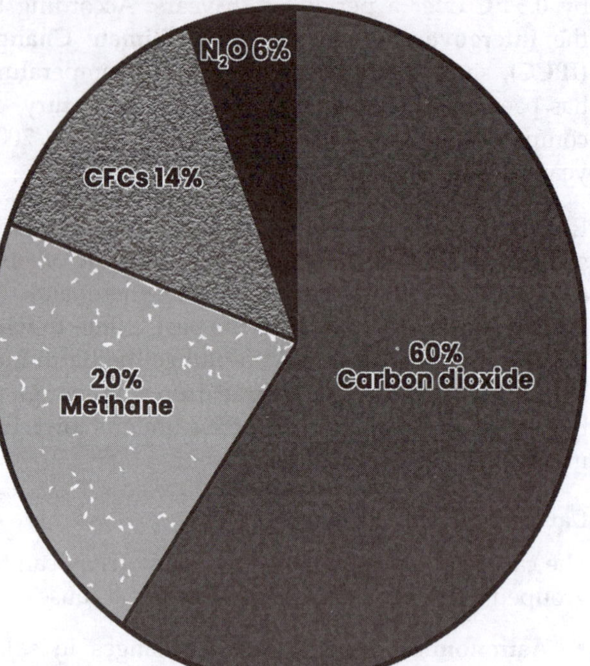

Relative Contribution of Various Greenhouse Gases to Total Global Warming

Green House Gases

The Main Greenhouse Gases

Compound	Pre-industrial concentration (ppmv*)	concentration in 2020 (ppmv)	Atmospheric lifetime (years)	Main human activity source	GWP**
Carbon dioxide (CO_2)	278	413	variable	Fossil fuels, cement production, land use change	1
Methane (CH_4)	0.722	1.889	12	Fossil fuels, rice paddies, waste dumps, livestock	28
Nitrous oxide (N_2O)	0.27	0.333	121	Fertilizers, combustion industrial processes	265
HFC 23 (CHF_3)	0	0.000024***	222	Electronics, refrigerants	12,400
HFC 134a (CF_3CH_2F)	0	0.000062***	13	Refrigerants	1,300
HFC 152a (CH_3CHF_2)	0	0.0000064***	1.5	Industrial processes	138
Perfluoromethane (CF_4)	0.00004	0.000079***	50,000	Aluminum production	6,630
Perfluoroethane (C_2F_6)	0	0.0000041***	10,000	Aluminum production	11,100
Sulphur hexafluoride (SF_6)	0	0.0000073***	3,200	Electrical insulation	23,500

*ppmv = parts per million by volume, **GWP = 100-year global warming potential, ***Concentration in 2011
Water vapour not included in table.

Greenhouse Gases Factsheet (Source Center for Sustainable Systems)

- The effectiveness of any given GHG molecule will depend on the magnitude of the **increase in its concentration, its lifetime** in the atmosphere and the **wavelength of radiation** that it absorbs.
  - ➢ Another important point is that the **more time** the GHG molecule remains in the atmosphere, the **longer it will take** for earth's atmospheric system **to recover** from any change brought about by the latter.
- **Ozone,** which absorbs ultraviolet radiation in the stratosphere, is very effective in absorbing terrestrial radiation when it is present in the lower troposphere.
  - ➢ Ozone occurs in the **stratosphere** where ultra-violet rays convert oxygen into ozone. Thus, ultraviolet rays do not reach the earth's surface. The CFCs which drift into the stratosphere destroy the ozone. Large depletion of ozone occurs over Antarctica.
  - ➢ The **depletion of ozone concentration** in the stratosphere is called the **Ozone Hole.** This allows the ultraviolet rays to pass through the troposphere.
- The **largest concentration** of GHGs in the atmosphere is **Carbon Dioxide**. The emission of CO_2 comes mainly from **fossil fuel combustion** (oil, gas and coal). Forests and oceans are the sinks for carbon dioxide. Forests use CO_2 in their growth. So, **deforestation** due to changes in land use, also increases the concentration of CO_2.
  - ➢ The time taken for atmospheric CO_2 to adjust to changes in sources to sinks is **20-50 years.** It is **rising at about 0.5 per cent annually**.
  - ➢ **Doubling of concentration of CO_2 over pre-industrial level** is used as an index for estimating the changes in climate in climatic models.
- International efforts have been initiated for reducing the emission of GHGs into the atmosphere through the UN Framework Convention on Climate Change.
- One such initiative was the Kyoto Protocol, which set binding climate targets for industrialised nations.
- Proclaimed in 1997. This Protocol went into effect for its First Phase from 2005-2012. Its Second Phase (2012-2020) was much less successful with many industrialised countries like USA and Canada

withdrawing, and many others like Russia and Middle Eastern economies not ratifying.

- Another ongoing effort is the Paris Agreement 2016, which seeks to set voluntary targets for climate change mitigation for all nations, with a goal to limit climate change to 1.5 degree Celsius from pre-industrial levels.
    - The increasing trend in the concentration of GHGs in the atmosphere may, **in the long run, warm up the earth.** Once global warming sets in, it won't be easy **to reverse** it.
    - The effect of global warming **may not be uniform** everywhere. Nevertheless, the adverse effect due to global warming will adversely affect the life supporting system.
    - **Rise in the sea level** due to **melting of glaciers and ice-caps and thermal expansion of the sea** may inundate large parts of the coastal area and islands, leading to **social problems.** This is another cause for serious concern for the world community.
    - Efforts have already been initiated to control the emission of GHGs and to arrest the trend towards global warming.
    - The **annual average near-surface air temperature** of the world is approximately **14°C.** An increasing trend in temperature was discernible in the 20th century.
        - The **most significant warming of the 20th century** was during the two periods, **1901-44 and 1977-99.** Over each of these two periods, global temperatures rose by about 0.4°C. In between, there was a slight cooling, which was more marked in the Northern Hemisphere.
    - The **globally averaged annual mean temperature** at the end of the 20th century was about **0.6°C above** that recorded at the end of the 19th century. The seven warmest years during the 1856-2000 were recorded in the last decade. The year **1998 was the warmest year for the 20th century and 2023 was the hottest year globally since records began in 1850.**

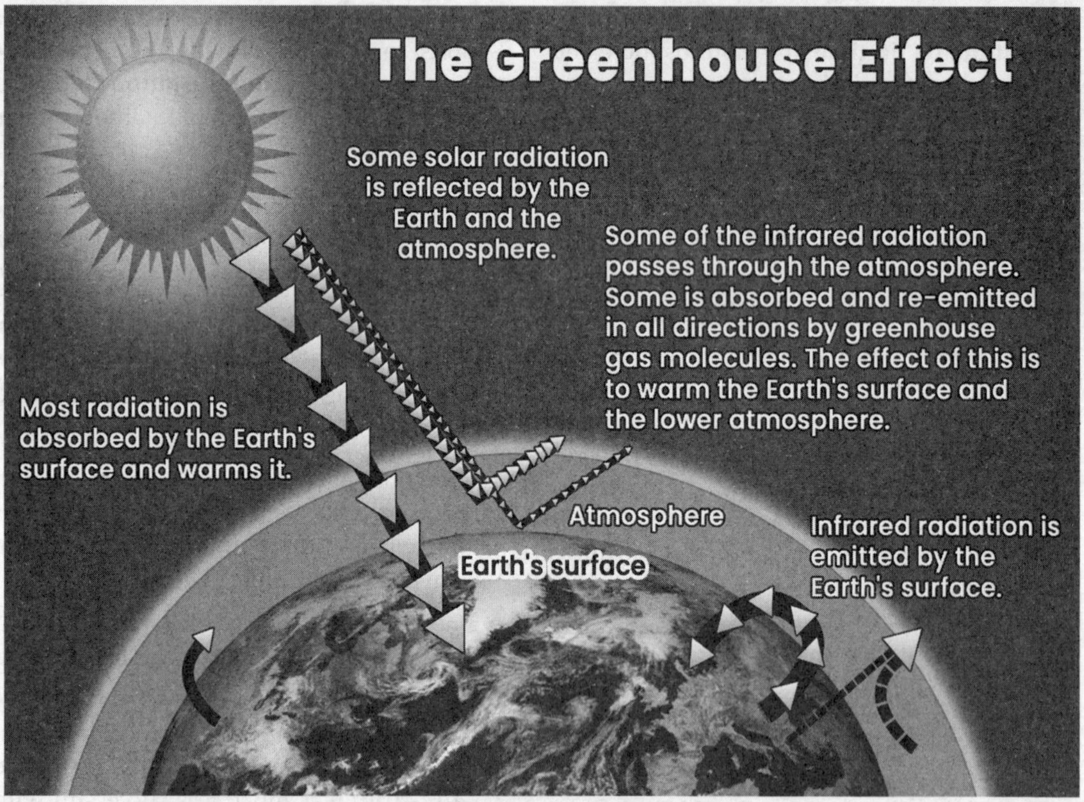

Greenhouse Effect

TEST YOURSELF

Multiple Choice Questions

Q1. The Koppen's classification system is based on:

(a) Temperature and rainfall

(b) Temperature and pressure

(c) Pressure and wind direction

(d) Wind direction and rainfall

Q2. Which of the following characteristics is typical of a tropical humid climate?

(a) Dry and hot weather throughout the year

(b) Seasonal variations with mild winters

(c) Freezing temperatures and heavy snowfall

(d) Extreme cold and arid conditions

Q3. In which belt is the tropical humid climate generally found?

(a) Equatorial belt (b) Subtropical belt

(c) Polar belt (d) Temperate belt

Q4. The main factor responsible for the high temperature in tropical humid regions is:

(a) Latitude (b) Altitude

(c) Ocean currents (d) Solar insolation

Q5. Which of the following is NOT a characteristic of mid-latitude climates?

(a) Moderate temperature ranges

(b) Abundant rainfall throughout the year

(c) Distinct seasons

(d) Variable weather patterns

Q6. Which type of mid-latitude climate is characterised by hot summers and cold winters, with a moderate amount of precipitation throughout the year?

(a) Mediterranean climate

(b) Marine west coast climate

(c) Humid continental climate

(d) Subarctic climate

Q7. Greenhouse gases trap heat in the Earth's atmosphere by:

(a) Reflecting sunlight back into space

(b) Absorbing heat from the Earth's surface

(c) Creating a protective layer around the planet

(d) Decreasing the concentration of oxygen in the atmosphere

Q8. Which gas is primarily responsible for the greenhouse effect?

(a) Carbon dioxide (CO_2)

(b) Methane (CH_4)

(c) Water Vapour (H_2O)

(d) Nitrous oxide (N_2O)

Q9. The region near the Equator experiences which type of climate?

(a) Tropical climate

(b) Mediterranean climate

(c) Continental climate

(d) Polar climate

Q10. The climate zone characterised by hot and humid conditions with abundant rainfall throughout the year is:

(a) Tropical rainforest (b) Mediterranean

(c) Desert (d) Tundra

Q11. The climate zone characterised by mild, wet winters and hot, dry summers is:

(a) Tropical rainforest (b) Mediterranean

(c) Desert (d) Tundra

Q12. The climate zone characterised by low rainfall and extreme temperature variations is:

(a) Tropical rainforest (b) Mediterranean

(c) Desert (d) Tundra

Q13. The climate zone characterised by extremely cold temperatures and low precipitation is:

(a) Tropical rainforest (b) Mediterranean

(c) Desert (d) Tundra

Q14. The increase in the Earth's average temperature due to human activities is referred to as:

(a) Weathering (b) Global Warming

(c) Plate tectonics (d) Erosion

Q15. The main greenhouse gas responsible for climate change is:

(a) Oxygen (O_2) (b) Nitrogen (N_2)

(c) Carbon dioxide (CO_2) (d) Argon (Ar)

Answers Key

Q1.	a	Q2.	b	Q3.	a
Q4.	d	Q5.	b	Q6.	c
Q7.	b	Q8.	a	Q9.	a
Q10.	a	Q11.	b	Q12.	c
Q13.	d	Q14.	b	Q15.	c

Model Questions for Main Examination

Q1. Explain the concept of the greenhouse effect and its role in shaping the Earth's climate.

Q2. Discuss the potential consequences of enhanced greenhouse effect due to human activities. Suggest measures that can be taken to mitigate the adverse effects of this phenomenon.

UNIT 15

Climate of India

In This Unit

Comprehensive and profound coverage of the following NCERTs' chapters:

- ✓ NCERT Class- 9th (Contemporary India-I), Chapter- 4
- ✓ NCERT Class- 11th (India Physical Environment), Chapter- 4

Climate refers to the sum total of weather conditions and variations over a large area for a long period of time (more than thirty years). **Weather** refers to the state of the atmosphere over an area at any point in time.

The common elements of Weather and Climate include temperature, atmospheric pressure, wind, humidity and precipitation.

Weather is the momentary state of the atmosphere, while **Climate** refers to the average of the weather conditions over a longer period of time. Weather changes quickly, maybe within a day or week, but climate changes are imperceptible and may be noted after 50 years or even more.

- The Climate of India is described as the **'Monsoon'** type. In **Asia**, this type of climate is found mainly in the **south and the southeast**.
- The word **'monsoon'** is derived from the **Arabic word 'mausim'**, which literally means **season**. **'Monsoon' refers to the seasonal reversal in the direction of the wind during a year.**
- The Climate of India is strongly influenced by monsoon winds. The sailors who came to India in historic times were one of the first to have noticed the phenomenon of the monsoon. They benefited from the reversal of the wind system as they came by sailing ships at the mercy of winds. The Arabs, who had also come to India as traders named this seasonal reversal of the wind system **'monsoon'**.

Unity and Diversity in the Monsoon Climate

This view of broad unity of the monsoon type of climate should not, however, lead one to ignore its **regional variations,** which differentiate the weather and climate of different regions of India.

The climate of India has many regional variations expressed in the **pattern of winds, temperature and rainfall, rhythm of seasons and the degree of wetness or dryness.** Let us take a closer look at these regional variations in temperature, winds and rainfall.

Variations in Temperature

- While in the summer, the mercury occasionally touches **55°C in the western Rajasthan**, it drops down to as low as **minus 45°C in winter around Leh**.
- On a December night, the temperature in Drass (Ladakh) may drop down to **minus 45°C** while Thiruvananthapuram or Chennai records **20°C or 22°C** on the same night. These examples confirm seasonal variations in temperature from place to place and region to region in India.

Variations in Rainfall

- While snowfall occurs in the Himalayas, it only rains over the rest of the country. Similarly, variations are noticeable not only in the type of precipitation but also in its amount. While **Cherrapunji and Mawsynram in the Khasi Hills of Meghalaya** receive rainfall over **1,080 cm in** a year, **Jaisalmer in Rajasthan** rarely gets more than **9 cm of rainfall** during the same period.

- **Tura** situated in the **Garo Hills of Meghalaya** may receive an amount of rainfall in a single day which is equal to **10 years of rainfall at Jaisalmer**.
- The **Ganga delta and the coastal plains of Odisha** are hit by strong **rain-bearing** storms almost every third or fifth day in July and August, while the **Coromandel coast,** a thousand km to the south, generally goes **dry** during these months.

In spite of these differences and variations, the climate of India is **monsoonal in rhythm and character.**

Factors Determining the Climate of India

India's climate is controlled by a number of factors, which can be broadly divided into two groups:

- Factors related to **Location and Relief**
- Factors related to **Air Pressure and Winds**

Factors Related to Location and Relief

- **Latitude:**
  - ➢ The **Tropic of Cancer** passes through the central part of India from the Rann of Kuchchh in the west to Mizoram in the east. Thus, the **northern part of India lies in a sub-tropical and temperate zone** and the part lying **south** of the Tropic of Cancer falls in the **tropical zone.**
    - ♦ The **Tropical Zone,** being nearer to the equator, experiences **high temperatures** throughout the year with **small daily and annual ranges.**
    - ♦ The area **north of the Tropic of Cancer,** which is away from the equator, experiences **an extreme climate** with a high daily and annual range of temperature.
- **The Himalayan Mountains**
  - ➢ **The lofty Himalayas in the north along with its extensions act as an effective 'Climatic Divide'.** The towering mountain chain provides an invincible shield to protect the subcontinent from the cold northern winds.
  - ➢ These **cold and chilly winds** originate near the **Arctic Circle** and blow across **central and eastern Asia**. The Himalayas also **trap the monsoon winds**, forcing them to shed their moisture within the subcontinent.
- **Distribution of Land and Water**
  - ➢ India is flanked by the Indian Ocean on **three sides** in the **south** and girdled by a **high and continuous mountain-wall in the north**. As compared to the landmass, water **heats up or cools down slowly.**
  - ➢ This **'Differential Heating of land and sea'** creates different air pressure zones in different seasons in and around the Indian subcontinent. Difference in air pressure causes **reversal in the direction** of monsoon winds.
- **Distance from the Sea**
  - ➢ With a long coastline, large coastal areas have an **equable climate**. Areas in the interior of India are far away from the moderating influence of the sea. Such areas have extremes of climate. That is why the people of **Mumbai and the Konkan coast** have hardly any idea of extremes of temperature and the seasonal rhythm of weather.
  - ➢ On the other hand, the **seasonal contrasts** in weather at places **in the interior** of the country, such as **Delhi, Kanpur and Amritsar,** affect the entire sphere of life.
- **Altitude**
  - ➢ Temperature decreases with height. Due to thin air, **places in the mountains** are **cooler than places on the plains.**
  - ➢ For example, **Agra and Darjeeling** are located at the **same latitude**, but the temperature in January in Agra is **16°C,** whereas it is only **4°C** in Darjeeling.
- **Relief**
  - ➢ The **physiography or relief** of India also affects the **temperature, air pressure, direction and speed of wind and the amount and distribution of rainfall.**
  - ➢ The **windward sides of Western Ghats and Assam** get **wet** during June-September whereas the **southern plateau** remains **dry** due to its **leeward situation** along the Western Ghats.

Factors Related to Air Pressure and Wind

To understand the **differences in local climates of India,** we need to understand the **mechanism of the following three factors:**

- **Distribution of Air Pressure and Winds** on the surface of the earth.
- **Upper-air circulation** is caused by factors **controlling global weather** and the **inflow of different Air Masses and Jet Streams.**
- **The inflow of western cyclones**, generally known as **'Western Disturbances'** during the **winter** season and **Tropical Depressions** during the **southwest monsoon** period in India, creates weather conditions favourable for rainfall.

The mechanism of these three factors can be understood with reference to winter and summer seasons of the year separately.

Mechanism of Weather in the Winter Season

- **Surface Pressure and Winds:** In winter months, the weather conditions over India are generally influenced by the distribution of pressure in Central and Western Asia.
    - A high pressure, centre in the region lying to the north of the Himalayas develops during winter. This centre of **high pressure** gives **rise to the flow of air** at the low level from the **north towards** the Indian subcontinent, south of the mountain range.
    - The surface winds blowing out of the high pressure centred over **Central Asia**, reach India in the form of a **Dry Continental Air Mass**. These continental winds come in contact with **Trade Winds over north-western India**.
    - The position of this contact zone is not, however, stable. Occasionally, it may shift its position as far east as the **middle Ganga valley** with the result that the whole of the **north-western and northern India** up to the middle Ganga valley comes under the influence of dry north-western winds.
- **Jet Stream and Upper Air Circulation:** The pattern of air circulation is witnessed only at the lower level of the atmosphere near the surface of the earth.
    - Higher up in the lower troposphere, about three km above the surface of the earth, a different pattern of air circulation is observed. All of Western and Central Asia remains under the influence of **westerly winds** along an altitude of 9-13 km from west to east.
    - These winds blow **across the Asian continent** at latitudes north of the Himalayas, roughly **parallel to the Tibetan highlands**. These are known as **Jet Streams**.

ROSSBY WAVES

Rossby Waves are a type of planetary jet-stream winds that **meander** from north to south and back again, while the usual jet stream generally travels at the same latitude. They are usually found near tropopause at very high velocities in sinusoidal movement. **The Coriolis Force** varies with latitude, which causes the Rossby wave to emerge in the planet's atmosphere and oceans. Rossby waves are formed when **polar air moves toward the Equator while tropical air is moving poleward**. Because of the temperature difference between the Equator and the poles due to differences in the amounts of solar radiation received, **heat tends to flow from low to high latitudes**; this is accomplished, in part, by these air movements. Rossby waves are a dominant component of the **Ferrel circulation**. The existence of these waves explains the **low-pressure cells (cyclones) and high-pressure cells (anticyclones)** that are important in producing the weather of the middle and higher latitudes.

- Tibetan highlands **act as a barrier** in the path of these jet streams. As a result, jet streams get **bifurcated**.
- One of its branches blows to the **north of the Tibetan highlands**, while the southern branch blows in an **eastward direction, south of the Himalayas**.
- It is believed that this southern branch of the jet stream has an important influence on winter weather in India.

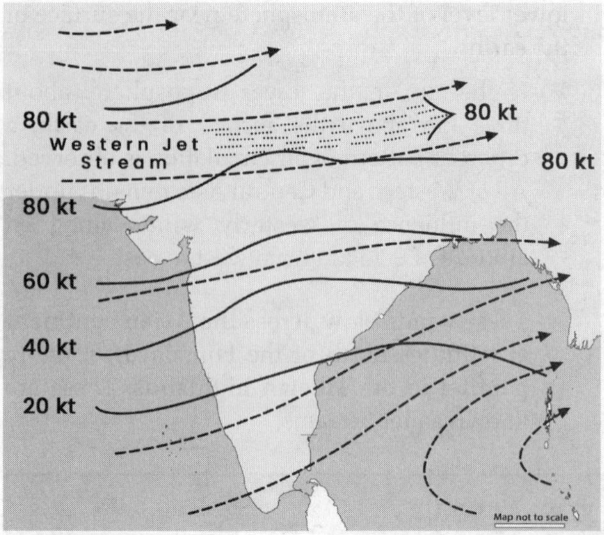

Direction of Winds in India in Winter at the Height of 9-13 km

- **Western Cyclonic Disturbance and Tropical Cyclones:** The western cyclonic disturbances that enter the Indian subcontinent from the west and the northwest during the **winter months** originate over the Mediterranean Sea and are brought into India by the **Westerly Jet Stream.**
    - ➢ An **increase in the prevailing night temperature** generally indicates an advance in the arrival of these cyclone disturbances.
    - ➢ **At this time, Tropical Cyclones** originate over the Bay of Bengal and the Indian Ocean. These tropical cyclones have **very high wind velocity and heavy rainfall** and hit the Tamil Nadu, Andhra Pradesh and Odisha coasts. Most of these cyclones are very destructive due to **high wind velocity and torrential rain** that accompanies them.

Inter Tropical Convergence Zone (ITCZ)

The **Inter Tropical Convergence Zone (ITCZ)** is a low-pressure, zone located at the equator where **trade winds converge**, and so, it is a zone where **air tends to ascend**.

In Summers in July, the ITCZ is located around **20°N-25°N** latitudes (over the Gangetic plain), sometimes called the **'Monsoon Trough'.** This monsoon trough encourages the development of **thermal low** over north and northwest India. Due to the shift of ITCZ, the **trade winds of the southern hemisphere cross the equator** between **40° and 60°E** longitudes and start blowing from **southwest to northeast** due to the **Coriolis Force**. It becomes **Southwest Monsoon**.

In Winters, the ITCZ moves southward, and so the **reversal of winds** from northeast to south and southwest, takes place. They are called **Northeast Monsoon.**

Coriolis Force

It is an **apparent force** caused by the **earth's rotation.** The Coriolis force is responsible for **deflecting winds** towards the right in the northern hemisphere and towards the left in the southern hemisphere. This is also known as **'Ferrel's Law'**.

Mechanism of Weather in the Summer Season

- **Surface Pressure and Winds:** As the summer sets in and the sun shifts northwards, the **wind circulation** over the subcontinent undergoes a **complete reversal at both the lower as well as the upper levels**.
    - ➢ In the middle of July, the **low-pressure belt** nearer the surface (termed as **Inter Tropical Convergence Zone (ITCZ)**) shifts northwards, roughly parallel to the Himalayas between **20° N and 25° N**. By this time, the **Westerly Jet Stream** withdraws from the Indian region.
    - ➢ In fact, meteorologists have found an **interrelationship between the northward shift of the equatorial trough (ITCZ) and the withdrawal of the westerly jet stream from over the North Indian Plain**. The ITCZ, being a zone of low pressure, attracts an inflow of winds from different directions.
    - ➢ The **Maritime Tropical Airmass (mT)** from the southern hemisphere, after crossing the equator, rushes to the low pressure area in the general **south-westerly direction**. It is this moist air current which is popularly known as the **'Southwest Monsoon'**.

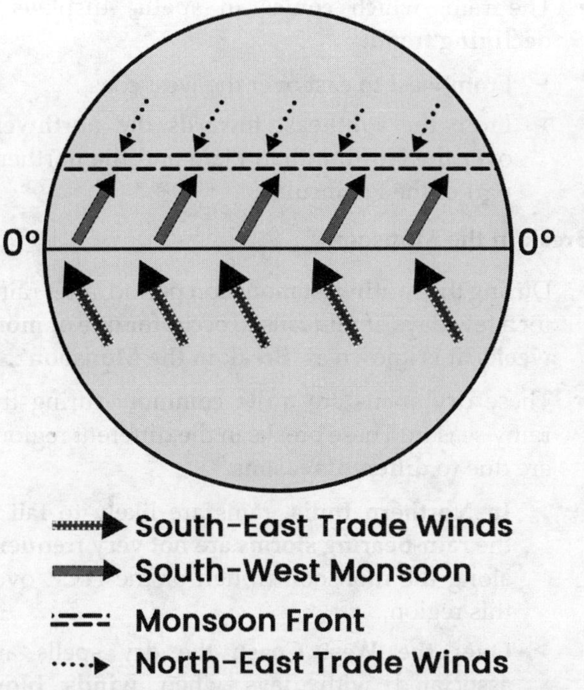

Northward shifting of ITCZ and the wind system in summer season of northern hemisphere.

- **Jet Streams and Upper Air Circulation:** The pattern of pressure and winds, as mentioned above is formed **only at** the level of the **troposphere**.
  - ➢ An **Easterly Jet Stream** flows over the southern part of the **Peninsula** in June and has a **maximum speed of 90 km per hour**.
  - ➢ In August, it is confined to **15°N latitude**, and in September up to **22°N latitude**. The easterlies normally do not extend to the north of 30°N latitude in the upper atmosphere.

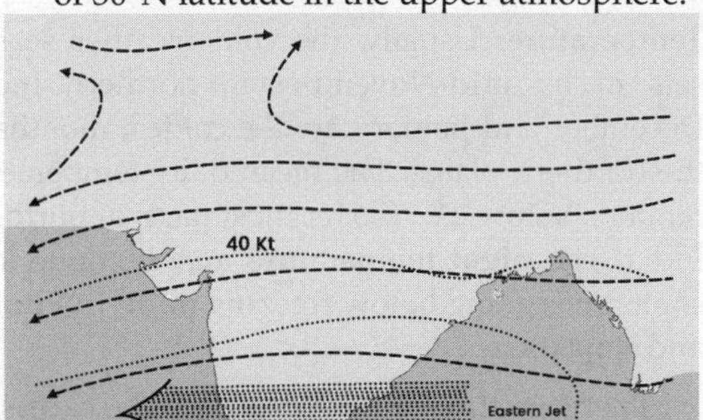

The Direction of Winds at 13 km Altitude in Summer Season

- **Easterly Jet Stream and Tropical Cyclones:** The easterly jet stream steers the **Tropical Depressions** into India. These depressions play a significant role in the **distribution of monsoon rainfall** over the Indian subcontinent. The tracks of these depressions are the areas of highest rainfall in India.

The Nature of Indian Monsoon

- Monsoons are a familiar, though **little-known**, climatic phenomenon. Many attempts have been made to discover the **exact nature and causation** of monsoons, but so far, **no single theory** has been able to explain the monsoon fully.
- A **real breakthrough** has come recently, when it was studied **at the global rather than at the regional level**. Systematic studies of the causes of rainfall in the South Asian region help to understand the **causes and salient features** of the monsoon, particularly some of its important aspects, such as:
  - ➢ The Onset of the Monsoon.
  - ➢ Rain-bearing Systems (e.g., tropical cyclones) and the Relationship between their Frequency and Distribution of Monsoon Rainfall.
  - ➢ Break in the Monsoon.

Onset of the Monsoon

- Towards the end of the nineteenth century, it was believed that the **differential heating of land and sea** during the summer months is the mechanism which sets the stage for the **monsoon winds to drift towards the subcontinent**.
  - ➢ During April and May, when the sun shines **vertically over the Tropic of Cancer**, the large **landmass** in the north of the Indian Ocean gets **intensely heated.** This causes the formation of an **intense low pressure** in the northwestern part of the subcontinent.
  - ➢ Since the pressure in the Indian Ocean in the south of the landmass is high as the **water gets heated slowly**, the **low-pressure cell** attracts the southeast trades across the Equator. **These conditions help in the northward shift in the position of the ITCZ.**
  - ➢ The southwest monsoon may thus be seen as a **continuation of the Southeast Trades**

deflected towards the Indian subcontinent after crossing the Equator. These winds **cross the Equator** between **40°E and 60°E** longitudes.

- The **shift in the position of the ITCZ** is also related to the phenomenon of the **withdrawal of the Westerly Jet Stream** from its position over the north Indian plain, south of the Himalayas.
  - The **Easterly Jet Stream sets in** along at a **15°N latitude** only after the westerly jet stream has withdrawn itself from the region. **This easterly jet stream is held responsible for the burst of the monsoon in India.**
- **Entry of Monsoon into India:** The southwest monsoon sets in over the **Kerala coast by 1st June** and moves swiftly to reach Mumbai and Kolkata between 10th and 13th June. By mid-July, southwest monsoon **engulfs the entire subcontinent**.

Rain-Bearing Systems and Rainfall Distribution

- There seem to be **two rain-bearing systems** in India.
  - **First** originates in the **Bay of Bengal,** causing rainfall over the **plains of north India**.
  - **Second** is the **Arabian Sea current** of the south- west monsoon which brings rain to the **west coast** of India.
- **Much of the rainfall** along the Western Ghats is **Orographic** as the moist air is obstructed and forced to rise along the Ghats. **The intensity of rainfall over the west coast of India is, however, related to two factors:**
  - **Offshore Meteorological Conditions**
  - **Position of the Equatorial Jet Stream** along the **eastern coast of Africa**
- The **frequency of the tropical depressions** originating from the Bay of Bengal **varies** from year to year. Their paths over India are mainly determined by the position of ITCZ which is generally termed as the **'Monsoon Trough'**.
- As the axis of the **monsoon trough oscillates**, there are fluctuations in the **track and direction** of these depressions, and the **intensity and the amount of rainfall** vary from year to year.
- The rain, which **comes in spells**, displays a **declining trend.**
  - **From west to east** over the west coast.
  - From the **southeast towards the northwest** over the North Indian Plain and the northern part of the Peninsula.

Break in the Monsoon

- During the **southwest monsoon** period, after rains for a few days, if rain fails to occur for **one or more weeks**, it is known as **'Break in the Monsoon'.**
- These dry spells are **quite common** during the rainy season. These breaks in the different regions are due to **different reasons:**
  - **In Northern India,** rains are likely to fail if the **rain-bearing storms are not very frequent** along the monsoon trough or the ITCZ over this region.
  - **Over the West Coast,** the dry spells are associated with days when **winds blow parallel** to the coast.

The Rhythm of Seasons

The climatic conditions of India can best be described in terms of an 'Annual Cycle of Seasons'. Meteorologists recognise the following **four seasons**:

- The Cold Weather Season
- The Hot Weather Season
- The Southwest Monsoon Season
- The Retreating Monsoon Season

The Cold Weather Season

- **Temperature:** Usually, the cold weather season sets in by **mid-November** in northern India. December and January are the coldest months in the northern plains. The mean daily temperature remains **below 21°°C** over most parts of northern India. The **night temperature** may be quite low, sometimes going **below freezing point in Punjab and Rajasthan.**
  - There are three main reasons for the excessive cold in north India during this season:
    - States like Punjab, Haryana and Rajasthan are **far away from the moderating influence of sea** experience **continental climate.**

- ♦ The **snowfall in the nearby Himalayan ranges** creates a cold wave situation.
- ♦ Around February, the **cold winds coming from the Caspian Sea and Turkmenistan** bring cold waves along with **frost and fog** over the northwestern parts of India.
- ➢ The **Peninsular region of India**, however, **does not have any well-defined cold weather season.** There is hardly any seasonal change in the distribution pattern of the temperature in coastal areas because of **moderating influence of the sea and the proximity to equator.**
    - ♦ For example, the mean maximum temperature for January at Thiruvananthapuram and temperatures at the hills of Western Ghats remain comparatively low.

- **Pressure and Winds:** By the end of December (22nd December), the sun shines vertically over the Tropic of Capricorn in the southern hemisphere. The weather in this season is characterised by **feeble high pressure** conditions over the northern plain. In south India, the air pressure is slightly lower. As a result, **winds start blowing from northwestern high pressure zone to the low air pressure zone** over the Indian Ocean in the south.
    - ➢ **Due to low pressure gradient,** the light winds with a low velocity of about 3-5 km per hour begin to blow outwards. By and large, the **topography of the region** influences the wind direction. They are **westerly or north-westerly** down the Ganga Valley. They become **northerly in the Ganga-Brahmaputra delta.** Free from the influence of topography, they are clearly **northeasterly over the Bay of Bengal.**
    - ➢ During the winter, the weather in India is pleasant. The pleasant weather conditions, however, at intervals, get disturbed by **shallow cyclonic depressions** originating over the **east Mediterranean Sea** and travelling eastwards across **West Asia, Iran, Afghanistan and Pakistan** before they reach the northwestern parts of India. On their way, the moisture content gets augmented from the Caspian Sea in the north and the Persian Gulf in the south.

- **Rainfall: Winter monsoons do not cause rainfall as they move from land to the sea**. This is because, **firstly**, they have little humidity; **secondly,** due to **anticyclonic circulation** on land the possibility of rainfall from them is reduced. So, most parts of India do not have rainfall in the winter season. However, there are some exceptions to it:
    - ➢ **In northwestern India**, some **weak temperate cyclones from the Mediterranean Sea** cause rainfall in Punjab, Haryana, Delhi and western Uttar Pradesh. Although the amount is meagre, it is **highly beneficial for rabi crops.** The precipitation is in the form of **snowfall in the lower Himalayas.** It is this snow that **sustains the flow of water** in the Himalayan rivers during the summer months.
        - ♦ The precipitation decreases **from west to east** in the plains and from **north to south** in the mountains.
    - ➢ **Central parts of India** and **northern parts of the southern peninsula** also get occasional winter rainfall.
    - ➢ **Arunachal Pradesh and Assam** in the northeastern parts of India also have rains between **25 mm and 50 mm** during these winter months.
    - ➢ During October and November, **northeast monsoon** while crossing over the Bay of Bengal, picks up moisture and causes **torrential rainfall over the Tamil Nadu coast, southern Andhra Pradesh, southeast Karnataka and southeast Kerala.**

The Hot Weather Season

- **Temperature:** With the apparent **northward movement of the sun** towards the Tropic of Cancer in March, temperatures start rising in north India. **April, May, and June** are the months of summer in northern India. In **most parts of India,** temperatures recorded are between **30°-32°C.**
    - ➢ In March, the highest day temperature of about **38°C** occurs in the Deccan Plateau while in April, temperature ranging between 38°C and 43°C are found in Gujarat and Madhya Pradesh. In May, the **heat belt moves further north**, and in the **north-western** part of India, temperatures around **48°C** are not uncommon.

➢ The hot weather season is **mild in south India** and **intense in north India.**

♦ The Peninsular situation of South India, with **the moderating effect of the oceans,** keeps the temperatures lower than that prevailing in North India. So, temperatures remain between **26°C and 32°C.**

♦ **Due to altitude**, the temperatures in the **hills of Western Ghats** remain **below 25°C.**

♦ **In the coastal regions**, the **north-south extent of Isotherms parallel to the coast** confirms that temperature does not decrease from **north to south.** Rather, it increases from the **coast to the interior**. The mean daily minimum temperature during the summer months also remains quite high and rarely goes below 26°C.

- **Pressure and Winds:** The summer months are a period of **excessive heat and falling air pressure in the northern half** of the country. Because of the heating of the subcontinent, the **ITCZ moves northwards** occupying a position **centred at 25°N** in July. The location of the ITCZ attracts a **surface circulation of the winds** which are **South Westerly on the west coast** as well as along the coast of West Bengal and Bangladesh. They are **Easterly or South-Easterly over north Bengal and Bihar.**

➢ In the heart of the ITCZ in the northwest, the **dry and hot winds** known as **'Loo'** blow in the afternoon, and very often, they continue well into midnight.

➢ **Dust Storms** in the evening are very common during May in **Punjab, Haryana, Eastern Rajasthan and Uttar Pradesh**. These temporary storms bring a welcome respite from the oppressing heat since they bring with them **light rains and a pleasant cool breeze**. Occasionally, the moisture-laden winds are attracted towards the periphery of the trough. A **sudden contact between dry and moist air masses** gives rise to local storms of great intensity. These local storms are associated with **violent winds, torrential rains and even hailstorms.**

Some Famous Local Storms of Hot Weather Season

1. **Mango Shower**: Towards the end of summer, there are **pre-monsoon showers,** which are a common phenomenon in **Kerala and coastal areas of Karnataka**. Locally, they are known as **'Mango Showers'** since they help in the early ripening of mangoes.
2. **Blossom Shower**: With this shower, coffee flowers blossom in **Kerala and nearby areas.**
3. **Nor Westers**: These are dreaded **evening thunderstorms** in **Bengal and Assam**. Their notorious nature can be understood from the local nomenclature of **'Kalbaisakhi'**, a calamity of the month of **Baisakh.** These showers are useful for **tea, jute and rice** cultivation. In Assam, these storms are known as **'Bardoisila' or 'Bardoli Cheerha'.**
4. **Loo**: **Hot, dry and oppressing** winds blowing in the Northern plains from **Punjab to Bihar** with higher intensity between **Delhi and Patna**.

The Southwest Monsoon Season

- As a result of **the rapid increase of temperature** in May over the northwestern plains, the low-pressure conditions over there get further intensified. By early June, they are powerful enough to **attract the trade winds of the Southern Hemisphere** coming from the Indian Ocean. These **southeast trade winds cross the equator** and enter the Bay of Bengal and the Arabian Sea, only to be caught up in the **air circulation over India**. Passing over the **equatorial warm currents**, these bring with them moisture in abundance. After crossing the equator, they follow a **south-westerly direction**. That is why they are known as **'Southwest Monsoon'**.
- The rain in the southwest monsoon season **begins rather abruptly**. One result of the first rain is that it **brings down the temperature** substantially. This sudden onset of the moisture-laden winds associated with **violent thunder and lightning** is often termed as the **"Break"** or **"Burst"** of the monsoons.

➢ The monsoon may **burst in the first week of June** in the coastal areas of **Kerala, Karnataka,**

Goa, and Maharashtra, while in the interior parts of the country, it may be delayed until the first week of July. The day temperature registers a decline of 5°C to 8°C between mid-June and mid-July.

- As these winds approach the land, their south westerly direction is modified by the **relief and thermal low pressure** over northwest India. **The monsoon approaches the landmass in Two Branches:**
  - ➢ The Arabian Sea Branch
  - ➢ The Bay of Bengal Branch

Wind Direction during Southwest Monsoon Season

Monsoon Winds of the Arabian Sea Branch

The monsoon winds originating over the Arabian Sea further **split into Three Branches**:

- **One branch of it** is obstructed by the Western Ghats. These winds climb the slopes of the Western Ghats from 900-1200 m. Soon, they become cool, and as a result, the **windward side of the Sahyadris and Western Coastal Plain** receives **very heavy rainfall** ranging between 250 cm and 400 cm. After **crossing the Western Ghats**, these winds **descend and get heated up**. This reduces humidity in the winds. As a result, these winds cause **little rainfall** east of the Western Ghats. This region of low rainfall is known as the **'Rain-Shadow Area'**.

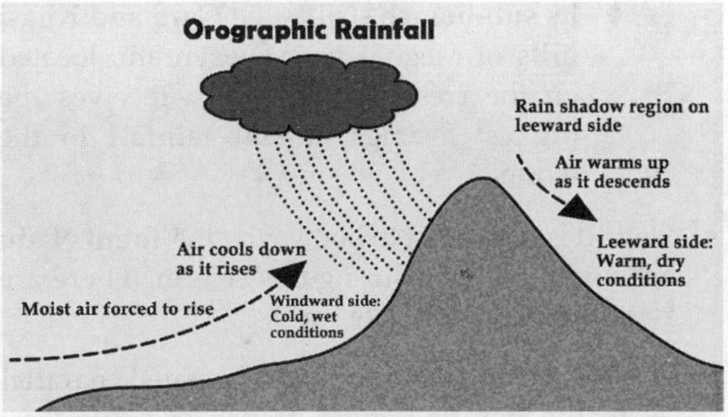

Orographic Rainfall during Monsoon Season

- **Second branch of the Arabian sea monsoon** strikes the coast **north of Mumbai**. Moving along the **Narmada and Tapi river valleys**, these winds cause rainfall in extensive areas of central India. The **Chotanagpur plateau** gets 15 cm rainfall from this part of the branch. Thereafter, they enter the Ganga plains and **mingle with the Bay of Bengal branch**.
- **The Third branch of this monsoon** wind strikes the **Saurashtra Peninsula and the Kachchh**. It then passes over **west Rajasthan and along the Aravalis**, causing only a **scanty rainfall**. In Punjab and Haryana, it too joins the Bay of Bengal branch. These two branches, reinforced by each other, cause **rains in the western Himalayas**.

Monsoon Winds of The Bay of Bengal Branch

- The **Bay of Bengal branch** strikes the coast of Myanmar and part of southeast Bangladesh. But the **Arakan Hills** along the coast of Myanmar **deflect a big portion** of this branch towards the Indian subcontinent. The monsoon, therefore, enters West Bengal and Bangladesh from the **south and southeast** instead of from the **south-westerly direction**.
- From here, this **branch 'splits into two'** under the influence of the Himalayas and the thermal low in Northwest India.
  - ➢ The First branch moves **westward along the Ganga plains** reaching, as far as the **Punjab plains.**
  - ➢ The Second branch **moves up the Brahmaputra valley in the north and the northeast**, causing widespread rains.

- Its **sub-branch** strikes the **Garo and Khasi hills** of Meghalaya. Mawsynram, located on the crest of Khasi hills, receives the **highest average annual rainfall** in the world.

- Here, it is important to know why the **Tamil Nadu coast remains dry** during this season. **There are two factors responsible for it:**

  - The Tamil Nadu coast is situated **parallel to the Bay of Bengal branch** of south-west monsoon.

  - It lies in the **rain-shadow area** of the Arabian Sea branch of the south-west monsoon.

Characteristics of Monsoonal Rainfall

- Rainfall received from the southwest monsoons is seasonal and occurs between **June and September.**
- Monsoonal rainfall is largely governed by **relief or topography**. For instance, the windward side of the Western Ghats register a rainfall of over 250 cm. Again, the heavy rainfall in the **north- eastern states** can be attributed to their hill ranges and the Eastern Himalayas.
- The monsoon rainfall has a **declining trend with increasing distance from the sea.** Kolkata receives 119 cm during the southwest monsoon period, Patna 105 cm, Allahabad 76 cm and Delhi 56 cm.
- The monsoon rains occur in **wet spells of few days**, duration at a time. The wet spells are interspersed with rainless interval known as **'Breaks'**. These breaks in rainfall are related to the cyclonic depressions mainly formed at the head of the Bay of Bengal, and their crossing into the mainland.
- Summer rainfall arrives in the form of **heavy downpours**, resulting in **significant runoff and soil erosion.**
- Monsoons hold a critical position in **India's agrarian economy as the southwest monsoon season** delivers over **three-quarters of the nation's total annual rainfall.**
- **The spatial distribution of rainfall is uneven,** ranging from as low as 12 cm to exceeding 250 cm.
- The commencement of the monsoon rains can be considerably delayed over the entire country or specific regions.
- The monsoons may occasionally conclude noticeably earlier than usual, inflicting substantial **damage on standing crops** and hindering the sowing of winter crops.

Season of Retreating Monsoon

- During the months of **October and November**, a period characterised by the retreat of the monsoon winds, a gradual weakening of the southwest monsoon becomes evident. This phenomenon coincides with the southward shift of **the low-pressure trough located over the Ganga Plain, a response to the sun's southward movement**.

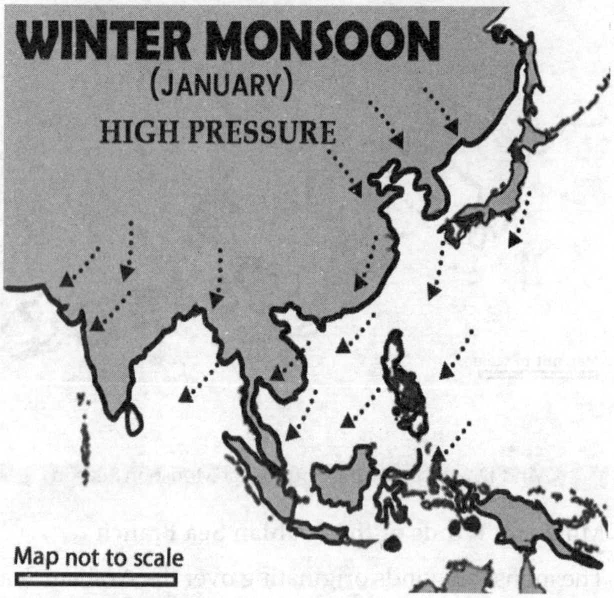

Wind Direction during Retreating Monsoon Season

- The monsoon retreats from **western Rajasthan** by the first week of September. It will withdraw from **Rajasthan, Gujarat, Western Ganga plain, and the Central Highlands** by the end of the month.

- By the beginning of October, the low pressure covers northern parts of the Bay of Bengal, and by early November, it will have moved over **Karnataka and Tamil Nadu. By the middle of December**, the centre of low pressure is completely removed from the Peninsula.

- The retreating southwest monsoon season is marked by **clear skies and a rise in temperature.** The land is still moist.
  - Owing to the conditions of **high temperature and humidity**, the weather becomes rather oppressive. This is commonly known as the **'October Heat'.**
- In the second half of October, the mercury begins to fall rapidly, particularly in northern India. The weather in the retreating monsoon is **dry in north India**, but it is associated with rain in the eastern part of the Peninsula. Here, October and November are the rainiest months of the year.
- The widespread rain in this season is associated with the **passage of cyclonic depressions** which originate over the Andaman Sea and manage to cross the eastern coast of the southern Peninsula. These **tropical cyclones** are very destructive.
  - The **thickly populated deltas** of the Godavari, Krishna and Kaveri are their preferred targets. Every year, cyclones bring disaster here.
  - A few cyclonic storms also strike the coast of **West Bengal, Bangladesh and Myanmar.**
  - A bulk of the rainfall of the Coromandel coast is derived from these depressions and cyclones. Such cyclonic storms are **less frequent in the Arabian Sea.**

Traditional Indian Seasons

In the Indian tradition, a year is divided into **six two-monthly seasons**. This cycle of seasons, which the common people in **north and central India** follow, is based on their **practical experience and age-old perception** of weather phenomena. However, this system **does not match the seasons of South India**, where there is little variation.

Seasons	Months (According to the Indian Calendar)	Months (According to the Gregorian Calendar)
Vasanta	Chaitra-Vaisakha	March-April
Grishma	Jyaistha-Asadha	May-June
Varsha	Sravana-Bhadra	July-August
Sharada	Asvina-Kartika	September -October
Hemanta	Margashirsa-Pausa	November -December
Shishira	Magha-Phalguna	January-February

Distribution and Variability of Rainfall

The average annual rainfall in India is about 125 cm, but it has great spatial variations.

- **Areas of High Rainfall:** The highest rainfall occurs along the west coast, on the Western Ghats, as well as in the sub-Himalayan areas of the northeast and the hills of Meghalaya. Here, the rainfall exceeds 200 cm. In some parts of Khasi and Jaintia hills, the rainfall exceeds 1,000 cm. In the Brahmaputra valley and the adjoining hills, the rainfall is less than 200 cm.
- **Areas of Medium Rainfall:** Rainfall between 100-200 cm is received in the southern parts of Gujarat, east Tamil Nadu, northeastern Peninsula covering Odisha, Jharkhand, Bihar, eastern Madhya Pradesh, northern Ganga plain along the sub-Himalayas and the Cachar Valley and Manipur.
- **Areas of Low Rainfall:** Western Uttar Pradesh, Delhi, Haryana, Punjab, Jammu and Kashmir, eastern Rajasthan, Gujarat and Deccan Plateau receive rainfall between 50-100 cm.
- **Areas of Inadequate Rainfall:** Parts of the Peninsula, especially in Andhra Pradesh, Karnataka and Maharashtra, Ladakh and most of western Rajasthan receive rainfall below 50 cm.
- **Snowfall** is restricted to the Himalayan region.

Variability of Rainfall

A characteristic feature of rainfall in India is its variability. The values of the coefficient of variation show the variability of rainfall in India. The variability of rainfall is computed with the help of the following formula:

C.V. = Standard Deviation / Mean × 100
where **C.V. is the coefficient of variation.**

- A variability of **less than 25 per cent** exists on the western coasts, Western Ghats, northeastern Peninsula, eastern plains of the Ganga, northeastern India, Uttarakhand and Himachal Pradesh and south-western part of Jammu and Kashmir. These areas have an annual rainfall of **over 100 cm.**

- A variability of **over 50 per cent** exists in the western part of Rajasthan, the northern part of Jammu and Kashmir and the interior parts of the Deccan plateau. These areas have an **annual rainfall of less than 50 cm.**
- Rest of India have a variability of **25-50 per cent** and these areas receive an annual rainfall between **50 -100 cm.**

Monsoons and the Economic Life in India

- Monsoon is that axis around which revolves the entire agricultural cycle of India. It is because about **64 per cent people of India depend on agriculture** for their livelihood and agriculture itself is based on southwest monsoon.
  - ➢ **Except for the Himalayas**, all the parts of the country have temperatures above the threshold level to grow the crops or plants throughout the year.
- **Regional variations** in monsoon climate help in growing various types of crops.
  - ➢ The variability of rainfall brings **droughts or floods** every year in some parts of the country.
  - ➢ The agricultural prosperity of India depends very much on **timely and adequately distributed rainfall**. If it fails, agriculture is adversely affected, particularly in regions where irrigation methods are not developed.
- Sudden monsoon bursts create a problem of soil erosion over large areas in India.
  - ➢ Winter rainfall by **temperate cyclones** in north India is highly beneficial for **rabi crops.**
- Regional climatic variation in India is reflected in the **vast variety of food, clothes and house** types.

TEST YOURSELF

Multiple Choice Questions

Q1. Which of the following states receives little rainfall from the southwest monsoon?

(a) Tamil Nadu (b) Kerala

(c) Rajasthan (d) Goa

Q2. The retreating Monsoon gives rainfall to

(a) Gujarat (b) Goa

(c) Tamil Nadu (d) Maharashtra

Q3. Consider the following statements regarding Jet streams.

1. They are also called Rossby waves.
2. They are usually found near tropopause.
3. They travel from west to east in the northern hemisphere and from east to west in the southern hemisphere.
4. They travel at very high velocity.
5. They are usually sinuous in character.

Which of the above statements are correct?

(a) 1, 2, 3 and 4 only (b) 1, 2, 3 and 5 only

(c) 1, 2 and 4 only (d) 1, 2, 4 and 5 only

Q4. Which of the following statements is/are true regarding ITCZ.

I. It is a low pressure, area near the equator.

II. It is at the convergence of NE and SE trade winds.

III. It shifts its position to the north of equator in the summer and to the south of equator in the winter season.

Choose the correct option

(a) I is true (b) II, III are true

(c) I, II, III are true (d) I, III are true

Q5. Which of the following statements is not true regarding Westerlies?

(a) They blow from sub-tropical high pressure belts to sub-polar low pressure belts.

(b) They cause heavy rainfall on the eastern margins of the continents.

(c) They are deflected due to the earth's rotation.

(d) They are best developed between 40° and 65° south latitudes.

Q6. Consider the following statements:

1. The duration of the monsoon decreases from southern India to northern India.
2. The amount of annual rainfall in the northern plains of India decreases from east to west.

Which of the statements given above is / are correct?

(a) 1 only (b) 2 only

(c) Both 1 and 2 (d) Neither 1 nor 2

Q7. Consider the following statements with respect to Distribution of Rainfall:

1. The monsoon rainfall has a declining trend with increasing distance from the sea.
2. Rainfall in Sub-Himalayan areas in the northeast and the hills of Meghalaya exceeds 200 cm.

Which of the above statements is / are correct?

(a) 1 only (b) 2 only

(c) Both 1 and 2 (d) Neither 1 nor 2

Q8. Which of the following statements is/are correct about Indian Monsoons?

1. Indian Monsoons are convection cells on a very large scale.
2. North-east monsoons are formed due to an intense low-pressure system formed over the Tibetan plateau.

Select the correct answers using the codes given below:

(a) 1 only (b) 2 only

(c) Both 1 and 2 (d) Neither 1 nor 2

Q9. The average weather conditions of a place over a long period of time are called:

(a) Weather system (b) Climate change

(c) Climate (d) Atmosphere

Q10. The primary factor influencing climate is:

(a) Latitude (b) Altitude

(c) Ocean currents (d) All of the above

Answer Key			
Q1.	a	Q2.	c
Q3.	d	Q4.	c
Q5.	b	Q6.	c
Q7.	c	Q8.	a
Q9.	c	Q10.	d

Model Questions for Main Examination

Q1. The troposphere is a very significant atmosphere layer that determines the Weather processes. How?

Q2. Discuss the nature and origin of the Indian monsoon and recent techniques of its prediction. (UPSC 2014)

UNIT 16 Water (Oceans)

In This Unit

Comprehensive and profound coverage of the following NCERTs' chapter:

✓ NCERT Class- 11th (Fundamentals of Physical Geography), Chapter- 12

Water is an essential component of all life forms that exist over the surface of the earth. The creatures on the earth are lucky that it is a water planet, otherwise we all would have no existence. Water is a rare commodity in our solar system. There is no water on the sun or anywhere else in the solar system. The earth, fortunately has an abundant supply of water on its surface. Hence, our planet is called the **'Blue Planet'**.

Hydrological Cycle

Water is a cyclic resource. It can be **used and re-used.** Water also undergoes a cycle from the ocean to land and land to ocean. The hydrological cycle describes the movement of water on, in, and above the earth. The water cycle has been working for billions of years and all the life on earth depends on it. **Next to air,** water is the most important element required for the **existence of life on earth.** The distribution of water on earth is **quite uneven.** Many locations have plenty of water while others have very limited quantity. The hydrological cycle, is the circulation of water within the earth's hydrosphere in different forms i.e., the liquid, solid and the gaseous phases. It also refers to the continuous exchange of water between the oceans, atmosphere, land surface and subsurface and the organisms.

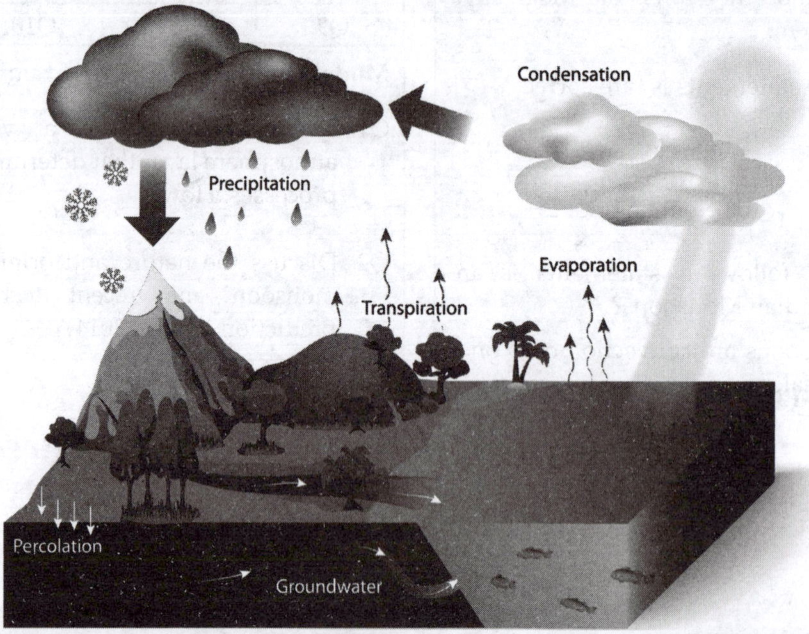

Hydrological Cycle

About 71 per cent of the planetary water is found in the oceans. The remaining is held as freshwater in glaciers and icecaps, groundwater sources, lakes, soil moisture, atmosphere, streams and within life. Nearly 59 per cent of the water that falls on land returns to the atmosphere through evaporation from over the oceans as well as from other places. The remainder runs-off on the surface, infiltrates into the ground or a part of it becomes glacier.

It is to be noted that the renewable water on the earth is constant while the demand is increasing tremendously. This leads to water crisis in different parts of the world — spatially and temporally. The pollution of river waters has further aggravated the crisis.

Reservoir	Volume (Million Cubic km)	Percentage of the Total
Oceans	1,370	97.25
Ice Caps and Glaciers	29	2.05
Groundwater	9.5	0.68
Lakes	0.125	0.01
Soil Moisture	0.065	0.005
Atmosphere	0.013	0.001
Streams and Rivers	0.0017	0.0001
Biosphere	0.0006	0.00004

Water on the Earth's surface

Components	Processes
Water storage in oceans	Evaporation, Evapotranspiration and Sublimation
Water in the atmosphere	Condensation, Precipitation
Water storage in ice and snow	Snowmelt runoff to streams
Surface runoff	Stream flow freshwater storage infiltration
Groundwater storage	Groundwater discharge springs

Components and Processes of the Water Cycle

Relief of the Ocean Floor

The Earth's vast oceans occupy the significant depressions of its outermost layer, known as the crust. This section will explore the characteristics and topography of the Earth's ocean basins. Unlike continents, which have distinct boundaries, the oceans transition seamlessly into one another, making precise demarcation challenging.

Geographers have conventionally divided the Earth's oceanic realm into five distinct entities: **the Pacific, Atlantic, Indian, Southern, and Arctic Oceans.** Notably, various smaller bodies of water, such as seas, bays, and gulfs, are considered subsidiary components of these five larger oceans.

The ocean floor is located 3–6 kilometres below sea level for the most part. The 'land' under the waters of the oceans, that is, the **ocean floor** exhibits complex and varied features as those observed over the land. The floors of the oceans are rugged with the world's largest mountain ranges, deepest trenches and the largest plains. These features are formed, like those of the continents, by the factors of tectonic, volcanic and depositional processes.

Divisions of The Ocean Floors

The ocean floors can be divided into four major divisions: (i) Continental Shelf; (ii) Continental Slope; (iii) Deep Sea Plain; (iv) Oceanic Deeps. Besides, these divisions there are also major and minor relief features in the ocean floors like ridges, hills, sea mounts, guyots, trenches, canyons, etc.

Continental Shelf

The continental shelf is the **extended margin of each continent** occupied by relatively shallow seas and gulfs. It is the shallowest part of the ocean showing an average gradient of 1° or even less. The shelf typically ends at a very steep slope, called the **shelf break.** The width of the continental shelves varies from one ocean to another. The **average width** of **continental shelves is about 80 km**. The shelves are almost absent or very narrow along some of the margins like the coasts of Chile, the west coast of Sumatra, etc. On the contrary, the Siberian shelf in the Arctic Ocean, the largest in the world, stretches to 1,500 km in width. The depth of the shelves also varies. It may be as shallow as 30 m in some areas while in some areas it is as deep as 600 m. The continental shelves are covered with variable thicknesses of sediments brought down by rivers, glaciers, wind, from the land and distributed by waves and currents. Massive sedimentary deposits received over a long time by the continental shelves, become the source of fossil fuels.

Continental Slope

The continental slope **connects the continental shelf and the ocean basins**. It begins where the bottom of the continental shelf sharply drops off into a steep slope. The gradient of the slope region varies between 2-5°. The depth of the slope region varies between 200 and 3,000 m. The slope boundary indicates the **end of the continents**. Canyons and trenches are observed in this region.

Deep Sea Plain

Deep Sea Plains are **gently sloping areas** of the ocean basins. These are the flattest and smoothest regions of the world. The depths vary between 3,000 and 6,000m. These plains are covered with **fine-grained sediments** like **clay and silt**.

Oceanic Deeps or Trenches

These areas are the **deepest parts of the oceans**. The trenches are relatively steep sided, narrow basins. They are some 3-5 km deeper than the surrounding ocean floor. They occur at the bases of continental slopes and along island arcs and are associated with active volcanoes and strong earthquakes. That is why they are very significant in the study of plate movements. As many as 57 deeps have been explored so far; of which 32 are in the Pacific Ocean; 19 in the Atlantic Ocean and 6 in the Indian Ocean.

> **SONAR (Sound Navigation and Ranging)** A system for the detection of objects under water by emitting sound pulses and detecting or measuring their return after being reflected.

Minor Relief Features

Apart from the above mentioned, major relief features of the ocean floor, some minor but significant features predominate in different parts of the oceans.

Mid-Oceanic Ridges

A mid-oceanic ridge is composed of two chains of mountains separated by a large depression. The mountain ranges can have peaks as high as 2,500 m and some even reach above the ocean's surface. Iceland, a part of the mid Atlantic Ridge, is an example.

Seamount

It is a mountain with pointed summits, rising from the seafloor that does not reach the surface of the ocean. Seamounts **are volcanic** in origin. These can be 3,000-4,500 m tall. The Emperor Seamount, an extension of the Hawaiian Islands in the Pacific Ocean, is a good example.

Submarine Canyons

These are deep valleys, some comparable to the Grand Canyon of the Colorado river. They are sometimes found cutting across the continental shelves and slopes, often extending from the mouths of large rivers. The Hudson Canyon is the best known, submarine canyon in the world.

Guyots

It is a flat topped seamount. They show evidences of gradual subsidence through stages to become flat topped submerged mountains. It is estimated that more than 10,000 seamounts and guyots exist in the Pacific Ocean alone.

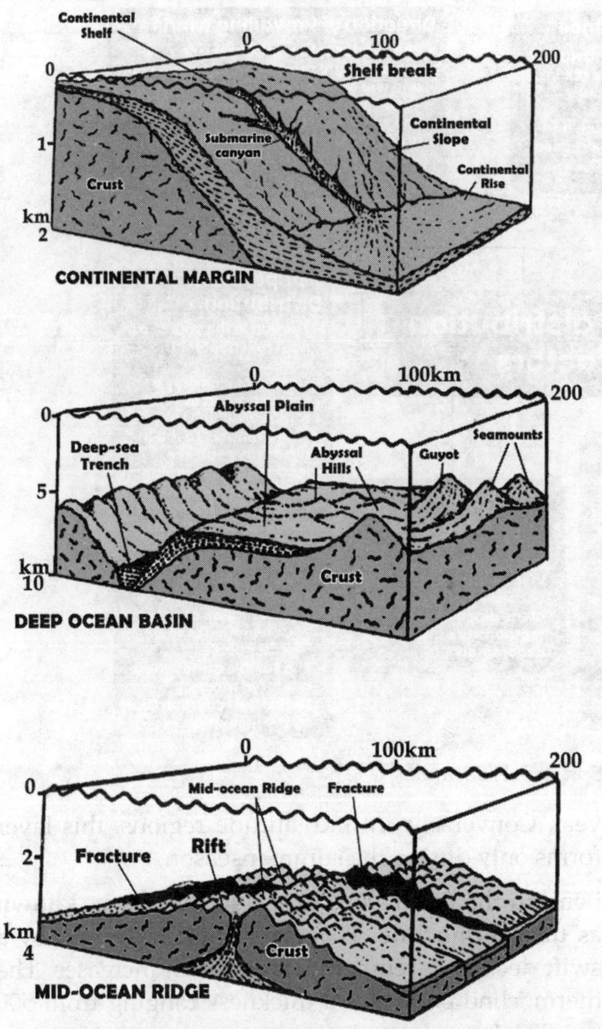

Relief Features of Ocean Floors

Atoll

Within the tropical regions of the world's oceans lie low-lying islands comprised of **coral reefs encircling a central depression**. This depression can either be a direct extension of the open ocean (lagoon) or, in some instances, enclose a body of freshwater, brackish water, or highly saline water.

Temperature of Ocean Waters

This section explores the spatial and vertical disparities in temperature that exist within various global oceans. Similar to land masses, solar energy serves as the primary heating mechanism for ocean waters. However, the process of thermal exchange, encompassing both heating and subsequent cooling, transpires at a slower pace within oceanic environments compared to terrestrial ones.

Factors Affecting Temperature Distribution

The factors which affect the distribution of temperature of ocean water are:

(i) **Latitude:** Surface water temperatures exhibit a marked decrease as one progresses from the equator towards the poles. This phenomenon can be attributed to the diminishing intensity of insolation received at higher latitudes.

(ii) **Unequal distribution of land and water:** A disparity exists in the heat distribution between the northern and southern hemispheres' oceans. The northern hemisphere's oceans experience a greater influx of heat due to their proximity to a larger landmass compared to their southern counterparts.

(iii) **Prevailing wind:** The winds blowing from the land towards the oceans drive warm surface water away from the coast resulting in the upwelling of cold water from below. It results into the longitudinal variation in the temperature. Contrary to this, the onshore winds pile up warm water near the coast and this raises the temperature.

(iv) **Ocean currents:** Warm ocean currents raise the temperature in cold areas while the cold currents decrease the temperature in warm ocean areas. Gulf stream (warm current) raises the temperature near the eastern coast of North America and the West Coast of Europe while the Labrador current (cold current) lowers the temperature near the north-east coast of North America.

A confluence of these factors exerts a localised influence on the temperature of ocean currents. Notably, enclosed seas situated within low latitudes exhibit comparatively higher temperatures than their counterparts in the open ocean. Conversely, enclosed seas at high latitudes demonstrate lower temperatures compared to the surrounding open waters.

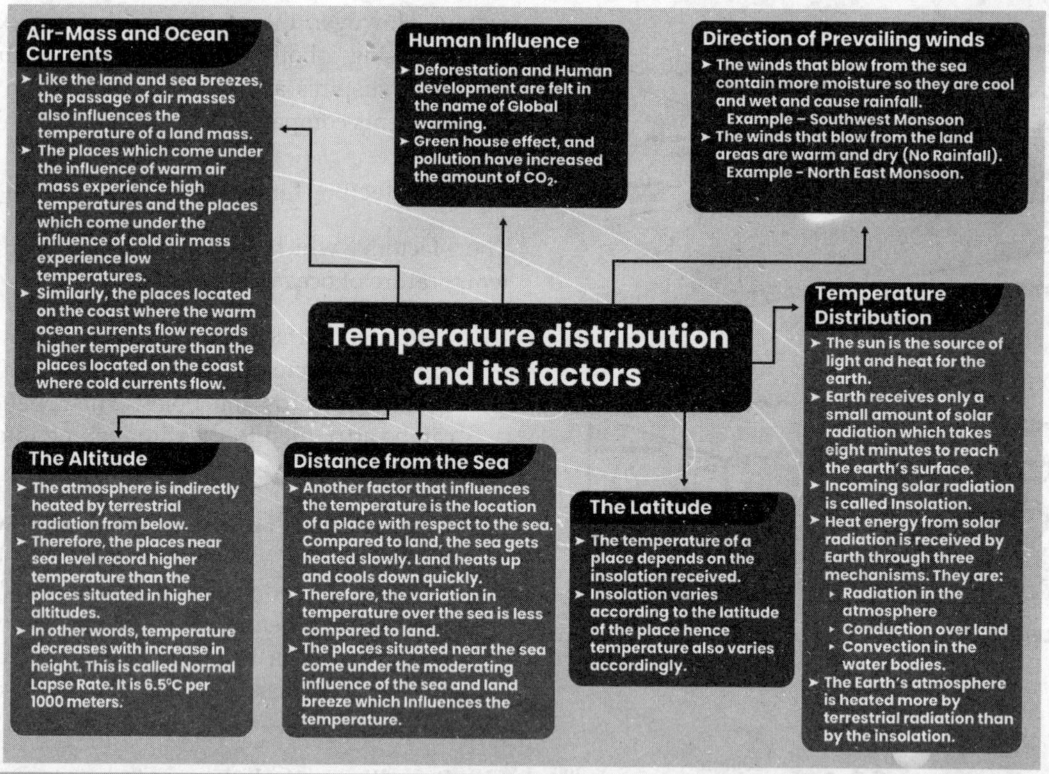

Temperature Distribution and its Factors

Horizontal and Vertical Distribution of Temperature

The vertical temperature distribution for the ocean water illustrates the manner in which the **temperature exhibits a decline with increasing depth**. The profile depicts an interfacial zone between the upper ocean layers and the bathypelagic zone. The boundary customarily commences approximately 100 - 400 meters inferior to the air-sea interface and spans for several hundreds of meters in a downward direction. Within the ocean, a distinct boundary region exists characterised by a rapid decline in temperature. This region is designated as the **thermocline**. Notably, approximately ninety percent of the total water volume resides beneath the thermocline, in the deep ocean depths. Here, temperatures progressively approach 0° C. In the middle and low latitudes, the thermal stratification of the ocean can be conceptualised as a three-layered system, progressing from the surface to the seabed.

In the uppermost portion of the ocean exists the **first layer**, comprised of **warm surface water**. This layer, approximately 500 meters thick, exhibits a temperature range of 20°C to 25°C. Notably, **within tropical regions**, this layer persists throughout the year. Conversely, in mid-latitude regions, this layer forms only during the summer season.

Beneath the first layer lies the **second layer, known as the thermocline**. This layer is characterised by a swift decline in temperature as depth increases. The thermocline possesses a thickness ranging from 500 to 1,000 meters.

The third layer, characterised by frigid temperatures, persists until reaching the profound depths of the ocean floor. Notably, within the Arctic and Antarctic circles, where surface water temperatures hover near 0°C, the temperature differential with increasing depth is minimal. Consequently, in these polar regions, a singular layer of frigid water prevails, encompassing the entirety of the water column from the surface to the abyssal depths.

On average, the surface water temperature of the oceans exhibits a latitudinal gradient, decreasing approximately 0.5°C per degree of latitude from the equator towards the poles. This translates to a mean temperature of 22°C at 20° latitude, 14°C at 40° latitude, and near freezing (0°C) at polar regions. Notably, the northern hemisphere oceans maintain a slightly warmer average annual temperature (approximately 19°C) compared to the southern hemisphere (approximately 16°C). This hemispheric disparity can be attributed to the unequal distribution of land and water masses between the two hemispheres.

A fundamental principle of oceanography is that surface waters exhibit the warmest temperatures. This is a direct consequence of solar radiation being absorbed at the surface, with subsequent transfer of heat to deeper layers via convection currents. As depth increases, a decrease in temperature is observed. However, this decrease is not uniform. A rapid decline in temperature characterises the upper 200 meters, followed by a more gradual decrease in deeper waters.

Salinity of Ocean Waters

All natural waters, including both precipitation and oceanic waters, possess **dissolved mineral salts.** The **total concentration** of these dissolved salts within seawater is referred to as salinity. It is determined by calculating the mass of salt (in grams) dissolved per kilogram (1,000 grams) of seawater. Salinity is typically expressed in parts per thousand (‰) or ppt. This property plays a significant role in the characteristics of seawater. A salinity level of 24.7 ‰ is considered the upper limit for **classifying water as "brackish.".**

The following factors influence the salinity of ocean waters:

(i) **Evaporation and precipitation** are the primary determinants of surface salinity. Increased evaporation concentrates dissolved salts, while precipitation dilutes them.

(ii) **Freshwater influx** from rivers in coastal regions and **freezing and thawing processes** in polar regions significantly impact surface salinity. River discharge adds freshwater, lowering salinity, while sea ice formation removes freshwater as ice crystals, increasing salinity.

(iii) **Wind patterns** can influence salinity by transporting surface water masses, leading to localised changes in concentration.

Ocean currents play a crucial role in distributing salinity throughout the global oceans. The interconnectedness of salinity, temperature, and density in seawater means that variations in one factor can influence the others. Consequently, changes in temperature or density driven by ocean circulation can also affect salinity levels.

> Among natural bodies of water, the highest salinity levels are observed in Lake Van, Turkey (330 ‰), followed by the Dead Sea (238 ‰) and the Great Salt Lake (220 ‰).

Dissolved Salts in Sea Water
(gm of Salt per kg of Water)

Salt	gm/kg
Chlorine	18.97
Sodium	10.47
Sulphate	2.65
Magnesium	1.28
Calcium	0.41
Potassium	0.38
Bicarbonate	0.14
Bromine	0.06
Borate	0.02
Strontium	0.01

Horizontal Distribution of Salinity

The salinity for normal open ocean ranges between 33 ‰ and 37 ‰. In the land locked Red Sea, it is as high as 41 ‰, while in the estuaries and the Arctic, the salinity fluctuates from 0 - 35 ‰, seasonally. In hot and dry regions, where evaporation is high, the salinity sometimes reaches to 70 ‰. The salinity variation in the Pacific Ocean is mainly due to its shape and larger areal extent. Salinity decreases from 35 ‰ - 31 ‰ on the western parts of the northern hemisphere because of the influx of melted water from the Arctic region. In the same way, after 15° - 20° south, it decreases to 33 ‰.

The average salinity of the Atlantic Ocean is around 36 ‰. The highest salinity is recorded between 15° and 20° latitudes. Maximum salinity (37 ‰) is observed between 20° N and 30° N and 20° W - 60° W. It gradually decreases towards the north. **North Sea**, inspite of its location in higher latitudes, records higher salinity due to **more saline water** brought by the North Atlantic Drift. **Baltic Sea** records low salinity due to influx of river waters in large quantity.

The Mediterranean Sea records **higher salinity** due to **high evaporation**. Salinity is, however, **very low in Black Sea** due to **enormous fresh water** influx by rivers.

The average salinity of the Indian Ocean is 35 ‰. The low salinity trend is observed in the Bay of Bengal due to influx of river water. On the contrary, the Arabian Sea shows higher salinity due to high evaporation and low influx of fresh water.

Vertical Distribution of Salinity

Salinity changes with depth, but the way it changes depends upon the **location of the sea**. Salinity at the surface increases by the loss of water to ice or evaporation, or decreased by the input of fresh waters, such as from the rivers. Salinity at depth is very much fixed, because there is no way that water is 'lost', or the salt is 'added.' There is a marked difference in the salinity between the surface zones and the deep zones of the oceans. **The lower salinity water rests above the higher salinity dense water**. Salinity, generally, increases with depth and there is a distinct zone called the **halocline**, where salinity increases sharply. Other factors being constant, increasing salinity of seawater causes its density to increase. High salinity seawater, generally, sinks below the lower salinity water. This leads to **stratification** by salinity.

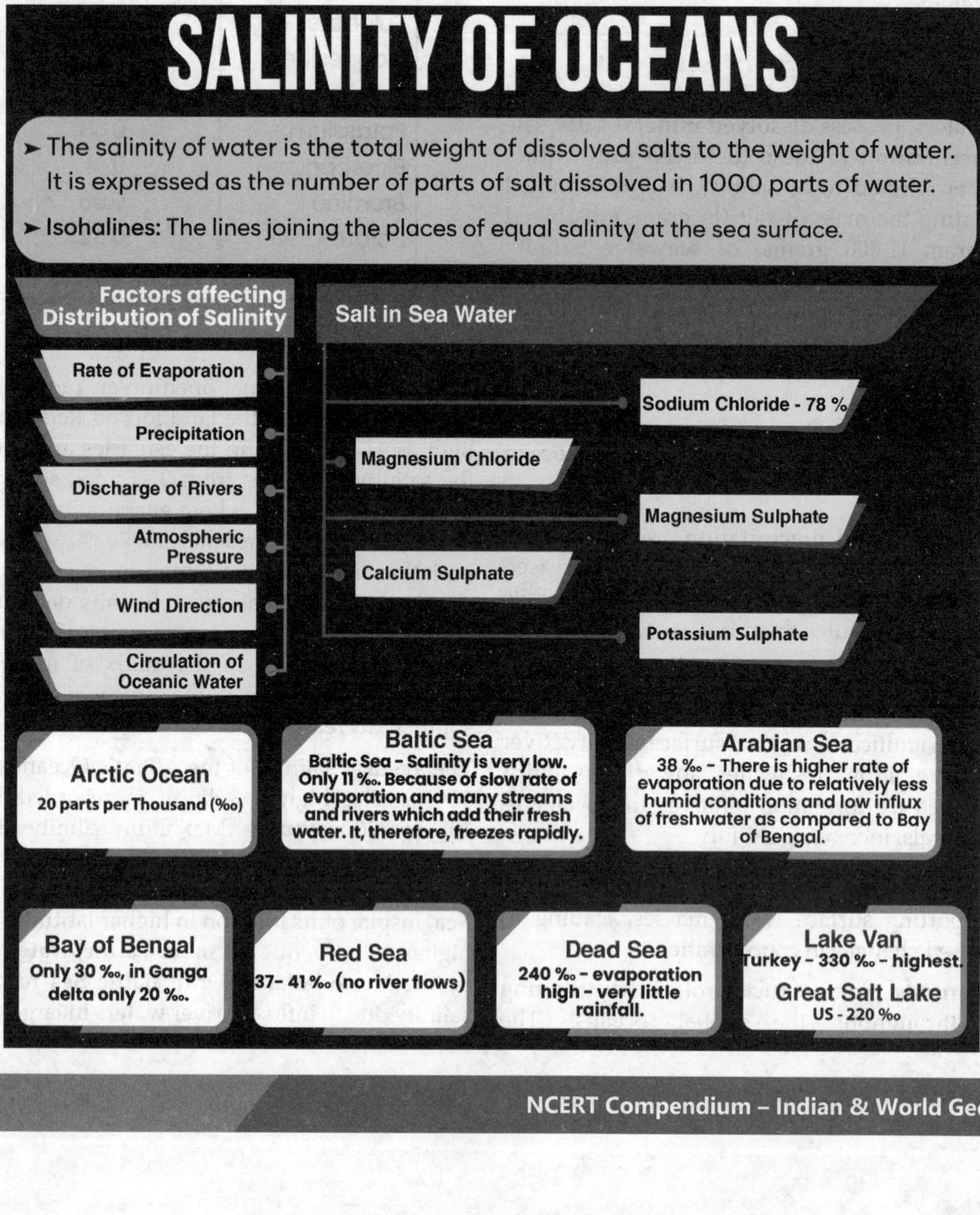

TEST YOURSELF

Multiple Choice Questions

Q1. Which factor primarily influences the vertical distribution of salinity in the ocean?

(a) Temperature (b) Depth

(c) Wind speed (d) Density

Q2. In the open ocean, the salinity generally:

(a) Decreases with increasing depth

(b) Increases with increasing depth

(c) Remains constant at all depths

(d) Varies randomly with depth

Q3. The region of the ocean with the highest salinity near the surface is typically:

(a) Polar regions (b) Equatorial regions

(c) Coastal regions (d) Mid-latitudes

Q4. Which of the following features is not typically found in the ocean floor?

(a) Mid-ocean ridges (b) Submarine canyons

(c) Coral reefs (d) Seamounts

Answer Key

Q1.	b	Q2.	b	Q3.	b	Q4.	c

Model Questions for Main Examination

Q1. Critically analyse the factors which affect the distribution of temperature of ocean water.

Q2. Write a short note on vertical distribution of salinity.

UNIT 17

Movements of Ocean Water

In This Unit

Comprehensive and profound coverage of the following NCERTs' chapter:

✓ NCERT Class- 11th (Fundamentals of Physical Geography), Chapter- 13

The ocean water is dynamic. Its physical characteristics like **temperature, salinity, density and the external forces like the sun, moon and the winds influence the movement of ocean water**. The horizontal and vertical motions are common in ocean water bodies. The horizontal motion refers to the **ocean currents** and **waves**. The vertical motion refers to **tides**. Ocean currents are the continuous flow of huge amount of water in a definite direction while the waves are the horizontal motion of water. Water moves ahead from one place to another through ocean currents while the water in the waves does not move, but the wave trains move ahead. The vertical motion refers to the rise and fall of water in the oceans and seas. **Due to attraction of the sun and the moon**, the ocean water is raised up and falls down twice a day. The upwelling of cold water from subsurface and the sinking of surface water are also forms of vertical motion of ocean water.

Waves

- Waves are actually the energy, not the water as such, which moves across the ocean surface. Water particles only travel in a small circle as a wave passes.
- Wind provides energy to the waves. Wind causes waves to travel in the ocean and the energy is released on shorelines. The motion of the surface water seldom affects the stagnant deep bottom water of the oceans.
- When the depth of water is less than half the wavelength of the wave, the wave breaks.
- The largest waves are found in the open oceans. Waves continue to grow larger as they move and absorb energy from the wind.
- Most of the waves are caused by the wind driving against water.
- When a breeze of two knots or less blows over calm water, small ripples form and grow as the wind speed increases until white caps appear in the breaking waves.
- A wave's size and shape reveal its origin. Steep waves are fairly young ones and are probably formed by local wind.
- Slow and steady waves originate from far-away places, possibly from another hemisphere.
- The maximum wave height is determined by the strength of the wind, i.e., how long it blows and the area over which it blows in a single direction.
- Waves travel because wind pushes the water body in its course while gravity pulls the crests of the waves downward.
- The falling water pushes the former troughs upward, and the wave moves to a new position.
- The actual motion of the water beneath the waves is circular. It indicates that things are carried up and forward as the wave approaches, and down and back as it passes.

Characteristics of Waves

Wave crest and trough: The highest and lowest points of a wave are called the crest and trough respectively.

> **Wave height:** It is the vertical distance from the bottom of a trough to the top of a crest of a wave.
>
> **Wave amplitude:** It is one-half of the wave height.
>
> **Wave period:** It is merely the time interval between two successive wave crests or troughs as they pass a fixed point.
>
> **Wavelength:** It is the horizontal distance between two successive crests.
>
> **Wave speed:** It is the rate at which the wave moves through the water, and is measured in knots.
>
> **Wave frequency:** It is the number of waves passing a given point during a one- second time interval.

Tides

- The periodical rise and fall of the sea level, once or twice a day, mainly due to the attraction of the sun and the moon, is called a **tide**.
- Movement of water caused by meteorological effects (winds and atmospheric pressure changes) are called **surges. Surges are not regular like tides.**
- The primary factors responsible for the occurrence of tides are the **gravitational attraction of the moon**, which is greater than that of the sun.
- The force acting to counterbalance gravity, known as **centrifugal force**, is another factor.
- The two main tidal bulges on Earth are the result of the combined action of centrifugal force and gravitational attraction.
- A tidal bulge develops on the side of the earth that faces the moon, whereas centrifugal force creates a tidal bulge on the opposite side even though the moon's gravitational pull is smaller as it gets farther away.
- The difference between these two forces—the centrifugal force and the moon's gravitational attraction—is the **"tide-generating"** force.
- When the moon's pull or attraction force exceeds the centrifugal force on Earth's surface closest to it, a net force results in a bulge in the direction of the moon.
- The centrifugal force is more powerful on the other side of the planet when the attraction is less because of the distance from the moon. As a result, the moon is being pulled away by a net force. It causes the moon's second bulge to form.

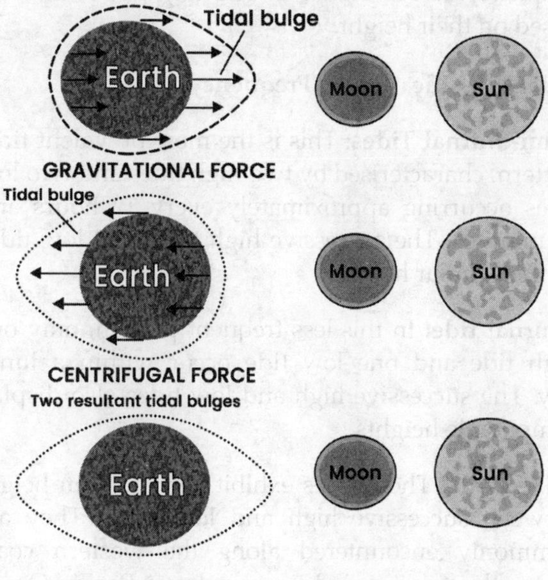

Relation between Gravitational Forces and Tides

- When it comes to creating tidal bulges on the surface of the planet, horizontal forces have a greater influence than vertical forces.
- On broad continental shelves, the tidal bulges are taller. The mid-oceanic islands get low when tidal bulges cause them to do so.
- The way bays and estuaries are shaped along a coastline can also intensify the tides.
- Large-scale tidal magnitude changes occur in funnel-shaped bays. Tidal currents are created when the tide channels into bays, estuaries, or between islands.

> **Tides of Bay of Fundy, Canada**
>
> The highest tides in the world occur in the Bay of Fundy in Nova Scotia, Canada. The tidal bulge is 15 - 16 m. Because there are two high tides and two low tides every day (roughly a 24 hours period); then a tide must come in within about a six hours period. As a rough estimate, the tide rises about 240 cm an hour.

Types of Tides

Tides vary in their frequency, direction and movement from place to place and also from time to time. Tides may be grouped into various types based on their frequency of occurrence in one day or 24 hours or based on their height.

Tidal Classification by Frequency

Semi-diurnal Tides: This is the most prevalent tidal pattern, characterised by two high tides and two low tides occurring approximately every 12 hours and 25 minutes. The successive high tides and low tides exhibit similar heights.

Diurnal tide: In this less frequent pattern, only one high tide and one low tide occur within a lunar day. The successive high and low tides also display comparable heights.

Mixed tide: These tides exhibit variations in height between successive high and low tides. They are commonly encountered along the western coast of North America and on numerous Pacific Ocean islands.

Tides based on the Sun, Moon and the Earth Positions

Spring tides: The relative positions of the Sun, Moon, and Earth exert a significant influence on the height of tides. When these celestial bodies are aligned, a phenomenon known as a **spring tide** occurs. Spring tides, characterised by **exceptionally high tides** and low tides, transpire twice per lunar month, coinciding with both the full and new moon phases.

Neap tides: Conversely, when the Sun and Moon are positioned at right angles to each other, a period of neap tides ensues. **During neap tides, which typically occur approximately one week after spring tides, the gravitational forces of the Sun and Moon partially counteract one another.** Although the Moon's gravitational pull remains dominant, exceeding the Sun's influence by more than a factor of two, the opposing force from the Sun's gravitational attraction diminishes the overall tidal effect, resulting in tides of lesser magnitude.

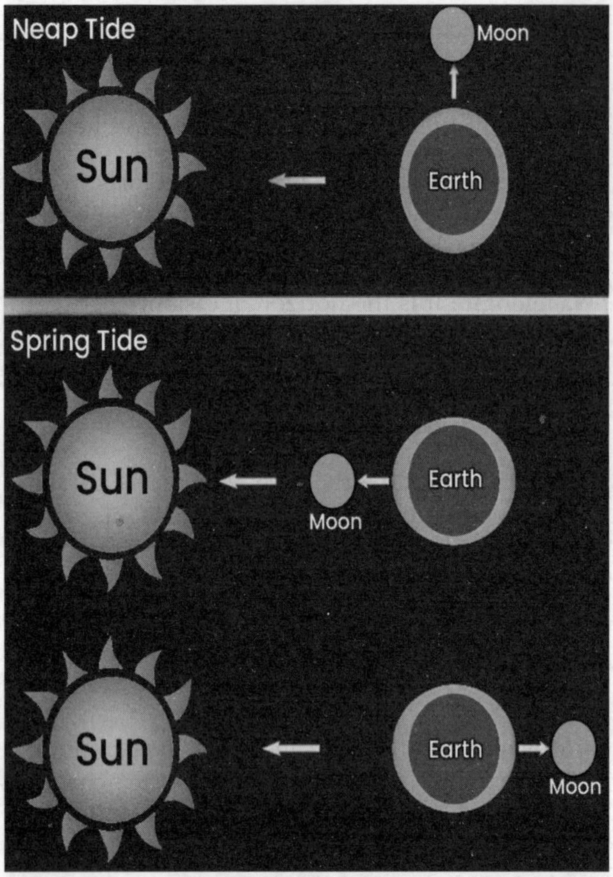

Neap and Spring Tides

- Once in a month, **when the moon's orbit is closest to the earth (perigee)**, unusually high and low tides occur. During this time the tidal range is greater than normal. Two weeks later, **when the moon is farthest from earth (apogee)**, the moon's gravitational force is limited and the tidal ranges are less than their average heights.
- **When the earth is closest to the sun (perihelion), around 3rd January each year,** tidal ranges are also much greater, with unusually high and unusually low tides. **When the earth is farthest from the sun (aphelion), around 4th July each year,** tidal ranges are much less than average.
- The time between the high tide and low tide, when the water level is falling, is called the **ebb**. The time between the low tide and high tide, when the tide is rising, is called the **flow** or **flood**.

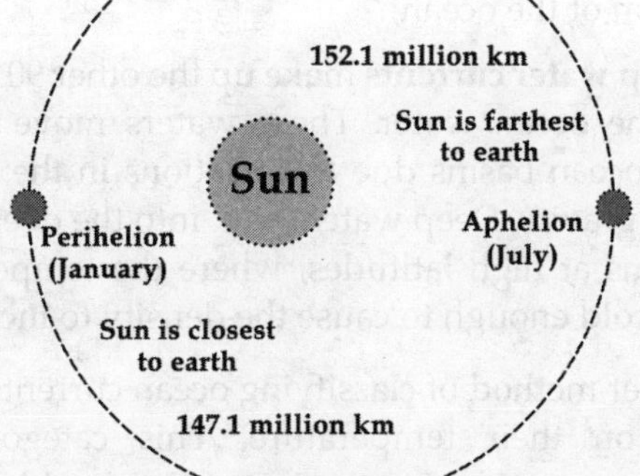

Perihelion and Aphelion

Importance of Tides

Since tides are caused by the earth-moon-sun positions which are known accurately, the tides can be predicted well in advance. This helps the navigators and fishermen plan their activities. Tidal flows are of great importance in navigation. Tidal heights are very important, especially for **harbours** near rivers and within estuaries having shallow 'bars' at the entrance, which prevent ships and boats from entering into the harbour. Tides are also helpful in desilting the sediments and in removing polluted water from river estuaries. Tides are used to generate electrical power.

Ocean Currents

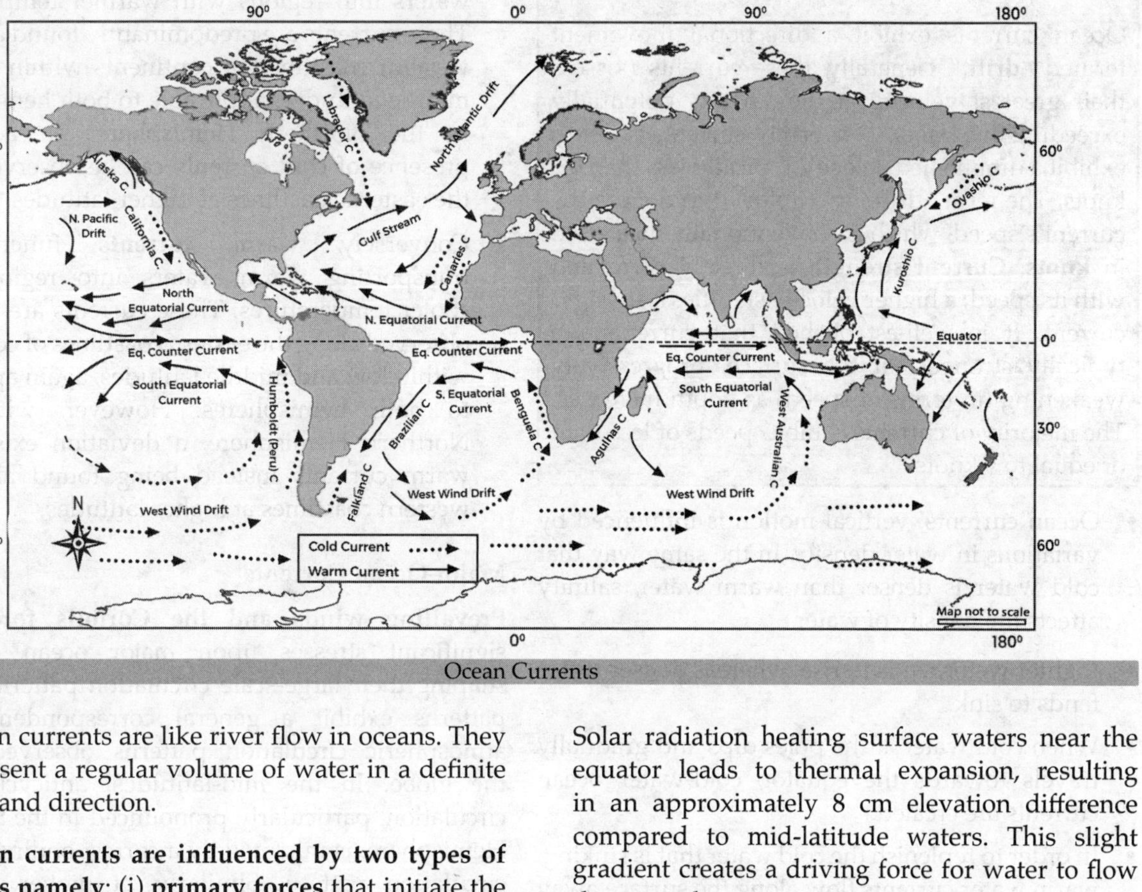

Ocean Currents

- Ocean currents are like river flow in oceans. They represent a regular volume of water in a definite path and direction.
- **Ocean currents are influenced by two types of forces namely**: (i) **primary forces** that initiate the movement of water; (ii) **secondary forces** that influence the currents to flow.

The primary forces that influence the currents are:

1. **Heating by solar energy:** The movement of ocean currents is influenced by a confluence of factors. Solar radiation heating surface waters near the equator leads to thermal expansion, resulting in an approximately 8 cm elevation difference compared to mid-latitude waters. This slight gradient creates a driving force for water to flow downwards.
2. **Wind:** Wind also plays a significant role, as sustained winds blowing across the ocean's surface create a frictional drag, propelling water bodies in the direction of the wind's movement.

3. **Gravity:** Gravity additionally exerts an influence, pulling water downward along slopes within the ocean floor's topography, further contributing to variations in water pressure and creating a driving force for movement.
4. **Coriolis force:** However, the Coriolis effect, arising from the Earth's rotation, introduces a crucial element. This force deflects the movement of water masses to the right in the Northern Hemisphere and to the left in the Southern Hemisphere. These deflected currents, along with large-scale accumulations of water, give rise to **gyres,** massive circular currents that dominate the flow patterns within each ocean basin.

Ocean Currents Properties

Ocean currents exhibit a directional movement termed **"drift."** Generally, these currents possess their greatest velocity at the surface, potentially exceeding five knots. Conversely, currents at depth exhibit a diminished velocity, typically less than 0.5 knots. The term "drift" is employed to denote the current's speed, which is conventionally measured in **knots. Current strength** is directly correlated with its speed; a higher velocity signifies a stronger current. It is well-established that currents are typically strongest at the surface, progressively weakening (in terms of speed) as depth increases. The majority of currents exhibit speeds of less than or equal to 5 knots.

- Ocean currents' vertical motion is influenced by variations in water density. In the same way that cold water is denser than warm water, salinity affects the density of water.
- Lighter water tends to rise, whereas denser water tends to sink.
- When cold water at the poles dips and gradually travels towards the equator, cold-water ocean currents are created.
- In order to replenish the cold water that is sinking, warm water currents flow along the surface away from the equator and towards the poles.

Types of Ocean Currents

Surface currents and deep-water currents are two categories into which the ocean currents can be divided based on their depth:

1. **Surface currents** constitute about 10 percent of all the water in the ocean, these waters are the upper 400 m of the ocean;
2. **Deep water currents** make up the other 90 percent of the ocean water. These waters move around the ocean basins due to variations in the density and gravity. Deep waters sink into the deep ocean basins at high latitudes, where the temperatures are cold enough to cause the density to increase.

A further method of classifying ocean currents exists, based on their temperature. This categorisation divides currents into two primary types: cold currents and warm currents:

1. **Cold currents** act as conduits, transporting frigid waters into regions with warmer temperatures. These currents are predominantly found along the western coastlines of continents within low and middle latitudes, applicable to both hemispheres. In the Northern Hemisphere, an additional presence of cold currents can be observed along the eastern coastlines at higher latitudes.
2. Conversely, **warm currents** function by transporting warm waters into regions with cooler temperatures. These currents are typically observed along the eastern coastlines of continents within low and middle latitudes, again applicable to both hemispheres. However, within the Northern Hemisphere, a deviation exists, with warm currents instead being found along the western coastlines at higher latitudes.

Major Ocean Currents

Prevailing winds and the Coriolis force exert significant stresses upon major ocean currents, shaping their large-scale circulation patterns. These patterns exhibit a general correspondence with atmospheric circulation patterns observed across the globe. In the mid-latitudes, anticyclonic air circulation, particularly pronounced in the Southern Hemisphere, is mirrored by a corresponding oceanic circulation pattern. Similarly, at higher latitudes where cyclonic wind flow dominates, the oceanic circulation aligns with this atmospheric pattern. Regions experiencing pronounced monsoonal winds further demonstrate this influence, as these seasonal winds directly impact current movements. Notably, the Coriolis force plays a crucial role in deflecting warm currents from low latitudes; these currents are deflected to the right in the Northern Hemisphere and to the left in the Southern Hemisphere.

Large-scale oceanic circulation patterns function as a **conveyor belt,** redistributing thermal energy between latitudinal bands in a similar manner to the heat transport observed within the general atmospheric circulation. Cold waters originating in the polar regions, specifically the Arctic and Antarctic Circles, migrate towards the warmer equatorial and tropical zones. Conversely, warm surface waters from lower latitudes are transported poleward.

Effects of Ocean Currents

- Ocean currents have a number of direct and indirect influences on human activities.
- West coasts of the continents in tropical and subtropical latitudes (except close to the equator) are bordered by cool waters. Their average temperatures are relatively low with a narrow diurnal and annual ranges. There is fog, but generally the areas are arid.
- West coasts of the continents in the middle and higher latitudes are bordered by warm waters which cause a distinct marine climate. They are characterised by cool summers and relatively mild winters with a narrow annual range of temperatures.
- Warm currents flow parallel to the east coasts of the continents in tropical and subtropical latitudes. This results in warm and rainy climates. These areas lie in the western margins of the subtropical anti-cyclones.
- The mixing of warm and cold currents helps to replenish the oxygen and favour the growth of planktons, the primary food for fish population. The best fishing grounds of the world exist mainly in these mixing zones.

TEST YOURSELF

Multiple Choice Questions

Q1. The horizontal movement of ocean water along the surface is called:

(a) Ocean currents (b) Tides
(c) Waves (d) Upwelling

Q2. The circular movement of water in the ocean caused by the combined effects of winds and the Earth's rotation is called:

(a) Upwelling (b) Gyres
(c) Tides (d) El Niño

Q3. The warm ocean current that flows northward along the eastern coast of North America is the:

(a) Gulf Stream (b) Labrador Current
(c) Kuroshio Current (d) Agulhas Current

Q4. The cold ocean current that flows southward along the eastern coast of North America is

(a) Gulf Stream (b) Labrador Current
(c) Kuroshio Current (d) Agulhas Current

Q5. The warm ocean current that flows North-eastward along the eastern coast of Japan is the:

(a) Gulf Stream (b) Labrador Current
(c) Kuroshio Current (d) Agulhas Current

Q6. The warm ocean current that flows southward along the eastern coast of Africa is the:

(a) Gulf Stream (b) Labrador Current
(c) Kuroshio Current (d) Agulhas Current

Q7. The periodic warming of the surface waters in the eastern Pacific Ocean, causing changes in weather patterns, is known as:

(a) Gulf Stream (b) Labrador Current
(c) Kuroshio Current (d) El Niño

Q8. The periodic cooling of the surface waters in the eastern Pacific Ocean, causing changes in weather patterns, is known as:

(a) Gulf Stream (b) Labrador Current
(c) Kuroshio Current (d) La Niña

Q9. The daily rise and fall of ocean water level caused by the gravitational pull of the moon and the sun is called:

(a) Ocean currents (b) Tides

(c) Waves (d) Upwelling

Q10. The vertical movement of cold, nutrient-rich water from the ocean depths to the surface is known as:

(a) Ocean currents (b) Tides

(c) Waves (d) Upwelling

Answer Key

Q1.	a	Q2.	b	Q3.	a	Q4.	b
Q5.	c	Q6.	d	Q7.	d	Q8.	d
Q9.	b	Q10.	d				

UNIT 18

Life on The Earth

In This Unit

Comprehensive and profound coverage of the following NCERTs' chapter:

✓ NCERT (Before Rationalisation) Class- 11th (Fundamentals of Physical Geography), Chapter- 15

The living organisms of the earth, constituting the **biosphere**, interact with other environmental realms. The biosphere encompasses the totality of Earth's living components. It comprises all flora and fauna, encompassing microscopic organisms, and their intricate interactions with the surrounding environment. The majority of these organisms reside within the lithosphere, hydrosphere, or atmosphere, with a significant number exhibiting mobility across these realms.

The biosphere and its components are very significant elements of the environment. These elements interact with other components of the natural landscape such as land, water and soil. They are also influenced by the atmospheric elements such as the temperature, rainfall, moisture and sunlight. The interactions of biosphere with land, air and water are important to the growth, development and evolution of the organism.

Ecology

The term ecology originates from the Greek word **"oikos," signifying "house,"** and is compounded with **"logy," meaning "the study of" or "the science of."** Literally interpreted, ecology is the scientific exploration of the Earth as a cohesive unit, encompassing plants, humans, animals, and microorganisms. These organisms coexist as interrelated components within this system. The German zoologist Ernst Haeckel is credited with the first use of the term "ecology" in 1869, having previously employed the variant "oekologie." Ecology can be formally defined as the scientific discipline concerned with the intricate interactions between **living organisms** (biotic factors) and the **non-living physical environment** (abiotic factors). Therefore, ecology can be understood as the comprehensive scientific investigation of how organisms interact with both their surroundings and with each other.

- An environment consists of both abiotic and biotic components. Within a specific habitat, the interactions between a particular group of organisms and the abiotic factors present define an **ecological system**. These systems are characterised by clearly delineated energy flows and material cycles occurring across terrestrial, aquatic, and atmospheric realms.
- In the ecological context, **a habitat** is defined as the entirety of the physical and chemical elements that collectively comprise the surrounding environment.
- **An ecological system**, or ecosystem for short, can be defined as a complex unity formed by the interaction of living organisms (biotic components) with their non-living environment (abiotic components). These components are inextricably linked and exhibit a high degree of interdependence.
- Different types of ecosystems exist with varying ranges of environmental conditions where various plants and animal species have got adapted through evolution. This phenomenon is known as **ecological adaptation.**

Types of Ecosystems

- Ecosystems are of two major types: **terrestrial** and **aquatic**.
- **Terrestrial ecosystem** can be further be classified into **'Biomes'**.
- A **biome** is a plant and animal community that covers a large geographical area.
  - ➢ The boundaries of different biomes on land are determined mainly by climate. Therefore, a biome can be defined as the **total assemblage of plant and animal** species interacting within **specific conditions**. These include rainfall, temperature, humidity and soil conditions.
- Some of the major biomes of the world are: forest, grassland, desert and tundra biomes.
- **Aquatic ecosystems** can be classed as marine and freshwater ecosystems.
- **Marine ecosystem** includes the oceans, estuaries and coral reefs. **Freshwater ecosystem** includes lakes, ponds, streams, marshes and bogs.

Structure and Functions of Ecosystems

- An understanding of an ecosystem's structure necessitates a description of the plant and animal species it encompasses. From a structural perspective, all ecosystems can be categorised by the presence of **abiotic and biotic factors**.
- **Abiotic factors** encompass a range of non-living elements that influence the ecosystem, including precipitation, temperature, solar radiation, atmospheric moisture, soil composition, and inorganic substances such as carbon dioxide, water, nitrogen, calcium, phosphorus, and potassium.
- **Biotic factors**, on the other hand, refer to the living components within an ecosystem. These can be further classified into producers, consumers (categorised as primary, secondary, and tertiary), and decomposers.
- **Producers,** primarily green plants, utilise photosynthesis to synthesise their own nourishment.
- **Primary consumers** consist of herbivorous animals such as deer, goats, mice, and all creatures that subsist on plant matter.
- **Carnivores,** including snakes, tigers, and lions, are defined by their consumption of flesh. Certain carnivores that prey on other carnivores, such as **hawks and mongooses, are categorised as top carnivores.**
- Within an ecosystem, **decomposers** fulfil the critical role of breaking down deceased organisms. This process can be initiated by scavengers, such as vultures and crows, who consume the remains. Subsequently, bacteria and various microorganisms further decompose the organic matter.
- **Producers** within the ecosystem serve as the primary food source, being consumed by herbivores, designated as primary consumers. These primary consumers then become **prey for secondary consumers,** often carnivores. The food chain can extend further, with tertiary consumers, such as apex predators, **feeding on secondary consumers.**
- **Decomposers** play a vital role at each trophic level, transforming the dead organic matter into essential nutrients, including organic and inorganic salts, which contribute to soil fertility.
- The interconnectedness of organisms within an ecosystem is established through the concept of a **food chain.** A classic example involves a plant-eating beetle consuming a paddy stalk. This beetle, in turn, becomes prey for a frog, which may be consumed by a snake. The snake itself might then fall victim to a hawk. This sequential process of consumption, from one organism to the next, facilitates the **transfer of energy throughout the ecosystem.**
- **The transfer of energy** from one trophic level to another within a food chain is known as **energy flow.**
- However, food chains exhibit a lack of isolation. For instance, a murid (mouse) consuming grain may be preyed upon by various secondary consumers (carnivores). These carnivores, in turn, may fall victim to a diverse range of tertiary consumers (top predators). In such scenarios, each carnivore might consume multiple prey types. Consequently, food chains become intricately interwoven.
- This interconnected network of species is designated as a **food web.**

- Broadly, two primary categories of food chains are recognised: the **grazing food chain (GFC)** and **the detritus food chain (DFC).**
- **Within a grazing food chain**, the initial level comprises producers, such as plants, and culminates with carnivores as the terminal level consumers, with herbivores occupying intermediate levels.
- It is important to note that energy loss occurs at each trophic level, potentially through respiration, excretion, or decomposition. The number of trophic levels within a food chain typically ranges from three to five, with energy dissipation occurring at each level.
- **A detritus food chain** is predicated upon the capture of energy by autotrophs, subsequently initiated by grazing animals. This chain involves the decomposition or breakdown of organic waste and deceased matter originating from the grazing food chain.

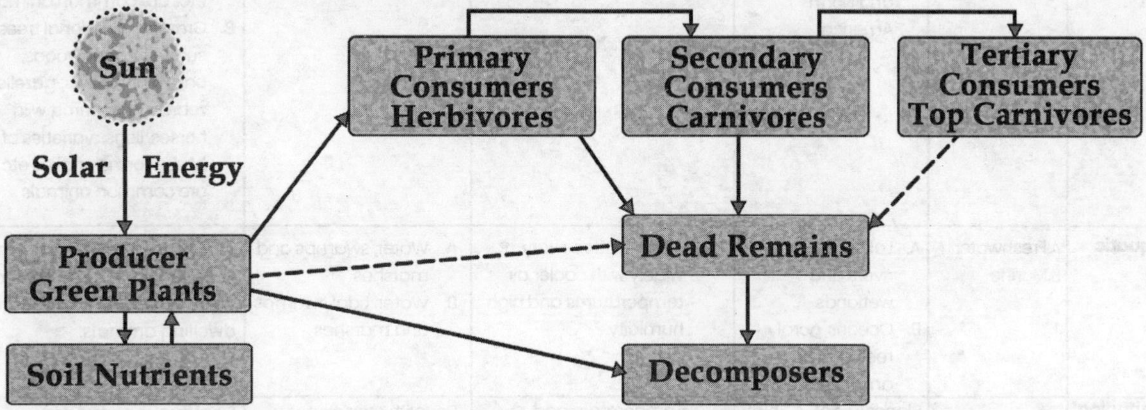

Structure and Functions of Ecosystems

Types of Biomes

The Earth's biosphere can be categorised into **five primary biomes**: forest, desert, grassland, aquatic, and altitudinal.

Biomes	Subtypes	Regions	Climatic Characteristics	Soil	Flora and Fauna
Forest	A. Tropical 1. Equatorial 2. Deciduous B. Temperate C. Boreal	A1. 10° N-S A2. 10°–25° N-S B. Eastern North America, N.E. Asia, Western and Central Europe C. Broad belt of Eurasia and North America (parts of Siberia, Alaska, Canada and Scandinavia)	A1. Temp. 20-25°C, evenly distributed A2. Temp. 25-30°C, Rainfall, ave, ann. 1,000mm, seasonal. B. Temp. 20-30°C, Rainfall evenly distributed 750 - 1,500mm, Well defined seasons and distinct winter C. Short moist moderately warm summers and long cold dry winter; very low temperatures. Precipitation mostly snowfall 400–1,000mm	A1. Acidic, poor in nutrients A2. Rich in nutrients B. Fertile. enriched with decaying litter C. Acidic and poor in nutrients. thin soil cover	A1. Multi-layered canopy tall and large trees A2. Less dense, trees of medium height; many varieties coexist. Insects, bats, birds and mammals are common species in both B. Moderately dense broad leaved trees With less diversity of plant species. Oak, Beach, Maple etc. are some common species Squirrels, rabbit, skunks, birds, black bears. mountain lions etc. C. Evergreen conifers like pine, fur and spruce etc. Wood peckers, hawks, bears, wolves, deer, hares and bats are common animals.

Desert	A. Hot and Dry desert B. Semi arid desert C. Coastal desert D. Cold desert	A. Sahara, Kalahari, Marusthali, Rub-el-Khali B. Marginal areas of hot deserts C. Atacama D. Tundra climatic regions	A. Temp. 20-45°C B. 21-38°C C. 15-35°C. D. 2-25°C A-D Rainfall is less than 50 mm	Rich in nutrients with little or no organic matter	A-C. Scanty vegetation: few large mammals. Insects, reptiles and birds D. Rabbits, rats, antelopes and ground squirrels
Grassland	A Tropical Savannah B. Temperate Steppe	A. Large areas of Africa, Australia. South America and India B. Parts of Eurasia and North America	A. Warm hot climate Rainfall 500-1,250 mm B. Hot summers and cold winter. Rainfall 500-900 mm	A. Porous with thin layer of humus. B. Thin flocculated soil, rich in bases	A. Grasses; trees and large shrubs absent; giraffes zebras, buffalos, leopards, hyenas, elephants, mice, moles, snakes and worms etc., are common animals B. Grasses; occasional trees such as cottonwoods, oaks and willows; gazelles, zebras, rhinoceros, wild horses, lions, varieties of birds, worms, snakes etc., are common animals
Aquatic	A. Freshwater B. Marine	A. Lakes, streams, rivers and wetlands B. Oceans, coral reefs, lagoons and estuaries	A-B Temperatures vary widely with cooler air temperatures and high humidity	A. Water, swamps and marshes B. Water, tidal swamps and marshes	Algal and other aquatic and marine plant communities with varieties of water dwelling animals.
Altitudinal		Slopes of high mountain ranges like the Himalayas, the Andes and the Rockies	Temperature and precipitation vary depending upon latitudinal zone	Regolith over slopes	Deciduous to tundra vegetation varying according to altitude

World Biomes

Biosphere – The Domain of Life

- **The biosphere** is the narrow region where air, water, and land meet.
- This is the region where life, which is exclusive to this planet, thrives. Numerous types of life exist, ranging in size from microscopic bacteria to enormous mammals.
- For survival, all living things, including people, are interdependent with the biosphere.
- The two kingdoms of organisms that make up the biosphere are the plant and animal kingdoms.

Biogeochemical Cycles

- The sun is the basic source of energy on which all life depends. This energy initiates life processes in the biosphere through photosynthesis, the main source of food and energy for green plants.
- During photosynthesis, carbon dioxide is converted into organic compounds and oxygen. Out of the total solar insolation that reaches the earth's surface, only a very small fraction (0.1 per cent) is fixed in photosynthesis. More than half is used for plant respiration and the remaining part is temporarily stored or is shifted to other portions of the plant.
- Life on earth consists of a great variety of living organisms. These living organisms exist and survive in a diversity of associations. Such survival involves the presence of systemic flows such as flows of energy, water and nutrients. These flows show variations in different parts of the world, in different seasons of the year and under varying local circumstances.
- Studies have shown that for the last one billion years, the atmosphere and hydrosphere have

been composed of approximately the same balance of chemical components. This balance of the chemical elements is maintained by a cyclic passage through the tissues of plants and animals.

- The cycle starts by absorbing the chemical elements by the organism and is returned to the air, water and soil through decomposition. These cycles are largely energised by solar insolation. These cyclic movements of chemical elements of the biosphere between the organism and the environment are referred to as **biogeochemical cycles. Bio refers to living organisms and geo to rocks, soil, air and water of the earth.**

There are two types of biogeochemical cycles: the **gaseous** and the **sedimentary** cycle. In the **gaseous cycle**, the main reservoir of nutrients is the atmosphere and the ocean. In the **sedimentary cycle**, the main reservoir is the soil and the sedimentary and other rocks of the earth's crust.

The Carbon Cycle

- **Carbon,** a fundamental element of life, constitutes the building blocks of all organic compounds. The biosphere harbours well over half a million distinct carbon-based molecules.
- The carbon cycle revolves primarily around the **transformation of carbon dioxide**. This process commences with the fixation of atmospheric carbon dioxide through photosynthesis. This conversion yields carbohydrates, most notably glucose, which can be further converted into other organic compounds such as sucrose, starch, and cellulose. Notably, a portion of these carbohydrates are directly utilised by the plant itself for its metabolic processes.
- However, this photosynthetic process also generates additional carbon dioxide, which is released through the plant's leaves or roots during daylight hours. The remaining carbohydrates that are not directly utilised by the plant are incorporated into its tissues. These plant tissues then serve as sustenance for herbivorous animals or undergo decomposition by microorganisms.
- Herbivores convert a portion of the consumed carbohydrates into carbon dioxide, which is subsequently released back into the atmosphere via respiration. Following the death of the animal, any remaining carbohydrates are decomposed by microorganisms.
- Finally, the carbohydrates broken down by microorganisms are oxidised into carbon dioxide, completing the cycle and returning this essential element to the atmosphere.

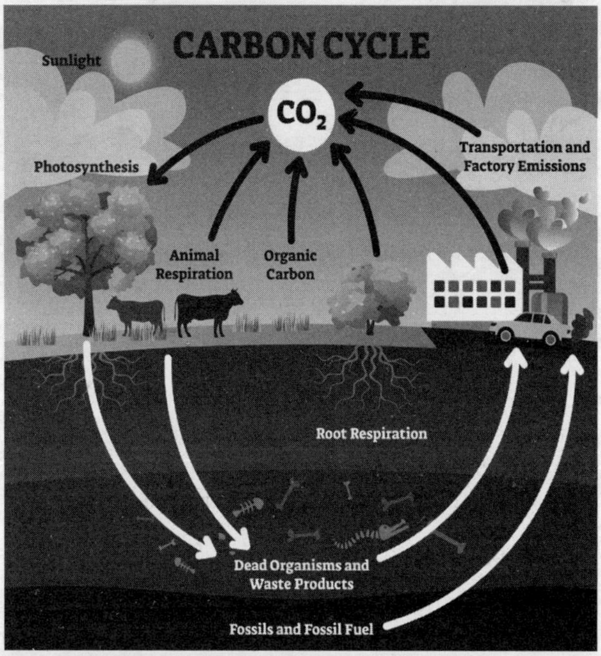

Carbon Cycle

The Oxygen Cycle

- Oxygen is one of the most vital elements on Earth and the most common element of the human body. Oxygen **constitutes about 65% of the mass of the human body** and most of this is in the form of water. Oxygen also **makes up about 30% of the Earth and 20% of the atmosphere.**
- **The primary byproduct** of photosynthesis is **oxygen**. Energy, carbon dioxide, and water are released during the oxidation of carbohydrates.
- The oxygen cycle is an extremely intricate operation. There are several chemical configurations and types of oxygen.
- It reacts with nitrogen to create nitrates, and it also reacts with a wide range of other minerals and elements to create different oxides, including aluminium oxide and iron oxide.

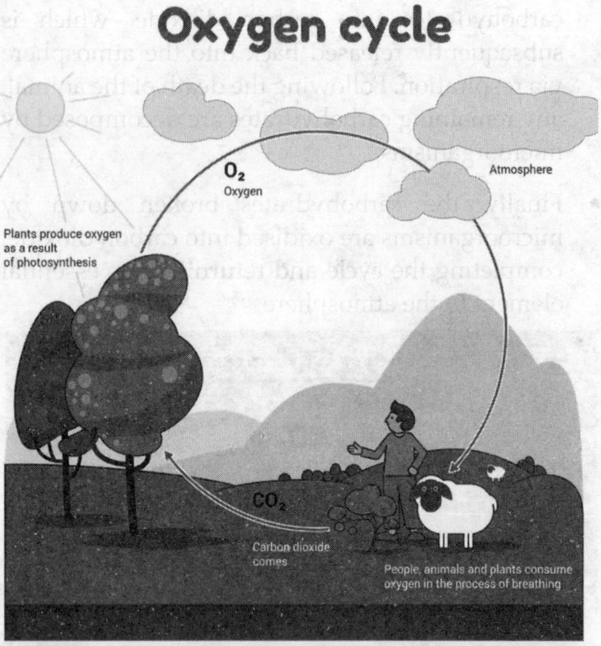

Oxygen Cycle

- During photosynthesis, sunlight breaks down water molecules, producing a large amount of oxygen that plants then release into the atmosphere through transpiration and respiration.

The Nitrogen Cycle

- **Approximately 78%** of the atmospheric gases are composed of **nitrogen**, making it a significant component of the atmosphere.
- Moreover, it is a necessary component of several chemical substances, including proteins, amino acids, nucleic acids, vitamins, and pigments.
- Merely a limited group of organisms, such as some types of **soil bacteria and blue-green algae, possess the ability to directly utilise it in its gaseous state**.
- Nitrogen is usually only useful once it has been corrected. Ninety percent is biological in origin for fixed nitrogen.
- The primary source of free nitrogen is the atmospheric nitrogen that is present in the soil's pore spaces, which is utilised by soil microorganisms and related plant roots.
- Furthermore, cosmic radiation and lightning have the ability to fix nitrogen in the atmosphere. Some aquatic organisms can repair it in the oceans.
- Green plants are able to absorb atmospheric nitrogen once it has been fixed into an accessible state. Part of it is then eaten by herbivorous animals that feed on plants.

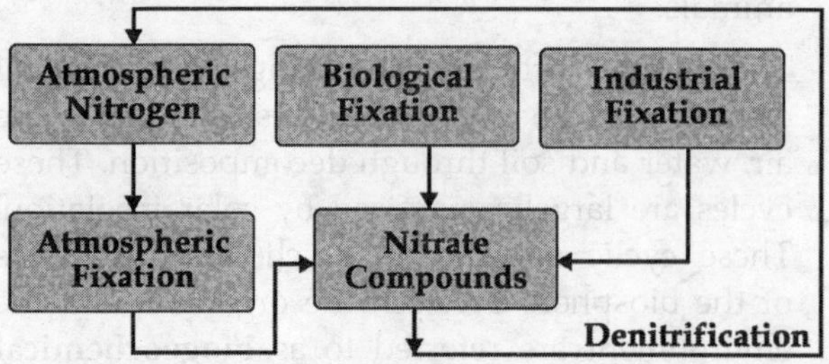

Nitrogen Cycle

- The bacteria found in the soil transform dead plants and animals excreted nitrogenous waste into nitrites.
- **Certain bacteria can even change nitrites into nitrates, which green plants can utilise again. Nitrates can be converted by other kinds of bacteria into free nitrogen** through a process called **denitrification.**

Other Mineral Cycles

- Other than carbon, oxygen, nitrogen and hydrogen being the principal geochemical components of the biosphere, many other minerals also occur as critical nutrients for plant and animal life.
- These **mineral elements** required by living organisms are obtained initially from inorganic sources such as phosphorus, sulphur, calcium and potassium.
- They usually occur as salts dissolved in soil water or lakes, streams and seas.
- **Mineral salts** come directly from the earth's crust by weathering where the soluble salts enter the water cycle, eventually reaching the sea.
- **Other salts** are returned to the earth's surface through sedimentation, and after weathering, they again enter the cycle.
- All living organisms fulfilled their mineral requirements from mineral solutions in their environments. Other animals receive their mineral needs from the plants and animals they consume.

- After the death of living organisms, the minerals are returned to the soil and water through decomposition and flow.

Ecological Balance

- **Ecological balance** is a state of dynamic equilibrium within a community of organisms in a habitat or ecosystem.
- It can happen when the diversity of the living organisms remains relatively stable.
- Gradual changes do take place but that happens only through natural succession.
- It can also be explained as a stable balance in the numbers of each species in an ecosystem. This occurs through competition and cooperation between different organisms where the population remains stable.
- This balance is brought about by the fact that certain species compete with one another determined by the environment in which they grow.
- This balance is also attained by the fact that some species depend on others for their food and sustenance.
- Such accounts are encountered in vast grasslands where the herbivorous animals (deer, zebras, buffaloes etc.,) are found in plenty. On the other hand, the carnivorous animals (tigers, lions, etc.) that are not usually in large numbers, hunt and feed on the herbivores, thereby controlling their population.
- In the plants, any disturbance in the native forests such as clearing the forest for shifting cultivation usually brings about a change in the species distribution. This change is due to competition where the secondary forest species such as grasses, bamboos or pines overtakes the native species changing the original forest structure. This is called **succession.**
- Ecological balance may be **disturbed due to the introduction of new species, natural hazards or human causes.**
- **Human interference** has affected the balance of plant communities leading to disturbances in the ecosystems. Such disturbances bring about numerous **secondary successions.**
- Ecological imbalances **have brought many natural calamities like floods, landslides, diseases, erratic climatic occurrences, etc.**
- There is a very close relationship between the plant and animal communities within particular habitats. Diversity of life in a particular area can be employed as an indicator of the habitat factor. Proper knowledge and understanding of such factors provide a strong base for protecting and conserving the ecosystems.

TEST YOURSELF

Multiple Choice Questions

Q1. Which of the following best defines an ecosystem?

(a) A group of organisms (biotic or abiotic) living together in a specific area

(b) A single organism interacting with its environment

(c) A collection of unrelated species living in a habitat

(d) A community of plants and animals sharing resources

Q2. What is the primary source of energy in most ecosystems?

(a) Sunlight (b) Fossil fuels

(c) Geothermal heat (d) Chemical reactions

Q3. Which of the following is an abiotic component of an ecosystem?

(a) Plants (b) Animals

(c) Rocks (d) Decomposers

Q4. Which of the following is an example of a decomposer in an ecosystem?

(a) Rabbit (b) Hawk

(c) Earthworm (d) Tree

Q5. What is the role of producers in an ecosystem?

(a) They consume other organisms for energy.

(b) They break down organic matter into simpler forms.

(c) They convert sunlight into chemical energy through photosynthesis.

(d) They regulate the population of other organisms.

Q6. Which trophic level is occupied by herbivores in a food chain?

(a) Primary consumers

(b) Secondary consumers

(c) Tertiary consumers

(d) Decomposers

Q7. What happens to energy as it flows through trophic levels in an ecosystem?

(a) It increases. (b) It remains constant.

(c) It decreases. (d) It is recycled.

Q8. Which of the following is an example of a biotic factor in an ecosystem?

(a) Temperature (b) Water availability

(c) Soil type (d) Predators

Q9. What is the main role of decomposers in an ecosystem?

(a) To produce oxygen through photosynthesis

(b) To break down dead organisms and recycle nutrients

(c) To provide energy to other organisms through predation

(d) To regulate the temperature of the ecosystem

Q10. Which of the following is an example of a natural ecosystem?

(a) A zoo (b) A garden

(c) A forest (d) A parking lot

Q11. Which of the following is not a major biogeochemical cycle?

(a) Carbon cycle (b) Nitrogen cycle

(c) Oxygen cycle (d) Energy cycle

Q12. The process by which carbon dioxide is converted into organic compounds by plants is called:

(a) Photosynthesis (b) Respiration

(c) Decomposition (d) Nitrogen fixation

Q13. Which element is primarily cycled through the phosphorus cycle?

(a) Carbon (b) Nitrogen

(c) Oxygen (d) Phosphorus

Q14. Nitrogen fixation is the process by which:

(a) Nitrogen gas is converted into ammonia

(b) Ammonia is converted into nitrogen gas

(c) Nitrate is converted into nitrogen gas

(d) Nitrogen gas is converted into nitrate

Q15. The main reservoir of water in the water cycle is:

(a) Oceans (b) Atmosphere

(c) Rivers (d) Groundwater

Q16. The process of converting atmospheric nitrogen gas into a usable form by bacteria is called:

(a) Denitrification (b) Nitrification

(c) Nitrogen fixation (d) Ammonification

Q17. Which of the following is not a step in the nitrogen cycle?

(a) Nitrogen fixation (b) Nitrification

(c) Photosynthesis (d) Denitrification

Q18. The phosphorus cycle does not involve a significant atmospheric component because:

(a) Phosphorus is not present in the atmosphere

(b) Phosphorus is rapidly cycled through the atmosphere

(c) Phosphorus is released from volcanic activity

(d) Phosphorus is primarily found in the oceans

Q19. The primary source of phosphorus for the phosphorus cycle is:

(a) Rocks and minerals

(b) Atmosphere

(c) Decomposing organic matter

(d) Nitrogen-fixing bacteria

Q20. The release of excess carbon dioxide into the atmosphere due to human activities is a major factor contributing to:

(a) Global warming (b) Ozone depletion

(c) Acid rain (d) Soil erosion

Answer Key

Q1.	a	Q2.	a	Q3.	c	Q4.	c
Q5.	c	Q6.	a	Q7.	c	Q8.	d
Q9.	b	Q10.	c	Q11.	d	Q12.	a
Q13.	d	Q14.	a	Q15.	a	Q16.	c
Q17.	c	Q18.	a	Q19.	a	Q20.	a

UNIT 19 Natural Vegetation and Wild Life of India and the World

In This Unit

Comprehensive and profound coverage of the following NCERTs' chapters:

- ✓ NCERT (Before Rationalisation) Class- 7th (Our Environment), Chapter- 6
- ✓ NCERT Class- 8th (Resources and Development), Chapter- 2
- ✓ NCERT Class- 9th (Contemporary India-I), Chapter- 5
- ✓ NCERT Class- 11th (India Physical Environment), Chapter- 5

Our country India is one of the **12 Mega Bio-Diverse** countries of the world. With about 47,000 plant species India occupies tenth place in the world and **fourth in Asia in plant diversity.** There are about 15,000 flowering plants in India, which account for 6 per cent in the world's total number of flowering plants. The country has many non- flowering plants, such as ferns, algae and fungi. India also has approximately 90,000 species of animals, as well as, a rich variety of fish in its fresh and marine waters.

Natural vegetation refers to a plant community, which has grown naturally without human aid and has been left undisturbed by humans for a long time. This is termed as **'Virgin Vegetation'.** Thus, cultivated crops and fruits, orchards form part of vegetation but not natural vegetation.

India is a land of great variety of natural vegetation. Himalayan heights are marked with temperate vegetation; the Western Ghats and the Andaman Nicobar Islands have tropical rain forests, the deltaic regions have tropical forests and mangroves; the desert and semi desert areas of Rajasthan are known for cacti, a wide variety of bushes and thorny vegetation. Depending upon the variations in the climate and the soil, the vegetation of India changes from one region to another.

The term 'Flora' is used to denote plants of a particular region or period. Similarly, the species of animals are referred to as **'Fauna'.** This huge diversity in the flora and fauna kingdom is due to the following factors.

Relief

- **Land-** Land affects the natural vegetation directly and indirectly. The nature of land influences the type of vegetation. The fertile level is generally devoted to agriculture. The undulating and rough terrains are areas where grassland and woodlands develop and give shelter to a variety of wildlife.
- **Soil-** Different types of soils provide basis for different types of vegetation. The sandy soils of the desert support cactus and thorny bushes, while wet, marshy, deltaic soils support mangroves and deltaic vegetation. The hill slopes with some depth of soil have conical trees.

Climate

- **Temperature-** The character and extent of vegetation are mainly determined by temperature along with humidity in the air, precipitation and soil. On the slopes of the Himalayas and the hills of the Peninsula above the height of 915 metres, the fall in the temperature affects the types of vegetation and its growth, and changes it from tropical to subtropical temperate and alpine vegetation.
- **Photoperiod (Sunlight)-** The variation in duration of sunlight at different places is due to differences in latitude, altitude, season and duration of the day. Due to the longer duration of sunlight, trees grow faster in summer.

- **Precipitation-** In India, almost the entire rainfall is brought in by the advancing southwest monsoon (June to September) and retreating northeast monsoons. **Areas of heavy rainfall have more dense vegetation as compared to areas of less rainfall.**

Types of Vegetation in India

The following major types of vegetation identified in our country are:

1. Tropical Evergreen and Semi Evergreen Forests
2. Tropical Deciduous Forests
3. Tropical Thorn Forests
4. Montane Forests
5. Littoral and Swamp Forests

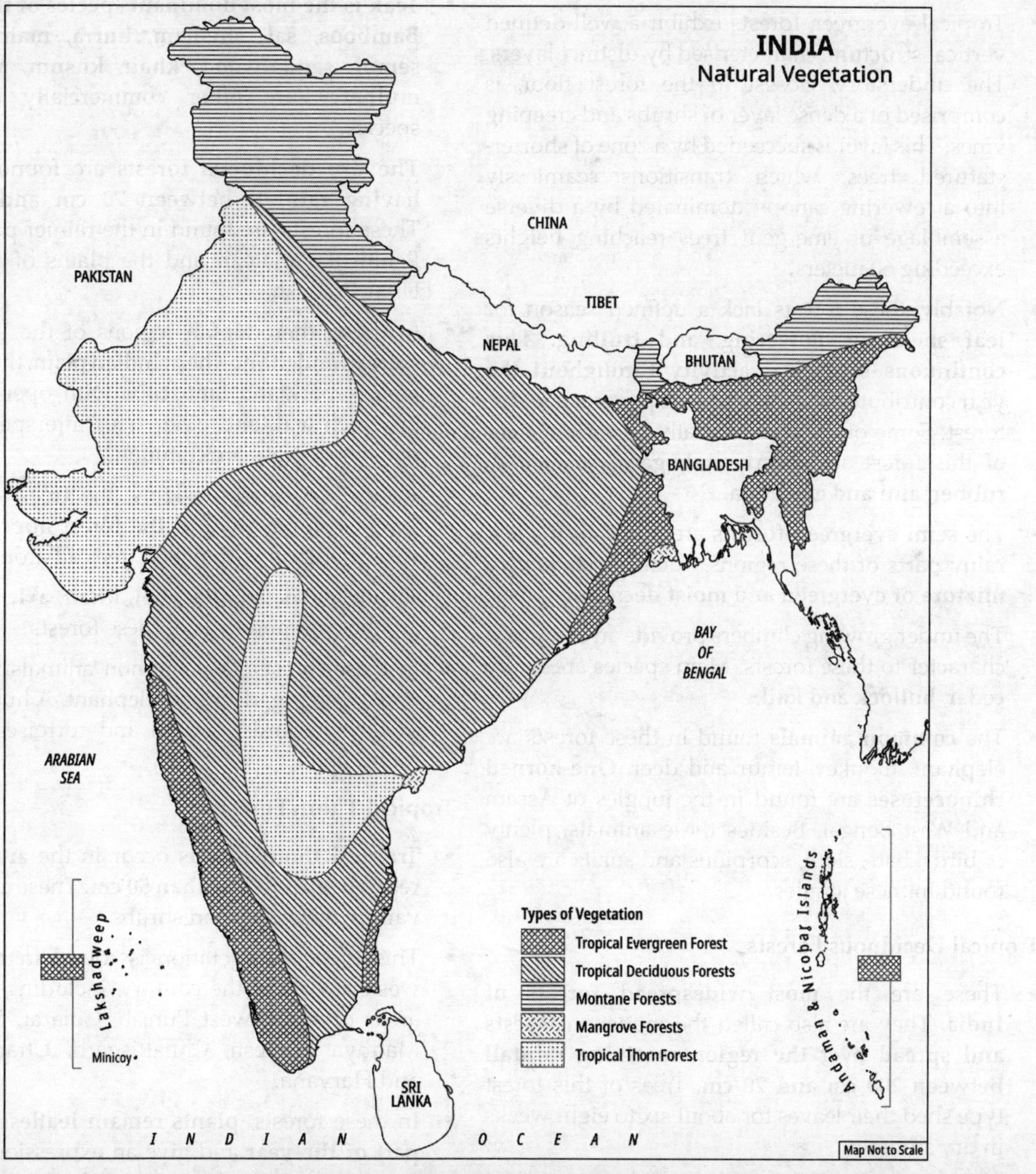

India: Natural Vegetation

Tropical Evergreen Forests and Semi Evergreen Forests

- These forests are **restricted to heavy rainfall areas** of the Western Ghats and the island groups of Lakshadweep, Andaman and Nicobar, upper parts of Assam and Tamil Nadu coast.
- They are found in areas having **more than 200 cm of rainfall and mean annual temperature above 22°C.**
- Tropical evergreen forests exhibit a well-defined vertical structure, characterised by distinct layers. The understory, closest to the forest floor, is comprised of a dense layer of shrubs and creeping vines. This layer is succeeded by a zone of shorter-statured trees, which transitions seamlessly into a towering canopy dominated by a diverse assemblage of emergent trees reaching heights exceeding 60 meters.
- Notably, these forests lack a defined season for **leaf shedding, flowering, and fruiting. This continuous biological activity throughout the year** contributes to the evergreen appearance of the forest. Some of the commercially important trees of this forest are **ebony, mahogany, rosewood, rubber, aini and cinchona.**
- The **semi evergreen forests** are found in the less rainy parts of these regions. Such forests have a **mixture of evergreen and moist deciduous** trees.
- The under growing climbers provide an evergreen character to these forests. Main species are **white cedar, hollock and kail.**
- The **common animals** found in these forests are elephant, monkey, lemur and deer. **One-horned rhinoceroses** are found in the jungles of Assam and West Bengal. Besides these animals, plenty of birds, bats, sloth, scorpions and snails are also found in these jungles.

Tropical Deciduous Forests

- These are the **most widespread forests of India.** They are also called the **monsoon forests and spread over the region receiving rainfall between 200 cm and 70 cm.** Trees of this forest type shed their leaves for about six to eight weeks in dry summer.
- **On the basis of the availability of water,** these forests are further divided into **moist and dry deciduous.**
- **The Moist deciduous forests** are more pronounced in the regions **which record rainfall between 100-200 cm.** These forests exist, therefore, mostly in the eastern part of the country northeastern states, along the foothills of the Himalayas, Jharkhand, West Odisha and Chhattisgarh, and on the eastern slopes of the Western Ghats.
- **Teak is the most dominant species of this forest. Bamboos, sal, shisham, hurra, mahua, amla, semul, sandalwood, khair, kusum, arjun and mulberry** are other commercially important species.
- **The dry deciduous forests** are found in areas **having rainfall between 70 cm and 100 cm.** These forests are found in the rainier parts of the Peninsular plateau and the plains of Bihar and Uttar Pradesh.
- In the higher rainfall regions of the Peninsular plateau and the northern Indian plain, these forests have a parkland landscape with open stretches in which teak and other trees interspersed with patches of grass are common.
- As the dry season begins, the trees shed their leaves completely and the forest appears like a vast grassland with naked trees all around.
- **Tendu, palas, amaltas, bel, khair, axlewood,** etc. are the common trees of these forests.
- In these forests, the common animals found are lion, tiger, pig, deer and elephant. A huge variety of birds, lizards, snakes and tortoises are also found here.

Tropical Thorn Forests

- **Tropical thorn forests** occur in the **areas which receive rainfall less than 50 cm**. These consist of a variety of grasses and shrubs.
- This type of vegetation is found in the north-western part of the country, including semi-arid areas of south west Punjab, Gujarat, Rajasthan, Madhya Pradesh, Chhattisgarh, Uttar Pradesh and Haryana.
- In these forests, **plants remain leafless for most part of the year** and give an expression of scrub vegetation. Important species found are **babool,**

ber, and wild date palm, khair, neem, khejri, palas, acacias, palms, euphorbias and cacti etc. **Tussocky grass** grows upto a height of 2 m as the undergrowth.

- Trees are scattered and have long roots penetrating deep into the soil in order to get moisture. The stems are succulent to conserve water. Leaves are mostly thick and small to minimise evaporation. These forests give way to thorn forests and scrubs in arid areas.
- In these forests, the common animals are **rats, mice, rabbits, fox, wolf, tiger, lion, wild ass, horses and camels.**

Montane Forests

- In mountainous areas, the decrease in temperature with increasing altitude leads to the corresponding change in natural vegetation. **Mountain forests can be classified into two types,** the **northern mountain forests and the southern mountain forests.**
- The Himalayan ranges show a succession of vegetation from the tropical to the tundra, which change with the altitude.
- Deciduous forests are found in the **foothills of the Himalayas.** It is succeeded by the **wet temperate type of forests** found between a height of **1000 and 2000 m**. In the higher hill ranges of northeastern India, hilly areas of West Bengal and Uttarakhand, **evergreen broad leaf trees such as oak and chestnut** are predominant.
- Between **1500 and 3000 m, temperate forests** containing **coniferous trees, like pine, deodar, silver fir, spruce and cedar,** are found. These forests cover mostly the southern slopes of the Himalayas, places having high altitude in southern and north-east India. Deodar, a highly valued endemic species grows mainly in the western part of the Himalayan range. Deodar is a durable wood mainly used in construction activity. Similarly, the **chinar and the walnut,** which sustain the famous Kashmir handicrafts, belong to this zone. **Blue pine and spruce** appear at altitudes of 2,225-3,048 m
- **At higher elevations, temperate grasslands** are common. At high altitudes, generally, more than 3,600 meters above the sea level, temperate forests and grasslands give way to the **Alpine Vegetation. Silver fir, junipers, pines and birches** are the common trees of these forests. However, they get progressively stunted as they approach the snow-line. These pastures are used extensively for grazing by **nomadic tribes, like the Gujjars and the Bakarwals.**
- The **southern slopes of the Himalayas** carry a thicker vegetation cover because of relatively **higher precipitation** than the drier north-facing slopes. At higher altitudes, mosses and lichens form part of tundra vegetation.
- The southern mountain forests include the forests found in **three distinct areas** of Peninsular India viz; **the Western Ghats, the Vindhyas and the Nilgiris**. As they are closer to the tropics, and only 1,500 m above the sea level, vegetation is temperate in the higher regions, and subtropical on the lower regions of the Western Ghats, especially in Kerala, Tamil Nadu and Karnataka.
- **The temperate forests are called Sholas in the Nilgiris, Anaimalai and Palani hills**. Some of the other trees of this forest of economic significance include, **magnolia, laurel, cinchona and wattle.** Such forests are also found in the Satpura and the Maikal ranges.
- The **common animals** found in these forests are Kashmir stag, spotted deer, wild sheep, jack rabbit, **Tibetan antelope, yak, snow leopard, squirrels, Shaggy horned wild ibex, bear and rare red panda,** sheep and goats with thick hair.

Littoral and Swamp Forests

- India has a rich variety of wetland habitats. About 70 percent of this comprises areas under paddy cultivation. The total area of wetland is 3.9 million hectares.
- Two sites - **Chilika Lake (Odisha) and Keoladeo National Park (Bharatpur)** are protected as water-fowl habitats under the Convention of Wetlands of International Importance (**Ramsar Convention**).
- **The country's wetlands have been grouped into Eight categories, viz.**
  - The **reservoirs of the Deccan Plateau** in the south together with the lagoons and other wetlands of the southern west coast;
  - The vast **saline** expanses of Rajasthan, Gujarat and the **Gulf of Kachchh;**

➢ **Freshwater lakes and reservoirs** from Gujarat eastwards through Rajasthan (Keoladeo National Park) and Madhya Pradesh;

➢ The delta wetlands and **lagoons of India's east coast** (Chilika Lake);

➢ The **freshwater marshes of the Gangetic** Plain;

➢ The **floodplains of the Brahmaputra;** the marshes and swamps in the hills of northeast India and the Himalayan foothills;

➢ The lakes and **rivers of the montane region of Kashmir and Ladakh;** and

➢ The **mangrove forest** and other wetlands of the island arcs of the Andaman and Nicobar Islands.

- **Mangroves grow along the coasts in the salt marshes, tidal creeks, mud flats and estuaries. They consist of a number of salt-tolerant species of plants.** In India, the mangrove forests spread over 6,740 sq. km which is 7 per cent of the world's mangrove forests. They are highly developed in the Andaman and Nicobar Islands and the Sunderbans of West Bengal. Other areas of significance are the Mahanadi, the Godavari and the Krishna deltas. These forests too, are being encroached upon, and hence, need conservation.

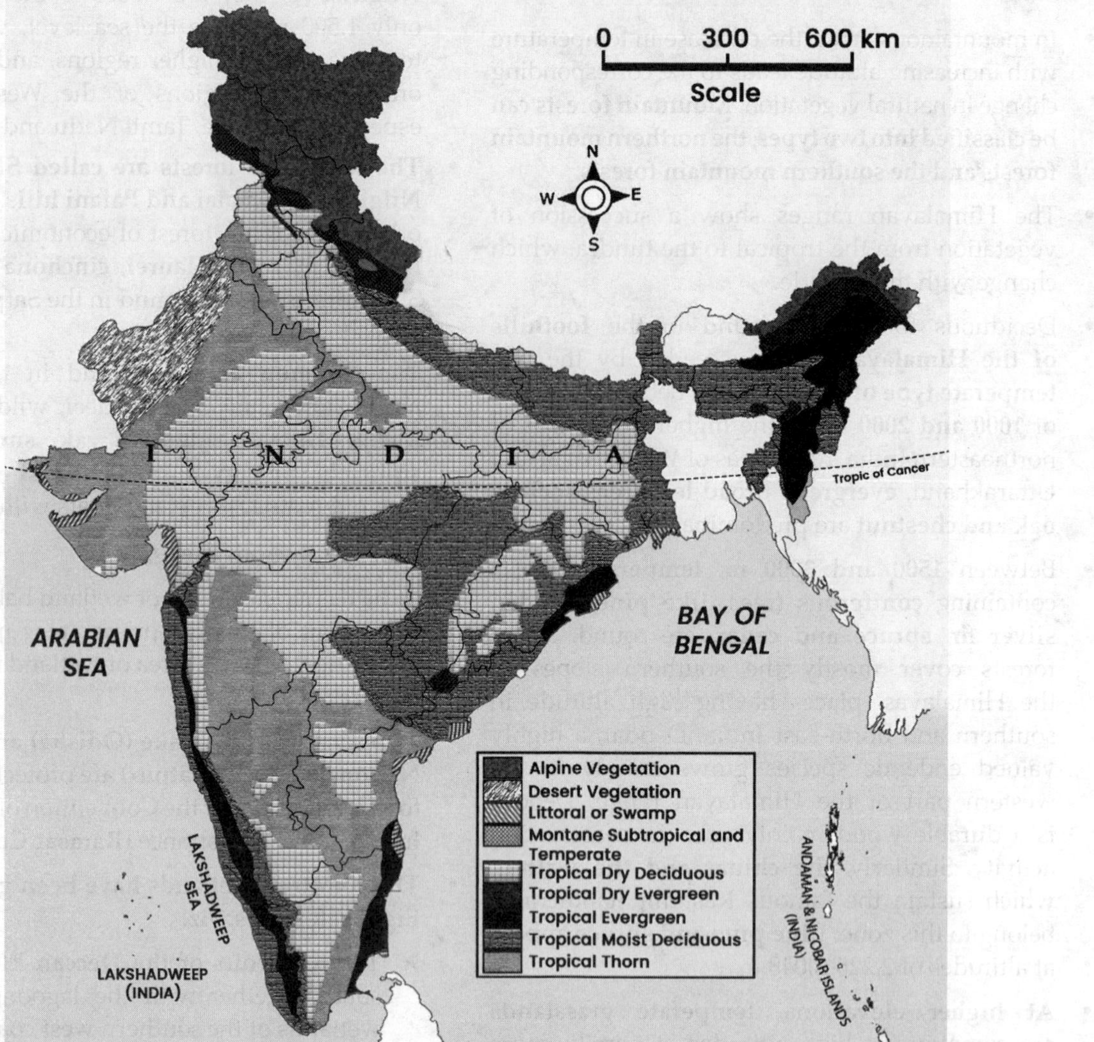

Types of Forests in India

- In the Ganga- Brahmaputra delta, **sundari trees** are found, which provide durable hard timber. **Palm, coconut, keora, agar,** etc., also grow in some parts of the delta. The Royal Bengal Tiger is the famous animal in Mangrove Forests. Turtles, crocodiles, gharials and snakes are also found in these forests.

World Distribution of Vegetation

Tropical Evergreen Forests: Found in Amazon, Congo and Malaysia. Hardwood trees like rosewood, ebony, mahogany are common here.

Tropical Deciduous Forests: Found in **northern Australia, central America, East Africa and Madagascar**. The hardwood trees found in these forests are sal, teak and acacia.

Temperate Evergreen Forests: The mid-latitude coastal region is home to the temperate evergreen forests. They usually belong in the easternmost regions of the continents, such as the southeast of the **United States, southeast China, and southeast Brazil**. They include trees with **both soft and hard wood,** such as eucalyptus, pine, and oak.

Temperate Deciduous Forests: There are more temperate deciduous woodlands in higher latitudes. These can be found in the **coastal regions of Western Europe as well as in China, New Zealand, Chile, and the northeastern United States**. During the dry season, they lose their leaves. Common trees include beeches, ash, and oaks. The most prevalent animals include wolves, foxes, and deer. This area is also home to birds like monals and pheasants.

Mediterranean Vegetation: Deciduous and temperate evergreen trees cover most of the east and northeastern edges of the continents. There are differences between the continents' west and south-west margins. Their vegetation is **Mediterranean.** As suggested by the name, it is **primarily found in regions of Europe, Africa, and Asia that are close to the Mediterranean Sea.** This type of vegetation can also be found in **South West Africa, South West Australia, South West Africa, and California in the United States,** all of which are located outside of the true Mediterranean region. The summers in these areas are hot and dry, and the winters are warm and rainy. Due to the removal of the native vegetation to make room for cultivation, citrus fruits including oranges, figs, grapes, and olives are frequently grown here.

Coniferous Forests: In the higher latitudes (50° - 70°) of the Northern hemisphere the spectacular Coniferous forests are found. **These are also called Taiga.** These are tall **evergreen trees with softwood.** These trees' woods are highly valuable for producing pulp, which is needed to make newsprint and paper. Softwood is also used to make packing boxes and match boxes. In these forests, the most significant tree varieties are **cedar, pine, and chir**. Polar bears, mink, and silver foxes are typical creatures in this area.

Grasslands Across the World

Tropical grasslands: They are found throughout the tropics and on **both sides of the equator.** This type of vegetation grows in regions with **moderate to little rainfall.** The grass has the potential to reach heights of three to four metres. These are the **Savannah grasslands** found in Africa. In tropical grasslands, one can frequently find elephants, zebras, giraffes, deer, and leopards.

Tropical Grasslands examples- **East Africa- Savanna, Brazil- Campos and Venezuela- Llanos**

Temperate grasslands: These can be found in the **interior regions of the continents** as well as the mid-latitudinal zones. Here, the **grass is often short and nutrient-rich.** In the temperate zone, antelopes, bison, and wild buffalo are common.

Temperate Grasslands examples- Argentina- **Pampas,** North America- **Prairie,** S. Africa- **Veld,** C. Asia- **Steppe** and Australia- **Down.**

Forest Cover in India

According to **Forest Survey of India Report 2021**, the forest area covers **24.62 per cent** of the total land area of the country. It is important to note that the forest area and the actual forest cover are not the same. The **Forest Area** is the area notified and recorded as the forest land irrespective of the existence of trees, while the **Actual Forest Cover** is the area occupied by forests with canopy. The former is based on the records of the State Revenue Department, while the latter is based on aerial photographs and satellite imageries.

The Region	Percentage Cover of the Forest
(i) The region of high concentration	> 40
(ii) The region of medium concentration	20–40
(iii) The region of low concentration	10–20
(iv) The region of very low concentration	< 10

Both forest area and forest cover **vary from state to state.** Lakshadweep has zero per cent forest area; **Andaman and Nicobar Islands have 86.93 per cent.** Most of the states with less than 10 per cent of the forest area lie in the north and northwestern part of the country. These are Rajasthan, Gujarat, Punjab, Haryana and Delhi. Most of the forests in Punjab and Haryana have been cleared for cultivation. States with **10-20 per cent forest area are Tamil Nadu and West Bengal.** In Peninsular India, excluding Tamil Nadu, Dadra and Nagar Haveli and Goa, the area under forest cover is 20-30 per cent. The **northeastern states have more than 30 per cent of the land under forest.** Hilly topography and heavy rainfall are good for forest growth. There is a lot of variation in actual forest cover, which ranges from 9.56 per cent in Jammu and Kashmir to 84.01 per cent in Andaman and Nicobar Islands. There are **15 states where the forest cover is more than one-third of the total area, which is the basic requirement for maintaining the ecological balance.**

Forest Conservation

Forests have an intricate interrelationship with life and environment. These provide numerous direct and indirect advantages to our economy and society. Hence, conservation of forest is of vital importance to the survival and prosperity of humankind.

The Government of India proposed to have a nation-wide forest conservation policy, and adopted a Forest Policy in 1952, which was further modified in 1988. According to the new forest policy, the **Government will emphasise sustainable forest management in order to conserve and expand forest reserve on the one hand, and to meet the needs of local people on the other.**

The National Forest Policy, 1988 aimed at:

- Bringing 33 per cent of the geographical area under forest cover;
- Maintaining environmental stability and to restore forests where ecological balance was disturbed;
- Conserving the natural heritage of the country, its biological diversity and genetic pool;
- Checks soil erosion, extension of the desert lands and reduction of floods and droughts;
- Increasing the forest cover through social forestry and afforestation on degraded land;
- Increasing the productivity of forests to make timber, fuel, fodder and food available to rural population dependent on forests, and encourage the substitution of wood;
- Creating of a massive people's movement involving women to encourage planting of trees, stop felling of trees and thus, reduce pressure on the existing forest.

Social Forestry

Social forestry means the management and protection of forests and afforestation on barren lands with the purpose of helping in the environmental, social and rural development.

There are 3 types of forestry- Urban forestry, Rural forestry and Farm forestry.

Urban forestry pertains to the raising and management of trees on public and privately owned lands in and around urban centres such as green belts, parks, roadside avenues, industrial and commercial green belts, etc.

Rural forestry lays emphasis on promotion of **Agro-Forestry and Community-Forestry.**

Agro-forestry is the raising of trees and agriculture crops on the same land inclusive of the waste patches. It combines forestry with agriculture, thus, altering the simultaneous production of food, fodder, fuel, timber and fruit.

Community forestry involves the raising of trees on public or community land such as the village pasture and temple land, roadside, canal bank, strips along railway lines, and schools etc.

Farm Forestry

It is a term applied to the process under which farmers **grow trees** for **commercial and non-commercial** purposes on their farm lands. Forest departments of various states distribute seedlings of trees free of cost to small and medium farmers. Several lands such as the margins of agricultural fields, grasslands and pastures, land around homes and cow sheds may be used for raising trees under non-commercial farm forestry.

Wildlife

Some of the important reasons of the decline of wildlife are as follows:

(i) Industrial and technological advancement brought about a rapid increase in the exploitation of forest resources.

(ii) More and more lands were cleared for agriculture, human settlement, roads, mining, reservoirs, etc.

(iii) Pressure on forests mounted due to lopping for fodder and fuelwood and removal of small timber by the local people.

(iv) Grazing by domestic cattle caused an adverse effect on wildlife and its habitat.

(v) Hunting was taken up as a sport by the elite and hundreds of wild animals were killed in a single hunt. **Now commercial poaching is rampant.**

(vi) Incidence of forest fire.

Thus, **conservation of wildlife is very important, steps taken for wildlife conservation are as follows:**

- In **1972**, a comprehensive **Wildlife Act** was enacted, which provides the main legal framework for conservation and protection of wildlife in India. **The two main objectives of the Act are**; to provide protection to the endangered species listed in the schedule of the Act and to provide legal support to the conservation areas of the country classified as National parks, sanctuaries and closed areas.
- In **1991**, this Act was amended making punishments more stringent and has also made provisions for the protection of specified plant species and conservation of endangered species of wild animals.
- For the purpose of effective conservation of flora and fauna, special steps have been initiated by the Government of India in collaboration with UNESCO's **'Man and Biosphere Programme'.**
- Special schemes like **Project Tiger (1973) and Project Elephant (1992)** and for various animals like **Crocodile Breeding Project, Project Hangul and conservation of Himalayan Musk deer** have also been launched to conserve these species and their habitat in a sustainable manner.
- **Project Tiger** has been implemented since 1973. The main objective of the scheme is to ensure maintenance of viable population of tigers in India for scientific, aesthetic, cultural and ecological and to preserve areas of biological importance as natural heritage for the benefit, education and enjoyment of the people.
- **Project Elephant** was launched in 1992 to assist states having free ranging population of wild elephants. It was aimed at ensuring long-term survival of identified viable population of elephants in their natural habitat. The project is being implemented in 16 states.

Biosphere Reserves-

A Biosphere Reserve is a unique and representative ecosystem of **terrestrial and coastal areas** which are internationally recognised within the framework of **UNESCO's Man and Biosphere (MAB) Programme.**

The Biosphere Reserve aims at achieving the three objectives-

1. **Conservation-** Conservation of biodiversity and ecosystem.

2. **Development-** Association of environment with development.

3. **Logistics-** International network for research and monitoring.

There are 18 Biosphere Reserves in India, 12 Biosphere Reserves have been recognised by the UNESCO on **World Network of Biosphere Reserves.**

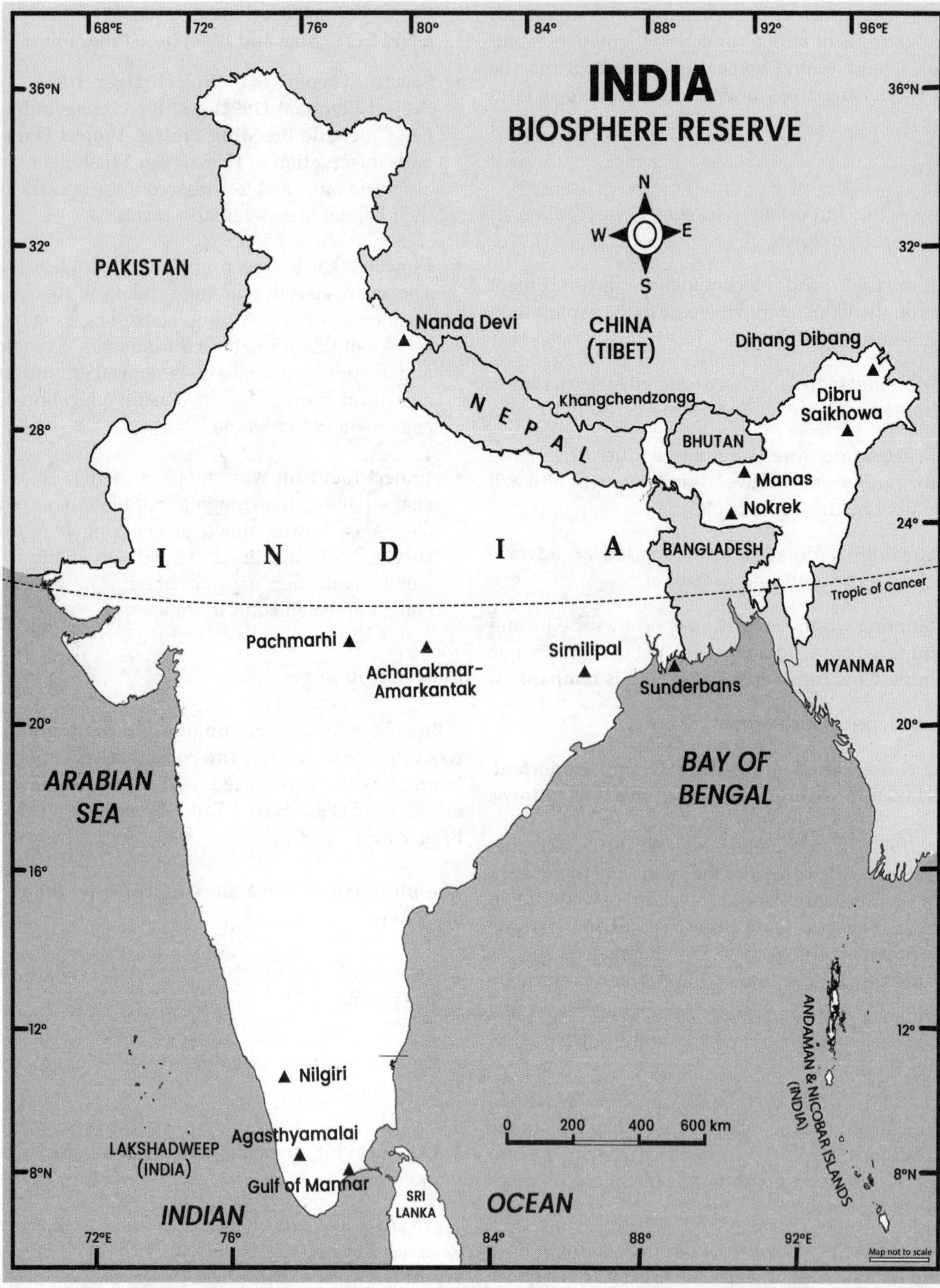

India: Biosphere Reserve

Sl.No.	Name of the Biosphere Reserve and Total Geographical Area (km²)	Date of Designation	Location in the States/UT
1.	**Nilgiri (5520)**	01.08.1986	Part of Wayanad, Nagarhole, Bandipur and Madumalai, Nilambur, Silent Valley and Siruvani Hills (Tamil Nadu, Kerala and Karnataka).
2.	**Nanda Devi (5860.69)**	18.01.1988	Part of Chamoli, Pithoragarh and Almora Districts in Uttarakhand.
3.	**Nokrek (820)**	01.09.1988	Part of East, West and South Garo Hill Districts in Meghalaya.
4.	**Manas (2837)**	14.03.1989	Part of Kokrajhar, Bongaigaon, Barpeta, Nalbari, Kamrup and Darang Districts in Assam
5.	**Sunderban (9630)**	29.03.1989	Part of delta of Ganga and Brahamaputra river system in West Bengal.
6.	**Gulf of Mannar (10500)**	18.02.1989	Indian part of Gulf of Mannar extending from Rameswaram island in the North to Kaniyakumari in the South of Tamil Nadu.
7.	**Great Nicobar (885)**	06.01.1989	Southern most island of Andaman and Nicobar Islands.
8.	**Similipal (4374)**	21.06.1994	Part of Mayurbhanj District in Odisha.
9.	**Dibru-Saikhowa (765)**	28.07.1997	Part of Dibrugarh and Tinsukia Districts in Assam
10.	**Dehang Debang (5111.5)**	02.09.1998	Part of Upper Siang, West Siang and Dibang Valley Districts in Arunachal Pradesh.
11.	**Pachmarhi (4981.72)**	03.03.1999	Part of Betul, Hoshangabad and Chhindwara Districts in Madhya Pradesh.
12.	**Khangchendzonga(2619.92)**	07.02.2000	Part of North and West Districts in Sikkim
13.	**Agasthyamalai (3500.36)**	12.11.2001	Part of Tirunelveli and Kanyakumari Districts in Tamil Nadu and Thiruvananthapuram, Kollam and Pathanamthitta districts in Kerala.
14.	**Achanakmar-Amarkantak (3835.51)**	**30.03.2005**	**Part of Anuppur and Dindori Districts of Madhya Pradesh** and Bilaspur district of Chhattisgarh
15.	**Kachchh (12,454)**	29.01.2008	Part of Kachchh, Rajkot, Surendranagar and Patan Districts in Gujarat.
16.	**Cold Desert (7770)**	28.08.2009	Pin Valley National Park and surroundings; Chandratal and Sarchu and Kibber Wildlife sanctuary in Himachal Pradesh.
17.	**Seshachalam (4755.997)**	20.09.2010	Seshachalam hill ranges in Eastern Ghats encompassing part of Chittoor and Kadapa Districts in Andhra Pradesh.
18.	**Panna (2998.98)**	25.08.2011	Part of Panna and Chhattarpur Districts in Madhya Pradesh.

Biosphere Reserves

TEST YOURSELF

Multiple Choice Questions

Q1. Which forests are situated in regions receiving rainfall between 70-200 cm?

(a) Tropical thorn forests

(b) Tropical deciduous forests

(c) Tropical evergreen forests

(d) Montane forests

Q2. Which biosphere reserves has been recognised by the UNESCO on world network of biosphere reserves?

1. Simlipal 2. Manas

3. Pachmarhi 4. Nilgiri

Which of the points given above is/are correct? –

(a) Only 1 (b) 2 and 3

(c) 1, 3 and 4 (d) 2 and 4

Q3. In which year was the Wildlife Act, 1972 amended?

(a) 1991 (b) 1990

(c) 1989 (d) 1993

Q4. Which type of forests are found in semi-arid areas of south west Punjab, Haryana, Rajasthan, Gujarat, Madhya Pradesh and Uttar Pradesh?

(a) Montane forest

(b) Dry deciduous forest

(c) Tropical thorn forest

(d) Moist deciduous forest

Q5. Khangchendzonga Biosphere Reserve is located in which state of India?

(a) Arunachal Pradesh (b) Nagaland

(c) Manipur (d) Sikkim

Q6. Which type of vegetation is found in the Himalayan region?

(a) Tropical rainforest (b) Deciduous forest

(c) Alpine vegetation (d) Mangrove forest

Q7. The Sundarbans, known for its mangrove forests, is located in which state of India?

(a) West Bengal (b) Assam

(c) Kerala (d) Tamil Nadu

Q8. Which type of forest is characterised by trees that shed their leaves seasonally?

(a) Evergreen forest (b) Mangrove forest

(c) Deciduous forest (d) Thorny forest

Q9. Which region in India is known for its tropical rainforests?

(a) Western Ghats (b) Eastern Ghats

(c) Western Himalayas (d) Eastern Himalayas

Q10. The type of vegetation found in the desert regions is:

(a) Tropical rainforest

(b) Deciduous forest

(c) Alpine vegetation

(d) Thorny bushes and shrubs

Q11. Which national park is known for its population of Indian one-horned rhinoceros?

(a) Kaziranga National Park

(b) Periyar National Park

(c) Gir National Park

(d) Jim Corbett National Park

Q12. The Great Indian Bustard, an endangered species, is found in which region of India?

(a) Western Ghats (b) Sundarbans

(c) Western Himalayas (d) Thar Desert

Q13. Which wildlife sanctuary is famous for its population of Asiatic lions?

(a) Bandipur Wildlife Sanctuary

(b) Gir Wildlife Sanctuary

(c) Ranthambore Wildlife Sanctuary

(d) Sariska Wildlife Sanctuary

Q14. The Silent Valley National Park is located in which state of India?

(a) Kerala (b) Tamil Nadu

(c) Karnataka (d) Andhra Pradesh

Q15. Which bird sanctuary is known for its population of migratory birds from Siberia?

(a) Keoladeo National Park

(b) Ranganathittu Bird Sanctuary

(c) Sultanpur Bird Sanctuary

(d) Bharatpur Bird Sanctuary

Answer Key							
Q1.	b	Q2.	c	Q3.	a	Q4.	c
Q5.	d	Q6.	c	Q7.	a	Q8.	c
Q9.	a	Q10.	d	Q11.	a	Q12.	d
Q13.	b	Q14.	a	Q15.	a		

Model Questions for Main Examination

Q1. State the ways to conserve forests in India.

Q2. Differentiate between tropical thorn and deciduous forest.

UNIT 20 Human-Environment Interactions

In This Unit

Comprehensive and profound coverage of the following NCERTs' chapters:

- ✓ NCERT Class- 7th (Our Environment), Chapter- 6 and 7
- ✓ NCERT (Before Rationalisation) Class- 7th (Our Environment), Chapter- 9

Life in The Amazon Basin: The Tropics

When Spanish explorers **discovered the Amazon River**, they were attacked by a **group of local tribes** wearing headgears and grass skirts. These people reminded them of the **fierce tribes of women warriors** known in ancient Roman Empire as the **Amazons**. Hence the name **Amazon.**

The tropical zone is located between **10°N and 10°S,** fairly near to the equator. That's why it is called the **equatorial region**. Through this area **runs the Amazon River**. It originates in the west in the highlands and empties into the Atlantic Ocean in the east. **The river mouth** is the location where a river empties into another body of water. The river basin drains portions of **Brazil, parts of Peru, Bolivia, Ecuador, Columbia and a small part of Venezuela.**

Climate

The Amazon Basin stretches directly on the equator and experiences year-round **hot and wet climate. The temperature** is nearly the same during the day and at night. The skin has a sticky feeling. Almost every day, and with little notice, it rains. During the day, there is a lot of heat and humidity. The temperature drops at night, but the humidity doesn't.

Rainforests

- **Thick forests develop** in this area due to heavy rainfall.
- The trees are actually so dense that sunlight cannot penetrate the thick "roof" made of branches and leaves.
- The earth persists damp and dark. Here, only plants tolerant of shade may flourish.
- **Bromeliads and orchids develop as plant parasites** (**Bromeliads** are special plants that store water in their leaves. Animals like frogs use these pockets of water for laying their eggs.)
- Wildlife abounds in the rainforest. Differentiated from other birds are birds like **toucans, hummingbirds, and macaws**, which have colourful plumage and large bills for food. In the woodlands, these birds also create a lot of noise.
- There are creatures like **tapirs that devour ants, sloths, and monkeys** in this area.
- The jungles also support a wide variety of snake and reptile species. There are several pythons, snakes, and crocodiles. A few of the species are the **boa constrictor and anaconda**.
- In addition, the basin is a home to thousands of insect species. There are also a number of fish species in the river, including the **flesh-eating piranha.**

People of the Rainforests

- After some forest trees are cleared, people grow the majority of their food in tiny spaces.
- Women take care of the crops while men do fish and hunt beside the rivers. **Sweet potatoes, pineapples, and tapiocas** are their principal crops.
- They practice **"slash and burn agriculture".**

Slash and Burn Cultivation

Slash and Burn is a way of cultivating land where farmers clear a piece of land by slashing or cutting down trees and bushes. These are then burnt, which **releases the nutrients** into the soil. Now crops are grown in this **cleared field for a few years**. After repeatedly using the patch of land, the soil loses its nutrients. So, it is **abandoned**. Then they clear another plot of land to plant. In the meantime, young trees grow in the old field. In this way, **soil fertility is restored**. People can then return to it and start cultivating it again.

- The main dietary mainstay is **manioc, or cassava**, which grows underground similarly to potatoes.
- Moreover, they consume egg sacs and queen ants. Additionally, **cash crops like cocoa, maize, and coffee** are also grown .
- A lot of timber for buildings is provided by the rainforests. Certain households reside in thatched homes designed to resemble beehives. Other big, apartment-like homes with a roof that slopes sharply are known as **"Maloca."**

Life in the Ganga-Brahmaputra Basin: The Subtropics

- The Indian subcontinent's Ganga-Brahmaputra basin is made up of the tributaries of the rivers Ganga and Brahmaputra.
- The basin is located in the **subtropical zone**, which spans latitudes from **10°N to 30°N.**
- The Ganga River is drained by its tributaries, including the Ghaghra, Son, Chambal, Gandak, Kosi, and Brahmaputra.
- The principal features of this basin include the **Sundarbans delta,** the mountains and foothills of the Himalayas, and the plains of the Ganga and Brahmaputra.
- **Numerous oxbow lakes** are scattered throughout the plains. The region experiences a predominantly **monsoonal climate,** characterised by seasonal rainfall concentrated between mid-June and mid-September. **Summers are hot, while winters are characterised by cool temperatures.**
- The Ganga-Brahmaputra basin exhibits a clear **correlation between topography and population distribution.** The mountainous regions, characterised by steep slopes and challenging terrain, are sparsely populated. Conversely, the vast plains offer fertile land ideal for human settlement.
- The flat topography and fertile soil of the plains create a highly suitable environment for agriculture, the primary occupation of the basin's inhabitants. This allows for the **cultivation of a diverse range of crops.**
- **Paddy** cultivation dominates the agricultural landscape, followed by **wheat, maize, sorghum, pulses (gram), and millets**. Additionally, cash crops like sugarcane and jute contribute significantly to the basin's economy.
- **Banana plantations** flourish in specific areas of the plains, while West Bengal and Assam are known for their **tea estates.** Notably, **Bihar and Assam practice sericulture**, involving the cultivation of silkworms for silk production.
- On gentler slopes in the mountains and hills, **terraced farming** practices enable crop cultivation despite the challenging terrain.
- The Ganga and Brahmaputra plains are characterised by **tropical deciduous forests**, with **teak, sal, and peepal trees** being prominent species.
- **Dense bamboo groves** are a common feature in the Brahmaputra plain, while the delta region boasts extensive mangrove forests.
- **The Himalayan foothills in regions like Uttarakhand, Sikkim, and Arunachal Pradesh exhibit a predominance of coniferous trees such as pine, deodar, and fir.** This adaptation thrives due to the prevailing cool climate and the steepness of the slopes.
- The basin boasts a diverse wildlife. Common sightings include elephants, tigers, deer, and monkeys. Notably, the one-horned rhinoceros inhabits the Brahmaputra plain, while the delta region provides a habitat for the **Bengal tiger and crocodiles.**

- **The freshwater ecosystem** of the rivers, lakes, and the Bay of Bengal teems with aquatic life. The **Rohu, Catla, and Hilsa** are particularly popular varieties of fish found in these waters.

> In the fresh waters of river Ganga and Brahmaputra, a variety of dolphin locally called **Susu (also called blind dolphin)** is found. The presence of Susu is an **indication of the health** of the river. The untreated industrial and urban wastes with high amount of chemicals are killing this species.

- The plain of the Ganga-Brahmaputra contains **numerous large towns and cities.** Along the Ganga river are the cities of Allahabad, Kanpur, Varanasi, Lucknow, Patna, and Kolkata, all with the population of more than ten lakhs.
- The **waterways** are an effective means of transport, particularly along the rivers. Kolkata is an important port on the **river Hooghly.**
- Tourism constitutes another significant economic activity within the Ganga Basin. Renowned historical landmarks such as the **Taj Mahal situated on the banks of the Yamuna River in Agra, and the confluence of the Ganga and Yamuna rivers** at Allahabad, attract a multitude of visitors. Additionally, the basin boasts a rich cultural heritage, exemplified by the Buddhist stupas scattered throughout Uttar Pradesh and Bihar. Lucknow, with its magnificent **Imambara,** offers a glimpse into Mughal architecture. **Assam's Kaziranga** and **Manas sanctuaries** provide opportunities to encounter diverse wildlife, while **Arunachal Pradesh beckons with its unique tribal culture**, further enriching the tourist experience within the Ganga Basin.

Life in the Temperate Grasslands

Climate is a primary influence in shaping grassland ecosystems. Due to this, a widely accepted classification system categorises the world's grasslands into two major types based on their geographical location and associated climatic regimes: **temperate grasslands and tropical grasslands.** Temperate grasslands occur within the temperate zone, while tropical grasslands are found in tropical regions.

The Prairies

- **Prairies** are the name given to North America's temperate grasslands. The word Prairie originated from the **Latin word 'Priata' which means meadow or grass field.**
- It is a region of flat, gently sloping or hilly land.
- **Predominantly treeless,** prairies occasionally give way to woodlands near the **low-lying plains** flanking river valleys. These vast grasslands are characterised by **towering** grasses that can reach up to two meters in height, aptly resembling a **sea of grass.**
- The western boundary of the prairies is delineated by the **Rocky Mountains,** while the **Great Lakes** form their eastern extent.
- **Encompassing regions within both the United States of America and Canada,** the prairies are drained by distinct river systems. In the USA, tributaries of the **Mississippi River** serve this function, while the **Saskatchewan River and its tributaries** perform the same role in the **Canadian prairies.**
- The grasslands of Prairies were the home of **native Americans often called "Red Indians".** They were the original inhabitants of the continent. The Prairies were home of other **tribes** also like the **Apache, the Crow, the Cree and the Pawnee.**

Climate

- Situated in the continental interior, the region experiences a dramatic climate characterised by **significant temperature fluctuations.**
- Summers are characterised by moderate warmth, with average temperatures hovering around 20°C. Conversely, winters are frigid, with records as low as -20°C observed in **Winnipeg, Canada. During this season, the region is blanketed by a thick layer of snow.**
- Annual precipitation levels are moderate, fostering the growth of grasslands. Notably, the absence of a north-south geographic barrier facilitates the occurrence of the local wind phenomenon known as the **Chinook.**
- **Chinook is a hot wind** that blows in winter and therefore raises the temperature within a short

time. This increase in temperature results in the melting of snow, making pasture land available for grazing of animals.

Flora and Fauna

- There are **hardly any trees in the prairies**. Trees like poplars, alders, and willows grow in areas with access to water.
- Because the soil is fertile, areas with rainfall over 50 cm are good for agriculture.
- Although **maize** is the predominant crop in this region, **potatoes, soybeans, cotton and alfa-alfa** are also cultivated.
- Grass is short and sparse in areas with very little or irregular rainfall. Cattle can be raised in these places.
- Sturdy males known as cowboys look after **cattle farms called ranches.**
- The **American buffalo, sometimes known as bison**, is the most significant animal in this area. **Gophers, prairie dogs, coyotes, and rabbits** are among the numerous creatures that inhabit this area.

People

- The inhabitants in this area work extremely hard. They have used technology to effectively use their abundant natural resources.
- This region is home to the **United States of America and Canada**, two of the world's most developed nations.
- Thanks to advanced farming techniques and the usage of tractors, harvesters, and combines, North America is now a surplus food producer.
- Because of the enormous excess of wheat produced, the Prairies are frequently referred to as the **"Granaries of the World."**
- **Dairy farming** is an additional significant industry. From the **Great Lakes to the Atlantic Coast** in the east is the dairy belt.
- Its **vast coal and iron reserves,** along with an efficient system of highways, trains, and canals, have made it the **world's most industrialised region.**

> Important cities in the **American prairies** are **Chicago, Minneapolis, Indianapolis, Kansas, and Denver. In the Canadian prairies** the important cities are **Edmonton, Saskatoon, Calgary and Winnipeg.**

The Velds

- The temperate grasslands of South Africa are called the **Velds**. The Veld name was given by the Dutch settlers before South Africa was colonised by the British.
- Velds are **rolling plateaus** that range in elevation from **600 to 1100 metres.**
- The **Drakensberg Mountains** encircle it on the east. The **Kalahari Desert** is to the west of it.
- There are **"High Velds"** on the northeastern side that, in certain areas, reach elevations of above **1600 metres.**
- The tributaries of **rivers Orange and Limpopo** drain the region.

Climate

- The Indian Ocean's influence gives the Velds a temperate climate.
- The winters are dry and chilly. There is a 5°C to 10°C temperature range, with July being the coldest month. The summers are warm and brief.
- The warmer months of November through February are when the Velds receive the most rainfall. **The warm ocean currents** that wash the Velds' shorelines are mostly to blame for this. Drought may arise if there is little rainfall during the winter months of June through August.

Flora and Fauna

- There is **not much vegetation cover.** The terrain is **dominated by grasses.**
- Bush Velds are home to **red grass. Acacia and maroola** are seen to be flourishing in the high Velds.
- The main inhabitants of the Velds include **cheetahs, lions, leopards, and kudu.**

People

- Velds are known for **cattle rearing an mining.**

- The Velds' uneven grass cover, which reveals a bare surface, makes the soils there less fruitful.
- Nonetheless, **crops are cultivated in areas with high fertility.** Maize, wheat, barley, oats, and potatoes are the **principal crops. Additionally, cash crops like cotton, sugarcane, and tobacco are farmed.**
- The most significant job for humans is **raising sheep**. The veldts' wool business was founded on the breeding of sheep primarily for their wool.
- **Merino sheep** are a popular breed and have particularly warm wool. The second essential job is **dairy farming.**
- The Velds are rich in mineral reserves. In areas where **coal and iron** are found, the iron and steel industry has grown.
- The **mining of gold and diamonds** is one of the main industries in this area. **Johannesburg** is renowned for being the global centre for gold mining. **Diamond mines** are the main attraction of Kimberley.
- South Africa's mining of gold and diamonds resulted in the development of trade relations with Britain, and the country eventually became a British colony.

Life in Deserts

Desert is an arid region characterised by extremely high or low temperatures and has scarce vegetation. Depending on the **temperatures** there can be **hot deserts or cold deserts.**

The Hot Desert – Sahara

- A sizeable portion of North Africa is covered by the Sahara Desert. It is the biggest desert in the planet. It covers about 8.54 million square km.
- Eleven nations are surrounded by the Sahara Desert. These include the **Western Sahara, Algeria, Chad, Egypt, Libya, Mali, Mauritania, Morocco, Niger, Sudan, and Tunisia.**
- In addition to the huge expanses of sand that fill the Sahara Desert, there are **elevated plateaus with bare rocky surfaces and gravel plains.** In certain instances, these rocky surfaces might be higher than 2500 metres.

The Present day, **Sahara once used to be a lush green plain.** Cave paintings in Sahara Desert show that there used to be rivers with crocodiles. Elephants, lions, giraffes, ostriches, sheep, cattle and goats were common animals. But the change in climate has changed it to a very hot and dry region.

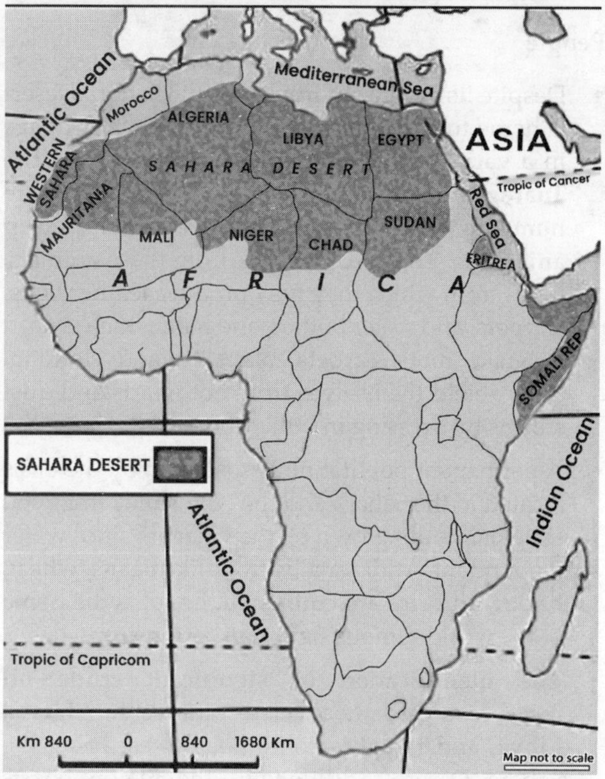

Sahara in Africa

Climate

- The Sahara Desert has an **extremely hot and dry climate**. There is a brief wet season there. There are no clouds and a clear sky. In this place, moisture evaporation exceeds condensation rate. The days are really hot.
- The daytime highs can reach up to 50°C, warming the naked rocks and sand. This heat then radiates outward, heating the surrounding area. The nights might be extremely cold, with lows close to zero.

Al Azizia in the Sahara Desert, south of Tripoli, Libya recorded the highest temperature of 57.7°C in 1922.

Flora and Fauna

- The Sahara Desert is home to **acacia, date palms, and cacti**. There are oasis in several locations, which are verdant islands encircled by date palms.
- There are numerous types of snakes, lizards, foxes, hyenas, jackals, scorpions, and camels among the notable animal inhabitants.

People

- Despite its severe environment, the Sahara Desert is home to a diverse range of people who engage in a variety of activities. **The Bedouins and the Tuaregs** are two among them. These people are **nomadic tribes that raise horses, camels, sheep and goats.** They receive milk from these animals, hides from which they may produce leather belts, slippers, and water bottles, and hair, which is used to make mats, carpets, blankets, and clothing. They shield themselves from hot winds and dust storms by dressing in bulky robes.
- A permanent population is sustained by the oasis located in the Sahara and the Nile Valley in Egypt. Date palms are grown by the villagers since water is abundant. Additionally, crops like **beans, wheat, barley, and rice are cultivated.** Egypt is the home of the world-famous **Egyptian cotton crop.**
- **The identification of significant crude oil reserves**, a globally coveted resource, in **Algeria, Libya, and Egypt** is continuously reshaping the Sahara Desert. Additionally, the region boasts deposits of other valuable minerals, including **iron, phosphorus, manganese, and uranium.**

> Depressions are formed when the wind blows away the sands. In the depressions where underground water reaches the surface, an **oasis** is formed. These areas are fertile. People may settle around these water bodies and grow date palms and other crops. Sometimes the oasis may be abnormally large. **Tafilalet Oasis in Morocco** is a large oasis with an area of about 13,000 sq.km.

The Cold Desert – Ladakh

- Ladakh, situated within the eastern confines of Jammu and Kashmir, constitutes a high-altitude desert region nestled amidst the majestic **Great Himalayas.** Encompassed by the formidable **Karakoram Range to the north and the Zanskar Mountains to the south, Ladakh is a land sculpted by powerful rivers**, the **Indus** being the most prominent. These rivers have carved deep valleys and dramatic gorges within the landscape. Additionally, Ladakh boasts several glaciers, including the renowned **Gangri glacier.**
- Ladakh's elevation exhibits significant variation, ranging from approximately 3000 meters in **Kargil** to exceeding 8000 meters within the Karakoram. As a consequence of this high altitude, the region experiences an **extremely cold and arid climate.** The thin atmosphere at such elevations allows for the sun's warmth to be felt intensely, despite the overall frigid temperatures.
- Summertime in Ladakh witnesses daytime temperatures hovering just above freezing, while nighttime temperatures plummet well below -30°C. Winters in the region are characterised by bone-chilling cold, with temperatures remaining below -40°C for extended periods.
- Because it is **located in the Himalayan rain shadow**, it receives as little as 10 cm of precipitation annually. There are chilling winds and scorching sun in this place.

> - Ladakh is made up of two words – **'La'** meaning 'mountain pass' and **'Dak'** meaning 'country'.
> - **Drass,** one of the coldest inhabited places on earth is located in Ladakh.
> - Ladakh is also known as **Khapa-chan** which means **snow land.**

Flora and Fauna

- High levels of aridity have left the vegetation sparse. There are not many places for animals to feed on grasses and plants. In the valleys are groves of poplars and willows.
- Fruit trees that bear **apples, apricots, and walnuts bloom in the summer**. In Ladakh, a variety of **bird** species have been observed. Common birds include **robins, redstarts, hoopoes, Tibetan snowcocks, and ravens.** A few of these are birds that migrate.
- **Ladakh is home to yaks, wild sheep, goats, and unique breeds of dogs**. The purpose of raising the

animals is to supply milk, meat, and hides. The milk from yaks is used to make butter and cheese. **Wool is made from the hair of sheep and goats.**

- The **Chiru or the Tibetan antelope** is an endangered species. It is hunted for its wool known as **shahtoosh,** which is light in weight and extremely warm.
- The **finest cricket bats** are made from the wood of the **willow trees.**

People

- Either **Buddhists or Muslims** make up the population here. Actually, with their distinctive **"gompas,"** a number of Buddhist monasteries dot the Ladakhi landscape. **Shey, Lamayuru, Hemis, and Thiksey are a few well-known monasteries.**
- People work hard to **cultivate barley, potatoes, peas, beans, and turnips** during the **summer months.** People keep themselves occupied with celebrations and rituals **during the winter** because of the extreme weather. The ladies work really hard. They operate stores and small businesses in addition to working in the fields and around the house.
- There are **good air and road connections** to Leh, the capital of Ladakh. Through **Zoji la Pass, National Highway 1A links Leh with the Kashmir Valley**.
- **Tourism** is a significant industry, drawing many visitors from both domestic and foreign travel destinations. Important activities include going on excursions to view the glaciers and meadows, visiting gompas, and taking in ceremonies and celebrations.

Manali – Leh highway crosses four passes, **Rohtang la, Baralacha la, Lungalacha la and Tanglang la.** The highway opens only between July and September when snow is cleared from the road.

TEST YOURSELF

Multiple Choice Questions

Q1. Which region is characterised by extremely high or low temperature and has scarce vegetation?

(a) Desert (b) Fertile land

(c) Grassland (d) None of these

Q2. What are two words by which Ladakh is made of?

(a) Lad and akh (b) Lad and hakh

(c) La and Dak (d) None of these

Q3. Ladakh is also known as

(a) Khapa-tuaregs (b) Khapa-chan

(c) Khapa-bedouins (d) Khapa-drass

Q4. What is the climate of Ganga-Brahmaputra Basin?

(a) Hot and wet (b) Hot and dry

(c) Monsoon type (d) Very cold

Q5. Consider the following statements regarding Amazon Forests:

1. Amazon Forest is one of the world's richest regions in terms of biodiversity and natural resources.
2. It is surrounded by the Guiana Highlands to the north, and the Andes Mountains to the west.

Which of the statements given above is/are correct?

(a) 1 only (b) 2 only

(c) Both 1 and 2 (d) Neither 1 nor 2

Q6. Big towns and cities on the Ganga-Brahmaputra plains those have population of more than ten lakhs are?

1. Allahabad
2. Varanasi
3. Kolkata
4. Agra

Choose the correct option/s given below?

(a) Only 1
(b) Only 2
(c) Only 3
(d) All of the above

Q7. Velds are grasslands of:

(a) Australia
(b) Africa
(c) America
(d) Asia

Answer Key

Q1.	a	Q2.	c	Q3.	b	Q4.	c
Q5.	c	Q6.	d	Q7.	b		

UNIT
21

Biodiversity and Conservation

In This Unit

Comprehensive and profound coverage of the following NCERTs' chapter:

✓ NCERT Class- 11th (Fundamentals of Physical Geography), Chapter- 14

Biodiversity itself is a combination of two words, **Bio (life) and diversity (variety).** In simple terms, biodiversity is the number and variety of organisms found within a specified geographic region. It refers to the varieties of plants, animals and microorganisms, the genes they contain and the ecosystems they form. It relates to the variability among living organisms on the earth, including the variability within and between the species and that within and between the ecosystems. Biodiversity is our living wealth.

Biodiversity can be discussed at three levels:

(i) Genetic diversity

(ii) Species diversity

(iii) Ecosystem diversity

Genetic Diversity

Genes are the basic building blocks of various life forms. Genetic biodiversity refers to the variation of genes within species. Groups of individual organisms having certain similarities in their physical characteristics are called **species.** Human beings genetically belong to the **homo sapiens** group and also differ in their characteristics such as height, colour, physical appearance, etc., considerably. This is due to genetic diversity. This **genetic diversity is essential for a healthy breeding population of species.**

Species Diversity

This refers to the variety of species. It relates to the **number of species in a defined area.** The diversity of species can be measured through its richness, abundance and types. Some areas are more rich in species than others. Areas rich in species diversity are called **hotspots of diversity**.

Ecosystem Diversity

The broad differences between ecosystem types and the **diversity of habitats and ecological processes** occurring within each ecosystem type constitute the ecosystem diversity. The 'boundaries' of communities (associations of species) and ecosystems are not very rigidly defined. Thus, the demarcation of ecosystem boundaries is difficult and complex. **Example:** Grasslands and sholas in Indira Gandhi National Park, Annamalai, Western Ghats.

Importance of Biodiversity

Biodiversity has contributed in many ways to the development of human culture and, in turn, human communities have played a major role in shaping the diversity of nature at the genetic, species and ecological levels. Biodiversity plays the following roles: **ecological, economic and scientific**.

Ecological Role of Biodiversity

Species of many kinds perform some function or the other in an ecosystem. Nothing in an ecosystem evolves and sustains without any reason. That means, every organism, besides extracting its needs, also contributes something useful to other organisms. Species capture and store energy, produce and decompose organic materials, help to cycle water and nutrients throughout the ecosystem, fix atmospheric gases and help regulate the climate. These functions are important for ecosystem function and human survival. The more diverse an ecosystem, better are the chances for the species to survive through adversities and attacks, and consequently, is more productive. Hence, the loss of species would decrease the ability of the system to maintain itself. Just like a species with a high genetic diversity, an ecosystem with high biodiversity may have a greater chance of adapting to environmental change. In other words, the more the variety of species in an ecosystem, the more stable the ecosystem is likely to be.

Economic Role of Biodiversity

For all humans, biodiversity is an important resource in their day-to-day life. One important part of biodiversity is **'Crop Diversity'**, which is also called **Agro-Biodiversity**. Biodiversity is seen as a reservoir of resources to be drawn upon for the manufacture of food, pharmaceutical, and cosmetic products. This concept of biological resources is responsible for the deterioration of biodiversity. At the same time, it is also the origin of new conflicts dealing with rules of division and appropriation of natural resources. Some of the **important economic commodities** that biodiversity supplies to humankind are: food crops, livestock, forests, fish, medicinal resources, etc.

Scientific Role of Biodiversity

Biodiversity is important because each species can give us some clue as to how life evolved and will continue to evolve. Biodiversity also helps in understanding how life functions and the role of each species in sustaining ecosystems of which we are also a species. **This fact must be drawn upon every one of us so that we live and let other species also live their lives.** It is our ethical responsibility to consider that each and every species along with us have an intrinsic right to exist. Hence, it is morally wrong to voluntarily cause the extinction of any species. The level of biodiversity is a good indicator of the state of our relationships with other living species. In fact, the concept of biodiversity is an integral part of many human cultures.

Loss of Biodiversity

- Since the last few decades, growth in the human population has increased the rate of consumption of natural resources. It has accelerated the loss of species and habitation in different parts of the world.
- **Tropical regions** which occupy only about one-fourth of the total area of the world, **contain about three-fourth of the world human population.** Over-exploitation of resources and deforestation have become rampant to fulfill the needs of a large population. As these tropical rain forests contain 50 per cent of the species on the earth, destruction of natural habitats have proved disastrous for the entire biosphere.
- **Natural calamities** such as earthquakes, floods, volcanic eruptions, forest fires, droughts, etc. cause damage to the flora and fauna of the earth, bringing change to the biodiversity of respective affected regions. **Pesticides and other pollutants** such as hydrocarbons and toxic heavy metals destroy the weak and sensitive species.
- Species which are not the natural inhabitants of the local habitat but are introduced into the system, are called **exotic species.** There are many examples when **a natural biotic community of the ecosystem suffered extensive damage because of the introduction of exotic species.**
- During the last few decades, some animals like tigers, elephants, rhinoceros, crocodiles, minks and birds were hunted mercilessly by poachers for their horn, tusks, hides, etc. It has resulted in the rendering of certain types of organisms as an endangered category.
- **The greatest damage inflicted on Indian forests was during the colonial period** due to the expansion of the railways, agriculture, commercial and scientific forestry and mining activities. Even after Independence, agricultural expansion continues to be one of the major causes of depletion of forest resources.
- Between **1951 and 1980**, according to the Forest Survey of India, over **26,200 sq. km. of forest area was converted into agricultural land** all over India. Substantial parts of the tribal belts, especially in the north- eastern and central India, have been deforested or degraded by shifting cultivation (jhum), a type of **'slash and burn' agriculture.**

Are colonial forest policies to be blamed?

The promotion of a few favoured species, in many parts of India, has been carried through the ironically-termed **"enrichment plantation"**, in which a **single commercially valuable species was extensively planted** and other species eliminated. For instance, **teak monoculture has damaged the natural forest** in South India and Chir Pine (Pinus roxburghii) plantations in the Himalayas have replaced the Himalayan oak (Quercus spp.) and Rhododendron forests.

- Large-scale development projects have also contributed significantly to the loss of forests. Since 1951, over 5,000 sq. km of forest was cleared for river valley projects.
- Clearing of forests is still continuing with projects like the **Narmada Sagar Project in Madhya Pradesh**, which would inundate 40,000 hectares of forest. Mining is another important factor behind deforestation. The **Buxa Tiger Reserve in West Bengal** is seriously threatened by the ongoing dolomite mining. It has disturbed the natural habitat of many species and blocked the migration route of several others, including the great Indian elephant.

The Himalayan Yew

The **Himalayan Yew (Taxus Wallichiana)** is a **medicinal plant** found in various parts of Himachal Pradesh and Arunachal Pradesh. A chemical compound called 'taxol' is extracted from the bark, needles, twigs and roots of this tree, and it has been successfully used to treat some cancers – the drug is now the biggest selling anti-cancer drug in the world. The species is under great threat due to over-exploitation. In the last one decade, thousands of yew trees have dried up in various parts of Himachal Pradesh and Arunachal Pradesh.

- Other important causes of environmental destruction are **unequal access, inequitable consumption of resources** and differential sharing of responsibility for environmental well-being.
- Overpopulation in third world countries is often cited as the cause of environmental degradation. However, an average American consumes 40 times more resources than an average Somalian. Similarly, the richest five per cent of Indian society probably cause more ecological damage because of the amount they consume than the poorest 25 per cent. The former shares minimum responsibilities for environmental well-being.
- The destruction of forests and wildlife is not just a biological issue. The **biological loss is strongly correlated with the loss of cultural diversity.** Such losses have increasingly marginalised and impoverished many indigenous and other forest-dependent communities, who directly depend on various components of the forest and wildlife for food, drink, medicine, culture, spirituality, etc.
- The indirect impact of degradation such as severe drought or deforestation-induced floods, etc. hits the poor the hardest. Poverty in these cases is a direct outcome of environmental destruction.

Classification of Species

Some estimates suggest that at **least 10 percent of India's recorded wild flora and 20 percent of its mammals are on the threatened list.** Many of these would now be categorised as **'critical'**, that is on the verge of extinction like the cheetah, pink-headed duck, mountain quail, forest spotted owlet, and plants like **Madhuca insignis** (a wild variety of mahua) and **Hubbardia heptaneuron**, (a species of grass). The **International Union for Conservation of Nature (IUCN)** has classified the threatened species of plants and animals into different categories for the purpose of their conservation.

Normal Species

Species whose population levels are considered to be normal for their survival, such as cattle, sal, pine, rodents, etc.

Endangered Species

It includes those species which are **in danger of extinction.** The survival of such species is difficult if the negative factors that have led to a decline in their population continue to operate. The examples of such species are black buck, crocodile, Indian wild ass, Indian rhino, lion tailed macaque, sangai (brow-antlered deer in Manipur), etc. **The IUCN publishes information about endangered species world-wide as the Red List of threatened species.**

Vulnerable Species

This includes the species which are **likely to be in danger of extinction in near future** if the factors threatening to their extinction continue. Survival of these species is not assured as their population has reduced greatly. The examples of such species are blue sheep, Asiatic elephant, Gangetic dolphin, etc.

Rare Species

Population of these species is very small in the world; they are **confined to limited areas or thinly scattered** over a wider area. The examples of such species are the Himalayan brown bear, wild Asiatic buffalo, desert fox and hornbill, etc.

Endemic Species

These are species which are **only found in some particular areas** usually isolated by natural or geographical barriers. Examples of such species are the Andaman teal, Nicobar pigeon, Andaman wild pig, mithun in Arunachal Pradesh and Humboldtia decurrens Bedd — highly rare endemic tree of Southern Western Ghats.

Extinct Species

These are species **which are not found** after searches of known or likely areas where they may occur. A species may be extinct from a local area, region, country, continent or the entire earth. Examples of such species are the Asiatic cheetah, pink head duck.

> **Asiatic Cheetah**
>
> The **world's fastest land mammal,** the cheetah (Acinonyx Jubatus), is a unique and specialised member of the cat family and can move at the speed of 112 km./hr. The cheetah is often mistaken for a leopard. Its distinguishing marks are the long teardrop- shaped lines on each side of the nose from the corner of its eyes to its mouth. Prior to the 20th century, cheetahs were widely distributed throughout Africa and Asia. Today, the Asian cheetah is nearly extinct due to a decline of available habitat and prey. The species was declared extinct in India long back in 1952.

Conservation of Biodiversity

- **Biodiversity is important for human existence**. All forms of life are so closely interlinked that disturbance in one give rise to imbalance in the others. If species of plants and animals become endangered, they cause degradation in the environment, which may threaten human being's own existence.
- There is an **urgent need to educate people to adopt environment-friendly** practices and reorient their activities in such a way that our development is harmonious with other life forms and is sustainable.
- There is an increasing consciousness of the fact that such conservation with sustainable use is possible only with the **involvement and cooperation of local communities** and individuals. For this, the development of institutional structures at local levels is necessary. The critical problem is not merely the conservation of species nor the habitat but the continuation of the process of conservation.
- **The Government of India along with 155 other nations have signed the Convention of Biodiversity at the Earth Summit held at Rio de Janeiro, Brazil in June 1992.**
- The world conservation strategy has suggested the following steps for biodiversity conservation:
  - Efforts should be made to preserve the species that are endangered.
  - Prevention of extinction requires proper planning and management.
  - Varieties of food crops, forage plants, timber trees, livestock, animals and their wild relatives should be preserved.
  - Each country should identify habitats of wild relatives and ensure their protection.
  - Habitats where species feed, breed, rest and nurse their young should be safeguarded and protected.
  - International trade in wild plants and animals be regulated.
- To **protect, preserve and propagate** the variety of species within natural boundaries, the Government of India passed the **Wild Life (Protection) Act, 1972, under which national parks and sanctuaries were established and biosphere reserves declared.**
- The central government also announced several projects for protecting specific animals, which

were gravely threatened, including the tiger, the one-horned rhinoceros, the Kashmir stag or hangul, three types of crocodiles – fresh water crocodile, saltwater crocodile and the Gharial, the Asiatic lion, and others. Most recently, the Indian elephant, black buck (chinkara), the great Indian bustard (godawan) and the snow leopard, etc. have been given full or partial legal protection against hunting and trade throughout India.

- In the notification under **Wildlife Act of 1980 and 1986**, several hundred butterflies, moths, beetles, and one dragonfly have been added to the list of protected species. **In 1991, for the first time, plants were also added to the list, starting with six species.**
- There are some countries which are situated in the tropical region; they possess a large number of the world's species diversity. They are called **mega diversity centres.** There are 12 such countries, namely **Mexico, Colombia, Ecuador, Peru, Brazil, Democratic Republic of Congo, Madagascar, China, India, Malaysia, Indonesia and Australia** in which these centres are located.
- In order to concentrate resources on those areas that are most vulnerable, the International Union for Conservation of Nature (IUCN) has identified certain areas as **biodiversity hotspots. Hotspots are defined according to their vegetation.** Plants are important because these determine the primary productivity of an ecosystem.
- Most, but not all, of the hotspots rely on species-rich ecosystems for food, firewood, cropland, and income from timber. In **Madagascar**, for example, about 85 percent of the plants and animals are found nowhere else in the world. Other, hotspots in wealthy countries are facing different types of pressures. The **islands of Hawaii** have many unique plants and animals that are threatened by introduced species and land development.

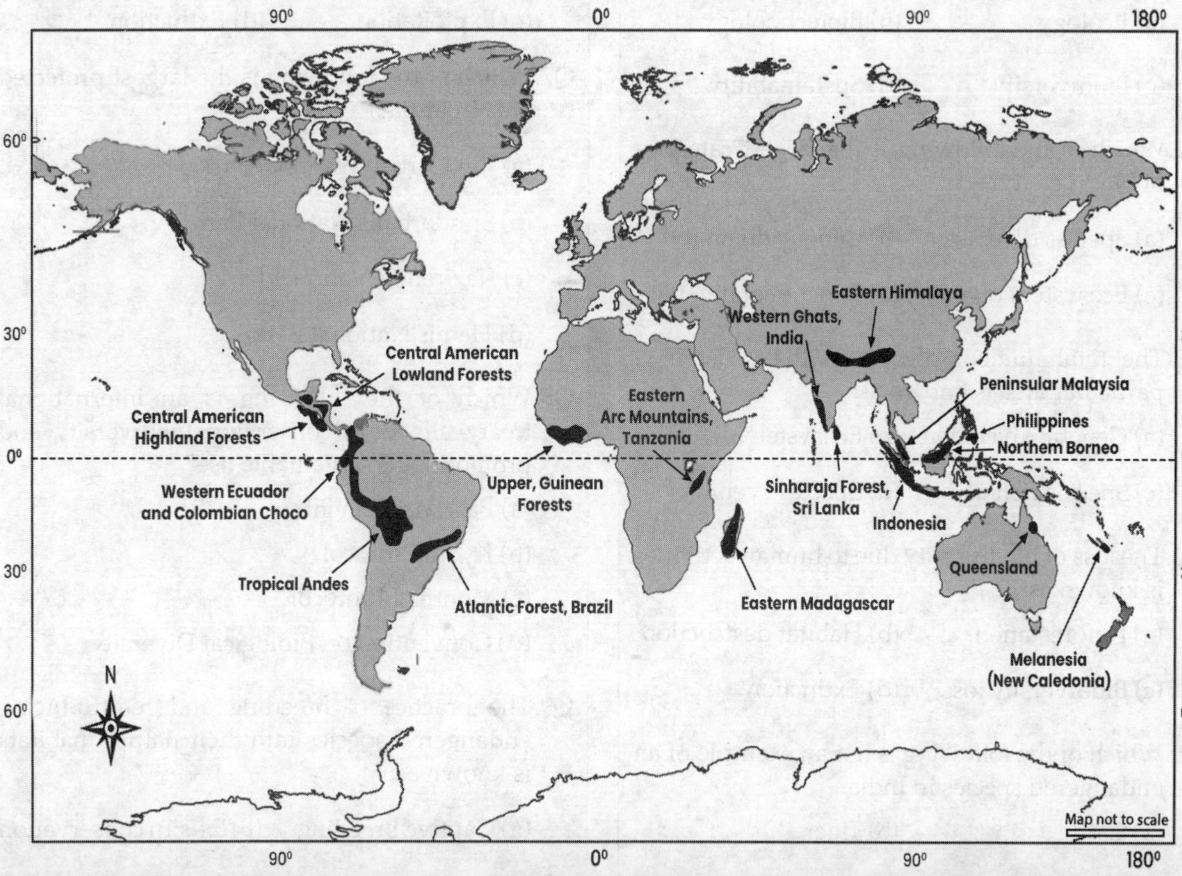

Some Ecological 'Hotspots' in the World

Project Tiger

Tiger is one of the key wildlife species in the faunal web. In 1973, the authorities realised that the **tiger population had dwindled** to 1,827 from an estimated 55,000 at the turn of the century. The major threats to tiger population are numerous, such as poaching for trade, shrinking habitat, depletion of prey base species, growing human population, etc. **The trade of tiger skins and the use of their bones in traditional medicines, especially in Asian countries, left the tiger population on the verge of extinction.** Since India and Nepal provide habitat to about two-thirds of the surviving tiger population in the world, these two nations became prime targets for poaching and illegal trading.

"Project Tiger", one of the well-publicised wildlife campaigns in the world, was launched in 1973. **Corbett National Park** in Uttarakhand, **Sundarbans National Park** in West Bengal, **Bandhavgarh National Park** in Madhya Pradesh, **Sariska Wildlife Sanctuary** in Rajasthan, **Manas Tiger Reserve** in Assam and **Periyar Tiger Reserve** in Kerala are some of the tiger reserves of India.

TEST YOURSELF

Multiple Choice Questions

Q1. Which of the following is the term used to describe the variety of living organisms in a given area?

(a) Ecology (b) Biotechnology

(c) Biodiversity (d) Sustainability

Q2. Which of the following is the largest category of biodiversity?

(a) Species diversity (b) Genetic diversity

(c) Ecosystem diversity (d) Functional diversity

Q3. The total number of species that exist in a particular area is known as:

(a) Genetic diversity (b) Ecosystem diversity

(c) Species richness (d) Species evenness

Q4. The loss of biodiversity due to human activities is known as:

(a) Deforestation (b) Habitat destruction

(c) Biodiversity loss (d) Extinction

Q5. Which of the following is not an example of an endangered species in India?

(a) Cattle (b) Tiger

(c) Elephant (d) Deer

Q6. The process of protecting and managing the natural resources and ecosystems to ensure their sustainability is known as:

(a) Conservation (b) Preservation

(c) Exploitation (d) Extinction

Q7. Which of the following is the largest protected area in India?

(a) Jim Corbett National Park

(b) Sundarbans National Park

(c) Kaziranga National Park

(d) Hemis National Park

Q8. Which of the following is an international treaty aimed at conserving biodiversity and promoting its sustainable use?

(a) Paris Agreement

(b) Kyoto Protocol

(c) Montreal Protocol

(d) Convention on Biological Diversity

Q9. The practice of breeding and reintroducing endangered species into their natural habitats is known as:

(a) Captive breeding (b) Ex-situ conservation

(c) In-situ conservation (d) Ecotourism

Q10. The process of restoring or reestablishing degraded ecosystems and habitats is known as:

(a) Conservation (b) Restoration

(c) Rehabilitation (d) Preservation

Answer Key

Q1.	c	Q2.	c	Q3.	c	Q4.	c
Q5.	a	Q6.	a	Q7.	d	Q8.	d
Q9.	a	Q10.	b				

Model Question for Main Examination

Q. Briefly explain the role of loss of biodiversity in tackling climate change?

UNIT 22

Population of India and The World

In This Unit

Comprehensive and profound coverage of the following NCERTs' chapters:

- ✓ NCERT Class- 8th (Resources and Development), Chapter- 6
- ✓ NCERT Class- 9th (Contemporary India-I), Chapter- 6
- ✓ NCERT Class- 12th (India People and Economy), Chapter- 1
- ✓ NCERT (Before Rationalisation) Class- 12th (Human Geography), Chapter- 3

The people are very important component of a country. India's population is **larger** than the **total population of North America, South America and Australia put together**. More often, it is argued that such a large population invariably puts pressure on its limited resources and is also responsible for many socio-economic problems in the country. At the same time, it is people with their **demands and abilities** that turn them into **resources**. Hence, human resources are the ultimate resource.

Sources of Population Data: Population data are collected through Census operations held **every 10 years** in our country. **The first population Census in India** was conducted in 1872 but its first complete Census was conducted only in 1881. The Census of 2021 has been **postponed** due to the outbreak of Covid-19 till further orders.

Distribution of Population- India

India has a **highly uneven** pattern of population distribution. **Uttar Pradesh has the highest population** followed by Maharashtra, Bihar and West Bengal. Ten states including U.P., Maharashtra, Bihar, West Bengal, Andhra Pradesh along with Tamil Nadu, Madhya Pradesh, Rajasthan, Karnataka and Gujarat, together account for **about 76 per cent** of the total population of the country. On the other hand, share of population is very small in the Union Territory of Jammu & Kashmir (1.04%), and states like Arunachal Pradesh (0.11%) and Uttarakhand (0.84%) in spite of this UT and states having **fairly large geographical area**.

- Such an **uneven spatial distribution** of population in India suggests a close relationship between population and **physical, socioeconomic and historical factors**.
- As far as the **Physical factors** are concerned, it is clear that **climate along with terrain and availability of water** largely determines the pattern of the population distribution.
  - ➢ Consequently, we observe that the **North Indian Plains, deltas and Coastal Plains** have higher proportion of population than the interior districts of southern and central Indian States, Himalayas, some of the north eastern and the western states.
- Among the **Socio-Economic and Historical Factors** of distribution of population, important ones are **evolution of settled agriculture** and agricultural development; pattern of human settlement; **development of transport network, industrialisation and urbanisation.**
  - ➢ For instance, development of **irrigation (Rajasthan),** availability of **mineral and energy resources (Jharkhand)** and development of **transport network (Peninsular States)** have resulted in moderate to high concentration of population in areas which were previously very sparsely populated.

- **It is observed** that the regions falling in the **river plains and coastal areas** of India have remained the regions of larger population concentration. Despite **signs of degradation of natural resources like land and water**, the concentration of population remains high because of an **early history of human settlement and development of transport network.**
- On the other hand, the **urban regions** of Delhi, Mumbai, Kolkata, Bengaluru, Pune, Ahmedabad, Chennai and Jaipur have high concentration of population due to **industrial development and urbanisation** drawing a large number of rural-urban migrants.

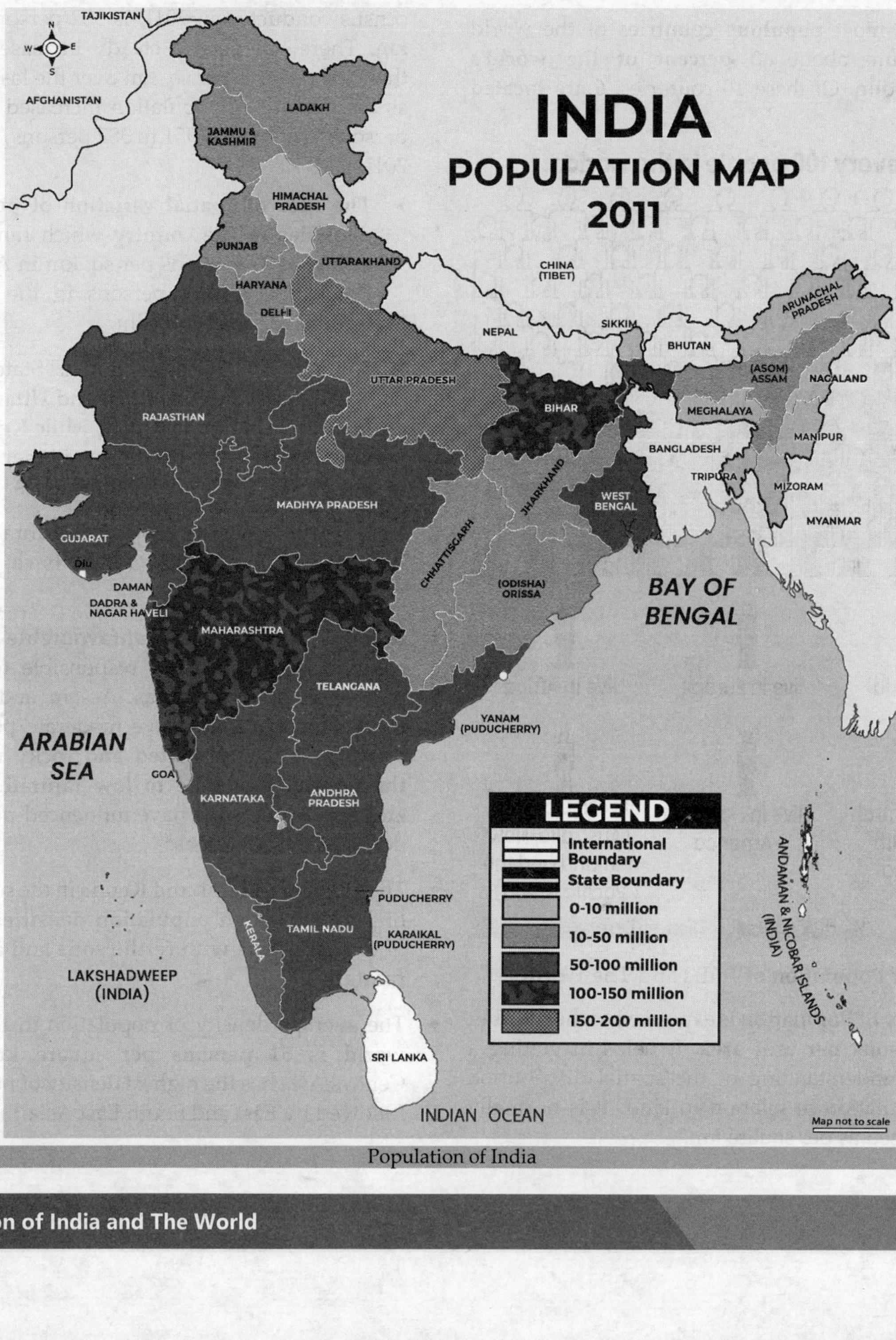

Population of India

Distribution of Population- World

- Patterns of population distribution and density help us to understand the demographic characteristics of any area.
- The term **'population distribution'** refers to the way people are spaced over the earth's surface. Broadly, **90 percent of the world population lives in about 10 percent of its land area.**
- The **10 most populous countries** of the world contribute about **60 percent of the world's population**. Of these 10 countries, **6 are located in Asia.**

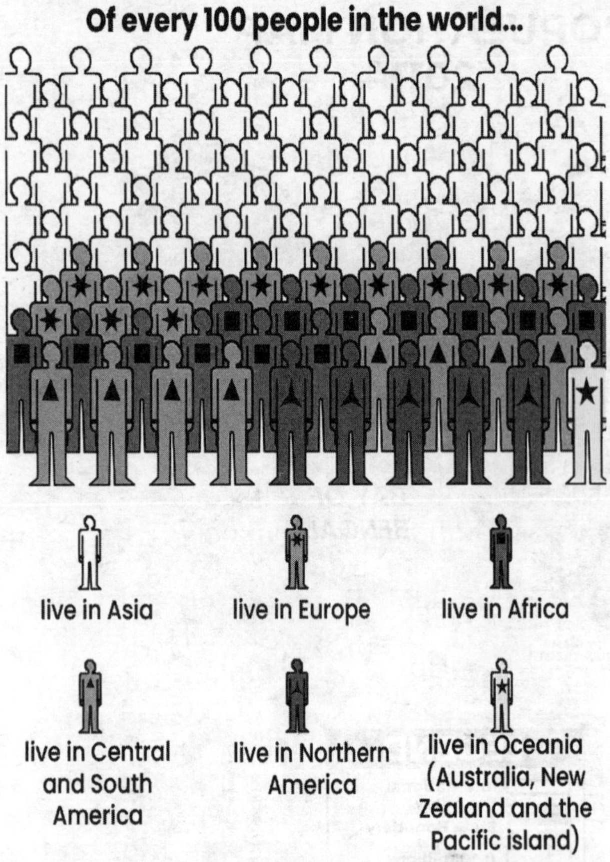

World Population Distribution

Density of Population of India and The World

- **Density of Population** is expressed as the **number of persons per unit area.** It helps in getting a better understanding of the spatial distribution of population in relation to land. It is normally expressed as per square km.

Density of Population = Population/Area

> **For example,** the area of Region X is 100 sq. km and the population is 1,50,000 persons. The density of population is calculated as:

Density = 1,50,000/ 100 = 1,500 person/sq. km

- The density of population in India as per the last census conducted in 2011, is 382 persons per sq. km. There has been a steady increase of more than 200 persons per sq. km over the last 50 years as the density of population increased from 117 persons/ sq. km in 1951 to 382 persons/sq. km in 2011.
  - **The idea of spatial variation of population densities in the country** which ranges from as low as 17 persons per sq. km in Arunachal Pradesh to 11,297 persons in the National Capital Territory of Delhi.
  - Among the northern Indian States, **Bihar (1102), West Bengal (1029) and Uttar Pradesh (828)** have higher densities, while **Kerala (859) and Tamil Nadu (555)** have higher densities among the peninsular Indian states.
  - States like Assam, Gujarat, Andhra Pradesh, Haryana, Jharkhand, Odisha have moderate densities.
- **Rugged terrain and unfavourable** climatic conditions are primarily responsible for sparse population in these areas. Assam and most of the Peninsular states have moderate population densities. **Hilly, dissected and rocky nature of the terrain, moderate to low rainfall, shallow and less fertile soils** have influenced population densities in these areas.
- The **Northern plains and Kerala** in the south have high to very **high population densities** because of the **flat plains with fertile soils and abundant rainfall.**
- The average density of population in the **whole world is 51 persons per square km.** South Central Asia has the highest density of population followed by East and South East Asia.

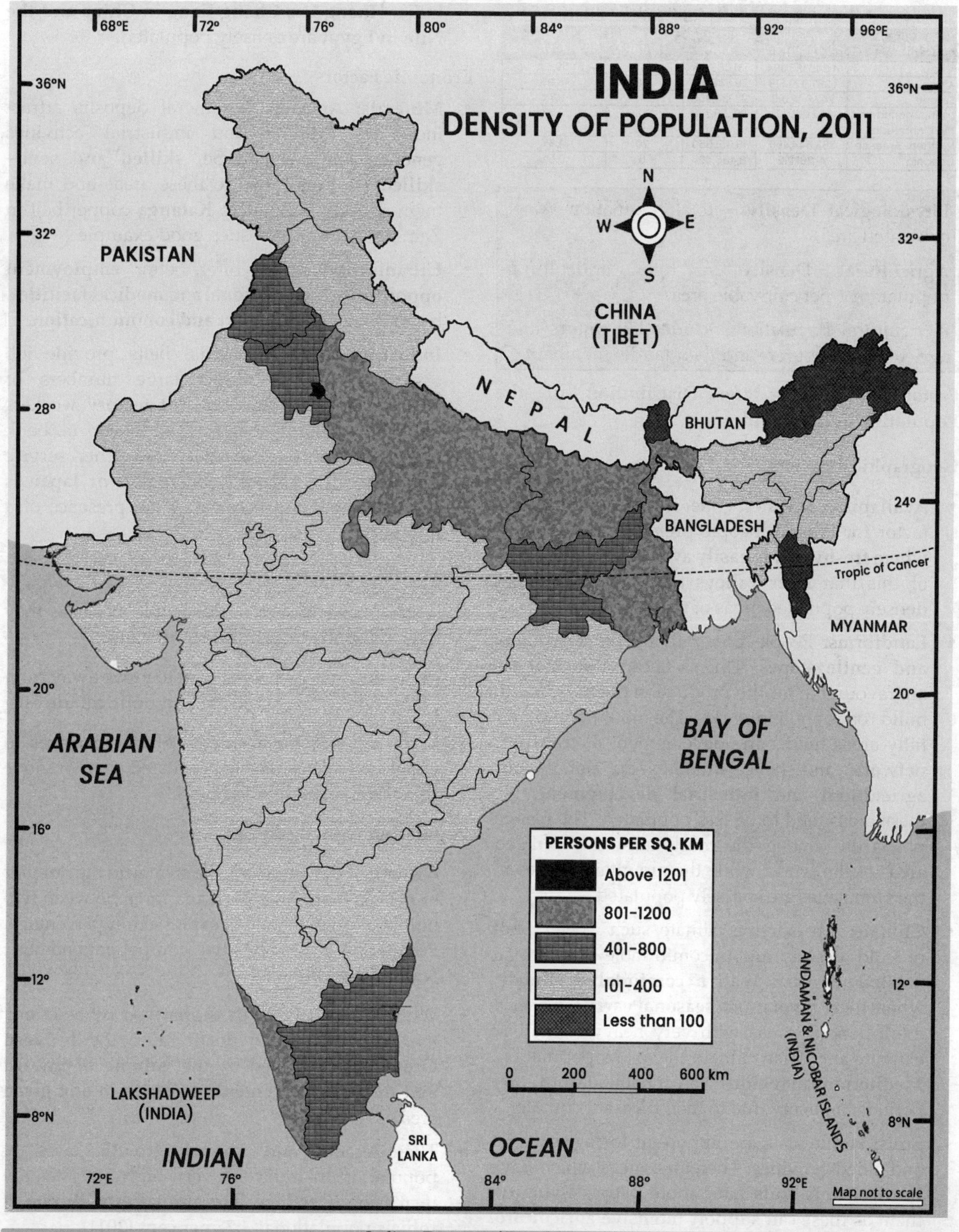

India – Density of Population

Region wise Density of Population

Region	Population (2018)	Land Area (Km²)	Density (P/Km²)	World Share (in percentage)
Asia	4,545,133,094	31,033,131	146	59.5%
Africa	1,287,920,518	29,648,481	43	16.9%
Europe	742,648,010	22,134,900	34	9.7%
Latin America and the Caribbean	652,012,001	20,139,378	32	8.5%
Northern America	363,844,490	18,651,660	20	4.8%
Oceania	41,261,212	8,486,460	5	0.5%

Physiological Density = total population / net cultivated area

Agricultural Density = total agricultural population / net cultivable area

Agricultural Population includes cultivators and agricultural labourers and their family members.

Factors Influencing the Distribution of the Population of the World

Geographical Factors

- **Availability of Water:** Water is the most important factor for life. So, people prefer to live in areas where **freshwater is easily available.** It is because of this that **river valleys** are among the most densely populated areas of the world.
- **Landforms:** People prefer living on **flat plains and gentle slopes.** This is because such areas are favourable for the production of crops and to build roads and industries. The mountainous and hilly areas hinder the development of **transport network** and hence initially do not favour **agricultural and industrial development**. So, these areas tend to be less populated. The Ganga plains are among the most densely populated areas of the world while the mountains zones in the Himalayas are sparsely populated.
- **Climate:** An extreme climate such as very hot or cold deserts are uncomfortable for human habitation. Areas with a **comfortable climate,** where there is **not much seasonal variation** attract more people. Areas with very heavy rainfall or extreme and harsh climates have low population. **Mediterranean regions** were inhabited from early periods in history due to their pleasant climate.
- **Soils:** Fertile soils are important for agricultural and allied activities. Therefore, areas which have **fertile loamy soils** have more people living on them as these can support **intensive agriculture.** Fertile plains such as Ganga and Brahmaputra in India, **Huang-He, Chang Jiang in China and the Nile in Egypt** are densely populated.

Economic Factors

- **Minerals:** Areas with mineral deposits attract industries. Mining and industrial activities generate employment. So, **skilled and semi–skilled workers** move to these areas and make them densely populated. **Katanga** copper belt in Zambia, Africa is one such good example.
- **Urbanisation:** Cities offer better **employment opportunities, educational and medical facilities,** better means of **transport and communication.**
- **Industrialisation:** Industrial belts provide job opportunities and attract large numbers of people. These include not just factory workers but also transport operators, shopkeepers, bank employees, doctors, teachers and other service providers. The **Osaka-Kobe region of Japan** is densely populated because of the presence of a number of industries.

Social and Cultural Factors

- Some places attract more people because they have **religious or cultural significance.**
- In the same way – people tend to move away from places where there is **social and political unrest.**
- Many a times, **governments offer incentives** to people to live in sparsely populated areas or move away from overcrowded place.

Population Growth- India

- **Growth of Population** is the change in the number of people living in a particular area between two points of time. Its rate is expressed in percentage. Population growth has two components namely; **Natural and Induced.**
- While **Natural Growth** is analysed by assessing the crude birth and death rates, the **Induced Growth** is explained by the **volume of inward and outward movement** of people in any given area.
- The **decadal and annual growth rates** of population in India are very high and steadily increasing over time. The **annual growth rate** of India's population is **1.77 per cent (2011).**

- The growth rate of population in India over the last one century has been caused by **annual birth rate and death rate and rate of migration** and thereby shows different trends. There are **Four distinct phases of growth** identified within this period:
    - **Phase 1:** The period from **1901-1921** is referred to as a **period of 'Stagnant or Stationary' phase of growth of India's population**, since in this period growth rate was very low, even recording a negative growth rate during 1911-1921. Both the birth rate and death rate were high keeping the rate of increase low. **Poor health and medical services, illiteracy** of people at large and **inefficient distribution system** of food and other basic necessities were largely responsible for high birth and death rates in this phase.
    - **Phase 2:** The decades **1921-1951** are referred to as the **period of 'Steady Population Growth'**. An overall improvement in **health and sanitation** throughout the country brought down the mortality rate. At the same time, a better **transport and communication** system improved the distribution system. The crude birth rate remained high in this period leading to higher growth rate than the previous phase. This is impressive at the backdrop of the **Great Economic Depression in 1920s and the World War II.**
        - The **year 1921** is taken as the **"Demographic Divide"** for the reason that before this year, the population was not stable, sometimes it increased and at other times it decreased. The growth rate of population was generally low before 1921. But after this year, there has been **'considerable and continuous' increase in the population.** Between 1901 and 1911, the total increase in population was 5.9% and between 1911 and 1921, there was a decrease of 0.39%. In the decade of 1921-1931, the increase was 11.1%, from 1931 to 1941, it was 14.00% and during 1941-1951, it was 13.5%. It is increasing since then. Hence, the **year 1921** is rightly called the **Demographic Divide.**
    - **Phase 3:** The decades **1951-1981** are referred to as the **period of 'Population Explosion' in India,** which was caused by a rapid fall in the mortality rate but a high fertility rate of population in the country. The **average annual growth rate** was as high as **2.2 per cent**. It is in this period, after the Independence, that developmental activities were introduced through a **centralised planning process and the economy** started showing up ensuring the improvement of living conditions of people at large. Consequently, there was a **high natural increase and higher growth rate.** Besides, increased **international migration** bringing in **Tibetans, Bangladeshis, Nepalese** and even people from **Pakistan** contributed to the high growth rate.
    - **Phase 4:** Post **1981 till present**, the growth rate of the country's population, though remained high, has started slowing down gradually. A **downward trend of crude birth rate** is held responsible for such a population growth. This was, in turn, affected by an increase in the mean age **at marriage, improved quality of life particularly education of females** in the country.

The growth rate of population is, however, still high in the country, and it has been projected by the **World Development Report** that the population of India will touch 1,350 million by 2025.

Regional Variation in Population Growth

- The growth rate of population during **1991- 2001** in Indian States and Union Territories shows very obvious pattern. The States like **Kerala, Karnataka, Tamil Nadu, Andhra Pradesh, Odisha, Puducherry, and Goa show a low rate of growth** not exceeding 20 percent over the decade. Kerala registered the lowest growth rate (9.4) not only in this group of states but also in the country as a whole.
- A **continuous belt of states from west to east in the north-west, north, and north central parts of the country has relatively high growth rate** than the southern states.
    - It is in this belt comprising Gujarat, Maharashtra, Rajasthan, Punjab, Haryana, Uttar Pradesh, Uttarakhand, Madhya Pradesh, Sikkim, Assam, West Bengal, Bihar, Chhattisgarh, and Jharkhand, the growth rate on the average remained 20-25 percent.

- During **2001-2011**, the growth rates of almost all States and Union Territories have registered a lower figure compared to the previous decade, namely, 1991-2001.
- The **percentage decadal growth rates** of the six most populous States, namely, Uttar Pradesh, Maharashtra, Bihar, West Bengal, Andhra Pradesh and Madhya Pradesh have all fallen during 2001-2011 compared to 1991-2001, **the fall being the lowest** for Andhra Pradesh (3.5% percentage points) and **highest** for Maharashtra (6.7 percentage points). Tamil Nadu (3.9 percentage points) and Puducherry (7.1 percentage points) have registered some **increase** during 2001-2011 over the previous decade.
- An important aspect of population growth in India is the **growth of its adolescents.** At present the share of adolescents i.e., up to the age group of **10-19 years** is about 20.9 per cent (2011), among which male adolescents constitute 52.7 percent and female adolescents constitute 47.3 percent.
- The growth rate of population is widely **variant over space and time** in the country and also highlights **various social problems** related to the growth of population.

Processes of Population Change/Growth

- There are three main processes of change of population: **birth rates, death rates and migration**. The natural increase of population is the difference between birth rates and death rates.
- **Birth rate** is the number of **live births per thousand persons in a year**. It is a major component of growth because in India, birth rates have always been higher than death rates.
- **Death rate** is the number of **deaths per thousand persons in a year**. The main cause of the rate of growth of the Indian population has been the rapid decline in death rates.
  - Till 1980, high birth rates and declining death rates led to a large difference between birth rates and death rates resulting in higher rates of population growth. Since 1981, birth rates have also started declining gradually, resulting in a gradual decline in the rate of population growth. Reasons for this trend is the third component of population growth i.e., **migration**.
- **Migration** is the **movement of people across regions and territories**. Migration can be **internal** (within the country) or **international** (between the countries). Internal migration does not change the size of the population, but influences the distribution of population within the nation. Migration plays a very **significant role** in changing the **composition and distribution of population.**
  - **In India**, most migrations have been **from rural to urban** areas because of the **"push"** factor in rural areas. These are adverse conditions of poverty and unemployment in the rural areas and the **"pull"** of the city in terms of **increased employment** opportunities and **better living conditions**. Migration is an important determinant of population change.
  - The urban population has increased from 17.29 per cent of the total population in 1951 to 31.80 per cent in 2011. There has been a significant increase in the number of **'million plus cities'** from 35 to 53 in just one decade, i.e., 2001 to 2011.

Adolescent Population

- The most significant feature of the Indian population is the size of its adolescent population. It constitutes one-fifth of the total population of India. Adolescents are, generally, grouped in the **age group of 10 to 19 years**. They are the most important resource for the future.
- The adolescent population, though, regarded as the **youthful population** having high potentials, but at the same time they are **quite vulnerable** if not guided and channelised properly.
  - **There are many challenges for the society as far as these adolescents are concerned,** some of which are lower age at marriage, illiteracy – particularly female illiteracy, school dropouts, low intake of nutrients, high rate of maternal mortality of adolescent mothers, high rate of HIV and AIDS infections, physical and mental disability or retardedness, drug abuse and alcoholism, juvenile delinquency etc.
  - **Nutrition requirements** of adolescents are higher than those of a normal child or adult. Poor nutrition can lead to deficiency and stunted growth. But in India, the diet available

to adolescents is inadequate in all nutrients. A large number of **adolescent girls suffer from anaemia.**

➢ In view of these, the **Government of India** has undertaken certain policies to impart proper education to the adolescent groups so that their talents are better channelised and properly utilised. The **National Youth Policy** is one example which has been designed to look into the overall development of our large youth and adolescent population.

➢ The **National Youth Policy (NYP–2014)** launched in February 2014 proposes a holistic 'vision' for the youth of India, which is "To empower the youth of the country to achieve their full potential, and through them enable India to find its rightful place in the community of nations." **The NYP–2014 has defined 'youth' as persons in the age group of 15–29 years.**

➢ The Government of India also formulated the **National Policy for Skill Development and Entrepreneurship in 2015** to provide an umbrella framework to all skilling activities being carried out within the country, and to align these to common standards and link skilling with demand centres.

- However, in general, their problems have so far not received adequate attention in the process of development. The **adolescent girls have to be sensitised** to the problems they confront. Awareness among them can be improved through the **spread of literacy and education**.

National Population Policy

Recognising that the planning of families would improve individual health and welfare, the Government of India initiated a **comprehensive Family Planning Programme in 1952**. The Family Welfare Programme has sought to promote **responsible and planned parenthood** on a **voluntary** basis.

The **National Population Policy (NPP) 2000** is a culmination of years of planned efforts. The NPP 2000 provides a policy framework for:

- Imparting **free and compulsory school education** up to 14 years of age.
- **Reducing infant mortality rate** to below 30 per 1000 live births.
- Achieving **universal immunisation** of children against all vaccine preventable diseases.
- Promoting **delayed marriage** for girls.
- Making family welfare a **people-centred** programme.

Population Growth of the World

The **'Population Growth' or 'Population Change'** refers to the change in number of inhabitants of a territory during a specific period of time. This change may be **positive as well as negative.** It can be expressed either in terms of **absolute numbers or in terms of percentage**. Population change in an area is an important indicator of **economic development, social upliftment and historical and cultural background** of the region.

Some Basic Concepts of Population Geography

- **Growth of Population:** Change of population in a particular area between two points of time is known as growth of population. For example, if we deduct the population of India 2001 (102.70 crore) from the population of 2011 (121.02 crore) then we shall get the growth of population (18.15 crores) in actual numbers.
- **Growth Rate of Population:** This is the change of population expressed in percentage.
- **Natural Growth of Population:** This is the population increased by difference between births and deaths in a particular region between two points of time.
  - ➢ **Natural Growth** = Births – Deaths
  - ➢ **Actual Growth of Population:** This is Births – Deaths + In Migration – Out Migration
- **Positive Growth of Population:** This happens when the birth rate is more than the death rate between two points of time or when people from other countries migrate permanently to a region.
- **Negative Growth of Population:** If the population decreases between two points of time it is known as negative growth of population. It occurs when the birth rate falls below the death rate or people migrate to other countries.

Components of Population Change

There are three components of population change – **births, deaths and migration.**

- The **Crude Birth Rate** (CBR) is expressed as the number of **live births in a year per thousand of population**. It is calculated as:
  - ➢ CBR = Bi/P*1000
  - ➢ Here, CBR = Crude Birth Rate; Bi = live births during the year; P = Mid-year, population of the area.
- **Crude Death Rate** (CDR) is a simple method of measuring mortality of any area. It plays an active role in population change. CDR is expressed in terms of the **number of deaths in a particular year per thousand of population in a particular region**. CDR is calculated as:
  - ➢ CDR = D/P*1000
  - ➢ Here, CDR=Crude Death Rate; D= Number of deaths; P=Estimated mid-year population of that year.
- **Migration-** Migration is the movement of people in and out of an area. When people move from one place to another, the place they move from is called the **Place of Origin** and the place they move to is called the **Place of Destination.**

Trends in Population Growth

According to the United Nations, on **15 November 2022**, the world's population is projected to reach **8 billion** people, a milestone in human development. This unprecedented growth is due to the gradual **increase in human lifespan** owing to improvements in **public health, nutrition, personal hygiene and medicine.** It is also the result of **high and persistent levels of fertility** in some countries.

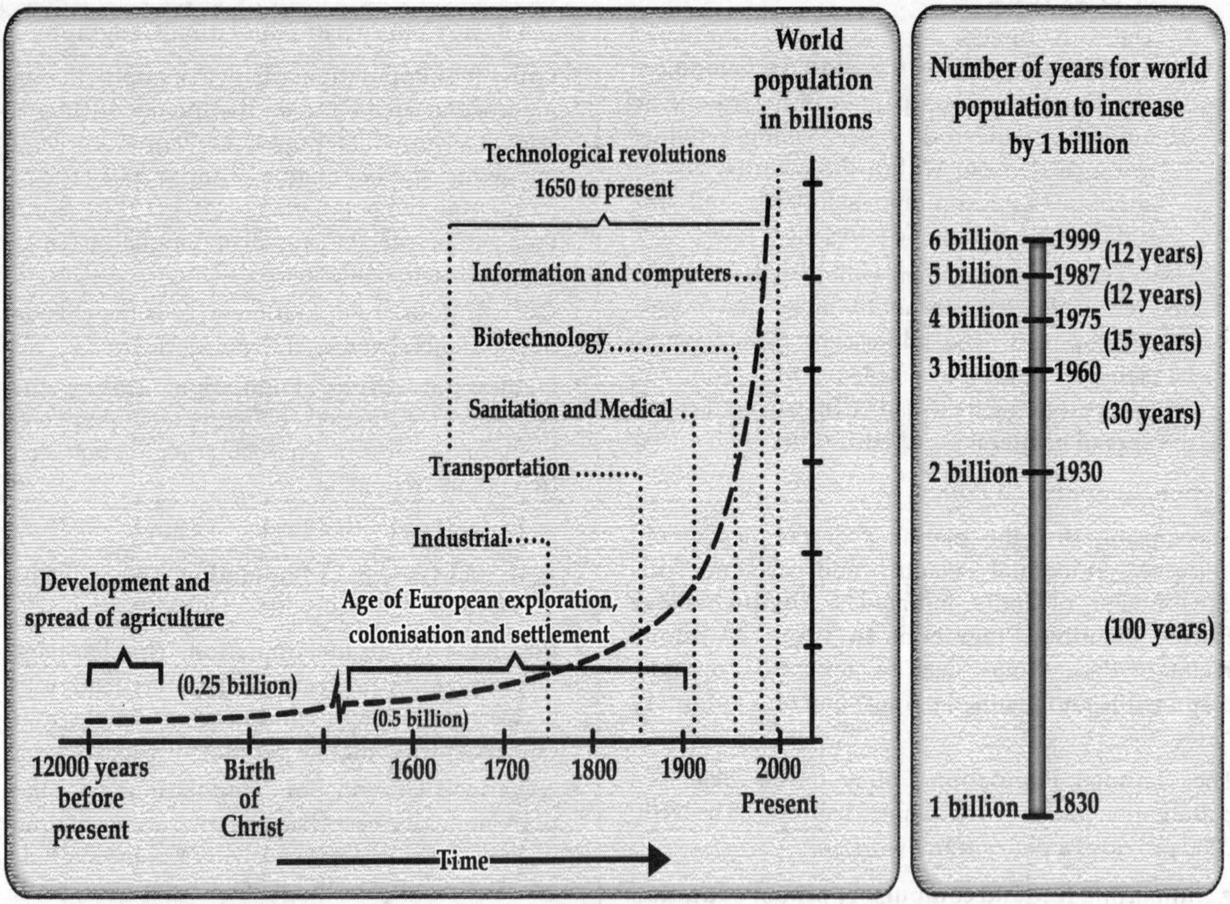

It took over **200,000 years of human prehistory and history** for the human population to reach **one billion** and **only 219 years more to reach 8 billion**. While it took the **global population 12 years to grow from 7 to 8 billion**, it will take approximately **15 years until 2037** for it to reach 9 billion, a sign that the overall growth rate of the global population is slowing.

In the early periods population of the world grew very slowly. It is only during the **last few hundred years** that population has increased at an **alarming rate**.

After the evolution and introduction of agriculture about **12,000 to 8,000 years ago**, the size of population was small – **roughly 8 million**. In the first century A.D. it was **below 300 million**. The expanding world trade during the **sixteenth and seventeenth century**, set the stage for rapid population growth. Around 1750, at the dawn of the Industrial Revolution, the world population was **550 million**. World population **exploded in the eighteenth century after the Industrial Revolution**. Technological advancement achieved so far helped in the reduction of death rate and provided a stage for accelerated population growth.

Doubling Time of World Population

Population Doubling Time is the time taken by any population to double itself at its current annual growth rate.

It took more than a million years for the human population to attain the one billion mark. But it took only 12 years for it to rise from 5 billion to 6 billion, similar to the trajectory from 7 billion to 8 billion.

This is double what the population was **just 48 years after 1975**, when it reached four billion people. When we compare growth rates over the selected periods, it took an average of 12 years per one billion people between 1975 and 2023, which is almost double the rate of the period between 1928 and 1975, and over ten times faster than growth between 1803 and 1928.

There is a **great variation among regions** in doubling their population. Developed countries take more time to double their population as compared to developing countries. Most of the population growth is taking place in the developing world, where the population is exploding.

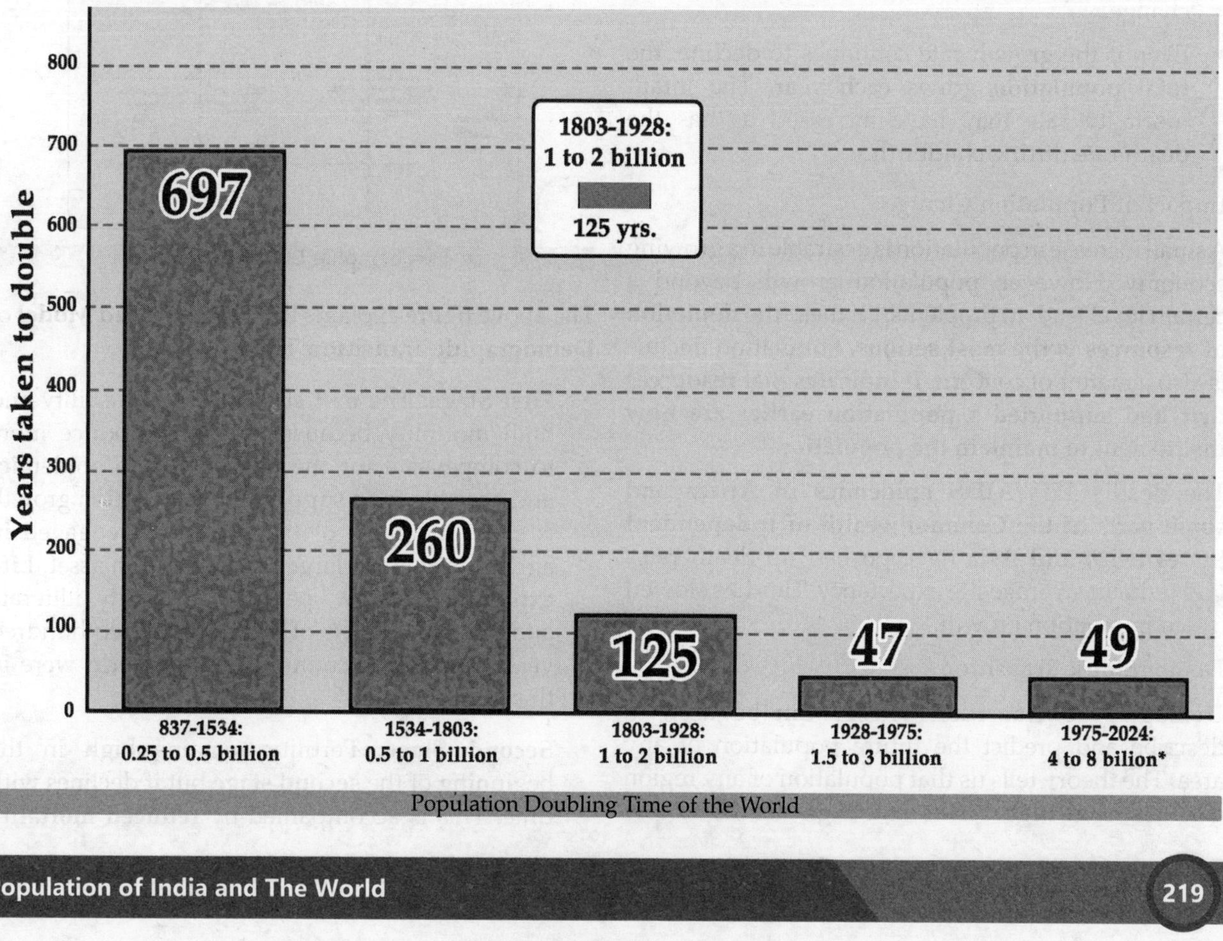

Population Doubling Time of the World

Period	Population	Time in which Population Doubles
10,000 B.C.	5 million	
1650 A.D.	500 million	1,500 years
1850 A.D.	1,000 million	200 years
1930 A.D.	2,000 million	80 years
1975 A.D.	4,000 million	45 years
2012 A.D.	8,000 million projected figure	37 years

Doubling Time of World Population

Spatial Pattern of Population Change

Population growth in different parts of the world can be compared. The growth of population is low in developed countries as compared to developing countries. There is a **negative correlation between economic development and population growth.**

Although the **annual rate of population change (1.4 per cent) seems to be low, it is actually not so.** This is because:

- When a small annual rate is applied to a very large population, it will lead to a large population change.
- Even if the growth rate continues to decline, the **total population grows each year**. The infant mortality rate may have increased as has the death rate during childbirth.

Impact of Population Change

A small increase in population is desirable in a growing economy. However, population growth beyond a certain level lead, to problems. Of these the **depletion of resources is the most serious**. Population decline is also a matter of concern. **It indicates that resources that had supported a population earlier are now insufficient to maintain the population.**

The deadly **HIV/AIDS epidemics in Africa and some parts of the Commonwealth of Independent States (CIS) and Asia** have pushed up death rates and reduced average life expectancy. This has slowed down population growth.

Demographic Transition

Demographic Transition Theory can be used to describe and predict the future population of any area. The theory tells us that population of any region changes from **high births and high deaths to low births and low deaths** as society progresses from **rural agrarian and illiterate to urban industrial and literate society.** These changes occur in stages which are collectively known as the **'Demographic Cycle'.**

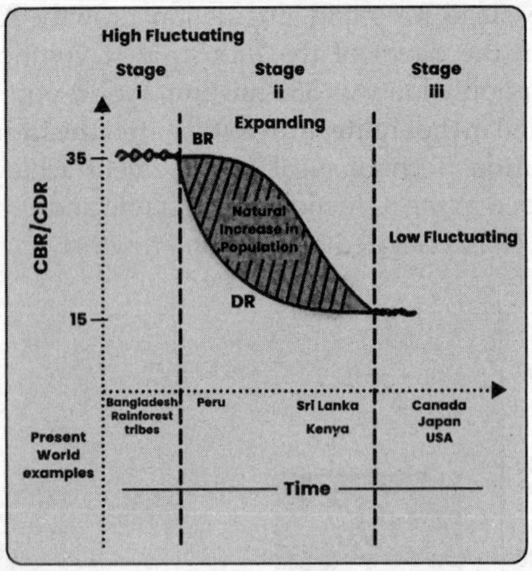

Demographic Transition Theory

The above figure explains the **Three-Staged Model** of **Demographic Transition Theory**:

- **First Stage:** The **first stage** has high fertility and high mortality because people reproduce more to compensate for the deaths due to epidemics and variable food supply. The population growth is slow and most of the people are engaged in agriculture where large families are an asset. **Life expectancy is low**, people are mostly illiterate and have low levels of technology. Two hundred years ago all the countries of the world were in this stage.
- **Second Stage:** Fertility remains high in the beginning of the **second stage** but it declines with time. This is accompanied by **reduced mortality**

rate. Improvements in sanitation and health conditions lead to decline in mortality. Because of this gap the net addition to population is high.

- **Third Stage:** In the **last stage,** both fertility and mortality decline considerably. The **population is either stable or grows slowly.** The population becomes **urbanised, literate** and has **high technical know-how** and deliberately controls the family size.

This shows that human beings are extremely flexible and are able to adjust their fertility.

Population Control Measures

Family Planning is the spacing or preventing the birth of children. Access to family planning services is a significant factor in limiting population growth and improving women's health. **Propaganda, free availability of contraceptives and tax disincentives** for large families are some of the measures which can help population control.

Thomas Malthus stated in 1798 that the number of people would increase faster than the food supply. He said further increase in population would result in a population crash caused by famine, disease and war. Hence he believed that preventive checks are necessary for the sustainable use of resources and the world will have to control the rapid population increase.

Population Composition of the World

People can be distinguished by their **age, sex and their place of residence**. Some of the other distinguishing attributes of the population are **occupation, education and life expectancy**.

Sex Composition

- The number of women and men in a country is an important demographic characteristic. The ratio between the number of women and men in the population is called the **'Sex Ratio'**. In some countries it is calculated by using the formula:
  - ➢ Male Population/ Female Population*1000 or the number of males per thousand females.
- In India, the sex ratio is worked out using the formula:
  - ➢ **Female Population/ Male Population*1000** or the number of females per thousand males.

> **Not gold but only (Wo)men can make a people great and strong.**
>
> (Wo)men who for truth and honour's sake, stand fast and suffer long. (Wo)men who toil while others sleep who dare while others flee they build a nation's pillars deep and lift it to the sky.
>
> -Ralph Waldo Emerson

The sex ratio is an important information about the **status of women** in a country. In regions where **gender discrimination** is rampant, the sex ratio is bound to be unfavourable to women. Such areas are those where the practice of **female foeticide, female infanticide and domestic violence** against women are prevalent. One of the reasons could be **lower socio-economic status** of women in these areas.

> **Natural Advantage vs Social Advantage**
>
> Females have a **biological advantage** over males as they tend to be more resilient than males yet this advantage is cancelled out by the **social disadvantages and discriminations** that they face.

- On an average, the **world population** reflects a sex ratio of **102 males per 100 females.**
  - ➢ The highest sex ratio in the world has been recorded in **Latvia** where there are **85 males per 100 females**. In contrast, in **Qatar** there are **311 males per 100 females.**
- The world pattern of sex ratio does not exhibit variations in the developed regions of the world. The sex ratio is **favourable for females in 139 countries** of the world and unfavourable for them in the remaining 72 countries listed by the United Nations.
- In general, **Asia has a low sex ratio. Countries like China, India, Saudi Arabia, Pakistan, Afghanistan had a lower sex ratio.**
- On the other extreme is **greater part of Europe (including Russia) where males are in minority**. A deficit of males in the populations of many European countries is attributed to **better status of women**, and an **excessively male-dominated out-migration** to different parts of the world in the past.

Age Structure

Age Structure represents the number of people of different age groups. This is an important indicator of population composition, since a large size of population in the age group of **15- 59** indicates a large working population. A greater proportion of population **above 60 years represents an ageing population** which requires more expenditure on health care facilities. Similarly, a high proportion of the **young population** would mean that the region has a **high birth rate** and the population is youthful.

Age-Sex Pyramid

The Age-Sex Structure of a population refers to the number of females and males in different age groups. A **Population Pyramid** is used to show the age-sex structure of the population.

The shape of the population pyramid reflects the characteristics of the population. The left side shows the percentage of males while the right side shows the percentage of women in each age group.

- **Expanding Population-** The age-sex pyramid of **Nigeria** as you can see is a **triangular shaped** pyramid with a wide base and is typical of **less developed** countries. These have larger populations in lower age groups due to high birth rates. Countries like **Bangladesh and Mexico** also show similar pyramid structure.

Expanding Population

- **Constant Population-** Australia's age-sex pyramid is **bell-shaped and tapered towards the top**. This shows **birth and death rates are almost equal** leading to a near constant population.

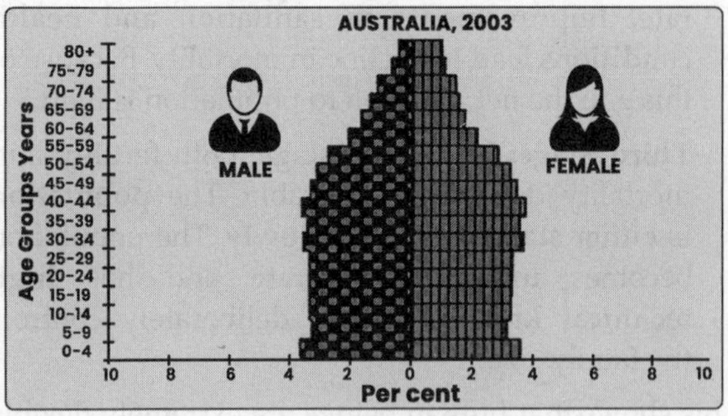

Constant Population

- **Declining Population-** The **Japan** pyramid has a **narrow base and a tapered top** showing low birth and death rates. The population growth in developed countries is usually zero or negative.

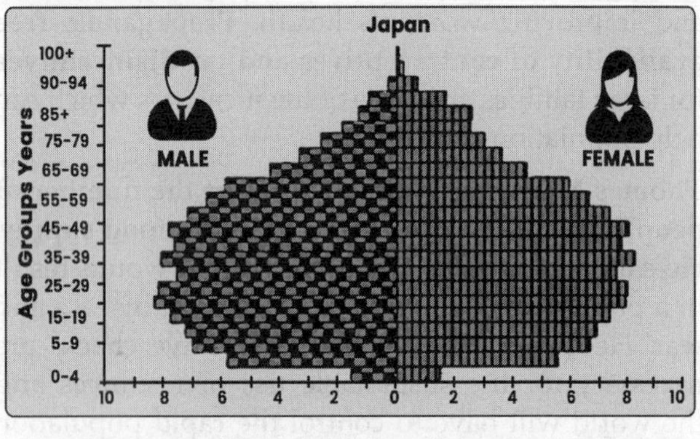

Declining Population

Population Composition- India

The composition of Indian population with respect to their **rural-urban characteristics, language, religion** and pattern of occupation is as follows:

Rural – Urban Composition

- Composition of population by their respective places of residence is an important indicator of **social and economic characteristics**. This becomes even more significant for a country where about 68.8 percent of its total population lives in villages (2011). The Distribution of the rural population is **not uniform** throughout the country.
  - The states like **Bihar and Sikkim** have a very high percentage of rural population.
  - The states of **Goa and Maharashtra** have only little over half of their total population residing in villages.

- The **Union Territories**, on the other hand, have a **smaller proportion** of rural population, except Dadra and Nagar Haveli (53.38 per cent).
- The **size of villages also varies** considerably. It is **less than 200 persons** in the **hill states of north-eastern India, Western Rajasthan and Rann of Kuchchh** and as high as **17 thousand persons** in the states of **Kerala and in parts of Maharashtra**.

- In contrast to rural population, **the proportion of urban population (31.16 per cent) in India is quite low but it is showing a much faster rate of growth over the decades.**
  - It is, however, noticed that in almost all the states and Union Territories, there has been a **considerable increase of urban population**. This indicates both development of urban areas in terms of **socio-economic conditions** and an increased rate of **rural-urban migration.**
  - The rural-urban migration is conspicuous in the case of urban areas **along the main road links and railroads** in the North Indian Plains, the **industrial areas** around Kolkata, Mumbai, Bengaluru – Mysuru, Madurai – Coimbatore, Ahmedabad – Surat, Delhi – Kanpur and Ludhiana – Jalandhar.
  - In the **agriculturally stagnant parts** of the middle and lower Ganga Plains, Telangana, non-irrigated Western Rajasthan, **remote hilly, tribal areas** of north- east, along the **flood-prone areas** of Peninsular India and along eastern part of Madhya Pradesh, the degree of urbanisation has remained low.

Linguistic Composition

- India is a land of linguistic diversity. According to Grierson (Linguistic Survey of India, 1903 – 1928), there were **179 languages and as many as 544 dialects in the country**.
- In the context of modern India, **there are about 22 Scheduled languages and a number of non-scheduled languages.**
- Among the **Scheduled languages**, the speakers of **Hindi** have the highest percentage. The smallest language groups are **Sanskrit, Bodo and Manipuri** speakers (2011).
- However, it is noticed that the linguistic regions in the country do not have a sharp and distinct boundary, rather they **gradually merge and overlap** in their respective frontier zones.

Linguistic Classification

The speakers of major Indian languages belong to **four language families**, which have their sub-families and branches or groups.

Family	Sub-Family	Branch/Group	Speech Areas
Austric (Nishada) 1.38%	Austro-Asiatic Austro-Nesian	Mon-Khmer Munda	Meghalaya, Nicobar Islands, West Bengal, Bihar, Odisha, Assam, Madhya Pradesh, Maharashtra, Outside India.
Dravidian (Dravida) 20%		South-Dravidian Central Dravidian North Dravidian	Tamil Nadu, Karnataka, Kerala, Andhra Pradesh, M.P., Odisha, Maharashtra Bihar, West Bengal, Madhya Pradesh.
Sino-Tibetan (Kirata) 0.85%	Tibeto-Myanmari Siamese -Chinese	Tibeto-Himalayan North Assam Assam-Myanmari	Jammu & Kashmir, Himachal Pradesh, Sikkim, Arunachal Pradesh, Assam, Nagaland, Manipur, Mizoram, Tripura, Meghalaya
Indo-European (Aryan) 73%	Indo-Aryan	Iranian Dardic Indo-Aryan	Outside India Jammu & Kashmiar, Punjab, Himachal Pradesh, U.P., Rajasthan, Haryana, M.P., Bihar, Odisha, West Bengal, Assam, Gujarat, Maharashtra, Goa.

Classification of Modern Indian Languages

Religious Composition

- The spatial distribution of religious communities in the country shows that there are certain states and districts having large numerical strength of one religion, while the same may be very negligibly represented in other states.
  - **Hindus** are distributed as a major group in many states (ranging from 70 - 90 per cent and above) except the districts of states along Indo-Bangladesh border, Indo-Pak border, Jammu & Kashmir, Hill States of North-East and in scattered areas of Deccan Plateau and Ganga Plain.
  - **Muslims,** the largest religious minority, are concentrated in Jammu & Kashmir, certain districts of West Bengal and Kerala, many districts of Uttar Pradesh, in and around Delhi and in Lakshadweep. They form a majority in Kashmir valley and Lakshadweep.
  - The **Christian population** is distributed mostly in rural areas of the country. The main concentration is observed along the Western coast around Goa, Kerala and also in the hill states of Meghalaya, Mizoram, Nagaland, Chotanagpur area and Hills of Manipur.
  - **Sikhs** are mostly concentrated in relatively small area of the country, particularly in the states of Punjab, Haryana and Delhi.
  - **Jains and Buddhists**, the smallest religious groups in India have their concentration only in selected areas of the country. **Jains** have major concentration in the urban areas of Rajasthan, Gujarat and Maharashtra, while the **Buddhists** are concentrated mostly in Maharashtra. The other areas of Buddhist majority are Sikkim, Arunachal Pradesh, Ladakh, Tripura, and Lahul and Spiti in Himachal Pradesh.
  - The other religions of India include **Zoroastrians, tribal and other indigenous faiths and beliefs**. These groups are concentrated in small pockets scattered throughout the country.

Religious Group	2011 Population (in million)	2011 % of Total
Hindus	966.3	79.8
Muslims	172.2	14.2
Christians	27.8	2.3
Sikhs	20.8	1.7
Buddhists	8.4	0.7
Jains	4.5	0.4
Other Religions and Persuasions (ORP)	7.9	0.7
Religion Not Stated	2.9	0.2

Religious Communities of India, 2011

Composition of Working Population

- The population of India according to their **economic status is divided into three groups,** namely;
  - Main Workers
  - Marginal Workers
  - Non-Workers
- It is observed that in India, the proportion of **workers (both main and marginal) is only 39.8 percent (2011)** leaving a vast majority of about 60 per cent as non-workers. This indicates an economic status in which there is a larger proportion of dependent population, further indicating possible existence of large number of unemployed or under employed people.
  - **The proportion of working population, of the states and Union Territories** show a moderate variation from about 39.6 per cent in Goa to about 49.9 per cent in Daman and Diu.
  - **The states with larger percentages of workers** are Himachal Pradesh, Sikkim, Chhattisgarh, Andhra Pradesh, Karnataka, Arunachal Pradesh, Nagaland, Manipur and Meghalaya.
  - Among the **Union Territories**, Dadra and Nagar Haveli and Daman and Diu have higher participation rate.
- The **Occupational Composition** of India's population (which actually means engagement of an individual in farming, manufacturing, trade,

services or any kind of professional activities) shows a **large proportion of primary sector workers** compared to secondary and tertiary sectors.

- About **54.6 per cent** of total working population are **cultivators and agricultural labourers,** whereas only **3.8%** of workers are engaged in **household industries** and **41.6%** are other workers in **non- household industries, trade, commerce, construction and repair and other services.**
- As far as the occupation of country's male and female population is concerned, **male workers out-number female** workers **in all the three sectors.**

Occupational Categories

The 2011 Census has divided the working population of India into four major categories:

1. Cultivators
2. Agricultural Labourers
3. Household Industrial Workers
4. Other Workers.

Standard Census Definition

- **Main Worker** is a person who works for at least 183 days or six months in a year.
- **Marginal Worker** is a person who works for less than 183 days or six months in a year.

TEST YOURSELF

Multiple Choice Questions

Q1. Human Resources refer to:

(a) Natural resources found in the Earth's crust

(b) The skills, knowledge, and abilities of individuals

(c) Physical infrastructure and facilities

(d) Financial Capital and investments

Q2. The term "Population Density" refers to:

(a) The number of people per unit area

(b) The distribution of population in rural and urban areas

(c) The age structure of a population

(d) The rate of population growth

Q3. Which of the following factors influences the distribution of human population?

(a) Climate and natural resources

(b) Migration patterns

(c) Government policies

(d) All of the above

Q4. The percentage of the population that is able to read and write is known as the:

(a) Literacy rate (b) Life expectancy

(c) Fertility rate (d) Urbanisation rate

Q5. The process of acquiring skills, knowledge, and attitudes necessary to participate effectively in society is known as:

(a) Education (b) Training

(c) Employment (d) Migration

Q6. The ratio of the economically active population to the total population is known as the:

(a) Dependency ratio

(b) Labour force participation rate

(c) Unemployment rate

(d) Population growth rate

Q7. The number of live births per 1,000 women in the reproductive age group (usually 15-49 years) is known as the:

(a) Infant mortality rate

(b) Crude birth rate

(c) Total fertility rate

(d) Maternal mortality rate

Q8. The process by which a country experiences a decline in its birth rate and death rate, leading to a slower population growth rate, is known as:

(a) Demographic Transition

(b) Population Explosion

(c) Population Pyramid

(d) Urbanisation

Q9. The concept that refers to the potential workforce that is available in a country or region is known as:

(a) Human Capital

(b) Demographic Dividend

(c) Brain Drain

(d) Population Density

Q10. Which of the following is the study of the spatial patterns and dynamics of human populations?

(a) Demography (b) Cartography

(c) Geopolitics (d) Topography

Answer Key

Q1.	b	Q2.	a	Q3.	d	Q4.	a
Q5.	a	Q6.	b	Q7.	c	Q8.	a
Q9.	b	Q10.	a				

Model Questions for Main Examination

Q1. Analyse the population distribution across India.

Q2. Assess the factors influencing the population distribution in India.

UNIT 23

Human Settlements

In This Unit

Comprehensive and profound coverage of the following NCERTs' chapters:

- ✓ NCERT Class- 12th (India-People and Economy), Chapter- 4
- ✓ NCERT (Before Rationalisation) Class- 12th (Human Geography), Chapter- 10

Human Settlement means **cluster of dwellings** of any type or size where human beings live. For this purpose, people may erect houses and other structures and command some area or territory as their economic support-base. Thus, the process of settlement inherently involves grouping of people and **apportioning of territory** as their resource base.

Settlements Vary in Size and Type

They range from a **hamlet to metropolitan** cities. With size, the **economic character and social structure** of settlements changes and so do its **ecology and technology**. Settlements could be small and sparsely spaced; they may also be large and closely spaced. The sparsely located small settlements are called **Villages**, specialising in agriculture or other **primary activities.** On the other hand, there are fewer but larger settlements which are termed as **Urban Settlements specialising in secondary and tertiary activities.**

The basic differences between rural and urban settlements are as follows:

- The **Rural Settlements** derive their life support or basic economic needs from land based primary economic activities, whereas, **Urban Settlements,** depend on processing of raw materials and manufacturing of finished goods on the one hand and a variety of services on the other.
- **Cities** act as **'nodes of economic growth'**, provide goods and services not only to urban dwellers but also to the people of the rural settlements in their hinterlands in return for food and raw materials. This **functional relationship** between the urban and rural settlements takes place through transport and communication network.
- **Rural and urban settlements differ in terms** of **social relationship, attitude and outlook.** Rural people are less mobile and therefore, social relations among them are intimate. In urban areas, on the other hand, way of life is complex and fast, and social relations are formal.

Rural Settlements

Rural settlements are most closely and directly related to land. They are dominated by primary activities such as agriculture, animal husbandry, fishing etc. The settlements size is relatively small. **Some factors affecting the location of rural settlements are:**

- **Water Supply:** Usually rural settlements are located near water bodies such as rivers, lakes, and springs where water can be easily obtained. Sometimes the need for water drives people to settle in otherwise disadvantaged sites such as islands surrounded by **swamps or low-lying river banks.**
  - ➢ Most water based **'Wet Point'** settlements have many advantages such as water for drinking, cooking and washing. Water bodies also have fish which can be caught for diet and navigable rivers and lakes can be used for transportation.
- **Land:** People choose to settle near fertile lands suitable for agriculture.
  - ➢ In Europe, villages grew up near rolling country avoiding **swampy, low-lying land**

while people in **South East Asia** chose to live near **low lying river valleys and coastal plains** suited for wet rice cultivation. **Early settlers** chose plain areas with fertile soils.

- **Upland:** Upland which is not prone to flooding was chosen to prevent damage to houses and loss of life. Thus, in low lying river basins people chose to settle on **terraces and levees** which are **"Dry Points."**
  - In tropical countries, people build their houses on stilts near marshy lands to protect themselves from **flood, insects and animal pests.**
- **Building Material:** The availability of building materials- **wood, stone** near settlements is another advantage. Early villages were built in forest clearings where wood was plentiful.
  - In **loess areas of China, cave dwellings** were important and **African Savanna's** building materials were **mud bricks** and the **Eskimos, in polar regions, use ice blocks** to construct **igloos.**
- **Defence:** During the times of **political instability, war, hostility** of neighbouring groups, villages were built on **defensive hills and islands.**
  - In **Nigeria, upstanding inselbergs** formed good defensive sites. **In India**, most of the forts are located on higher grounds or hills.
- **Planned Settlements:** Sites that are not spontaneously chosen by villagers themselves, planned settlements are constructed by governments by providing **shelter, water and other infrastructure** on acquired lands.
  - The scheme of **villagisation in Ethiopia** and the **canal colonies in Indira Gandhi canal command area** in India are some good examples.

Rural Settlement Patterns

Rural settlements may be classified on the basis of a number of criteria:

- **On the basis of Setting:** The main types are plain villages, plateau villages, coastal villages, forest villages and desert villages.
- **On the basis of Functions:** There may be farming villages, fishermen's villages, lumberjack villages, pastoral villages etc.
- **On the basis of Forms or Shapes of the settlements:** These may be a number of geometrical forms and shapes such as Linear, rectangular, circular star like, T-shaped village, double village, cross-shaped village etc.
- **Linear pattern:** In such settlement houses are located along a road, railway line, river, canal edge of a **valley or along a levee.**
- **Rectangular pattern:** Such patterns of rural settlements are found in plain areas or wide inter montane valleys. The roads are rectangular and **cut each other at right angles.**
- **Circular pattern:** Circular villages develop around lakes, tanks and sometimes the village is planned in such a way that the central part remains open and is used for keeping the animals to protect them from wild animals.
- **Star-like pattern:** Where several roads converge, star shaped settlements develop by the houses built along the roads.
- **T-shaped, Y-shaped, Cross-shaped or Cruciform settlements:** T-shaped settlements develop at tri-junctions of the roads, while Y-shaped settlements emerge at the places where two roads converge on the third one and houses are built along these roads. Cruciform settlements develop on the cross-roads and houses extend in all the four directions.
- **Double Village:** These settlements extend on both sides of a river where there is a **bridge or a ferry.**

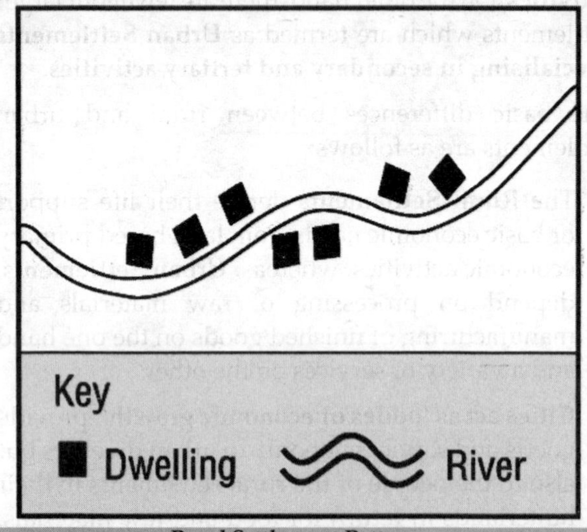

Rural Settlement Patterns

Types of Rural Settlement- India

Types of the settlement are determined by the extent of the **built-up area and inter-house distance**. In India, **compact or clustered village** of a few hundred houses is a rather universal feature, particularly in the northern plains. However, there are several areas, which have other forms of rural settlements. **There are various factors and conditions responsible for having different types of rural settlements in India.**

These include:

- **Physical Features** – nature of terrain, altitude, climate and availability of water
- **Cultural and Ethnic Factors** – social structure, caste and religion
- **Security Factors** – defence against thefts and robberies

Rural Settlements in India can broadly be put into Four Types:

1 Clustered, Agglomerated or Nucleated

2 Semi-clustered or Fragmented

3 Hamleted

4 Dispersed or Isolated

Clustered Settlements

- ➢ The clustered rural settlement is a **compact or closely built up**, area of houses.
- ➢ In this type of village, the general living area is **distinct and separated** from the surrounding farms, barns and pastures.
- ➢ The closely built-up area and its intervening streets present some recognisable **pattern or geometric shape**, such as rectangular, radial, linear, etc.
- ➢ Such settlements are generally found in **fertile alluvial plains and in the northeastern states.**
- ➢ Sometimes, people live in compact villages for **security or defence reasons**, such as in the Bundelkhand region of central India and in Nagaland.
- ➢ In Rajasthan, **scarcity of water** has necessitated compact settlement for maximum utilisation of available water resources.

Semi-Clustered Settlements

- ➢ Semi-clustered or fragmented settlements may result from tendency of **clustering in a restricted area of dispersed settlement.**
- ➢ More often such a pattern may also result from **segregation or fragmentation of a large compact village.**
- ➢ In this case, one or more sections of the village society **choose or is forced to live a little away** from the main cluster or village.
- ➢ In such cases, generally, the **land-owning and dominant community occupies the central part** of the main village, whereas people of lower strata of society and menial workers settle on the outer flanks of the village.
- ➢ Such settlements are widespread in the **Gujarat plain and some parts of Rajasthan**.

Hamleted Settlements

- ➢ Sometimes settlement is fragmented into **several units physically separated** from each other bearing a common name. These units are locally called **panna, para, palli, nagla, dhani, etc.** in various parts of the country.
- ➢ This segmentation of a large village is often motivated by **social and ethnic factors.** Such villages are more frequently found in the **middle and lower Ganga plain, Chhattisgarh and lower valleys of the Himalayas.**

Dispersed Settlements

- ➢ Dispersed or isolated settlement pattern in India appears in the form of **isolated huts or hamlets** of few huts in remote jungles, or on small hills with farms or pasture on the slopes.
- ➢ **Extreme dispersion** of settlement is often caused by **extremely fragmented nature of the terrain and land resource** base of habitable areas.
- ➢ Many areas of **Meghalaya, Uttarakhand, Himachal Pradesh and Kerala** have this type of settlement.

Problems of Rural Settlements

- Rural settlements in the developing countries are **large in number and poorly equipped** with infrastructure. They represent a great challenge and opportunity for planners.

- Supply of water to rural settlements in developing countries is not adequate. People in villages, particularly in mountainous and arid areas have to walk long distances to fetch drinking water.
  - **Water borne diseases** such as cholera and jaundice tend to be a common problem.
- The countries of South Asia face conditions of **drought and flood** very often.
  - Crop cultivation sequences, in the absence of irrigation, also suffer.
  - The general **absence of toilet and garbage disposal facilities** cause health related problems.
- The design and use of building materials of houses vary from one ecological region to another. The **houses made up of mud, wood and thatch, remain susceptible to damage** during heavy rains and floods, and require proper maintenance every year.
  - Most house designs are typically **deficient in proper ventilation.**
- **Unmetalled roads and lack of modern communication network** creates a unique problem.
  - During rainy season, the settlements remain cut off and pose serious **difficulties in providing emergency services.** It is also difficult to provide adequate health and educational infrastructure for their large rural population.
- The problem is particularly serious where proper villagisation has not taken place and houses are scattered over a large area.

Urban Settlements

The **first urban settlement** to reach a population of one million was the **city of London** by around 1810 A.D. By 1982, approximately 175 cities in the world had crossed the one million population mark. Presently, 54 percent of the world's population lives in urban settlements compared to only 3 per cent in the year 1800.

Classification of Urban Settlements

The definition of urban areas varies from one country to another. Some of the **common basis** of classification are **size of population, occupational structure and administrative setup.**

Population Size

- It is an important criterion used by most countries to define urban areas. The lower limit of the population size for a settlement to be designated as urban is 1,500 in Colombia, 2,000 in Argentina and Portugal, 2,500 in U.S.A. and Thailand, **5,000 in India** and 30,000 in Japan. Besides the size of population, density of 400 persons per sq. km and share of non-agricultural workers are taken into consideration in India.
- **In Denmark, Sweden and Finland**, all places with a population size of **250 persons** are called **Urban**. The minimum population for a city is 300 in Iceland, whereas in Canada and Venezuela, it is 1,000 persons.

Occupational Structure

- In some countries, such as India, the **major economic activities** in addition to the size of the population in designating a settlement as urban are also taken as a criterion. Similarly, **in Italy**, a settlement is called **Urban**, if more than 50 per cent of its economically productive population is engaged in non-agricultural pursuits. India has set this criterion at **75 per cent**.

Administration

- The administrative setup is a criterion for classifying a settlement as urban in some countries. For example, in India, a settlement of any size is classified as **urban, if it has a municipality, Cantonment Board or Notified Area Council.** Similarly, in **Latin American** countries, such as **Brazil and Bolivia**, any administrative centre is considered urban irrespective of its population size.

Types of Urban Settlements

Depending on the size and the services available and functions rendered, urban centres are designated as town, city, Million city, conurbation, megalopolis.

- **Town:** The concept of **'town'** can best be understood with reference to **'village'**. Population size is not the only criterion. Functional contrasts between towns and villages may not always be clear-cut, but specific functions such as, manufacturing, retail and wholesale trade, and professional services exist in towns.

- **City:** A city may be regarded as a **leading town, which has outstripped its local or regional rivals.** Cities are **much larger than towns** and have a greater number of economic functions. They tend to have **transport terminals, major financial institutions and regional administrative offices.** When the population crosses the one million mark it is designated as a million city.
- **Conurbation: The term conurbation was coined by Patrick Geddes in 1915** and applied to a large area of urban development that **resulted from the merging of originally separate towns** or cities. Greater London, Manchester, Chicago and Tokyo are examples.
- **Million City:** London reached the Million mark in 1800, followed by Paris in 1850, New York in 1860, and by 1950 there were around 80 such cities. There were 162 million cities in Mid 70's and there was threefold increase in 2005 and the number reached to 438. In 2016, there were 512 cities with at least 1 million inhabitants globally. By 2030, a projected 662 cities will have at least 1 million residents. This Greek word meaning **"Great City,"** was popularised by Jean Gottman (1957) and signifies 'super-metropolitan' region extending, as union of conurbations. The urban landscape stretching from Boston in the north to south of Washington in U.S.A. is the best known, example of a **Megalopolis**.

The **Census of India, 1991 defines Urban Settlements as** all places which have:

- Municipality, corporation, cantonment board or **notified** town area committee
- A minimum population of **5000 persons**
- At least **75 per cent** of Male Workers are engaged in **Non-Agricultural pursuits**
- A Density of Population of at least **400 persons per square kilometres**

Evolution of Towns In India

Towns flourished since prehistoric times in India. Even at the time of Indus valley civilisation, towns like **Harappa and Mohenjodaro** were in existence. The following period has witnessed the evolution of towns. It continued with periodic ups and downs until the arrival of Europeans in India in the eighteenth century.

On the basis of their evolution in different periods, Indian towns may be classified as:

- Ancient towns
- Medieval towns
- Modern towns

Ancient Towns

- There are number of towns in India having historical background spanning over 2000 years. Most of them developed as **religious and cultural centres**. Varanasi is one of the important towns among these. **Prayag (Allahabad), Pataliputra (Patna), Madurai** are some other examples of ancient towns in the country.

Medieval Towns

- About 100 of the existing towns have their roots in the medieval period. Most of them developed as **headquarters of principalities and kingdoms**. These are **fort towns** which came up on the ruins of ancient towns. Important among them are **Delhi, Hyderabad, Jaipur, Lucknow, Agra and Nagpur**.

Modern Towns

- The **British and other Europeans** have developed a number of towns in India. Starting their foothold on coastal locations, they first developed some **trading ports** such as Surat, Daman, Goa, Pondicherry, etc. The British later consolidated their hold around three principal nodes **Mumbai (Bombay), Chennai (Madras), and Kolkata** (Calcutta) and built them in the British style. Rapidly extending their domination either directly or through control over the princely states, they established their administrative centres, hill towns as summer resorts, and added new **civil, administrative and military** areas to them. **Towns based on modern industries also evolved after 1850. Jamshedpur** can be cited as an example.

After independence, a large number of towns have been developed as **Administrative Headquarters**, e.g., Chandigarh, Bhubaneswar, Gandhinagar, Dispur, etc., and **Industrial Centres**, such as Durgapur, Bhilai, Sindri, Barauni. Some old towns also developed as **Satellite Towns** around metropolitan cities, such as Ghaziabad, Rohtak, Gurugram around Delhi. With increasing investment in rural areas, a large number of medium and small towns have developed all over the country.

Urbanisation in India

The **Level of Urbanisation** is measured in terms of percentage of urban population to total population. The level of urbanisation in India in 2011 was **31.16 per cent**, which is **quite low** in comparison to developed countries. Total urban population has increased eleven-fold during the twentieth century. Enlargement of urban centres and **emergence of new towns** have played a significant role in the growth of urban population and urbanisation in the country. But the growth rate of urbanisation has slowed down during the last two decades.

Classification of Towns on the basis of Population Size

- **Census of India** classifies urban centres into **six classes** as presented in Table below.
  - ➢ Urban centre with a population of more than one lakh is called a **City or Class I Town.**
  - ➢ Cities accommodating population size between one to five million are called **Metropolitan Cities.**
  - ➢ Cities having population more than five million are **Mega Cities.**
  - ➢ **Majority of metropolitan and mega cities are Urban Agglomerations.**
- An urban agglomeration may consist of any one of the following three combinations:
  - ➢ A town and its adjoining urban outgrowths
  - ➢ Two or more contiguous towns with or without their outgrowths
  - ➢ A city and one or more adjoining towns with their outgrowths together forming a contiguous spread

Class	Population Size	Number of Cities	Total Urban Population (in thousand)	% of Total Urban Population
I	1,00,000 and more	468	2,27,899	60.45
II	50,000-99,999	474	41,328	10.96
III	20,000-49,999	1,373	58,174	15.43
IV	10,000-19,999	1,683	31,866	8.45
V	5,000-9,999	1,749	15,883	4.21
VI	Less than 5,000	424	1,956	0.51

India: Class-wise Number of Towns and Cities and their Population, 2011

It is evident from Table that more than **60 percent of urban population in India lives in Class I towns**. Out of 468 cities, 53 cities/ urban agglomerations are metropolitan cities. Six of them are mega cities with a population over five million each. More than one-fifth (21.0%) of urban population lives in these mega cities. Among them, Greater Mumbai is the largest agglomeration with 18.4 million people. Delhi, Kolkata, Chennai, Bengaluru and Hyderabad are other mega cities in the country.

Functional Classification of Towns

- Apart from their role as central or nodal places, many towns and cities perform specialised services. Some towns and cities specialise in certain functions and they are known for some specific activities, products or services. However, each town performs a number of functions. **On the basis of dominant or specialised functions, Indian cities and towns can be broadly classified as follows:**

- **Administrative towns and cities**
  - ➢ Towns supporting administrative headquarters of higher order are administrative towns, such as Chandigarh, New Delhi, Bhopal, Shillong, Guwahati, Imphal, Srinagar, Gandhinagar, Jaipur, Chennai, etc.
- **Industrial towns**
  - ➢ Industries constitute the prime motive force of these cities, such as Mumbai, Salem, Coimbatore, Modinagar, Jamshedpur, Hugli, Bhilai, etc.
- **Transport Cities**
  - ➢ They may be ports primarily engaged in export and import activities such as Kandla, Kochi, Kozhikode, Vishakhapatnam, etc., or hubs of inland transport, such as Agra, Dhulia, Mughalsarai, Itarsi, Katni, etc.
- **Commercial towns**
  - ➢ Towns and cities specialising in trade and commerce are kept in this class. Kolkata, Saharanpur, Satna, etc., are some examples.
- **Mining towns**
  - ➢ These towns have developed in mineral rich areas such as Raniganj, Jharia, Digboi, Ankaleshwar, Singrauli, etc.
- **Garrison Cantonment towns**
  - ➢ These towns emerged as to station armed forces such as Ambala, Jalandhar, Mhow, Babina, Udhampur, etc.
- **Educational towns**
  - ➢ Starting as centres of education, some of the towns have grown into major campus towns, such as Roorkee, Varanasi, Aligarh, Pilani, Allahabad, etc.
- **Religious and cultural towns**
  - ➢ Varanasi, Mathura, Amritsar, Madurai, Puri, Ajmer, Pushkar, Tirupati, Kurukshetra, Haridwar, Ujjain came to prominence due to their religious/cultural significance.
- **Tourist towns**
  - ➢ Nainital, Mussoorie, Shimla, Pachmarhi, Jodhpur, Jaisalmer, Udagamandalam (Ooty), Mount Abu are some of the tourist destinations.

The cities are not static in their function. The functions change due to their dynamic nature.

Smart Cities Mission

The aims are to ensures access to housing, transport, education, healthcare, and recreational facilities, tailored to the diverse needs of city inhabitants by focusing on three key pillars: liveability, economic-ability, and sustainability.

The strategy includes transforming existing areas (through retrofitting and redevelopment), developing new areas (greenfield development), and applying smart solutions city-wide (Pan-city initiatives). All Smart Cities are expected to complete their projects by June 2024.

Problems of Human Settlements in Developing Countries

- The settlements in developing countries, suffer from various problems, such as **unsustainable concentration of population, congested housing and streets, lack of drinking water facilities. They also lack infrastructure such as, electricity, sewage disposal, health and education facilities.**

Problems of Urban Settlements include:

- **Economic Problems**
  - ➢ The **decreasing employment opportunities** in the rural as well as smaller urban areas of the developing countries consistently push the population to the urban areas. The enormous migrant population generates a pool of **un-skilled and semi-skilled** labour force, which is **already saturated** in urban areas.
- **Socio-Cultural Problems**
  - ➢ Cities in the developing countries suffer from several social ills. **Insufficient financial resources** fail to create adequate social infrastructure catering to the basic needs of the huge population. The available educational and health facilities remain **beyond the reach of the urban poor**. Health indices also, present a gloomy picture in cities of developing countries. **Lack of employment and education** tends to aggravate the crime rates. **Male selective migration** to the urban areas distorts the sex ratio in these cities.

- **Environmental Problems**
  - The large urban population in developing countries not only uses but also disposes off a huge quantity of **water and all types of waste materials**. Many cities of the developing countries even find it extremely difficult to provide the minimum required **quantity of potable water and water for domestic and industrial uses**. An **improper sewerage system** creates unhealthy conditions. **Massive use of traditional fuel** in the **domestic as well as the industrial** sector severely pollutes the air. The domestic and industrial wastes are either let into the general **sewerages or dumped without treatment** at unspecified locations. **Huge concrete structures** erected to accommodate the population and economy play a very conducive role to create **Heat Islands.**

TEST YOURSELF

Multiple Choice Questions

Q1. Which of the following factors is NOT considered while selecting a site for human settlement?

(a) Availability of water
(b) Proximity to natural resources
(c) Presence of fertile soil
(d) Population density

Q2. A settlement that is primarily involved in agricultural activities is called:

(a) Rural settlement
(b) Urban settlement
(c) Industrial settlement
(d) Commercial settlement

Q3. The largest and most dominant settlement in a country or region is known as:

(a) Metropolis (b) Million City
(c) Capital City (d) Urban Agglomeration

Q4. A settlement pattern that is characterised by clustered and compact settlements is known as:

(a) Dispersed settlement
(b) Nucleated settlement
(c) Linear settlement
(d) Satellite settlement

Q5. The process by which people move from rural areas to urban areas in search of better economic opportunities is known as:

(a) Urbanisation
(b) Industrialisation
(c) Rural-urban migration
(d) Suburbanisation

Q6. A planned city that is designed to be self-contained and sustainable is called a:

(a) Satellite city (b) Eco-city
(c) Garden city (d) Smart city

Q7. A residential area located on the outskirts of a city is called:

(a) Central Business District (b) Urban Sprawl
(c) Suburb (d) Slum

Q8. The process by which an urban area expands into the surrounding rural areas is known as:

(a) Urban decay (b) Urban renewal
(c) Urban sprawl (d) Urban planning

Q9. A settlement pattern that is characterised by settlements located along a transportation route, such as a road or river, is known as:

(a) Dispersed settlement
(b) Nucleated settlement
(c) Linear settlement
(d) Satellite settlement

Q10. The area within a city or town where economic activities such as commerce, trade, and services are concentrated is known as:

(a) Residential area (b) Industrial area

(c) Central business district (d) Green Belt

Q11. The movement of people from rural areas to urban areas is known as:

(a) Urbanisation (b) Migration

(c) Industrialisation (d) Globalisation

Answer Key

Q1.	d	Q2.	a	Q3.	a	Q4.	b
Q5.	a	Q6.	b	Q7.	c	Q8.	c
Q9.	c	Q10.	c	Q11.	a		

Model Questions for Main Examination

Q1. Small towns in India have problems and prospects of their own. Elaborate.

Q2. Write a note on the emergence of urbanisation in colonial India and also discuss the factors contributing to urbanisation in post-independence period.

UNIT 24

Resources in India

In This Unit

Comprehensive and profound coverage of the following NCERTs' chapters:

- ✓ NCERT Class- 8th (Resources and Development), Chapter- 1
- ✓ NCERT Class- 10th (Contemporary India-II), Chapter- 1
- ✓ NCERT Class- 12th (India-People and Economy), Chapter- 3

- Everything available in our environment which can be used to satisfy our needs, provided it is technologically accessible, economically feasible and culturally acceptable can be termed as **'Resource'**.

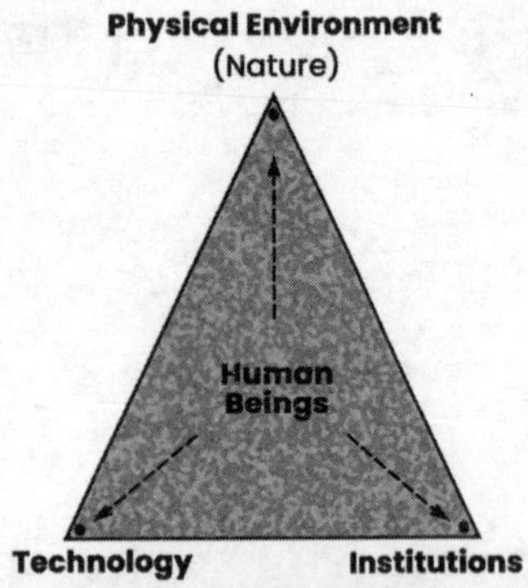

Interdependent Relationship between Nature, Technology and Institutions

- The process of transformation of things available in our environment involves an interactive relationship between nature, technology and institutions. Human beings interact with nature through technology and create institutions to accelerate their economic development.
- Resources are a function of human activities. Human beings themselves are essential components of resources. They transform material available in our environment into resources and use them. **These resources can be classified in the following ways –**
  - ➢ On the basis of **origin**: biotic and abiotic.
  - ➢ On the basis of **exhaustibility**: renewable and non-renewable.
  - ➢ On the basis of **ownership**: individual, community, national and international.
  - ➢ On the basis of **status of development**: potential, developed stock and reserves.
  - ➢ On the basis of **distribution**: ubiquitous and localised.

Classification of Resources

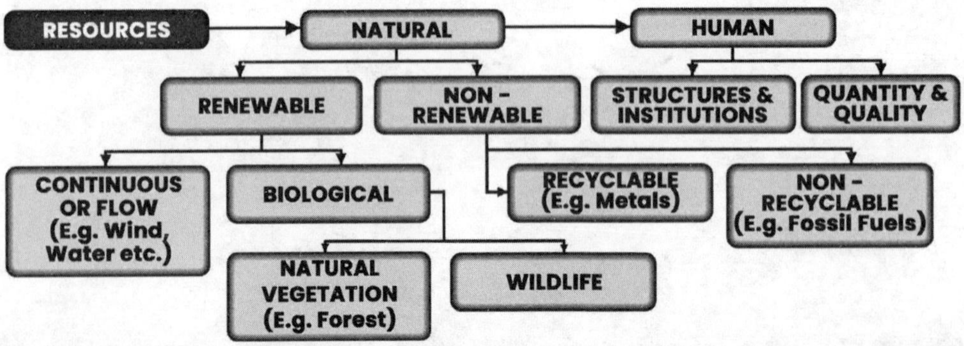

Types of Resources

On the Basis of Origin

- **Biotic Resources:** These are obtained from the biosphere and have life such as human beings, flora and fauna, fisheries, livestock etc.
- **Abiotic Resources:** All those things which are composed of non-living things are called abiotic resources. For example, rocks and metals.

On the Basis of Exhaustibility

- **Renewable Resources:** The resources which can be renewed or reproduced by physical, chemical or mechanical processes are known as renewable or replenishable resources. For example, solar and wind energy, water, forests and wildlife, etc. The renewable resource may further be divided into **continuous or flow resources like wind and biological resources like vegetation and wildlife.**
- **Non-Renewable Resources:** These occur over a very long geological time. Minerals and fossil fuels are examples of such resources. These resources take millions of years in their formation. Some of the resources like metals are recyclable and some like fossil fuels cannot be recycled and get exhausted with their use.

On the Basis of Ownership

- **Individual Resources:** These are also owned privately by individuals. Many farmers own land which is allotted to them by the government against the payment of revenue. In villages there are people with land owned but there are many who are landless. Urban people own plots, houses and other property. Plantation, pasture lands, ponds, water in wells etc. are some of the examples of resources owned by individuals.
- **Community Owned Resources:** There are resources which are accessible to all the members of the community. **Village commons** (grazing grounds, burial grounds, village ponds, etc.) public parks, picnic spots, playgrounds in urban areas are de facto accessible to all the people living there.
- **National Resources:** Technically, all the resources belong to the nation. The country has legal powers to acquire even private property for public good. Some roads, canals, railways are being constructed on fields owned by some individuals. Urban Development Authorities get empowered by the government to acquire land. All the **minerals, water resources, forests, wildlife, land within the political boundaries and oceanic area up to 12 nautical miles (22.2 km) from the coast termed as territorial water and resources therein belong to the nation.**
- **International Resources:** There are international institutions which regulate some resources. **The oceanic resources beyond 200 nautical miles of the coastline of the country belong to the open ocean and no individual country can utilise these without the concurrence of international institutions.**

> India has got the right to mine manganese nodules from the bed of the Indian Ocean from that area which lies beyond the exclusive economic zone.

On the Basis of the Status of Development

- **Potential Resources:** Resources which are found in a region, but have not been utilised. For example, the western parts of India particularly Rajasthan and Gujarat have enormous potential for the development of wind and solar energy, but so far these have not been developed properly.
- **Developed Resources:** Resources which are surveyed and their quality and quantity have been determined for utilisation. The development of resources depends on technology and level of their feasibility.
- **Stock:** Materials in the environment which have the potential to satisfy human needs but human beings do not have the appropriate technology to access these, are included among stock. For example, water is a compound of two gases; hydrogen and oxygen. Hydrogen can be used as a rich source of energy. But we do not have advanced technical 'know-how' to use it for this purpose. Hence, it can be considered as stock.
- **Reserves:** These are the **subset of the stock**, which can be put into use with the help of existing technical 'know-how' but their use has not been started. These can be used for meeting future requirements. River water can be used for

generating hydroelectric power but presently, it is being utilised only to a limited extent. Thus, the water in the dams, forests etc. is a reserve which can be used in the future.

On the basis of distribution

- **Ubiquitous:** Resources that are found everywhere like air we breathe are ubiquitous.
- **Localised:** Resources that are found only in certain places are localised like copper and iron ore.

Development of Resources

Resources are vital for human survival as well as for maintaining the quality of life. It was believed that resources are free gifts of nature. As a result, human beings used them indiscriminately and this has led to the following major problems.

- **Depletion of resources** for satisfying the greed of a few individuals.
- **Accumulation of resources** in few hands, which, in turn, divided the society into two segments i.e., haves and have nots or rich and poor.
- Indiscriminate exploitation of resources has led to **global ecological crises** such as, global warming, ozone layer depletion, environmental pollution and land degradation.

An equitable distribution of resources has become essential for a sustained quality of life and global peace. If the present trend of resource depletion by a few individuals and countries continues, the future of our planet is in danger. Therefore, resource planning is essential for the sustainable existence of all forms of life. **Sustainable existence is a component of sustainable development.**

- **Sustainable development:** Sustainable economic development means 'development should take place without damaging the environment, and development in the present should not compromise with the needs of the future generations.
- **Rio de Janeiro Earth Summit, 1992:** In June 1992, more than 100 Heads of States met in Rio de Janeiro in Brazil, for the first International Earth Summit. The Summit was convened for addressing urgent problems of environmental protection and socio- economic development at the global level. The assembled leaders signed the Declaration on Global Climatic Change and Biological Diversity. The Rio Convention endorsed the **Global Forest Principles and adopted Agenda 21 for achieving Sustainable Development** in the 21st century.
- **Agenda 21:** It is the declaration signed by world leaders in 1992 at the United Nations Conference on Environment and Development (UNCED), which took place at Rio de Janeiro, Brazil. It aims at achieving global sustainable development. It is an agenda to combat environmental damage, poverty, disease through global co-operation on common interests, mutual needs and shared responsibilities. One major objective of Agenda 21 is that every local government should draw its own local Agenda 21.

Resource Planning

- Planning is the widely accepted strategy for judicious use of resources. It has importance in a country like India, which has enormous diversity in the availability of resources. There are regions which are rich in certain types of resources but are deficient in some other resources.
- There are some regions which can be considered self-sufficient in terms of the availability of resources and there are some regions which have acute shortage of some vital resources. For example, the states of Jharkhand, Chhattisgarh and Madhya Pradesh are rich in minerals and coal deposits. Arunachal Pradesh has abundance of water resources but lacks in infrastructural development.
- The state of Rajasthan is very well endowed with solar and wind energy but lacks in water resources. The cold desert of Ladakh is relatively isolated from the rest of the country. It has very rich cultural heritage but it is deficient in water, infrastructure and some vital minerals. This calls for balanced resource planning at the national, state, regional and local levels.

Resource Planning in India

- **Resource planning is a complex process which involves:**
  - ➤ **Identification and inventory** of resources across the regions of the country. This involves

surveying, mapping and qualitative and quantitative estimation and measurement of the resources.

- Evolving a **planning structure** endowed with appropriate technology, skill and institutional set up for implementing resource development plans.
- Matching the **resource development plans** with overall **national development plans.**

- India has made concerted efforts for achieving the goals of resource planning right from the **First Five Year Plan launched after Independence.**
- The availability of resources is a necessary condition for the development of any region, but mere availability of resources in the absence of corresponding changes in technology and institutions may hinder development.
- There are many regions in our country that are rich in resources but these are included in economically backward regions. On the contrary there are some regions which have a poor resource base but they are economically developed.
- The history of colonisation reveals that rich resources in colonies were the main attractions for the foreign invaders. It was primarily the higher level of technological development of the colonising countries that helped them to exploit resources of other regions and establish their supremacy over the colonies. Therefore, **resources can contribute to development only when they are accompanied by appropriate technological development and institutional changes.**
- India has experienced all this in different phases of colonisation. Therefore, in India, development, in general, and resource development in particular does not only involve the availability of resources, but also the technology, quality of human resources and the historical experiences of the people.

Conservation of Resource

- Resources are vital for any developmental activity. But irrational consumption and over-utilisation of resources may lead to socio-economic and environmental problems. To overcome these problems, resource conservation at various levels is important.
- Using resources carefully and giving them time to get renewed is called **resource conservation**. Balancing the need to use resources and also conserve them for the future is called **sustainable development.**

At the international level, the Club of Rome advocated resource conservation for the first time in a more systematic way in 1968. Subsequently, in 1974, Gandhian philosophy was once again presented by Schumacher in his book **Small is Beautiful**. The seminal contribution with respect to resource conservation at the global level was made by the Brundtland Commission Report, 1987. This report introduced the concept of 'Sustainable Development' and advocated it as a means for resource conservation, which was subsequently published in a book entitled **Our Common Future.** Another significant contribution was made at the Earth Summit at Rio de Janeiro, Brazil in 1992.

Land Resources

- Land is among the most important natural resources. It covers only about thirty percent of the total area of the earth's surface and all parts of this small percentage are not habitable.
- It supports natural vegetation, wild life, human life, economic activities, transport and communication systems. However, land is an asset of a finite magnitude, therefore, it is important to use the available land for various purposes with careful planning.
- India has land under a variety of relief features, namely; mountains, plateaus, plains and islands. About 43 per cent of the land area is plain, which provides facilities for agriculture and industry. Mountains account for 30 per cent of the total surface area of the country and ensure perennial flow of some rivers, providing facilities for tourism and ecological aspects.
- About 27 percent of the area of the country is the plateau region. It possesses rich reserves of minerals, fossil fuels and forests.

Ninety per cent of the world population occupies only thirty per cent of land area. The remaining seventy per cent of the land is either sparsely populated or uninhabited.

Land Utilisation

Land resources are used for the following purposes:

- Forests
- Land not available for cultivation
  - ➢ **Barren** and waste land
  - ➢ Land put to **Non-agricultural uses,** e.g., buildings, roads, factories, etc.
- Other uncultivated land (excluding fallow land)
  - ➢ **Permanent Pastures** and Grazing Land,
  - ➢ Land under **miscellaneous tree crops** and groves (not included in net sown area),
  - ➢ **Culturable waste land** (left uncultivated for more than 5 agricultural years).
- Fallow lands
  - ➢ **Current fallow-** (left without cultivation for one or less than one agricultural year)
  - ➢ Other than current fallow-(left uncultivated for the past 1 to 5 agricultural years).
- The physical extent of land on which crops are sown harvested is known as **net sown area.**
- Area sown more than once in an agricultural year. plus net sown area is known as **gross cropped area.**

General land use categories-1960-61

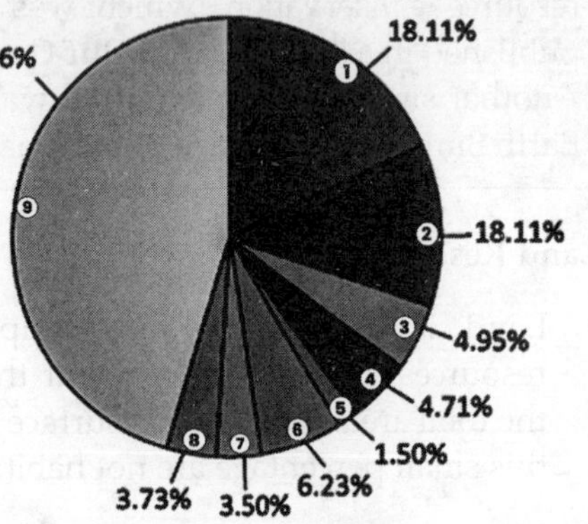

General land use categories-2014-15

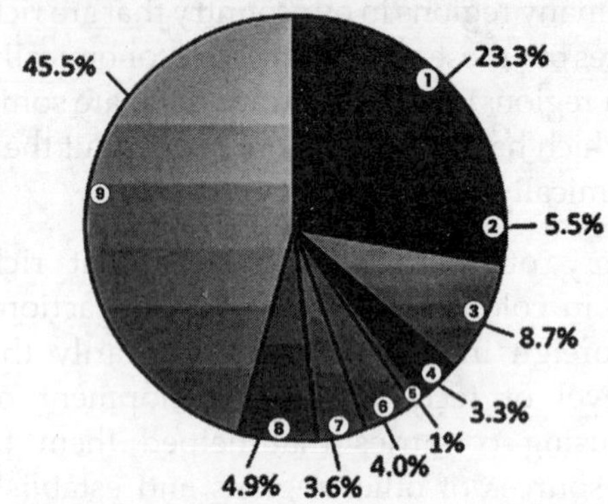

1 ■ **Forest**
2 ■ **Barren and unculturable waste land**
3 ■ **Area under non-agricultural uses**
4 ■ **Permanent pasture and grazing land**
5 ■ **Area under misc. tree crops and groves**
6 ■ **Culturable waste land**
7 ■ **Fallow other than current fallow**
8 ■ **Current fallow**
9 ■ **Net sown area**

Comparison of Land use Pattern in India

Land Use Pattern in India

- The use of land is determined both by physical factors such as topography, climate, soil types as well as human factors such as population density, technological capability and culture and traditions etc.
- **Total geographical area of India is 3.28 million sq. km**. Land use data, however, is available only for 93 per cent of the total geographical area because the land use reporting for most of the north-east states except Assam has not been done fully. Moreover, some areas of Jammu and Kashmir occupied by Pakistan and China have also not been surveyed.
- The **land under permanent pasture has also decreased.** Most of the other than the current fallow lands are either of poor quality or the cost of cultivation of such land is very high. Hence, these

lands are cultivated once or twice in about two to three years and if these are included in the net sown area then the percentage of NSA in India comes to about 54 per cent of the total reporting area.

- The **pattern of net sown area varies greatly from one state to another.** It is over 80 per cent of the total area in Punjab and Haryana and less than 10 per cent in Arunachal Pradesh, Mizoram, Manipur and Andaman Nicobar Islands.
- **Forest area** in the country is far lower than the desired 33 percent of geographical area, as it was outlined in the National Forest Policy (1952). It was considered essential for maintenance of the ecological balance. The livelihood of millions of people who live on the fringes of these forests depends upon it.
- A part of the land is termed as **waste land and land put to other non-agricultural uses.** Waste land includes rocky, arid and desert areas and land put to other non-agricultural uses includes settlements, roads, railways, industry etc.
- Continuous use of land over a long period of time without taking appropriate measures to conserve and manage it, has resulted in **land degradation.** This, in turn, has serious repercussions on society and the environment.

Countries	Percentage of area in			
	Cropland	Pasture	Forest	Other Use
Australia	6	56	14	24
Brazil	9	20	66	5
Canada	5	4	39	52
China	10	34	14	42
France	35	21	27	17
India	57	4	22	17
Japan	12	2	67	19
Russia	8	5	44	44
UK	29	46	10	16
USA	21	26	32	21
World	11	26	31	32

Land Used in Selected Countries

Reasons of Land Degradation

- Ninety-five per cent of our basic needs for food, shelter and clothing are obtained from land. Human activities have not only brought about degradation of land but have also aggravated the pace of natural forces to cause damage to land.
- Some human activities such as deforestation, overgrazing, mining and quarrying too have contributed significantly in land degradation.
- **Mining sites** are abandoned after excavation work is complete leaving deep scars and traces of over-burdening. In states like Jharkhand, Chhattisgarh, Madhya Pradesh and Odisha deforestation due to mining have caused severe land degradation.
- In states like Gujarat, Rajasthan, Madhya Pradesh and Maharashtra **overgrazing** is one of the main reasons for land degradation.
- In the states of Punjab, Haryana, western Uttar Pradesh, **over irrigation is responsible for land degradation** due to water logging leading to increase in salinity and alkalinity in the soil.
- The **mineral processing** like grinding of limestone for cement industry and calcite and soapstone for ceramic industry generate huge quantities of dust in the atmosphere. It retards the process of infiltration of water into the soil after it settles down on the land.
- In recent years, industrial effluents as waste have become a major source of land and water pollution in many parts of the country.

Conservation Measures

- There are many ways to solve the problems of land degradation. **Afforestation and proper management of grazing** can help to some extent.
- Planting of **shelter belts of plants, control on overgrazing, stabilisation of sand dunes** by growing thorny bushes are some of the methods to check land degradation in arid areas.
- **Proper management** of waste lands, control of mining activities, proper discharge and disposal of industrial effluents and wastes after treatment can reduce land and water degradation in industrial and suburban areas.

Land Use Categories

- **Land-use records are maintained by the land revenue department.** The land use categories add up to the reporting area, which is somewhat different from the geographical area.
- The Survey of India is responsible for measuring the geographical area of administrative units in India.
- The difference between the two concepts is that while the former changes somewhat depending on the estimates of the land revenue records, the latter does not change and stays fixed as per Survey of India measurements.
- The land-use categories as maintained in the Land Revenue Records are as follows:
  - **Forests:** It is important to note that the area under actual forest cover is different from the area classified as forest. The latter is the area which the Government has identified and demarcated for forest growth. The land revenue records are consistent with the latter definition. Thus, there may be an increase in this category without any increase in the actual forest cover.
  - **Barren and Wastelands:** The land which may be classified as a wasteland such as barren, hilly terrains, desert lands, ravines, etc. normally cannot be brought under cultivation with the available technology.
  - **Land put to Non-agricultural Uses:** Land under settlements (rural and urban), infrastructure (roads, canals, etc.), industries, shops, etc., are included in this category. An expansion in the secondary and tertiary activities would lead to an increase in this category of land-use.
  - **Area under Permanent Pastures and Grazing Land:** Most of this type land is owned by the village 'Panchayat' or the Government. Only a small proportion of this land is privately owned. The **land owned by the village panchayat comes under 'Common Property Resources'.**
  - **Area under Miscellaneous Tree Crops and Groves (Not included in Net sown Area):** The land under orchards and fruit trees are included in this category. Much of this land is privately owned.
  - **Culturable Wasteland: Any land which is left fallow (uncultivated) for more than five years is included in this category**. It can be brought under cultivation after improving it through reclamation practices.
  - **Current Fallow**: **This is the land which is left without cultivation for one or less than one agricultural year.** Fallowing, is a cultural practice adopted for giving the land rest. The land recoups the lost fertility through natural processes.
  - **Fallow other than Current Fallow:** This is also a cultivable land which is left uncultivated for more than a year but less than five years. If the land is left uncultivated for more than five years, it would be categorised as a culturable wasteland.
  - **Net Area Sown:** The physical extent of land on which crops are sown and harvested is known as net sown area.

TEST YOURSELF

Multiple Choice Questions

Q1. Which of the following is a non-renewable resource?

(a) Solar energy (b) Wind energy

(c) Natural gas (d) Hydroelectric power

Q2. Which type of resource is derived from living organisms and can be replenished within a relatively short period of time?

(a) Renewable resource

(b) Non-renewable resource

(c) Fossil fuel

(d) Metallic mineral

Q3. Which of the following is an example of a metallic mineral?

(a) Coal (b) Natural gas

(c) Iron ore (d) Petroleum

Q4. The process of extracting minerals from the Earth's crust is known as:

(a) Deforestation (b) Afforestation

(c) Mining (d) Agriculture

Q5. Which type of resource is a result of the interaction between technology, human skills, and human knowledge?

(a) Human resource

(b) Natural resource

(c) Physical resource

(d) Human-made resource

Q6. The process of cutting down trees in a forest for commercial purposes is known as:

(a) Afforestation (b) Desertification

(c) Deforestation (d) Reforestation

Q7. Which type of resource is obtained from the Earth's crust and has economic value?

(a) Natural resource

(b) Renewable resource

(c) Non-renewable resource

(d) Human-made resource

Q8. Which of the following is an example of a renewable resource?

(a) Coal (b) Natural gas

(c) Solar energy (d) Crude oil

Q9. The development that meets the needs of the present without compromising the ability of future generations to meet their own needs is known as:

(a) Sustainable development

(b) Industrial development

(c) Economic development

(d) Urban development

Q10. The process of converting waste materials into reusable materials is known as:

(a) Recycling (b) Mining

(c) Deforestation (d) Extraction

Answer Key							
Q1.	c	Q2.	a	Q3.	c	Q4.	c
Q5.	d	Q6.	c	Q7.	a	Q8.	c
Q9.	a	Q10.	a				

Model Question for Main Examination

Q. Correlate the price of land, vertical growth of cities and the growth of slums in large cities of India. (UPSC 2019)

UNIT 25

Water Resources

In This Unit

Comprehensive and profound coverage of the following NCERTs' chapter:

✓ NCERT Class- 12th (India-People and Economy), Chapter- 4

Water is a **cyclic resource** with abundant supplies on the globe. Approximately, 71 per cent of the earth's surface is covered with it but **freshwater constitutes only about 3 percent of the total water.** In fact, a very small proportion of freshwater is effectively available for human use.

Water Resources of India

India accounts for about 2.45 per cent of the world's surface area, 4 percent of the world's water resources and about 16 percent of the world's population. The total water available from precipitation in the country in a year is about 4,000 cubic km. The availability from surface water and replenishable groundwater is 1,869 cubic km. Out of this, only 60 per cent can be put to beneficial uses. Thus, the total utilisable water resource in the country is only 1,122 cubic km.

Surface Water Resources

- **There are four major sources of surface water**. These are **rivers, lakes, ponds and tanks**.
- In the country, there are about 10,360 rivers and their tributaries are longer than 1.6 km each. The mean annual flow in all the river basins in India is estimated to be 1,869 cubic km.
- However, due to topographical, hydrological and other constraints, only about 690 cubic km **(32 per cent) of the available surface water can be utilised.** Water flow in a river depends on the size of its catchment area or river basin and rainfall within its catchment area.
- Given that precipitation is relatively high in the catchment areas of the Ganga, the Brahmaputra and the Barak rivers, these rivers, although account for only about one-third of the total area in the country, have 60 per cent of the total surface water resources. Much of the annual water flow in south Indian rivers like the Godavari, the Krishna, and the Kaveri has been harnessed, but it is yet to be done in the Brahmaputra and the Ganga basins.

Groundwater Resources

- The total replenishable groundwater resources in the country are about 432 cubic km. The level of groundwater utilisation is relatively high in the river basins lying in north-western region and parts of south India.
- The **groundwater utilisation** is very high in the states of Punjab, Haryana, Rajasthan, and Tamil Nadu.
- However, there are States like Chhattisgarh, Odisha, Kerala, etc., which utilise only a small proportion of their groundwater potentials. states like Gujarat, Uttar Pradesh, Bihar, Tripura and Maharashtra are utilising their groundwater resources at a moderate rate.

Lagoons and Backwaters

- India has a vast coastline and the coast is very indented in some states. Due to this, a number of **lagoons and lakes have formed.**
- The States like Kerala, Odisha and West Bengal have vast surface water resources in these lagoons and lakes. Although, water is generally **brackish** in these water bodies, it is used for **fishing and irrigating** certain varieties of paddy crops, coconut, etc.

Water Demand and Utilisation

India has traditionally been an agrarian economy, and about two-third of its population have been dependent on agriculture. Hence, development of irrigation to increase agricultural production has been assigned a very high priority in the **Five-Year Plans, and multipurpose river valleys projects, like the Bhakra-Nangal, Hirakud, Damodar Valley, Nagarjuna Sagar, Indira Gandhi Canal Project, etc., have been taken up.** In fact, India's water demand at present is dominated by irrigational needs.

- **Agriculture** accounts for most of the surface and groundwater utilisation, it accounts for 89 per cent of the surface water and 92 per cent of the groundwater utilisation.
- While the share of the **industrial sector** is limited to 2 per cent of the surface water utilisation and 5 percent of the ground-water, the **share of the domestic sector is higher (9 per cent) in surface water utilisation as compared to groundwater.**
- The share of the agricultural sector in total water utilisation is much higher than other sectors.

Demand of Water for Irrigation

- In agriculture, water is mainly used for irrigation. Irrigation is needed because of spatio-temporal variability in rainfall in the country.
- The large tracts of the country are deficient in rainfall and are drought prone. North-western India and Deccan plateau constitute such areas.
- Winter and summer seasons are more or less dry in most part of the country. Hence, it is difficult to practise agriculture without assured irrigation during dry seasons. Even in the areas of ample rainfall like West Bengal and Bihar, breaks in monsoon or its failure creates dry spells detrimental for agriculture.
- Water need of certain crops also makes irrigation necessary. For instance, water requirement of rice, sugarcane, jute, etc. is very high which can be met only through irrigation.
- It has also been found that irrigated lands have higher agricultural productivity than unirrigated land. Further, the high yielding varieties of crops need regular moisture supply, which is made possible only by developed irrigation systems. In fact, this is why that green revolution strategy of agriculture development in the country has largely been successful in Punjab, Haryana and western Uttar Pradesh.
- In Punjab, Haryana and western Uttar Pradesh, more than 85 percent of their net sown area is under irrigation. **Wheat and rice** are grown mainly with the help of irrigation in these states. Of the total net irrigated area 76.1 per cent in Punjab and 51.3 per cent in Haryana is irrigated through **wells and tube-wells**. This shows that these states utilise large proportion of their groundwater potential which has resulted in groundwater depletion in these states.
- The **over-use of groundwater resources has led to decline in groundwater table** in these states. In fact, over withdrawals in some states, like Rajasthan and Maharashtra, has increased fluoride concentration in groundwater, and this practice has led to increase in concentration of arsenic in parts of West Bengal and Bihar.

Emerging Water Problems

The per capita availability of water is dwindling day-by-day due to increase in population. The available water resources are also getting polluted with industrial, agricultural and domestic effluents, and this, in turn, is further limiting the availability of usable water resources.

Deterioration of Water Quality

Water quality refers to purity of water, or water without unwanted foreign substances. Water gets polluted by foreign matters, such as micro-organisms, chemicals, industrial and other wastes. Such matters deteriorate the quality of water and render it unfit for human use. When toxic substances enter lakes, streams, rivers, ocean and other water bodies, they get dissolved or lie suspended in water. This results in pollution of water, whereby quality of water deteriorates affecting aquatic systems. Sometimes, these pollutants also seep down and pollute groundwater. **The Ganga and the Yamuna** are the two highly polluted rivers in the country.

Water Conservation and Management

Given that water availability from sea/ocean, due to high cost of desalinisation, is considered negligible,

India has to take quick steps and make effective policies and laws, and adopt effective measures for its conservation. Besides developing water-saving technologies and methods, attempts are being made to prevent the pollution. There is need to encourage watershed development, rainwater harvesting, water recycling and reuse, and conjunctive use of water for sustaining water supply in long run.

Prevention of Water Pollution

The **Central Pollution Control Board (CPCB)** in collaboration with **State Pollution Control Boards** has been monitoring water quality of national aquatic resources at 507 stations. The data obtained from these stations show that **organic and bacterial contamination continues to be the main source of pollution** in rivers. **The Yamuna River** is the most polluted river in the country between Delhi and Etawah. Other severely polluted rivers are: the Sabarmati at Ahmedabad, the Gomti at Lucknow, the Kali, the Adyar, the Cooum throughout its entire stretch, the Vaigai at Madurai and the Musi of Hyderabad and the Ganga at Kanpur and Varanasi.

Groundwater pollution has occurred due to **high concentrations of heavy/toxic metals, fluoride and nitrates in different parts of the country.**

The **legislative provisions** such as the **Water (Prevention and Control of Pollution) Act 1974**, and **Environment Protection Act 1986** have not been implemented effectively. The result is that in 1997, 251 polluting industries were located along the rivers and lakes. The **Water Cess Act, 1977**, meant to reduce pollution has also made marginal impacts. There is a strong need to **generate public awareness about importance of water** and impacts of water pollution. The public awareness and action can be very effective in reducing the pollutants from agricultural activities, domestic and industrial discharges.

Recycle and Reuse of Water

Another way through which we can improve fresh water availability is **by recycle and reuse**. Use of water of lesser quality such as reclaimed wastewater would be an attractive option for industries for cooling and firefighting to reduce their water cost. Similarly, in urban areas water after bathing and washing utensils can be used for gardening. Water used for washing vehicle can also be used for gardening. This would conserve better quality of water for drinking purposes. Currently, recycling of water is practised on a limited scale. However, there is enormous scope for replenishing water through recycling.

Multi-Purpose River Projects and Integrated Water Resources Management

Archaeological and historical records show that from ancient times we have been constructing sophisticated hydraulic structures like dams built of stone rubble, reservoirs or lakes, embankments and canals for irrigation. Not surprisingly, we have continued this tradition in modern India by building dams in most of our river basins.

> A dam is a barrier across flowing water that obstructs, directs or retards the flow, often creating a reservoir, lake or impoundment. **"Dam" refers to the reservoir rather than the structure.** Most dams have a section called a **spillway or weir** over which or through which it is intended that water will flow either intermittently or continuously. Dams are classified according to structure, intended purpose or height. Based on structure and the materials used, dams are classified as timber dams, embankment dams or masonry dams, with several subtypes. According to the height, dams can be categorised as large dams and major dams or alternatively as low dams, medium height dams and high dams.

- Dams were traditionally built to impound rivers and rainwater that could be used later to irrigate agricultural fields.
- Today, dams are built not just for irrigation but for electricity generation, water supply for domestic and industrial uses, flood control, recreation, inland navigation and fish breeding.
- Hence, **dams are now referred to as multi-purpose projects** where the many uses of the impounded water are integrated with one another.
- For example, in the Sutlej-Beas River basin, the Bhakra Nangal project water is being used both for hydel power production and irrigation. Similarly, the Hirakud project in the Mahanadi basin integrates conservation of water with flood control.
- **Jawaharlal Nehru** proudly proclaimed **the dams as the 'temples of modern India'**; the reason being that it would integrate development

of agriculture and the village economy with rapid industrialisation and growth of the urban economy.

Hydraulic Structures in Ancient India

- In the **first century B.C., Sringaverapura** near Allahabad had a sophisticated water harvesting system channelling the flood water of the river Ganga.
- During the time of **Chandragupta Maurya**, dams, lakes and irrigation systems were extensively built.
- Evidence of sophisticated irrigation works have also been found in Kalinga, (Odisha), Nagarjunakonda (Andhra Pradesh), Bennur (Karnataka), Kolhapur (Maharashtra), etc.
- In the **11th Century, Bhopal Lake,** one of the largest artificial lakes of its time was built.
- In the 14th Century, the **tank in Hauz Khas,** Delhi was constructed by **Iltutmish** for supplying water to Siri Fort area.

Challenges

In recent years, multi-purpose projects and large dams have come under great scrutiny and opposition for a variety of reasons.

- Regulating and damming of rivers affect their natural flow causing poor sediment flow and **excessive sedimentation** at the bottom of the reservoir, resulting in rockier stream beds and **poorer habitats for the rivers' aquatic life.**
- Dams also **fragment rivers** making it difficult for aquatic fauna to migrate, especially for spawning.
- The reservoirs that are created on the floodplains also **submerge the existing vegetation** and soil leading to its decomposition over a period of time.
- Multi-purpose projects and large dams have also been the cause of many new environmental movements like the 'Narmada Bachao Andolan' and the 'Tehri Dam Andolan' etc. Resistance to these projects has primarily been due to the **large-scale displacement of local communities.**

Sardar Sarovar Dam

Sardar Sarovar Dam has been built over the **Narmada River in Gujarat.** This is one of the largest water resource projects of India covering four states—Maharashtra, Madhya Pradesh, Gujarat and Rajasthan. The Sardar Sarovar project would meet the requirement of water in drought-prone and desert areas of Gujarat (9,490 villages and 173 towns) and Rajasthan (124 villages).

Narmada Bachao Andolan

Narmada Bachao Andolan or Save Narmada Movement is a Non-Governmental Organisation (NGO) that mobilised tribal people, farmers, environmentalists and human rights activists against the Sardar Sarovar Dam being built across the Narmada River in Gujarat. It originally focused on the environmental issues related to trees that would be submerged under the dam water. Recently it has re-focused the aim to **enable poor citizens, especially the oustees (displaced people) to get full rehabilitation** facilities from the government.

Krishna-Godavari Dispute

Krishna-Godavari dispute is due to the objections raised by Karnataka and Andhra Pradesh governments. It is regarding the diversion of more water from Koyna dam by the Maharashtra government for a multipurpose project. This would reduce downstream flow in their states with adverse consequences for agriculture and industry.

Watershed Management

- **Watershed management** basically refers to efficient management and conservation of surface and groundwater resources.
- It involves prevention of runoff and storage and recharge of groundwater through various methods like percolation tanks, recharge wells, etc.
- In broad sense watershed management includes **conservation, regeneration and judicious use of all resources** – natural (like land, water, plants and animals) and human with in a watershed.
- Watershed management aims at bringing about balance between natural resources on the one hand and society on the other. The success of

watershed development largely depends upon **community participation.**

Role of Government in Watershed Management

The **Central and State Governments** have initiated many watershed development and management programmes in the country.

- **Haryali** is a watershed development project sponsored by the Central Government which aims at enabling the rural population to conserve water for drinking, irrigation, fisheries and afforestation. The Project is being executed by Gram Panchayats with people's participation.
- **Neeru-Meeru** (Water and You) programme in Andhra Pradesh and **Arvary Pani Sansad** in Alwar, Rajasthan have taken up construction of various water-harvesting structures such as percolation tanks, dug out ponds *(Johad)*, check dams, etc., through people's participation.

> **Tamil Nadu** has made water harvesting structures in the houses compulsory. No building can be constructed without making structures for water harvesting.
>
> **A Case Study:**
>
> **Watershed Development in Ralegan Siddhi, Ahmednagar, Maharashtra**
>
> Ralegan Siddhi is a small village in the district of Ahmednagar, Maharashtra. It has become an example for watershed development throughout the country.
>
> In 1975, this village was caught in a web of poverty and illicit liquor trade. The transformation took place when a retired army personnel settled down in the village and took up the task of watershed development. He convinced villagers about the importance of family planning and voluntary labour; preventing open grazing, felling trees, and liquor prohibition.

Rainwater Harvesting

- Rainwater (***palar pani***) harvesting is a method to capture and store rainwater for various uses.
- It is also used to **recharge groundwater** aquifers. It is a **low cost and eco-friendly technique** for preserving every drop of water by guiding the rain water to borewell, pits and wells.
- Rainwater harvesting increases water availability, checks the declining groundwater table, **improves the quality of groundwater** through dilution of contaminants, like fluoride and nitrates, **prevents soil erosion, and flooding** and arrests salt water intrusion in coastal areas if used to recharge aquifers.
- Traditional rainwater harvesting in rural areas is done by using surface storage bodies, like lakes, ponds, irrigation tanks, etc.
- In **Rajasthan,** rainwater harvesting structures locally known as **Kund or Tanka (a covered underground tank)** are constructed near or in the house or village to store harvested rainwater.
- It can be done by harvesting rainwater on rooftops and open spaces. Harvesting rainwater also decreases the community dependence on groundwater for domestic use.
- Besides bridging the demand-supply gap, it can also **save energy to pump groundwater** as recharge leads to rise in groundwater table.
- Urban areas can specially benefit from rainwater harvesting as water demand has already outstripped supply in most of the cities and towns.

Apart from rainwater harvesting, desalination of water particularly in coastal areas and brackish water in arid and semi-arid areas, transfer of water from water surplus areas to water deficit areas through inter-linking of rivers can be important remedies for solving water problems in India. However, the most important issue from the point of view of individual users, household and communities is **pricing of water.**

> **Rooftop Rainwater Harvesting- Tamil Nadu** is the first state in India which has made rooftop rainwater harvesting structure compulsory to all the houses across the state. There are legal provisions to punish the defaulters.
>
> **Bamboo Drip Irrigation System-** In **Meghalaya,** a 200-year-old system of tapping stream and spring water by using bamboo pipes, is prevalent. About 18-20 litres of water enters the bamboo pipe system, gets transported over hundreds of metres, and finally released at 20-80 drops per minute at the site of the plant.

Highlights of India's National Water Policy, 2002

The National Water Policy 2002 stipulates water allocation priorities broadly in the following order: drinking water, irrigation, hydro-power, navigation, industrial and other uses. The policy stipulates progressive new approaches to water management. **Key features include-**

- Irrigation and multi-purpose projects should invariably include drinking water component, wherever there is no alternative source of drinking water.
- Providing **drinking water** to all human beings and animals should be the **first priority.**
- Measures should be taken to **limit and regulate the exploitation of groundwater.**
- Both surface and groundwater should be **regularly monitored for quality.** A phased programme should be undertaken for improving water quality.
- The **efficiency of utilisation** in all the diverse uses of water should be improved.
- Awareness of **water as a scarce resource** should be fostered.
- **Conservation consciousness** should be promoted through education, regulation, incentives and disincentives.

TEST YOURSELF

Multiple Choice Questions

Q1. Which of the following is the primary source of freshwater on Earth?

(a) Oceans (b) Lakes

(c) Rivers (d) Groundwater

Q2. The largest river in India, which flows through multiple states and empties into the Bay of Bengal, is:

(a) Ganges (b) Yamuna

(c) Brahmaputra (d) Godavari

Q3. The process of removing salt and other impurities from seawater to make it suitable for human consumption is known as:

(a) Desalination (b) Purification

(c) Filtration (d) Distillation

Q4. The process of storing excess water during the monsoon season for use during the dry season is known as:

(a) Irrigation

(b) Damming

(c) Watershed management

(d) Rainwater harvesting

Q5. The largest freshwater lake in India, located in the state of Jammu and Kashmir, is:

(a) Lake Pichola (b) Dal Lake

(c) Chilika Lake (d) Wular Lake

Q6. The process of water seeping into the ground and replenishing the groundwater is known as:

(a) Runoff (b) Infiltration

(c) Erosion (d) Percolation

Q7. The percentage of Earth's total water that is available as freshwater for human use is approximately:

(a) 10% (b) 25%

(c) 50% (d) 75%

Q8. The process of recharging groundwater by redirecting and collecting rainwater is known as:

(a) Watershed management

(b) Rainwater harvesting

(c) Aquifer depletion

(d) Surface water diversion

Q9. With reference to the water on the planet Earth, consider the following statements: (UPSC 2021)

1. The amount of water in the rivers and lakes is more than the amount of groundwater.
2. The amount of water in polar ice caps and glaciers is more than the amount of groundwater.

Which of the statements given above is / are correct?

(a) 1 only (b) 2 only

(c) Both 1 and 2 (d) Neither 1 nor 2

Answer Key

Q1.	d	Q2.	a	Q3.	a
Q4.	d	Q5.	d	Q6.	b
Q7.	a	Q8.	b	Q9.	b

Model Questions for Main Examination

Q1. Highlight the emerging water problem in India. Also give suggestion regarding water conservation and management system present in India.

Q2. Write a short note on Watershed Management in India.

UNIT 26 Minerals and Energy Resources of India and The World

In This Unit

Comprehensive and profound coverage of the following NCERT's chapters:

- ✓ NCERT (Before Rationalisation) Class- 8th (Resources and Development), Chapter- 3
- ✓ NCERT Class- 10th (Contemporary India-II), Chapter- 5
- ✓ NCERT Class- 12th (India-People and Economy), Chapter- 5

What is a Mineral?

A Bright Smile from Toothpaste and Minerals

Toothpaste cleans your teeth. **Abrasive minerals** like **Silica, Limestone, Aluminium Oxide** and various phosphate minerals do the cleaning. **Fluoride,** which is used to reduce cavities, comes from a mineral fluorite. Most toothpastes are made white with **Titanium Oxide**, which comes from minerals called **Rutile, Ilmenite and Anatase**. The sparkle in some toothpastes comes from **Mica.** The toothbrush and tube containing the paste are made of **plastics from petroleum**.

Geologists define **mineral** as a **"homogenous, naturally occurring substance with a definable internal structure."** Minerals are found in varied forms in nature, ranging from the hardest diamond to the softest talc.

Mode of Occurrence of Minerals

Where are these minerals found?

Minerals are usually found in **"Ores"**. The term **'ore'** is used to describe an accumulation of any mineral mixed with other elements.

Minerals generally occur in these forms

- **In Igneous and Metamorphic rocks,** minerals may occur in the cracks, crevices, faults or joints. The smaller occurrences are called **Veins** and the larger are called **Lodes**. In most cases, they are formed when minerals in liquid/molten and gaseous forms are forced upward through cavities towards the earth's surface. They cool and solidify as they rise.
  - ➢ Major metallic minerals like tin, copper, zinc and lead etc. are obtained from veins and lodes.
- In **Sedimentary rocks,** a number of minerals occur in **beds** or **layers**. They have been formed as a result of **Deposition, Accumulation and Concentration** in horizontal strata. **Coal and some forms of iron ore** have been concentrated as a result of long periods under great heat and pressure.
  - ➢ Another group of sedimentary minerals include **gypsum, potash salt and sodium salt**. These are formed as a result of evaporation, especially in arid regions.
- Another mode of formation involves the **Decomposition of surface rocks,** and **the removal of soluble constituents**, leaving a **residual mass of weathered material containing ores.**
  - ➢ Bauxite is formed this way.
- Certain minerals may occur as **Alluvial Deposits** in sands of valley floors and the base of hills. These deposits are called **'Placer Deposits'** and generally contain minerals, which are not corroded by water.

- Gold, silver, tin and platinum are most important among such minerals.

- The ocean waters contain vast quantities of minerals, but most of these are too **widely diffused** to be of economic significance.
  - However, **common salt, magnesium and bromine** are largely derived from ocean waters. The ocean beds, too, are rich in manganese nodules.

On the basis of **chemical and physical properties**, minerals may be grouped under two main categories of **Metallics and Non-Metallics which may further be classified as follows:**

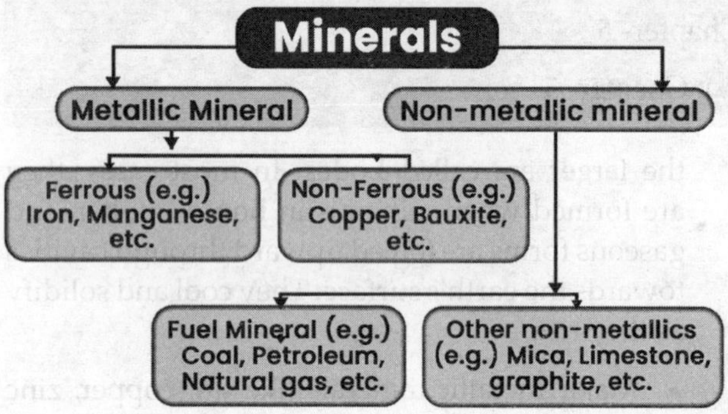

Metallic Minerals

These minerals contain **metal** content and can be **sub-divided into three types:**

- **Precious metals**: gold, silver, platinum etc.
- **Ferrous minerals**: **Iron ore** and other metals like **manganese and chromites** which contain iron and are often mixed with iron to form various kinds of steel.
- **Non-ferrous minerals**: Include metals, which do not contain iron, like **copper, lead, zinc, tin, aluminium, gold, silver** etc.

Non-Metallic Minerals

- These minerals do not contain metal content. **Limestone, Mica, Gypsum, Sulphur, phosphates and nitrates** are examples of non-metallic minerals. Coal and Petroleum are also non-metallic minerals. Cement is a mixture of non-metallic minerals.

Extraction of Minerals

Mining, drilling and quarrying are methods of extraction. Mining is a process of extraction of taking out minerals from rocks under the earth's surface.

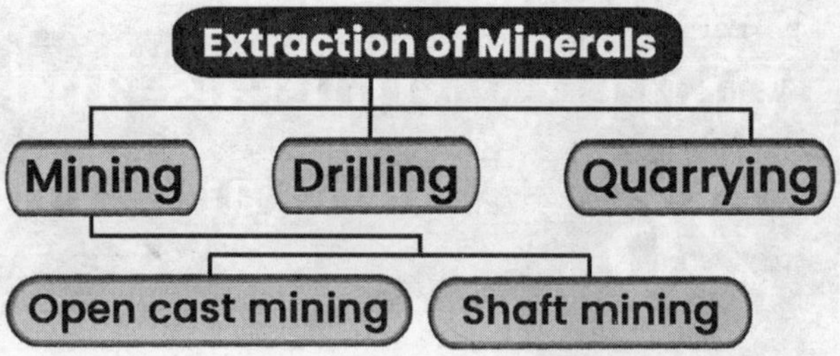

- **Open Cast Mining:** In this, minerals lying at shallow depths are taken out by removing the surface layer.
- **Shaft Mining:** In this, deep bores (called shafts) are made to reach mineral deposits lying at large depths.
- **Drilling:** In this, deep wells are bored to take out minerals.
- **Quarrying:** It is the process of extraction in which minerals lying very close to the surface are extracted just by digging them out.

Rat-Hole Mining

In most of **the tribal areas of north-east India**, minerals are owned by individuals or communities. In Meghalaya, there are large deposits of coal, iron ore, limestone and dolomite etc. Coal mining in Jowai and Cherapunjee is done by family members in the form of a long narrow tunnel, known as **'Rat hole'** mining. **The National Green Tribunal** has declared such activities illegal and recommended that these should be stopped forthwith.

Distribution of Minerals In India

Most of the metallic minerals in India occur in the peninsular plateau region in the old crystalline rocks. **Over 97 per cent of coal reserves** occur in the valleys of Damodar, Sone, Mahanadi and Godavari. Petroleum reserves are located in the **sedimentary basins of Assam, Gujarat and Mumbai High** i.e off-shore region in the Arabian Sea. Most of the major mineral resources occur to the east of a line linking Mangaluru and Kanpur.

Minerals are generally concentrated in three broad belts in India. There may be some sporadic occurrences here and there in isolated pockets. These belts are:

- **The North-Eastern Plateau Region**
  - This belt covers **Chhotanagpur (Jharkhand), Odisha Plateau, West Bengal** and **parts of Chhattisgarh**. It has a variety of minerals viz. **iron ore, coal, manganese, bauxite, mica**. Due to this reason major iron and steel industries are located in this region.
- **The South-Western Plateau Region**
  - This belt extends over **Karnataka, Goa and contiguous Tamil Nadu uplands and Kerala**. This belt is rich in **ferrous metals and bauxite**. It also contains high grade iron ore, manganese and limestone. This belt lacks coal deposits **except Neyveli lignite**.
  - This belt does not have as diversified mineral deposits as the **north-eastern belt. Kerala** has deposits of **monazite and thorium, bauxite clay**. Goa has iron ore deposits.
- **The North-Western Region**
  - This belt extends along **Aravali in Rajasthan and parts of Gujarat** are associated with the Dharwar system of rocks. Rajasthan is rich in building stones i.e., sandstone, granite, marble. **Gypsum and Fuller's earth deposits** are also extensive. **Dolomite and limestone** provide raw materials for the cement industry.
  - Gujarat is known for its **petroleum deposits**. Gujarat and Rajasthan both have rich sources of **salt.**
- **The Himalayan belt** is another mineral belt where **copper, lead, zinc, cobalt and tungsten** are known to occur. They occur in both the eastern and western parts. **Assam valley** has mineral oil deposits.

Spatial Pattern of Ferrous Minerals

Ferrous minerals account for about **three-fourths of the total value of the production of metallic minerals**. Ferrous minerals such as **iron ore, manganese, chromite**, etc., provide a strong base for the development of **metallurgical industries**.

Iron Ore

- Iron ore is the **basic mineral and the backbone of industrial development**. India is endowed with fairly abundant resources of iron ore. It has the **largest reserve of iron ore in Asia**.
- The **two main types** of ore found in our country are **haematite and magnetite**.
  - **Magnetite** is the finest iron ore with a **very high content of iron up to 70 per cent**. It has excellent magnetic qualities, especially valuable in the electrical industry.
  - **Haematite** ore is the most important industrial iron ore in terms of the quantity used, but has a slightly **lower iron content than magnetite (50-60 per cent).**
- The iron ore mines occur in **close proximity to the coal fields** in the north- eastern plateau region of the country which adds to their advantage.
- **Distribution of Iron ore -** About 95 per cent of total reserves of iron ore located in the States of Odisha, Jharkhand, Chhattisgarh, Karnataka, Goa, Telangana, Andhra Pradesh and Tamil Nadu. The major iron ore belts in India are:

Odisha-Jharkhand belt

- In **Odisha,** high grade haematite ore is found in **Sundergarh, Mayurbhanj district**. The important mines are Gurumahisani, Sulaipet, Badampahar (Mayurbhaj), Kiruburu (Kendujhar) and Bonai (Sundergarh).
- **Jharkhand** has some of the oldest iron ore mines and most of the **iron and steel plants** are located around them. Most of the important mines such as **Noamundi and Gua** are located in **Poorbi and Pashchimi Singhbhum** districts.

Durg-Bastar-Chandrapur belt

- This belt lies in **Chhattisgarh and Maharashtra. Very high grade haematites** are found in the famous **Bailadila range of hills** in the **Bastar district** of Chhattisgarh. The range of hills comprises 14 deposits of super high grade haematite iron ore. It has the best physical properties needed for steel making. Iron ore from these mines is **exported to Japan and South Korea** via Visakhapatnam port.
- This belt further extends to Durg, Dantewada and Bailadila. **Dalli and Rajhara in Durg** are the important mines of iron ore in the country.

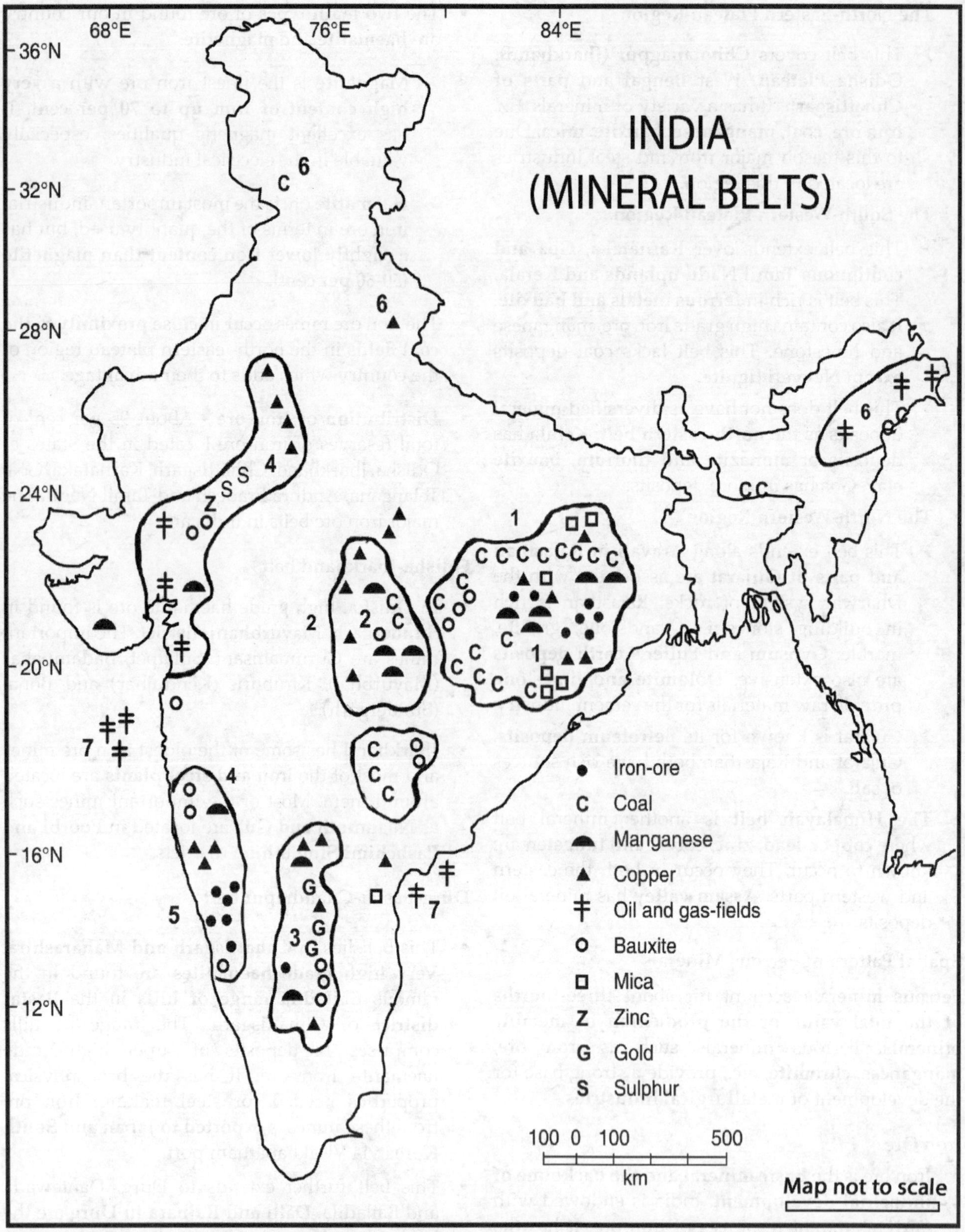

India-Metallic Minerals (Ferrous)

Bellary-Chitradurga-Chikkmagaluru-Tumakuru belt

- In **Karnataka,** iron ore deposits occur in **Sandur -Hospet area of Ballari district, Baba Budan hills and Kudremukh** in Chikkmagaluru district and parts of Shivamogga, Chitradurga and Tumakuru districts.
- The **Kudremukh mines** located in the **Western Ghats of Karnataka** are a 100 percent export unit. Kudremukh deposits are known to be one of the largest in the world. The ore is transported as slurry through a pipeline to a port near Mangaluru.

Maharashtra-Goa belt

- It includes the state of Goa and Chandrapur, Bhandara, Ratnagiri districts of Maharashtra. Though, the ores are not of very high quality, yet they are efficiently exploited. Iron ore is exported through Mormugao port.
- **Karimnagar and Warangal districts** of Telangana, **Kurnool, Cuddapah and Anantapur** districts of Andhra Pradesh, **Salem and Nilgiris** districts of Tamil Nadu are other iron mining regions.
- Goa has also emerged as an important producer of iron ore.

Manganese

Manganese is an important raw material for smelting of iron ore and also used for manufacturing ferro alloys. Manganese deposits are found in almost all geological formations however, it is mainly associated with the **Dharwar system**.

Distribution of Manganese

- **Odisha** is the leading producer of Manganese. Major mines in **Odisha** are located in the central part of the iron ore belt of India, particularly in **Bonai, Kendujhar, Sundergarh, Gangpur, Koraput, Kalahandi and Bolangir.**
- **Karnataka** is another major producer and here the mines are located in **Dharwar, Ballari, Belagavi, North Canara, Chikkmagaluru, Shivamogga, Chitradurg and Tumakuru.**
- **Maharashtra** is also an important producer of manganese, which is mined in **Nagpur, Bhandara and Ratnagiri** districts.
- The manganese belt **of Madhya Pradesh extends** in Balaghat-Chhindwara-Nimar-Mandla and Jhabua districts.
- **Telangana, Goa, and Jharkhand** are other minor producers of manganese.
- The disadvantage of these mines is that they are **located far from steel plants**.
    - ➢ Nearly 10 kg of manganese is required to manufacture one tonne of steel. It is also used in manufacturing bleaching powder, insecticides and paints.
- Madhya Pradesh 33%, Maharashtra 27%, Odisha 16%, Karnataka 12%, Andhra Pradesh 10% and Others 2%.

Spatial Pattern of Non-Ferrous Minerals

India's reserves and production of non-ferrous minerals is not very satisfactory. However, these minerals, which include **copper, bauxite, lead, zinc and gold** play a vital role in a number of metallurgical, engineering and electrical industries.

Copper

- India is **critically deficient** in the reserve and production of copper. **Being malleable, ductile and a good conductor**, copper is mainly used in **electrical cables, electronics and chemical industries.**
- It is also **mixed with gold** to provide strength to jewellery.

Distribution of copper

- The **Balaghat mines** in Madhya Pradesh, **Khetri mines** in Rajasthan and **Singhbhum district** of Jharkhand are **leading producers of copper.**
- **Minor producers of Copper** are **Agnigundala** in Guntur District (Andhra Pradesh), **Chitradurga and Hasan** districts (Karnataka) and **South Arcot** district (Tamil Nadu).

Bauxite

- Bauxite is the ore, which is used in the **manufacturing of aluminium**. Bauxite deposits are formed by the **decomposition of a wide variety of rocks** rich in **aluminium silicates**.
- Aluminium is an important metal because it **combines the strength of metals** such as iron, with **extreme lightness and also with good conductivity and great malleability**.

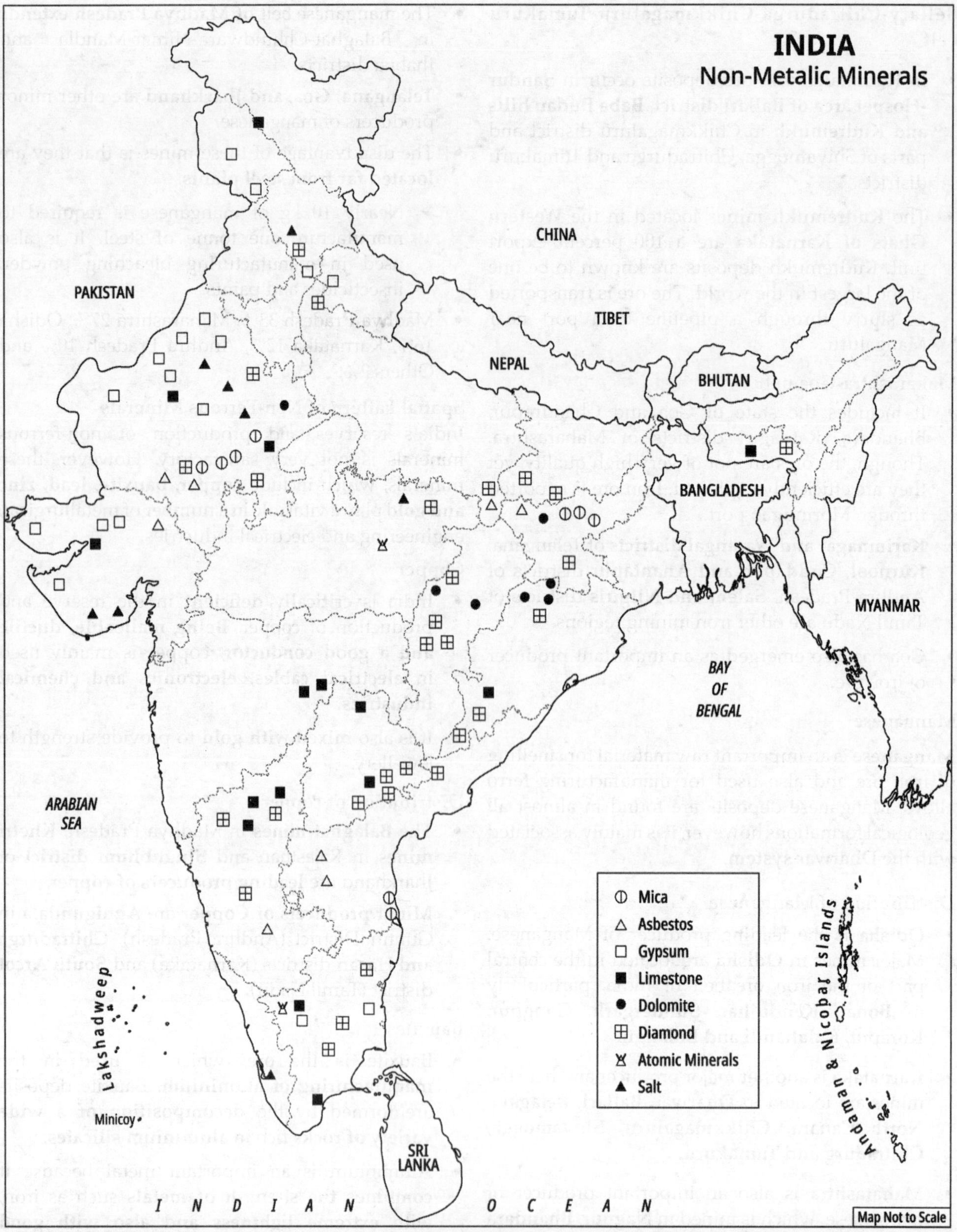

India-Minerals (Non-Ferrous)

Distribution of Bauxite

- Bauxite is found mainly in **tertiary deposits** and is associated with **laterite rocks** occurring extensively either on the plateau or hill ranges of peninsular India and also in the coastal tracts of the country.
- **Odisha** happens to be the largest producer of Bauxite. **Kalahandi and Sambalpur** are the leading producers. The other two areas which have been increasing their production are **Balangir district and Panchpatmali in Koraput district**.
- The **patlands of Lohardaga** in Jharkhand have rich deposits. Gujarat, Chhattisgarh, Madhya Pradesh and Maharashtra are other major producers. **Bhavanagar, and Jamnagar** in Gujarat have the major deposits. Chhattisgarh has bauxite deposits in **Amarkantak plateau** while **Katni-Jabalpur area and Balaghat** in M.P. have important deposits of bauxite.
- **Kolaba, Thane, Ratnagiri, Satara, Pune and Kolhapur** in Maharashtra are important producers.
- Tamil Nadu, Karnataka and Goa are minor producers of bauxite.
- **Major porducers of Bauxite include: Odisha 65%, Jharkhand 10%, Gujarat 9%, Chhattisgarh 6%, Maharashtra 6%, Madhya Pradesh 3% and Others 1%.**

Gold

- Kolar in Karnataka has deposits of gold in India. These mines are among the deepest in the world which makes mining of this ore a very expensive process.

Spatial Pattern of Non-Metallic Minerals

Mica

- **Mica** is a mineral made up of a series of plates or leaves. It splits easily into **thin sheets.** These sheets can be so thin that a thousand can be layered into a mica sheet of a few centimeters high. Mica can be clear, black, green, red, yellow or brown.
- Due to its excellent **di-electric strength, low power loss factor, insulating properties** and resistance to high voltage, mica is one of the most indispensable minerals used in electric and electronic industries.

Distribution of Mica

- Mica in India is produced in **Jharkhand, Andhra Pradesh, Telangana and Rajasthan followed by Tamil Nadu, West Bengal and Madhya Pradesh.**
- **Koderma-Gaya–Hazaribagh** belt of Bihar-Jharkhand is the leading producer. In Andhra Pradesh, Nellore district produces the best quality mica.
- **In Rajasthan**, the mica belt extends for about 320 kms from Jaipur to Bhilwara and around Udaipur. Mica deposits also occur in Mysuru and Hasan districts of Karnataka, Coimbatore, Tiruchirapalli, Madurai and Kanyakumari in Tamil Nadu, Alleppey in Kerala, Ratnagiri in Maharashtra, Purulia and Bankura in West Bengal.

Spatial Pattern of Rock Minerals

Limestone is found in association with rocks composed of calcium carbonates or calcium and magnesium carbonates. It is found in **sedimentary rocks** of most geological formations. Limestone is the basic raw material for the cement industry and essential for smelting iron ore in the blast furnace.

Production of Limestone showing state-wise share in percent, **Rajasthan 20%**, Madhya Pradesh 13%, Andhra Pradesh 13%, Chhattisgarh 11%, Karnataka 9%, Telangana 8%, Gujarat 7%, Tamil Nadu 6%, Maharashtra 4% and Others 8%.

Salt: It is obtained from seas, lakes and rocks. India is one of the world's leading producers and exporters of salt.

Distribution of Minerals in the World

Minerals are found in different types of rocks. Metallic minerals are usually found in igneous and metamorphic rocks that form large plateaus. Examples: iron ore is found in north Sweden, copper and nickel in Canada. In igneous and metamorphic rocks in South Africa, iron, nickel, chromites and platinum are found. Non-metallic minerals are found in sedimentary rock formations. Limestone deposits are found in France. Mineral fuels such as coal and petroleum are found in sedimentary strata.

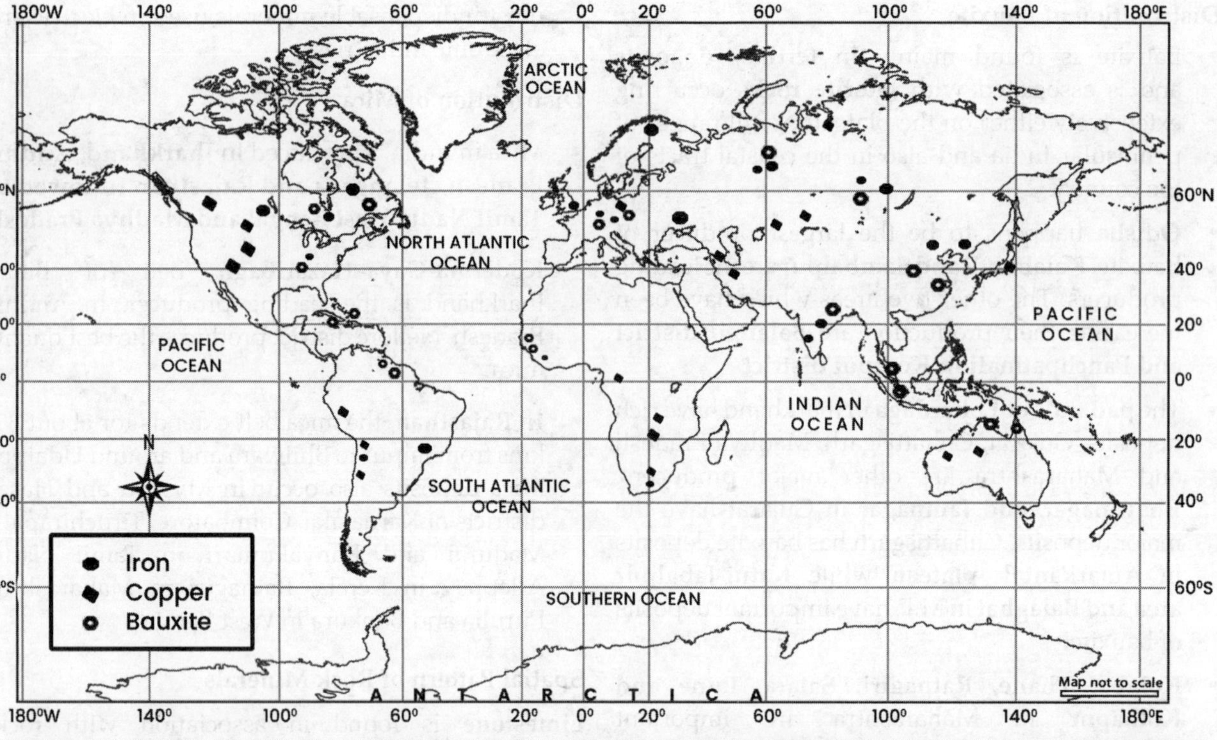

World: Distribution of Iron, Copper and Bauxite

Asia

China and India have large iron ore deposits. The continent **produces more than half of the world's tin.** China, Malaysia and Indonesia are among the world's leading tin producers. China also leads in production of lead, antimony and tungsten. Asia also has deposits of manganese, bauxite, nickel, zinc and copper

Europe

Europe is the leading producer of iron-ore in the world. The countries with large deposits of iron ore are Russia, Ukraine, Sweden and France. Mineral deposits of copper, lead, zinc, manganese and nickel are found in eastern Europe and European Russia.

North America

The mineral deposits in North America are located in three zones: the Canadian region north of the Great Lakes, the Appalachian region and the mountain ranges of the west. Iron ore, nickel, gold, uranium and copper are mined in the Canadian Shield Region, coal in the Appalachian region. Western Cordilleras have vast deposits of copper, lead, zinc, gold and silver.

South America

Brazil is the **largest producer of high grade iron-ore** in the world. Chile and Peru are leading producers of copper. Brazil and Bolivia are among the world's largest producers of tin. South America also has large deposits of gold, silver, zinc, chromium, manganese, bauxite, mica, platinum, asbestos and diamond. Mineral oil is found in Venezuela, Argentina, Chile, Peru and Colombia.

Africa

Africa is rich in mineral resources. It is the world's **largest producer of diamonds, gold and platinum.** South Africa, Zimbabwe and Zaire produce a large portion of the world's gold. The other minerals found in Africa are copper, iron ore, chromium, uranium, cobalt and bauxite. Oil is found in Nigeria, Libya and Angola.

Australia

Australia is the **largest producer of bauxite** in the world. It is a leading producer of gold, diamond, iron ore, tin and nickel. It is also rich in copper, lead, zinc and manganese. Kalgoorlie and Coolgardie areas of western Australia have the **largest deposits of gold.**

Antarctica

The geology of Antarctica is sufficiently well known to predict the existence of a variety of mineral deposits, **some probably large.** Significant size of deposits of **coal** in the Transantarctic Mountains and **iron near** the Prince Charles Mountains of East Antarctica is forecasted. Iron ore, gold, silver and oil are also present in commercial quantities.

Energy Resources

Energy can be generated from fuel minerals like coal, petroleum, natural gas, uranium and from electricity. Energy resources can be classified as **conventional and non-conventional sources.**

- **Conventional sources** Conventional sources of energy are those which have been in common use for a long time. **Firewood and fossil fuels** are the two main conventional energy sources which include firewood, cattle dung cake, coal, petroleum, natural gas and electricity (both hydel and thermal).
- **Non-conventional sources** include solar, wind, tidal, geothermal, biogas and atomic energy.

Conventional Sources of Energy

Mineral fuels are essential for generation of power, required by agriculture, industry, transport and other sectors of the economy. Mineral fuels like coal, petroleum and natural gas (known as fossil fuels), nuclear energy minerals, are the conventional sources of energy. These conventional sources are **exhaustible resources.**

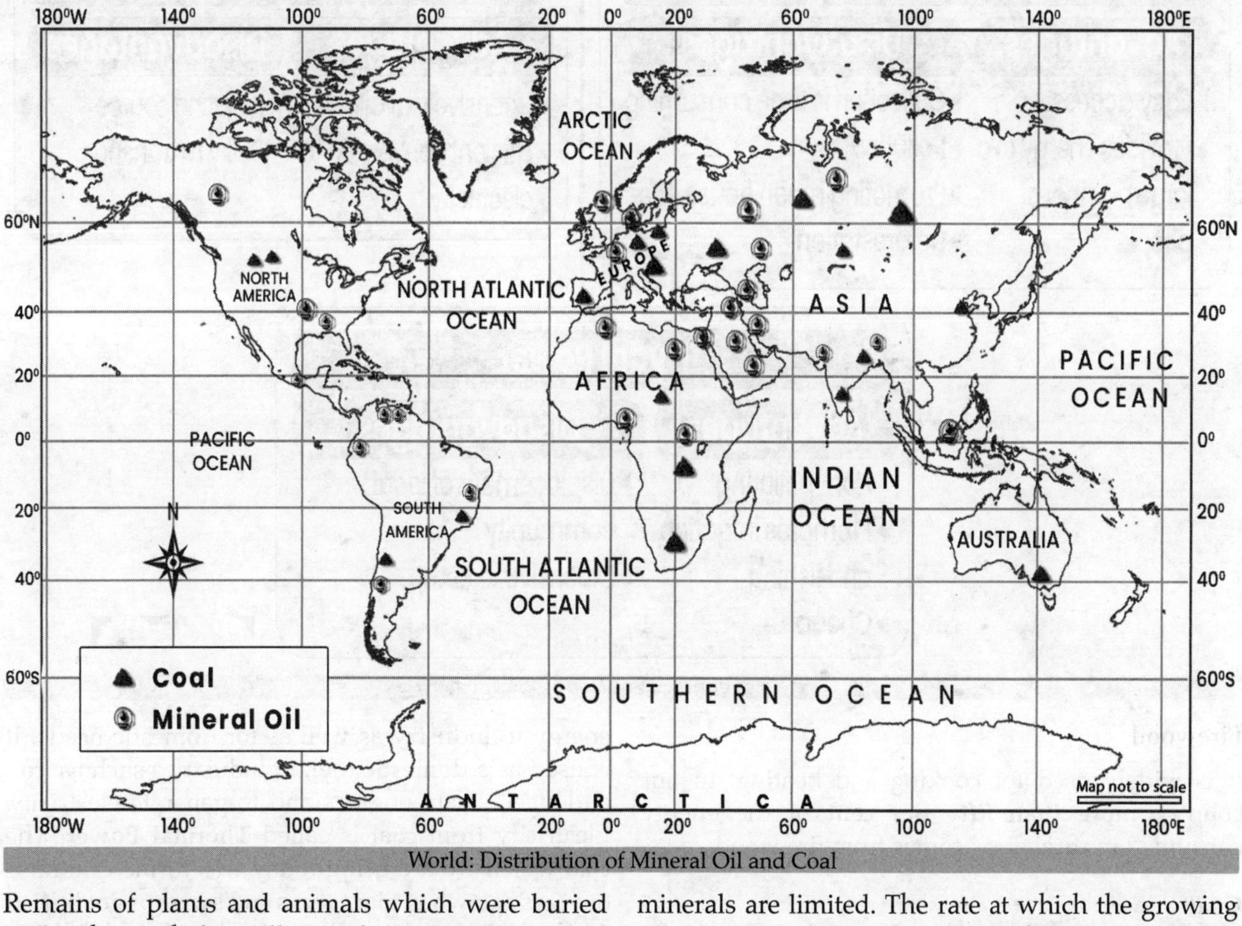

World: Distribution of Mineral Oil and Coal

Remains of plants and animals which were buried under the earth for millions of years got converted by the heat and pressure into fossil fuels. Fossil fuel such as coal, petroleum and natural gas are the main sources of conventional energy. The reserves of these minerals are limited. The rate at which the growing world population is consuming them is far greater than the rate of their formation. So, these are likely to be exhausted soon.

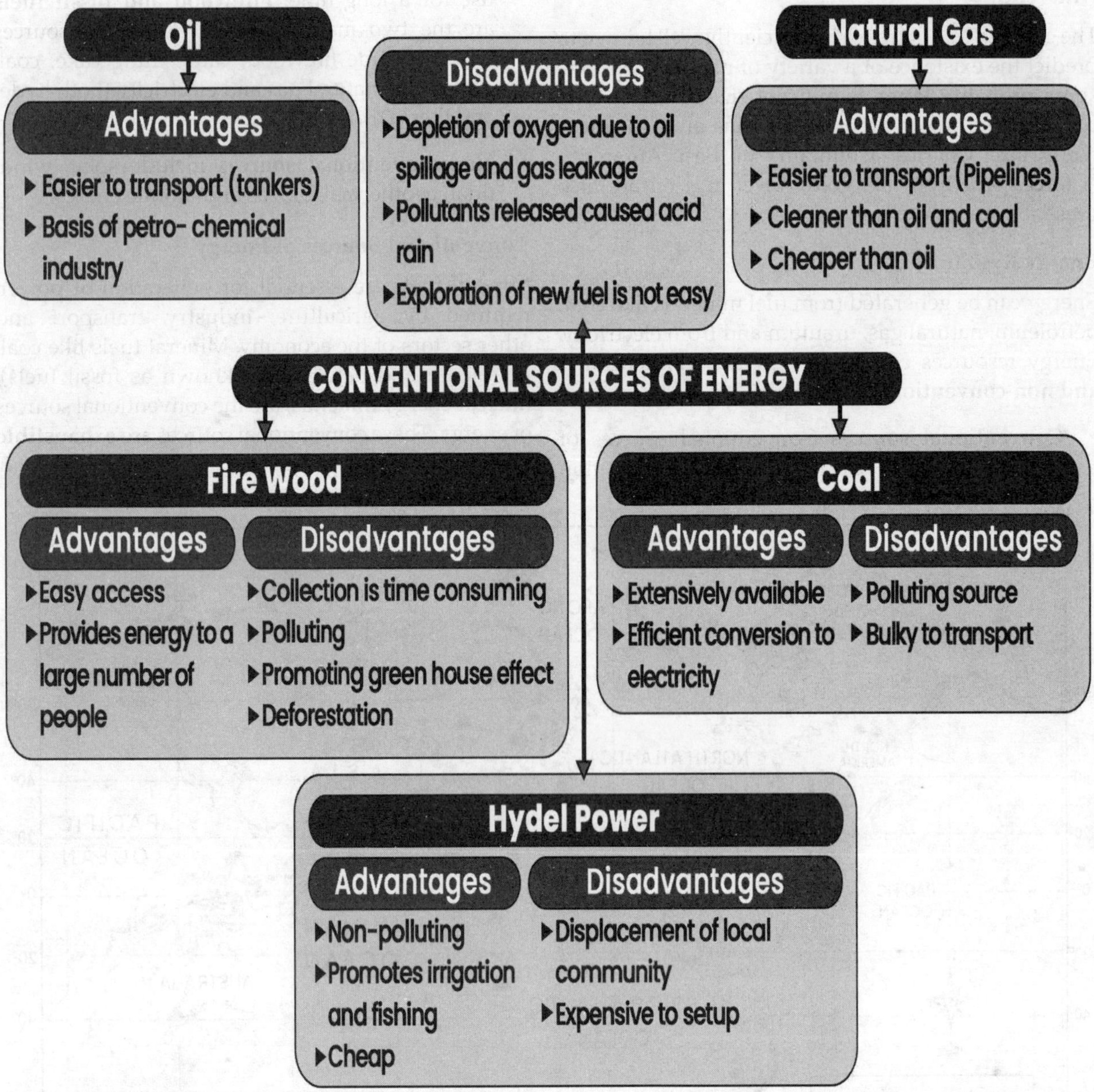

Conventional Sources of Energy

Firewood

It is widely used for cooking and heating. In our country **more than fifty per cent** of the energy consumed in rural areas comes from fire wood.

Coal

In India, coal is the most abundantly available fossil fuel. It provides a substantial part of the nation's energy needs. It is used for power generation, to supply energy to industry as well as for domestic needs. It is used as a domestic fuel, in industries such as iron and steel, steam engines and to generate electricity. Electricity from coal is called **Thermal Power**. The coal which we are using today was formed millions of years ago when giant ferns and swamps got buried under the layers of earth. Coal is therefore referred to as **Buried Sunshine**. The leading coal producers of the world are **China, USA, Germany, Russia, South Africa and France.**

India-Conventional Energy Resources

Formation of coal

Coal is formed due the compression of plant material over millions of years. Coal, therefore, is found in a variety of forms depending on the degrees of compression and the depth and time of burial.

- Decaying plants in swamps produce **peat**, which has a low carbon and high moisture content low heating capacity.
- **Lignite** is a low grade, **brown coal,** which is soft with high moisture content. The principal lignite reserves are in Neyveli in Tamil Nadu and are used for generation of electricity.
- Coal that has been buried deep and subjected to increased temperatures is **bituminous** coal. It is the most **popular coal for commercial use**. Metallurgical coal is high grade bituminous coal which has a special value for smelting iron in blast furnaces.
- **Anthracite is the highest quality hard coal.**

Distribution of Coal

In India coal occurs in rock series of two main geological ages, namely **Gondwana**, a little over 200 million years in age and in **Tertiary Deposits** which are only about 55 million years old.

- The most important Gondwana coal fields of India are located in **Damodar Valley**. They lie in the **Jharkhand-Bengal Coal Belt** and the important coal fields in this region are Raniganj, Jharia, Bokaro, Giridih, Karanpura.
- **Jharia is the largest coal field followed by Raniganj**. The other river valleys associated

with coal are Godavari, Mahanadi and Sone. The most important coal mining centers are Singrauli in Madhya Pradesh (part of Singrauli coal field lies in Uttar Pradesh), Korba in Chhattisgarh, Talcher and Rampur in Odisha, Chanda-Wardha, Kamptee and Bander in **Maharashtra,** Singareni in Telangana and Pandur in Andhra Pradesh.

- **Tertiary coals** occur in Assam, Arunachal Pradesh, Meghalaya and Nagaland. It is extracted from Darangiri, Cherrapunji, Mewlong and Langrin (Meghalaya); Makum, Jaipur and Nazira in upper Assam, Namchik – Namphuk (Arunachal Pradesh) and Kalakot (Jammu and Kashmir).
- **Brown Coal or Lignite** occurs in the coastal areas of Tamil Nadu, Puducherry, Gujarat and Jammu and Kashmir.

Coal is a bulky material, which loses weight on use as it is reduced to ash. Hence, heavy industries and thermal power stations are located on or near the coalfields.

Petroleum

Petroleum or mineral oil is the next major energy source in India after coal. It provides fuel for heat and lighting, lubricants for machinery and raw materials for a number of manufacturing industries. Petroleum refineries act as a **"nodal industry"** for synthetic textile, fertiliser and numerous chemical industries. Petroleum is referred to as **Liquid Gold** because of its scarcity and diversified uses. Petroleum and its derivatives are called **Black Gold** as they are very valuable.

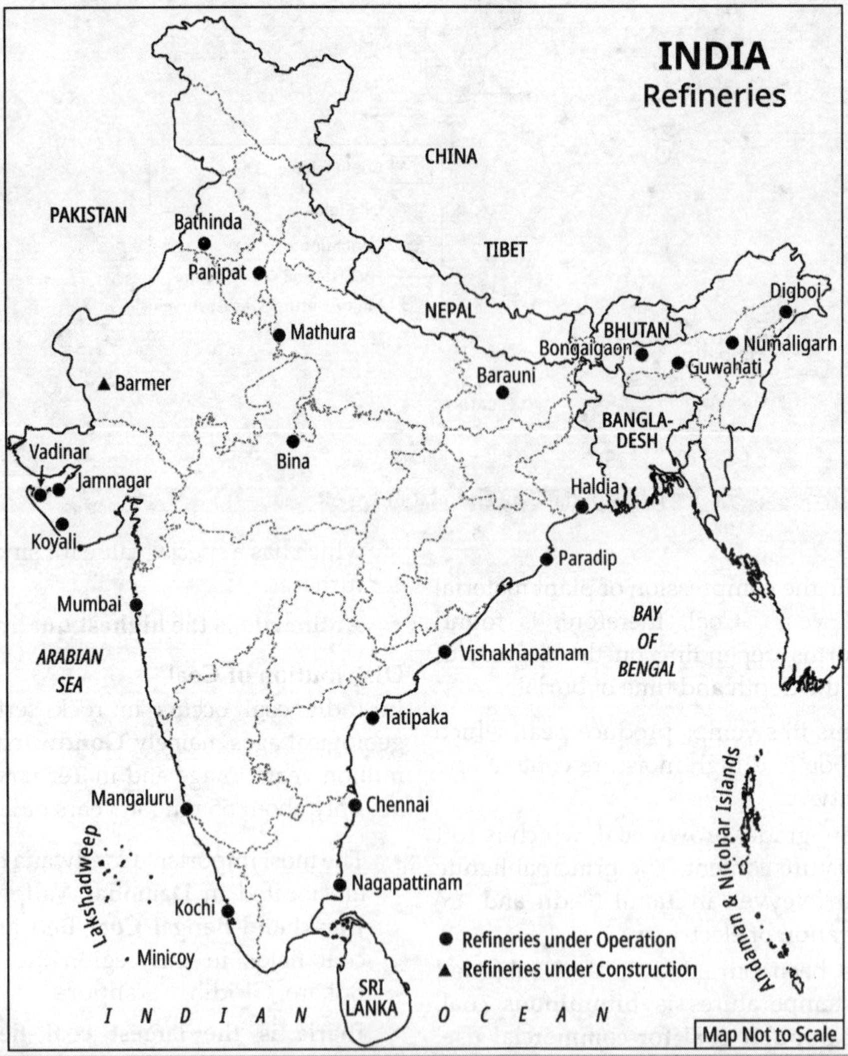

India-Oil Refineries

Most of the petroleum occurrences in India are associated with anticlines and fault traps in the rock formations of the tertiary age. In regions of folding, anticlines or domes, it occurs where oil is trapped in the crest of the upfold. The oil bearing, layer is a porous limestone or sandstone through which oil may flow. The oil is prevented from rising or sinking by intervening non-porous layers.

Petroleum is also found in fault traps between porous and non-porous rocks. Gas, being lighter, usually occurs above the oil. The chief petroleum producing countries are **Iran, Iraq, Saudi Arabia and Qatar. The other major producers are USA, Russia, Venezuela, and Algeria.**

Distribution

- **In Assam**, Digboi, Naharkatiya and Moran are important oil producing areas.
- The major oil fields of **Gujarat** are Ankaleshwar, Kalol, Mehsana, Nawagam, Kosamba and Lunej.
- **Mumbai High** which lies 160 km off Mumbai was discovered in 1973 and production commenced in 1976.
- Oil and natural gas have been found in exploratory wells in **Krishna-Godavari and Kaveri basin** on the east coast.

Oil extracted from the wells is crude oil and contains many impurities. It cannot be used directly. It needs to be refined. **There are two types of refineries in India**:

- Field-based and
- Market-based

Digboi is an example of field- based and Barauni is an example of market- based refinery.

Natural Gas

Natural Gas is **found with petroleum deposits and is released when crude oil is brought to the surface.** It can be used as a domestic and industrial fuel. It is used as fuel in power sector to generate electricity, for heating purpose in industries, as raw material in chemical, petrochemical and fertiliser industries, as transport fuel and as cooking fuel. **Russia, Norway, UK and the Netherlands** are the major producers of natural gas.

Natural gas is also emerging as a preferred transport fuel (CNG) and cooking fuel (PNG) at homes.

Distribution

- India's major gas reserves are found in the **Mumbai High** and allied fields along the west coast which are supplemented by finds in the **Cambay basin**.
- Along the East Coast, new reserves of natural gas have been discovered in the **Krishna-Godavari basin.**
- The first 1,700 Km long **Hazira-Vijaipur-Jagdishpur (HVJ)** cross country gas pipeline, constructed by GAIL (India), linked Mumbai High and Bassein gas fields with various fertiliser, power and industrial complexes in western and northern India. This has been done under **'One Nation One Grid' Programme of the Government**.

Electricity

Electricity is generated mainly in two ways: by running water which drives hydro turbines to generate **hydro-electricity**; and by burning other fuels such as coal, petroleum and natural gas to drive turbines to produce **thermal power.**

- **Hydro Electricity** is generated by fast flowing water, which is a renewable resource. The water discharged after the generation of electricity is used for irrigation. India has a number of multi-purpose projects like the Bhakra Nangal, Damodar Valley corporation, the Kopili Hydel Project etc. producing hydroelectric power. **One fourth of the world's electricity** is produced by hydel power. Norway was the first country in the world to develop hydroelectricity. The leading producers of hydel power in the world are **Paraguay, Norway, Brazil, and China.**
- **Thermal Electricity** is generated by using coal, petroleum and natural gas. The thermal power stations use non-renewable fossil fuels for generating electricity.

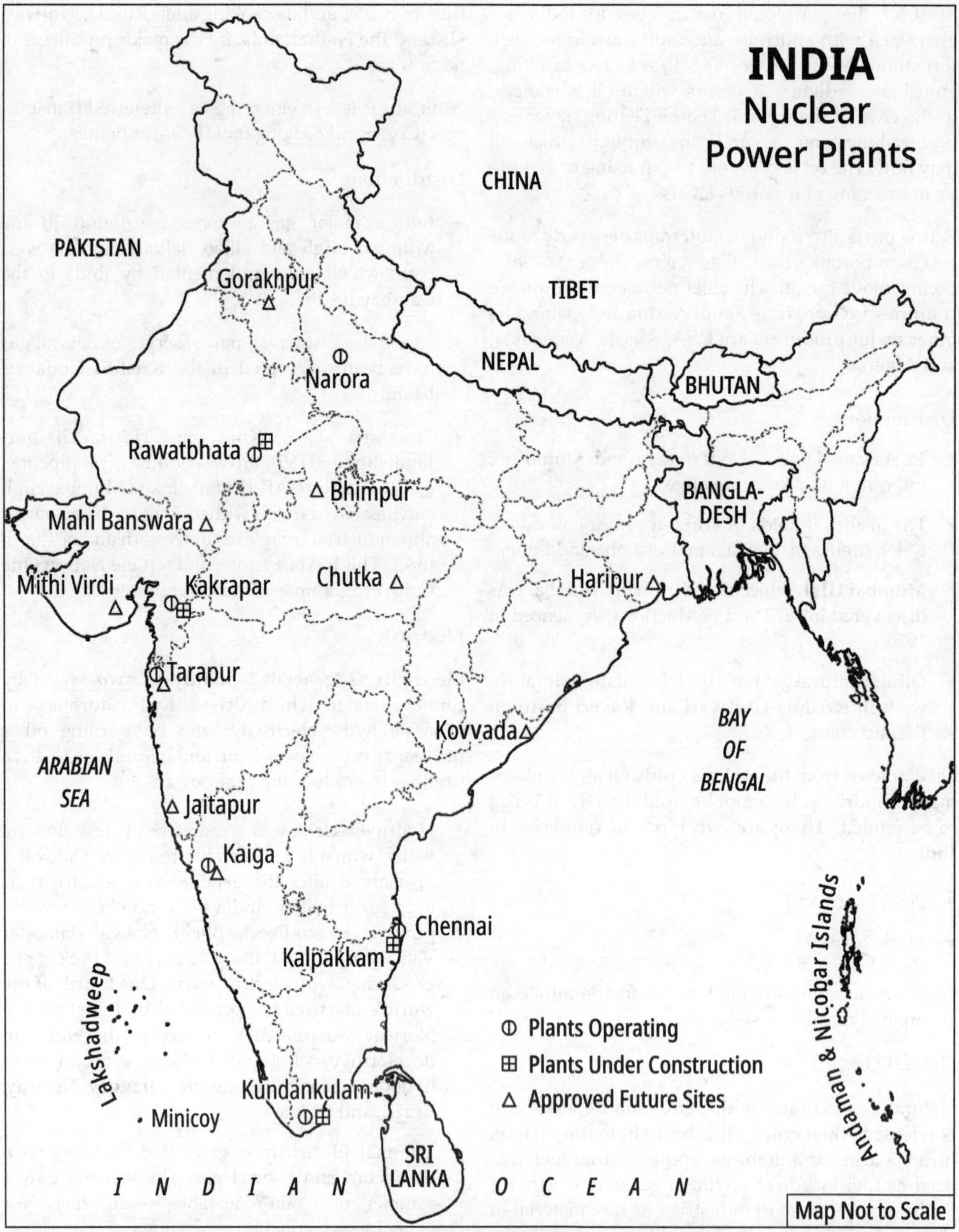

India: Distribution of Nuclear Power Plants

Non-Conventional Sources of Energy

Fossil fuel sources, such as coal, petroleum, natural gas and nuclear energy use exhaustible raw materials. **Sustainable energy resources** are only the renewable energy sources like solar, wind, hydro-geothermal and biomass. These energy sources are more equitably distributed and environment-friendly. These non-conventional energy sources will provide more sustained, eco-friendly cheaper energy after the initial cost is taken care of.

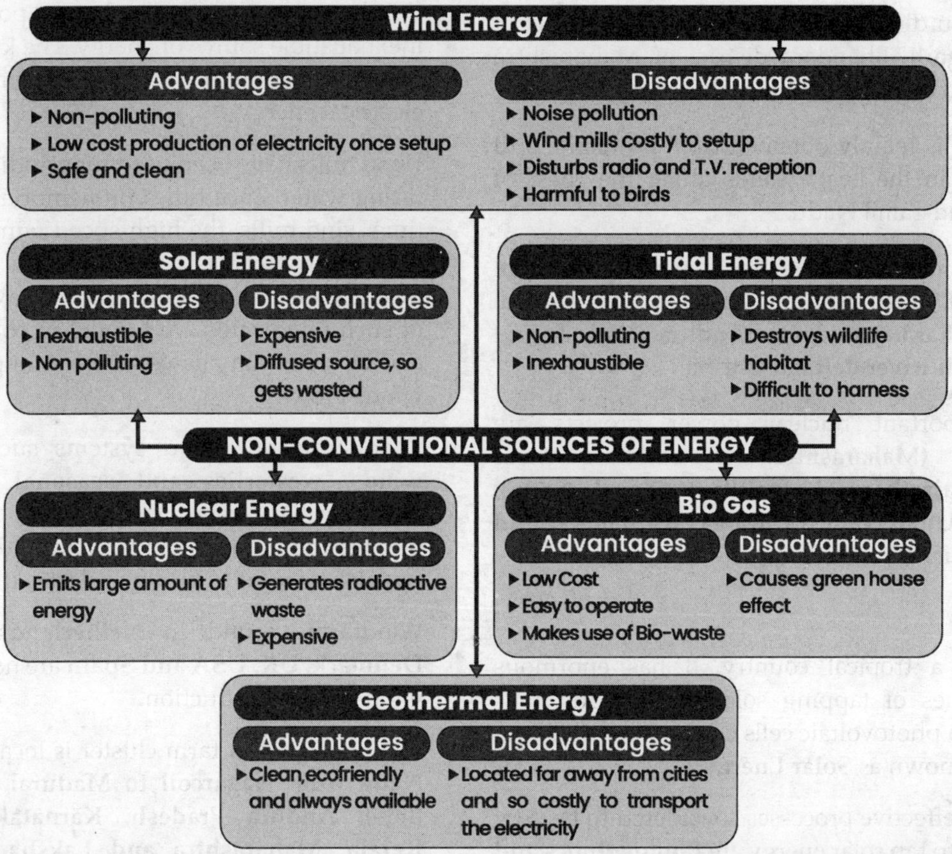

Non-conventional Sources of Energy

Nuclear or Atomic Energy

- It is obtained by altering the structure of atoms. When such an alteration is made, much energy is released in the form of heat and this is used to generate electric power.

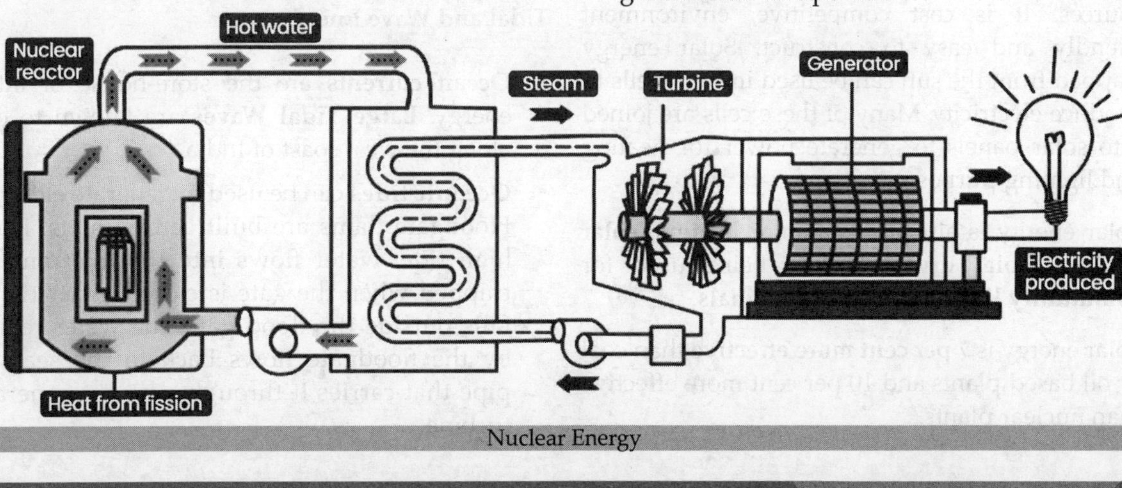

Nuclear Energy

- **Uranium deposits** occur in the Dharwar rocks. Geographically, uranium ores are known to occur in several locations along the Singhbhum Copper belt of Jharkhand.
- It is also found in Udaipur, Alwar and Jhunjhunu districts of Rajasthan, Durg district of Chhattisgarh, Bhandara district of Maharashtra and Kullu district of Himachal Pradesh.
- **Thorium** is mainly obtained from **monazite and ilmenite** in the beach sands along the coast of Kerala and Tamil Nadu.
- **World's richest monazite** deposits occur in **Palakkad and Kollam districts of Kerala**, near **Vishakhapatnam** in Andhra Pradesh and **Mahanadi River delta** in Odisha.
- The important nuclear power projects are **Tarapur (Maharashtra), Rawatbhata near Kota (Rajasthan), Kalpakkam (Tamil Nadu), Narora (Uttar Pradesh), Kaiga (Karnataka) and Kakarapara (Gujarat).**

Solar Energy

- India is a tropical country. It has enormous possibilities of tapping solar energy. Sun rays tapped in photovoltaic cells can be converted into energy, known as **Solar Energy**.
- The two effective processes considered to be very effective to tap solar energy are **Photovoltaics and Solar Thermal Technology.**
- Solar thermal technology has some relative advantages over all other non-renewable energy sources. It is cost competitive, environment friendly and easy to construct. Solar energy trapped from the sun can be used in solar cells to produce electricity. Many of these cells are joined into solar panels to generate power for heating and lighting purpose.
- Solar energy is also used in **solar heaters, solar cookers, solar dryers** besides being used for **community lighting and traffic signals**.
- Solar energy is **7 per cent more effective** than coal or oil based plants and 10 per cent more effective than nuclear plants.
- The western part of India has greater potential for the development of solar energy in **Gujarat and Rajasthan.**

Wind Power

- Wind energy is an absolutely pollution free, inexhaustible source of energy. The kinetic energy of wind, through turbines is converted into electrical energy.
- Wind mills have been used for grinding grain and lifting water since times immemorial. In modern time wind mills, the high-speed winds rotate the wind mill which is connected to a generator to produce electricity. Wind farms having clusters of such wind mills are located in coastal regions and in mountain passes where strong and steady winds blow.
- The permanent wind systems such the **trade winds, westerlies and seasonal winds** like monsoon have been used as a source of energy. Besides these, local winds, land and sea breezes can also be used to produce electricity.
- Windfarms found in **Netherlands, Germany, Denmark, UK, USA and Spain** are noted for their wind energy production.
- The largest wind farm cluster is located in **Tamil Nadu from Nagarcoil to Madurai**. Apart from these, **Andhra Pradesh, Karnataka, Gujarat, Kerala, Maharashtra and Lakshadweep** have important wind farms. **Nagarcoil and Jaisalmer** are well known for effective use of wind energy in the country.

Tidal and Wave Energy

- **Ocean currents** are the store-house of infinite energy. **Large Tidal Waves** are known to occur along the west coast of India.
- **Oceanic tides** can be used to generate electricity. Floodgate dams are built across inlets. During high tide, water flows into the inlet and gets trapped when the gate is closed. After the tide falls outside the flood gate, the water retained by the floodgate flows back to the sea via a pipe that carries it through a power-generating turbine.

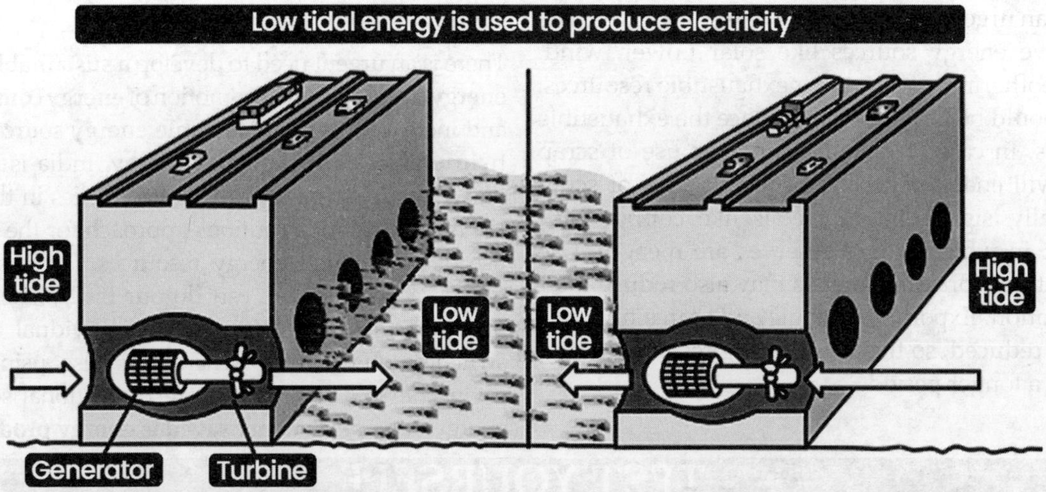

Tidal Energy

- **Russia, France and the Gulf of Kachchh** in India have huge tidal mill farms.
- In India the **Gulf of Khambhat, the Gulf of Kachchh** in Gujarat on the western coast and Gangetic delta in **Sunderban** regions of West Bengal provide ideal conditions for utilising tidal energy.

Geo Thermal Energy

- Geo thermal energy refers to the electricity produced by using the heat from the interior of the Earth.
- When the magma from the interior of earth, comes out on the surface, tremendous heat is released. This heat energy can successfully be tapped and converted to electrical energy.
- Apart from this, the hot water, that gushes out through the **Geyser Wells,** is also used in the generation of thermal energy.
- Groundwater in such areas absorbs heat from the rocks and becomes hot. It is so hot that when it rises to the earth's surface, it turns into steam. This steam is used to drive turbines and generate electricity.
- **USA has the world's largest geothermal power plants** followed by **New Zealand, Iceland, Philippines and Central America.** The first successful (1890) attempt to tap the underground heat was made in the city of Boise, Idaho (U.S.A.), where a hot water pipe network was built to give heat to the surrounding buildings. This plant is still working.
- **There are several hundred Hot Springs in India,** which could be used to generate electricity. Two experimental projects have been set up in India to harness geothermal energy. One is located in the **Parvati valley near Manikaran in Himachal Pradesh** and the other is located in the **Puga Valley, Ladakh**.

Bio-Energy

- Bio-energy refers to energy derived from biological products which includes agricultural residues, municipal, industrial and other wastes.
- Bio-energy is a potential source of energy conversion. It can be converted into electrical energy, heat energy or gas for cooking.
- It will also process the waste and garbage and produce energy. This will improve the economic life of rural areas in developing countries, reduce environmental pollution, enhance self-reliance and reduce pressure on fuel wood.
- One such project converting municipal waste into energy is **Okhla in Delhi.**

Conservation of Minerals Resources

Sustainable development requires integration of economic development with environmental concerns. Traditional methods of resource use result into generating enormous quantity of waste as well as create other environmental problems. Hence, sustainable development calls for the protection of resources for the future generations.

There is an urgent need to conserve the resources. The alternative energy sources like solar power, wind, wave, geothermal energy are inexhaustible resources. These should be developed to replace the exhaustible resources. In case of metallic minerals, use of scrap metals will enable recycling of metals. Use of scrap is specially, significant in metals like copper, lead and zinc in which India's reserves are meagre. Use of substitutes for scarce metals may also reduce their consumption. Export of strategic and scarce minerals must be reduced, so that the existing reserve may be used for a longer period.

Conservation of Energy Resources

There is an urgent need to develop a **sustainable path of energy development**. Promotion of **energy conservation** and increased use of **renewable energy** sources are the **twin planks of sustainable energy**. India is presently one of the least energy efficient countries in the world. We have to adopt a cautious approach for the judicious use of our limited energy resources. For example, as concerned citizens we can do our bit by using public transport systems instead of individual vehicles; switching off electricity when not in use, using power-saving devices and using non-conventional sources of energy. After all, **"energy saved is energy produced".**

TEST YOURSELF

Multiple Choice Questions

Q1. Which of the following is a non-metallic mineral?

(a) Iron ore (b) Bauxite
(c) Manganese (d) Limestone

Q2. Which state in India is the leading producer of coal?

(a) Jharkhand (b) Odisha
(c) Chhattisgarh (d) West Bengal

Q3. Which mineral is used as a fuel in nuclear power plants?

(a) Coal (b) Uranium
(c) Lignite (d) Natural gas

Q4. The largest producer of petroleum in India is:

(a) Gujarat (b) Rajasthan
(c) Assam (d) Maharashtra

Q5. Which state is the largest producer of iron ore in India?

(a) Odisha (b) Jharkhand
(c) Chhattisgarh (d) Karnataka

Q6. Which mineral is used as a reducing agent in metallurgical processes?

(a) Copper (b) Zinc
(c) Iron (d) Aluminium

Q7. Which energy resource is obtained from biomass?

(a) Coal (b) Natural gas
(c) Solar energy (d) Bioenergy

Q8. The major coalfields of India belong to which geological age?

(a) Carboniferous period (b) Cenozoic era
(c) Archean eon (d) Mesozoic era

Q9. The largest reserves of thorium in India are found in which state?

(a) Kerala (b) Tamil Nadu
(c) Jharkhand (d) Odisha

Q10. Which of the following minerals is used as a fertiliser?

(a) Limestone (b) Bauxite
(c) Potash (d) Gypsum

Q11. Consider the following minerals; Bentonite, Chromite, Kyanite, and Sillimanite. In India, which of the above is/are officially designated as major minerals? (UPSC 2020)

(a) Bentonite and Chromite only

(b) Sillimanite only

(c) Bentonite and Kyanite only

(d) Chromite, Kyanite, and Sillimanite only

Q12. Consider the following statements: (UPSC 2020)

1. Coal ash contains arsenic, lead, and mercury.
2. Coal-fired power plants release sulphur dioxide and oxides of nitrogen into the environment.
3. High ash content is observed in Indian coal.

Which of the statements given above is/are correct?

(a) 1 only

(b) 2 and 3 only

(c) 3 only

(d) 1, 2 and 3

Answer Key

Q1.	d	Q2.	a	Q3.	b	Q4.	b
Q5.	a	Q6.	d	Q7.	d	Q8.	a
Q9.	d	Q10.	c	Q11.	d	Q12.	d

UNIT 27

Primary Activities

In This Unit

Comprehensive and profound coverage of the following NCERTs' chapters:

- ✓ NCERT Class- 8th (Resources and Development), Chapter- 3
- ✓ NCERT Class- 10th (Contemporary India-II), Chapter- 3
- ✓ NCERT Class- 12th (India-People and Economy), Chapter- 3
- ✓ NCERT Class- 12th (Fundamentals of Human Geography), Chapter- 4

Human activities which generate income are known as **economic activities.** Economic activities are broadly grouped into **primary, secondary, tertiary and quaternary activities**. **Primary activities** are directly dependent on the environment as these refer to utilisation of earth's resources such as land, water, vegetation, building materials and minerals. It thus includes hunting and gathering, pastoral activities, fishing, forestry, agriculture, and mining and quarrying.

People engaged in primary activities are called **red-collar workers** due to the outdoor nature of their work.

Hunting and Gathering

- The earliest human beings depended on their immediate environment for their sustenance. They subsisted on:
  - ➢ Animals which they hunted;
  - ➢ The edible plants which they gathered from forests in the vicinity.

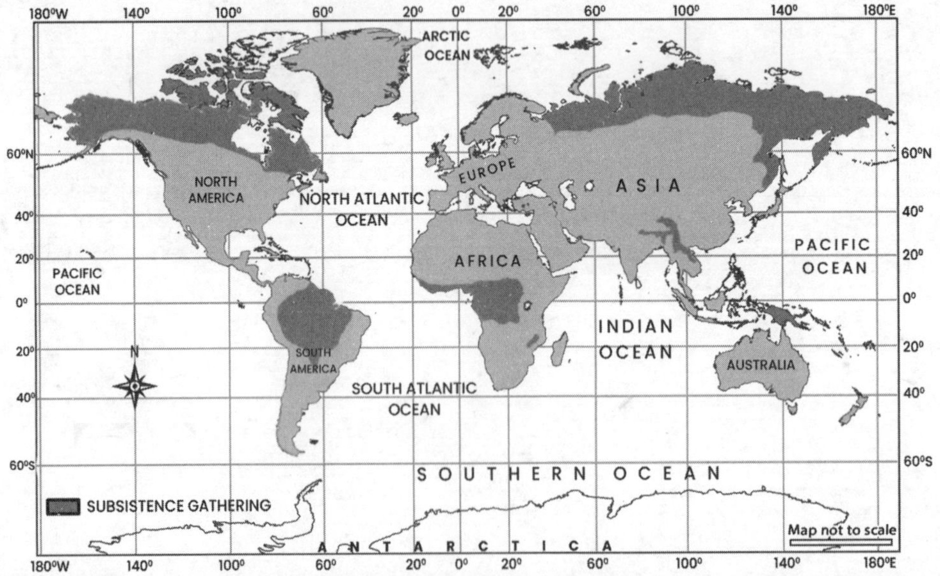

Areas of Subsistence Gathering

- Primitive societies depended on wild animals. People located in very cold and extremely hot climates survived on hunting.
- The people in the coastal areas still catch fish though fishing has experienced modernisation due to technological progress.
- The early hunters used primitive tools made of stones, twigs or arrows so the number of animals killed was limited.
- Gathering and hunting are the **oldest economic activities known**. These are carried out at different levels with different orientations.
- Gathering is **practised in regions with harsh climatic conditions**. It often involves primitive societies, who extract both plants and animals to satisfy their needs for food, shelter and clothing.
- This type of activity requires a small amount of capital investment and operates at a very low level of technology. The yield per person is very low and **little or no surplus is produced.**
- Gathering is practised in
  - ➢ **High Latitude zones** which include northern Canada, northern Eurasia and southern Chile;
  - ➢ **Low Latitude zones** such as the Amazon Basin, tropical Africa, Northern fringe of Australia and the interior parts of Southeast Asia.
- In modern times, some gathering is market-oriented and has become commercial.

Pastoralism

At some stage in history, with the realisation that hunting is an unsustainable activity, human beings might have thought of domestication of animals. People living in different climatic conditions selected and domesticated animals found in those regions. **Depending on the geographical factors,** and **technological development**, animal rearing today is practised either at the subsistence or at the commercial level.

Nomadic Herding

- Nomadic herding or **pastoral nomadism** is a primitive subsistence activity, in which the **herders rely on animals for food, clothing, shelter, tools and transport.**

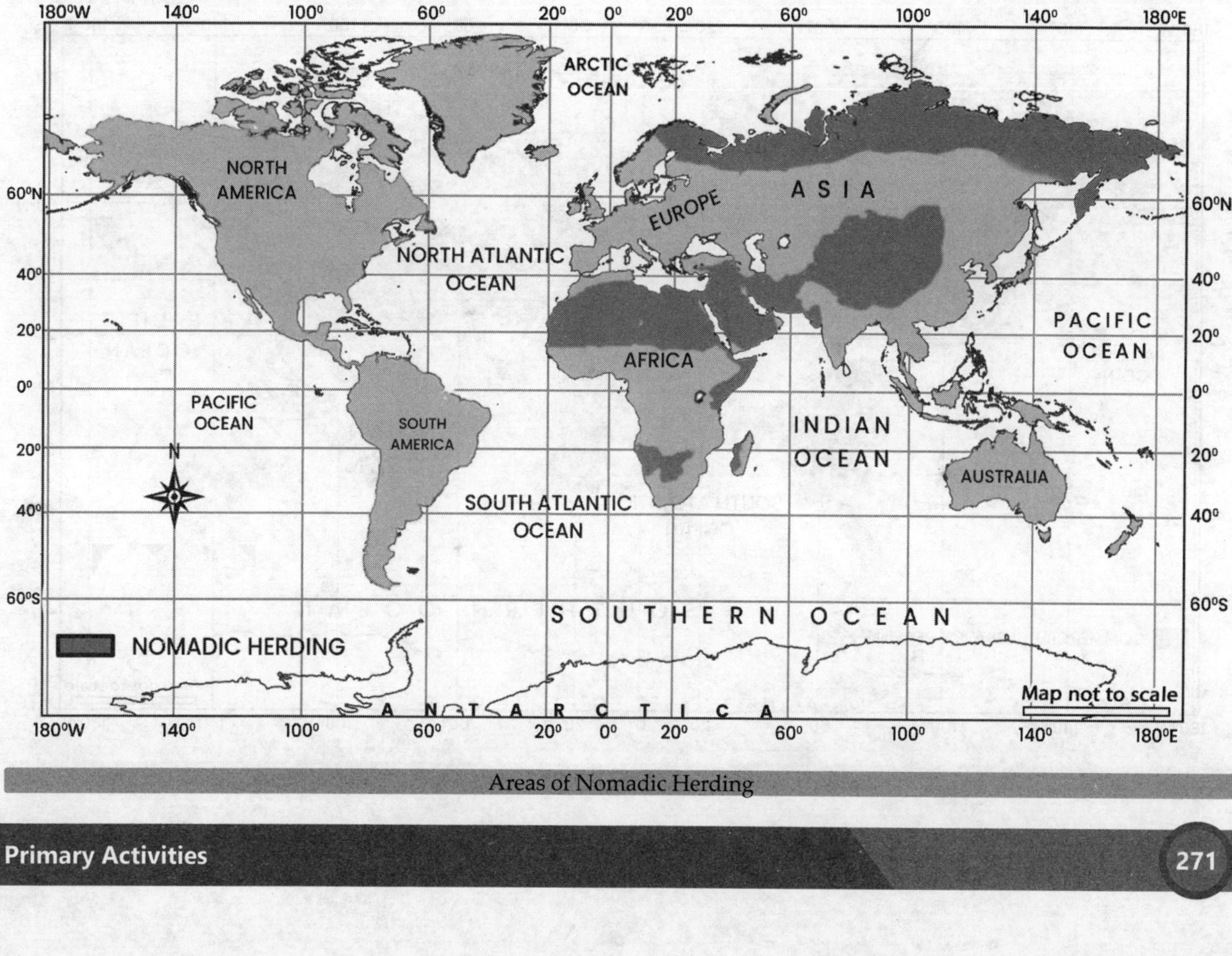

Areas of Nomadic Herding

- They move from one place to another along with their livestock, depending on the amount and quality of pastures and water.
- Each nomadic community occupies a well-identified territory as a matter of tradition.
- A wide variety of animals is kept in different regions. **In tropical Africa**, cattle are the most important livestock, while in **Sahara and Asiatic deserts**, sheep, goats and camel are reared.
- In the **mountainous areas of Tibet and Andes**, yak and llamas and in the **Arctic and Sub Arctic areas**, reindeer are the most important animals.
- Movement in search of pastures is undertaken either over vast horizontal distances or vertically from one elevation to another in the mountainous regions.
- **The process of migration from plain areas to pastures on mountains during summers and again from mountain pastures to plain areas during winters** is known as **transhumance**.
- In regions, such as **Himalayas,** Gujjars, Bakarwals, Gaddis and Bhotiyas migrate from plains to the mountains in summers and to the plains from the high altitude, pastures in winters.
- **Pastoral nomadism is associated with three important regions**. The core region extends from the **Atlantic shores of North Africa eastwards across the Arabian Peninsula into Mongolia and Central China.** The **second region** extends over the **tundra region of Eurasia.** In the **southern hemisphere there are small areas in South-west Africa and on the island of Madagascar.**
- The number of **pastoral nomads has been decreasing** and the areas operated by them shrinking. This is due to:
  - ➢ Imposition of political boundaries;
  - ➢ New settlement plans by different countries.

Commercial Livestock Rearing

- Unlike nomadic herding, commercial livestock rearing is more **organised and capital** intensive.
- Commercial livestock ranching is essentially associated with western cultures and is practised on permanent ranches.

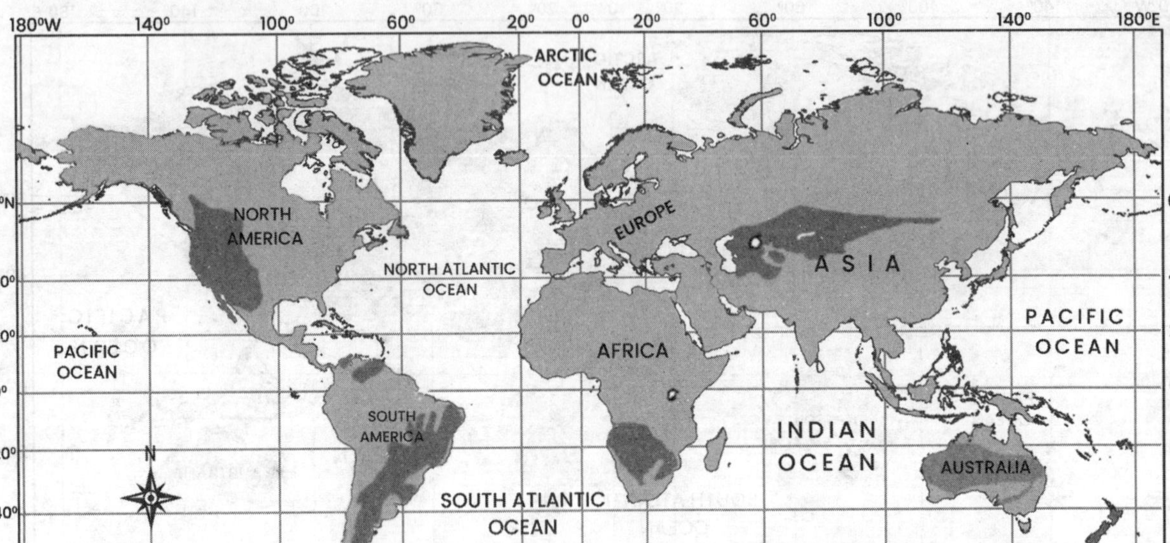

Areas of Commercial Livestock Rearing

- These **ranches cover large areas and are divided into a number of parcels, which are fenced** to regulate the grazing.
- When the grass of one parcel is grazed, animals are moved to another parcel. The number of animals in a pasture is kept according to the carrying capacity of the pasture.
- This is a specialised activity in which **only one type of animal is reared.** Important animals include sheep, cattle, goats and horses. Products such as **meat, wool, hides and skin** are processed and packed scientifically and exported to different world markets.
- Rearing of animals in ranching is organised on a scientific basis. The main emphasis is on breeding, genetic improvement, disease control and health care of the animals.
- **New Zealand, Australia, Argentina, Uruguay and United States of America** are important countries where commercial livestock rearing is practised.

Agriculture

Agriculture is practised under multiple combinations of physical and socio-economic conditions, which gives rise to different types of agricultural systems.

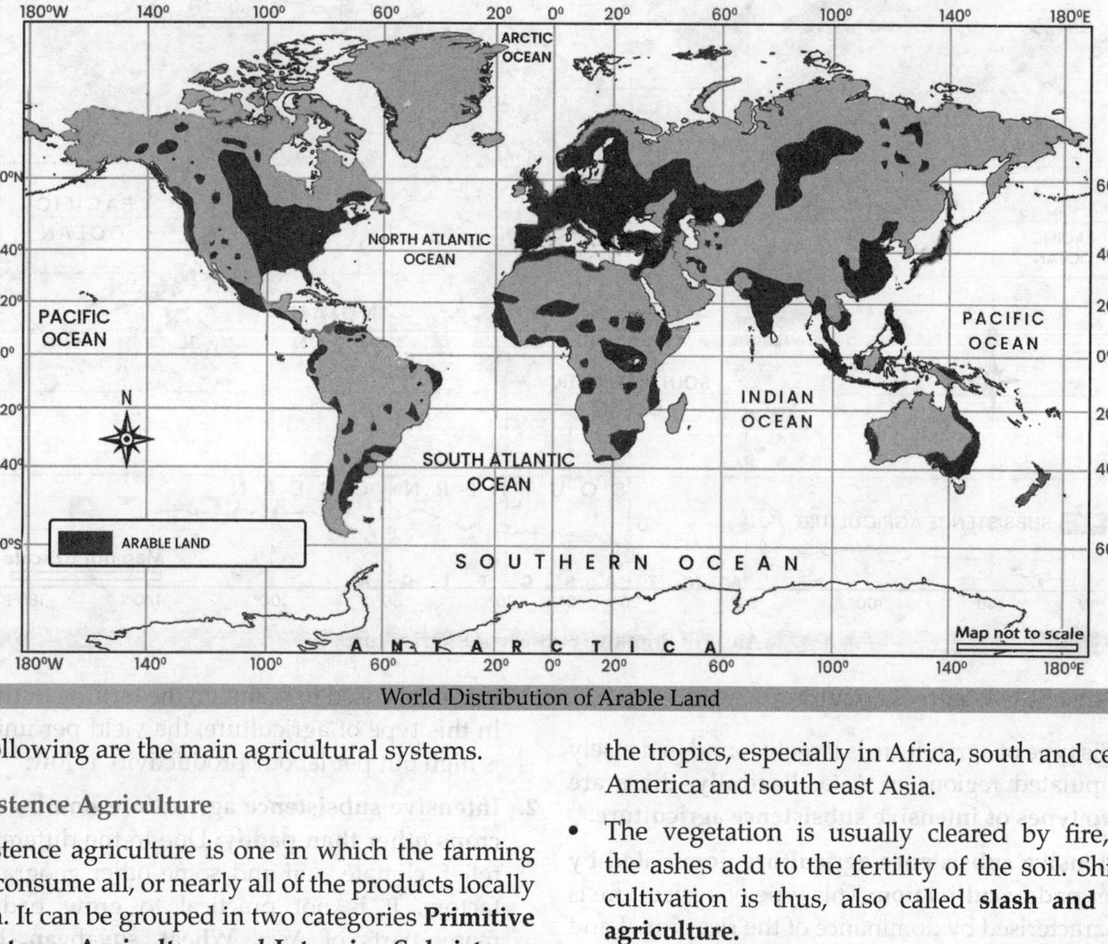

World Distribution of Arable Land

The following are the main agricultural systems.

Subsistence Agriculture

Subsistence agriculture is one in which the farming areas consume all, or nearly all of the products locally grown. It can be grouped in two categories **Primitive Subsistence Agriculture and Intensive Subsistence Agriculture.**

Primitive Subsistence Agriculture

- Primitive subsistence agriculture or shifting cultivation is widely practised by many tribes in the tropics, especially in Africa, south and central America and south east Asia.
- The vegetation is usually cleared by fire, and the ashes add to the fertility of the soil. Shifting cultivation is thus, also called **slash and burn agriculture.**
- The cultivated patches are very small and cultivation is done with very primitive tools such as sticks and hoes.
- After sometime (3 to 5 years) the soil loose its fertility and the farmer shifts to another

parts and clears other patch of the forest for cultivation.

- One of the major problems of shifting cultivation is that the cycle of **jhum** becomes less and less due to loss of fertility in different parcels.

- The **'slash and burn'** agriculture is known as 'Milpa' in Mexico and Central America, 'Conuco' in Venzuela, 'Roca' in Brazil, 'Masole' in Central Africa, 'Ladang' in Indonesia, 'Ray' in Vietnam.
- In India, this primitive form of cultivation is called 'Bewar' or 'Dahiya' in Madhya Pradesh, 'Podu' or 'Penda' in Andhra Pradesh, 'Pama Dabi' or 'Koman' or Bringa' in Odisha, 'Kumari' in Western Ghats, 'Valre' or 'Waltre' in South-eastern Rajasthan, 'Khil' in the Himalayan belt, 'Kuruwa' in Jharkhand, and 'Jhumming' in the North-eastern region.

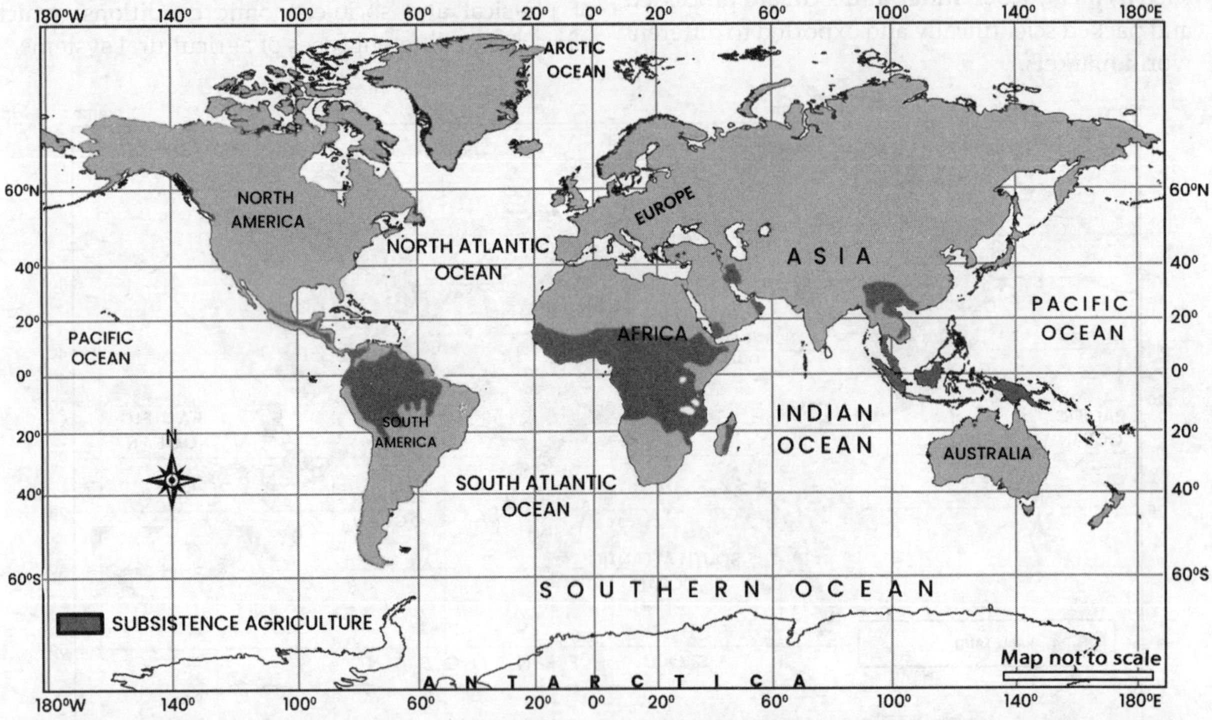

Areas of Primitive Subsistence Agriculture

Intensive Subsistence Agriculture

- This type of agriculture is largely found in densely populated regions of Asia. **Basically, there are two types of intensive subsistence agriculture.**

1. **Intensive subsistence agriculture dominated by wet paddy cultivation:** This type of agriculture is characterised by dominance of the rice crop. Land holdings are very small due to the high density of population. Farmers work with the help of family labour leading to intensive use of land. **Use of machinery is limited** and most of the agricultural operations are done by **manual labour**. Farm yard manure is used to maintain the fertility of the soil. In this type of agriculture, the yield per unit area is high but per labour productivity is low.
2. **Intensive subsistence agriculture dominated by crops other than paddy:** Due to the difference in relief, climate, soil and some other geographical factors, it is not practical to grow paddy in many parts of Asia. **Wheat, soyabean, barley and sorghum** are grown in northern China, Manchuria, North Korea and North Japan. In India wheat is grown in western parts of the Indo-Gangetic plains and **millets** are grown in dry parts of western and southern India.

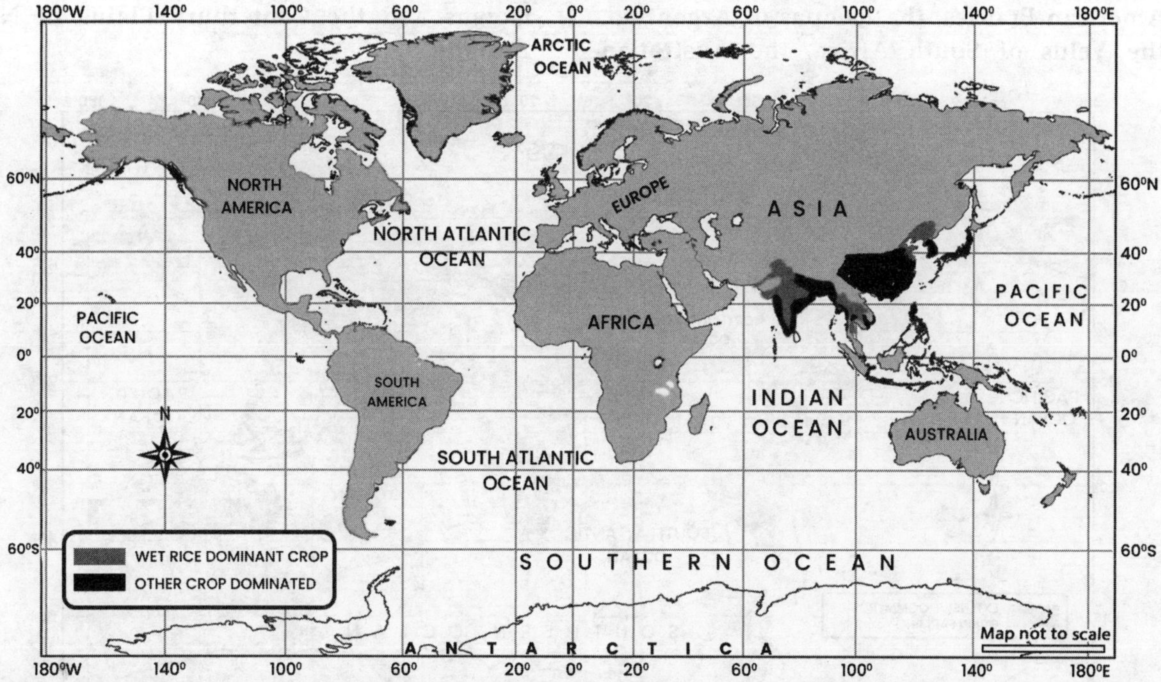

Areas of Intensive Subsistence Farming

The Europeans colonised many parts of the world and introduced some other forms of agriculture such as plantations which were mainly profit-oriented large scale production systems.

Plantation Agriculture

- Plantation agriculture as mentioned above was introduced by the Europeans in colonies situated in the tropics.
- Some of the important plantation crops are **tea, coffee, cocoa, rubber, cotton, oil palm, sugarcane, bananas and pineapples.**
- The characteristic features of this type of farming are large estates or plantations, large capital investment, managerial and technical support, scientific methods of cultivation, single crop specialisation, cheap labour, and **a good system of transportation** which links the estates to the factories and markets for the export of the products.
- The **French** established cocoa and coffee plantations in west Africa. The **British** set up large tea gardens in India and Sri Lanka, rubber plantations in Malaysia and sugarcane and banana plantations in West Indies.
- **Spanish and Americans** invested heavily in coconut and sugarcane plantations in the Philippines.
- The **Dutch** once had monopoly over sugarcane plantation in Indonesia. Some **coffee fazendas** (large plantations) in Brazil are still managed by Europeans.
- Today, ownership of the majority of plantations has passed into the hands of the government or the nationals of the countries concerned.

Extensive Commercial Grain Cultivation

- Commercial grain cultivation is practised in the interior parts of semi-arid lands of the mid-latitudes.
- **Wheat** is the principal crop, though other crops like **corn, barley, oats and rye** are also grown.
- The **size of the farm is very large,** therefore entire operations of cultivation from ploughing to harvesting are **mechanised.**
- There is low yield per acre but high yield per person.
- This type of agriculture is best developed in **Eurasian steppes, the Canadian and**

American Prairies, the Pampas of Argentina, the Velds of South Africa, the Australian Downs and the Canterbury Plains of New Zealand.

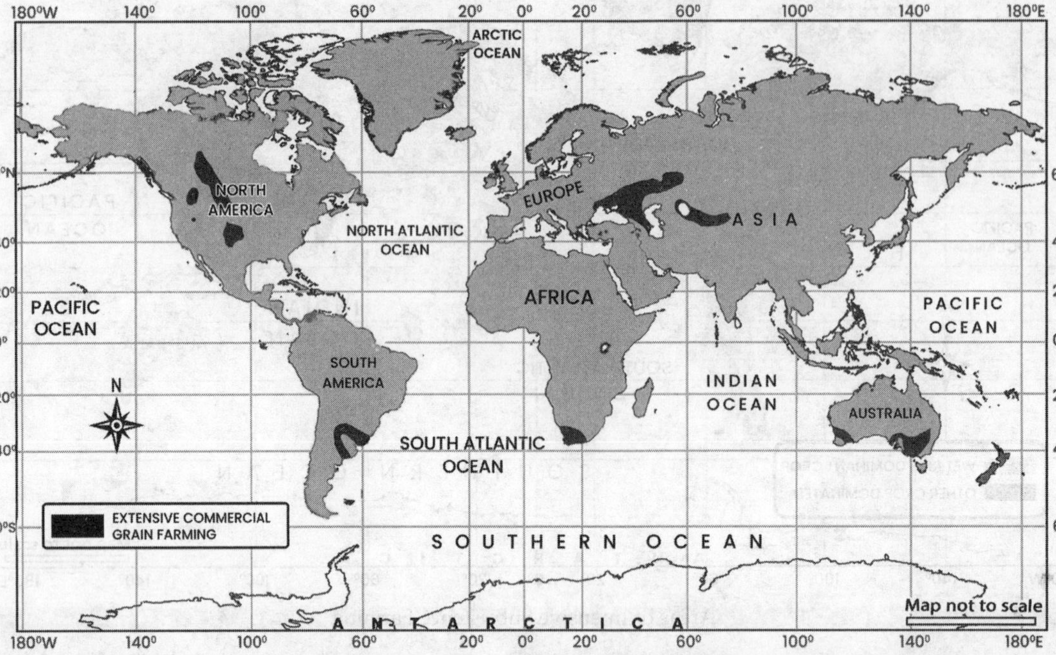

Areas of Extensive Commercial Grain Farming

Mixed Farming

- This form of agriculture is found in the highly developed parts of the world, e.g., **North-western Europe, Eastern North America, parts of Eurasia and the temperate latitudes of Southern continents.**

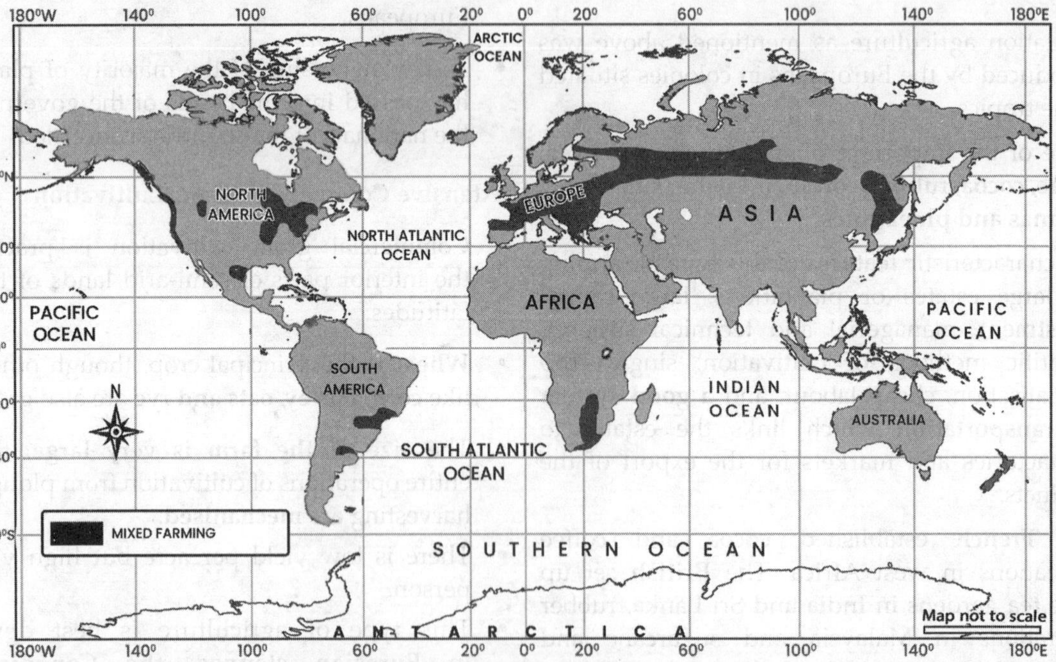

Areas of Mixed Farming

- Mixed farms are moderate in size and usually the crops associated with it are w**heat, barley, oats, rye, maize, fodder and root crops.**
- Fodder crops are an important component of mixed farming. **Crop rotation and intercropping** play an important role in maintaining soil fertility.
- Equal emphasis is laid on **crop cultivation and animal husbandry**. Animals like cattle, sheep, pigs and poultry provide the main income along with crops.

Dairy Farming

- Dairy is **the most advanced and efficient type of rearing of milch animals. It is highly capital intensive.**
- Animal sheds, storage facilities for fodder, feeding and milching machines add to the cost of dairy farming.
- Special emphasis is laid on cattle breeding, health care and veterinary services.
- It is **highly labour intensive** as it involves rigorous care in feeding and milching. There is **no off season** during the year as in the case of crop raising.
- It is practised mainly near urban and industrial centres which provide neighbourhood market for fresh milk and dairy products
- The development of **transportation, refrigeration, pasteurisation and other preservation** processes have increased the duration of storage of various dairy products.
- **There are three main regions of commercial dairy farming**. The largest is **North Western Europe,** the second is **Canada** and the third belt includes **South Eastern Australia, New Zealand and Tasmania.**

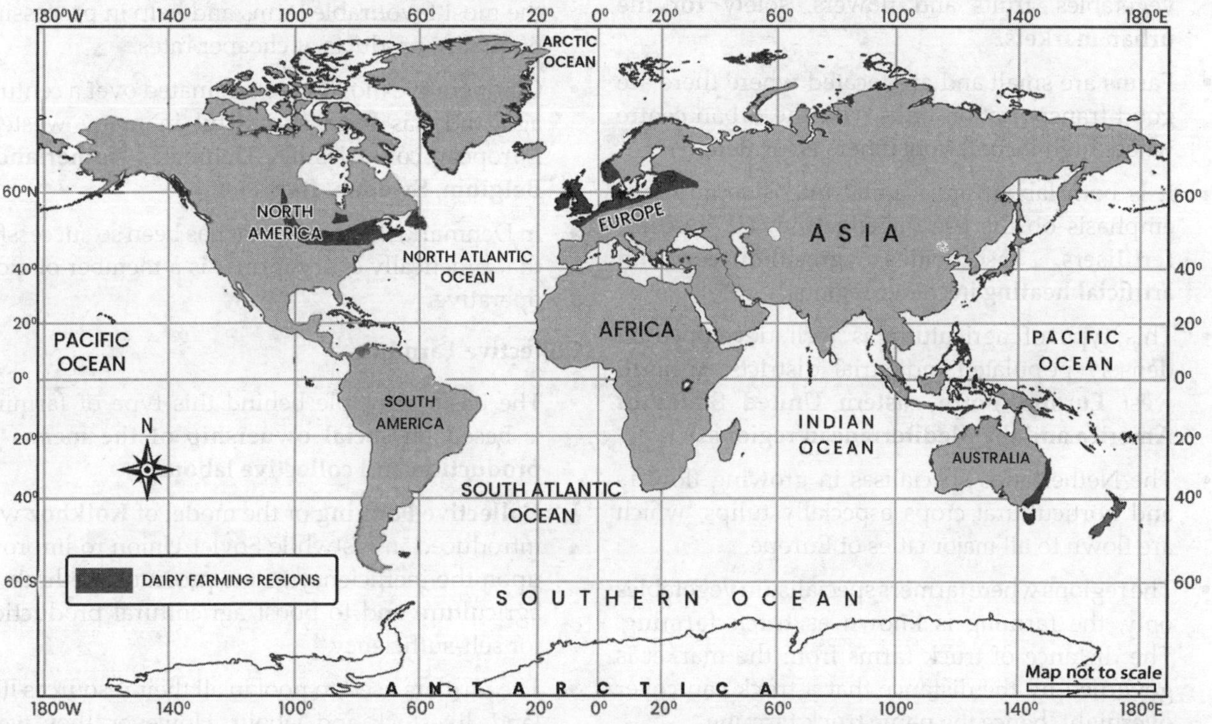

Areas of Dairy Farming

Mediterranean Agriculture

- Mediterranean agriculture is **highly specialised commercial agriculture.**
- It is practised in the countries on either side of **the Mediterranean Sea in Europe and in north Africa from Tunisia to Atlantic coast, southern California, central Chile, south western parts of South Africa and south western parts of Australia.**

- This region is an important supplier of **citrus fruits**.
- **Viticulture** or grape cultivation is a speciality of the Mediterranean region.
- **Best quality wines** in the world with distinctive flavours are produced from high quality grapes in various countries of this region.
- The inferior grapes are dried into **raisins and currants.** This region also produces **olives and figs.**
- The advantage of Mediterranean agriculture is that more valuable crops such as fruits and vegetables are grown in winters when there is great demand in European and North American markets.

Market Gardening and Horticulture

- Market gardening and horticulture specialise in the cultivation of **high value crops** such as vegetables, fruits and flowers, solely **for the urban markets.**
- Farms are small and are located where there are good transportation links with the urban centre where high income consumers is located.
- It is both labour and capital intensive and lays emphasis on the use of **irrigation, HYV seeds, fertilisers, insecticides, greenhouses and artificial heating** in colder regions.
- This type of agriculture is well developed in densely populated industrial districts of north west **Europe, north eastern United States of America and the Mediterranean regions.**
- The Netherlands specialises in growing flowers and horticultural crops especially tulips, which are flown to all major cities of Europe.
- The regions where farmers specialise in vegetables only, the farming is known as **truck farming.** The distance of truck farms from the market is governed by the distance that a truck can cover overnight, hence the name truck farming.
- In addition to market gardening, a modern development in the industrial regions of Western Europe and North America is **Factory Farming.**
- Livestock, particularly poultry and cattle rearing, is done in stalls and pens, fed on manufactured feedstuff and carefully supervised against diseases.
- This requires heavy capital investment in terms of building, machinery for various operations, **veterinary services and heating and lighting.**

Types of farming can also be categorised according to the **farming organisation.** Farming organisation is affected by the way in which farmers own their farms and various policies of the government which help to run these farms.

Co-operative Farming

- A group of farmers form a co-operative society by pooling in their resources voluntarily for more efficient and profitable farming.
- **Individual farms remain intact** and farming is a matter of cooperative initiative.
- Co-operative societies help farmers, to procure all important inputs of farming, sell the products at the most favourable terms and help in processing of quality products at cheaper rates.
- Co-operative movement originated over a century ago and has been successful in many western European countries like **Denmark, Netherlands, Belgium, Sweden, Italy** etc.
- In Denmark, the movement has been so successful that practically every farmer is a member of a co-operative.

Collective Farming

- The basic principle behind this type of farming is based on **social ownership of the means of production and collective labour.**
- **Collective Farming** or the model of **Kolkhoz** was introduced in erstwhile Soviet Union to improve upon the inefficiency of the previous methods of agriculture and to boost agricultural production for self-sufficiency.
- The farmers used to pool in all their resources like land, livestock and labour. However, they were allowed to retain very small plots to grow crops in order to meet their daily requirements.

Mining

The discovery of minerals in the history of human development, is reflected in many stages in terms of copper age, bronze age and iron age. The actual development of mining began with the industrial revolution and its importance is continuously increasing.

Factors Affecting Mining Activity

The profitability of mining operations thus, **depends on two main factors:**

1. **Physical factors** include the size, grade and the mode of occurrence of the deposits.
2. **Economic factors** such as the demand for the mineral, technology available and used, capital to develop infrastructure and the labour and transport costs.

Methods of Mining

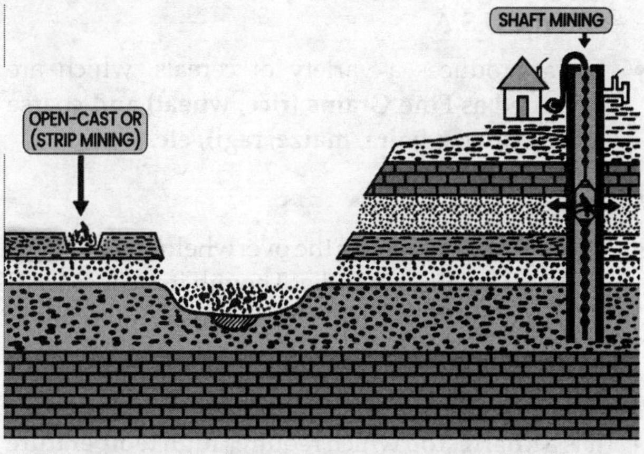

Methods of Mining

Depending on the **mode of occurrence** and the **nature of the ore, mining is of two types: surface and underground mining.**

Surface mining - The **surface mining** also known as **open-cast mining** is the easiest and the cheapest way of mining minerals that occur close to the surface. Overhead costs such as safety precautions and equipment is relatively low in this method. The output is both large and rapid.

Underground mining - When the ore lies deep below the surface, **underground mining method** (shaft method) has to be used. In this method, vertical shafts have to be sunk, from where underground galleries radiate to reach the minerals. Minerals are extracted and transported to the surface through these passages. It requires specially designed lifts, drills, haulage vehicles, ventilation system for safety and efficient movement of people and material. This method is risky. Poisonous gases, fires, floods lead to fatal accidents.

The developed economies are retreating from **mining, processing and refining** stages of production due to high labour costs and developing countries with large labour force are striving for higher standard of living. Several countries of Africa and few of south America and Asia have over **fifty per cent of the earnings** from minerals alone.

Agriculture in India: Cropping Seasons

There are three distinct crop seasons in the northern and interior parts of the country, namely **kharif, Rabi and Zaid.**

Kharif Season

It largely coincides with **Southwest Monsoon** in different parts of the country and these are harvested in **September-October**. Important crops grown during this season are paddy, maize, jowar, bajra, tur (arhar), moong, urad, cotton, jute, groundnut and soybean.

Rabi Season

The rabi season begins with the onset of **Winter** in **October-November** and ends in **March-April**. The low temperature conditions during this season facilitate the cultivation of **Temperate and Subtropical Crops** such as wheat, barley, peas, gram and mustard. Availability of precipitation during winter months due to the **western temperate cyclones** helps in the success of these crops.

Zaid Season

It is a **short duration Summer** cropping season beginning after harvesting of rabi crops. The cultivation of watermelons, cucumbers, vegetables and fodder crops during this season is done on irrigated lands.

However, this type of distinction in the cropping season **does not exist in southern parts** of the country. Here, the temperature is high enough to grow tropical crops during any period of the year provided the soil moisture is available. Therefore, in this region **same crops can be grown thrice in an agricultural year** provided there is sufficient soil moisture.

Cropping Season	Major Crops Cultivated	
	Northern States	Southern States
Kharif June-September	Rice, Cotton, Bajra, Maize, Jowar, Tur	Rice, Maize, Ragi, Jowar, Groundnut
Rabi October- March	Wheat, Gram, Rapeseeds, Mustard and Barley	Rice, Maize, Ragi, Groundnut, Jowar
Zaid April-June	Vegetables, Fruits, Fodder	Rice, Vegetables, Fodder

Cropping Seasons in India

Types of Farming

On the basis of the main source of moisture for crops, farming can be classified as **Irrigated and Rainfed (barani).**

Irrigated Farming

- Irrigated Farming can be divided into two parts based on the objective of irrigation, i.e., **protective or productive**.
- The objective of **Protective Irrigation** is to protect the crops from adverse effects of soil moisture deficiency which often means that irrigation acts as a supplementary source of water over and above the rainfall. The strategy of this kind of irrigation is to provide soil moisture to the maximum possible area.
- **Productive Irrigation** is meant to provide sufficient soil moisture in the cropping season to achieve high productivity. In such irrigation the water input per unit area of cultivated land is higher than protective irrigation.

Rainfed Farming

Rainfed farming is further classified on the basis of adequacy of soil moisture during cropping season into dryland and wetland farming.

- The **Dryland Farming** is largely confined to the regions having annual rainfall less than 75 cm. These regions grow **hardy and drought resistant crops** such as ragi, bajra, moong, gram and guar (fodder crops) and practice various measures of soil moisture conservation and rainwater harvesting.
- In **Wetland Farming**, the rainfall is in excess of soil moisture requirements of plants during the rainy season. Such regions may face **Flood and Soil Erosion hazards**. These areas grow various water intensive crops such as rice, jute and sugarcane and practice **aquaculture** in the freshwater bodies.

Food Grains

The importance of foodgrains in the Indian agricultural economy may be gauged from the fact these crops occupy about two-third of total cropped area in the country. **On the basis of the structure of grain the foodgrains are classified as Cereals and Pulses.**

Cereals

- The cereals occupy about **54 per cent of total cropped area** in India.
- The country produces about 11 percent of the world and ranks **third in production** after **China and the U.S.A.**
- India produces a variety of cereals, which are classified as **Fine Grains (rice, wheat) and coarse grains (jowar, bajra, maize, ragi), etc.**

Rice

- Rice is a staple food for the overwhelming majority of the population in India. Though it is considered to be a crop of **Tropical Humid** areas, it has about 3,000 varieties which are grown in different **agro-climatic regions.**
- It is a **kharif crop** which requires **high temperature (above 25°C) and high humidity** with **annual rainfall above 100 cm.** In the areas of less rainfall, it grows with the help of irrigation.
- It grows best in alluvial clayey soil, which can retain water.
- These are successfully grown from sea level to about 2,000 m altitude and from humid areas in eastern India to dry but irrigated areas of **Punjab, Haryana, western U.P. and northern Rajasthan.**
- In southern states and West Bengal, the climatic conditions allow the cultivation of two or three crops of rice in an agricultural year.
- In West Bengal, farmers grow three crops of rice called **'aus'**, **'aman'** and **'boro'**.
- In Himalayas and northwestern parts of the country, it is grown as a kharif crop during the southwest Monsoon season.

- **About one-fourth of the total cropped area** in the country is under rice cultivation.
- **West Bengal, Uttar Pradesh, and Punjab** are the leading rice producing states in the country.
- The yield level of rice is high in **Punjab, Tamil Nadu, Haryana, Andhra Pradesh, Telangana, West Bengal and Kerala.**
- Punjab and Haryana are not traditional rice growing areas. Rice cultivation in the irrigated areas of Punjab and Haryana was introduced in 1970s following the Green Revolution.
- **India contributes 22.07 per cent of rice production** in the world and **ranked second after China** in 2018.

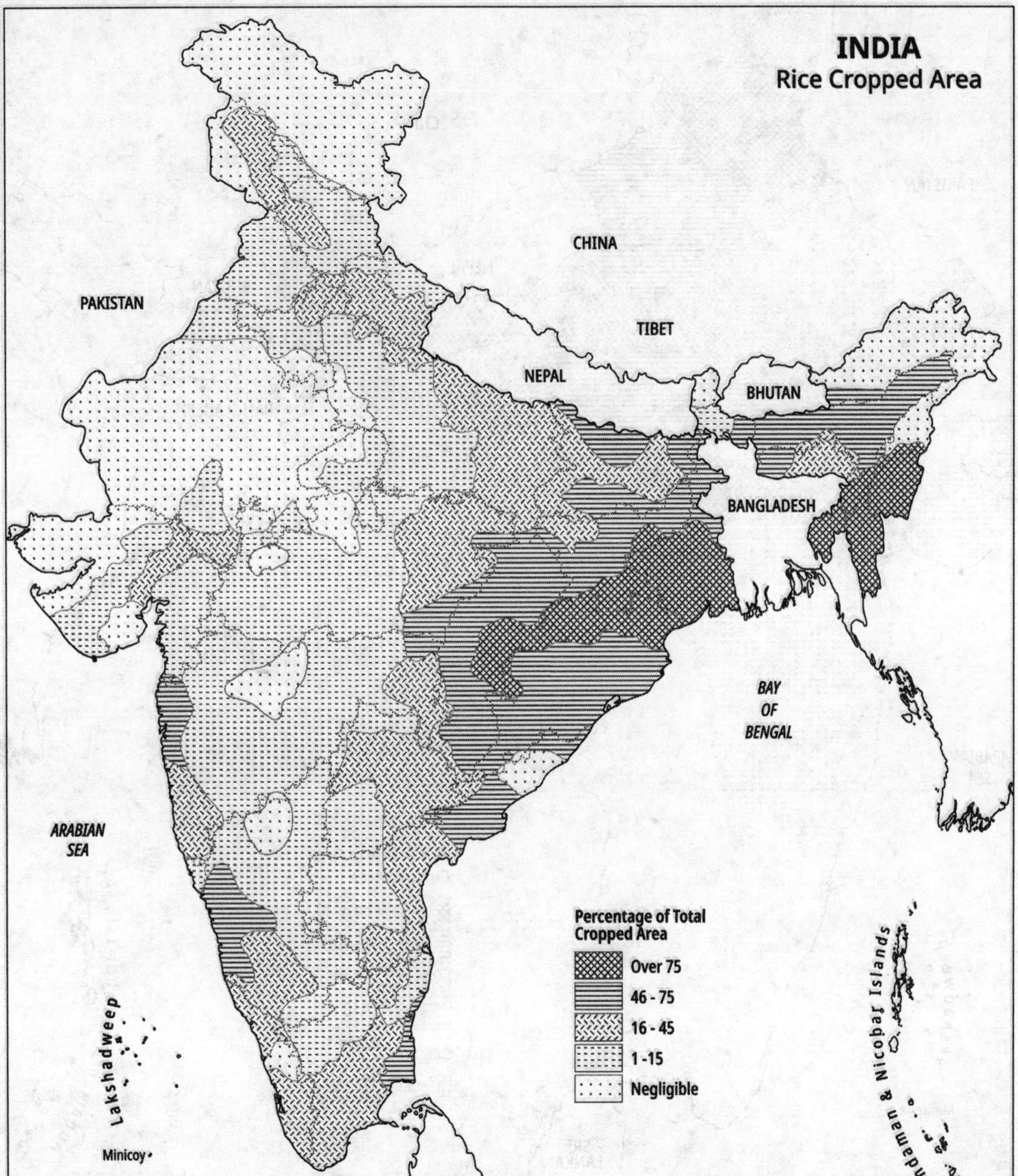

India: Distribution of Rice

Wheat

- **Wheat** is the second most important cereal crop in India after rice. India produces about 12.8 per cent of the world's total wheat production (2017).

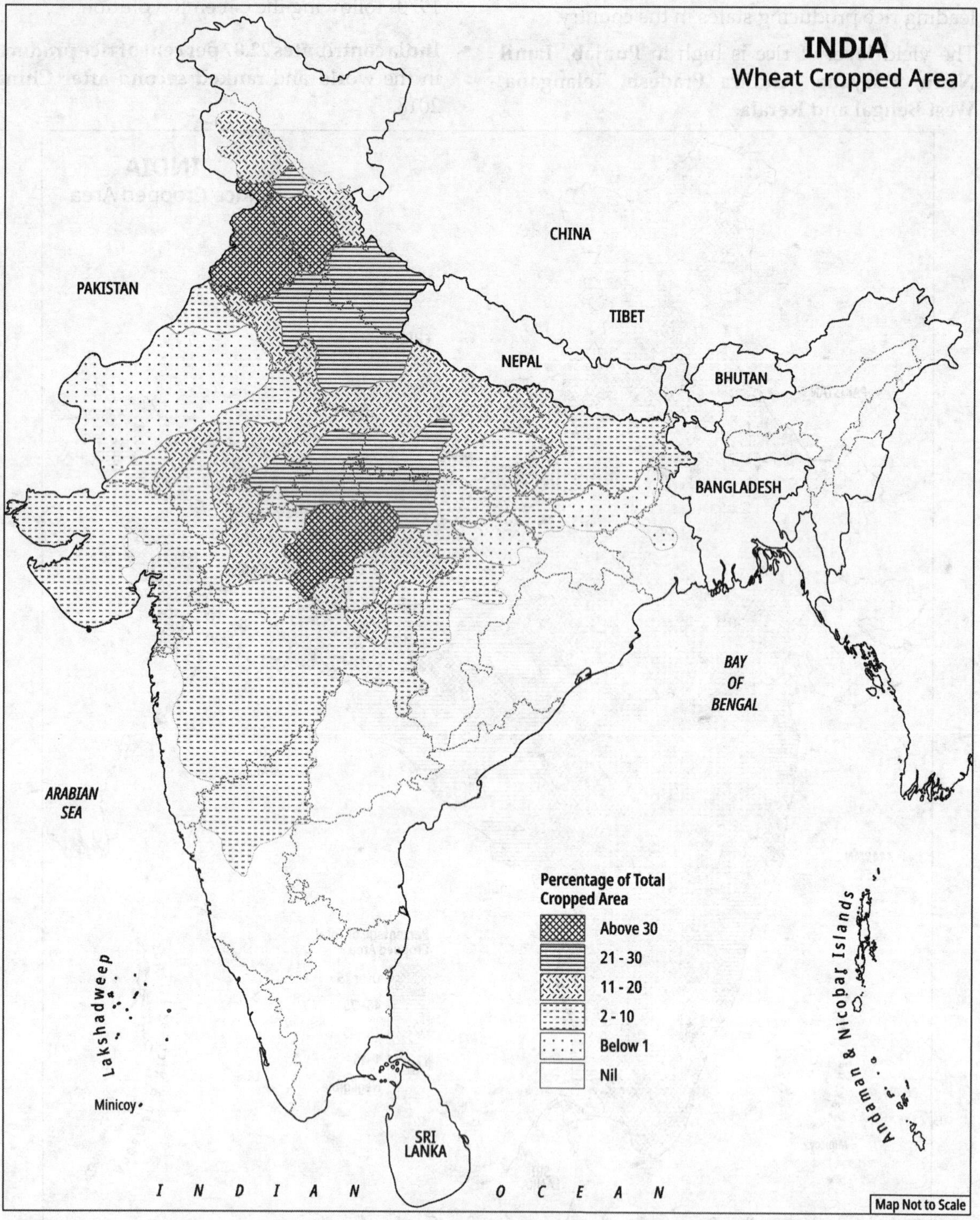

India: Distribution of Wheat

- It is primarily a crop of **Temperate** zone. Hence, its cultivation in India is done during winter i.e. **rabi season.**
- This crop requires a **cool growing season and bright sunshine** at the time of ripening. It requires **50 to 75 cm of annual rainfall** evenly- distributed over the growing season.
- About **85 percent of total area** under this crop is concentrated in north and central regions of the country i.e., Indo- Gangetic Plain, Malwa Plateau and Himalayas up to 2,700 m altitude.
- **Being a rabi crop**, it is mostly grown under irrigated conditions. But it is a rainfed crop in Himalayan highlands and parts of Malwa plateau in Madhya Pradesh.
- About **14 per cent of the total cropped area** in the country is under wheat cultivation.
- **Uttar Pradesh, Madhya Pradesh, Punjab, Haryana and Rajasthan** are leading wheat producing states.
- The yield level of wheat is very high (above 4,000 k.g. per ha) in Punjab and Haryana whereas Uttar Pradesh, Rajasthan and Bihar have moderate yields.
- Apart from India, it is extensively grown in **USA, Canada, Argentina, Russia, Ukraine, Australia.**

Jowar

- The **Coarse Cereals** together occupy about **16.50 per cent of total cropped area** in the country.
- Among these, **jowar or sorghum** alone accounts for about **5.3 per cent of total cropped area.**
- It is **main food crop** in semi-arid areas of central and southern India. Maharashtra alone produces **more than half of the total jowar production of the country.**
- Other leading producer states of jowar are **Karnataka, Madhya Pradesh, Andhra Pradesh and Telangana.**
- **It is sown in both kharif and rabi seasons in southern states.** But it is a **kharif crop in northern India where it is mostly grown as a fodder crop.**
- South of Vindhyachal it is a rainfed crop and its yield level is very low in this region.

Bajra

- **Bajra** is sown in **hot and dry** climatic conditions in northwestern and western parts of the country.
- Bajra grows well on sandy soils and shallow black soil.
- It is a hardy crop which resists frequent **dry spells and drought** in this region.
- It is cultivated alone as well as part of mixed cropping. This coarse cereal occupies about **5.2 per cent of total cropped area** in the country.
- Leading producers of bajra are the states of Maharashtra, Gujarat, Uttar Pradesh, Rajasthan and Haryana.
- Being a rainfed crop, the yield level of this crop is low in Rajasthan and fluctuates a lot from year to year.

Ragi

- **Ragi** is a crop of **dry** regions and grows well on red, black, sandy, loamy and shallow black soils.
- Major ragi producing states are: **Karnataka, Tamil Nadu, Himachal Pradesh, Uttarakhand, Sikkim, Jharkhand and Arunachal Pradesh.**

Maize

- **Maize** is a food as well as **fodder crop** grown under **Semi-Arid** climatic conditions and over **inferior soils.**
- This crop occupies only about **3.6 per cent of total cropped area.**
- It is a **kharif crop** which requires temperature between **21°C to 27°C** and grows well in old **alluvial soil.** In some states like Bihar maize is grown in rabi season also.
- Maize cultivation is not concentrated in any specific region. It is sown all over India except Punjab and eastern and north-eastern regions.
- The leading producers of maize are the states of **Karnataka, Madhya Pradesh, Bihar, Andhra**

Pradesh, Telangana, Rajasthan and Uttar Pradesh.

- Yield level of maize is higher than other coarse cereals. It is high in southern states and declines towards central parts.
- In the world it is grown in **North America, Brazil, China, Russia, Canada, and Mexico.**

Pulses

- **Pulses** are a very important ingredient of vegetarian food as these are rich sources of proteins.
- These are legume crops which increase the natural fertility of soils through nitrogen fixation.
- **India is a leading producer of pulses in the world.**
- The cultivation of pulses in the country is largely concentrated in the **drylands of Deccan and central plateaus and northwestern** parts of the country.
- Pulses occupy about **11 per cent of the total cropped area** in the country.
- Being the rainfed crops of drylands, the yields of pulses are low and fluctuate from year to year. **Gram** and **tur** are the main pulses cultivated in India.

Gram

- **Gram** is cultivated in **Subtropical areas.** It is mostly a rainfed crop cultivated during rabi season in central, western and northwestern parts of the country.
- Just one or two light showers are required to grow this crop successfully.
- It has been displaced from the cropping pattern by wheat in **Haryana, Punjab and northern Rajasthan** following the green revolution.
- At present, gram covers only about **2.8 per cent of the total cropped area** in the country.
- **Madhya Pradesh, Uttar Pradesh, Maharashtra, Andhra Pradesh, Telangana and Rajasthan** are the main producers of this pulse crop.

Tur (Arhar)

- **Tur** is the second important pulse crop in the country. It is also known as **red gram** or **pigeon pea.**
- It is cultivated over marginal lands and under rainfed conditions in the dry areas of central and southern states of the country.
- This crop occupies only about **2 percent of the total cropped area** of India.
- **Maharashtra alone contributes about one-third** of the total production of tur.
- Other leading producer states are **Uttar Pradesh, Karnataka, Gujarat and Madhya Pradesh.**
- Per hectare output of this crop is very low and its performance is inconsistent.

Food Crops other than Grains

Sugarcane

- **Sugarcane** is a crop of **Tropical areas.** Under rainfed conditions, it is cultivated in sub-humid and humid climates. But it is **largely an irrigated crop** in India.
- In the Indo-Gangetic plain, its cultivation is largely concentrated in Uttar Pradesh. Uttar Pradesh produces about **two-fifth of sugarcane** of the country.
- Sugarcane growing area in western India is spread over Maharashtra and Gujarat.
- In southern India, it is cultivated in irrigated tracts of **Karnataka, Tamil Nadu, Telangana and Andhra Pradesh.**
- **India was the second largest producer of sugarcane after Brazil in 2018.** It accounts for about 19.7 percent of the world production of sugarcane. But it occupies only 2.4 per cent of total cropped area in the country.
- The yield level of sugarcane is high in southern India. Its yield is low in northern India.

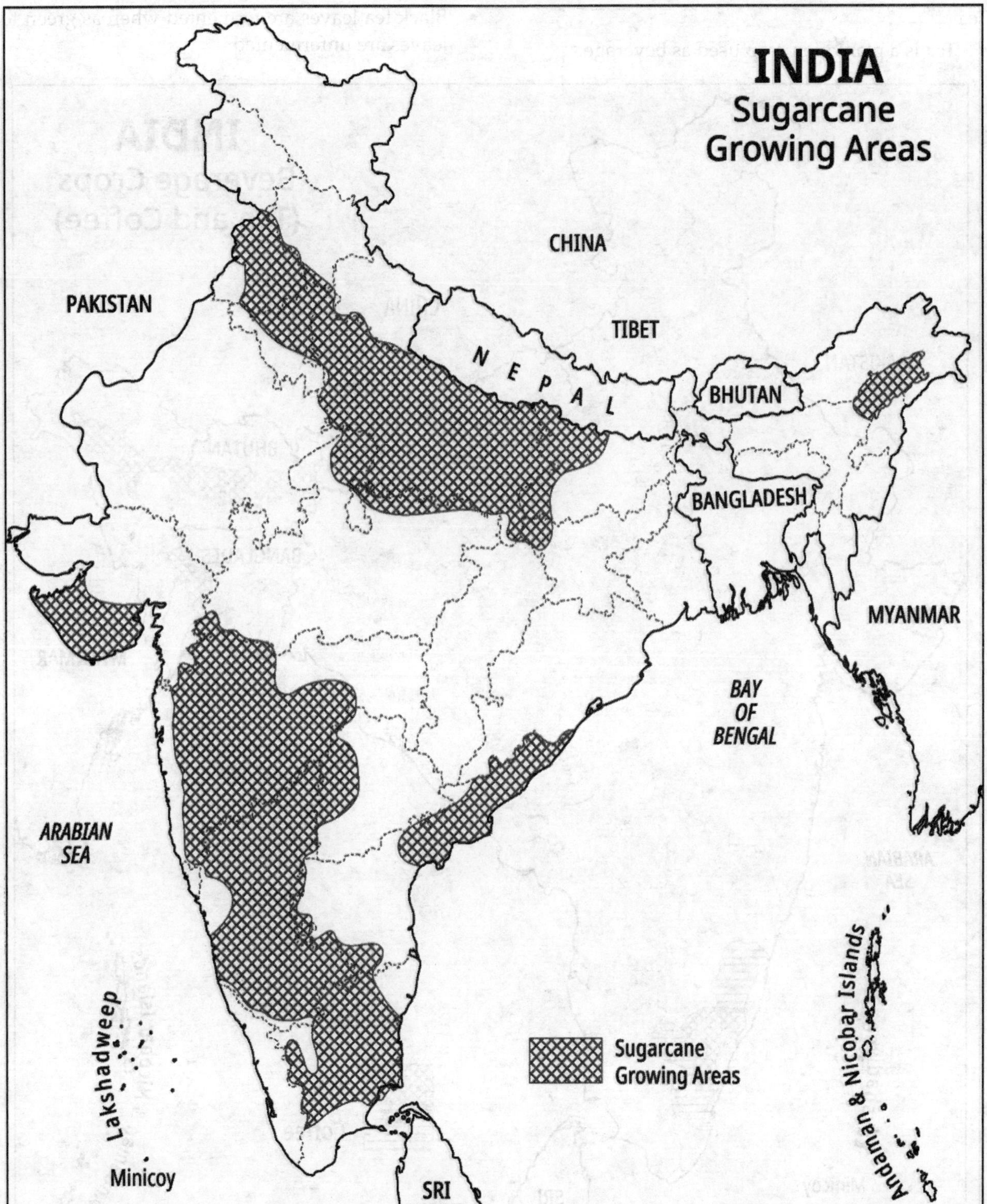

India: Distribution of Sugarcane

Tea

- **Tea** is a plantation crop used as beverage.
- Black tea leaves are fermented whereas green tea leaves are unfermented.

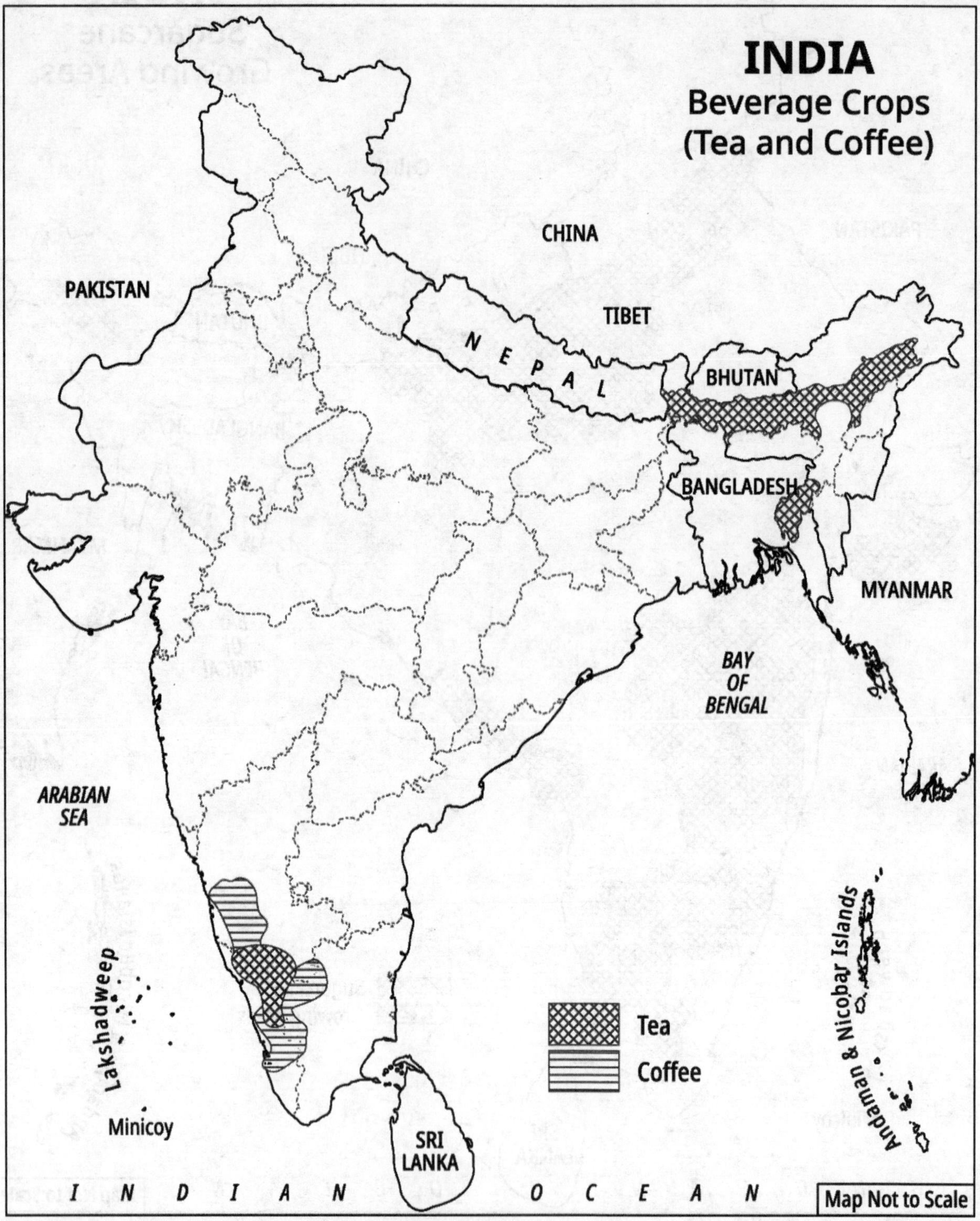

India: Distribution of Tea and Coffee

- Tea leaves have rich content of caffeine and tannin.
- It is an indigenous crop of hills in northern China.
- The tea plant grows well in **Tropical and Sub-Tropical climates** endowed with deep and fertile well-drained soil, rich in humus and organic matter.
- Tea bushes require warm and moist, frost-free climate all through the year. Frequent showers evenly distributed over the year ensure continuous growth of tender leaves.
- In India, tea plantations started in the 1840s in Brahmaputra valley of Assam which still is a major tea growing area in the country.
- Later on, its plantation was introduced in the sub-Himalayan region of **West Bengal (Darjeeling, Jalpaiguri and Cooch Behar districts).**
- Tea is also cultivated on the **lower slopes of Nilgiri.**
- **Assam** accounts for about 53.2 per cent of the total cropped area and contributes more than half of total production of tea in the country.
- **West Bengal and Tamil Nadu** are the other leading producers of tea.
- **Kenya, India, China, Sri Lanka** produce the best quality tea in the world.

Coffee

- **Coffee** is a tropical plantation crop. Coffee requires a warm and wet climate and well- drained loamy soil. Hill slopes are more suitable for the growth of this crop.
- Coffee is a beverage brewed from the roasted and ground seeds.
- **There are three varieties of coffee** i.e., **arabica, robusta** and **liberica**. The Arabica variety initially brought from Yemen.
- India mostly grows superior quality coffee, arabica, which is in great demand in the international market.
- But **India produces only about 3.17 percent coffee of the world and ranks eighth after Brazil, Vietnam, Indonesia, Colombia, Honduras, Ethiopia and Peru in 2018.**
- Coffee is cultivated in the highlands of Western Ghats in **Karnataka, Kerala and Tamil Nadu.**
- **Karnataka alone accounts for more than two-third** of total production of coffee in the country.

Oilseeds

- The **oilseeds** are produced for extracting edible oils. Drylands of Malwa plateau, Marathwada, Gujarat, Rajasthan, Telangana, Rayalaseema region of Andhra Pradesh and Karnataka plateau are oilseeds growing regions of India.
- These crops together **occupy about 14 percent of the total cropped area in the country. Groundnut, rapeseed and mustard, soyabean and sunflower** are the main oilseed crops grown in India.

Groundnut

- India produces about 18.8 per cent of the total groundnut production of the world. It is largely a **rainfed kharif** crop of drylands. But in southern India, it is cultivated during rabi season as well.
- It covers about 3.6 per cent of total cropped area in the country. Gujarat, Rajasthan, Tamil Nadu, Telangana, Andhra Pradesh, Karnataka and Maharashtra are the leading producers.
- Yield of groundnut is comparatively high in Tamil Nadu where it is partly irrigated. But its yield is low in Telangana, Andhra Pradesh and Karnataka.
- In 2018 India was the **second largest producer of groundnut** in the world after China.

Rapeseed and Mustard

- **Rapeseed and mustard** comprises several oilseed such as **rai, sarson, toria and taramira**. These are subtropical crops cultivated during rabi season in north-western and central parts of India.
- These are **frost sensitive crops** and their yields fluctuate from year to year. But with the expansion of irrigation and improvement in seed technology, their yields have improved and stabilised to some extent.
- About two-third of the cultivated area under these crops is irrigated. These oilseeds together occupy only about 2.5 percent of total cropped area in the country.
- Rajasthan contributes about one-third production while other leading producers are Haryana and Madhya Pradesh. Yields of these crops are comparatively high in Haryana and Rajasthan.

- In rapeseed production **India was third largest producer in the world after Canada and China in 2018.**

Other Oilseeds

- **Soyabean and sunflower** are other important oilseeds grown in India. Soyabean is mostly grown in Madhya Pradesh and Maharashtra. These two states together produce about 90 per cent of total output of soyabean in the country.

- **Sunflower** cultivation is concentrated in Karnataka, Andhra Pradesh, Telangana and adjoining areas of Maharashtra. It is a minor crop in northern parts of the country where its yield is high due to irrigation.

Horticulture Crops

- In 2018, India was the second largest producer of fruits and vegetables in the world after China. India is a producer of tropical as well as temperate fruits.

- Mangoes of Maharashtra, Andhra Pradesh, Telangana, Uttar Pradesh and West Bengal, oranges of Nagpur and Cherrapunji (Meghalaya), bananas of Kerala, Mizoram, Maharashtra and Tamil Nadu, lichi and guava of Uttar Pradesh and Bihar, pineapples of Meghalaya, grapes of Andhra Pradesh, Telangana and Maharashtra, apples, pears, apricots and walnuts of Jammu and Kashmir and Himachal Pradesh are in great demand the world over.

Non-Food Crops

Rubber

- It is an equatorial crop, but under special conditions, it is also grown in tropical and sub-tropical areas.

- It requires a moist and humid climate with rainfall of more than 200 cm. and temperature above 25°C.

- Rubber is an important **industrial raw material.** It is mainly grown in Kerala, Tamil Nadu, Karnataka, Andaman and Nicobar Islands and Garo hills of Meghalaya.

Fibre Crops

These crops provide us fibre for preparing cloth, bags, sacks and a number of other items. Cotton, jute, hemp and natural silk are the four major fibre crops grown in India. The first three are derived from the crops grown in the soil, the latter is obtained from cocoons of the silkworms fed on green leaves especially mulberry. Rearing of silk worms for the production of silk fibre is known as **sericulture.**

Cotton

- **Cotton** is a tropical crop grown in **kharif season** in semi-arid areas of the country. India lost a large proportion of cotton growing area to Pakistan during partition.

- However, its acreage has increased considerably during the last 50 years. India grows both **short staple (Indian) cotton as well as long staple (American) cotton called 'narma'** in north-western parts of the country. Cotton requires a clear sky during the flowering stage.

- India ranks **second in the world** in the production of cotton after China. Cotton occupies about 4.7 per cent of total cropped area in the country.

- Cotton grows well in drier parts of the **black cotton soil** of the Deccan plateau. It requires **high temperature, light rainfall or irrigation, 210 frost-free days and bright sun-shines** for its growth. It requires 6 to 8 months to mature.

- There are **three cotton growing areas**, i.e. parts of Punjab, Haryana and northern Rajasthan in north-west, Gujarat and Maharashtra in the west and plateaus of Andhra Pradesh, Karnataka and Tamil Nadu in south.

- Leading producers of this crop are Gujarat, Maharashtra and Telangana. Per hectare output of cotton is high under irrigated conditions in north-western region of the country. Its yield is very low in Maharashtra where it is grown under rainfed conditions.

- In the world, the U.S, China, Pakistan, Brazil and Egypt are the leading producers of cotton.

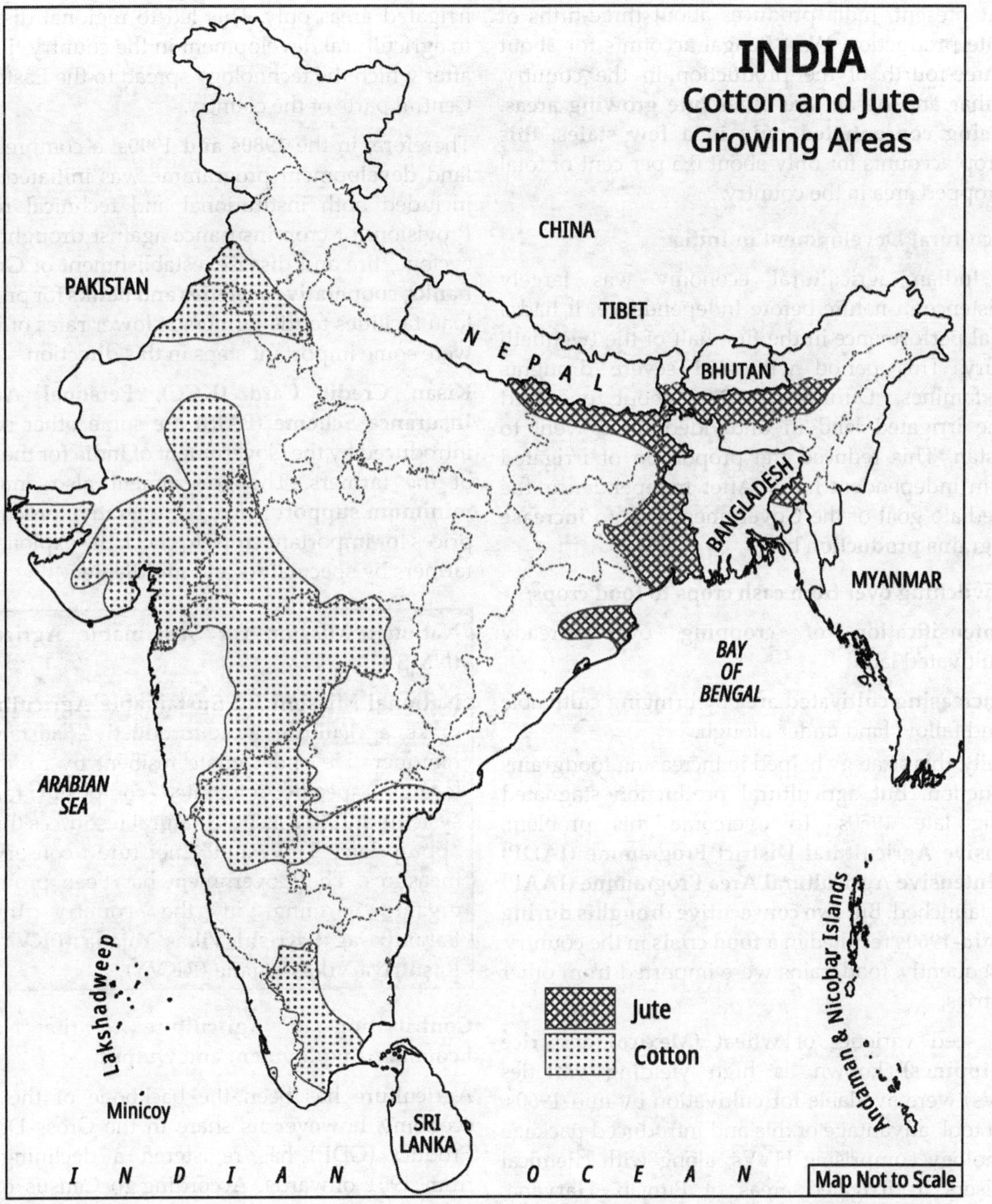

India: Distribution of Cotton and Jute

Jute

- **It is known as the golden fibre**. Jute grows well on **well-drained fertile soils** in the flood plains where soils are renewed every year.
- Jute is used for making coarse cloth, bags, sacks and decorative items. Due to its **high cost,** it is losing market to synthetic fibres and packing materials, particularly the nylon.
- It is a cash crop in West Bengal and adjoining eastern parts of the country. India lost large jute growing areas to East Pakistan (Bangladesh) during partition.

- At present, India produces about three-fifths of jute production. West Bengal accounts for about three-fourth of the production in the country. Bihar and Assam **are other jute growing areas. being concentrated only in a few states, this** crop accounts for only about 0.5 per cent of total cropped area in the country.

Agricultural Development in India

The Indian agricultural economy was largely subsistence in nature before Independence. It had a dismal performance in the first half of the twentieth century. This period witnessed severe droughts and famines. During partition about one-third of the irrigated land in undivided India went to Pakistan. This reduced the proportion of irrigated area in Independent India. After Independence, the immediate goal of the Government was to **increase foodgrains production** by:

- **Switching over from cash crops to food crops;**
- **Intensification of cropping** over already cultivated land;
- **Increasing cultivated area** by bringing cultivable and fallow land under plough.

Initially, this strategy helped in increasing foodgrains production. But agricultural production stagnated during late 1950s. To overcome this problem, **Intensive Agricultural District Programme (IADP) and Intensive Agricultural Area Programme (IAAP)** were launched. But **two consecutive droughts during the mid-1960s** resulted in a **food crisis** in the country. Consequently, foodgrains were imported from other countries.

New seed varieties of **wheat (Mexico)** and **rice (Philippines)** known as high yielding varieties (HYVs) were available for cultivation by mid-1960s. India took advantage of this and introduced package technology comprising HYVs, along with chemical fertilisers in irrigated areas of Punjab, Haryana, Western Uttar Pradesh, Andhra Pradesh and Gujarat. This strategy of agricultural development paid dividends instantly and increased the foodgrains production at a fast rate. This spurt of agricultural growth came to be known as **'Green Revolution'.**

This strategy of agricultural development made the country self-reliant in foodgrain production. But the Green Revolution was initially confined to irrigated areas only. This led to regional disparities in agricultural development in the country till 1970s, after which the technology spread to the Eastern and Central parts of the country.

Therefore, in the **1980s and 1990s**, a comprehensive land development programme was initiated, which included both institutional and technical reforms. Provision for crop insurance against drought, flood, cyclone, fire and disease, establishment of **Grameen banks, cooperative societies and banks** for providing loan facilities to the farmers at lower rates of interest were some important steps in this direction.

Kisan Credit Card (KCC), Personal Accident Insurance Scheme (PAIS) are some other schemes introduced by the Government of India for the benefit of the farmers. The government also announces **minimum support price,** remunerative procurement prices for important crops to check the exploitation of farmers by speculators and middlemen.

National Mission for Sustainable Agriculture (NMSA)

National Mission for Sustainable Agriculture to make agriculture more productive, sustainable, remunerative and climate resilient by promoting location specific integrated/composite farming systems and to conserve natural resources through appropriate soil and moisture conservation measures. The Government has been promoting organic farming in the country through **Paramparagat Krishi Vikas Yojana (PKVY) and Rashtriya Vikas Yojana (RKVY).**

Contribution of Agriculture to the National Economy, Employment and Output

Agriculture has been the backbone of the Indian economy, however its share in the Gross Domestic Product (GDP) has registered a declining trend from 1951 onwards. According to Census of India 2011, about **54.6 percent of the total work force** was engaged in agriculture and allied sector activities which makes more than half of the Indian population dependent on agriculture for sustenance.

The declining share of agriculture in the GDP is a **matter of serious concern** because any decline in agriculture will lead to a decline in other spheres of the economy having wider implications for society. In order to strengthen and support agricultural sector, several initiatives have been taken by government of India under the **Atma Nirbhar Bharat Abhiyan**.

Growth of Agricultural Output and Technology

There has been a significant increase in agricultural output and improvement in technology during the last 50 years.

- Production and yield of many crops, such as **Rice and Wheat,** have increased at an impressive rate. Among the other crops, the production of sugarcane, oilseeds and cotton has also increased appreciably.
- **Expansion of irrigation** has played a crucial role in enhancing agricultural output in the country. It provided basis for introduction of modern agricultural technology, such as high yielding varieties of **seeds, chemical fertilisers, pesticides and farm machinery**. The net irrigated area in the country has also increased.
- **Modern agricultural technology** has diffused very fast in various areas of the country. Consumption of chemical fertilisers has increased by 15 times since mid-sixties. Since the high yielding varieties are highly susceptible to pests and diseases, the use of pesticides has increased significantly since 1960s.

Impact of Globalisation on Agriculture

- **Globalisation** is not a new phenomenon. It was there at the time of colonisation. In the nineteenth century when European traders came to India, at that time too, Indian spices were exported to different countries of the world and farmers of south India were encouraged to grow these crops. Till today it is one of the important items of export from India.
- **During the British period cotton belts of India attracted the British** and ultimately cotton was exported to Britain as a raw material for their textile industries. Cotton textile industry in Manchester and Liverpool flourished due to the availability of good quality cotton from India.
- Under globalisation, particularly after **1990**, the farmers in India have been exposed to new challenges. Despite being an important producer of rice, cotton, rubber, tea, coffee, jute and spices our agricultural products are not able to compete with the developed countries because of the highly subsidised agriculture in those countries.
- **Today, Indian agriculture finds itself at the crossroads.** To make agriculture successful and profitable, proper thrust should be given to the improvement of the condition of marginal and small farmers. The Green Revolution promised much. It is being alleged that it has caused land degradation due to overuse of chemicals, drying aquifers and vanishing biodiversity.
- A few economists think that Indian farmers have a bleak future if they continue growing foodgrains on the holdings that grow smaller and smaller as the population rises. India's **rural population** is about 833 million (2011) which depends upon 250 million (approximate) hectares of agricultural land, an **average of less than half a hectare per person.**
- **Indian farmers should diversify their cropping pattern** from **cereals to high-value crops**. This will increase incomes and reduce environmental degradation simultaneously. **Fruits, medicinal herbs, flowers, vegetables, bio-diesel crops** like **jatropha and jojoba** need much less irrigation than rice or sugarcane. India's diverse climate can be harnessed to grow a wide range of high-value crops.

Problems of Indian Agriculture

The nature of problems faced by Indian agriculture varies according to **agro-ecological and historical experiences** of its different regions. Hence, most of the agricultural problems in the country are region specific. Yet, there are some problems which are common and range from physical constraints to institutional hindrances. A detailed discussion on these problems is as follows:

Dependence on Erratic Monsoon

- Irrigation covers only about **33 per cent of the cultivated area** in India. The crop production in the rest of the cultivated land directly depends on rain.
- Poor performance of south-west monsoon also adversely affects the supply of canal water for irrigation. On the other hand, the rainfall in Rajasthan and other drought- prone areas is **too meagre and highly unreliable.**

- Even the areas receiving high annual rainfall experience considerable fluctuations. This makes them vulnerable to both **droughts and floods**.
- Drought is a common phenomenon in the low rainfall areas, which may also experience occasional floods. The **Flash Floods** in drylands of **Maharashtra, Gujarat and Rajasthan** in 2006 and 2017 are examples of this phenomenon. Droughts and floods continue to be the twin menace in Indian agriculture.

Low Productivity

- Per hectare output of most of the crops such as **rice, wheat, cotton and oilseeds** in India is much lower than that of **USA, Russia and Japan**.
- Because of high pressure on land resources, the labour productivity in Indian agriculture is also very low in comparison to other countries.
- The vast rainfed areas of the country, particularly drylands which mostly grow **coarse cereals, pulses and oilseeds** have low yields.

Constraints of Financial Resources and Indebtedness

- The inputs of modern agriculture are very expensive. This resource intensive approach has become unmanageable for marginal and small farmers as they have very meagre or no savings to invest in agriculture.
- To tide over these difficulties, most of such farmers have resorted to availing credit from various institutions and moneylenders. Crop failures and low returns from agriculture have forced them to fall in the trap of indebtedness.

Lack of Land Reforms

- Indian peasantry had been exploited for a long time as there had been unequal distribution of land. Among the three revenue systems operational during the British period, i.e., **Mahalwari, Ryotwari and Zamindari,** the last one was most exploitative for the peasants.
- After Independence, land reforms were accorded priority, but these reforms were not implemented effectively due to lack of strong political will.
- Most of the state governments avoided taking politically tough decisions which went against strong political lobbies of landlords.
- Lack of implementation of land reforms has resulted in continuation of iniquitous distribution of cultivable land which is detrimental to agricultural development.

Small Farm Size and Fragmentation of Landholdings

- There are a large number of marginal and small farmers in the country. The average size of land holding is **shrinking under increasing population pressure**.
- Furthermore, in India, the land holdings are mostly fragmented. There are some states where consolidation of holding has not been carried out even once.
- Even in the states where it has been carried out once, **second consolidation is required** as land holdings have fragmented again in the process of division of land among the owners of the next generations. The small size of **fragmented landholdings is uneconomic**.

Lack of Commercialisation

- A large number of farmers produce crops for self-consumption. These farmers do not have enough land resources to produce more than their requirement.
- Most of the small and marginal farmers grow foodgrains, which are meant for their own family consumption. **Modernisation and commercialisation** of agriculture have, however, taken place in the irrigated areas.

Vast Underemployment

- There is a massive underemployment in the agricultural sector in India, particularly in the unirrigated tracts. In these areas, there is **seasonal unemployment** ranging from 4 to 8 months.
- Even in the cropping season, work is not available throughout as agricultural operations are labour intensive. Hence, the people engaged in agriculture do not have the opportunity to work round the year.

Degradation of Cultivable Land

- One of the serious problems that arises out of **faulty strategy** of irrigation and agricultural development is **degradation of land resources**. It may lead to depletion of soil fertility. The situation is particularly alarming in irrigated areas.

- A large tract of agricultural land has lost its fertility due to **alkalisation, salinisation of soils and waterlogging**. Excessive use of chemicals such as **insecticides and pesticides** has led to their concentration in toxic amounts in the soil profile.
- **Leguminous crops** have been displaced from the cropping pattern in the irrigated areas and duration of fallow has substantially reduced owing to **multiple cropping**. This has obliterated the process of **natural fertilisation** such as nitrogen fixation.
- Rainfed areas in **Humid and Semi-Arid Tropics** also experience degradation of several types like soil erosion by water and wind erosion which are often induced by human activities.

Bhoodan – Gramdan

Mahatma Gandhi declared Vinoba Bhave as his spiritual heir. He also participated in Satyagraha as one of the foremost satyagrahis. He was one of the votaries of Gandhi's concept of **Gram Swarajya**. After Gandhi's martyrdom, Vinoba Bhave undertook padyatra to spread Gandhiji's message. Once, when he was delivering a lecture at Pochampalli in Andhra Pradesh, some poor landless villagers demanded some land for their economic well-being. Vinoba Bhave could not promise it to them immediately but assured them to talk to the Government of India regarding provision of land for them if they undertook cooperative farming. Suddenly, Shri Ram Chandra Reddy stood up and offered 80 acres of land to be distributed among 80 land-less villagers. This act was known as **'Bhoodan'**. Later he travelled and introduced his ideas widely all over India. Some zamindars, owners of many villages offered to distribute some villages among the landless. It was known as **Gramdan**. However, many land-owners chose to provide some part of their land to the poor farmers due to the fear of land ceiling act. This Bhoodan-Gramdan movement initiated by **Vinoba Bhave** is also known as the **Blood-less Revolution.**

TEST YOURSELF

Multiple Choice Questions

Q1. Which of the following activities belongs to the primary sector?

(a) Manufacturing automobiles

(b) Banking and finance

(c) Farming

(d) Software development

Q2. The primary sector is primarily concerned with:

(a) Extracting and utilising natural resources

(b) Processing raw materials into finished goods

(c) Providing services to consumers

(d) Conducting research and development activities

Q3. Which of the following is an example of primary sector activity?

(a) Operating a call-centre

(b) Building construction

(c) Fishing

(d) Teaching in a school

Q4. Which of the following best defines the primary sector?

(a) It involves the production of goods using machinery and technology.

(b) It involves the extraction of raw materials from nature.

(c) It involves the distribution and exchange of goods and services.

(d) It involves the provision of financial and banking services.

Q5. Which of the following is not an example of primary sector activity?

(a) Mining coal from underground mines

(b) Cultivating crops on a farm

(c) Manufacturing clothing in a factory

(d) Drilling for oil in offshore locations

Q6. Which sector forms the base for all other sectors of the economy?

(a) Primary sector (b) Secondary sector

(c) Tertiary sector (d) Quaternary sector

Q7. Which of the following is an example of a primary sector occupation?

(a) Civil engineering

(b) Software programming

(c) Mining engineer

(d) Marketing manager

Q8. In which sector do forestry and logging activities belong?

(a) Primary sector (b) Secondary sector

(c) Tertiary sector (d) Quaternary sector

Q9. Which of the following activities is not associated with the primary sector?

(a) Animal husbandry

(b) Quarrying of stones

(c) Advertising and promotion

(d) Fishing in a river

Q10. Which sector is characterised by a direct interaction with nature?

(a) Primary sector (b) Secondary sector

(c) Tertiary sector (d) Quaternary sector

Q11. Which of the following is the main occupation of the majority of people in India?

(a) Fishing (b) Mining

(c) Agriculture (d) Manufacturing

Q12. The practice of growing crops and raising livestock on a large scale for commercial purposes is known as:

(a) Subsistence farming

(b) Commercial farming

(c) Mixed farming

(d) Shifting cultivation

Q13. Which of the following is a traditional method of irrigation where water is supplied to the fields by a series of small channels?

(a) Sprinkler irrigation

(b) Drip irrigation

(c) Canal irrigation

(d) Rainwater harvesting

Q14. The process of growing crops without the use of synthetic fertilisers and pesticides is known as:

(a) Organic farming (b) Hydroponics

(c) Greenhouse farming (d) Agroforestry

Q15. The cultivation of a single crop on a large scale is known as:

(a) Monocropping (b) Poly cropping

(c) Mixed cropping (d) Crop rotation

Q16. The practice of shifting agricultural activities from one area to another in search of fertile land is known as:

(a) Terrace farming

(b) Plantation farming

(c) Shifting cultivation

(d) Commercial farming

Q17. The process of rearing animals for milk, meat, wool, and other products is known as:

(a) Horticulture (b) Poultry farming

(c) Animal husbandry (d) Sericulture

Q18. The method of irrigation that involves providing water to plants drop by drop near their roots is known as:

(a) Sprinkler irrigation (b) Drip irrigation

(c) Canal irrigation (d) Tube well irrigation

Q19. The practice of growing fruits, vegetables, and flowers in controlled environments such as greenhouses is known as:

(a) Horticulture (b) Poultry farming

(c) Animal husbandry (d) Sericulture

Q20. Among the following, which one is the least water-efficient crop? (UPSC 2021)

(a) Sugarcane (b) Sunflower

(c) Pearl millet (d) Red gram

Q21. In the context of India, which of the following is/are considered to be a practice(s) of eco-friendly agriculture?

1. Crop diversification
2. Legume intensification
3. Tensiometer use
4. Vertical farming

Select the correct answer using the code given below:

(a) 1, 2 and 3 only (b) 3 only

(c) 4 only (d) 1, 2, 3 and 4

Q22. With reference to pulse production in India, consider the following statements: (UPSC 2020)

1. Black gram can be cultivated as both Kharif and rabi crops.
2. Green gram alone accounts for nearly half of the pulse production.
3. In the last three decades, while the production of Kharif pulses has increased, the production of rabi pulses has decreased.

Which of the statements given above is/are correct?

(a) 1 only (b) 2 and 3 only

(c) 2 only (d) 1, 2 and 3

Answer Key

Q1.	c	Q2.	a	Q3.	c	Q4.	b
Q5.	c	Q6.	a	Q7.	c	Q8.	a
Q9.	c	Q10.	a	Q11.	c	Q12.	b
Q13.	c	Q14.	a	Q15.	a	Q16.	c
Q17.	c	Q18.	b	Q19.	a	Q20.	a
Q21.	d	Q22.	a				

Model Questions for Main Examination

Q1. What are the major factors responsible for making the rice-wheat system a success? In spite of this success, how has this system become a bane in India? (UPSC-2020)

Q2. What is water-use efficiency? Describe the role of micro-irrigation in increasing water-use efficiency. (UPSC-2018)

UNIT 28

Secondary Activities

In This Unit

Comprehensive and profound coverage of the following NCERTs' chapters:

- ✓ NCERT Class- 8th (Resources and Development), Chapter- 4
- ✓ NCERT Class- 10th (Contemporary India-II), Chapter- 6
- ✓ NCERT (Before Rationalisation) Class- 12th (India-People and Economy), Chapter- 8
- ✓ NCERT Class- 12th (Fundamentals of Human Geography), Chapter- 5

All economic activities namely primary, secondary, tertiary and quaternary, revolve around obtaining and utilising resources necessary for survival. **Secondary activities add value to natural resources by transforming raw materials into valuable products.** Cotton in the boll has limited use but after it is transformed into yarn, becomes more valuable and can be used for making clothes. Iron ore cannot be used; directly from the mines, but after being converted into steel it gets its value and can be used for making many valuable machines, tools, etc. The same is true of most of the materials from the farm, forest, mine and the sea. Secondary activities, therefore, are concerned with manufacturing, processing and construction (infrastructure) industries.

Manufacturing

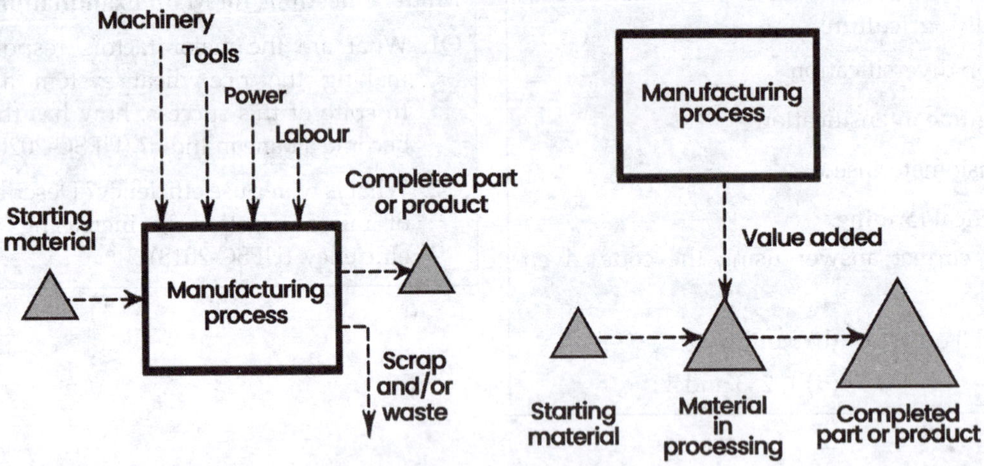

Manufacturing

- Manufacturing involves a full array of production from handicrafts to moulding iron and steel and stamping out plastic toys to assembling delicate computer components or space vehicles.
- In each of these processes, the common characteristics are the **application of power, mass production** of identical products and **specialised labour in factory settings** for the production of **standardised commodities.**

- Manufacturing may be done with modern power and machinery or it may still be very primitive. More emphasis is given to the kind of 'industrial' activity which involves less complicated systems of production.

Characteristics of Modern Large Scale, Manufacturing

Modern large scale, manufacturing has the following characteristics:

Specialisation of Skills/Methods of Production

Under the 'craft' method factories produce only a few pieces which are made-to-order. So the costs are high. On the other hand, mass production involves production of large quantities of standardised parts by each worker performing only one task repeatedly.

Mechanisation

Mechanisation refers to using gadgets which accomplish tasks. Automation (without aid of human thinking during the manufacturing process) is the advanced stage of mechanisation. Automatic factories with feedback and closed-loop computer control systems where machines are developed to 'think', have sprung up all over the world.

Technological Innovation

Technological innovations through research and development strategy are an important aspect of modern manufacturing for quality control, eliminating waste and inefficiency, and combating pollution.

Organisational Structure and Stratification

Modern manufacturing is characterised by:

- A complex machine technology
- Extreme specialisation and division of labour for producing more goods with less effort, and low costs
- Vast capital
- Large organisations
- Executive bureaucracy.

Uneven Geographic Distribution

Major concentrations of modern manufacturing have flourished in a few numbers of places. These cover less than 10 per cent of the world's land area. These nations have become the centres of economic and political power. However, in terms of the total area covered, manufacturing sites are much less conspicuous and concentrated on much smaller areas than that of agriculture due to greater intensity of processes. For example, 2.5 sq. km of the American corn belt usually includes about four large farms employing about 10-20 workers supporting 50-100 persons. But this same area could contain several large integrated factories and employ thousands of workers.

Industry and 'Manufacturing Industry'

Manufacturing literally means 'to make by hand'. However, now it includes goods 'made by Machines'. It is essentially a process which involves transforming raw materials into finished goods of higher value for sale in local or distant markets. Conceptually, an industry is a geographically located manufacturing unit maintaining books of accounts and, records under a management system. As the term **industry is comprehensive, it is also used as synonymous with 'manufacturing'** When one uses terms like 'steel industry' and 'chemical industry' one thinks of factories and processes. But there are many secondary activities which are not carried on in factories such as what is now called the 'entertainment industry' and Tourism industry, etc.

Manufacturing Industries in India and the World

Production of goods in large quantities after processing from raw materials to more valuable products is called **manufacturing**. People employed in the secondary activities manufacture the primary materials into finished goods. The workers employed in steel factories, car, breweries, textile industries, bakeries etc. fall into this category. **The economic strength of a country is measured by the development of manufacturing industries.**

Importance of Manufacturing

Manufacturing sector is considered the backbone of development in general and economic development in particular mainly because:

- Manufacturing industries not only help in modernising agriculture, which forms the backbone of our economy, they also reduce the heavy dependence of people on agricultural income by providing them jobs in secondary and tertiary sectors.
- Industrial development is a precondition for eradication of unemployment and poverty from our country. This was the main philosophy behind public sector industries and joint sector ventures in India. It was also aimed at bringing down regional disparities by establishing industries in tribal and backward areas.
- Export of manufactured goods expands trade and commerce, and brings in much needed foreign exchange.
- Countries that transform their raw materials into a wide variety of finished goods of higher value are prosperous.

Contribution of Industry to National Economy

- Over the last two decades, the share of the **manufacturing sector has stagnated at 17 percent** of GDP–out of a **total of 27 percent of the industry** which includes 10 per cent for mining, quarrying, electricity and gas. This is much **lower in comparison to some East Asian economies**, where it is 25 to 35 per cent.
- Since 2003, manufacturing is once again growing at the rate of 9 to 10 per cent per annum.

Location of Industries

Location of industries is influenced by several factors like access to raw materials, power, market, capital, transport and labour, etc. Relative significance of these factors varies with time and place. There is a strong relationship between raw material and type of industry. It is economical to locate the manufacturing industries at a place where cost of production and delivery cost of manufactured goods to consumers are the least. Transport costs, to a great extent, depend on the nature of raw materials and manufactured products. A brief description of factors influencing the location of industries are given below:

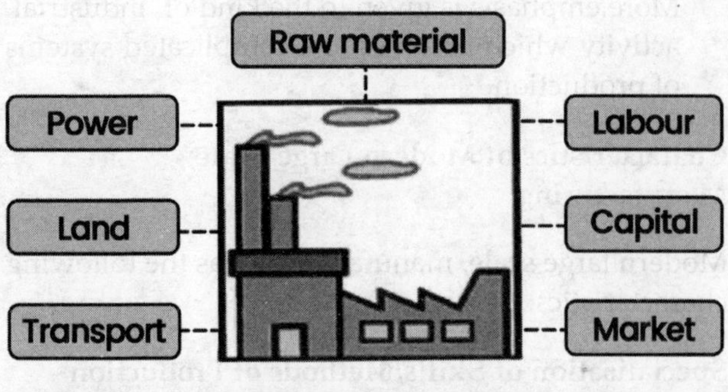

Locational Factors for Industries

Raw Materials

- Raw material used by industries should be cheap and easy to transport. Industries using weight-losing raw materials are located in the regions where raw materials are located. Similarly, the locations of pulp industry, copper smelting and pig iron industries are located near their raw materials.
- **In iron and steel industries,** iron ore and coal both are weight-losing raw materials. Therefore, an optimum location for iron and steel industries should be near raw material sources. This is why most of the iron and steel industries are located either near coalfields (Bokaro, Durgapur, etc.) or near sources of iron ore (Bhadravati, Bhilai, and Rourkela).
- Similarly, industries **based on perishable raw materials** are also located close to raw material sources. Agro-processing and dairy products are processed close to the sources of farm produce or milk supply respectively.

Power

- **Power** provides the motive force for machines, and therefore, its supply has to be ensured before the location of any industry.
- However, certain industries, like **aluminium and synthetic nitrogen manufacturing industries** tend to be located near sources of power because they are power intensive and require a huge quantum of electricity.

Market

- **Market** means people who have a demand for these goods and also have the purchasing power to be able to purchase from the sellers at a place. Remote areas inhabited by a few people offer small markets.
- Markets provide the outlets for manufactured products. Heavy machine, machine tools, heavy chemicals are located near the high demand areas as these are market orientated.
- **Cotton textile industry** uses a **non-weight-losing raw material** and is generally located in large urban centre, e.g., **Mumbai, Ahmedabad, Surat**, etc.
- **Petroleum refineries** are also located near the markets as the transport of crude oil is easier and several products derived from them are used as raw material in other industries. **Koyali, Mathura and Barauni** refineries are typical examples. Ports also play a crucial role in the location of oil refineries.
- In the world, developed regions of **Europe, North America, Japan and Australia** provide large global markets as the purchasing power of the people is very high. The densely populated regions of South and South-east Asia also provide large markets. Some industries, such as aircraft manufacturing, have a global market. The arms industry also has global markets.

Transport

- Speedy and efficient transport facilities to carry raw materials to the factory and to move finished goods to the market are essential for the development of industries. The cost of transport plays an important role in the location of industrial units.
- In the world, **Western Europe and eastern North America** have a highly developed transport system which has always induced the concentration of industries in these areas.
- Modern industry is inseparably tied to transportation systems. Improvements in transportation led to integrated economic development and regional specialisation of manufacturing.

Labour

- **Labour supply** is an important factor in the location of industries. Some types of manufacturing still require skilled labour. Increasing mechanisation, automation and flexibility of industrial processes have reduced the dependence of industry upon labour.
- In India, labour is quite mobile and is available in large numbers due to our large population.

Government Policy

- Governments adopt 'regional policies' to promote 'balanced' economic development and hence set up industries in particular areas.
- Establishment of iron and steel industry in Bhilai and Rourkela were based on decision to develop backward tribal areas of the country. At present, the government of India provides lots of incentives to industries in backward areas.

Access to Agglomeration Economies/ Links between Industries

- Many industries benefit from nearness to a leader-industry and other industries. These are termed as agglomeration economies. Savings are derived from the linkages which exist between different industries.

Historical Factors

- The reasons for Mumbai, Kolkata and Chennai emerging as industrial nodes is that these locations were greatly influenced by our colonial past. During the initial phase of colonisation, manufacturing activities received new impetus provided by the European traders. Places like Murshidabad, Bhadohi, Surat, Vadodara, Kozhikode, Coimbatore, Mysuru etc., emerged as important manufacturing centres.
- In the subsequent industrial phase of colonialism, these manufacturing centres experienced rapid growth due to competition from the goods manufactured in Britain and the discriminatory policies of colonial power.
- In the last phase of colonialism, the British promoted few industries in selected areas. This led to larger spatial coverage by different types of industries in the country.

Footloose Industries

Footloose industries can be located in a wide variety of places. They are not dependent on any specific raw material, weight losing or otherwise. They largely depend on component parts which can be obtained anywhere. They produce in small quantities and also employ a small labour force. These are generally not polluting industries. The important factor in their location is accessibility by road network.

Classification of Industries

Manufacturing industries are classified on the basis of their **size, inputs/raw materials, output/products and ownership.**

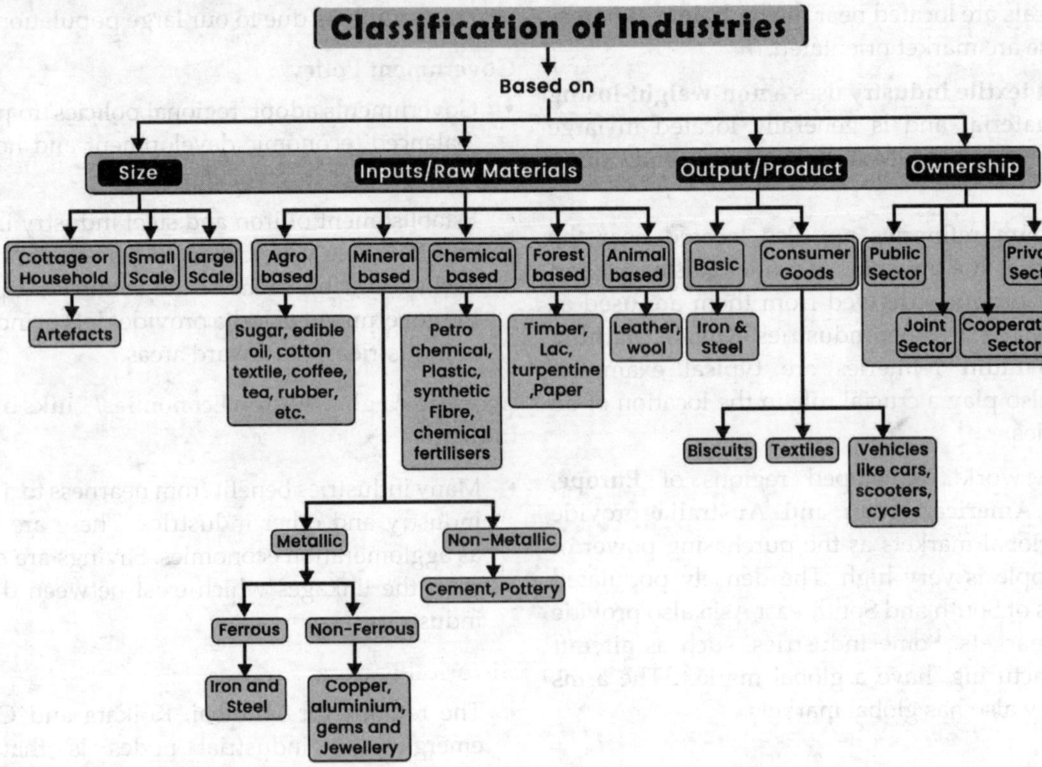

Industries Based on Size

The amount of capital invested, number of workers employed and volume of production determine the size of industry. Accordingly, industries may be classified into household or cottage, small-scale and large-scale.

Household Industries or Cottage Manufacturing

- It is the smallest manufacturing unit. The artisans use local raw materials and simple tools to produce everyday goods in their homes with the help of their family members or part- time labour.
- Finished products may be for consumption in the same household or, for sale in local (village) markets, or, for barter.
- Capital and transportation **do not wield** much influence as this type of manufacturing has low commercial significance and most of the tools are devised locally.
- Some common everyday products produced in this sector of manufacturing include foodstuffs, fabrics, mats, containers, tools, furniture, shoes, and figurines from wood lot and forest, shoes etc.

Small Scale Manufacturing

- Small scale manufacturing is distinguished from household industries by its production techniques and place of manufacture (a workshop outside the home/ cottage of the producer).

- This type of manufacturing uses local raw material, simple power-driven machines and semi-skilled labour.
- It provides employment and raises local purchasing power.
- Countries like India, China, Indonesia and Brazil, etc. have developed labour-intensive small-scale manufacturing in order to provide employment to their population.

Large Scale Manufacturing

- Large scale manufacturing involves a large market, various raw materials, enormous energy, specialised workers, advanced technology, assembly-line mass production and large capital.
- This kind of manufacturing developed in the last 200 years, in the United Kingdom, north-eastern USA and Europe. Now it has diffused to almost all over the world.

On the basis of the system of large-scale manufacturing, the world's major industrial regions may be grouped under two broad types, namely:

1. traditional large-scale industrial regions which are thickly clustered in a few more developed countries.
2. high-technology large scale industrial regions which have diffused to less developed countries.

Industries Based on Inputs/Raw Materials

On the basis of the raw materials used, the industries are classified as: **(a) agro-based; (b) mineral based; (c) chemical based; (d) forest based: and (e) animal based.**

(a) Agro-based Industries

Agro processing involves the processing of raw materials from the field and the farm into finished products for rural and urban markets. Major agro-processing industries are food processing, sugar, pickles, fruits juices, beverages (tea, coffee and cocoa), spices and oils, fats and textiles (cotton, jute, silk), rubber, etc.

(b) Mineral-based Industries

These industries use **minerals as a raw material.** Some industries use ferrous metallic minerals which contain ferrous (iron), such as iron and steel industries but some use non-ferrous metallic minerals, such as aluminium, copper and jewellery industries. Many industries use non-metallic minerals such as cement and pottery industries.

(c) Chemical-based Industries

Such industries use natural chemical minerals, e.g., mineral-oil (petroleum) is used in Petro Chemical industry. Salts, sulphur and potash industries also use natural minerals. Chemical industries are also based on raw materials obtained from wood and coal. Synthetic fibre, plastic, etc. are other examples of chemical-based industries.

(d) Forest-based Raw Material using Industries

The forests provide many major and minor products which are used as raw material. Timber for furniture industry, wood, bamboo and grass for paper industry, lac for lac industries come from forests.

(e) Animal-based Industries

Leather for the leather industry and wool for woollen textiles are obtained from animals. Besides, ivory is also obtained from elephant's tusks.

Industries Based on Output/Product

- Some machines and tools are made of iron or steel. The raw material for such machines and tools is iron and steel. Which is itself an industry. The industry whose products are used to make other goods by using them as raw materials are **Basic Industries.**
- The consumer goods industries produced goods which are consumed by consumers directly. For example, industries producing breads and biscuits, tea, soaps and toiletries, paper for writing, televisions, etc. are consumer goods or **Non-Basic Industries.**

Industries Based on Ownership

- **Public Sector Industries** are owned and managed by governments. In India, there were a number of Public Sector Undertakings (PSUs). Socialist countries have many state-owned industries. **Mixed economies have both Public and Private sector enterprises**. Examples- BHEL, SAIL etc.
- **Private Sector Industries** are owned by individual investors. These are managed by private

organisations. In capitalist countries, industries are generally owned privately. Examples- TISCO, Bajaj Auto Ltd., Dabur Industries.

- **Joint Sector Industries** are managed by joint stock companies or sometimes the private and public sectors together establish and manage the industries. Oil India Ltd. (OIL) is jointly owned by public and private sector.
- **Cooperative sector industries** are owned and operated by the producers or suppliers of raw materials, workers or both. They pool in the resources and share the profits or losses proportionately. Such examples are the **sugar industry in Maharashtra, the coir industry in Kerala.**

Major Industries

Agro-Based Industries

Textile Industry: The textile industry occupies a unique position in the Indian economy, because it contributes significantly to industrial production, employment generation and foreign exchange earnings.

Cotton Textiles:

The cotton textile industry is one of the traditional industries of India. In ancient India, cotton textiles were produced with hand spinning and handloom weaving techniques. After the 18th century, power-looms came into use. India was famous worldwide for the production of muslin, a very fine variety of **cotton cloth, calicos, chintz** and other different varieties of fine cotton cloth.

Cotton is a **'pure' raw material** which **does not lose weight** in the manufacturing process so other factors, like, power to drive the looms, labour, capital or market may determine the location of the industry. At present, the trend is to locate the industry at or close to markets, as it is the market that decides what kind of cloth is to be produced. Also, the market for the finished products is extremely variable, therefore, it becomes important to locate the mills close to the market.

- **Development of Textile Industry in India**
  - ➢ One, it is a tropical country and cotton is the most comfortable fabric for a hot and humid climate.
  - ➢ Second, large quantity of cotton was grown in India.
  - ➢ Abundant skilled labour required for this industry was available in this country.
- **Role of Britishers**
  - ➢ Initially, the British did not encourage the development of the indigenous cotton textile industry. They exported raw cotton to their mills in **Manchester and Liverpool** and brought back the finished products to be sold in India.
  - ➢ Our traditional industries suffered a setback during the colonial period because they could not compete with the mill-made cloth from England.

In the early years, the cotton textile industry was concentrated in the cotton growing belt of Maharashtra and Gujarat. In **1854**, the first modern cotton mill was established in Mumbai. This city had several advantages as a cotton textile manufacturing centre. They are as follows:

- It was very close to the cotton producing areas of **Gujarat and Maharashtra**. Raw cotton used to be brought to Mumbai port to be transported to England.
- Mumbai even then was the financial centre and the capital needed to start an industry was available there.
- As a large town, providing employment opportunities attracted labour in large numbers. Hence, cheap and abundant labour too was available locally.
- The machinery required for a cotton textile mill could be directly imported from England.

Subsequently, **two more mills, the Shahpur Mill and the Calico Mill were established in Ahmedabad**. By 1947, the number of mills in India went up to 423 but the scenario changed after partition, and this industry suffered a major recession. This was due to the fact that the most of the good quality cotton growing areas had gone to West Pakistan and India was left with 409 mills and only 29 per cent of the cotton producing area.

After Independence, this industry gradually recovered and eventually flourished.

The **cotton textile industry in India** can be **broadly divided into two sectors**, the **organised sector and the unorganised sector**. The **unorganised or decentralised sector** includes cloth produced in handlooms (including Khadi) and power looms. The production of the organised sector has drastically fallen from 81 per cent in the mid-twentieth century to only about 6 per cent in 2000. At present, the power looms in the decentralised sector produce more than the handloom sector.

After the first mills were set up in Mumbai and Ahmedabad in the second half of the nineteenth century, the cotton textile industry expanded very rapidly. The number of units increased dramatically. The **Swadeshi movement** gave a major impetus to the industry as there was a call for boycotting all British made goods in favour of Indian goods. After 1921, with the development of the railway network other cotton textile centres expanded rapidly.

Distribution

- In **southern India,** mills were set up at Coimbatore, Madurai and Bengaluru. In **central India,** Nagpur, Indore, Solapur and Vadodara became cotton textile centres.
- **Cotton textile mills** were set up at Kanpur based on local investment. Mills were also set up at Kolkata due to its port facilities.
- The development of **hydro-electricity** also favoured the location of the cotton textile mills away from the cotton producing areas. The rapid development of this industry in **Tamil Nadu** is the result of the abundant availability of hydel power for the mills.
- Lower labour costs at centres like **Ujjain, Bharuch, Agra, Hathras, Coimbatore and Tirunelveli** also caused industries to be located away from cotton producing areas.
- Presently, the major centres of the **cotton textile industry** are **Ahmedabad, Bhiwandi, Solapur, Kolhapur, Nagpur, Indore and Ujjain**. All these centres are the traditional centres and are located close to the cotton producing regions.
- **Maharashtra, Gujarat and Tamil Nadu** are the leading cotton producing states. **West Bengal, Uttar Pradesh, Karnataka, and Punjab** are the other important cotton textile producers.
- **Tamil Nadu has the largest number of mills** and most of them produce yarn rather than cloth. Coimbatore has emerged as the most important centre with nearly half the mills located there. **Chennai, Madurai, Tirunelveli, Tuticorin, Thanjavur, Ramanathapuram and Salem** are the other important centres.
- In Karnataka, the cotton textile industry has developed in the cotton producing areas in the north-eastern part of the state. **Davangere, Hubballi, Ballari, Mysuru and Bengaluru** are important centres.
- The cotton textile industry is located in the cotton producing Telengana region, where most of the mills are spinning mills producing yarn. The important centres are **Hyderabad, Secunderabad and Warangal in Telangana and Guntur in Andhra Pradesh.**
- In Uttar Pradesh, **Kanpur** is the largest centre. Some of the other important centres are **Modinagar, Hathras, Saharanpur, Agra and Lucknow.**
- In West Bengal, the cotton mills are located in the **Hugli region.** Howrah, Serampore, Kolkata and Shyamnagar are the important centres.

India has world class production in spinning, but weaving supplies **low quality of fabric** as it cannot use much of the high-quality yarn produced in the country. India exports yarn to **Japan**. Other importers of cotton goods from India are **USA, UK, Russia, France, East European countries, Nepal, Singapore, Sri Lanka, and African countries**. There are some large and modern factories in these segments, but most of the production is in fragmented small units, which cater to the local market. **This mismatch is a major drawback for the industry.**

Why is it important for us to improve our weaving sector instead of exporting yarn in large quantities?

Although, we have made significant increase in the production of **good quality long staple cotton**, the need to import is still felt. **Power supply is erratic and machinery needs to be upgraded** in the weaving and processing sectors in particular. Other problems are the low output of labour and stiff competition with the synthetic fibre industry.

Important Textile Centres

Ahmedabad:

- It is located in Gujarat on the banks of the Sabarmati River. The first mill was established in this city in 1861. It soon became the second largest textile city of India, after Mumbai. Ahmedabad was therefore often referred to as the 'Manchester of India.'
- Favourable locational factors were responsible for the development of the textile industry in Ahmedabad. Ahmedabad is situated very close to cotton growing area. This ensures easy availability of raw material. The climate is ideal for spinning and weaving. The flat terrain and easy availability of land is suitable for the establishment of the mills.
- The densely populated states of Gujarat and Maharashtra provide both skilled and semi-skilled labour. Well developed, road and railway network permit easy transportation of textiles to different parts of the country, thus providing easy access to the market. Mumbai port nearby facilitates import of machinery and export of cotton textiles.
- But in the recent years, Ahmedabad textile mills have been having some problems. Several textile mills have closed down. This is primarily due to the emergence of new textile centers in the country as well as non-upgradation of machines and technology in the mills of Ahmedabad.

Osaka:

- It is an important textile center of Japan which is also known as the 'Manchester of Japan'. The textile industry developed in Osaka due to several geographical factors. The extensive plain around Osaka ensured that land was easily available for the growth of cotton mills.
- Warm humid climate is well suited to spinning and weaving. The river Yodo provides sufficient water for the mills. Labour is easily available. Location of port facilitates import of raw cotton and for exporting textiles.
- The textile industry at Osaka depends completely upon imported raw materials. Cotton is imported from Egypt, India, China and USA. The finished product is mostly exported and has a good market due to good quality and low price.
- Though it is one of the important textile cities in the country, of late, the cotton textile industry of Osaka has been replaced by other industries, such as iron and steel, machinery, shipbuilding, automobiles, electrical equipment and cement.

Important facts

- The **first textile mill** in the country was established at **Fort Gloster near Kolkata in 1818** but it closed down after some time.
- The first successful textile mill was established in Mumbai in 1854.
- The two World Wars were fought in Europe, India was a British colony. There was a demand for cloth in UK hence, they gave a boost to the development of the cotton textile industry.
- About one-third of the Indian textile industry's total production is exported.

Jute Textiles

India is the largest producer of raw jute and jute goods and stands at second place as an exporter after Bangladesh. Most of the mills are located in West Bengal, mainly along the banks of the Hugli River, in a narrow belt. **Factors responsible for their location in the Hugli basin are:**

- Inexpensive water transport.
- A good network of railways, roadways and waterways to facilitate movement of raw material to the mills.
- Abundant water for processing raw jute.
- Cheap labour from West Bengal and adjoining states of Bihar, Odisha and Uttar Pradesh.
- Kolkata as a large urban centre provides banking, insurance and port facilities for export of jute goods.

Challenges faced by the industry include stiff competition in the international market from synthetic substitutes and from other competitors like **Bangladesh, Brazil, Philippines, Egypt and Thailand.** However, the internal demand has been on the rise due to the Government policy of mandatory use of jute packaging. To stimulate demand, the products need to be diversified. The main markets are **USA, Canada, Ghana, Saudi Arabia, UK and Australia**. The growing global concern for environment friendly, biodegradable materials, has once again opened the opportunity for jute products.

The first jute mill was set up near Kolkata in 1855 at Rishra. After Partition in 1947, the jute mills remained in India but three-fourth of the jute producing area went to Bangladesh (erstwhile East Pakistan).

Sugar Industry

The sugar industry is the second most important agro-based industry in the country. **India is the largest producer of both sugarcane and cane sugar** and contributes about 8 percent of the total sugar production in the world. Besides, **Khandasari and Gur or Jaggery** are also prepared from sugarcane. This industry provides employment for more than 4 lakh persons directly and a large number of farmers indirectly. Sugar industry is a seasonal industry because of the seasonality of raw materials.

Development of the industry on modern lines dates back to 1903, when a sugar mill was started in Bihar. Subsequently, sugar mills were started in other parts of Bihar and Uttar Pradesh. In 1950-51, 139 factories were in operation. The number of sugar factories rose to 662 in 2010-11.

Location of the Sugar Industry

Sugarcane is a weight-losing crop. The ratio of sugar to sugarcane varies between 9 to 12 per cent depending on its variety. Its **sucrose content begins to dry during haulage** after it has been harvested from the field. Better recovery of sugar is dependent upon it being crushed within 24 hours of its harvesting. Sugar factories hence, are located within the cane producing regions.

Distribution

- **Maharashtra** has emerged as a leading sugar producer in the country and produces more than one-third of the total production of the sugar in the country.
- **Uttar Pradesh** is the second largest producer of sugar. The **sugar factories are concentrated in two belts – the Ganga-Yamuna doab and the tarai region**. The major sugar producing centres in the Ganga -Yamuna doab is Saharanpur, Muzaffarnagar, Meerut, Ghaziabad, Baghpat and Bulandshahr districts; while Lakhimpur Kheri, Basti, Gonda, Gorakhpur, Bahraich are important sugar producing districts in the Tarai region.
- **In Tamil Nadu**, sugar factories are located in Coimbatore, Vellore, Tiruvannamalai, Villupuram and Tiruchchirappalli districts. Belagavi, Ballari, Mandya, Shivamogga, Vijayapura and Chitradurg districts are the major producers in Karnataka. The industry is distributed in the coastal regions i.e., East Godavari, West Godavari, Visakhapatnam districts of Andhra Pradesh and Nizamabad and Medak districts of Telangana.
- The other States which produce sugar are **Bihar, Punjab, Haryana, Madhya Pradesh and Gujarat. Saran, Champaran, Muzaffarpur, Siwan, Darbhanga, and Gaya** are the important sugarcane producing districts in **Bihar**.
- **The relative significance of Punjab has declined**, although Gurdaspur, Jalandhar, Sangrur, Patiala and Amritsar are major sugar producers.
- In **Haryana,** sugar factories are located in **Yamuna Nagar, Rohtak, Hisar and Faridabad** districts.
- Sugar industry is comparatively new in **Gujarat**. Sugar mills are located in the cane growing tracts of **Surat, Junagarh, Rajkot, Amreli, Valsad and Bhavnagar** districts.

In recent years, there is a tendency for the mills to shift and concentrate in the southern and western states, especially in Maharashtra. This, is because the cane produced here has a higher sucrose content. The cooler climate also ensures a longer crushing season. Moreover, the cooperatives are more successful in these states.

Major Challenges

The seasonal nature of the industry, old and inefficient methods of production, transport delay in reaching cane to factories and the need to maximise the use of baggase.

Mineral-Based Industries

The Iron and Steel Industry

- The **iron and steel industry** forms the base of all other industries and, therefore, it is called a **basic industry**. It is basic because it provides raw material for other industries such as machine tools used for further production. It may also be called a **heavy industry because it uses large quantities of bulky raw materials and its products are also heavy.**

- Iron is extracted from iron ore by smelting in a blast furnace with carbon (coke) and limestone. The molten iron is cooled and moulded to form pig iron which is used for converting iron into steel by adding strengthening materials like manganese.

Smelting: It is the process in which metals are extracted from their ores by heating beyond the melting point.

- The other raw materials besides iron ore and coking coal, essential for iron and steel industry are limestone, dolomite, manganese and fire clay. All these raw materials are weight losing, therefore, the best location for the iron and steel plants is near the source of raw materials.
- In **India**, there is a crescent shaped region comprising **parts of Chhattisgarh, Northern Odisha, Jharkhand and western West Bengal,** which is extremely rich in high grade iron ore, good quality coking coal and other supplementing raw materials.
- The Indian iron and steel industry consists of large integrated steel plants as well as mini steel mills. It also includes **secondary producers, rolling mills and ancillary industries.**
- In India, **Chota Nagpur Plateau** region has the maximum concentration of iron and steel industries. It is largely, because of the relative advantages this region has for the development of this industry. These include **low cost of iron ore, high grade raw materials in proximity, cheap labour** and vast growth potential in the home market.
- **Distribution**: The industry is one of the most **complex and capital-intensive industries** and is concentrated in the advanced countries of **North America, Europe and Asia.**
  - ➢ In **USA,** most of the production comes from the **north Appalachian region (Pittsburgh), Great Lake region (Chicago-Gary, Erie, Cleveland, Lorain, Buffalo and Duluth) and the Atlantic Coast (Sparrows Point and Morissville).**
  - ➢ The industry has also moved towards the southern state of **Alabama. Pittsburgh** area is now losing ground. It has now become the **"Rust Bowl"** of USA
  - ➢ In **Europe**, the **UK, Germany, France, Belgium, Luxembourg, the Netherlands and Russia** are the leading producers.
  - ➢ The important steel producing areas are **Scunthorpe, Port Talbot, Birmingham and Sheffield in the UK; Duisburg, Dortmund, Dusseldorf and Essen in Germany; Le Creusot and St. Etienne in France; and Moscow, St. Petersburgh, Lipetsk, Tula, in Russia and Krivoi Rog, and Donetsk in Ukraine.**
  - ➢ In **Asia,** the important areas include **Nagasaki and Tokyo-Yokohama in Japan; Shanghai, Tientsin and Wuhan in China; and Jamshedpur, Kulti-Burnpur, Durgapur, Rourkela, Bhilai, Bokaro, Salem, Visakhapatnam and Bhadravati in India.**
- Though, India is an important iron and steel producing country in the world yet, we are not able to perform to our full potential largely due to:
  - ➢ High costs and limited availability of coking coal
  - ➢ Lower productivity of labour
  - ➢ Irregular supply of energy and
  - ➢ Poor infrastructure.

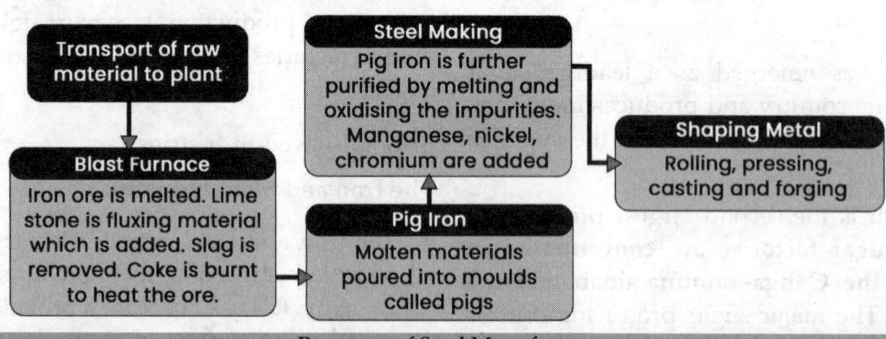

Processes of Steel Manufacture

TISCO (The Tata Iron and Steel Company)

The **Tata Iron and Steel plant** lies very close to the Mumbai-Kolkata railway line and about 240 km away from Kolkata, which is the nearest port for the export of steel. The **rivers Subarnarekha and Kharkai** provide water to the plant. The iron ore for the plant is obtained from **Noamundi and Badam Pahar** and coal is brought from **Joda mines in Odisha**. Coking coal comes from **Jharia and west Bokaro** coalfields.

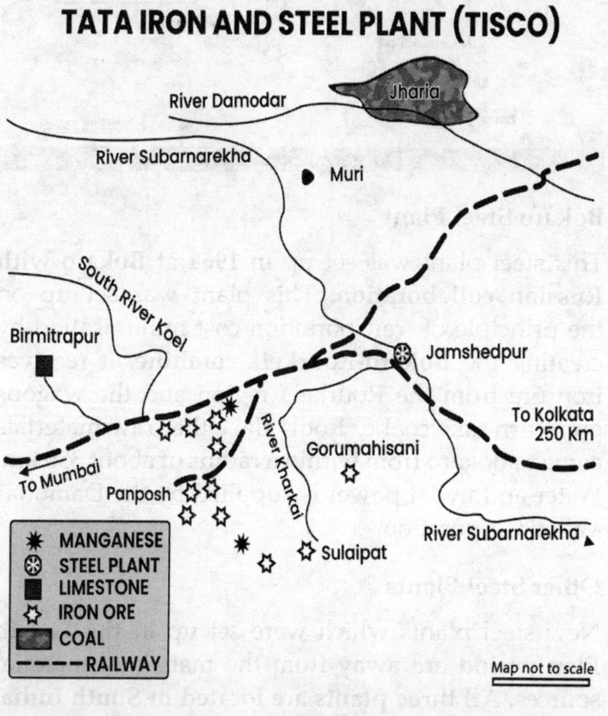

Tata Iron and Steel Plant (TISCO)

IISCO (Indian Iron and Steel Company)

It set up its first factory at Hirapur and later on another at Kulti. In **1937**, the Steel corporation of Bengal was constituted in association with IISCO and set up another iron and steel producing unit at Burnpur (West Bengal). **All the three plants under IISCO** are located very close to Damodar valley coalfields (Raniganj, Jharia, and Ramgarh). Iron ore comes from Singhbhum in Jharkhand. Water is obtained from the Barakar River, a tributary of the Damodar. All the plants are located along the **Kolkata-Asansol railway line.** Unfortunately, steel production from IISCO fell considerably in 1972-73 and the plants were taken over by the government.

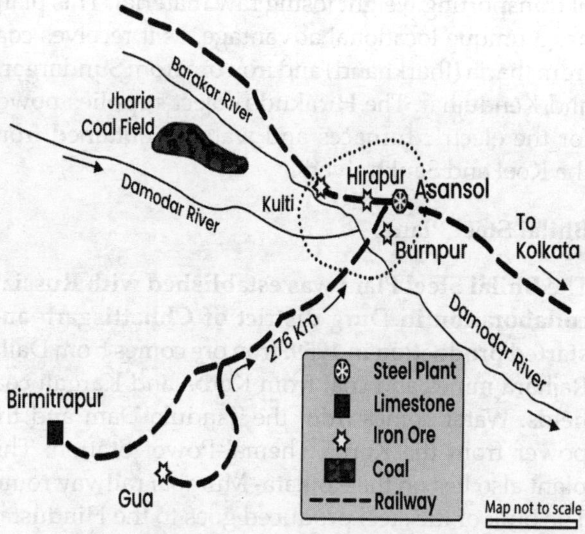

Indian Iron and Steel Company

Visvesvaraya Iron and Steel Plant (VISL)

The third integrated steel plant, the **Visvesvaraya Iron and Steel Plant**, initially called the Mysore Iron and Steel Works, is located close to an iron ore producing area of **Kemmangundi** in the **Baba Budan hills.** Limestone and manganese are also locally available. **But this region has no coal.** At the beginning, charcoal obtained by burning wood from nearby forests was used as fuel till 1951. Afterwards, electric furnaces were installed which use hydroelectricity from the Jog Falls hydel power project. The **Bhadravati River** supplies water to the plant. This plant produces **specialised steels and alloys.**

After independence, during the **Second Five Year Plan (1956-61), three new integrated steel plants were set up with foreign collaboration:** Rourkela in Odisha, Bhilai in Chhattisgarh and Durgapur in West Bengal. These were public sector plants under **Hindustan Steel Limited (HSL). In 1973, the Steel Authority of India Limited (SAIL) was created to manage these plants.**

Rourkela Steel Plant

The **Rourkela Steel plant was set up in 1959** in the **Sundargarh district of Odisha in collaboration with Germany**. The plant was located on the basis of proximity to raw materials, thus, minimising the cost of transporting weight losing raw material. This plant has a unique locational advantage, as it receives coal from Jharia (Jharkhand) and iron ore from Sundargarh and Kendujhar. The Hirakud project supplies power for the electric furnaces and water is obtained from the Koel and Sankh rivers.

Bhilai Steel Plant

The **Bhilai Steel Plant was established with Russian collaboration in Durg district of Chhattisgarh and started production in 1959.** Iron ore comes from Dalli-Rajhara mines and coal from Korba and Kargali coal fields. Water comes from the Tandula Dam and the power from the Korba Themal-Power Station. This plant also lies on the Kolkata- Mumbai railway route. The bulk of the steel produced goes to the Hindustan Shipyard at Visakhapatnam.

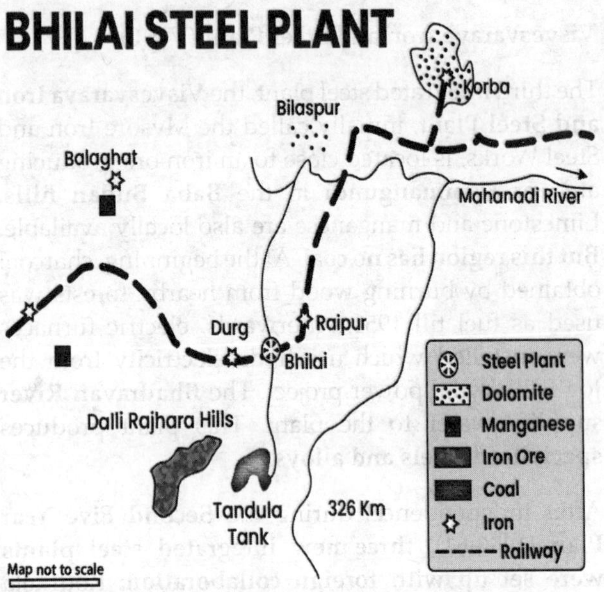

Bhilai Steel Plant

Durgapur Steel Plant

Durgapur Steel Plant in West Bengal **was set up in collaboration with the government of the United Kingdom and started production in 1962.** This plant lies in Raniganj and Jharia coal belt and gets iron ore from Noamundi. Durgapur lies on the main **Kolkata-Delhi railway route.** Hydel power and water is obtained from the **Damodar Valley Corporation (DVC).**

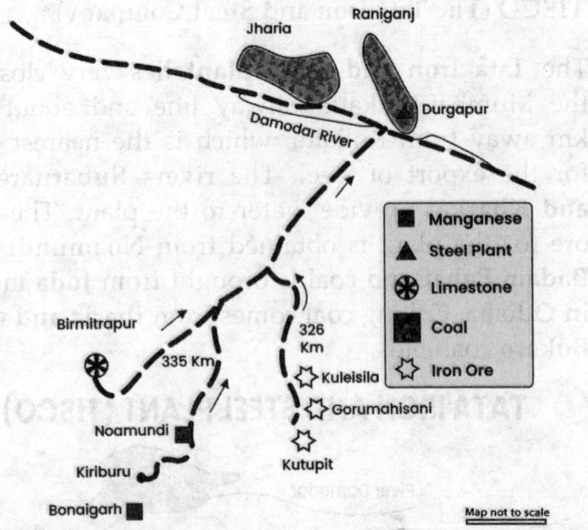

Durgapur Steel Plant

Bokaro Steel Plant

This steel plant was set up in **1964 at Bokaro with Russian collaboration.** This plant was set up on the principle of transportation cost minimisation by creating the **Bokaro-Rourkela combine.** It receives iron ore from the Rourkela region and the wagons on return take coal to Rourkela. Other raw materials come to Bokaro from within a radius of about 350 km. Water and hydel power is supplied by the Damodar Valley Corporation.

Other Steel Plants

New steel plants which were set up in **the Fourth Plan period** are away from the main raw material sources. **All three plants are located in South India.** The **Vizag Steel Plant, in Visakhapatnam in Andhra Pradesh is the first port-based plant which started operating in 1992.** Its port location is of advantage. The **Vijayanagar Steel Plant at Hospet in Karnataka** was developed using indigenous technology. This uses local iron ore and limestone. The **Salem Steel Plant in Tamil Nadu was commissioned in 1982.**

> **Pittsburg Steel City**
>
> **Pittsburgh:** It is an important steel city of the United States of America. The steel industry at Pittsburgh enjoys locational advantages. Some of the raw material such as coal is available locally, while the iron ore comes from the iron mines at Minnesota, about 1500 km from Pittsburgh. Between these mines and Pittsburgh is one of the

world's best routes for shipping ore, cheaply – the famous Great Lakes waterway. Trains carry the ore from the **Great Lakes to the Pittsburgh area. The Ohio, the Monongahela and Allegheny rivers** provide adequate water supply.

Today, very few of the large steel mills are in Pittsburgh itself. They are located in the valleys of the Monongahela and Allegheny rivers above Pittsburgh and along the Ohio River below it. Finished steel is transported to the market by both land and water routes.

The Pittsburgh area has many factories other than steel mills. These use steel as their raw material to make many different products such as railroad equipment, heavy machinery and rails.

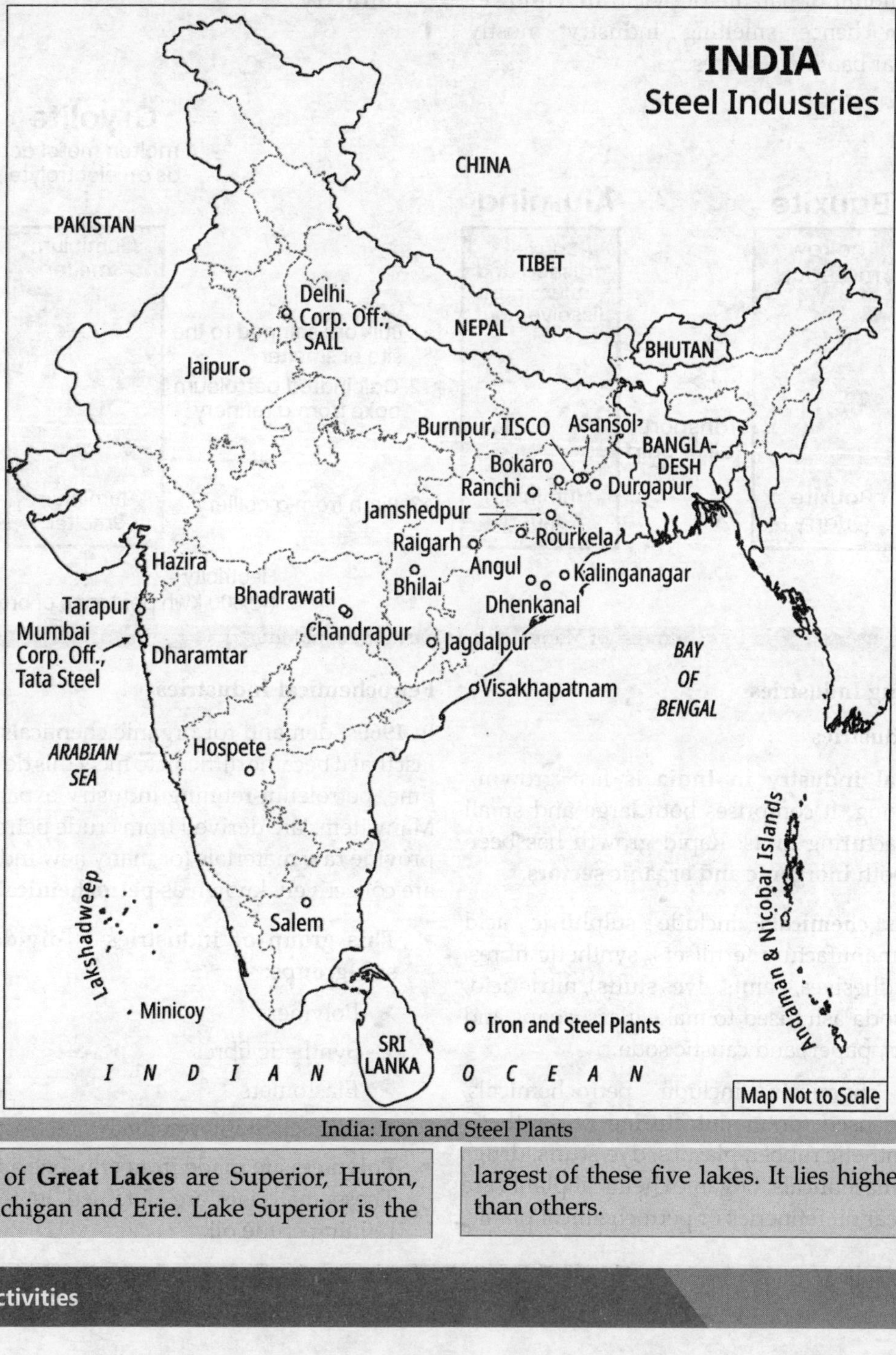

India: Iron and Steel Plants

The names of **Great Lakes** are Superior, Huron, Ontario, Michigan and Erie. Lake Superior is the largest of these five lakes. It lies higher upstream than others.

Aluminium Smelting

- **Aluminium smelting** is the second most important metallurgical industry in India. It is light, resistant to corrosion, a good conductor of heat, malleable and becomes strong when it is mixed with other metals. It is used to manufacture aircraft, utensils and wires. It has gained popularity as a substitute of steel, copper, zinc and lead in a number of industries.
- A large amount of bauxite ore yield much lower aluminium hence smelting industry mostly located near bauxite reserves.
- Aluminium smelting plants in the country are located in Odisha, West Bengal, Kerala, Uttar Pradesh, Chhattisgarh, Maharashtra and Tamil Nadu.
- **Bauxite**, the raw material used in the smelters, is a very bulky, dark reddish coloured rock. **Regular supply of electricity and an assured source of raw material** at minimum cost are the **two prime factors for location of the industry**.

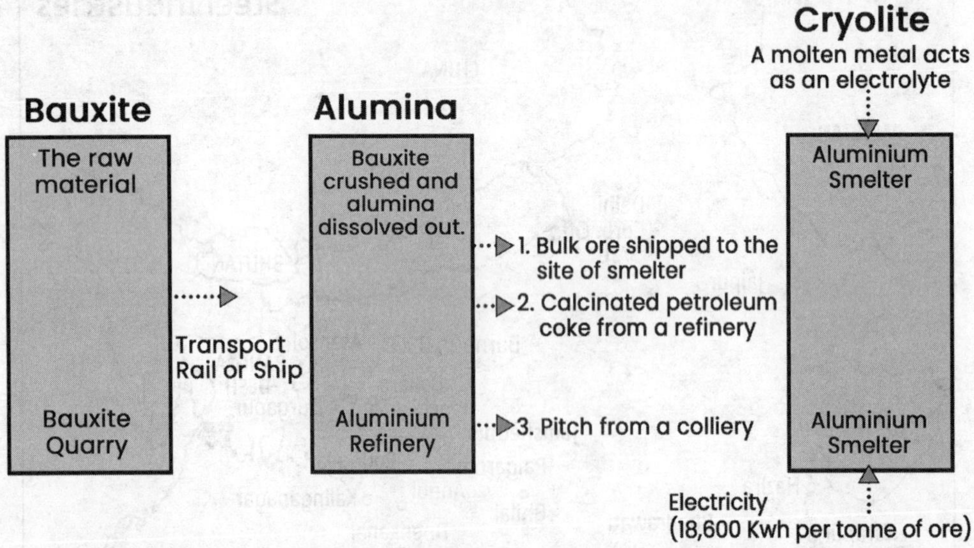

Process of Manufacturing in Aluminium Industry

Manufacturing Industries

Chemical Industries

The **Chemical industry in India** is fast growing and diversifying. It comprises both large and small scale, manufacturing units. Rapid growth has been recorded in both **inorganic and organic sectors.**

- **Inorganic chemicals** include sulphuric acid (used to manufacture fertilisers, synthetic fibres, plastics, adhesives, paints, dyes stuffs), nitric acid, alkalies, soda ash (used to make glass, soaps and detergents, paper) and caustic soda.
- **Organic chemicals** include petrochemicals, which are used for manufacturing of synthetic fibers, synthetic rubber, plastics, dye-stuffs, drugs and pharmaceuticals. Organic chemical plants are located near oil refineries or petrochemical plants.

Petrochemical Industries

In **1960s**, demand for organic chemicals increased so fast that it became difficult to meet this demand. At that time, petroleum refining industry expanded rapidly. Many items are derived from crude petroleum, which provide raw materials for many new industries, these are collectively known as **petrochemical industries.**

- **This group of industries is divided into four sub-groups**:
  - Polymers
  - Synthetic fibres
  - Elastomers
  - Surfactant intermediate
- **Polymers** are made from ethylene and propylene. These materials are obtained in the process of refining crude oil.

- Polymers are used as raw materials in the plastic industry. Among polymers, polyethylene is a widely used thermoplastic. Plastic is first converted into sheets, powder, resin and pellets, and then used in manufacturing plastic products.
- Production of plastic polymers started in India in the late fifties and the early sixties using other organic chemicals.
- The **National Organic Chemicals Industries Limited (NOCIL),** established in private sector in 1961, started the first naphtha based chemical industry in Mumbai.
- The plants located at Mumbai, Barauni, Mettur, Pimpri and Rishra are the major producers of plastic materials. About 75 per cent of these units are in small scale sector.
- **Synthetic fibres** are widely used in the manufacturing of fabrics because of their inherent strength, durability, washability, and resistance to shrinkage.
- Industries manufacturing nylon and polyester yarns are located at **Kota, Pimpri, Mumbai, Modinagar, Pune, Ujjain, Nagpur and Udhna.** Acrylic staple fibre is manufactured at Kota and Vadodara.

Distribution

- Mumbai is the hub of the petrochemical industries.
- **Cracker units** are also located in **Auraiya (Uttar Pradesh), Jamnagar, Gandhinagar and Hazira (Gujarat), Nagothane, Ratnagiri (Maharashtra), Haldia (West Bengal) and Visakhapatnam (Andhra Pradesh).**

Organisations

Three organisations are working in the petrochemical sector under the administrative control of the Department of Chemicals and Petrochemicals.

- **First** is the **Indian Petrochemical Corporation Limited (IPCL),** a public sector undertaking. It is responsible for the manufacture and distribution of the various petrochemicals like polymers, chemicals, fibres and fibre intermediates.
- **Second** is the **Petrofils Cooperative Limited (PCL),** a joint venture of the Government of India and Weaver's Cooperative Societies. It produces polyester filament yarn and nylon chips at its two plants located at Vadodara and Naldhari in Gujarat.
- **Third** is the **Central Institute of Plastic Engineering and Technology (CIPET),** involved in imparting training in petro-chemical industry.

Fertiliser Industry

The fertiliser industry is centred around the production of nitrogenous fertilisers (mainly urea), phosphatic fertilisers and ammonium phosphate (DAP) and complex fertilisers which have a combination of **nitrogen (N), phosphate (P), and potash (K).** The third, i.e., **potash is entirely imported** as the country does not have any reserves of commercially usable potash or potassium compounds in any form.

After the Green Revolution the industry expanded to several other parts of the country. **Gujarat, Tamil Nadu, Uttar Pradesh, Punjab and Kerala** contribute towards half of the fertiliser production. Other significant producers are Andhra Pradesh, Odisha, Rajasthan, Bihar, Maharashtra, Assam, West Bengal, Goa, Delhi, Madhya Pradesh and Karnataka.

Cement Industry

Cement is essential for construction activity such as building houses, factories, bridges, roads, airports, dams and for other commercial establishments. This industry requires bulky and heavy raw materials like **Limestone, Silica and Gypsum**. Coal and electric power are needed apart from rail transportation.

The industry has strategically located plants in Gujarat that have suitable access to the market in the Gulf countries. The first cement plant was set up in Chennai in 1904.

Improvement in the quality has found the produce a readily available market in **East Asia, Middle East, Africa and South Asia** apart from a large demand within the country.

Automobile Industry

Automobiles provide vehicle for quick transport of goods, services and passengers. Trucks, buses, cars, motor cycles, scooters, three-wheelers and multi-utility vehicles are manufactured in India at various centres. After the liberalisation, the coming in of new and contemporary models stimulated the demand for vehicles in the market, which led to the healthy growth of the industry including passenger cars, two and three-wheelers. **The industry is located around Delhi, Gurugram, Mumbai, Pune, Chennai, Kolkata, Lucknow, Indore, Hyderabad, Jamshedpur and Bengaluru.**

Electronics Industry

The **electronics industry** covers a wide range of products from transistor sets to television, telephones, cellular telecom, telephone exchange, radars, computers and many other equipments required by the telecommunication industry. **Bengaluru has emerged as the Electronic Capital of India.** Other important centres for electronic goods are Mumbai, Delhi, Hyderabad, Pune, Chennai, Kolkata, Lucknow and Coimbatore. The major industry concentration is at **Bengaluru, Noida, Mumbai, Chennai, Hyderabad and Pune**. A major impact of this industry has been on employment generation. The continuing growth in the hardware and software is the key to the success of IT industry in India.

The advancement in information technology has had a profound influence on the country's economy. The **Information Technology (IT)** revolution opened up new possibilities of economic and social transformation. The **IT and IT enabled business process outsourcing (ITES- BPO)** services continue to be on a robust growth path. Indian software industry has emerged as one of the fastest growing sectors in the economy. The software industry has surpassed electronic hardware production. The Indian government has created a number of software parks in the country. A major impact of this growth has been on employment creation, which has almost doubled every year.

Liberalisation, Privatisation, Globalisation (LPG) and Industrial Development in India

The new Industrial Policy was announced in 1991. The major objectives of this policy were to build on the gains already made, correct the distortions or weaknesses that have crept in, maintain a sustained growth in productivity and gainful employment and attain international competitiveness. **Within this policy, measures initiated are:**

- Abolition of industrial licensing,
- Free entry to foreign technology,
- Foreign investment policy,
- Access to capital market,
- Open trade,
- Abolition of phased manufacturing programme, and
- Liberalised industrial location programme.

The policy has three main dimensions: **liberalisation**, **privatisation** and **globalisation**.

- The **industrial licensing system** has been abolished for all except six industries related to security, strategic or environmental concerns.
- At the same time, the number of industries reserved for public sector since 1956 have been reduced from 17 to 4.
- Industries related to atomic energy substances specified in the Schedule of the Department of Atomic Energy as well as Railways have remained under the public sector.
- The government also has decided to offer a part of the shareholdings in the public enterprises to financial institutions, general public and workers.
- The threshold limits of assets have been scrapped and no industry requires prior approval for investing in the delicensed sector. They only need to submit a memorandum in the prescribed format.
- In the new industrial policy, **Foreign Direct Investment (FDI)** has been seen as a supplement to domestic investment for achieving a higher level of economic development.
- FDI benefits the domestic industry as well as the consumers by providing technological upgradation, access to global managerial skills and practices, optimum use of natural and human resources, etc. Keeping all this in mind, foreign investment has been liberalised and the government has permitted access to an automatic route for Foreign Direct Investment.
- The government has also announced changes in the industrial location policies. Industries are discouraged in or very close to large cities due to environmental reasons.

- The industrial policy has been liberalised to attract private investor both domestic and multi-nationals.
- New sectors like, **mining, telecommunications, highway construction and management** have been thrown open to private companies.
- **Globalisation means integrating the economy of the country with the world economy. Under this process, goods and services along with capital, labour and resources can move freely from one nation to another.**
- The thrust of globalisation has been to increase the **domestic and external competition** through extensive application of market mechanism and facilitating dynamic relationship with the foreign investors and suppliers of technology.

In the Indian context, this implies

- Opening of the economy to foreign direct investment by providing facilities to foreign companies to invest in different fields of economic activity in India;
- Removing restrictions and obstacles to the entry of multi- national companies in India;
- Allowing Indian companies to enter into foreign collaboration in India and also encouraging them to set up joint-ventures abroad;
- Carrying out massive import liberalisation programmes by switching over from quantitative restrictions to tariffs in the first place, and then bringing down the level of import duties considerably; and
- Instead of a set of export incentives, opting for exchange rate adjustments for promoting export.

Industrial Regions in India

Industries are not evenly distributed in the country. They tend to concentrate on certain locations because of the favourable locational factors. Several indices are used to identify the clustering of industries, important among them are:

- The number of industrial units,
- Number of industrial workers,
- Quantum of power used for industrial purposes,
- Total industrial output, and
- Value added by manufacturing, etc.

Major industrial regions of the country are given below:

Mumbai-Pune Industrial Region

- It extends from Mumbai-Thane to Pune and in adjoining districts of Nashik and Solapur. Besides, industrial development has been rapid in **Kolaba, Ahmednagar, Satara, Sangli and Jalgaon** districts. Development of this region started with the location of the cotton textile industry in Mumbai.
- Mumbai, with cotton hinterland and moist climate favoured the location of the cotton textile industry. Opening of the Suez Canal in 1869 provided impetus to the growth of Mumbai port. Machineries were imported through this port. Hydro-electricity was developed in the Western Ghat region to meet the requirements of this industry.
- With the development of the cotton textile industry, the chemical industry also developed. Opening of the Mumbai High petroleum field and erection of nuclear energy plants added additional pull to this region.
- Besides, engineering goods, petroleum refining, petrochemicals, leather, synthetic and plastic goods, drugs, fertilisers, electrical, shipbuilding, electronics, software, transport equipment and food industries also developed.
- **Important Industrial Centres** are Mumbai, Kolaba, Kalyan, Thane, Pune, Pimpri, Nashik, Manmad, Solapur, Kolhapur, Ahmednagar, Satara and Sangli.

Hugli Industrial Region

- Located along the **Hugli River,** this region extends from Bansberia in the north to Birlanagar in the south for a distance of about 100 km. Industries also have developed in Medinipur in the west.
- **Kolkata-Howrah** form the nucleus of this industrial region. Historical, geographical, economic and political factors have contributed much to its development. It developed with the opening of the river port on Hugli.
- Kolkata emerged as a leading centre of the country. Later, Kolkata was connected with interior parts by railway lines and road routes.

- Development of **tea plantations in Assam and northern hills of West Bengal**, the processing of indigo earlier and jute later coupled with the opening of coalfields of the Damodar Valley and iron ore deposits of the Chotanagpur plateau, contributed to the industrial development of the region.
- Cheap labour available from thickly populated parts of Bihar, eastern Uttar Pradesh and Odisha also contributed to its development.
- Kolkata, being the capital city of British India (1773-1911), attracted the British capital. **The establishment of first jute mill at Rishra in 1855 ushered in the era of modern industrial clustering in this region.**
- The major concentration of jute industry is at Howrah and Bhatapara. The partition of the country in 1947 adversely affected this industrial region. Cotton textile industry also grew along with jute industry, paper, engineering, textile machinery, electrical, chemical, pharmaceuticals, fertiliser and petrochemical industries have also developed within this region. Factory of the Hindustan Motors Limited at Konnagar and the **Diesel Engine factory at Chittaranjan** are landmarks of this region.
- Location of petroleum refinery at Haldia has facilitated the development of a variety of industries.
- Important industrial centres of this region are Kolkata, Howrah, Haldia, Serampore, Rishra, Shibpur, Naihati, Kakinara, Shyamnagar, Titagarh, Sodepur, Budge Budge, Birlanagar, Bansberia, Belgharia, Triveni, Hugli, Belur, etc.
- However, industrial growth of this region has slowed down in comparison to other regions. **Decline of the jute industry is one of the reasons.**

Bengaluru-Chennai Industrial Region

- This region witnessed the most rapid industrial growth in the post-Independence period. Till 1960, industries were confined to Bengaluru, Salem and Madurai districts but now they have spread over all the districts of **Tamil Nadu except Viluppuram**. Since this region is away from the coalfields, its development is dependent on the **Pykara hydroelectric plant, which was built in 1932.**
- Cotton textile industry was the first to take roots due to the presence of cotton growing areas. Along with cotton mills, the loom industry spread very rapidly.
- Several heavy engineering industries converged at Bengaluru. **Aircraft (HAL), machine tools, telephone (HTL) and Bharat Electronics** are industrial landmarks of this region.
- Important industries are textiles, rail wagons, diesel engines, radio, light engineering goods, rubber goods, medicines, aluminium, sugar, cement, glass, paper, chemicals, film, cigarette, match box, leather goods, etc.
- Petroleum refinery at Chennai, iron and steel plant at Salem and fertiliser plants are recent developments.

Gujarat Industrial Region

- The **nucleus** of this region lies between Ahmedabad and Vadodara but this region extends upto Valsad and Surat in the south and to Jamnagar in the west.
- **Development of this region** is also associated with the location of the cotton textile industry since the 1860s. This region became an important textile region with the decline of the cotton textile industry at Mumbai. Located in a cotton growing area, this region has the double advantage of the proximity of raw materials as well as of market.
- The discovery of oilfields led to the establishment of petrochemical industries around **Ankleshwar, Vadodara and Jamnagar.** The port at Kandla helped in the rapid growth of this region.
- Petroleum refinery at Koyali provided raw materials to a host of petrochemical industries. The industrial structure is now diversified.
- Besides, **textiles (cotton, silk and synthetic fabrics) and petrochemical industries**, other industries are heavy and basic chemicals, motor, tractor, diesel engines, textile machinery, engineering, pharmaceuticals, dyes, pesticides, sugar, dairy products and food processing.

Recently, **the largest petroleum refinery has been set up at Jamnagar.**

- Important industrial centres of this region are Ahmedabad, Vadodara, Bharuch, Koyali, Anand, Khera, Surendranagar, Rajkot, Surat, Valsad and Jamnagar.

Chotanagpur Region

- This region extends over **Jharkhand, northern Odisha and western West Bengal** and is known for the heavy metallurgical industries. This region owes its development to the discovery of coal in the Damodar Valley and metallic and non-metallic minerals in Jharkhand and northern Odisha. Proximity to coal, iron ore and other minerals facilitated the location of heavy industries in this region.
- Six large integrated iron and steel plants at Jamshedpur, **Burnpur-Kulti, Durgapur, Bokaro and Rourkela** are located within this region. To meet the power requirement, thermal and hydroelectric plants have been constructed in the Damodar Valley. Densely populated surrounding regions provide cheap labour and Hugli region provides a vast market for its industries.
- Heavy engineering, machine tools, fertilisers, cement, paper, locomotives and heavy electricals are some of the important industries in this region.
- Important centres are **Ranchi, Dhanbad, Chaibasa, Sindri, Hazaribag, Jamshedpur, Bokaro, Rourkela, Durgapur, Asansol and Dalmianagar.**

Visakhapatnam-Guntur Region

- This industrial region extends from Visakhapatnam district to **Kurnool and Prakasam** districts in the south. Industrial development of this region hinged upon **Visakhapatnam and Machilipatnam ports** developed agriculture and rich reserves of minerals in their hinterlands.
- **Coalfields of the Godavari basin** provide energy. The shipbuilding industry was started at **Visakhapatnam in 1941.**
- Petroleum refineries based on imported petroleum facilitated the growth of several petrochemical industries. Sugar, textile, jute, paper, fertiliser, cement, aluminium and light engineering are principal industries of this region.
- One lead- zinc smelter is functioning in Guntur district. Iron and steel plant at Visakhapatnam uses the **Bailadila iron ore. Visakhapatnam, Vijayawada, Vijaynagar, Rajahmundry, Guntur, Eluru and Kurnool** are important industrial centres.

Gurugram-Delhi-Meerut Region

- Industries located in this region have shown very fast growth in the recent past. **This region is located far away from the mineral and power resources, and therefore, the industries are light and market-oriented.**
- Electronics, light engineering and electrical goods are major industries of this region. Besides, there are cotton, woolen and synthetic fabrics, hosiery, sugar, cement, machine tools, tractor, cycle, agricultural implements, chemical and vanaspati industries which have developed on a large scale. Software industry is a recent addition.
- To the south lies the **Agra-Mathura industrial area**, which specialises in glass and leather goods. Mathura with an oil refinery is a petrochemical complex. Among industrial centers, mention be made of Gurugram, Delhi, Faridabad, Meerut, Modinagar, Ghaziabad, Ambala, Agra and Mathura.

Kollam-Thiruvananthapuram Region

- This industrial region is spread over Thiruvananthapuram, Kollam, Alwaye, Ernakulam and Alappuzha districts. Plantation, agriculture and hydropower provide industrial base to this region.
- Located far from the mineral belt of the country, agricultural products processing and market-oriented light industries predominate the region. Among them, cotton textile, sugar, rubber, matchbox, glass, chemical fertiliser and fish-based industries are important.
- Food processing, paper, coconut coir products, aluminium and cement industries are also significant. Location of petroleum refinery at Kochchi has added a vista of new industries to this region.
- Important industrial centres are **Kollam, Thiruvananthapuram, Alluva, Kochchi, Alappuzha and Punalur.**

Industrial Pollution and Environmental Degradation

Although industries contribute significantly to India's economic growth and development, the increase in pollution of land, water, air, noise and resulting degradation of the environment that they have caused, cannot be overlooked. The polluting industries also include thermal power plants. **Industries are responsible for four types of pollution**:

- **Air**
- **Water**
- **Land**
- **Noise.**

Air pollution is caused by the presence of high proportion of undesirable gases, such as sulphur dioxide and carbon monoxide. Air- borne particulate materials contain both solid and liquid particles like dust, sprays mist and smoke. Smoke is emitted by **chemical and paper factories, brick kilns, refineries and smelting plants, and burning of fossil fuels in big and small factories** that ignore pollution norms. Toxic gas leaks can be very hazardous with long-term effects. Air pollution adversely affects human health, animals, plants, buildings and the atmosphere as a whole.

Water pollution is caused by organic and inorganic industrial wastes and affluents discharged into rivers. The main culprits in this regard are paper, pulp, chemical, textile and dyeing, petroleum refineries, tanneries and electroplating industries that let out **dyes, detergents, acids, salts and heavy metals like lead and mercury pesticides, fertilisers, synthetic chemicals with carbon, plastics and rubber,** etc. into the water bodies. **Fly ash, phosphogypsum and iron and steel slags** are the major solid wastes in India.

Thermal pollution of water occurs when hot water from factories and thermal plants is drained into rivers and ponds before cooling. Wastes from nuclear power plants, nuclear and weapon production facilities cause **cancers, birth defects and miscarriages**. Soil and water pollution are closely related. Dumping of wastes specially **glass, harmful chemicals, industrial effluents, packaging, salts and garbage** renders the soil useless. Rain water percolates to the soil carrying the pollutants to the ground and the ground water also gets contaminated.

Noise pollution not only results in irritation and anger, it can also cause hearing impairment, increased heart rate and blood pressure among other physiological effects. Unwanted sound is an irritant and a source of stress. Industrial and construction activities, machinery, factory equipment, generators, saws and pneumatic and electric drills also make a lot of noise.

Control of Environmental Degradation

Every litre of waste water discharged by our industry pollutes eight times the quantity of freshwater. How can the industrial pollution of fresh water be reduced?

Some suggestions are

- Minimising use of water for processing by reusing and recycling it in two or more successive stages.
- Harvesting of rainwater to meet water requirements.
- Treating hot water and effluents before releasing them in rivers and ponds. **Treatment of industrial effluents can be done in three phases.**
  - **Primary treatment** by mechanical means. This involves screening, grinding, flocculation and sedimentation.
  - **Secondary treatment** by biological process.
  - **Tertiary treatment** by biological, chemical and physical processes. This involves recycling of wastewater.

Overdrawing of groundwater reserves by industry where there is a threat to groundwater resources also needs to be regulated legally. **Particulate matter in the air** can be reduced by fitting smoke stacks to factories with electrostatic precipitators, fabric filters, scrubbers and inertial separators. Smoke can be reduced by using oil or gas instead of coal in factories. Machinery and equipment can be used and generators should be fitted with silencers. Almost all machinery can be redesigned to increase energy efficiency and reduce noise. Noise absorbing material may be used apart from personal use of earplugs and earphones. **The challenge of sustainable development requires integration of economic development with environmental concerns.**

TEST YOURSELF

Multiple Choice Questions

Q1. Modern manufacturing is characterised by which of the following?

(a) A complex machine technology

(b) Huge amount of capital

(c) Large organisations and infrastructure

(d) All of the above

Q2. Manufacturing industry is

(a) Primary (b) Secondary

(c) Tertiary (d) Quaternary

Q3. The dependence of industries on labour has reduced because of:

(a) Quality control (b) Hydro-electricity

(c) Infrastructure (d) Automation

Q4. Which activities transform raw materials into valuable products?

(a) Primary (b) Secondary

(c) Tertiary (d) Quaternary

Q5. Which of the following is not a factor affecting location of industry?

(a) Raw material (b) Capital

(c) Internet (d) Transport

Q6. Which of the following is an example of basic industry?

(a) Chemical industry

(b) Automobile industry

(c) Iron and steel industry

(d) All of these

Q7. What makes the household industries the smallest manufacturing units?

(a) It is based on local raw materials

(b) It is based on modernised tools

(c) Everyday goods are produced at homes

(d) Both (a) and (c)

Q8. The industry which is managed by Government is known as:

(a) Private sector (b) Public Sector

(c) Joint Sector (d) Cooperative sector

Q9. Consider the following statement regarding Footloose Industries:

1. Footloose industries can be located in a wide variety of places.

2. These are generally not polluting industries.

Which of the following statement(s) is / are correct?

(a) 1 only (b) 2 only

(c) Both 1 and 2 (d) None

Answer Key

Q1.	d	Q2.	b	Q3.	d	Q4.	b
Q5.	c	Q6.	c	Q7.	d	Q8.	b
Q9.	c						

Model Questions for Main Examination

Q1. Write a short note on classification of manufacturing industries in India.

Q2. Discuss the factors that are responsible for locating industries in a particular place.

UNIT 29
Tertiary and Quaternary Activities

In This Unit

Comprehensive and profound coverage of the following NCERTs' chapter:

✓ NCERT Class- 12th (Fundamentals of Human Geography), Chapter- 6

Health, education, law, governance and recreation etc. require professional skills. These services require other theoretical knowledge and practical training. Tertiary activities are related to the service sector. Manpower is an important component of the service sector as most of the tertiary activities are performed by skilled labour, professionally trained experts and consultants.

- In the initial stages of economic development, larger proportion of people worked in the primary sector. In a developed economy, the majority of workers get employment in tertiary activity and a moderate proportion is employed in the secondary sector.
- Tertiary activities include **both production and exchange.** In production, the output is indirectly measured in terms of wages and salaries. Exchange, involves trade, transport and communication facilities that are used to overcome distance.
- Tertiary activities, therefore, involve the commercial output of services rather than the production of tangible goods. They are not directly involved in the processing of physical raw materials. Common examples are the work of a plumber, electrician, technician, launderer, barber, shopkeeper, driver, cashier, teacher, doctor, lawyer and publisher etc.
- **The main difference between secondary activities and tertiary activities** is that the expertise provided by services relies more heavily on specialised skills, experience and knowledge of the workers rather than on the production techniques, machinery and factory processes.

Types of Tertiary Activities

TERTIARY SECTOR
(aka "The Service sector")

Services are non-physical products that cannot be touched or stored.

The Portion of the economy that produces services rather than physical goods.

EXAMPLES: Transport, Advertising, Retail, Teaching, Healthcare, Hospitality etc.

Trade and Commerce

- Trade is essentially **buying** and **selling** of items produced elsewhere. All the services in retail and wholesale trading or commerce are specifically intended for profit. The towns and cities where all these works take place are known as **Trading Centres.**
- Trading centres may be divided into rural and urban marketing centres.
- **Rural Marketing** centres cater to nearby settlements. These are quasi-urban centres. They serve as trading centres of the most rudimentary type. Here personal and professional services are not well-developed. These form local collecting and distributing centres.
  - **Periodic Markets** in rural areas are found where there are no regular markets and local periodic markets are organised at different temporal intervals. These may be weekly, bi-weekly markets from where people from the surrounding areas meet their temporally accumulated demand.

- **Urban Marketing** centres have more widely specialised urban services. They provide ordinary goods and services as well as many of the specialised goods and services required by people. Urban centres, therefore, offer manufactured goods as well as many specialised markets develop, e.g. markets for **labour, housing, semi or finished products**.

Retail Trading

- This is the business activity concerned with the **sale of goods directly to the consumers.**
- Most of the retail trading takes place in fixed establishments or stores solely devoted to selling.
- **Street peddling, handcarts, trucks, door-to-door, mail-order, telephone, automatic vending machines and internet** are examples of non-store retail trading.

Wholesale Trading

- Wholesale trading constitutes bulk business through numerous **intermediary merchants and supply houses** and not through retail stores.
- Wholesalers often extend **credit to retail stores** to such an extent that the retailer operates very largely on the wholesaler's capital.

Transport

- Transport is a service or facility by which people, materials and manufactured goods are physically carried from one location to another.
- **Factors Affecting Transport-**
  - **Demand** for transport is influenced by the size of population. The larger the population size, the greater is the demand for transport.
  - **Routes** depend on: location of cities, towns, villages, industrial centres and raw materials, pattern of trade between them, nature of the landscape between them, type of climate, and funds available for overcoming obstacles along the length of the route.

Communication

Communication services involve the transmission of words and messages, facts and ideas. Some of the communication services are discussed below.

Telecommunications

The use of telecommunications is linked to the development of modern technology. It has revolutionised communications because of the speed with which messages are sent. The time is reduced from weeks to minutes. Besides, the recent advancements like mobile telephony have made communications direct and instantaneous at any time and from anywhere.

Radio and television also help to relay news, pictures, and telephone calls to vast audiences around the world and hence they are termed as **mass media. Newspapers** are able to cover events in all corners of the world. Satellite communication relays information of the earth and from space. The **internet** has truly revolutionised the global communication system.

Services

Services occur at many different levels. Some are geared to industry, some to people, and some to both industry and people, e.g., the transport systems. **Low-order services**, such as grocery shops and laundries, are more common and widespread than **high-order services** or more specialised ones like those of accountants, consultants and physicians.

Many services have now been regulated. Making and maintaining highways and bridges, maintaining fire-fighting departments and supplying or supervising education and customer-care are among the important services most often supervised or performed by governments or companies.

Tourism

- Tourism is travel undertaken for purposes of recreation rather than business. It has become the **world's single largest tertiary activity** in total registered jobs (250 million) and total revenue (40 percent of the total GDP).
- Besides, many local persons are employed to provide services like accommodation, meals, transport, entertainment and special shops serving the tourists. Tourism fosters the growth of infrastructure industries, retail trading, and craft industries (souvenirs).
- In some regions, tourism is seasonal because the vacation period is dependent on favourable weather conditions, but many regions attract visitors all year round.

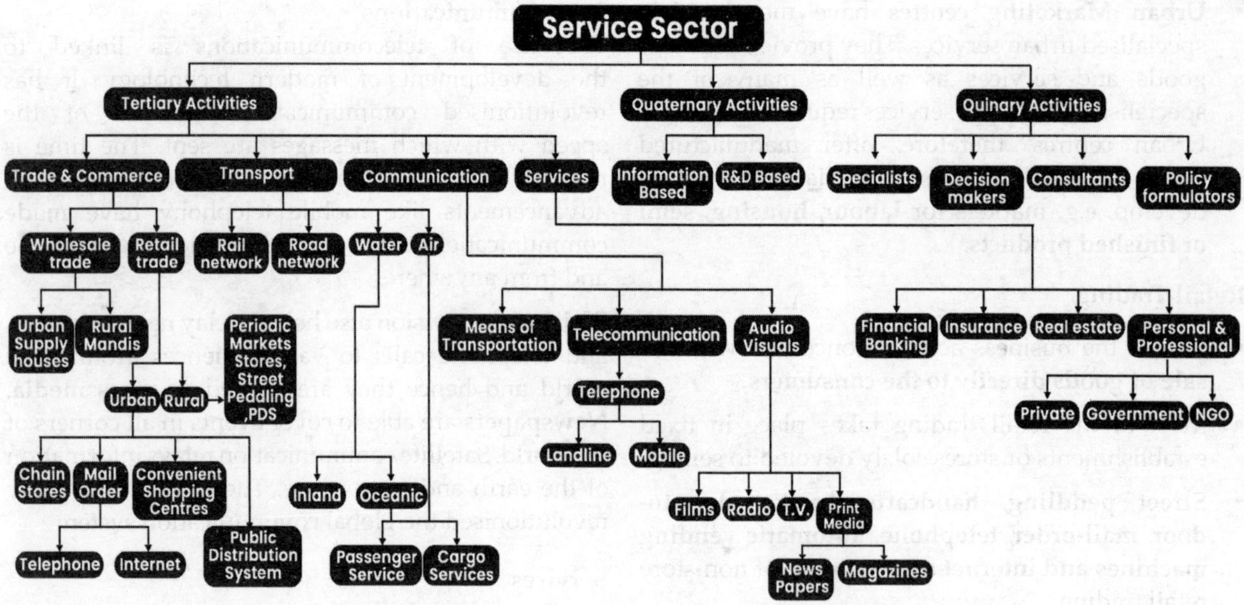

Tourist Regions

- The warmer places around the Mediterranean Coast and the West Coast of India are some of the popular tourist destinations in the world.
- Others include winter sports regions, found mainly in mountainous areas, and various scenic landscapes and national parks, which are scattered. Historic towns also attract tourists, because of the monuments, heritage sites and cultural activities.

Factors Affecting Tourism

Demand: Since the last century, the demand for holidays has increased rapidly. Improvements in the standard of living and increased leisure time, permit many more people to go on holidays for leisure.

Transport: The opening-up of tourist areas has been aided by improvement in transport facilities. Travel is easier by car, with better road systems. More significant in recent years has been the expansion in air transport. For example, air travel allows one to travel anywhere in the world in a few hours of flying- time from their homes. The advent of package holidays has reduced the costs.

Tourist Attractions

Climate: Most people from colder regions expect to have **warm and sunny weather for beach holidays.** This is one of the main reasons for the importance of tourism in Southern Europe and the Mediterranean region. The Mediterranean climate offers almost consistently higher temperatures than in other parts of Europe, long hours of sunshine and low rainfall throughout the peak holiday season. People taking winter holidays have specific climatic requirements, either higher temperatures than their own homelands, or snow cover suitable for skiing.

Landscape: Many people like to spend their holidays in an attractive environment, which often means mountains, lakes, spectacular sea coasts and landscapes not completely altered by man.

History and Art: The history and art of an area have potential attractiveness. People visit ancient or picturesque towns and archaeological sites, and enjoy exploring castles, palaces and churches.

Culture and Economy: These attract tourists with a penchant for experiencing ethnic and local customs. Besides, if a region provides for the needs of tourists at a cheap cost, it is likely to become very popular. Home-stay has emerged as a profitable business such as heritage homes in **Goa, Madikeri and Coorg in Karnataka.**

Medical Services for Overseas Patients in India

- About 55,000 patients from USA visited India in 2005 for treatment. This is still a small number compared with the millions of surgeries performed each year in the US healthcare system.

- India has emerged as the **leading country of medical tourism** in the world. World class hospitals located in metropolitan cities cater to patients all over the world. Medical tourism brings abundant benefits to developing countries like India, Thailand, Singapore and Malaysia.
- Beyond medical tourism, is the trend of outsourcing of medical tests and data interpretation. **Hospitals in India, Switzerland and Australia** have been performing certain medical services – ranging from reading radiology images, to interpreting Magnetic Resonance Images (MRIs) and ultrasound tests. Outsourcing holds tremendous advantages for patients, if it is focused on improving quality or providing specialised care.

> **Medical Tourism**
>
> When medical treatment is combined with international tourism activity, it lends itself to what is commonly known as medical tourism.

Quaternary Activities

People like the **CEO of an MNC or a medical transcriptionist** work in a segment of the service sector that is knowledge oriented. This sector can be divided into quaternary and quinary activities.

Quaternary activities involve some of the following: the **collection, production and dissemination** of information or even the production of information. Quaternary activities centre around research, development and may be seen as an advanced form of services involving **specialised knowledge and technical skills**. Personnel working in office buildings, elementary schools and university classrooms, hospitals and doctors' offices, theatres, accounting and brokerage firms all belong to this category of services.

Quinary Activities

The highest level of **decision makers or policy makers** perform quinary activities. These are subtly different from the knowledge based, industries that the quinary sector in general deals with. Quinary activities are services that focus on the **creation, re-arrangement and interpretation of new and existing ideas; data interpretation and the use and evaluation of new technologies**. Often referred to as **'Gold Collar'** professions, they represent another subdivision of the tertiary sector representing special and highly paid skills of **senior business executives, government officials, research scientists, financial and legal consultants**, etc. Their importance in the structure of advanced economies far outweighs their numbers.

Outsourcing- Outsourcing or contracting out is giving work to an outside agency to improve efficiency and to reduce costs. **When outsourcing involves transferring work to overseas locations**, it is described by the term **off - shoring,** although both off - shoring and outsourcing are used together. Business activities that are outsourced include information technology (IT), human resources, customer support and call centre services and at times also manufacturing and engineering. Outsourcing has resulted in the opening up of a large number of call centres in **India, China, Eastern Europe, Israel, Philippines and Costa Rica**. It has created new jobs in these countries. Outsourcing is coming to those countries where cheap and skilled workers are available. These are also out-migrating countries. With the work available though, outsourcing, the migration in these countries may come down. Outsourcing countries are facing resistance from job-seeking youths in their respective countries.

New trends in quinary services include **knowledge processing outsourcing (KPO)** and **'Home Shoring'**, the latter as an alternative to outsourcing. The KPO industry is distinct from Business Process Outsourcing (BPO) as it involves highly skilled workers. It is information driven knowledge outsourcing. KPO enables companies to create additional business opportunities. Examples of KPOs include **research and development (R and D) activities, e-learning, business research, intellectual property (IP) research, legal profession and the banking sector**.

The Digital Divide

Opportunities emerging from Information and Communication Technology based development are unevenly distributed across the globe. There are wide ranging economic, political and social differences among countries. How quickly countries can provide

ICT access and benefits to its citizens is the deciding factor. While developed countries in general have surged forward, the developing countries have lagged behind and this is known as the digital divide. Similarly, digital divides exist within countries. For example, in a large country like India or Russia, it is inevitable that certain areas like metropolitan centres possess better connectivity and access to the digital world versus peripheral rural areas.

TEST YOURSELF

Multiple Choice Questions

Q1. Which of the following is an example of a business activity in the tertiary sector?

(a) Farming
(b) Manufacturing cars
(c) Providing banking services
(d) Mining coal

Q2. The tertiary sector is also known as the:

(a) Agricultural sector (b) Industrial sector
(c) Service sector (d) Construction sector

Q3. Which of the following is NOT a characteristic of the tertiary sector?

(a) It involves the production of goods.
(b) It involves providing services to consumers.
(c) It focuses on customer satisfaction.
(d) It requires a skilled workforce.

Q4. Which of the following is an example of a service provided by the tertiary sector?

(a) Growing crops
(b) Manufacturing smartphones
(c) Repairing electronic devices
(d) Extracting minerals from mines

Q5. The tertiary sector is a significant contributor to a country's:

(a) Agricultural output
(b) Industrial production
(c) Gross Domestic Product (GDP)
(d) Natural resource extraction

Q6. Which of the following is an example of a profession in the tertiary sector?

(a) Farmer (b) Architect
(c) Factory worker (d) Miner

Q7. Which sector includes activities related to education, healthcare, and entertainment?

(a) Primary sector (b) Secondary sector
(c) Tertiary sector (d) Quaternary sector

Q8. Which sector of the economy has shown significant growth in developed countries?

(a) Primary sector (b) Secondary sector
(c) Tertiary sector (d) Quaternary sector

Q9. Which of the following is NOT a subsector of the tertiary sector?

(a) Retail trade (b) Hospitality and tourism
(c) Manufacturing (d) Financial Services

Q10. The tertiary sector plays a crucial role in:

(a) Extracting natural resources
(b) Producing raw materials
(c) Distributing goods and services
(d) Manufacturing products

Q11. Quinary activities are primarily associated with:

(a) Agriculture (b) Manufacturing
(c) Services (d) Research and development

Q12. Quaternary activities involve:

(a) Extraction of natural resources

(b) High-tech manufacturing

(c) Information processing and management

(d) Retail and wholesale trade

Q13. Which of the following is an example of a quinary activity?

(a) Mining (b) Education

(c) Construction (d) Textile production

Q14. Quaternary activities are characterised by:

(a) Direct involvement with raw materials

(b) High level of skill and expertise

(c) Physical labour-intensive tasks

(d) Mass production techniques

Q15. Which of the following is an example of a quaternary activity?

(a) Farming (b) Banking

(c) Fishing (d) Logging

Q16. Quinary activities are often associated with:

(a) Unskilled labour

(b) Traditional farming methods

(c) Government and decision-making roles

(d) Small-scale retail businesses

Q17. Research and development, consulting, and scientific research are examples of:

(a) Primary activities (b) Secondary activities

(c) Tertiary activities (d) Quaternary activities

Q18. Which of the following is NOT a characteristic of quaternary activities?

(a) Reliance on advanced technology

(b) Knowledge-intensive tasks

(c) Highly specialised skills

(d) Physical extraction of resources

Q19. Which sector of the economy is primarily associated with quinary activities?

(a) Primary sector (b) Secondary sector

(c) Tertiary sector (d) Quaternary sector

Q20. Which of the following is an example of a quinary activity?

(a) Manufacturing automobiles

(b) Providing healthcare services

(c) Performing manual labour

(d) Conducting market research

Answer Key

Q1.	c	Q2.	c	Q3.	a	Q4.	c
Q5.	c	Q6.	b	Q7.	c	Q8.	c
Q9.	c	Q10.	c	Q11.	d	Q12.	c
Q13.	b	Q14.	b	Q15.	b	Q16.	c
Q17.	d	Q18.	d	Q19.	c	Q20.	d

UNIT 30 Transport and Communication in India and the World

In This Unit

Comprehensive and profound coverage of the following NCERTs' chapters:

- ✓ NCERT Class- 10th (Contemporary India-II), Chapter- 7
- ✓ NCERT Class- 12th (Fundamentals of Human Geography), Chapter- 7

Transport is a service or facility for the carriage of persons and goods from one place to the other using humans, animals and different kinds of vehicles. Such movements take place over land, water and air. Roads and railways form part of **land transport**; while **shipping and waterways and airways** are the other two modes. Pipelines carry materials like petroleum, natural gas, and ores in liquified form.

Moreover, transportation is an organised service industry created to satisfy the basic needs of society. It includes transport arteries, vehicles to carry people and goods, and the organisation to maintain arteries, and to handle loading, unloading and delivery.

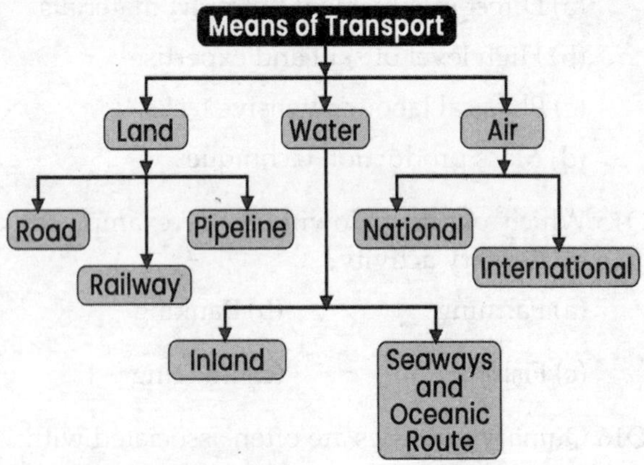

Major Means of Transportation

Modes of Transportation

The principal modes of world transportation, as already mentioned are land, water, air and pipelines. These are used for **inter-regional and intra-regional** transport, and each one (except pipelines) carries both passengers and freight.

The significance of a mode depends on the **type** of goods and services to be transported, **costs** of transport and the **mode** available. International movement of goods is handled by ocean freighters. **Road transport** is cheaper and faster over short distances and for door-to- door services. **Railways** are most suited for large volumes of bulky materials over long distances within a country. High-value, light and perishable goods are best moved by **Airways.**

Land Transport

- Most of the movement of goods and services takes place over land.
- In early days, humans themselves were carriers. Later animals were used as beasts of burden. With the invention of the wheel, the use of carts and wagons became important.
- The revolution in transport came about only after the invention of the steam engine in the eighteenth century. Perhaps the first public railway line was opened in 1825 between Stockton and Darlington in northern England.
- It opened up continental interiors for commercial grain farming, mining and manufacturing in USA.
- The invention of the internal combustion engine revolutionised road transport in terms of road

quality and vehicles (motor cars and trucks) plying over them.

- Among the newer developments in land transportation are pipelines, ropeways and cableways.
- Liquids like mineral oil, water, sludge and sewers are transported by pipelines.

Roads

- Road transport is the most economical for short distances compared to railways. Freight transport by road is gaining importance because it offers door-to-door service.
- India has one of the second largest road networks in the world with a total length of about 62.16 lakh km (Annual Report 2020-21). About 85 percent of passenger and 70 percent of freight traffic are carried by roads every year.
- Road transport in modern sense was very limited in India before World War-II. **The first serious attempt was made in 1943 when 'Nagpur Plan' was drawn.** This plan could not be implemented due to lack of coordination among the princely states and British India.
- After Independence, **twenty-year road plan (1961)** was introduced to improve the conditions of roads in India.
- **Traffic Flows:** Traffic on roads has increased dramatically in recent years. Peaks (high points) and troughs (low points) of traffic flow can be seen on roads at particular times of the day, for example, peaks occurring during the rush hour before and after work. Most of the cities in the world have been facing the problem of congestion.

Grand Trunk Road

Sher Shah Suri built the Shahi (Royal) road to strengthen and consolidate his empire from the **Indus Valley to the Sonar Valley in Bengal**. This road was renamed the Grand Trunk (GT) road during the British period, connecting **Calcutta and Peshawar**. At present, it extends from **Amritsar to Kolkata**. It is bifurcated into 2 segments:

- National Highway (NH)-1 from Delhi to Amritsar
- NH- 2 from Delhi to Kolkata.

For the purpose of construction and maintenance, roads are classified as **National Highways (NH), State Highways (SH), Major District Roads and Rural Roads.**

India Road Network 2020

Serial No.	Road Category	Length in Km
1.	National Highways	136440
2.	State Highways	176818
3.	Other Roads	5902539
	Total	**6215797**

India Road Network 2020

National Highways

- The main roads which are constructed and maintained by the Central Government are known as the National Highways.
- These roads are meant for inter-state transport and movement of defence personnel and material in strategic areas.
- The length of the National Highways has increased from 19,700 km in 1951 to 1,36,440 km in 2020.
- The National Highways constitute only about 2 **per cent of the total road length** but carry **40 per cent of the road traffic.**
- The **National Highways Authority of India (NHAI)** was operationalised in 1995. It is an autonomous body under the Ministry of Road Transport & Highways. It is entrusted with the responsibility of development, maintenance and operation of National Highways. This is also the apex body to improve the quality of the roads designated as National Highways.

National Highways Development Projects

Golden Quadrilateral: It comprises construction of 5,846-km long 4/6 lane, high density traffic corridor, to connect India's four big metro cities of **Delhi-Mumbai-Chennai-Kolkata**. With the construction of Golden Quadrilateral, the time, distance and cost of movement among the mega cities of India will be considerably minimised.

North-South and East-West Corridors: North-South corridor aims at connecting **Srinagar in Jammu and Kashmir with Kanniyakumari in Tamil Nadu** (including Kochchi-Salem Spur) with 4,076-km long road. The **East-West Corridor** has been planned to connect Silchar in Assam with the port town of Porbandar in Gujarat with 3,640- km of road length.

State Highways

- These are constructed and maintained by state governments. They join the state capitals with district headquarters and other important towns.
- These roads are connected to the National Highways. These constitute 4 per cent of total road length in the country.

District Roads

- These roads are the connecting link between District Headquarters and the other important nodes in the district.
- They account for 14 per cent of the total road length of the country.

Rural Roads

- These roads are vital for providing links in the rural areas. About 80 per cent of the total road length in India are categorised as rural roads.

Other Roads

- Other roads include Border Roads and International Highways.
- The **Border Road Organisation (BRO)** was established in May 1960 for accelerating economic development and strengthening defence preparedness through rapid and coordinated improvement of strategically important roads along the northern and north-eastern boundary of the country.
- It is a premier multifaceted construction agency. It has constructed roads in high altitude mountainous terrain joining Chandigarh with Manali (Himachal Pradesh) and Leh (Ladakh). This road runs at an average altitude of 4,270 metres above the mean sea level.
- Apart from the construction and maintenance of roads in strategically sensitive areas, the **BRO also undertakes snow clearance in high altitude areas.**

The World's longest High Altitude tunnel — **Atal Tunnel** (9.02 Km) has been built by Border Road Organisation. This tunnel connects Manali to Lahaul-Spiti valley throughout the year. Earlier the valley was cut off for about 6 months each year owing to heavy snowfall. The Tunnel is built with ultra-modern specifications in the Pir Panjal range of Himalayas at an altitude of 3000 metres from the Mean Sea Level (MSL).

Road Transport- World Scenario

The world's total motorable road length is only about 15 million km, of which **North America** accounts for 33 per cent. The highest road density and the highest number of vehicles are registered in this continent compared to Western Europe.

Highways

- In North America, highway density is high, about 0.65 km per sq. km. Every place is within 20 km distance from a highway.
- Likewise, the cities of Canada in the north are linked with those of Mexico in the south.
- The **Trans-Canadian Highway** links Vancouver in British Columbia (west coast) to St. John's City in Newfoundland (east coast) and the Alaskan Highway links Edmonton (Canada) to Anchorage (Alaska).
- The **Pan-American Highway**, a large portion of which has been constructed, will connect the countries of South America, Central America, USA and Canada.
- The **Trans-Continental Stuart Highway** connects Darwin (north coast) and Melbourne via Tennant Creek and Alice Springs in Australia.

- **Europe** has a large number of vehicles and a well-developed highway network. But highways face a lot of competition from railways and waterways.
- In **Russia**, a dense highway network is developed in the industrialised region west of the Urals with Moscow as the hub. The important **Moscow-Vladivostok Highway** serves the region to the east.
- In **China,** highways criss-cross the country connecting all major cities such as Tsungtso (near Vietnam boundary), Shanghai (central China), Guangzhou (south) and Beijing (north). A new highway links Chengdu with Lhasa in Tibet.
- In **Africa**, a highway joins Algiers in the north to Conakry in Guinea. Similarly, Cairo is also connected to Cape Town.

Rail Transport

- The Indian Railways network is one of the longest in the world. It facilitates the movement of both freight and passengers and contributes to the growth of the economy.
- The Indian Railway was introduced in 1853, when **a line was constructed from Bombay to Thane covering a distance of 34 km.**
- Indian Railways is the largest government undertaking in the country. The length of the Indian Railways network was 67,956 km. It is very large size puts a lot of pressure on a centralised railway management system. Thus, in India, the railway system has been divided into 17 zones.

Zonal Railways	Headquarters
Central	Mumbai
Eastern	Kolkata
East Coast	Bhubaneshwar
East Central	Hajipur
Northern	New Delhi
North Central	Allahabad
North Eastern	Gorakhpur
Northest Frontier	Maligaon (Guwahati)
North Western	Jaipur
Southern	Chennai
South Central	Secunderabad
South Eastern	Kolkata
South East Central Railway	Bilaspur
South Western Railway	Hubli
Western	Mumbai
West Central Railway	Jabalpur
Metro Railway	Kolkata

- On the basis of the width of track of the Indian Railways, three categories have been made:
  - **Broad gauge:** The distance between rails in broad gauge is 1.676 meter. The total length of broad gauge, lines was 63950 km (2019-20).
  - **Metre gauge:** The distance between rails is one meter. Its total length was 2402 km (2019-20).
  - **Narrow gauge:** The distance between the rails in this case is 0.762 meter or 0.610 meter. The total length of the narrow guage was 1604 km (2019-20). It is generally confined to hilly areas.
- Indian Railways has launched an extensive programme to **convert the meter and narrow gauges to broad gauge.** Moreover, **steam engines have been replaced by diesel and electric engines.** This step has increased the speed, as well as, the haulage capacity.
- The replacement of steam engines run by coal has also improved the environment of the stations.

Metro rail has revolutionised the urban transport system in India. Replacement of diesel buses by CNG-run vehicles along with the introduction of metro is a welcome step towards **controlling the air pollution in urban areas.**

- Areas around towns, raw material producing areas and of plantations and other commercial crops, hill stations and cantonment towns were well-connected by railways from the British colonial era. These were mostly developed for the exploitation of resources.
- After the Independence of the country, railway routes have been extended to other areas too. The most significant development has been the development of Konkan Railway along the western coast providing a direct link between Mumbai and Mangalore.
- Railway continues to remain the main means of transport for the masses. Railway network is relatively less dense in the hill states, north eastern states, central parts of India and Rajasthan.

Konkan Railway

One of the important achievements of the Indian Railways has been the construction of Konkan Railway in 1998. It is 760-km long rail route connecting **Roha in Maharashtra to Mangalore in Karnataka.** It is considered an engineering marvel. It crosses 146 rivers, streams, nearly 2000 bridges and 91 tunnels. Asia's largest tunnel which is nearly 6.5 km long, also lies on this route. The states of Maharashtra, Goa and Karnataka are partners in this undertaking.

Rail Transport - World Scenario

- The railway gauges vary in different countries and are roughly classified as **broad** (more than 1.5 m), **standard** (1.44 m), **meter gauge** (1 m) and **smaller gauges**. The standard gauge is used in the UK.
- Commuter trains are very popular in the UK, Europe has one of the dense rail networks in the world. There are about 4,40,000 km of railways, most of which is double or multiple-tracked. These carry millions of passengers daily to and fro in the city. There are about 13 lakh km of railways open for traffic in the world.
- **Belgium** has the highest density of 1 km of railway for every 6.5 sq. kms area.
- The industrial regions exhibit some of the highest densities in the world. The important rail heads are London, Paris, Brussels, Milan, Berlin and Warsaw.
- Passenger transport is more important than freight in many of these countries. Underground railways are important in **London and Paris.** Channel Tunnel, operated by Euro Tunnel Group through **England, connects London with Paris.**
- Trans-continental railway lines have now lost their importance to quicker and more flexible transport systems of airways and roadways.
- In **Russia**, railways account for about 90 percent of the country's total transport with a very dense network west of the Urals. Moscow is the most important rail head with major lines radiating to different parts of the country's vast geographical area. Underground railways and commuter trains are also important in Moscow.
- **North America** has one of the most extensive rail networks. It account for nearly 40 per cent of the world's total. In contrast to many European countries, the **railways are used more for long-distance bulky freight** like ores, grains, timber and machinery than for passengers. A very dense rail network is found in the highly industrialised and urbanised region **of East Central USA and adjoining Canada.**
- In **Canada**, railways are in the public sector and distributed all over the sparsely populated areas. The transcontinental railways carry the bulk of wheat and coal tonnage.
- **Australia** has about 40,000 km of railways, of which 25 per cent are found in New South Wales alone. The west-east Australian National Railway line runs across the country from Perth to Sydney. **New Zealand's** railways are mainly in the North Island to serve the farming areas.
- In **South America**, the rail network is very dense in two regions, namely, the **Pampas** of Argentina and the **coffee growing region of Brazil** which together account for 40 per cent of South America's total railway length.

- Only **Chile**, among the remaining countries has a considerable route length linking coastal centres with the mining sites in the interior. **Peru, Bolivia, Ecuador, Colombia and Venezuela** have short single-track rail-lines from ports to the interior with no inter-connecting links.

- There is only one trans-continental rail route linking **Buenos Aires (Argentina) with Valparaiso (Chile)** across the Andes Mountains through the Uspallatta Pass located at a height of 3,900 m.
- In **Asia**, rail networks are very dense in the thickly populated areas of **Japan, China and India**. Other countries have relatively few rail routes. **West Asia** is the least developed in rail facilities because of vast deserts and sparsely populated regions.
- **Africa continent,** has only 40,000 km of railways with South Africa alone accounting for 18,000 km due to the concentration of gold, diamond and copper mining activities.
- The important routes of the continent are:
  - ➢ The Benguela Railway through Angola to Katanga-Zambia Copper Belt;
  - ➢ The Tanzania Railway from the Zambian Copper Belt to Dar-es-Salaam on the coast;
  - ➢ The Railway through Botswana and Zimbabwe linking the landlocked states to the South African network; and
  - ➢ The Blue Train from Cape Town to Pretoria in the Republic of South Africa.
- Elsewhere, as in **Algeria, Senegal, Nigeria, Kenya and Ethiopia**, railway lines connect port cities to interior centres but do not form a good network with other countries.

Trans–Continental Railways

Trans–continental railways run across the continent and link its two ends. They were constructed for economic and political reasons to facilitate long runs in different directions. The following are the most important of these:

Trans–Siberian Railway

- This is a major rail route of Russia. It runs from St. Petersburg in the west to Vladivostok on the Pacific Coast in the east passing through Moscow, Ufa, Novosibirsk, Irkutsk, Chita and Khabarovsk. It is the most important route in Asia and the longest (9,332 km) double-tracked and electrified trans– continental railway in the world.
- It has helped in opening up its Asian region to West European markets. It runs across the Ural Mountains Ob and Yenisei rivers Chita is an important agro-centre and Irkutsk, a fur centre.
- There are connecting links to the south, namely, to Odessa (Ukraine), Baku on the Caspian Coast, Tashkent (Uzbekistan), Ulan Bator (Mongolia), Shenyang (Mukden) and Beijing in China.

Trans–Canadian Railways

- This 7,050 km long rail-line in Canada runs from **Halifax** in the east to Vancouver on the Pacific Coast passing through **Montreal, Ottawa, Winnipeg and Calgary.**
- It was constructed in 1886, initially as part of an agreement to make British Columbia on the west coast join the Federation of States. Later on, it gained economic significance because it connected the Quebec-Montreal Industrial Region with the wheat belt of the Prairie Region and the Coniferous Forest region in the north. Thus, each of these regions became complementary to the other.
- A loop line from Winnipeg to Thunder Bay (Lake Superior) connects this rail-line with one of the important waterways of the world. This line is the economic artery of Canada. Wheat and meat are the important exports on this route.

The Union and Pacific Railway

- This rail-line connects New **York on the Atlantic Coast to San Francisco** on the Pacific Coast passing through Cleveland, Chicago, Omaha, Evans, Ogden and Sacramento.
- The most valuable exports on this route are **ores, grain, paper, chemicals and machinery.**

The Australian Trans–Continental Railway

- This rail-line runs west-east across the southern part of the continent from **Perth** on the west coast, to **Sydney** on the east coast. passing through Kalgoorlie, Broken Hill and Port Augusta.
- Another major north-south line connects Adelaide and Alice Spring and to be joined further to the Darwin–Birdum line.

The Orient Express

- This line runs from **Paris to Istanbul** passing through Strasbourg, Munich, Vienna, Budapest and Belgrade. The journey time from London to Istanbul by this Express is now reduced to 96 hours as against 10 days by the sea-route. The chief exports on this rail-route are **cheese, bacon, oats, wine, fruits, and machinery.**
- There is a proposal to build a Trans–Asiatic Railway linking Istanbul with Bangkok via Iran, Pakistan, India, Bangladesh and Myanmar.

Water Transport

Waterways is an important mode of transport for both passenger and cargo traffic in India. It is the cheapest means of transport and is most suitable for carrying heavy and bulky material. It is a fuel-efficient and eco-friendly mode of transport.

The water transport is of two types:

- Inland waterways, and
- Oceanic waterways.

Inland Waterways

- It was the chief mode of transport before the advent of railways. It, however, faced tough competition from road and railway transport.
- Moreover, **diversion of river water for irrigation purposes made them non-navigable** in large parts of their courses.
- India has **14,500 km of navigable waterways, contributing about 1% to the country's transportation.** It comprises rivers, canals, backwaters, creeks, etc. At present, 5,685 km of major rivers are navigable by mechanised flat bottom vessels.
- For the development, maintenance and regulation of national waterways in the country, the **Inland Waterways Authority of India (IWAI) was set up in 1986.**

The following waterways have been declared as the National Waterways by the Government:

Waterway	Stretch	Specification
NW 1	Allahabad-Haldia stretch (1,620 km)	It is one of the most important waterways in India, which is navigable by mechanical boats up to Patna and by ordinary boats up to Haridwar. It is divided into three parts for developmental purposes (1) Haldia-Farakka (560 km), (ii) Farakka-Patna (460 km), (iii) Patna- Allahabad (600 km).
NW 2	Sadiya-Dhubri stretch (891 km)	Brahmaputra is navigable by steamers up to Dibrugarh (1,384 km) which is shared by India and Bangladesh
NW 3	Kottapuram-Kollam stretch (205 km)	It includes 168 km of west coast canal along with Champakara canal (14 km) and Udyogmandal canal (23 km).
NW 4	Specified streches of Godavari and Krishna rivers along with Kakinada Puducherry stretch of canals (1078 km)	
NW 5	Specified stretches of river Brahmani along with Matai river, delta channels of Mahanadi and Brahmani rivers and East Coast canals (588km).	

National Waterways of India

- There are some other inland water ways on which substantial transportation takes place. These are Mandavi, Zuari, Cumberjua, Sunderbans, Barak and backwaters of Kerala. The famous Nehru Trophy Boat Race (Vallamkali) is also held in the backwaters.

Oceanic Routes

- India has a vast coastline of approximate 7,517 km, including islands. **Twelve major and 185 minor ports** provide infrastructural support to these routes.
- Approximately 95 per cent of India's foreign trade by volume and 70 per cent by value moves through ocean routes.

Major Sea Ports

The capacity of Indian ports increased from 20 million tonnes of cargo handling in 1951 to more than 837 million tonnes in 2016.

Some of the Indian ports along with their hinterlands are as follows:

Kandla Port

- **Kandla Port** situated at the head of Gulf of Kachchh has been developed as a major port to cater to the needs of western and north western parts of the country and also to reduce the pressure at Mumbai port.
- Kandla, also known as the **Deendayal Port, is a tidal port**.
- The port is specially designed to receive large quantities of petroleum and petroleum products and fertiliser.
- The offshore terminal at Vadinar has been developed to reduce the pressure at Kandla port.

Mumbai Port

- Mumbai is a natural harbour and the biggest port of the country.
- The port is situated closer to the general routes from the countries of Middle East, Mediterranean countries, North Africa, North America and Europe where the major share of country's overseas trade is carried out.
- The port is 20 km long and 6-10 km wide with 54 berths and has the **country's largest oil terminal.**
- M.P., Maharashtra, Gujarat, U.P. and parts of Rajasthan constitute the main hinterlands of Mumbai port.

Jawaharlal Nehru Port

- Jawaharlal Nehru Port at Nhava Sheva was developed as a **satellite port** to relieve the pressure at the Mumbai port.
- It is the **largest container port** in India.

Mormugao Port

- Mormugao Port, situated at the entrance of the Zuari estuary, is a **natural harbour in Goa.**
- It gained significance after its remodelling in 1961 to handle **iron-ore exports to Japan.** It is the premier iron ore exporting port of the country. This port accounts for about fifty per cent of India's iron ore export.
- Construction of Konkan railway has considerably extended the hinterland of this port. Karnataka, Goa, Southern Maharashtra constitute its hinterland.

New Mangalore Port

- New Mangalore Port is located in the state of Karnataka and caters to the needs of the **export of iron-ore and iron-concentrates from Kudremukh mines.**
- It also handles fertilisers, petroleum products, edible oils, coffee, tea, wood pulp, yarn, granite stone, molasses, etc.
- **Karnataka is the major hinterland for this port**.

Kochi Port

- Kochi Port, situated at the head of **Vembanad Kayal,** popularly known as the 'Queen of the Arabian Sea', is also a **natural harbour.**
- This port has an advantageous location being **close to the Suez-Colombo route.**
- It caters to the needs of Kerala, southern-Karnataka and south western Tamil Nadu.

Kolkata Port

- Kolkata Port is located on the **Hugli River,** 128 km inland from the Bay of Bengal. Kolkata is an **inland riverine port.**

- Like the Mumbai port, this port was also developed by the British. Kolkata had the initial advantage of being the capital of British India.
- **The port has lost its significance** considerably on account of the diversion of exports to the other ports such as Visakhapatnam, Paradip and its satellite port, Haldia.
- Kolkata port is also confronted with the **problem of silt accumulation** in the Hugli River which provides a link to the sea.
- Its hinterland covers U.P., Bihar, Jharkhand, West Bengal, Sikkim and the north-eastern states.
- Apart from this, it also extends ports facilities to our neighbouring land-locked countries such as **Nepal and Bhutan**.

Haldia Port

- Haldia Port is located 105 km downstream from Kolkata. It has been **constructed to reduce the congestion at Kolkata port.**
- It handles bulk cargo like iron ore, coal, petroleum, petroleum products and fertilisers, jute, jute products, cotton and cotton yarn, etc.

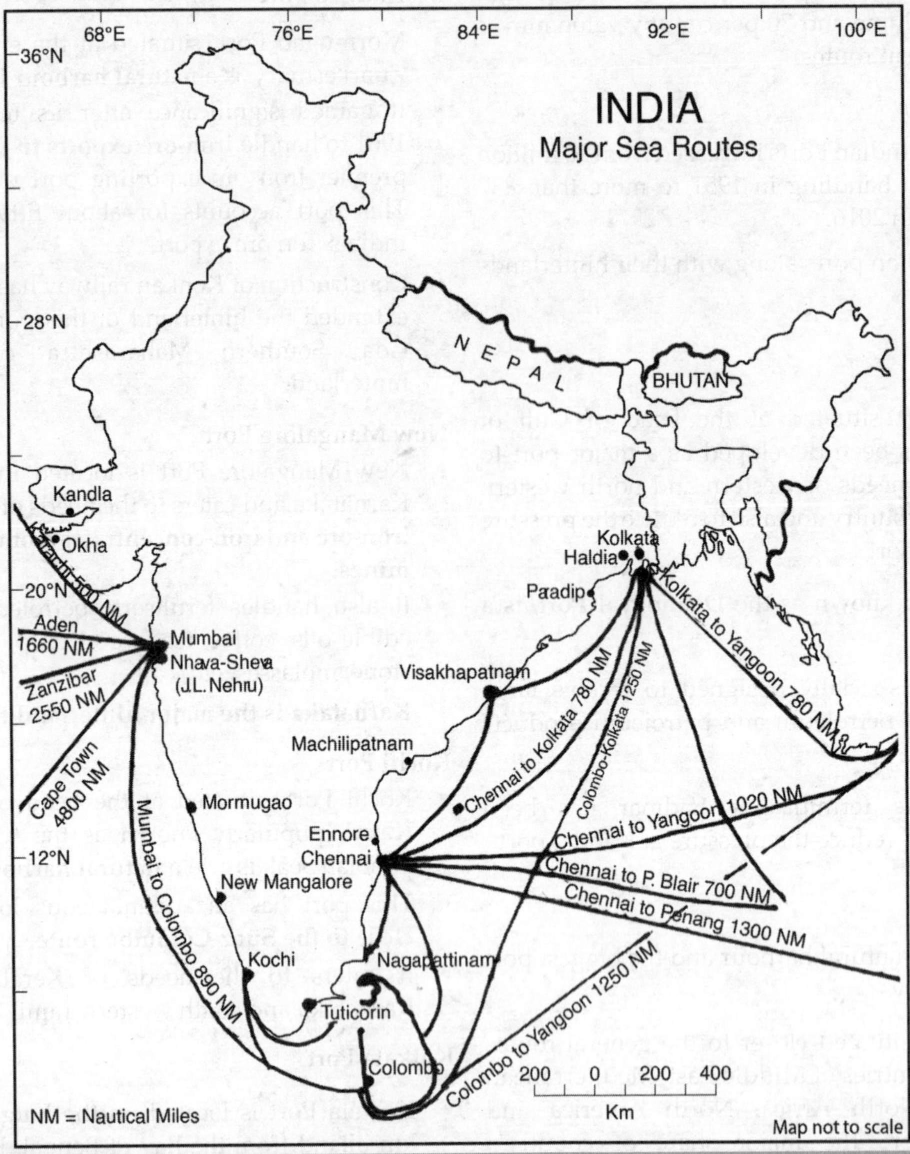

India – Major Ports and Sea Routes

Visakhapatnam Port

- Visakhapatnam Port in Andhra Pradesh is a **deepest land-locked harbour,** connected to the sea by a channel cut through solid rock and sand.
- **An outer harbour has been developed** for handling iron-ore, petroleum and general cargo.
- Andhra Pradesh and Telangana are the main hinterland for this port.

Chennai Port

- Chennai Port is one of the **oldest ports** on the eastern coast.
- It is ranked next to Mumbai in terms of the volume of trade and cargo.
- **It is an artificial harbour built in 1859.**
- It is not suitable for large ships because of the shallow waters near the coast.
- Tamil Nadu and Puducherry are its hinterland.

Ennore

- Ennore, a **newly developed port in Tamil Nadu,** has been constructed 25 km north of Chennai to relieve the pressure at Chennai port.

Tuticorin Port

- Tuticorin Port was also developed to relieve the pressure of Chennai port.
- It deals with a variety of **cargo, including coal, salt, food grains, edible oils, sugar, chemicals and petroleum products.**

Water Transport - World Scenario

Inland Waterways

The following river waterways are some of the world's important **highways of commerce.**

The Rhine Waterways

- The Rhine flows through **Germany and the Netherlands**. It is navigable for 700 km from Rotterdam, at its mouth in the Netherlands to Basel in Switzerland. Ocean-going vessels can reach up to Cologne. The **Ruhr River** joins the Rhine from the east.
- It flows through a rich coalfield and the whole basin has become a prosperous **manufacturing area**. Dusseldorf is the Rhine port for this region. Huge tonnage moves along the stretch south of the Ruhr. This waterway is the **world's most heavily used.**
- Each year more than 20,000 ocean-going ships and 2,00,000 inland vessels exchange their cargoes. It connects the industrial areas of **Switzerland, Germany, France, Belgium and the Netherlands with the North Atlantic Sea Route.**

The Danube Waterway

- This important inland waterway serves **Eastern Europe.** The Danube River rises in the **Black Forest** and flows eastwards through many countries.
- It is navigable up to **Taurna Severin**. The chief export items are **wheat, maize, timber, and machinery.**

The Volga Waterway

- Russia has a large number of developed waterways, of which the Volga is one of the most important. It provides a navigable waterway of 11,200 km and drains into the Caspian Sea.
- The **Volga-Moscow Canal** connects it with the Moscow region and the **Volga-Don Canal** with the Black Sea.

The Great Lakes – St. Lawrence Seaway

- The **Great Lakes of North America Superior, Huron, Erie and Ontario** are connected by Soo Canal and Welland Canal to form an inland waterway.
- The estuary of **St. Lawrence River**, along with the Great Lakes, forms a unique commercial waterway in the northern part of North America.
- The ports on this route like **Duluth and Buffalo** are equipped with all facilities of ocean ports. As such large ocean going vessels are able to navigate up the river deep inside the continent to Montreal.
- But here goods have to be trans-shipped to smaller vessels due to the presence of rapids. Canals have been constructed up to 3.5 m deep to avoid these.

The Mississippi Waterways

- The **Mississippi-Ohio waterway** connects the interior part of USA with the Gulf of Mexico in the south. Large steamers can go through this route up to Minneapolis.

Important Sea Routes

Some important sea routes are as follows:

The Northern Atlantic Sea Route

- This links **North-eastern USA and North-western Europe,** the two industrially developed regions of the world. The foreign trade over this route is greater than that of the rest of the world combined.
- One fourth of the world's foreign trade moves on this route. It is, **therefore, the busiest in the world and otherwise, called the 'Big Trunk Route.'** Both the coasts have highly advanced ports and harbour facilities.

The Mediterranean–Indian Ocean Sea Route

- This sea route passes through the heart of the Old World and serves more countries and people than any other route. **Port Said, Aden, Mumbai, Colombo and Singapore** are some of the important ports on this route.
- The construction of **Suez Canal** has greatly reduced the distance and time as compared to the earlier route through the **Cape of Good Hope,** which was longer than the route through Suez Canal.

The Cape of Good Hope Sea Route

- This trade route connects the highly industrialised **Western European region with West Africa, South Africa, South-east Asia** and the commercial agriculture and livestock economies of Australia and New Zealand.
- The volume of trade and traffic between both East and West Africa is on the rise due to the development of the rich natural resources such as gold, diamond, copper, tin, groundnut, oil palm, coffee and fruits.

The Southern Atlantic Sea Route

- This sea route is another important one across the Atlantic Ocean which connects **West European and West African countries with Brazil, Argentina and Uruguay** in South America.
- The traffic is far less on this route because of the limited development and population in South America and Africa. Only southeastern Brazil and Plata estuary and parts of South Africa have large-scale industries.
- There is also little traffic on the route between **Rio de Janeiro and Cape Town** because both South America and Africa have similar products and resources.

The North Pacific Great Circle Sea Route

- The shortest distance between any two points on a spherical object (such as the Earth) is known as a **"Great Circle Route."** The North Pacific Great Circle Route that connects the **west coast of the United States with major ports in Asia** transiting directly through the Aleutian archipelago.
- Trade across the vast North Pacific Ocean moves by several routes which converge at Honolulu. The direct route on the **Great Circle links Vancouver and Yokohama** and reduces the travelling distance (2,480 km) by half.
- This sea route links the ports on the west coast of North America with those of Asia. These are **Vancouver, Seattle, Portland, San Francisco and Los Angeles** on the American side and **Yokohama, Kobe, Shanghai, Hong Kong, Manila and Singapore** on the Asian side.

The South Pacific Sea Route

- This sea route connects Western Europe and North America with Australia, New Zealand and the scattered Pacific islands via the Panama Canal.
- This route is also used for reaching Hong Kong, Philippines and Indonesia. The distance covered between Panama and Sydney is 12,000 km. **Honolulu is an important port on this route.**

Coastal Shipping

- It is obvious that water transport is a cheaper mode. While oceanic routes connect different countries, coastal shipping is a convenient mode of transportation with long coastlines, e.g. **USA, China and India.**

- **Shenzhen States in Europe** are most suitably placed for coastal shipping connecting one member's coast with the other. If properly developed, coastal shipping can reduce the congestion on the land routes.

Shipping Canals

The Suez and the Panama Canals are two vital man-made navigation canals or waterways which serve as gateways of commerce for both the eastern and western worlds.

The Suez Canal

- This canal had been constructed in 1869 in Egypt between **Port Said in the north and Port Suez in the south** linking the Mediterranean Sea and the Red Sea.
- It gives Europe a new gateway to the Indian Ocean and reduces direct sea-route distance between **Liverpool and Colombo** compared to the Cape of Good Hope route.
- It is a sea-level canal without locks which is about 160 km and 11 to 15 m deep. About 100 ships travel daily and each ship takes 10-12 hours to cross this canal.
- The tolls are so heavy that some find it cheaper to go by the longer Cape Route whenever the consequent delay is not important.
- A railway follows the canal to Suez, and from Ismailia there is a branch line to Cairo. A navigable fresh-water canal from the Nile also joins the Suez Canal in Ismailia to supply fresh-water to Port Said and Suez.

The Panama Canal

- This canal connects the **Atlantic Ocean in the east to the Pacific Ocean in the west**. It has been constructed across the **Panama Isthmus between Panama City and Colon** by the US government which purchased 8 km of area on either side and named it the **Canal Zone.**
- The Canal is about 72 km long and involves a very deep cutting for a length of 12 km. It has a **six-lock system** and ships cross the different levels (26 m up and down) through these locks before entering the Gulf of Panama.
- It shortens the distance between **New York and San Francisco** by 13,000 km by sea. Likewise, the distance between Western Europe and the West-coast of USA; and North-eastern and Central USA and East and South-east Asia is shortened.
- The economic significance of this Canal is relatively less than that of the Suez. However, it is vital to the economies of Latin America.

Air Transportation

- Air transport is the fastest means of movement from one place to the other. It has reduced distances by minimising the travel time.
- It is essential for a vast country like India, where distances are large and the terrain and climatic conditions are diverse.
- Air transport in India made a beginning **in 1911** when airmail operation commenced over a little distance of 10 km between **Allahabad and Naini.**
- Its real development took place in the Post-Independence Period. **The Airport Authority of India** is responsible for providing safe, efficient air traffic and aeronautical communication services in the Indian Air Space. The authority manages 125 airports.
- The air transport in India is managed by **Directorate General of Civil Aviation (DGCA).** Now, many private companies have also started passenger services.
- Air Services are for both passengers and cargo traffic. It connects all the continents of the world.
- Pawanhans Helicopters Ltd. provides helicopter services to Oil and Natural Gas Corporation in its off-shore operations, to inaccessible areas and difficult terrains like the north-eastern states and the interior parts of Jammu and Kashmir, Himachal Pradesh and Uttarakhand.
- In north-eastern states special provisions are made to extend the services to the common people.
- There were **25 major airports functioning in the country** (Annual Report 2016-17). They are Ahmedabad, Bengaluru, Chennai, Delhi,

Goa, Guwahati, Hyderabad, Kolkata, Mumbai, Thiruvananthapuram, Srinagar, Jaipur, Calicut, Nagpur, Coimbatore, Cochin, Lucknow, Pune, Chandigarh, Mangaluru, Visakhapatnam, Indore, Patna, Bhubaneswar and Kannur.

History of Indian Airlines

- 1911 – Air transport in India was launched between Allahabad and Naini.
- 1947 – Air transport was provided by four major companies namely Indian National Airways, Tata Sons Limited, Air Services of India and Deccan Airways.
- 1951 – Four more companies joined the services, Bharat Airways, Himalayan Aviation Limited, Airways India and Kalinga Airlines.
- 1953 – Air transport was nationalised and two Corporations, Air India International and Indian Airlines were formed.
- 2007 – Air India and Indian Airlines were merged under Air India Limited.
- 2022 – was privatised and officially handed over to Tata Group.

Inter-Continental Air Routes

- In the **Northern Hemisphere**, there is a distinct east-west belt of inter-continental air routes. Dense network exists in **Eastern USA, Western Europe and Southeast Asia.**
- USA alone accounts for 60 per cent of the airways of the world.
- **New York, London, Paris, Amsterdam, Frankfurt Rome, Moscow, Karachi, New Delhi, Mumbai, Bangkok, Singapore, Tokyo, San Francisco, Los Angeles and Chicago** are the nodal points where air routes converge or radiate to all continents.
- **Africa, Asiatic part of Russia and South America lack air services**. There are limited air services between 10-35 latitudes in the Southern hemisphere due to sparser population, limited landmass and economic development.

Oil and Gas Pipelines

- Pipelines are the most convenient and efficient mode of transporting liquids and gases over long distances. Even solids can also be transported by pipelines after converting them into slurry.
- The far inland locations of refineries like **Barauni, Mathura, Panipat** and gas-based fertiliser plants could be thought of only because of pipelines.
- **Oil India Limited (OIL)** under the administrative set up of the Ministry of Petroleum and Natural Gas is engaged in the exploration, production and transportation of crude oil and natural gas. It was incorporated in **1959 as a company.**
- **GAIL (India) Ltd**. was set up in 1984 as a public sector undertaking to transport, process and market natural gas for its economic use.

There are three important networks of pipeline transportation in the country.

- From oil field in **upper Assam (Naharkatiya oilfield) to Kanpur (Uttar Pradesh),** via Guwahati, Barauni and Allahabad. It has branches from Barauni to Haldia, via Rajbandh, Rajbandh to Maurigram and Guwahati to Siliguri. It was constructed by **Oil India Limited** (OIL).
- From **Salaya in Gujarat to Jalandhar in Punjab**, via Viramgam, Mathura, Delhi and Sonipat. It has branches to connect Koyali (near Vadodara, Gujarat) Chakshu and other places. It was constructed by **Indian Oil Corporation Limited** (IOCL).
- The first 1,700 km long **Hazira-Vijaipur-Jagdishpur (HVJ) cross country gas pipeline**, linked Mumbai High and Bassein gas fields with various fertiliser, power and industrial complexes in western and northern India. It was constructed by **GAIL (India).**

Overall, India's gas infrastructure has expanded over ten times from 1,700 km to 18,500 km of cross-country pipelines and is expected to soon reach over 34,000 km as Gas Grid by linking all the gas sources across the country including North Eastern States.

World Scenario

- In **New Zealand**, milk is being supplied through pipelines from farms to factories.
- In **USA** there is a dense network of oil pipelines from the producing areas to the consuming areas.
- Big Inch is one such famous pipeline, which carries petroleum from the oil wells of the **Gulf of Mexico to the North-eastern States**.

- About 17 per cent of all freight per tonne. is carried through pipelines in USA.
- In **Europe, Russia and West Asia** pipelines are used to connect oil wells to refineries, and to ports or domestic markets. **Turkmenistan in central Asia** has extended pipelines to Iran and also to parts of China.
- The proposed **Iran-India via Pakistan** international oil and natural gas pipeline will be the longest in the world.

Communication Networks

Human beings have evolved different methods of communication over time. In earlier times, the messages were delivered by beating the drum or hollow tree trunks, giving indications through smoke or fire or with the help of fast runners. Initially, the means of communication were also the means of transportation. Invention of post office, telegraph, printing press, telephone, satellite, etc has made communication much faster and easier. Development in the field of science and technology has significantly contributed in bringing about revolution in the field of communication. People use different modes of communication to convey the messages. **On the basis of scale and quality, the modes of communication can be divided into:**

Personal Communication System

- Among all the personal communication systems, the internet is the most effective and advanced one. It is widely used in urban areas. It enables the user to establish direct contact through email to get access to the world of knowledge and information.
- **Cyberspace** is the world of electronic computerised space. It is encompassed by the Internet such as the **World Wide Web (www).** In simple words, it is the electronic digital world for communicating or accessing information over computer networks without physical movement of the sender and the receiver. It is also referred to as the Internet. Cyberspace exists everywhere. It may be in an office, sailing boat, flying plane and virtually anywhere.
- It is increasingly used for e-commerce and carrying out money transactions. The internet is like a huge central warehouse of data, with detailed information on various items.
- The network through internet and e-mail provides an efficient access to information at a comparatively low cost. It enables us with the basic facilities of direct communication.
- The **Indian Postal Network** is the largest in the world. It handles parcels as well as personal written communications.
  - Cards and envelopes are considered **first-class mail** and are airlifted between stations covering both land and air.
  - The **second-class mail** includes book packets, registered newspapers and periodicals. They are carried by surface mail, covering land and water transport.
  - To facilitate quick delivery of mail in large towns and cities, **six mail channels** have been introduced recently. They are called Rajdhani Channel, Metro Channel, Green Channel, Business Channel, Bulk Mail Channel and Periodical Channel.
- India has one of the largest telecom networks in Asia. Excluding urban places more than two-thirds of the villages in India have already been covered with **Subscriber Trunk Dialing (STD)** telephone facility.
- In order to strengthen the flow of information from the grassroot to the higher level, the government has made special provision to extend the twenty-four hours STD facility to every village in the country. There is a uniform rate of STD facilities all over India. It has been made possible by integrating the development in space technology with communication technology.

World Scenario

- In the last few years, there has been a shift among global users from **USA** to the developing countries. The percentage share of USA has dropped from 66 in 1995 to only 25 in 2005. Now, the majority of the world's users are in **USA, UK, Germany, Japan, China and India.**
- As billions use the Internet each year, cyberspace will expand the contemporary economic and social space of humans through **e-mail, e-commerce, e-learning and e-governance.** The Internet

together with **fax, television and radio** will be accessible to more and more people cutting across place and time. It is these modern communication systems, more than transportation, that has made the concept of **global village** a reality.

Mass Communication System

Radio

- **Radio broadcasting started in India in 1923 by the Radio Club of Bombay**. Since then, it gained immense popularity and changed the socio-cultural life of people.
- Within no time, it made a place in every household of the country. Government took this opportunity and brought this popular mode of communication under its control in 1930 under the Indian Broadcasting System. It was changed to **All India Radio in 1936 and to Akashwani in 1957.**
- All India Radio broadcasts a variety of programmes related to information, education and entertainment. Special news bulletins are also broadcasted on specific occasions like sessions of parliament and state legislatures.

Television (T.V.)

- Television broadcasting has emerged as the most effective audio-visual medium for disseminating information and educating masses.
- Initially, the T.V. services were limited only to the National Capital where it began in 1959. After 1972, several other stations became operational.
- In 1976, TV was delinked from All India Radio (AIR) and got a separate identity as Doordarshan (DD). After **INSAT-IA**, National Television-DD1 became operational, **Common National Programmes (CNP)** were started for the entire network and its services were extended to the backward and remote rural areas.

Satellite Communication

- Satellites are modes of communication in themselves as well as they regulate the use of other means of communication. However, the use of satellites in getting a continuous and synoptic view of a larger area has made satellite communication very vital for the country due to the economic and strategic reasons.
- Satellite images can be used for the weather forecast, monitoring of natural calamities, surveillance of border areas, etc. On the basis of configuration and purposes, **satellite system in India can be grouped into two: Indian National Satellite System (INSAT) and Indian Remote Sensing Satellite System (IRS).**
- The **INSAT**, which was established in 1983, is a multi-purpose satellite system for telecommunication, meteorological observation and for various other data and programmes.
- The **IRS** satellite system became operational with the launching of IRS-IA in March 1988 from Vaikanour in Russia.
- India has also developed her own Launching Vehicle, PSLV (Polar Satellite Launch Vehicle). These satellites collect data in several spectral bands and transmit them to the ground stations for various uses.
- The **National Remote Sensing Centre (NRSC)** at Hyderabad provides facilities for acquisition of data and its processing. These are very useful in the management of natural resources.
- India has also made great strides in satellite development. **Aryabhatt** was launched on 19 April 1979, Bhaskar-I in 1979 and Rohini in 1980. On 18 June 1981, **APPLE (Ariane Passenger Payload Experiment)** was launched through an **Arian rocket. Bhaskar, Challenger and INSAT I-B** have made long-distance communication, television and radio very effective.

Digital India is an umbrella programme to prepare India for a knowledge based, transformation. The focus of Digital India Programme is on being transformative to realise – IT (Indian Talent) + IT (Information Technology) = IT (India's Tomorrow) and is on making technology central to enabling change.

World scenario

- Communication through satellites emerged as a new area in communication technology since the **1970s after USA and former USSR pioneered space research.**
- **Artificial satellites**, now, are successfully deployed in the earth's orbit to connect even the

remote corners of the globe with limited on-site verification.

- These have rendered the unit cost and time of communication invariant in terms of distance. This means it costs the same to communicate over 500 km as it does over 5,000 km via satellites.

TEST YOURSELF

Multiple Choice Questions

Q1. Which mode of transport is the most suitable for the transportation of bulky and heavy goods over long distances?

(a) Air transport (b) Road transport
(c) Rail transport (d) Water transport

Q2. The system that enables the transmission of messages and information over long distances is known as:

(a) Communication (b) Transportation
(c) Infrastructure (d) Logistics

Q3. The main mode of transportation used for the movement of goods and passengers within cities and towns is:

(a) Air transport (b) Road transport
(c) Rail transport (d) Water transport

Q4. Which of the following is an example of an air transport infrastructure?

(a) Roads and highways
(b) Airports and airstrips
(c) Railway stations
(d) Seaports and harbours

Q5. The mode of transportation that is the fastest but also the most expensive is:

(a) Air transport (b) Road transport
(c) Rail transport (d) Water transport

Q6. The transmission of information through written or printed materials is known as:

(a) Oral communication
(b) Written communication
(c) Telecommunication
(d) Mass communication

Q7. Which mode of transport is the most suitable for transporting perishable goods like fruits and vegetables?

(a) Air transport (b) Road transport
(c) Rail transport (d) Water transport

Q8. The mode of transportation that is the most energy-efficient and environment-friendly is:

(a) Air transport (b) Road transport
(c) Rail transport (d) Water transport

Q9. The process of sending and receiving messages or information through electronic devices is known as:

(a) Telecommunication
(b) Oral communication
(c) Mass communication
(d) Written communication

Q10. The network of roads, railways, airports, and seaports that facilitates the movement of goods and people is known as:

(a) Transportation system
(b) Communication system
(c) Trade network
(d) Logistics network

Answer Key

Q1.	d	Q2.	a	Q3.	b	Q4.	b
Q5.	a	Q6.	b	Q7.	a	Q8.	d
Q9.	a	Q10.	a				

Model Question for Main Examination

Q. Indian railways had been the lifeline of India's growth story. Analyse the challenges, advantages and disadvantages of its privatisation. (250 words) (UPSC 2019)

UNIT 31

International Trade

In This Unit

Comprehensive and profound coverage of the following NCERTs' chapter:

✓ NCERT Class- 12th (Fundamentals of Human Geography), Chapter- 8

Trade means the voluntary exchange of goods and services. **Trade may be conducted at two levels: international and national**. International trade is the exchange of goods and services among countries across national boundaries. Countries need to trade to obtain commodities, they cannot produce themselves or they can purchase elsewhere at a lower price.

The initial form of trade in primitive societies was the barter system, where direct exchange of goods took place. **The difficulties of the barter system were overcome by the introduction of money.**

> The word **'salary'** comes from the Latin word **Salarium** which means **payment by salt**. As in those times producing salt from sea water was unknown and could only be made from rock salt which was rare and expensive. That is why it became a mode of payment.

History of International Trade

In ancient times, transporting goods over long distances was risky, hence trade was restricted to local markets. The Silk Route is an early example of long distance, trade **connecting Rome to China** – along the 6,000 km route. The traders transported Chinese silk, Roman wool and precious metals and many other high value commodities from intermediate points in **India, Persia and Central Asia.**

Slave Trade- Fifteenth century onwards, the European colonialism began and along with trade of exotic commodities, a new form of trade emerged which was called **Slave Trade**. The Portuguese, Dutch, Spaniards, and British captured African natives and forcefully transported them to the newly discovered Americas for their labour in the plantations. Slave trade was a lucrative business for more than two hundred years till **it was abolished in Denmark in 1792, Great Britain in 1807 and United States in 1808.**

Industrial Revolution — After the Industrial Revolution the demand for raw materials like grains, meat, wool also expanded, but their monetary value declined in relation to the manufactured goods. The industrialised nations imported primary products as raw materials and exported the value-added finished products back to the non-industrialised nations. In the later, half of the nineteenth century, regions producing primary goods were no more important, and industrial nations became each other's principal customers.

Why Does International Trade Exist?

International trade is the result of **specialisation in production**. It benefits the world economy if different countries practise specialisation and division of labour in the production of commodities or provision of services. Each kind of specialisation can give rise to trade. Thus, international trade is based on the **principle of comparative advantage, complementarity and transferability** of goods and services and in principle, should be **mutually beneficial** to the trading partners.

Basis of International Trade

- **Difference in National Resources:** The world's national resources are unevenly distributed because of differences in their physical make up i.e., geology, relief soil and climate.

- **Geological structure:** It determines the mineral resource base and topographical differences ensure diversity of crops and animals raised. Lowlands have greater agricultural potential. Mountains attract tourists and promote tourism.
- **Mineral resources:** They are unevenly distributed the world over. The availability of mineral resources provides the basis for industrial development.
- **Climate:** It influences the type of flora and fauna that can survive in a given region. It also ensures diversity in the range of various products, e.g., wool production can take place in cold regions, bananas, rubber and cocoa can grow in tropical regions.

- **Population factors:** The size, distribution and diversity of people between countries affect the type and volume of goods traded.
    - **Cultural factors:** Distinctive forms of art and craft develop in certain cultures which are valued the world over, e.g., China produces the finest porcelains and brocades. Carpets of Iran are famous while North African leather work and Indonesian batik cloth are prized handicrafts.
    - **Size of population:** Densely populated countries have large volume of internal trade but little external trade because most of the agricultural and industrial production is consumed in the local markets. Standard of living of the population determines the demand for better quality imported products because with low standard of living, only a few people can afford to buy **costly imported goods.**
- **Stage of Economic Development:** At different stages of economic development of countries, the nature of items traded undergo changes. In agriculturally important countries, agro-products are exchanged for manufactured goods whereas industrialised nations export machinery and finished products and import food grains and other raw materials.
- **Extent of Foreign Investment:** Foreign investment can boost trade in developing countries which lack in capital required for the development of **mining, oil drilling, heavy engineering, lumbering and plantation agriculture.** By developing such **capital-intensive industries** in developing countries, the industrial nations ensure import of food stuffs, minerals and create markets for their finished products. This entire cycle steps up the volume of trade between nations.
- **Transport:** In olden times, lack of adequate and efficient means of transport restricted trade to local areas. Only high value items, e.g., gems, silk and spices were traded over long distances. With expansions of rail, ocean and air transport, better means of **refrigeration and preservation**, trade has experienced **spatial expansion.**

Important Aspects of International Trade

International trade has three very important aspects. These are volume, sectoral composition and direction of trade.

Volume of Trade

The actual tonnage of goods traded makes up the volume. However, services traded cannot be measured in tonnage. Therefore, the **total value of goods and services traded is considered to be the volume of trade.**

Composition of Trade

The nature of goods and services imported and exported by countries have undergone changes during the last century. Trade of primary products was dominant in the beginning of the last century. Later, **manufactured goods gained prominence** and currently, though the manufacturing sector commands the bulk of the global trade, service sector which includes **travel, transportation and other commercial services** have been showing an **upward trend.** The volume of imports and exports of world merchandise has been **growing consistently** over the years. There is change in the share of continents in the **world's Merchandise Trade** as **Europe's contribution is declining** while the contribution of **Asian countries is growing**.

Direction of Trade

Historically, the developing countries of the present used to **export valuable goods and artefacts**, etc., which were exported to European countries. During the nineteenth century, there was a reversal in the direction of trade. European countries started exporting manufactured goods for exchange of foodstuffs and raw materials from their colonies. The world trade pattern underwent a drastic change during the second half of the twentieth century.

Balance of Trade

Balance of Trade records the volume of goods and services imported as well as exported by a country to other countries. If the value of imports is more than the value of a country's exports, the country has a **negative or unfavourable balance of trade**. If the value of exports is more than the value of imports, then the country has **a positive or favourable balance of trade**.

Balance of Trade and Balance of Payments have serious implications for a country's economy. A negative balance would mean that the country spends more on buying goods than it can earn by selling its goods. This would ultimately lead to exhaustion of its financial reserves.

Types of International Trade

International trade may be categorised into two types:

1. **Bilateral trade:** Bilateral trade is done by two countries with each other. They enter into agreement to trade specified commodities amongst them. For example, country A may agree to trade some raw material with agreement to purchase some other specified item to country B or vice versa.
2. **Multi-lateral trade:** As the term suggests multi-lateral trade is conducted with many trading countries. The same country can trade with a number of other countries. The country may also grant the status of the **"Most Favoured Nation" (MFN)** for some of the trading partners.

Case for Free Trade

The act of opening up economies for trading is known as **Free Trade** or **Trade Liberalisation.** This is done by bringing down trade barriers like tariffs. Trade liberalisation allows goods and services from everywhere to compete with domestic products and services.

Globalisation along with Free Trade can adversely affect the economies of developing countries by not giving equal playing field by imposing conditions which are unfavourable. With the development of transport and communication systems goods and services can travel faster and farther than ever before. But free trade should not only let rich countries enter the markets, but allow the developed countries to keep their own markets protected from foreign products.

Countries also need to be cautious about **Dumped Goods**; as along with free trade dumped goods of cheaper prices can harm the domestic producers.

> **Dumping:** The practice of selling a commodity in two countries at a price that differs for reasons not related to costs is called **dumping**. Dumping is considered a form of price discrimination. It occurs when a manufacturer lowers the price of an item entering a foreign market to a level that is less than the price paid by domestic customers in the originating country.

International Trade in the Context of India

India's international trade has undergone a sea change in recent years in terms of volume, composition as well as direction. Although India's contribution in the world trade is as low as one per cent of the total volume, yet it plays a significant role in the world economy.

Changing Pattern of India's International Trade

- In **1950-51**, India's external trade was worth Rs.1,214 crore, which rose to Rs. 44,29,762 crore in 2016-17.
- There are numerous reasons for this sharp rise in overseas trade, such as the momentum picked up by the **manufacturing sectors**, the **liberal policies** of the government and the **diversification of markets.**
- The nature of India's foreign trade has changed over the years. Though there has been an **increase in the total volume of import and export, the value of import continued to be higher** than that of exports.
- The **composition of commodities** in India's international trade has been undergoing a change

over the years. The share of **agriculture and allied products has declined**, whereas, shares of petroleum and crude products and other commodities have increased.

- The shares of **ore minerals and manufactured goods have largely remained constant** over the years from 2009-10 to 2010-11and 2015-16 to 2016-17.
- The **decline in traditional items** is largely due to the **tough international competition**. Amongst the agricultural products, there is a decline in the export of traditional items, such as coffee, cashew, etc., though an **increase has been registered in floricultural products, fresh fruits, marine products and sugar**, etc.
- Manufacturing sector alone accounted for 73.6 per cent of India's total value of export in 2016-17. Engineering goods have shown a significant growth in exports.
- **China and other East Asian countries** are our major competitors. **Gems and jewellery** contribute a larger share of India's foreign trade.

Changing Patterns of the Composition of India's Import

- India faced serious food shortage during the 1950s and 1960s. The major item of import at that time was foodgrain, capital goods, machinery and equipment.
- The balance of payment was adverse as imports were more than export in spite of all the efforts of import substitution.
- After 1970s, foodgrain import was discontinued due to the success of Green Revolution but the energy crisis of 1973 pushed the prices of petroleum.
- Foodgrain import was replaced by fertilisers and petroleum. Machine and equipment, special steel, edible oil and chemicals largely make the import basket.
- There is a steep rise in the import of petroleum products. It is used not only as a fuel but also as an industrial raw material.
- Import of capital goods maintained a steady increase due to rising demand in the export-oriented industrial and domestic sectors. Non-electrical machinery, transport equipment, manufacturers of metals and machine tools were the main items of capital goods.

World Trade Organisation

- In **1948,** to liberalise the world from high customs tariffs and various other types of restrictions, **General Agreement for Tariffs and Trade (GATT)** was formed by some countries.
- In **1994**, it was decided by the member countries to set up a permanent institution for looking after the promotion of free and fair trade amongst nation and the GATT was transformed into the **World Trade Organisation from 1st January 1995.**
- WTO Headquarters are located in Geneva, Switzerland. **India has been one of the founder members of WTO.**
- WTO is the only international organisation dealing with the global rules of trade between nations.
- It sets the **rules for the global trading system and resolves disputes** between its member nations.
- WTO also covers trade in services, such as telecommunication and banking, and others issues such as intellectual rights.

Regional Trade Blocs

Regional Trade Blocs have come up in order to encourage trade between countries with geographical proximity, similarity and complementarities in trading items and to curb restrictions on trade of the developing world. Today, **120 regional trade blocs generate 52 per cent of the world trade.** These trading blocs developed as a **response to the failure** of the global organisations to speed up intra-regional trade.

Regional Blocs	Head Quarter	Member nations	Origin	Commodities	Other Areas of Cooperation
ASEAN (Association of South East Asian Nations)	Jakarta, Indonesia	Brunei Darussalam, Cambodia, Indonesia, Laos, Malaysia, Myanmar, Philippines, Singapore, Thailand and Vietnam	Aug. 1967	Agro products, rubber, palm oil, rice, copra, coffee, minerals-copper, coal, nickel and tungsten. Energy - petroleum and natural gas and Software products	Accelerate economic growth, cultural development, peace and regional stability
CIS (Commonwealth of Independent States)	Minsk, Belarus	Armenia, Azerbaijan, Belarus, Georgia, Kazakhstan, Kyrgyzstan, Moldova, Russia, Tajikistan, Turkmenistan, Ukraine and Uzbekistan.	-	Crude oil, natural gas, gold, cotton, fibre, aluminium	Integration and cooperation on matters of economics, defence and foreign policy
EU (European Union)	Brussels, Belgium	Austria, Belgium, Bulgaria, Croatia, Cyprus, Czech Republic, Denmark, Estonia, Finland, France, Germany, Greece, Hungary, Ireland, Italy, Latvia, Lithuania, Luxembourg, Malta, Poland, Portugal, Romania, Slovakia, Slovenia, Spain, Sweden, Netherlands and United Kingdom	EEC - March 1957 EU - Feb. 1992	Agro products, minerals, chemicals, wood, paper, transport vehicles, optical instruments, clocks - works of art, antiques	Single market with single currency
LAIA (Latin American Integration Association)	Montevideo, Uruguay	Argentina, Bolivia, Brazil, Colombia, Ecuador, Mexico, Paraguay, Peru, Uruguay and Venezuela	1994	-	-
NAFTA (North American Free Trade Association)		USA, Canada and Mexico	1949	Agro products, motor vehicles. automotive parts, computers, textiles	-
OPEC (Organisation of Petroleum Exporting Countries)	Vienna, Austria	Algeria, Indonesia, Iran, Iraq, Kuwait, Libya, Nigeria, Qatar, Saudi Arabia, UAE and Venezuela		Crude petroleum	Coordinate and unify petroleum policies.
SAFTA (South Asian Free Trade Agreement)		Bangladesh, Maldives, Bhutan, Nepal, India, Pakistan and Sri Lanka	Jan-2006	-	Reduce tariffs on inter- regional trade

Major Regional Trade Organisation

Gateways of International Trade

Ports

The chief gateways of the world of international trade are Harbours and Ports.

Types of Port

Generally, **ports are classified according to the types of traffic which they handle.**

Types of ports according to cargo handled:

1. **Industrial Ports:** These ports specialise in bulk cargo-like grain, sugar, ore, oil, chemicals and similar materials.
2. **Commercial Ports**: These ports handle general cargo-packaged products and manufactured goods. These ports also handle passenger traffic.
3. **Comprehensive Ports:** Such ports handle bulk and general cargo in large volumes. Most of the world's great ports are classified as comprehensive ports.

Types of port on the basis of location:

1. **Inland Ports:** These ports are located away from the sea coast. They are linked to the sea through a river or a canal. Such ports are accessible to **flat bottom ships or barges.** For example, Manchester is linked with a canal; Memphis is located on the river Mississippi; Rhine has several ports like Mannheim and Duisburg; and Kolkata is located on the river Hugli, a branch of the river Ganga.
2. **Out Ports:** These are **deep** water ports built away from the actual ports. These serve the parent ports by receiving those ships which are unable to approach them due to their large size. For example, **Athens and its out-port Piraeus in Greece.**

Types of port on the basis of specialised functions:

1. **Oil Ports:** These ports deal in the processing and shipping of oil. Some of these are tanker ports and some are refinery ports. Maracaibo in Venezuela, Esskhira in Tunisia, Tripoli in Lebanon are tanker ports. Abadan on the Gulf of Persia is a refinery port.
2. **Ports of Call:** These are the ports which originally developed as calling points on main sea routes where ships used to anchor for refuelling, watering and taking food items. Later on, they developed into commercial ports. Aden, Honolulu and Singapore are good examples.
3. **Packet Station:** These are also known as **ferry ports**. These packet stations are exclusively concerned with the transportation of passengers and mail across water bodies covering short distances. These stations occur in pairs located in such a way that they face each other across the water body, e.g., **Dover in England and Calais in France across the English Channel.**
4. **Entrepot Ports:** These are collection centres where the goods are brought from different countries for export. **Singapore is an entrepot for Asia. Rotterdam for Europe, and Copenhagen for the Baltic region.**
5. **Naval Ports:** These are ports which have only strategic importance. **These ports serve warships and have repair workshops for them. Kochi and Karwar** are examples of such ports in India.

Concerns Related to International Trade

- Undertaking international trade is mutually beneficial to nations if it leads to:
  - Regional specialisation
  - Higher level of production
  - Better standard of living
  - Worldwide availability of goods and services
  - Equalisation of prices and wages
  - Diffusion of knowledge and culture
- International trade can prove to be detrimental to nations if it leads to **dependence on other countries, uneven levels of development, exploitation, and commercial rivalry** leading to wars.
- Global trade affects many aspects of life; it can impact everything from the **environment to health and well-being** of the people around the world.
- As countries compete to trade more, production and the use of natural resources spiral up, resources get **used up faster than they can be replenished**. As a result, marine life is also depleting fast, forests are being cut down and river basins sold off to private drinking water companies.
- Multi-national corporations trading in **oil, gas mining, pharmaceuticals and agri-business** keep expanding their operations at all costs creating

more pollution – their mode of work does not follow the norms of sustainable development.

- If organisations are geared **only towards profit making**, and environmental and health concerns are not addressed, then it could lead to serious implications in the future.

TEST YOURSELF

Multiple Choice Questions

Q1. International trade refers to the exchange of goods and services:

(a) Between two countries across their national boundaries

(b) Within the same country

(c) Between countries located in different continents

(d) Within a specific region or state

Q2. Which of the following is NOT a motive for international trade?

(a) Access to resources and raw materials

(b) Economic development and growth

(c) Political domination and control

(d) Expanding market opportunities

Q3. The difference between a country's total exports and total imports is known as:

(a) Trade surplus (b) Trade deficit

(c) Balance of trade (d) Current account

Q4. The removal of trade barriers, such as tariffs and quotas, between countries is known as:

(a) Protectionism (b) Import substitution

(c) Free trade (d) Mercantilism

Q5. Which of the following organisations is responsible for regulating and promoting international trade?

(a) World Trade Organisation (WTO)

(b) International Monetary Fund (IMF)

(c) United Nations (UN)

(d) Organization for Economic Cooperation and Development (OECD)

Q6. The total value of a country's exports and imports of goods and services is known as its:

(a) Gross Domestic Product (GDP)

(b) Gross National Product (GNP)

(c) Balance of trade

(d) Current account balance

Q7. Which of the following is an example of a trade barrier?

(a) Export subsidies

(b) Foreign direct investment

(c) Free trade agreements

(d) Trade liberalisation

Q8. The theory that suggests that countries should specialise in producing goods and services in which they have a comparative advantage is known as:

(a) Mercantilism

(b) Protectionism

(c) Comparative advantage theory

(d) Absolute advantage theory

Q9. If the value of exports is more than the value of imports, then the country's state shows:

(a) Trade surplus (b) Trade deficit

(c) Balance of payments (d) Current account

Q10. The process of selling goods and services to customers in another country is known as:

(a) Importing (b) Exporting

(c) Outsourcing (d) Offshoring

Answer Key

Q1.	a	Q2.	c	Q3.	c	Q4.	c
Q5.	a	Q6.	d	Q7.	a	Q8.	c
Q9.	a	Q10.	b				

Model Questions for Main Examination

Q1. Explain the two types of international trade. Examine any three possible negative impacts of globalisation along with free trade in the world.

Q2. Explain any two functions of WTO. Why has this organisation been criticised? Give three arguments in this regard.

UNIT 32 Migration in Indian Context

In This Unit

Comprehensive and profound coverage of the following NCERTs' chapter:

✓ NCERT (Before Rationalisation) Class- 12th (India-People and Economy), Chapter- 2

Actually, **migration was recorded beginning from the first Census of India conducted in 1881.** This data was recorded on the basis of place of birth. However, the first major modification was introduced in 1961 Census by bringing in two additional components viz; **place of birth** i.e., **village or town** and **duration of residence (if born elsewhere).** Further in **1971**, additional information on place of last residence and duration of stay at the place of enumeration were incorporated.

In the Census of India migration is enumerated on two bases:

- **Place of Birth**, if the place of birth is different from the place of enumeration (known as life-time migrant);
- **Place of Residence**, if the place of last residence is different from the place of enumeration (known as migrant by place of last residence). As per 2011 census, out of 1,210 million people in the country, 455.8 million (about 37%) were reported as migrants of place of last residence.

Indian Diaspora

During colonial period millions of **indentured labourers** were sent to Mauritius, Caribbean islands (Trinidad, Tobago and Guyana), Fiji and South Africa from **Uttar Pradesh and Bihar**; to Reunion Island, Guadeloupe, Martinique and Surinam by French Dutch and by Portuguese from **Goa, Daman and Diu** to work as plantation workers. All such migrations were covered under the time-bound contract known as **Girmit Act (Indian Emigration Act)**. However, the living conditions of these indentured labourers were not better than the slaves.

The second wave of migrants ventured out into the neighbouring countries in recent times as professionals, artisans, traders and factory workers, in search of economic opportunities to **Thailand, Malaysia, Singapore, Indonesia, Brunei and African countries**, etc. and the trend still continues. There was a steady outflow of India's **semi-skilled and skilled labour** in the wake of the oil boom in West Asia in the 1970s. There was also some outflow of **entrepreneurs, storeowners, professionals, businessmen** to Western Countries.

Third wave of migrants comprised professionals like doctors, engineers (1960s onwards), software engineers, management consultants, financial experts, media persons (1980s onwards), and others migrated to countries such as **USA, Canada, UK, Australia, New Zealand and Germany**, etc. These professionals enjoy the distinction of being one of highly educated, the highest earning and prospering groups. After liberalisation, in the 90s, **education and knowledge–based** Indian emigration has made Indian Diaspora one of the most powerful diasporas in the world.

Indian diaspora has been playing an important role in the development of the respective countries.

Streams of Migration

Under internal migration, four streams are identified:

- Rural to Rural (R-R);
- Rural to Urban (R-U);
- Urban to Urban (U-U);
- Urban to Rural (U-R).

In India, during 2011, out of 455.0 million migrants, enumerated on the basis of the last residence, 141.9 million had changed their place of residence in the last ten years. Out of these, 118.7 million were intra-state migrants. The stream was **dominated by female migrants**. Most of these were migrants related to marriage.

The distribution of **male and female migrants** in different streams of **intra-state and inter-state migration** is presented in the figure given below. It is clearly evident that females predominate the streams of short distance rural to rural migration in both types of migration. Contrary to this, men predominate the rural to urban stream of inter-state migration due to **economic reasons.**

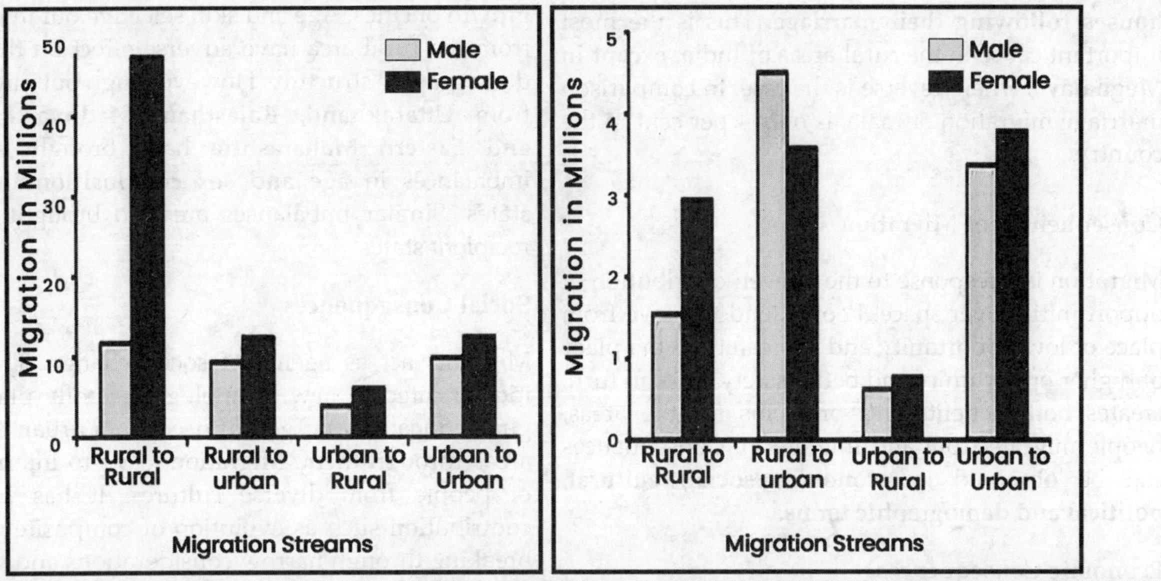

Graph Showing Intra-state and Inter-state Migration by Place of Last Residence Indicating Migration Streams in India, 2011

Apart from these streams of internal migration, India also experiences immigration from and emigration to the neighbouring countries. Indian Census 2011 has recorded that **more than 5 million** people have migrated to India from other countries. Out of these, about 88.9 percent came from the neighbouring countries: **Bangladesh followed by Nepal and Pakistan.**

Spatial Variation in Migration

Some states like **Maharashtra, Delhi, Gujarat and Haryana** attract migrants from other states such as **Uttar Pradesh, Bihar, Rajasthan**, etc. Maharashtra occupied first place in migrants, followed by **Delhi, Gujarat and Haryana**. On the other hand, Uttar Pradesh was the state, which had the largest number of net out-migrants from the state.

Causes of Migration

There could be a variety of reasons that millions of people leave their places of birth and residence. **These reasons can be put into two broad categories:**

Push Factors

These cause people to leave their place of residence or origin. In India people migrate from rural to urban areas mainly due to poverty, high population pressure on the land, lack of basic infrastructural facilities like health care, education, etc. Apart from these factors, natural disasters such as, **flood, drought, cyclonic storms, earthquake, tsunami, wars and local conflicts** also give extra push to migrate.

Pull Factors

The factor which attracts people from different places. The most important pull factor for the majority of the rural migrants to urban areas is the better opportunities, availability of regular work and relatively higher wages. Better opportunities for **education, better health facilities and sources of entertainment**, etc., are also quite important pull factors.

It can be seen that the reasons for migration of males and females are different. For example, work and employment have remained the main cause for male migration (26 percent) while it is only 2.3 percent for the females. Contrary to this, **about 67 percent of females move out from their parental houses following their marriage.** This is the most important cause in the rural areas of India, **except in Meghalaya,** where reverse is the case. In comparison marriage migration of male, is only 4 per cent in the country.

Consequences of Migration

Migration is a response to the uneven distribution of opportunities over space. People tend to move from place of low opportunity and low safety to the place of higher opportunity and better safety. This, in turn, creates both benefits and problems for the areas, people migrate from and migrate to. Consequences can be observed in **economic, social, cultural, political and demographic terms.**

Economic Consequences

A major benefit for the source region is the remittance sent by migrants. Remittances from international migrants are one of the major sources of foreign exchange. In 2002, India received **US$ 11 billion** as remittances from international migrants. **Punjab, Kerala and Tamil Nadu** receive a very significant amount from their international migrants. The sum of remittances sent by the internal migrants is very meagre as compared to international migrants, but it plays an important role in the growth of the economy of the source area. Remittances are mainly used for food, repayment of debts, treatment, marriages, children's education, agricultural inputs, construction of houses, etc. Migration from rural areas of **Eastern Uttar Pradesh, Bihar, Madhya Pradesh and Odisha to the rural areas of Punjab, Haryana, Western Uttar Pradesh** accounted for the success of their Green Revolution strategy for agricultural development. Besides this, unregulated migration to the metropolitan cities of India has caused overcrowding. Development of slums in industrially developed states such as **Maharashtra, Gujarat, Karnataka, Tamil Nadu and Delhi** are a negative consequence of **unregulated migration** within the country.

Demographic Consequences

Migration leads to the redistribution of the population within a country. **Rural Urban Migration** is one of the important factors contributing to the population growth of cities. Age and skill selective out migration from the rural area have adverse effect on the rural demographic structure. However, high out migration from **Uttarakhand, Rajasthan, Madhya Pradesh and Eastern Maharashtra** have brought serious imbalances in **age and sex composition** in these states. Similar imbalances are also brought in the recipient states.

Social Consequences

Migrants act as agents of social change. The new ideas related to new technologies, family planning, girl's education, etc. get diffused from urban to rural areas through them. Migration leads to intermixing of people from diverse cultures. It has positive contribution such as evolution of composite culture breaking through narrow considerations and widens up the mental horizon of people at large. But it also has serious negative consequences such as anonymity, which creates social vacuum and sense of dejection among individuals. Continued feeling of dejection may motivate people to fall in the trap of **anti-social activities like crime and drug abuse.**

Environmental Consequences

Overcrowding of people due to rural-urban migration has put pressure on the existing social and physical infrastructure in the urban areas. This ultimately leads to unplanned growth of urban settlements and formation of slums shanty colonies.

Apart from this, due to over-exploitation of natural resources, cities are facing the acute problem of depletion of **ground water, air pollution, disposal of sewage and management of solid wastes.**

Others

Migration (even excluding the marriage migration) affects the status of women directly or indirectly. In the rural areas, **male selective out migration** leaving their wives behind puts extra physical as well mental pressure on the women. **Migration of 'women' either for education or employment** enhances their autonomy and role in the economy.

If remittances are the major benefits of migration from the point of view of the source region, the loss of human resources, particularly highly skilled people are the most serious cost. The market for advanced skills has become truly a global market and the most dynamic industrial economies are admitting and recruiting significant proportions of the highly trained professionals from poor regions. Consequently, the existing underdevelopment in the source region gets reinforced.

TEST YOURSELF

Multiple Choice Questions

Q1. The movement of people from one place to another with the intention of settling in a new location is known as:

(a) Emigration (b) Immigration

(c) Migration (d) Repatriation

Q2. Which of the following is a push factor for migration?

(a) Better Job Opportunities

(b) Improved living standards

(c) Political stability

(d) Conflict and violence

Q3. The movement of people within the boundaries of a country is known as:

(a) International migration

(b) Internal migration

(c) Rural-urban migration

(d) Seasonal migration

Q4. A person who is forced to leave their home country due to persecution or violence is called a:

(a) Migrant worker (b) Refugee

(c) Immigrant (d) Tourist

Q5. The process by which individuals or families move back to their home country after residing in another country is known as:

(a) Return migration (b) Reverse migration

(c) Circular migration (d) Repatriation

Q6. A migration pattern in which people move from urban areas to rural areas is known as:

(a) Urban-urban migration

(b) Rural-rural migration

(c) Urban-rural migration

(d) Rural-urban migration

Q7. The movement of people across international borders for the purpose of employment is known as:

(a) Forced migration

(b) Economic migration

(c) Seasonal migration

(d) Environmental migration

Q8. The concept that describes the process of cultural, social, and economic integration between migrants and the host society is known as:

(a) Assimilation (b) Acculturation

(c) Integration (d) Segregation

Q9. The movement of people from one country to another in search of better economic opportunities is known as:

(a) International migration

(b) Internal migration

(c) Forced migration

(d) Voluntary migration

Q10. The movement of people from rural areas to urban areas is known as:

(a) Urbanisation

(b) Industrialisation

(c) Rural-urban migration

(d) Suburbanisation

Q11. The movement of people from one country to another in search of better job opportunities is known as:

(a) Migration (b) Immigration

(c) Repatriation (d) Remittances

Answer Key

Q1.	c	Q2.	d	Q3.	b	Q4.	b
Q5.	a	Q6.	c	Q7.	b	Q8.	c
Q9.	a	Q10.	c	Q11.	a		

Model Question for Main Examination

Q. Highlight the various factors that causes migration in India. Also highlight the consequences of spatial migration in India.

UNIT 33
Human Development

In This Unit

Comprehensive and profound coverage of the following NCERTs' chapter:

✓ NCERT (Before Rationalisation) Class- 12th (India-People and Economy) Chapter- 4

Growth and Development

- Both **Growth and Development** refer to changes over a period of time.
  - **Growth** is **quantitative and value neutral**. It may have a positive or a negative sign. This means that the change may be either positive (showing an increase) or negative (indicating a decrease).
  - **Development** means a qualitative change which is **always value positive**. This means that development cannot take place unless there is an increment or addition to the existing conditions.
- Development occurs when positive growth takes place. Yet, positive growth does not always lead to development. Development occurs when there is a positive change in quality.
  - For example, if the population of a city grows from one lakh to two lakhs over a period of time, we say the city has grown. However, if facilities like housing, provision of basic services and other characteristics remain the same, then this growth has not been accompanied by development.

Human Development

"Human Development is a process of **enlarging the range of people's choices,** increasing their opportunities for **education, health care, income and empowerment** and covering the full range of human choices from a sound physical environment to **economic, social and political freedom."**

The concept of human development was introduced by **Dr Mahbub-ul-Haq**. Dr Haq has described human development as development that enlarges people's choices and improves their lives. People are central to all development under this concept. He created the **Human Development Index in 1990**. The **United Nations Development Programme** has used his concept of human development to publish the Human Development Report annually **since 1990**.

Four Pillars of Human Development

The idea of human development is supported by the concepts of **equity, sustainability, productivity** and **empowerment**.

- **Equity** refers to equal access to opportunities **available to everybody.** The opportunities available to people must be equal irrespective of their gender, race, income and in the Indian case, caste. Yet this is very often not the case and happens in almost every society.
  - For example, in any country, it is interesting to see from **which group the most of the school dropouts belong to**. In India, a large number of women and persons belonging to socially and economically backward groups drop out of school.
- **Sustainability** means continuity in the availability of opportunities. To have sustainable human development, each generation must have the same opportunities. All **environmental, financial and human resources** must be used keeping in mind the future. Misuse of any of these resources will lead to fewer opportunities for future generations.

- A good example is about the **importance of sending girls to school**. If a community does not stress the importance of sending its girl children to school, many opportunities will be lost to these young women when they grow up. Their career choices will be severely curtailed and this would affect other aspects of their lives.

- **Productivity** here means **human labour productivity** or productivity in terms of human work. Such productivity must be constantly enriched by **building capabilities** in people. Ultimately, it is people who are the real wealth of nations.
  - Therefore, efforts to increase their **knowledge, or provide better health facilities** ultimately leads to better work efficiency.
- **Empowerment** means to have the power to make choices. Such power comes from increasing **freedom and capability**.
  - **Good governance and people-oriented policies** are required to empower people. The empowerment of socially and economically disadvantaged groups is of special importance.

Approaches to Human Development

There are many ways of looking at the problem of human development. Some of the important approaches are:

- The income approach
- The welfare approach
- Minimum needs approach
- Capabilities approach

- **Income Approach-** This is one of the oldest approaches to human development. Human development is seen as being linked to income. The idea is that the **level of income reflects the level of freedom** an individual enjoys. Higher the level of income, the higher is the level of human development.
- **Welfare Approach-** This approach looks at **human beings as beneficiaries or targets** of all development activities. The approach argues for higher government expenditure on **education, health, social welfare and amenities**. People are not participants in development but only **passive recipients**. The government is responsible for increasing levels of human development by maximising expenditure on welfare.
- **Basic Needs Approach-** This approach was initially **proposed by the International Labour Organisation (ILO).** Six basic needs i.e.: **health, education, food, water supply, sanitation, and housing** were identified. The question of human choices is ignored and the emphasis is on the provision of basic needs of defined sections.
- **Capability Approach-** This approach is associated with **Prof. Amartya Sen**. Building human capabilities in the areas of **health, education and access to resources** is the key to increasing human development.

Measuring Human Development

The Human Development Index (HDI) ranks the countries based on their performance in the key areas of **Health, Education and Access to Resources**. These rankings are based on a **score between 0 to 1** that a country earns from its record in the key areas of human development.

- The indicator chosen to assess health is the **life expectancy at birth**. A higher life expectancy means that people have a greater chance of living longer and healthier lives.
- The **Adult Literacy Rate and the Gross Enrolment Ratio** represent access to knowledge. The number of adults who are able to read and write and the number of children enrolled in schools show how easy or difficult it is to access knowledge in a particular country.
- Access to resources is measured in terms of **Purchasing Power** (in US dollars).
- Each of these dimensions is given a **weightage of 1/3**. The Human Development Index is a **sum total of the weights** assigned to all these dimensions.
- The human development index measures **attainments** in human development. It reflects what has been achieved in the key areas of human development. **Yet it is not the most reliable** measure. This is because it does **not say anything about the distribution.**
- The **Human Poverty Index** is related to the human development index. This index measures the **shortfall** in human development.

Gross National Happiness (GNH)

Bhutan is the only country in the world to officially proclaim the **Gross National Happiness (GNH)** as the measure of the country's progress. **Material progress and technological developments** are approached more cautiously taking into consideration the possible harm they might bring to the **environment** or the other aspects of **cultural and spiritual life** of the Bhutanese. This simply means material progress cannot come at the cost of happiness. GNH encourages us to think of the **spiritual, non-material and qualitative aspects of development.**

Human Development in India

India, with a population of over 1.42 billion, is **ranked 132 among 191 countries** of the world in terms of the **Human Development Index (HDI) Report 2023** with a **score of 0.633**. Low scores in the HDI is a matter of serious concern but, some reservations have been expressed about the approach as well as indicators selected to calculate the index values and ranking of the states/countries. Lack of sensitivity to the **historical factors** like colonisation, imperialism and neo-imperialism, **socio-cultural factors** like human rights violation, social discrimination on the basis of race, religion, gender and caste, social problems like crimes, terrorism, and war and **political factors** like nature of the State, forms of the government, (democracy or dictatorship) level of empowerment are some factors that are very crucial in determining the nature of human development. These aspects have **special significance in case of India** and many other developing countries.

Using the indicators selected by the UNDP, the **Planning Commission of India** also prepared the **Human Development Report for India in 2002**. It used states and the Union Territories as the units of analysis. Subsequently, each state government also started preparing the state level Human Development Reports, using districts as the units of analysis. Although, the final HDI by the Planning Commission of India has been calculated by taking the three indicators. Yet, this report also discussed other indicators like **economic attainment, social empowerment, social distributive justice, accessibility, hygiene and various welfare measures** undertaken by the state.

Indicators of Economic Attainments

- **Rich resource base and access to these resources by all**, particularly the poor, down trodden and the marginalised is the key to productivity, well-being and human development.
- **Gross National Product (GNP) and its per capita availability** are taken as measures to assess the resource base/ endowment of any country. Economic attainment and the well-being of individuals depend on economic growth, employment opportunities and access to assets.
- Over the years the **Per Capita Income and Consumption Expenditure** in India has increased. As a result, there has been a consistent decline in the proportion of population living below the poverty line.
  - ➢ The percentage of persons **below the poverty line in 2011-12** has been estimated as 25.7% in rural areas, 13.7% in urban areas and **21.9%** for the country as a whole.
  - ➢ The data of poverty for the states show that there are States like Chhattisgarh, Jharkhand, Manipur, Arunachal Pradesh, Assam, Bihar, Jharkhand, Madhya Pradesh, Manipur and Odisha, Dadra and Nagar Haveli which have recorded **more than 30 percent** of their population living below the poverty line.
  - ➢ Other states like Gujarat, Haryana, Maharashtra, Meghalaya, Nagaland Rajasthan, Tamil Nadu, Tripura, Uttarakhand and West-Bengal have recorded between **10 to 20 percent** of their population below poverty line.
  - ➢ Andhra Pradesh, Delhi, Goa, Himachal Pradesh, Kerala, Punjab, Sikkim, Puducherry, Andaman and Nicobar Islands, Daman and Diu, Lakshadweep have **below 10 percent** of their population living below poverty line.
- **Poverty** is a state of deprivation. In absolute terms, it reflects the inability of an individual to satisfy certain basic needs for a sustained, healthy and reasonably productive living.

- **Gross Domestic Product (GDP)** of a country does **not fully reflect the quality of life** of a country. There are **other factors** like housing, access to public transport, air, quality and access to drinking water which also determine the standard of living. Jobless growth and rampant unemployment are some of the important reasons for higher incidences of poverty in India.

Indicators of Healthy Life

- **Life free from illness and ailment and living a reasonably long-life span** are indicative of a **healthy life**. Availability of **Pre and Post Natal healthcare** facilities in order to reduce **infant mortality** and **Post Delivery deaths** among mothers, old age health care, adequate nutrition and safety of individuals are some important measures of a healthy and reasonably long life.
  - ➢ According to Central Institute of Educational Technology document India has done reasonably well in some of the health indicators like **decline in death rate** from 25.1 per thousand in 1951 to 6.5 per thousand in 2015 and infant mortality from 148 per thousand to 37 during the same period.
  - ➢ Similarly, it also succeeded in **increasing life expectancy at birth** from 37.1 years to 66.9 years for males and 36.2 to 70 years for females from 1951 to 2015.
  - ➢ Though these are great achievements, a lot needs to be done. Similarly, it has also done reasonably well in bringing down **birth rate** from 40.8 to 20.8 during the same years, but it still is much higher than many developed countries.
- The situation is more alarming when seen in the context of gender specific and rural and urban health indicators. India has recorded a **declining female sex ratio**. The findings of the 2011 Census of India are very disturbing particularly in the case of **child sex ratio** in the age group of **0-6 years**.
  - ➢ The other significant features of the report are, with the **exception of Kerala**, the child sex ratio has declined in all the states and it is the most alarming in the developed state of **Haryana and Punjab** where it is below **850 female children per thousand male children**.

Swachh Bharat Mission

The release of **toxic and non-biodegradable** wastes from **industries and urban sewerages,** and **open defecation**, etc, have created many health hazards. The Government of India has initiated many steps to address these problems and the Swachh Bharat Mission is one of these. The Government of India with its flagship programme Swachh Bharat Mission (SBM) aims at a pollution-free environment. Its **objectives are:**

- Making India **open defecation-free and achieving 100 per cent scientific management of municipal solid waste, construction of individual household latrines** (IHHL), community toilet (CT) seats and **public toilet** (PT) seats.
- Making provisions for the supply of **clean energy fuel LPG** to all households in rural India to reduce domestic pollution.
- Providing **potable drinking water** to every household to control the spread of water-borne diseases.
- Promoting the use of non-conventional energy resources, like **wind and solar energy.**

Indicators of Social Empowerment

- **Amartya Sen said that "Development is Freedom."**. Freedom from **hunger, poverty, servitude, bondage, ignorance, illiteracy** and any other forms of domination is the key to human development.
- **Freedom**, in the real sense of the term, is possible only with the **empowerment and participation** of the people in the exercise of their **capabilities and choices** in the society.
- **Access to knowledge** about the society and environment are fundamental to freedom. **Literacy** is the beginning of access to such a world of knowledge and freedom.
- The percentage of literates in India reveals some interesting features:
  - ➢ **Overall literacy** in India is approximately **74.04 per cent (2011),** while **female literacy is 65.46 per cent.**
  - ➢ Total literacy as well as female literacy is **higher than the national average** in most of the states from **south India.**

- ➢ There are **wide regional disparities** in literacy rate across the states of India. There is a state like **Bihar** which has very low (63.82 per cent) literacy and there are states like **Kerala and Mizoram** which have literacy rates of 93.91 and 91.58 per cent respectively.

- Apart from the spatial variations, the percentage of **literates in the rural areas** and among the marginalised sections of our society such as **females, scheduled castes, scheduled tribes, agricultural labourers**, etc. is very low.

- It is worth mentioning here that though, there has been improvement in the percentage of literates among the marginalised section, yet the **gap between the richer and the marginalised sections** of the population has **increased over the years**.

International Comparison

- International comparisons of human development are interesting. **Size of the territory and per capita income** are not directly related to human development. Often smaller countries have done better than larger ones in human development. Similarly, **relatively poorer nations have been ranked higher** than richer neighbours in terms of human development.
  - ➢ For example, **Sri Lanka, Trinidad and Tobago** have a higher rank than India in the human development index despite having smaller economies.
  - ➢ Similarly, within India, **Kerala performs much better than Punjab and Gujarat** in human development despite having lower per capita income.
- **Often people tend to blame low levels of human development on the culture** of the people.
  - ➢ For example, X country has lower human development because its people follow Y religion, or belong to Z community. Such statements are misleading.
  - ➢ To understand why a particular region keeps reporting low or high levels of human development it is important to look at the **pattern of government expenditure on the social sector.** The **political environment** of the country and the **amount of freedom** people have is also important.
  - ➢ Countries with high levels of human development **invest more in the social sectors** and are generally **free from political turmoil and instability**. Distribution of the country's resources is also far more equitable.

- On the other hand, places with **low levels of human development tend to spend more on defence** rather than social sectors. This shows that these countries tend to be located in areas of **political instability** and have not been able to initiate **accelerated economic development.**

Population, Environment and Development

Development in general and human development in particular is a complex concept used in social sciences. It is complex because for ages it was thought that development is a substantive concept and once it is achieved it will address all the **socio-cultural and environmental** ills of the society. Though, development has brought in significant improvement in the quality of life in more than one way but increasing **regional disparities, social inequalities, discriminations, deprivations, displacement of people, abuse of human rights and undermining human values and environmental degradation** have also increased.

Indian culture and civilisation have been very sensitive to the issues of **population, resource and development** for a long time. **Mahatma Gandhi**, advocated for the **reinforcement of the harmony and balance** between the two. His views were also re-echoed in the **Club of Rome Report "Limits to Growth" (1972), Schumacher's book "Small is Beautiful" (1974), Brundtland Commission's Report "Our Common Future" (1987) and finally in the "Agenda-21 Report of the Rio Conference" (1993).**

TEST YOURSELF

Model Questions for Main Examination

Q1. Explain the factors that helps to sustain a healthy life.

Q2. What is human development and how to measure it?

UNIT 34

Planning and Sustainable Development in Indian Context

In This Unit

Comprehensive and profound coverage of the following NCERTs' chapter:

✓ NCERT Class- 12th (India-People and Economy), Chapter- 6

Introduction

Planning involves the process of thinking, formulation of a scheme or programme and implementation of a set of actions to achieve some goal.

- Generally, there are two approaches to planning, i.e., **sectoral planning and regional planning.**
- **Sectoral Planning** means formulation and implementation of the sets of schemes or programmes aimed at development of various **sectors of the economy**, such as agriculture, irrigation, manufacturing, power, construction, transport, communication, social infrastructure and services.
- There is **no uniform economic development** over space in any country. Some areas are more developed and some lag behind. This **uneven pattern** of development over space necessitates that the planners have a **spatial perspective** and draw the plans to reduce regional imbalance in development. This type of planning is termed as **Regional Planning.**

Target Area Planning

- The planning process has to take special care of those areas which have remained economically backward.
- In order to arrest the accentuation of **regional and social disparities**, the Planning Commission introduced the **'target area'** and **'target group'** approaches to planning.
    - ➢ Some of the examples of programmes directed towards the development of target areas are:
        - ♦ Command Area Development Programme,
        - ♦ Drought Prone Area Development Programme,
        - ♦ Desert Development Programme and
        - ♦ Hill Area Development Programme.
- In the **8th Five Year Plan,** special area programmes were designed to develop infrastructure in **hill areas, north-eastern states, tribal areas and backward areas.**

Hill Area Development Programme

- **Hill Area Development Programme** was initiated during the **Fifth Five Year Plan** covering **15 districts** comprising all the hilly districts of Uttar Pradesh (present Uttarakhand), Mikir Hill and North Cachar hills of Assam, Darjeeling district of West Bengal and Nilgiri district of Tamil Nadu.
- **The National Committee on the Development of Backward Area in 1981** recommended that all the hill areas in the country having height above 600 m and not covered under tribal sub-plan be treated as backward hill areas.
- The detailed plans for the development of hill areas were drawn keeping in view their **Topographical, Ecological, Social and Economic conditions**.
- These programmes aimed at harnessing the indigenous resources of the hill areas through development of **horticulture, plantation, agriculture, animal husbandry, poultry, forestry and small-scale and village industry**.

Drought Prone Area Programme

- This programme was initiated during the **Fourth Five Year Plan** with the objectives of providing employment to the people in drought-prone areas and creating productive assets.
- Initially, this programme laid emphasis on the construction of **labour-intensive civil works**. But later on, it emphasised on **irrigation projects, land development programmes, afforestation, grassland development and creation of basic rural infrastructure**, such as electricity, roads, market, credit and services.
- The **National Committee on Development of Backward Areas** reviewed the performance of this programme.
- It has been observed that this programme is largely confined to the development of agriculture and allied sectors with major focus on **restoration of ecological balance.**
- **The Planning Commission of India (1967)** identified 67 districts (entire or partly) of the country prone to drought.
- **The Irrigation Commission (1972)** introduced the criterion of 30 per cent irrigated area and demarcated the drought-prone areas.
- Broadly, the drought- prone area in India spread over **semi-arid and arid tract** of Rajasthan, Gujarat, Western Madhya Pradesh, Marathwada region of Maharashtra, Rayalseema and Telangana plateaus of Andhra Pradesh, Karnataka plateau and highlands and interior parts of Tamil Nadu.

Case Study – Integrated Tribal Development Project in Bharmaur Region(HP)

Bharmaur tribal area comprises Bharmaur and Holi tehsils of Chamba district of Himachal Pradesh. It is a notified tribal area since 21 November 1975. Bharmaur is inhabited by **'Gaddi', a tribal community** who have maintained a distinct identity in the **Himalayan region as they practised transhumance and conversed through Gaddiali dialect.**

Bharmaur tribal region has **harsh climate conditions, low resource base and fragile environment**. These factors have influenced the **society and economy** of the region.

The process of development of tribal area of Bharmaur started in 1970s when Gaddis were included among **'Scheduled Tribes'**. Under the Fifth Five Year Plan, the **Tribal Sub-Plan** was introduced in 1974 and Bharmaur was designated as one of the five **Integrated Tribal Development Projects (ITDP)** in Himachal Pradesh. This area development plan was aimed at improving the quality of life of the Gaddis and narrowing the gap in the level of development between Bharmaur and other areas of Himachal Pradesh. This plan laid the highest priority on development of **transport and communications, agriculture and allied activities, and social and community services**. The most significant contribution of tribal sub-plan in Bharmaur region is the **development of infrastructure** in terms of schools, healthcare facilities, potable water, roads, communications and electricity.

The **social benefits** derived from ITDP include tremendous **increase in literacy rate, improvement in sex ratio and decline in child marriage.** The **female literacy rate** in the region increased from 1.88 per cent in 1971 to **65 per cent in 2011**. Traditionally, the Gaddis had **subsistence agricultural-cum-pastoral economy** having emphasis on **foodgrains and livestock production**. But during the last three decades of twentieth century, the cultivation of pulses and other cash crops has increased in Bharmaur region. The declining importance of pastoralism in the economy of the region can be gauged from the fact that at present only about **one-tenth of the total Households practise transhumance.**

Sustainable Development

The notion of sustainable development emerged in the wake of general rise in the awareness of environmental issues in the late 1960s in Western World. It reflected the concern of people about undesirable effects of industrial development on the environment.

The publication of **'The Population Bomb'** by **Ehrlich in 1968** and **'The Limits to Growth'** by **Meadows and others in 1972** further raised the level of fear among environmentalists in particular and people in general. This sets the scenario for the emergence of new models of development under a broad phrase **'Sustainable Development'.**

Concerned with the growing opinion of world community on the environmental issues, the United Nations established a **World Commission on Environment and Development (WCED)** headed by the Norwegian Prime Minister Gro Harlem Brundtland. The Commission gave its report (also known as **Brundtland Report**) entitled **'Our Common Future'** in **1987**. The report defines Sustainable Development as a **"development that meets the needs of the present without compromising the ability of future generations to meet their own needs."**

Sustainable development takes care of **ecological, social and economic** aspects of development during the present times and pleads for conservation of resources to enable the future generations to use these resources. **It takes into account the development of the whole human kind which have a common future.**

Case Study - Indira Gandhi Canal (Nahar) Command Area

Indira Gandhi Canal, previously known as the Rajasthan Canal, is one of the largest canal systems in India. Conceived by Kanwar Sain in 1948, the canal project was launched on 31 March, 1958. The canal originates at Harike barrage in Punjab and runs parallel to Pakistan border at an average distance of 40 km in Thar Desert (Marusthali) of Rajasthan.

Introduction of canal irrigation has brought about a perceptible transformation in the agricultural economy of the region. Soil moisture has been a limiting factor in successful growing of crops in this area. Spread of **canal irrigation led to increase in cultivated area and intensity of cropping.** The traditional crops sown in the area, gram, bajra and jowar have been replaced by wheat, cotton, groundnut and rice. This is the result of intensive irrigation. This intensive irrigation, no doubt, initially has led to tremendous increase in agricultural and livestock productivity. However, it has also caused waterlogging and soil salinity, and thus, in the long run, it hampers the sustainability of agriculture.

Measures for Promotion of Sustainable Development

Measures proposed to promote sustainable development in the command area are meant to **restore ecological balance.** They are:

- The first requirement is strict implementation of **Water Management Policy.**
- In general, the **cropping pattern** shall not include water intensive crops. It shall be adhered to and people shall be encouraged to **grow plantation crops** such as citrus fruits.
- The **Command Area Development programmes** such as **lining of water courses, land development and levelling and warabandi system** (equal distribution of canal water in the command area of outlet) shall be effectively implemented to reduce the conveyance loss of water.
- The areas affected by **water logging and soil salinity** shall be reclaimed.
- The **eco-development** through **afforestation, shelterbelt plantation and pasture development** is necessary particularly in the fragile environment.
- **Social sustainability** in the region can be achieved only if the land allottees having poor economic background are provided adequate **financial and institutional support** for cultivation of land.
- **The Economic Sustainability** in the region cannot be attained only through development of agriculture and animal husbandry. The agricultural and allied activities have to develop along with other sectors of the economy. This shall lead to **diversification of economic base** and establishment of **functional linkages** between **basic villages, agro-service centres and market centres.**

UNIT 35

Natural Hazards and Disasters

In This Unit

Comprehensive and profound coverage of the following NCERTs' chapter:

✓ NCERT Class- 11th (India-Physical Environment), Chapter- 6

Introduction

"**Disaster** is an undesirable occurrence resulting from forces that are largely outside human control, strikes quickly with little or no warning, which causes or threatens serious disruption of life and property including death and injury to a large number of people, and requires therefore, mobilisation of efforts in excess of that which are normally provided by statutory emergency services."

Natural Hazards are elements of circumstances in the Natural environment that have the potential to cause harm to people or property or both. These may be swift or permanent aspects of the respective environmental settings like currents in the oceans, steep slope and unstable structural features in the Himalayas or extreme climatic conditions in deserts or glaciated areas.

Natural disasters have caused widespread loss of life and property. Concerted efforts are on at various levels to take appropriate measures to deal with the situation. It is also being felt that the damages caused by natural disasters have global repercussions that are beyond the means and capabilities of individual nation-states to cope up with. Hence, this issue was raised at the **U.N. General Assembly** in **1989** and it was finally formalised at the **World Conference on Disaster Management** in **May 1994 at Yokohama, Japan.** This was subsequently called the **Yokohama Strategy and Plan of Action for a Safer World.**

Yokohama Strategy and Plan of Action for a Safer World

All the member States of the United Nations and other States met at the **World Conference on Natural Disaster Reduction in the city of Yokohama** from May 23rd-27th 1994. It acknowledged that the impact of natural disasters in terms of human and economic losses has risen in recent years, and society, in general, has become vulnerable to natural disasters. It also accepted that these disasters affected the poor and disadvantageous groups the worst, particularly in the developing countries, which are ill-equipped to cope with them. Hence, the conference adopted the Yokohama strategy as a guide to rest of the decade and beyond, to mitigate the losses due to these disasters.

The resolution of the World Conference on Natural Disasters Reduction is as mentioned below:

- It will note that each country has the sovereign responsibility to protect its citizens from natural disasters;
- It will give priority attention to the developing countries, particularly the least developed, land-locked countries and small-island developing States;
- It will develop and strengthen national capacities and capabilities and, where appropriate, national legislation for natural and other disaster prevention, mitigation and preparedness, including the mobilisation of non-governmental organisations and participation of local communities;
- It will promote and strengthen sub-regional, regional and international cooperation in

activities to prevent, reduce and mitigate natural and other disasters, with particular emphasis on:

- Human and institutional capacity-building and strengthening
- Technology sharing: the **collection, the dissemination and utilisation** of information
- Mobilisation of resources

It also declared the decade **1990-2000** as the **International Decade for Natural Disaster Reduction (IDNDR).**

Hyogo Framework for Action (2005-2015)

The Hyogo Framework for Action (2005–2015): Building the Resilience of Nations and Communities to Disasters was an outcome of the 2005 conference. The Hyogo Framework (HFA) was the first plan to explain, describe and detail the work required from all different sectors and actors to reduce disaster losses. It was developed and agreed on with the many partners needed to reduce disaster risk – governments, international agencies, disaster experts and many others – bringing them into a common system of coordination. The HFA, which ran from 2005 to 2015, set five specific priorities for action:

- Making disaster risk reduction a priority;
- Improving risk information and early warning;
- Building a culture of safety and resilience;
- Reducing the risks in key sectors;
- Strengthening preparedness for response.

Sendai Framework for Disaster Risk Reduction (2015–2030)

The **Sendai Framework for Disaster Risk Reduction (2015–2030)** is an international document that was adopted by the United Nations (UN) member States between 14 and 18 March 2015 at the World Conference on Disaster Risk Reduction held in Sendai, Japan, and endorsed by the **UN General Assembly in June 2015**. It is the **successor agreement** to the Hyogo Framework for Action (2005–2015), which had been the **most encompassing** international accord to date on disaster risk reduction.

Priority Areas: The Sendai Framework sets four specific priorities for action:

- Understanding disaster risk;
- Strengthening disaster risk governance to manage disaster risk;
- Investing in disaster risk reduction for resilience;
- Enhancing disaster preparedness for effective response, and to "Building Back Better" in recovery, rehabilitation and reconstruction.

Global Targets: To support the assessment of global progress in achieving the outcome and goal of the Sendai Framework, seven global targets have been agreed:

- Substantially **reduce global disaster mortality** by 2030, aiming to lower average per 100,000 global mortalities between 2020 and 2030 compared to 2005–2015;
- Substantially **reduce the number of affected people** globally by 2030, aiming to lower the average global figure per 100,000 between 2020 and 2030 compared to 2005–2015;
- **Reduce direct disaster economic loss** in relation to global gross domestic product by 2030;
- Substantially **reduce disaster damage to critical infrastructure and disruption of basic services,** among them health and educational facilities, including through developing their resilience by 2030;
- Substantially **increase the number of countries with national and local disaster risk reduction strategies** by 2020;
- Substantially **enhance international cooperation** to developing countries through adequate and sustainable support to complement their national actions for implementation of the framework by 2030;
- Substantially **increase the availability of and access to multi-hazard early warning systems and disaster risk information and assessments** to the people by 2030.

Links with Global Goals: Member States emphasised the need to tackle disaster risk reduction and climate change adaptation when setting the **17 Sustainable Development Goals in 2015 (to be achieved by 2030),** particularly in light of an insufficient focus on risk reduction and resilience in the original Millennium Development Goals. For example, Indicator 13.1.2 of **Sustainable Development Goal 13** on climate action tracks the "number of countries that adopt and implement national disaster risk reduction strategies in line with the Sendai Framework for Disaster Risk Reduction 2015–2030".

Classification of Natural Disasters

Identification and classification of disasters is being considered as an effective and scientific step to deal promptly and efficiently with the disasters. Broadly, natural disasters can be classified under **four categories.**

Atmospheric	Terrestrial	Aquatic	Biological
Blizzards Thunderstorms Lightning Tornadoes Tropical Cyclone Drought Hailstorm Frost, Heat Wave or Loo, Cold Waves, etc.	Earthquakes Volcanic Eruptions Avalanches Subsidence Soil Erosion Landslides Eruptions	Floods Tidal Waves Ocean Currents Storm Surge Tsunami	Plants and Animals as colonisers (Locusts, etc.). Insects infestation-fungal, bacterial and viral diseases such as bird flu, dengue, etc.

Classification of Natural Disasters

India is one of those countries which has experienced most of the natural disasters. Every year it loses thousands of lives and property worth millions of rupees due to these natural calamities.

Earthquakes

National Geophysical Laboratory, Geological Survey of India, Department of Meteorology, Government of India, along with the recently formed National Institute of Disaster Management, have made an intensive analysis of more than 1,200 earthquakes that have occurred in India in different years in the past, and based on these, **they divided India into the following four earthquake zones:**

- Very high damage risk zone
- High damage risk zone
- Low damage risk zone
- Very low damage risk zone

Out of these, the **first two zones** have experienced some of the most devastating earthquakes in India. The areas vulnerable to these earthquakes are the North-east states, areas to the north of Darbhanga and Araria along the Indo-Nepal border in Bihar, Uttarakhand, Western Himachal Pradesh (around Dharamshala) and Kashmir Valley in the Himalayan region and the Kachchh (Gujarat). These are included in the **Very High Damage Risk Zone**. Similarly, the remaining parts of Jammu and Kashmir, Ladakh, Himachal Pradesh, Northern parts of Punjab, Eastern parts of Haryana, Delhi, Western Uttar Pradesh, and Northern Bihar fall under the **High Damage Risk Zone**. Remaining parts of the country fall under Moderate to **Very Low Damage Risk Zone**. Most of the areas that can be considered safe are from the stable landmass covered under the Deccan plateau.

Earthquake Hazard Mitigation

Unlike other disasters, the damages caused by earthquakes are more devastating. Since it also destroys most of the transport and communication links, providing timely relief to the victims becomes difficult. It is not possible to prevent the occurrence of an earthquake; hence, the next best option is to emphasise on disaster preparedness and mitigation rather than curative measures such as:

- Establishing **Earthquake Monitoring Centres (Seismological Centres)** for regular monitoring and fast dissemination of information among the people in the vulnerable areas. Use of **Geographical Positioning System (GPS)** can be of great help in monitoring the movement of tectonic plates.
- Preparing a vulnerability map of the country and dissemination of vulnerability risk information among the people and educating them about the ways and means minimising the adverse impacts of disasters.
- Modifying the **house types and building-designs** in the vulnerable areas and discouraging construction of **high-rise buildings, large industrial establishments and big urban centres** in such areas.
- Finally, making it mandatory to adopt **earthquake-resistant designs and use light materials** in major construction activities in the vulnerable areas.

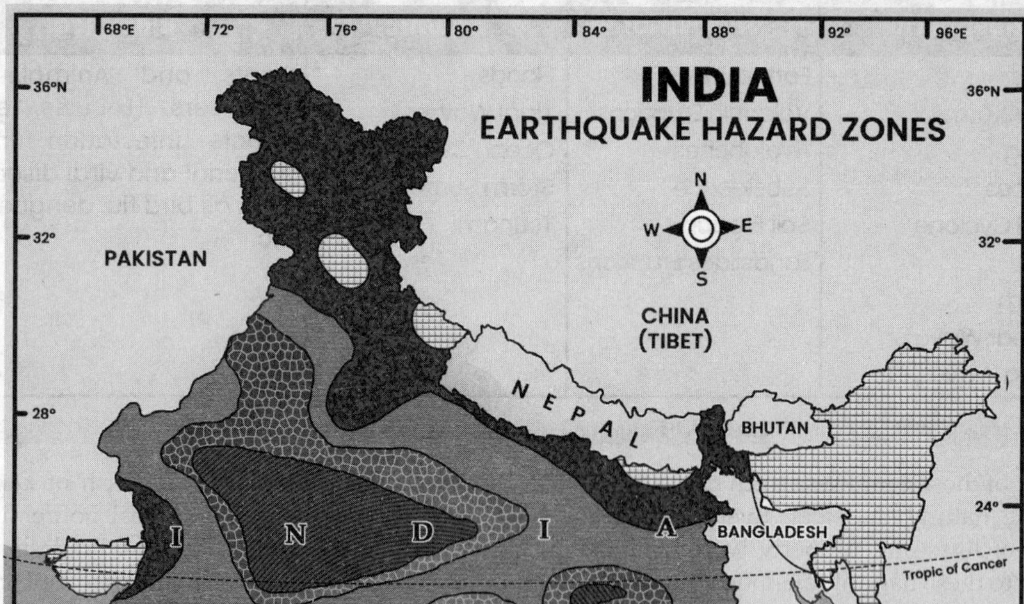

India: Earthquake Hazard Zones

Tsunami

Earthquakes and volcanic eruptions that cause the sea-floor to move abruptly resulting in sudden displacement of ocean water in the form of high vertical waves are called **Tsunamis (Harbour Waves)** or **Seismic Sea Waves.** The seismic waves cause only one instantaneous vertical wave; but, after the initial disturbance, a series of after waves are created in the water that oscillate between high crest and low trough in order to restore the water level.

The speed of wave in the ocean depends upon the depth of water. It is more in the shallow water than in the deep ocean. As a result of this, the impact of tsunami is less over the ocean and more near the coast where they cause large-scale devastations. Therefore, a ship at sea is not much affected by tsunami and it is difficult to detect a tsunami in the deeper parts of sea. It is so because over deep water the tsunami has very **long wave-length and limited wave-height**. Thus, a tsunami wave raises the ship only a metre or two and each rise and fall takes several minutes. As opposed to this, when a tsunami enters shallow water, its wave-length gets reduced and the period remains unchanged, which increases the wave-height. Sometimes, this height can be up to 15m or more, which causes large-scale destructions along the shores. Thus, these are also called **Shallow Water Waves.** Tsunamis are frequently observed along the **Pacific Ring of Fire**, particularly along the **coast of Alaska, Japan, Philippines, and other islands of South-east Asia, Indonesia, Malaysia, Myanmar, Sri Lanka, and India** etc.

After reaching the coast, the tsunami waves **release enormous energy** stored in them and water flows turbulently onto the land destroying **port-cities and towns, structures, buildings and other settlements.** Since the coastal areas are densely populated the world over, and these are also centres of intense human activity, the loss of life and property is likely to be much higher by a tsunami as compared to other natural hazards in the coastal areas. Unlike other natural hazards, the mitigation of hazards created by tsunami is difficult, mainly because of the fact that losses are on a much larger scale.

It is beyond the capacity of individual State or government to mitigate the damage. Hence, combined efforts at the international levels are the possible ways of dealing with these disasters as has been in the case of the tsunami that occurred on 26th December 2004 in which more than 300,000 people lost their lives. India has volunteered to join the **International Tsunami Warning System** after the December 2004 tsunami disaster.

Tropical Cyclone

Tropical cyclones are intense low-pressure areas confined to the area lying between 30° N and 30° S latitudes, in the atmosphere around which high velocity winds blow. Horizontally, it extends up to 500-1,000 km and vertically from surface to 12-14 km. A **Tropical Cyclone or Hurricane** is like a **Heat Engine** that is energised by the release of latent heat on account of the condensation of moisture that the wind gathers after moving over the oceans and seas. **However, some initial conditions for the emergence of a tropical cyclone are:**

- **Large and continuous supply of warm and moist air** that can release enormous latent heat.
- **Strong Coriolis force** that can prevent filling of low pressure at the centre (absence of Coriolis force near the equator prohibits the formation of tropical cyclone between 0°-5° latitude).
- **Unstable condition** through the troposphere that creates local disturbances around which a cyclone develops.
- Finally, **absence of strong vertical wind wedge**, which disturbs the vertical transport of latent heat.

Structure of Tropical Cyclone

Tropical cyclones are characterised by large pressure gradients. The centre of the cyclone is mostly a **warm and low-pressure**, cloudless core known as **Eye of the Storm.** Generally, the isobars are closely placed to each other showing high-pressure gradients. Normally, it varies between 14-17mb/100 km, but sometimes it can be as high as 60mb/100km. Expansion of the wind belt is about 10-150 km from the centre.

Spatial-Temporal Distribution of Tropical Cyclone in India

Owing to its Peninsular shape surrounded by the **Bay of Bengal in the east and the Arabian Sea in the west**, the tropical cyclones in India also originate in these two important locations. Though most of the cyclones originate between 10°-15° north latitudes during the monsoon season, yet in case of the Bay of Bengal, cyclones mostly develop during the months of October and November. Here, they originate between 16°-2° N latitudes and to the west of 92° E. By July the place of origin of these storms shifts to around 18° N latitude and west of 90°E near the **Sundarban Delta**.

Consequences of Tropical Cyclones

It was mentioned that the energy to the tropical cyclone comes from the latent heat released by the warm moist air. Hence, with the increase in distance from the sea, the force of the cyclone decreases. In India, the force of the cyclone decreases with increase in distance from the Bay of Bengal and the Arabian Sea. So, the coastal areas are often struck by severe cyclonic storms with an average velocity of 180 km/h. Often, this results in abnormal rise in the sea level known as **Storm Surge.** This results in inundation of human settlements, agricultural fields, damaging crops and destruction of structures created by human beings.

A Storm Surge is generated due to interaction of air, sea and land. The cyclone provides the driving force in the form of **very high horizontal pressure-gradient and very strong surface winds.** The sea water flows across the coast along with strong winds and heavy downpour.

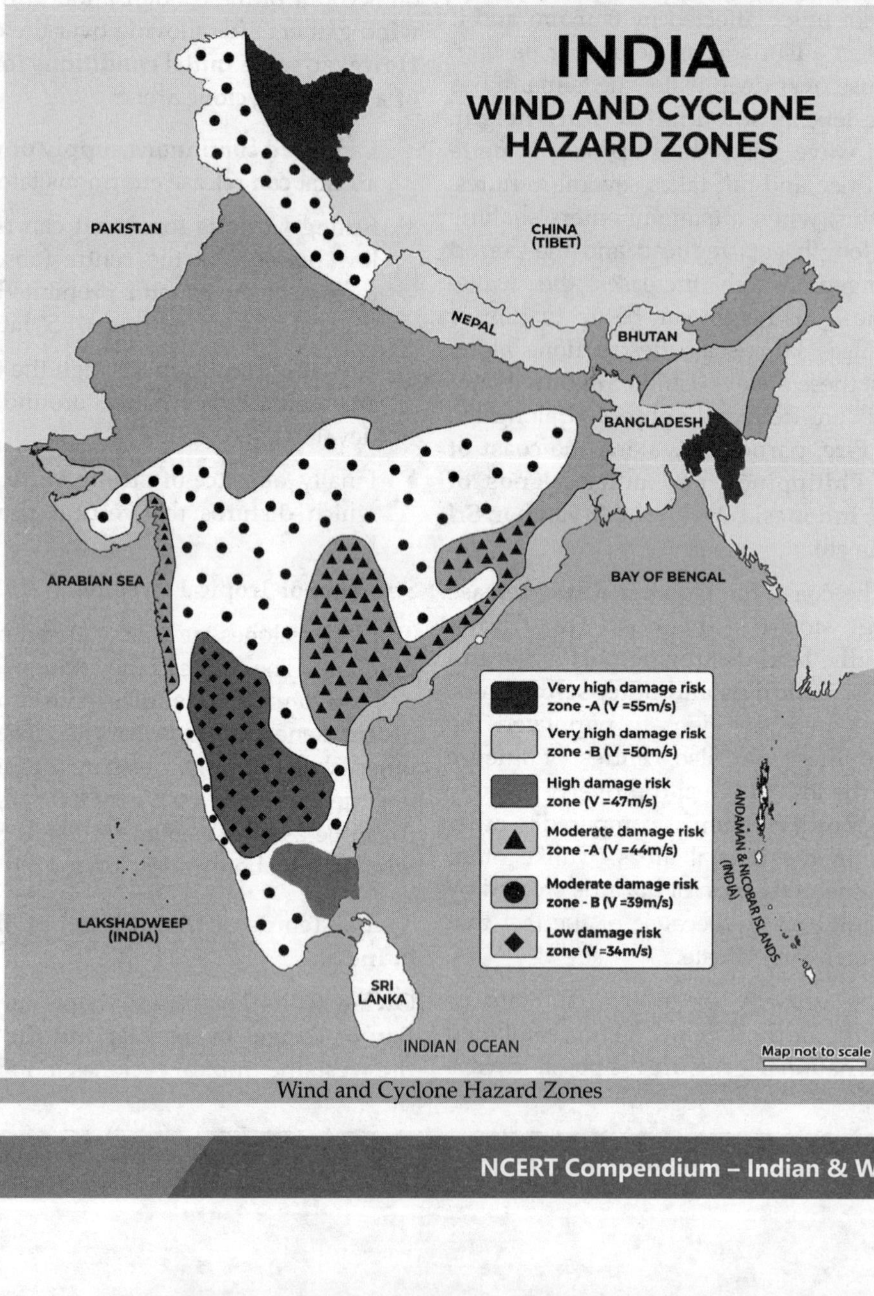

Wind and Cyclone Hazard Zones

Floods

Flooding is inundation of land and human settlements by the rise of water in the channels and its spill-over. Unlike other natural disasters, the causes of floods are well established. Floods are **relatively slow in occurrences** and often, occur in **well-identified regions and within expected time** in a year. Floods occur commonly when water in the form of surface run-off **exceeds the 'carrying capacity'** of the river channels and streams and flows into the neighbouring low-lying flood plains. At times, this even goes beyond the capacity of lakes and other inland water bodies in which they flow.

Floods can also be caused due to a **storm surge (in the coastal areas), high intensity rainfall for a considerably longer time period, melting of ice and snow, reduction in the infiltration rate and presence of eroded material** in the water due to higher rate of soil erosion. Though floods occur frequently over wide geographical area having disastrous ramifications in many parts of the world, floods in the **South, Southeast and East Asian countries, particularly in China, India and Bangladesh**, are frequent and equally disastrous.

Unlike other natural disasters, human beings play an important role in the genesis as well as spread of floods. **Indiscriminate deforestation, unscientific agricultural practices, disturbances along the natural drainage channels and colonisation of flood-plains and river-beds** are some of the human activities that play an important role in increasing the **intensity, magnitude and gravity** of floods.

Flood Hazard Zones

Droughts

The term **'drought'** is applied to an extended period when there is a shortage of water availability due to **inadequate precipitation, excessive rate of evaporation and over-utilisation of water** from the reservoirs and other storages, including the ground water.

Drought is a complex phenomenon as it involves elements of meteorology like **precipitation, evaporation, transpiration, ground water, soil moisture, storage and surface run-off, agricultural practices,** particularly the types of crops grown, socio-economic practices and ecological conditions.

Types of Droughts

Meteorological Drought: It is a situation when there is a prolonged period of inadequate rainfall marked with mal-distribution of the same over time and space.

Agricultural Drought: It is also known as **soil moisture drought**, characterised by low soil moisture that is necessary to support the crops, thereby resulting in crop failures. Moreover, if an area has more than 30 percent of its gross cropped area under irrigation, the area is excluded from the drought-prone category.

Hydrological Drought: It results when the availability of water in different storages and reservoirs like aquifers, lakes, reservoirs, etc. falls below what the precipitation can replenish.

Ecological Drought: When the productivity of a natural ecosystem fails due to shortage of water and as a consequence of ecological distress, damages are induced in the ecosystem.

Drought Prone Areas in India

Indian agriculture has been heavily dependent on the monsoon rainfall. Droughts and floods are the two accompanying features of Indian climate. According to some estimates, nearly 19 per cent of the total geographical area of the country and **12 per cent of its total population** suffer due to drought every year. About **30 per cent of the country's total area** is identified as drought prone affecting around 50 million people. It is a common experience that while some parts of the country reel under floods, there are regions that face severe drought during the same period. Moreover, it is also a common sight to witness that one region suffers due to floods in one season and experiences drought in the other. This is mainly because of the large-scale variations and unpredictability in the behaviour of the monsoon in India. Thus, droughts are widespread and common phenomena in most parts of the country, but these are most recurrent and severe in some and not so in others. **On the basis of severity of droughts, India can be divided into the following regions:**

Extreme Drought Affected Areas: Most parts of Rajasthan, particularly areas to the west of the Aravali hills, i.e., Marusthali and Kachchh regions of Gujarat fall in this category. Included here are also the districts like Jaisalmer and Barmer from the Indian desert that receive less than 90 mm average annual rainfall.

Severe Drought Prone Area: Parts of eastern Rajasthan, most parts of Madhya Pradesh, eastern parts of Maharashtra, interior parts of Andhra Pradesh and Karnataka Plateau, northern parts of interior Tamil Nadu and southern parts of Jharkhand and interior Odisha are included in this category.

Moderate Drought Affected Area: Northern parts of Rajasthan, Haryana, southern districts of Uttar Pradesh, the remaining parts of Gujarat, Maharashtra except Konkan, Jharkhand and Coimbatore plateau of Tamil Nadu and interior Karnataka are included in this category. The remaining parts of India can be considered either free or less prone to the drought.

Consequences of Drought

- Droughts have cascading effects on various other aspects of environment and society.
- Large-scale death of cattle and other animals, migration of humans and livestock are the most common sight to be seen in the drought-affected areas.
- Scarcity of water compels people to consume contaminated water resulting in spread of many waterborne diseases like **gastro-enteritis, cholera, hepatitis, etc.**

Measures

Droughts have both immediate as well as long-term disastrous consequences on the social and physical environments. Consequently, planning for drought has to take both aspects into consideration. Provision for the distribution of safe drinking water, medicines for the victims and availability of fodder and water for the cattle and shifting of the people and their livestock to safer places, etc. are some steps that need to be taken immediately. Identification of ground water potential in the form of aquifers, transfer of river water from the surplus to the deficit areas, and particularly planning for **inter-linking of rivers and construction of reservoirs and dams**, etc. should be given a serious thought. Remote sensing and satellite imageries can be useful in identifying the possible river-basins that can be inter-linked and in identifying the ground water potential.

Dissemination of knowledge about **drought-resistant crops and proper training** to practise the same can be some of the long-term measures that will be helpful in drought-mitigation. Rainwater harvesting can also be an effective method in minimising the effects of drought.

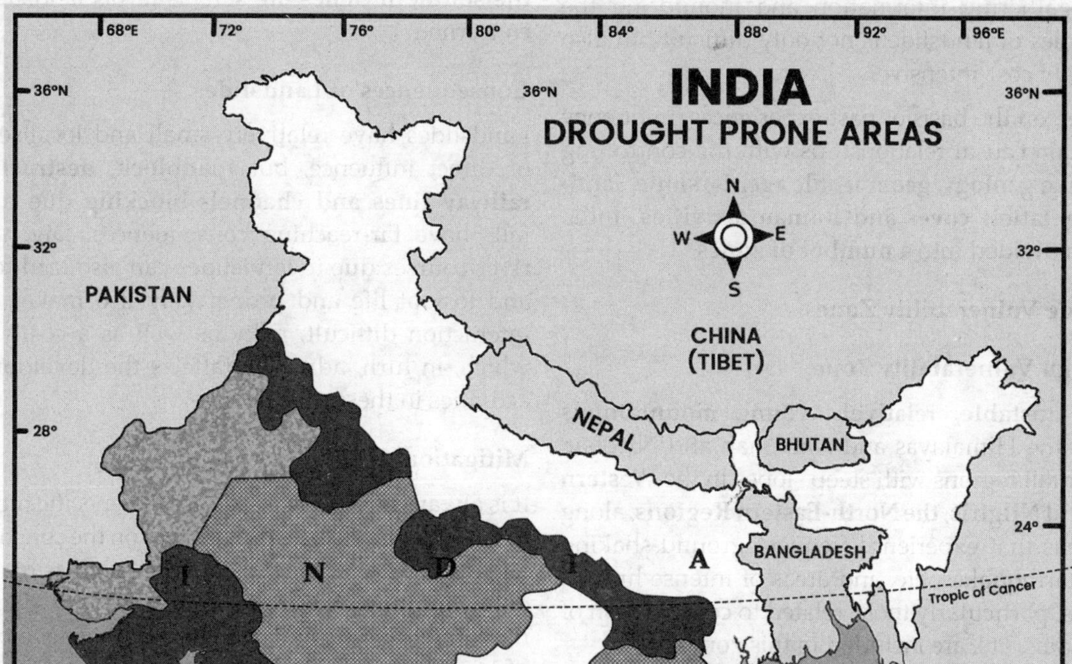

Drought Prone Areas

Landslides

Disasters due to landslides, are in general, far less dramatic than due to **earthquakes, volcanic eruptions, tsunamis and cyclones** but their impact on the natural environment and national economy is in no way less severe. Unlike other disasters that are **sudden, unpredictable and are largely controlled by macro or regional factors**, landslides are largely controlled by **highly localised** factors. Hence, gathering information and monitoring the possibilities of landslide is not only difficult but also immensely cost-intensive.

However, on the basis of past experiences, frequency and certain causal relationships with the controlling factors like **geology, geomorphic agents, slope, land-use, vegetation cover and human activities**, India has been divided into a **number of zones.**

Landslide Vulnerability Zones

Very High Vulnerability Zone

Highly unstable, relatively young mountainous areas in the Himalayas and Andaman and Nicobar, high rainfall regions with steep slopes in the **Western Ghats and Nilgiris, the North-Eastern Regions,** along with areas that experience frequent ground-shaking due to earthquakes, etc. and areas of intense human activities, particularly those related to construction of roads, dams, etc. are included in this zone.

High Vulnerability Zone

Areas that have almost similar conditions to those included in the very high vulnerability zone are also included in this category. The only difference between these two is the combination, intensity and frequency of the controlling factors. All the Himalayan states and the states from the north-eastern regions except the plains of Assam are included in the high vulnerability zones.

Moderate to Low Vulnerability Zone

Areas that receive less precipitation such as **Trans-Himalayan areas of Ladakh and Spiti (Himachal Pradesh)**, undulated yet stable relief and low precipitation areas in the Aravali, rain shadow areas in the Western and Eastern Ghats and Deccan plateau also experience occasional landslides. Landslides due to mining and subsidence are most common in states like **Jharkhand, Odisha, Chhattisgarh, Madhya Pradesh, Maharashtra, Andhra Pradesh, Karnataka, Tamil Nadu, Goa and Kerala.**

Other Areas

The remaining parts of India, particularly states like **Rajasthan, Haryana, Uttar Pradesh, Bihar, West Bengal (except district Darjiling), Assam (except district Karbi Anglong) and Coastal regions of the southern States** are safe as far as landslides are concerned.

Consequences of Landslides

Landslides have relatively small and localised area of direct influence, but **roadblock, destruction of railway lines and channel- blocking** due to rock-falls have far-reaching consequences. Diversion of river courses due to landslides can also lead to flood and loss of life and property. It also makes spatial interaction difficult, risky as well as a costly affair, which, in turn, adversely affects the developmental activities in these areas.

Mitigation

It is always advisable to adopt area-specific measures to deal with landslides. Restriction on the construction and other developmental activities such as roads and dams, limiting agriculture to valleys and areas with moderate slopes, and control on the development of large settlements in the high vulnerability zones, should be enforced. This should be supplemented by some positive actions like promoting **large-scale afforestation programmes** and **construction of bunds** to reduce the flow of water. Terrace farming should be encouraged in the northeastern hill states where **Jhumming (Slash and Burn/Shifting Cultivation)** is still prevalent.

Disaster Management

Disasters due to cyclones, unlike the ones caused by earthquakes, tsunamis and volcanic eruptions are more predictable in terms of the time and place of their occurrences. Moreover, with the help of development of techniques to monitor the behaviour of cyclones, their intensity, direction and magnitude, it has become possible to manage the cyclonic hazard to some extent. Construction of cyclone- **Shelters, Embankments, Dykes, Reservoirs and Afforestation** to reduce the speed of the winds are some of the steps that can help in minimising the damages.

Conclusion

It can be concluded that disasters can be natural or the results of human activities, and all hazards need not turn into disasters since it is difficult to eliminate disasters, particularly natural disasters. Then the next best option is mitigation and preparedness. **There are three stages involved in disaster mitigation and management:**

1. **Pre-Disaster Management** involves generating data and information about the disasters, preparing vulnerability zoning maps and spreading awareness among the people about these. Apart from these, disaster planning, preparedness and preventive measures are other steps that need to be taken in the vulnerable areas.
2. **During disasters**, rescue and relief operations such as evacuation, construction of shelters and relief camps, supplying of water, food, clothing and medical aids etc. should be done on an emergency basis.
3. **Post-Disaster Operations** should involve rehabilitation and recovery of victims. It should also concentrate on capacity- building in order to cope up with future disasters, if any.

These measures have special significance for a country like India, which has about two-third of its geographical area and equal proportion of its population, vulnerable to disasters.

TEST YOURSELF

Multiple Choice Questions

Q1. Which of the following natural hazards is a result of the collision between the Indian and Eurasian tectonic plates?

(a) Floods (b) Cyclones

(c) Earthquakes (d) Landslides

Q2. The northeastern region of India is prone to which of the following natural hazards?

(a) Droughts (b) Earthquakes

(c) Cyclones (d) Avalanches

Q3. The process of the gradual sinking of coastal land due to various factors, including subsidence and sea level rise, is known as:

(a) Coastal erosion (b) Desertification

(c) Coastal flooding (d) Coastal subsidence

Q4. The southeastern coast of India is prone to which of the following natural hazards?

(a) Earthquakes (b) Floods

(c) Cyclones (d) Tsunamis

Q5. The process of wearing away of the Earth's surface by natural forces such as wind, water, and ice is known as:

(a) Erosion (b) Deposition

(c) Weathering (d) Landslides

Q6. The state of Uttarakhand in India is prone to which of the following natural hazards?

(a) Cyclones (b) Earthquakes

(c) Floods (d) Landslides

Q7. The process of the gradual increase in the Earth's average temperature due to human activities, leading to climate change, is known as:

(a) Global warming (b) Ozone depletion

(c) Desertification (d) Deforestation

Q8. The state of Assam in India is prone to which of the following natural hazards?

(a) Cyclones (b) Droughts

(c) Earthquakes (d) Floods

Q9. The occurrence of excessive rainfall in a short period of time, leading to rapid runoff and waterlogging, is known as:

(a) Drought (b) Flood

(c) Landslide (d) Tsunami

Q10. The process of the sudden release of energy in the Earth's crust, causing seismic waves and shaking of the ground, is known as:

(a) Flood (b) Cyclone

(c) Earthquake (d) Landslide

Answer Key

Q1.	c	Q2.	b	Q3.	d	Q4.	c
Q5.	a	Q6.	d	Q7.	a	Q8.	d
Q9.	b	Q10.	c				

Model Questions for Main Examination

Q1. Disaster preparedness is the first step in any disaster management process. Explain how hazard zonation mapping will help disaster mitigation in the case of landslides. (UPSC 2019)

Q2. Describe the various causes and the effects of landslides. Mention the important components of the National Landslide Risk Management Strategy. (UPSC 2021)

UNIT 36 Human Geography

In This Unit

Comprehensive and profound coverage of the following NCERTs' chapter:

- ✓ NCERT Class- 12th (Fundamentals of Human Geography), Chapter- 1

Human geography studies the inter-relationship between the physical environment and socio- cultural environment created by human beings through mutual interaction with each other.

Naturalisation of Humans and Humanisation of Nature

Human beings interact with their physical environment with the help of technology. It is not important what human beings produce and create but it is extremely important 'with the help of what tools and techniques do they produce and create'.

Technology indicates the level of cultural development of society. Human beings were able to develop technology after they developed better understanding of natural laws. For example, the understanding of concepts of friction and heat helped us discover fire. Similarly, understanding of the **secrets of DNA and genetics** enabled us to conquer many diseases.

The knowledge about Nature is extremely important to develop technology and technology loosens the shackles of environment on human beings. In the early stages of their interaction with their natural environment humans were greatly influenced by it. They adapted to the dictates of Nature. This is so because the level of technology was very low and the stage of human social development was also primitive. This type of interaction between primitive human society and strong forces of nature was termed as **Environmental Determinism.**

The people begin to understand their environment and the forces of nature with the passage of time. With social and cultural development, humans develop better and more efficient technology. They move from a state of necessity to a state of freedom. They create possibilities with the resources obtained from the environment. The human activities create a **Cultural Landscape**. The imprints of human activities are created everywhere; health resorts on highlands, huge urban sprawls, fields, orchards and pastures in plains and rolling hills, ports on the coasts, oceanic routes on the oceanic surface and satellites in the space. The earlier scholars termed this as **Possibilism**.

A geographer, **Griffith Taylor** introduced another concept which reflects a middle path (Madhyam Marg) between the two ideas of **Environmental Determinism** and **Possibilism**. He termed it as **Neo determinism** or **Stop and Go Determinism.** Those of you who live in cities and those who have visited a city, might have seen that traffic is regulated by lights on the cross-roads. Red light means **'stop'**, amber light provides a gap between red and green lights **'to get set'** and green light means **'go'.** The concept shows that neither is there a situation of absolute necessity (environmental determinism) nor is there a condition of **absolute freedom (possibilism).** It means that human beings can conquer nature by obeying it. The neo-determinism conceptually attempts to bring a balance, nullifying the either or dichotomy.

Human Geography Through the Corridors of Time

The process of **Adaptation**, **Adjustment with and Modification** of the environment started with the appearance of human beings over the surface of the earth in different ecological niches. Thus, if we imagine the beginning of human geography with the interaction of environment and human beings, it has its roots deep in history. Thus, the concerns of human geography have a long temporal continuum though the approaches to articulate them have changed over time. This dynamism in approaches and thrusts shows the vibrant nature of the discipline.

Earlier there was little interaction between different societies and the knowledge about each other was limited. Travellers and explorers used to disseminate information about the areas of their visits. Navigational skills were not developed and voyages were fraught with dangers. The late fifteenth century witnessed attempts of explorations in Europe and slowly the myths and mysteries about countries and people started to open up. The colonial period provided impetus to further explorations in order to access the resources of the regions and to obtain inventorised information. This shows the processes of steady development of human geography.

Fields and Sub-Fields of Human Geography

Human Geography develops close interface with other sister disciplines in social sciences in order to understand and explain human elements on the surface of the earth.

Broad Stages and Thrust of Human Geography

Period	Approaches	Broad Features
Early Colonial period	Exploration and description	Imperial and trade interests prompted the discovery and exploration of new areas. An encyclopaedic description of the area formed an important aspect of the geographer's account.
Later Colonial period	Regional analysis	Elaborate description of all aspects of a region were undertaken. The idea was that all the regions were part of a whole, i.e. (the earth); so, understanding the parts in totality would lead to an understanding of the whole.
1930s through the inter-War period	Areal differentiation	The focus was on identifying the uniqueness of any region and understanding how and why it was different from others.
Late 1950s to the late 1960s	Spatial organisation	Marked by the use of computers and sophisticated statistical tools. Laws of physics were often applied to map and analyse human phenomena. This phase was called the quantitative revolution. The main objective was to identify mappable patterns for different human activities.
1970s	Emergence of humanistic, radical and behavioural schools	Discontentment with the quantitative revolution and its dehumanised manner of doing geography led to the emergence of three new schools of thought of human geography in the 1970s. Human geography was made more relevant to the socio-political reality by the emergence of these schools of thought.
1990s	Post-modernism in geography	The grand generalisations and the applicability of universal theories to explain the human conditions were questioned. The importance of understanding each local context in its own right was emphasised.

Fields of Human Geography	Sub-fields	Interface with Sister Disciplines of Social Sciences
Social Geography	-	Social Sciences - Sociology
	Behavioural Geography	Psychology
	Geography of Social Well-being	Welfare Economics
	Geography of Leisure	Sociology
	Cultural Geography	Anthropology
	Gender Geography	Sociology, Anthropology, Women's Studies
	Historical Geography	History
	Medical Geography	Epidemiology
Urban Geography	-	Urban Studies and Planning
Political Geography	-	Political Science
	Electoral Geography	Psephology
	Military Geography	Military Science
Population Geography	-	Demography
Settlement Geography	-	Urban/Rural Planning
Economic Geography	-	Economics
	Geography of Resources	Resource Economics
	Geography of Agriculture	Agricultural Sciences
	Geography of Industries	Industrial Economics
	Geography of Marketing	Business Studies, Economics, Commerce
	Geography of Tourism	Tourism and Travel Management
	Geography of International Trade	International Trade

Human Geography and Sister Disciplines of Social Sciences

Geographical Perspective on Selected Issues and Problems

Environmental Pollution

Environmental pollution results from 'the release of substances and energy from waste products of human activities. **There are many types of pollution**. They are classified on the basis of medium through which pollutants are transported and diffused. **Pollution can be classified into: air pollution, water pollution, land pollution and noise pollution.**

Water Pollution

Indiscriminate use of water by increasing population and industrial expansion has led to degradation of the quality of water considerably. Surface water available from rivers, canals, lakes, etc. is never pure. It contains small quantities of suspended particles, organic and inorganic substances. When concentration of these substances increases, the water becomes polluted, and hence becomes unfit for use. In such a situation, **the self-purifying capacity of water is unable to purify the water.**

Though water pollutants are also created from natural sources (erosion, landslides, decay and decomposition of plants and animals, etc.) **pollutants from human activities** are the real causes of concern. Human beings pollute the water through industrial, agricultural and cultural activities. **Among these activities, industry is the most significant contributor.**

Industries produce several undesirable products including industrial wastes, polluted waste water, poisonous gases, chemical residuals, numerous heavy metals, dust, smoke, etc. Most of the industrial wastes are disposed-off in running water or lakes. Consequently, **poisonous elements reach the reservoirs, rivers and other water bodies, which destroy the bio-system of these waters. Major water polluting industries are leather, pulp and paper, textiles and chemicals.**

Various types of chemicals used in modern agriculture such as inorganic fertilisers, pesticides and herbicides are also pollution generating components. These chemicals are washed down to rivers, lakes and tanks. These chemicals also infiltrate the soil to reach the ground water. Fertiliser induces an increase in the nitrate content of surface waters. **Cultural activities** such as pilgrimage, religious fairs, tourism, etc. also cause water pollution. In India, almost all surface water sources are contaminated and unfit for human consumption.

Water Pollution is a source of various water- borne diseases. The diseases commonly caused due to contaminated water are diarrhoea, intestinal worms, hepatitis, etc. The World Health Organization shows that about one-fourth of the communicable diseases in India are water-borne. Though river pollution is common to all rivers, yet pollution of river Ganga flowing through one of the most populous regions of India has caused great concerns among all. **To improve the condition of the river, the National Mission for Clean Ganga was initiated. The Namami Gange Programme has been launched for the same.**

Namami Gange Programme

Ganga, as a river, has national importance but the river requires cleaning by effectively controlling the pollution for its water. The Union Government has launched the **'Namami Gange Programme'** with the following objectives:

- Developing sewage treatment systems in towns
- Monitoring of industrial effluents
- Development of riverfront
- Afforestation along the bank to increase biodiversity
- Cleaning the river surface
- Development of **'Ganga Grams'** in Uttarakhand, UP, Bihar, Jharkhand and West Bengal
- Creating public awareness to avoid adding pollutants into the river even in the form of rituals

River and State	Polluted Stretches	Nature of Pollution	Main Polluters
Ganga Uttar Pradesh, Bihar and West Bengal	(a) Downstream of Kanpur (b) Downstream of Varanasi (c) Farrakka Barrage	1. Industrial pollution from towns like Kanpur 2. Domestic wastes from urban centres 3. Dumping of carcasses in the river	Cities of Kanpur, Allahabad. Varanasi, Patna and Kolkata release domestic waste into the river
Yamuna Delhi and Uttar Pradesh	(a) Delhi to confluence with Chambal (b) Mathura and Agra	1. Extraction of water by Haryana and Uttar Pradesh for irrigation 2.Agricultural run off resulting in high levels of micro-pollutants in the Yamuna 3. Domestic and industrial waste of Delhi flowing into the river	Delhi dumping its domestic waste

Sources of Pollution in the Ganga and the Yamuna Rivers

Air Pollution

Air pollution is taken as an addition of contaminants, like dust, fumes, gas, fog, odour, smoke or vapour to the air in substantial proportion and duration that may be harmful to flora & fauna and to property. With increasing use of varieties of fuels as the source of energy, there is a marked increase in emission of toxic gases into the atmosphere resulting in the pollution of air. Combustion of fossil fuels, mining and industries are the main sources of air pollution. These processes release oxides of sulphur and nitrogen hydrocarbons, carbon dioxide, carbon monoxide, lead and asbestos. Air pollution causes various diseases related to respiratory, nervous and circulatory systems.

Smoky fog over cities called **urban smog** is caused by atmospheric pollution. It proves very harmful to human health. **Air pollution can also cause acid rains.** Rainwater analysis of urban environment has indicated that the pH value of the first rain after summer is always lower than the subsequent rains.

Noise Pollution

Noise pollution refers to unbearable and uncomfortable noise from different sources.

The main sources of noise pollution are various factories, mechanised construction and demolition works, automobiles and aircraft, etc. They may include periodical but polluting noise from sirens, loudspeakers used in various festivals, programmes associated with community activities. The level of steady noise is measured by sound level expressed in terms of **decibels (dB).**

Of all these sources, **the biggest nuisance is the noise produced by traffic**, because its intensity and nature depend upon factors, such as the type of aircraft, vehicle, train and the condition of road, as well as, that of vehicle (in case of automobiles). **In sea traffic**, the noise pollution is confined to the harbour due to loading and unloading activities being carried. Industries cause noise pollution but with varying intensity depending upon the type of industry.

Noise pollution is location specific and its intensity declines with increase in distance from the source of pollution, i.e., industrial areas, arteries of transportation, airport, etc. Noise pollution is hazardous in many metropolitan and big cities in India.

Pollution Types	Pollutiing Agents/Substances	Sources of Pollution
Air Pollution	Oxides of sulphur (SO_2 , SO_3), Oxides of nitrogen, carbon monoxide, hydro-carbon, ammonia, lead, aldehydes, asbestos and beryllium.	Combustion of coal, petrol and diesel, industrial processes, solid waste disposal, sewage disposal, etc.
Water Pollution	Odour, dissolved and suspended solids, ammonia and urea, nitrate and nitrites, chloride, fluoride, carbonates, oil and grease, Insecticide and pesticide residue, tannin, coliform MPM (bacterial count) sulphates and sulphides, heavy metals e.g. lead, aresenic, mercury, manganese, etc, radioactive substances.	Sewage disposal, urban run-off, toxic effluents from industries, run-off over cultivated lands and nuclear power plants.
Land Pollution	Human and animal excreta viruses and bacteria, garbage and vectors therein, pesticides and fertiliser-residue alkalinity, fluorides, radio-active substances.	Improper human activities, disposal of untreated industrial waste, use of pesticides and fertilisers.
Noise Pollution	High level of noise above tolerance level.	Aircrafts, automobiles, trains, industrial processing and advertising media.

Types and Sources of Pollution

Urban Waste Disposal

Urban areas are generally marked by overcrowding, congestion, inadequate facilities to support the fast-growing population and consequent poor sanitary conditions and foul air. Environmental pollution by solid wastes has now got significance because of enormous growth in the quantity of wastes generated from various sources. Solid waste refers to a variety of old and used articles, for example, stained small pieces of metals, broken glassware, plastic containers, polythene bags, ash, floppies, CDs, etc., dumped at different places. These discarded materials are also termed as refuse, garbage and rubbish, etc., and are disposed of from two sources:

- **Household or Domestic Establishments**
- **Industrial or Commercial Establishments**

The **household wastes** are disposed-off either on public lands or on private contractors' sites, whereas the solid wastes of industrial units are collected and disposed-off through public (municipal) facilities at low lying public grounds (landfill areas). The huge turnout of ashes and debris from industries, thermal power houses and building constructions or demolitions have posed problems of serious consequences. Solid wastes cause health hazard through creation of obnoxious smell, and harbouring of flies and rodents, which act as carriers of diseases like typhoid, diphtheria, diarrhoea, malaria and cholera, etc. These wastes cause frequent nuisance as and when these are carelessly handled, spread by wind and splittered through rain water.

Concentration of Industrial Units in and around urban centres gives rise to disposal of industrial wastes. The dumping of industrial waste into rivers leads to water pollution. River pollution from city-based industries and untreated sewage leads to serious health problems downstream.

Urban waste disposal is a serious problem in India. In metropolitan cities like Mumbai, Kolkata, Chennai, Bengaluru, etc., about 90 per cent of the solid waste is collected and disposed. But in most other cities and towns in the country, about 30 to 50 per cent of the waste generated are left uncollected which accumulate on streets, in open spaces between houses and in wastelands leading to serious health hazards. These wastes should be treated as resource and utilised for generating energy and compost. **Untreated wastes ferment slowly and release toxic biogas to the atmosphere, including methane.**

Problems of Slums

Slums and colonies of shanty structures in urban areas are inhabited by those people who were forced to migrate from the rural areas to these urban centres in search of livelihood but could not afford proper housing due to high rent and high costs of land. They occupy environmentally incompatible and degraded areas.

Slums are residential areas of the least choice, dilapidated houses, poor hygienic conditions, poor ventilation, lack of basic amenities, like drinking water, light and toilet facilities, etc. Open defecation, unregulated drainage system and overcrowded narrow street patterns are serious health and socio-environmental hazards.

Moreover, most of the slum population works in low-paid, high risk-prone, unorganised sectors of the urban economy. Consequently, they are the undernourished, prone to different types of diseases and illness and cannot afford to give proper education to their children. The poverty makes them vulnerable to drug abuse, alcoholism, crime, vandalism, escapism, apathy and ultimately social exclusion.

Land Degradation

The pressure on agricultural land increases not only due to the limited availability but also by deterioration of quality of agricultural land. **Soil erosion, waterlogging, salinisation and alkalinisation of land lead to land degradation**. Land degradation is generally understood either as a temporary or a permanent decline in productive capacity of the land.

There are two processes that induce land degradation. These are natural and created by human beings. **National Remote Sensing Centre (NRSC)** has classified wastelands by using remote sensing techniques and it is possible to categorise these wastelands according to the processes that have created them. There are a few types of wastelands such as gullied or ravenous-land, desertic or coastal sands, barren rocky areas, steep sloping land, and glacial areas, which are primarily caused by **natural agents**. There are other types of degraded lands such as waterlogged and marshy areas, land affected by salinity and alkalinity and land with or without scrub, which have largely been caused by **natural as well as human factors.** There are some other types of wastelands such as degraded shifting cultivation area, degraded land under plantation crops, degraded forests, degraded pastures, and mining and industrial wastelands, are caused by **human action.**

A Case Study

Jhabua district is located in the westernmost agro climatic zone in Madhya Pradesh. It is, in fact, one of the five most backward districts of the country. It is characterised by high concentration of tribal population (mostly Bhils). The people suffer due to poverty which has been accentuated by the high rate of resource degradation, both forest and land. The **watershed management programmes** funded by both the ministries of "Rural Development" and "Agriculture", Government of India, have been successfully implemented in Jhabua district which has gone a long way in preventing land degradation and improving soil quality. Watershed Management Programmes acknowledge the linkage between land, water and vegetation and attempts to improve livelihoods of people through natural resource management and community participation.

TEST YOURSELF

Multiple Choice Questions

Q1. Which one of the following concepts describe the interaction between human societies and their physical environment?

(a) Environmentalism

(b) Human ecology

(c) Cultural geography

(d) Environmental geography

Q2. Which one of the following processes is known for spreading cultural traits and ideas from one society to another?

(a) Assimilation (b) Acculturation

(c) Cultural diffusion (d) Cultural relativism

Q3. When a city is divided into different zones based on land use and function, such as residential, commercial, and industrial zones, is described as:

(a) Urban sprawl (b) Urban planning

(c) Zoning (d) Gentrification

Q4. The study of the interaction between human societies and their physical environment, including natural resources, is known as:

(a) Political geography

(b) Economic geography

(c) Environmental geography

(d) Urban geography

Q5. Which one of the following economic system that is based on private ownership and profit-making is described as:

(a) Capitalism (b) Socialism

(c) Communism (d) Mercantilism

Q6. The process by which a previously functioning city or urban area declines in social and economic terms is known as:

(a) Urbanisation (b) Suburbanisation

(c) Urban decay (d) Urban renewal

Answer Key

Q1.	b	Q2.	c	Q3.	c	Q4.	c
Q5.	a	Q6.	c				

Model Question for Main Examination

Q. Justify the statement "Humanisation of nature and naturalisation of human".